Souls

ille, U.S.A.

The Story of
STAX RECORDS

Rob Bowman

SCHIRMER
TRADE
BOOKS

NEW YORK/LONDON/PARIS/SYDNEY/TOKYO
BERLIN/COPENHAGEN/MADRID

Schirmer Trade Books
A Division of Music Sales Corporation, New York

Design by Brady McNamara
Set in 9/11 Simoncini Garamond
Schirmer Trade Books paperback edition 2003

Printed in the United States of America

Exclusive Distributors:
Music Sales Corporation
257 Park Avenue South, New York, NY 10010 USA
Music Sales Limited
8/9 Frith Street, London W1D 3JB England
Music Sales Pty. Limited
120 Rothschild Street, Rosebery, Sydney, NSW 2018, Australia

Order No. SCH 10122
International Standard Book Number: 0.8256.7284.8
Library of Congress Catalog Card Number: 97-19812

Library of Congress Cataloging-in-Publication Data:

Bowman, Robert M.J. (Robert Maxwell James)
      Soulsville, U.S.A. : the story of Stax Records / Rob Bowman.
      p.   cm.
      Includes biographical references and index.
      ISBN 0-02-860268-4 (hard cover)
      ISBN 0-8256-7284-8 (paperback)
      1. Rhythm and blues music—History and criticism. 2. Memphis (Tenn.)—History, I.
Stax Records. II. Title.
   ML3792.B69   1997
   781.643'09768'19—dc21   97-19812
                                                                      CIP
                                                                      MN

In Memoriam

To those who gave me interviews and have since passed on:

Dave Clark
Dick Cane Cole
Willie Gordon
Monk Higgins
R. B. Hudmon
Allen Jones
Major Lance
O. B. McClinton
Dave Prater

Contents

Preface

When I first began researching the story of Stax Records in the summer of 1985, little did I know that 12 years later I would still be working at bringing this project to a conclusion. My initial motivation was simple. Although born and bred in Toronto, I had long been intoxicated by the music, black and white, of the Southern United States. Consequently, when it came time to do my Ph.D. in ethnomusicology, I enrolled at the University of Memphis. I chose a Southern school because I wanted to live within the culture that had produced wave upon wave, genre upon genre of the most exciting music I had ever known. It seemed obvious to me that I might just get that much closer to grokking the essence of this music if I actually lived within the culture that had produced it. It was the best decision I have ever made.

For those who have never lived in Memphis, let me state emphatically that it is a very odd city. Lying at the heart of the mid-South, everything moves at a much slower pace in Memphis than I was certainly used to. To make any headway at all, I had to learn to gear down. It is also a city where some of the rawest, most exciting music humans have ever created might be heard on any given weekend night. But, just as likely, nothing will be happening. The great musical moments in Memphis happen infrequently and, especially in the case of black Memphis, are often not publicized outside of a small sector of the community. Tourists rarely see any of it. Most locals are totally oblivious to either its existence or its magic.

All of this is a long way of saying that if I hadn't lived in Memphis, this book could never have been written. In fact, it never would have been written because I had never planned to devote a decade of my life to Stax Records. Stax was only one of several topics that fascinated me. What led me ultimately down the long winding path that has culminated in this book was a growing disgust I had with the fact that most Memphians seemed blissfully unaware of the importance of the legacy of Stax Records. While most people at least had some vague notion that it had existed, very few had any sense of the impact the records produced by Stax had on the popular music of the last 35 years, and just as few realized the importance this company had for the local African-American populace.

While I found this lack of knowledge and interest particularly galling in Memphis itself, the general neglect of Stax extended well beyond the Memphis city limits. At the time that I began this project, there were eight books out on Motown, but not a single volume had been written about Stax. Having worked my way into the local music community, I had already met a number of the people who had worked at Stax. Hence, I decided that I was the right person in the right place to do something about this injustice. I set out to document with as much richness, dignity, and grace as I could muster the story of those that had created the mighty Stax Records.

And so began an incredible journey. In the intervening dozen years, my Stax activities have included: innumerable lectures; academic and popular press articles on various Stax artists; a four-part radio special; over 65 compact disc reissues of Stax material; and a film. In some respects, Stax had become a full-time job, dominating a significant number of my waking hours. I conducted over 200 interviews with those who in one way or another were involved with Stax, including virtually every artist, songwriter, session musician, engineer, and producer as well as all three owners and several of the key office personnel. These interviews have taken me into a wide variety of milieus, ranging from roach-infested homes, reflecting the most abject poverty you could imagine, to mansions in the East Hamptons. The former was the site for a fascinating interview with one of the members of one of the great vocal groups at Stax; the latter was where I interviewed Atlantic Records co-owner Jerry Wexler, whose company distributed Stax. The two interviews were conducted within days of each other and provided a perfect insight as to who makes money in the music industry and who does not!

In the process of doing all of these interviews, I was graciously allowed into the lives of dozens of people, many of whom remain friends of mine to this day. My life has been that much richer for all these experiences. I consider myself blessed. Much of this book is derived from those interviews, and as often as possible I have tried to tell the story of Stax in the words of those that lived it.

Working on a project over this length of time has impressed upon me the urgency of conducting historical research earlier rather than later. Nine people that I interviewed for this book have passed away. Another five passed away before I found the time to talk to them and, of course, a very few such as Otis Redding and Al Jackson had passed away while the story was still unfolding. I have also become aware of a significant erosion in the memories of many of the people whom I have interviewed more than once. Details that in 1985 or 1986 came readily had all but vanished by 1996. Thank God for Maxell tape!

When I first began writing the history of Stax, I thought I was writing about a bunch of records that I loved. I quickly realized the story was much richer than that. As an integrated company in Memphis, Tennessee, in the 1960s, Stax was a political and /social phenomenon. As its ownership passed from being white to half-white/half-black to 100 percent black, Stax also became important as an innovative black business enterprise. The tale of its gradual unraveling at the hands of the United States government, CBS Records, and Memphis's Union Planters National Bank begged to be told.

Throughout its two very distinctive periods, Stax was a very special place to work. In the 1960s there was clearly the feeling of a Stax family. In the 1970s, as the company grew to include over 200 employees, the nature of that family changed, but for those who still toiled away at the McLemore Studio the family feeling remained. Most of those who were lucky enough to be a part of the company in either period describe their time at Stax as the best years of their lives. Several people got positively teary-eyed during the course of our interviews as they recalled the joy and occasionally the heartbreak of their time at Stax.

Doing justice to such a multifaceted story was much more difficult than I ever imagined it might be. The book you currently hold in your hands is two-and-a-half times as long as my publisher wanted. It is also longer than I had envisioned, and yet I found that, even at this length, I had to leave out dozens and dozens of interesting stories that people had shared with me over the years. While I have used footnotes throughout the book to include as much detail, for those who want it, as possible, it became impossible to work in the stories and recordings of a host of artists who never achieved fame but made truly great records. Amongst that group I include Wendy Rene, Ruby Johnson, Mable John, Linda Lyndell, Hot Sauce, and many others. It was also impossible to give adequate space to several artists with an extended series of records issued at Stax, including the Mad Lads, the Bar-Kays, the Emotions, the Temprees, and the Soul Children.

The decision to leave this material out was made somewhat easier because I had the opportunity to write booklets that accompany three boxed sets that feature every rhythm and blues single issued by Stax. For those who crave details about these records, the boxed sets have it all, the combined liner notes being about half the length of this book.

I initially planned to have absolutely no duplication between my liner notes for the boxed sets and the current book. A number of people, including some of those who were part of the Stax story, talked me out of that approach, reasoning that not everyone who would buy this book would have all three boxed sets. For those that do, about 15 percent of the material included here has been recycled from the boxed sets. Please accept my apologies. The vast majority, though, of what you will read here is brand-new material, never before published.

By and large, *Soulsville U.S.A.* is the *story of a company* that produced records. While I never would have written this book if it hadn't been for those records, the focus in this text is squarely on the incredible saga of the corporation that made possible the production of those records.

Those who have read much of what has been written on Stax will notice that at various points facts, stories, and perspectives differ in this account from what I and others have previously published. In all cases, that is because as I have continued to dig at this story from every conceivable angle I have uncovered a wealth of new information, contradictory facts, and/or more reliable facts than I or anyone else had found previously. I assume that this process will continue and that I will have at least a few corrections to make for the second edition. Anyone with corrections and/or further information can write to me care of the Music Department at York University, 4700 Keele Street, Toronto, Ontario, Canada M3J 1P3. As well, despite my best efforts, there are a few people that I have never been able to interview. Anyone knowing the whereabouts of Tom Nixon, Rhonda Washington a.k.a. Hot Sauce, Barbara Stephens, Earl Cage, or Prince Conley, please contact me at the above address.

While I like a good tale as much as anybody else, personally I am obsessed with accuracy. For a variety of reasons, much that is and has been propagated about Stax Records is impregnated with an awful lot of fanciful fiction. Myth making is part of the local Memphis psyche and has been developed into a fine art by a handful of quotable individuals who, although being important players in the history of Memphis rock and roll, were never an important part of Stax Records. I interviewed these people and over time found that much of what they told me was just plain wrong, consisting of little more than third-hand knowledge filtered through too many years, a fair bit of substance abuse, and too many agendas, the latter often as not connected to the fact that they never were able to work their way into Stax. Despite the fact that a lot of what I was told were often great stories and/or insights, if they didn't pan out through the corroboration of other individuals or documentary evidence, I didn't use them. As best as I can do it, then, this is the truth, much of it less romantic than what has been written before, but all of it in the service of telling accurately the story of Stax Records.

In addition to the interviews that I conducted, in the course of my research I have had access to all of the Stax-related files in the hands of Fantasy Records, which purchased Stax in 1977. This includes most of the company's press releases, artist bios, sessions sheets, royalty statements, artist and producer contracts, distribution contracts, inter-company memos, and so on. I have also been able to audition just under 200 hours of Stax recordings that have never been issued. A significant percentage of the detail that is found in this book comes from the access Fantasy and their European licensee, Ace Records, have granted me.

The end of Stax was wrapped up in an inordinate number of lawsuits. The records retained by the courts pertaining to those lawsuits contain, in between more legalese than I ever cared to read, a wealth of hard data in the form of trial transcripts, affidavits, depositions, and interrogatories. In addition to providing a fascinating window on the events that eventually destroyed the company, these documents included a wealth of hard factual detail about the company's operations that is not in the files owned by Fantasy Records and that would be otherwise inaccessible. Much of this material is cited in the body of this text. Other hard data came through the largesse of a few key individuals who had kept company memos, speeches, and other materials that they graciously lent to me.

Which brings me to those that I need to thank. First and foremost are all those who participated in the Stax experience and have put up with my constant entreaties for multiple interviews over the past 12 years. This book is dedicated to them. Unless noted in the text, every quote is from an interview conducted by myself from 1985 to 1997. They are, in alphabetical order: James Alexander, Ron Alexenburg, Joe Arnold, Clarence Avant, Estelle Axton, Homer Banks, James Banks, Ron Banks, Al Bell, William Bell, Earlie Biles, Pete Bishop, J. Blackfoot, Eddie Bond, Eddie Braddock, Bertram Brown, Randy Brown, Veda Brown, William Brown, Henry Bush, Sam Byrnes, Gilbert Caple, Ron Capone, Randle Catron, Ben Cauley, the late Dave Clark, Judy Clay, the late Dick "Cane" Cole, Dee Cotton, Steve Cropper, James Cross, Mary Cross (Wendy Rene), Bettye Crutcher, Jeanne Darling, Don Davis, Theresa Davis, Larry Dodson, Tom Dowd, Duck Dunn, Eddie Floyd, the late Willie Gordon, Julius Green, Sandra Hall, Carl Hampton, Robert Harris, Roger Hawkins, Isaac Hayes, the late Monk Higgins, David Hood, Ollie Hoskins, the late R. B. Hudmon, Sheila Hutchinson, Wanda Hutchinson, Luther Ingram, Reverend Jesse Jackson, Robert Jackson, Wayne Jackson, Mable John, Curtis Johnson, Jimmy Johnson, L. V. Johnson, the late Allen Jones, Booker T. Jones, E. Rodney Jones, Samuel Jones, Margie Joseph, John KaSandra, Johnny Keyes, Frederick Knight, Jean Knight, Little Milton, Little Sonny, Andrew Love, Benny Mabone, Terry Manning, Bobby Manuel, Eddie Marion, the late O. B. McClinton, Barbara McCoy, Larry McKinley, Chips Moman, Sam Moore, Floyd Newman, Larry Nix, Deanie Parker, Jasper Phillips, David Porter, the late Dave Prater, Dave Purple, Zelma Redding, Mack Rice, Rudy Robinson, Joe Rock, Ewell Roussell, Harvey Scales, Harold Scott, Ray Scott, Joe Shamwell, Larry Shaw, Alvin Standard, Mark Stansbury, Mavis Staples, Pops Staples, Lewie Steinberg, Jim Stewart, Randy Stewart, Ronnie Stoots, Henry Stone, Ronnie Stoots, Ted Storey, Tommy Tate, Johnnie Taylor, Henderson Thigpen, Carla Thomas, Marvell Thomas, Rufus Thomas, Michael Toles, Jim Tyrrell, Phil Walden, Hy Weiss, Norman West, Logan Westbrooks, Jerry Wexler, Carson Whitsett, Tim Whitsett, Bill Williams, John Gary Williams, Mike Williams, Ronnie Williams, and Dino Woodard. A number of other individuals who made a solitary record for Stax or who crossed paths with Stax for a brief minute were also interviewed. They are also due my thanks.

Extra special thanks are due to a few individuals who have spent an inordinate number of hours talking to me over the years and/or helped out in other ways far above and beyond the call of duty. In alphabetical order they are Al Bell, Steve Cropper, Isaac Hayes, Bobby Manuel, Sam Moore, Deanie Parker, David Porter, Marvell Thomas, Michael Toles, and Tim Whitsett. This book could not have been written without their participation.

For the use of photographs in this book, thanks go out to API Photography in Memphis, Bill Belmont at Fantasy Records, Ron Capone, Hugh Jeffreys, Deanie Parker, Don Paulsen,

Mark Stansbury, Tim Whitsett, and Muhammed Ziyad and the Stax Historical Preservation Commission.

In the Stax world, one interview often led to one or more other interviews as various people gave me phone numbers, suggestions as to how to find people, and/or vouched for me to those who might have been hesitant to speak on the record. Thanks to all those already cited who contributed in this manner. Thanks in this regard are also due to a few non-Stax people, specifically Don Dortch, Dan Greer, Peter Guralnick, and Muhammed Ziyad, who helped to set up interviews with a couple of key players who otherwise might not have been willing to talk to me.

A few individuals that were absolutely key to my accessing of the court records and other documents have asked that their names not be mentioned. They know who they are and they know how indebted I am to them.

Bill Belmont and Roger Armstrong at Fantasy and Ace Records, respectively, have bent over backwards to assist my research. I am truly eternally grateful to both, and I consider them to be ongoing friends. Terri Hinte and Lisa Gifford at Fantasy also are due many thanks. For the funneling of articles from reams of rare fanzines and/or for tapes of rare Stax recordings, inordinate thanks are due to Rene Wu, Terry Riley, Robert Pruter, Eddie Richardson, and my dear friend Paul Williams. (Be sure to check out Paul's Audiomania Record Shop when visiting Memphis.) For various tapes and some of the records that were used for the cover shot, thanks go out to Martin Koppel. For runnings around of various natures in the Memphis area when I couldn't be there I need to thank Deborah Camp, Jim Cole, and Ruth Youngblood. David Sanjek also deserves many thanks for absolutely indispensable research assistance.

Much of my earliest research was carried out as cheaply as possible. That meant imposing on a lot of people's hospitality. For homes away from home, thanks are due to Jay Orr, Jo Ttanna, and Nis Hansen, and especially Ross and Lauren Johnson. One couldn't ever hope for better friends.

For my first major Stax-related liner note assignment, thank you Kim Cooke. For constant perspective when I sorely needed it, thank you Matt Vander Woude. For financial assistance at the very end of the project I am grateful for a grant from the Social Sciences and Humanities Research Council of Canada. Thanks to my agent Dick McDonough for continuing to work the book when it appeared no one wanted it. Extra special thanks to my editor Richard Carlin, who went to bat for me once I realized this book was far bigger than anything he had contracted for.

Finally, thanks to Payne's Bar BQ and the Four Way Grill in Memphis: ribs and soul food simply don't come any finer than what one will find at these two Memphis eateries. And, thanks to my family, Susan, Ryland, and Miranda, for putting up with everything Stax.

ROB BOWMAN
Toronto, September 1997

1

Cause I Love You: 1957–1960

We often think of America in the late 1950s as a drab, dreary, and uninspiring place. Gray was the dominant color, politics were largely conservative, the great move to suburban cookie-cutter housing was in full swing, fast-food chains were on the rise, and television was the new entertainment medium of choice. The nation appeared to be moving toward a consensus culture: one grand, homogeneous wasteland with a Howard Johnson's, Holiday Inn, and McDonald's at every freeway exit.

In hindsight, it is obvious that, although all of these forces were undeniably in effect, their combined impact was not as overwhelming as we might believe. Moreover, this cultural homogenization was not evenly distributed throughout the country. Memphis, Tennessee, in particular, seemed largely unaffected by these developments. Even today, as we near the close of the twentieth century, parts of Memphis seem to be little different from what they were at the end of World War II.

Memphis had always been a land apart. Majestically perched on a bluff on the eastern bank of the Mississippi River, in terms of cartography Memphis is situated in the southwest corner of Tennessee; in terms of culture, Memphis has long been symbolically viewed as the capital of Mississippi. While Tennessee is a land of rolling hills and genteel country music, Memphis is as flat as the Delta and has historically served as a fertile breeding ground for blues, jug bands, black gospel, and rockabilly. The differences between Memphis and the rest of Tennessee are those that separate night from day.

Claiming more churches per person than any other city in the Union, Memphis has long served as a magnet for anyone who grew up within a two- or three-hundred-mile radius and had dreams bigger than a cotton field. The city also served as a stopping-off point for whites and blacks participating in the great migration north to St. Louis or Chicago. Many such migrants put down roots in Memphis and never left.

Despite such growth, Memphis in the late 1950s remained underdeveloped, backward, insular, and reactionary. Urban by definition, the city was rural in terms of mind-set and, although not completely impervious to national developments, it tended to march to a drummer of its own. How else can you explain Gus Cannon, Rev. Robert Wilkins, Ike Turner, Howlin' Wolf, Mattie Wigley, Sam Phillips, or Elvis Presley? Significantly, none of these cultural icons was actually born in Memphis. Rather, each in his or her own way migrated to the Bluff City, attracted by the bright lights and what in relative terms must have appeared to be economic and cultural opportunity.

For most of the twentieth century, Memphis has been a vibrant musical center, nurturing and supporting more musical genres than perhaps any other city in the United States. The home base of the Church of God in Christ, Memphis has long been a center for the recording of some of the most intense Pentecostal music-making imaginable. In the 1920s and 1930s, the city also served as a common site for the recording of country blues and jug-band music, and for a brief period was home to famed blues composer and society dance band leader W. C. Handy. Shortly thereafter, Memphis produced, in Rev. Herbert Brewster and Lucy Campbell, two of the most important gospel composers of all time. In the postwar era, the urbanized, sophisticated, big-band blues of B. B. King stood side by side with the harsh city-meets-the-country proto-metal of Howlin' Wolf and the newly emergent shouting gospel quartet style of the Spirit of Memphis and Southern Wonders. With the emergence of rockabilly in the mid-1950s, Memphis music stood poised at the root of a worldwide cataclysm. Finally, in the 1960s and 1970s, with Stax, Goldwax, and Hi Records, Memphis served up what is arguably the richest soul music the world has ever known.

There was obviously never a shortage of music in the city, much of it made by icono-clasts who simply wouldn't have had a chance in most other more "sophisticated" or "developed" music centers. Significantly, there were also a cast of what we might think of as *facilitators,* people who were often as colorful and very nearly as important as the musicians themselves, such as Nat D. Williams, Dewey Phillips, Martha Jean Steinberg, and Sam Phillips. Beginning in 1948, Williams and then in 1954 Steinberg helped pioneer the emergence of black radio via the legendary WDIA, "the mother station of the Negro." Across town, both figuratively and literally, Dewey Phillips was as close as a white guy could get to the hepness and cool and visceral energy that radiated from the black music he chose to program nightly on WHBQ. All three of these individuals figure into the Stax story, influencing and/or promoting the odd amalgam of black and white musical cross-pollination that lay at the bedrock of Stax.

Sam Phillips, on the other hand, had all but withdrawn from the record industry by the time Satellite Records, the precursor to Stax, came into fruition. As the essentially one-man operator of Sun Records, Phillips had recorded a Who's Who of black and white mid-South-based artists, including Howlin' Wolf, B. B. King, Ike Turner, Jackie Brenston, Little Milton, Junior Parker, Elvis Presley, Johnny Cash, Jerry Lee Lewis, Roy Orbison, Carl Perkins, and Charlie Rich. Collectively, this cavalcade of stars simply changed the very rules of American music-making.

A musical milieu populated by these musicians and facilitators must have been mind-boggling to behold. For Memphians in the know, each day must have seemed infinitely bright, with each new record seeming to hold the very possibility of self-definition and/or reinvention. One of the promises this music communicated was that anything was possible, the game was wide open. No one (at least that was the myth) had to be constrained by his or her position at birth. Consequently, thousands were bitten by the music-making bug, including the man most responsible for this story, James F. Stewart.

In 1957 the demure Stewart was a bank teller by vocation and a country fiddler by avocation. Not too surprisingly, the reality for Stewart was that the latter was much more interesting than the former. However, as much as he might have wanted to be, it was clear that he was not destined for fame or fortune as a practicing musician. But, what about this Sam Phillips guy? As far as Stewart knew, Phillips couldn't play an instrument at all. Maybe there was more than one way to crack this nut. "I never really became a proficient or professional musician," mused Stewart, nearly three decades after the fact. "I knew I was not gonna be able to make it in that field. I just didn't have the ability. [Starting a record company] was like another way of being involved in the music business so to speak.

It was like if I can't be a singer or a musician, maybe I can *make* a record. Not *produce* a record, because I didn't know what a producer was. That was a term that was completely unknown then. I wanted to *make* a record."

Born July 29, 1930, about seventy miles east of Memphis near the Mississippi border in the farming community of Middleton, Tennessee (population around 800), Stewart grew up intoxicated by postwar country music. His parents, Ollie and Dexter Stewart, ran a farm, with Dexter supplementing the family income with carpentry and bricklaying work. When Stewart was ten, his daddy bought him a guitar. "I didn't really care that much about it," recalls Jim. "Then he bought me a three-quarter-size violin and I got really interested. On Saturday night I would turn the radio on to the Grand Ole Opry and I'd try to play along with it." Practicing constantly when he wasn't in the field working, Stewart learned by ear and eventually developed enough facility that he and a friend were able to form a band that regularly provided the entertainment at square dances in that part of the country.

Once finished with school, there was little to keep a budding musician in Middleton, and so, at age eighteen, he headed for the big city an hour-and-a-half down the road, hoping to further develop his career as a country fiddler. Heavily influenced by the Western Swing of Bob Wills and the Texas Playboys, Spade Cooley, Pee Wee King, and Tex Williams, as well as by the honky-tonk sounds of Hank Williams, Moon Mullican, and Ernest Tubb, Stewart picked up the odd playing job around town while working for Sears Roebuck during the day. Prior to WDIA switching to an all-black format, Stewart could also be heard on that legendary station, regularly playing his fiddle in the early morning hours of the day as a member of Don Powell's Canyon Cowboys.[1]

By late 1950 Stewart had moved into banking with First National Bank (now First Tennessee Bank) only to be drafted in the new year into the armed forces. In 1953, following the requisite two-year term, Stewart returned to the bank and got a job playing in the house band at the Eagle's Nest out on Lamar Avenue. When Stewart was still in the house band, Elvis Presley would often play during the intermissions at the club. "I got interested in recording then as Elvis got to be a giant," recalls Stewart. At the same time as this new interest was taking shape, Stewart took advantage of the GI Bill and got his B.A. degree at Memphis State University (now the University of Memphis), majoring in business management and minoring in music.

By 1957 Stewart's interest in recording led him to tape a couple of songs which he then attempted to take to Sun as well as to a few other local record companies. With the exception of Erwin Ellis, Stewart's barber, who also happened to own a small concern dubbed Erwin Records, nobody would give Stewart the time of day. Ellis loaned Stewart his first recording equipment, educated him about the value of publishing, and taught Stewart the basic mechanics of running a small independent record label and establishing an affiliated publishing company.

Undaunted by the lack of interest everyone else exhibited towards his recording efforts, under Ellis's guidance Stewart started a label and recorded two sides by local country disc jockey, bass player, and singer Fred Byler.[2] Issued as Satellite 100[3] in January 1958, Byler's recording of "Blue Roses" b/w "Give Me Your Love" was an inauspicious debut.

---

1. Not "Don Paul," as has been previously printed.

2. Stewart was not involved in the Jaxon label as has been printed a number of times over the years.

3. Stewart hated the name Satellite, but with the Russian satellite Sputnik the latest rage and no better ideas forthcoming, he finally agreed to it.

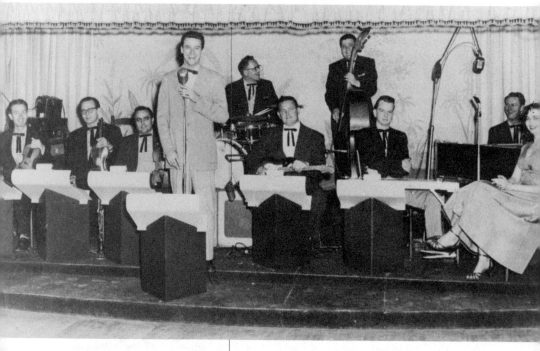

House band at the Eagle's Nest: (*left to right*) Jim Stewart, Speedy NcNatt, Joe Bracciante, WHHM disc jockey Sleepy-Eyed John Lepley, Ed Morgan, Tiny Dixon, Dan McHugh, Hugh Jeffreys, Thurmon Enlow, Ginnie Ford. COURTESY HUGH JEFFREYS.

At the time of its release Stewart was an equal partner in the new label with Byler and a rhythm guitarist named Neil Herbert, as all three had put in three or four hundred dollars of start-up capital. In total, they probably pressed less than three hundred copies of the Byler record.[4] The record is best described as undistinguished. Stewart wrote the A-side (his only composition ever to be recorded), which Byler croons his way through in a style somewhat reminiscent of Jim Reeves. The backing track is dominated by a weak and weepy imitation of the Anita Kerr Singers[5] and a somewhat heavy-handed sock rhythm backbeat. Virtually no copies were sold as, according to Jim, the only play the record received was on KWEM, the station where Byler worked.

Satellite's next release came within the month. This time Stewart was much more successful aesthetically, if not commercially. Neil Herbert brought rockabilly singer Don Willis to the label, and Stewart recorded him on one of the all-time killer rockabilly records. To this day "Boppin' High School Baby" backed with "Warrior Sam" (Satellite 101) remains a much sought-after collector's item in Europe.

After the Byler and Willis 45s, Stewart recorded and Satellite released a couple of undistinguished (Stewart describes them as "washed-out pop") country-pop records by Donna Rae and the Sunbeams (103) and Ray Scott (104), both most likely issued in

4. Until 1986, although Jim referred to it in a couple of interviews, its existence had never been confirmed because no copy had ever been found. That summer a single copy turned up in the back of a Memphis warehouse. More recently a second copy was discovered which is currently housed in the Memphis Music Museum.

5. Referred to as the Tunetts (sic) on the record label.

1958.[6] Donna Rae was the hostess of Wink Martindale's popular Memphis teen television show, "Dance Party." Erwin Ellis introduced Jim to Chips Moman, who played lead guitar on Donna Rae's record. Chips, in turn, was responsible for soliciting Ray Scott, in whose band Chips often played, to pen both sides for Donna Rae.[7] Scott then cut a deal with Stewart where he would hire the musicians, pay for the pressing of his own record, and give Stewart the publishing if Stewart would provide the studio and engineering duties free of charge. Scott's band included noted Memphis musicians Gene Chrisman on drums and Lee Adkins on lead guitar. As with the first two Satellite releases, Stewart pressed a few hundred copies of the Donna Rae and Ray Scott 45s (Scott is quite sure that only 300 were pressed of his record), selling somewhere between one and two hundred of each. "I couldn't get the stores to stock them," laments the then-frustrated entrepreneur.

Stewart, Byler, and Herbert had been recording Satellite's releases in Stewart's wife's uncle's two-car garage on Orchi Street[8] using a portable reel-to-reel tape recorder owned by Erwin Ellis. However, Stewart wanted to buy a state-of-the-art Ampex 350 monaural tape recorder—which at the time cost $1,300—but the partners lacked the needed capital to make the purchase. Stewart appealed to his sister, Estelle Axton, for help, asking her to mortgage her house for what he remembers as eight or nine thousand dollars.[9]

Axton was intrigued. For a while now, she had wanted to be involved with something other than her current job at the bank. At the same time she had the unenviable job of convincing her husband, Everett, that mortgaging the seventeen years of equity they had built up in their house to finance a recording label that had heretofore enjoyed absolutely no success somehow made sense. At the time, Everett Axton was only making eighteen dollars a week, their house note was already twenty-one dollars a month, and they had two teenagers still living at home. Nonetheless, in due time Estelle wore Everett down and they took out a second mortgage that was used to buy out Herbert and Byler's original investment, to finance the purchase of the Ampex tape recorder, and to provide badly needed operating capital.

Twelve years older than Jim (a sister, Lucille, had been born in-between), Estelle Stewart had always been strongly interested in music. As a teenager she had been a fan of pop music and had played the organ and sung soprano in a family gospel quartet. First coming to Memphis in 1935 to get her teaching certificate—teaching being the only career at the time readily open to women—she met her husband-to-be, Everett Axton, while attending Memphis State University. Teaching certificate in hand, Estelle went back to Middleton where, ironically, her younger brother Jim was one of her students. In 1941 Estelle married Everett and moved back to Memphis. For nearly a decade Estelle stayed

---

6. Although no one can remember why at this late date, there was never a Satellite 102 issued.

7. Rockabilly fans will be interested in knowing that this is the same Ray Scott who wrote Billy Lee Riley's manic "Flyin' Saucers Rock and Roll," released a year earlier on Sun Records.

8. Not "Orchard Street" as has been previously printed.

9. Estelle believes she contributed $2,500 at this point and another $4,000 in 1961. She also believes that she came into the company in February 1958, after the Byler and Willis releases, not in early 1959. (In an interview in *Goldmine* magazine in 1979, Willis stated that Estelle was involved with the company at the time of his recording.) However, the fact that Satellite's numbering system was begun again in 1959 with the company's fifth release, the Veltones' "Fool in Love," suggests that something significant happened after the first four records were issued, such as a partnership change. In addition, Stewart is quite certain that the Veltones' release was the first record cut with the new equipment that was purchased with the money Estelle brought into the company. Therefore, it seems most likely that Estelle joined the fold in February 1959 rather than February 1958.

at home raising two children, reentering the workforce in 1950 as an employee of Union Planters National Bank. She would remain at Union Planters until 1961 when she opened the Satellite Record Shop.

Estelle recalls being attracted to the record industry because she liked the idea of working with younger people. With Jim in charge of the recording end of the business, Estelle got busy augmenting Satellite's income by buying records wholesale from a local One-Stop[10] distributor in Memphis, which she would then resell at a mark-up to people she worked with, neighbors, and anyone else who might possibly be interested. Over the next few years, she would take this activity several steps further.

With the acquisition of new equipment, Stewart and Axton needed a permanent place to record other than a garage. As fate would have it, a barber friend of Stewart's by the name of Jimmy Mitchell had a vacant store building about thirty miles outside of Memphis in Brunswick, Tennessee. Mitchell was a country-and-western freak and was happy to let Stewart and Axton use his building free of charge until they made a profit if, in return, they would make a record with his daughter. At this point no one remembers who his daughter was but, evidently, although some effort was expended attempting to record her, she was not good enough to gain a record release.

In the late 1950s Brunswick was a sleepy rural enclave. Not surprisingly, the locals were pretty suspicious of this new-fangled enterprise called Satellite Records. As Stewart recalls events, he and Estelle were summoned to a town meeting at the local church. "Some of the local townspeople did not really understand what a recording studio was all about. They didn't know if it was legal, if it was a business, or what kind of business. They wanted to know more about us. You have to remember this is rural, it's southern, and it's a very close-knit community. They didn't understand why a recording studio would come to Brunswick. We had to answer a lot of questions, explain who we were and what making a record was all about."

Once the townspeople were satisfied, Jim and Estelle—with help from Chips Moman and a bass-playing compadre named Jimbo Hale—proceeded to set up shop. Ever resourceful, Stewart's wife, Evelyn, established a malt shop in a small adjoining structure that she operated on the weekends to help defray expenses. The studio itself was about as bad as it got. Mitchell's store was little more than a long wooden frame building.[11] The space was already divided at the two-thirds mark, so Stewart put a little window in the partition allowing the former storeroom at the back to serve as the control room, housing Satellite's newly purchased Ampex recorder and mixers. Equipped with eight inputs (seven used for microphones and one for echo) all of which went straight to one channel, in Jim Stewart's words, "it was the best machine we could get at the time."

The equipment may have been halfway decent but the studio was something else again, housing a Silvertone amplifier and little more. No acoustical work of any kind was done to this section of the building, aside from hanging a kind of burlap on the walls. "It was a horrible studio," admits Stewart. "I mean horrible! It was totally empty with wooden floors and the sound bounced all over the place. It had so much reverb it would go on forever." Further complicating matters was the fact that within thirty or forty yards of the

10. A One-Stop is a distributor that offers records from various labels at a discount to stores; the store owner can buy everything he or she needs from one place.

11. In 1994 Jim and I went out to Brunswick as part of the shooting of the film *The Soul of Stax*. This was the first time Jim had made the trek since 1960. The Satellite building was gone, but pretty well everything else, including the sign on the combination general store/cafe/post office across the street, remained the same.

nascent studio lay a railroad track. Trains blew by about every three hours, halting sessions and more than once ruining a recording.

In the spring of 1959 while still in Brunswick, Stewart recorded his first black group, the Veltones. Samuel Jones, Alvin Standard, Kenneth Patterson, George Powell, and Jimmy Ellis[12] had sung in and around Memphis since 1952, for eight years enjoying a residency at Curry's Club Tropicana with the Ben Branch Band. Stewart does not precisely remember how a country fiddler, who he freely admits did not know the first thing about rhythm and blues, came into contact with the group. He is reasonably certain that one Earl Cage, who would later surface as a songwriter on one side of the first release on Goldwax Records, was somehow involved, and has vague recollections that, via Cage, he had already attempted recording a black group by the name of the Keytones. According to Chips Moman, "Earl Cage was in and out of every studio in town all the time. He would always have somebody that could sing or somebody that he was pitching. He was into everything and never did really get nothing going." All Veltone members Sam Jones and Alvin Standard can recall is that it was Jim who contacted them.

In any event, after a month of biweekly journeys out to Brunswick, the Veltones' "Fool in Love" backed with "Someday" was deemed ready to release. The A-side of the Veltones record was cowritten and produced by session guitarist Chips Moman with Jimbo Hale on bass and Jerry "Satch" Arnold on drums. It would provide Stewart with his first hint of the possibility of success. Released in the summer of 1959 as the second record to bear the number Satellite 100, in September it was picked up for national distribution by Mercury Records for an advance somewhere in the neighborhood of four or five hundred dollars. "I thought that was a major coup at the time," muses Jim. "That was the first real money we made in the record business." Unfortunately, the Veltones were not to have their day in the sun and the record stiffed. Stewart received not a further penny from Mercury and found himself back at the drawing board.

After a year in Brunswick and only two record releases (the Veltones record and Charles Heinz's "Prove Your Love" b/w "Destiny"—Satellite 101—the latter artist brought to the company by Moman and Hale with accompaniment provided again courtesy of Moman, Hale, and Arnold), Stewart realized the neophyte operation had to make a move. "Brunswick was way out of the city. It was isolated and it was very inconvenient. We couldn't attract any artists because it was too far away from the center of the city. We decided we had to move back into town and either get very serious about the business or get out of it."

By early 1960, Stewart and Axton had given up on Brunswick and begun a search for a suitable location back in town. Acoustics and affordability being their two primary concerns, the would-be entrepreneurs quickly decided that the two types of buildings that might be most suitable were an old church or one of the old neighborhood movie theaters that had been abandoned in the late 1950s. Both types of facility would have the high ceiling and general room size that Stewart thought so acoustically desirable.

---

12. The Veltones had recorded a couple of demos at Sun in 1958 that would remain unissued until the 1980s, they recorded as the Canes on Stax in 1962, and in 1966, they would cut two sides for Goldwax Records. In my liner notes to both *The Complete Stax/Volt Singles 1959–1968* and *4000 Volts of Stax and Satellite* I list the personnel for the Veltones as Samuel Jones, Willie Mull, Alvin Standard, and George Reed. At the time I wrote those notes I had been unable to locate any of the Veltones and this information was obtained from the files of Goldwax Records. In April 1996 I finally tracked down Samuel Jones and Alvin Standard, from whom I got the information printed here. Apparently Mull and Reed replaced Patterson, Powell, and Ellis sometime after the Canes record. In the same two sets of liner notes I indicated that Don Bryant thought that the Canes record was another Memphis group, the Largoes, recording under a different name. It turns out the Canes were the Veltones recording during a period in which they were managed by Dick "Cane" Cole.

The first location that they looked at seriously was the old Capitol Theatre located at the corner of College and McLemore.[13] Owned by Paul Zerilla, the Capitol, as was the case with most of the city's neighborhood movie theaters, had been supplanted by the new, more modern movie palaces downtown.[14] Consequently, by 1960 it had been relegated to little more than hosting the occasional country-and-western performance (Jimbo Hale remembers both Mel Tillis and Eddie Bond being among the featured attractions); and as the neighborhood began to shift from white to black, even the country rentals had begun to fall off. According to Chips Moman, it was he and songwriting friend Paul Richey who found the theater while deliberately scouring black neighborhoods looking for a suitable building. "I wanted it in a black community," claims Moman. "That's the music that I wanted to do."

The fledgling owners of Satellite Records leased the Capitol for what Stewart remembers as $150 a month.[15] Given the fact that Stewart was only making about $350 a month at First National Bank and that Satellite was bringing in no income, this was no trifling amount. Estelle immediately came up with the bright idea that they would generate at least some cash flow if they could convert the candy counter of the theater into a record shop. With the lobby serving as display space for the LPs, the Satellite Record Shop was born. The record store would prove important in a number of respects.

The lease signed, Jim, Chips, Everett Axton, Estelle's son Packy, and Jim's wife set about renovating the theater. The most onerous task, pulling the seats out, had already been taken care of by Zerilla as part of the lease agreement. The rest of the work took a couple of months. Everyone pitched in after their regular workday and on weekends, hanging acoustical drapes (handmade by Estelle), building a control room on the stage, putting a few carpets on the floor, building baffles with burlap and ruffle insulation on the one outside plaster wall to cut down on the echo, and building a drum stand. The only thing professionals were hired to do was to hang the baffles from the ceiling.

Even with all this work, 926 E. McLemore remained a very "live" recording environment, having a reverberation effect akin to that of a concert hall. This would be an important component of what eventually became known as the Stax sound. Perhaps the oddest thing about the studio was that the original theater's sloping floor was never leveled. "I wasn't going to spend the money to level the damn floor," exclaims Stewart. "We didn't have the money to do those things." In typical Stax happenstance fashion, not leveling the floor turned out to be an acoustical plus as it meant the studio had no surfaces that were directly opposite each other.

In addition to all this acoustical work, a zigzag false partition was constructed that divided the theater in half, because, to put it mildly, the building was enormous. At its highest point, the ceiling was twenty-five feet high and, even when cut in half, the studio measured forty by forty-five feet.

Although the renovations cost a grand total of between two and three hundred dollars, Stewart and Axton found themselves strapped for funds. In a move that could have decidedly changed this whole story, they tried to find local investors but were unsuccessful. Consequently, according to Axton, she refinanced her house one more time to get another four thousand dollars of badly needed operating capital. As luck would have it, their very next recording would provide them with their first hit.

13. Before deciding on the Capitol, the principals in Satellite had also looked at the Handy Theatre on Park just east of Airways and the Lamar Theatre, still standing on Lamar a bit west of McLean.

14. Zerilla also owned the New and Old Daisy Theaters on Beale.

15. Axton says $100; Moman thinks $75.

Although the Veltones recording was ultimately not a commercial success, the fact that it was an R&B record with a bit of potential led Stewart to make promotional visits to all the local black media. No outlet was as important as WDIA where, among others, Stewart came into contact with one hepcat of a disc jockey named Rufus Thomas. If not a local legend by this point, Thomas was certainly part of the Who's Who of Memphis's black community. Married by Aretha Franklin's father, Reverend C. L. Franklin, Thomas's career had been long and varied, encompassing work as a dancer, comedian, emcee, vocalist, and radio announcer. One of his earliest gigs was as part of the dance team "Rufus and Johnny" with the Rabbit Foot Minstrels. He later forged a distinguished career as a comic ("Rufus and Bones") and master of ceremonies at all the black theaters in Memphis, including the Handy, Harlem, Savoy, Hyde Park, and, most significantly, the Palace. Most important as far as Stewart was concerned, in addition to hosting the daily "Sepia Swing Club" and "Hoot 'n' Holler" shows on 'DIA, Thomas was a singer and songwriter who had recorded for Star Talent, Meteor, Chess, and, most notably, Sun Records going back to 1949. His most successful recording had been an answer song conceived as a response to Big Mama Thornton's R&B hit "Hound Dog." Entitled "Bear Cat" and released in 1953, the record had been Sun's first bona fide hit, peaking at number 3 on *Billboard*'s R&B Best Seller and Juke Box charts.

When Thomas drove down to Satellite's new studio on McLemore he hadn't really made the connection that he would be seeing the same guy who brought him the Veltones' record. Instead, he had been prompted by a friend of his, a pianist named Bob Talley, who had already ventured into the theater, made Stewart's acquaintance, and felt that there were some possibilities here. Thomas eventually took tapes of himself, his daughter Carla, and a duet they had sung together down to the new studio. Stewart suggested he would be interested in recording the latter.

Thus, Rufus and Carla Thomas became the first artists recorded at the newly renovated theater-cum-studio. Issued in late summer 1960 as Satellite 102 under the sobriquet "Carla and Rufus," "Cause I Love You" b/w "Deep Down Inside" (the latter written by Rufus in the studio) changed the lives of everyone concerned. The recording, as with all of Stewart and Axton's previous efforts, was a nonunion session, because they simply could not afford to pay union rates.[16] Among those who gladly accepted the lower fee were a sixteen-year-old Booker T. Jones on baritone sax, Rufus's son Marvell Thomas on piano, and Wilbur Steinberg on bass. Collectively they conjured up a jumping New Orleans–influenced rhythm that Steinberg claims was his idea, and was borrowed from New Orleans artist Jesse Hill's recently released Top 5 R&B and Top 30 pop hit "Ooh Poo Pah Doo."

After three years of plugging without "even a smell of a hit," Jim Stewart suddenly found that he had a successful record. "We put that record out," Stewart remembered, smiling, "and it was like, surprise! People [were] actually buying this record and we weren't having to give them away. It was a great feeling. I really felt like I was in the record business. I had actually done something that the public was buying."

The success of "Cause I Love You" could not have been more timely because, by this point, Estelle's money was rapidly evaporating and, aside from the record shop, there was absolutely no money coming in. In addition to providing much-needed cash flow, "Cause I Love You" also provided direction. Although half of the next eight Satellite releases were either pop or country, for Jim Stewart life had irrevocably changed. As he himself puts it, "Prior to that I had no knowledge of what black music was about. Never

---

16. At the time union scale in Memphis was $51 per man for a three-song session with the leader being paid double. Satellite could only pay $15 per musician, and even this was a stretch.

heard black music and never even had an inkling of what it was all about. It was like a blind man who suddenly gained his sight. You don't want to go back, you don't even look back. It just never occurred to me [to keep recording country or pop]." From that moment on, Satellite became a rhythm and blues label.

The label benefited from a number of fortuitous circumstances with regard to this new-found direction. Perhaps the most important was the fact that Satellite's studio was located in the heart of what was fast becoming a black ghetto. Significantly, Satellite's first salaried songwriter, David Porter, worked at the Jones' Big D grocery right across the street from the studio. Two other early arrivals, Booker T. Jones and saxophonist Gilbert Caple also lived in the neighborhood.[17] Similar stories abound with regard to the arrival of other Satellite/Stax singers, instrumentalists, songwriters, producers, engineers, and office staff. Stax was an integral part of the community and, conversely, much of what became the heart of Stax came straight out of that same community.

The record store also played a key role in aiding and abetting neighborhood relations. One of the hipper local hangouts, the store also served as a conduit for talent recruitment, a number of future session musicians, songwriters, and vocalists making their initial contact with the company via the store. Among the customers was keyboardist and namesake of Booker T. and the MG's, Booker T. Jones. "I think there would have been no Stax Records without the Satellite Record Shop," declares Booker. "Estelle Axton will tell you we all came in there. Every Saturday I was at the Satellite Record Shop [and] that's where I went after school. After I threw my papers that's where I hung out. It was important to me as a young kid. I got to go in there and listen to everything. I'd spend three hours in the evening in there. I maybe bought one record a week, just enough so they'd let me back in. I'd hear that music behind the curtain so I just kind of hung around there. It was an important influence." Chips Moman recalls seeing Booker at the shop on a number of occasions, fresh out of school in his ROTC uniform.[18]

Although future MG Duck Dunn was white and consequently did not live in the neighborhood, the Satellite Record Shop was similarly important for him. "I used to live out east," relates Duck. "We had a little record shop there but if you wanted a rhythm and blues record, you had to special order it and it would take a week. Or, you'd have to get on a bus and go down to Beale Street to the Home of the Blues Record Shop. But they'd run you out if you [just] wanted to look."

"They wouldn't let you browse," adds MG guitarist and early Satellite clerk Steve Cropper. "Satellite was not that way. Estelle was very trusting of the people that came in and she'd let people browse. If they wanted to hear anything, we'd play it and let them hear it. They didn't have to buy it if they didn't want to. It was also amazing [in that] the local people who came by the record shop, they'd go, 'I write songs or I sing.' And we used to listen to them. It was good for everybody to have that sort of relationship with the people who lived around there." A number of future Stax employees, including Steve Cropper, Deanie Parker, Homer Banks, James Cross, William Brown, Johnny Keyes, and Henry Bush, started out as counter help in the record store. By 1961, its success inspired Stewart and Axton to expand their retail activity beyond the candy area at the front of the theater. Axton quit the bank to run the store on a full-time basis and they rented the recently vacated King's Barbershop next door. This was to serve as the home of the Satellite Record Shop through May 1968.

17. Caple, not Caples as has often been printed.

18. Steve Cropper recalls more than once picking up Booker from his ROTC training sessions for a recording date.

In addition to serving as a recruitment center and fostering neighborhood relations, the store also provided a vehicle for staying current with the listening tastes of Memphis black youth, providing a ready-made test market for just-cut Stax releases. It was not uncommon for Axton to take songs that had just been recorded and play them in the record shop for the local populace; many were changed, and some were not released, depending on their reaction. Even in the case of already-released product, the opinion of local youngsters could inform Stewart and Axton whether a record had a chance of becoming a hit, and consequently would be worth the hefty promotion expenses and the pressing of large quantities of records. Presumably a lot of money, time, and energy were saved by this method. "I gained a lot of knowledge from that," testifies Stewart. "A lot of record executives in their ivory towers could come down into a record shop and work on Saturday night in the ghetto behind the counter and learn a hell of a lot about the record business. That was the best test market in the world. We literally took demos up there, put them on the turntable, and watched the reaction." Atlantic Records co-owner and future Stax distributor Jerry Wexler was suitably impressed. "The theater on McLemore, the little store they had, the way they interacted with the street . . . I thought that was great."

The Satellite Record Shop had at least two other functions. It provided immediate access to a library of sounds whenever anyone cutting a session or writing a song needed to hear something currently out on the market. This proved useful for any number of Booker T. and the MG's covers, as well as at least Otis Redding's covers of "Satisfaction" and "Try a Little Tenderness" and Steve Cropper's writing of "(In the) Midnight Hour." Perhaps even more important, for aspiring writers the store functioned, in Estelle word's, as a workshop of sorts. "When a record would hit on another label," explains Estelle, "we would discuss what makes this record sell. We analyzed it. That's how the writers in the Stax studio got lessons from the record shop. That's why we had so many good writers. They knew what would sell. It was the workshop for Stax Records."

Booker T. concurs: "Most all our musical ideas and influences came out of that little record shop in the first couple of years. The Ray Charles records we listened to, the Bill Justis records . . . they had all that there. I can't see Stax being what it was without the Satellite Record Shop and Estelle Axton saying 'Why don't you guys try something like this?' She was always doing that. We'd leave the studio and go up there and stand around. I'd be listening to Motown up there. It was like having a library right next to the studio."

Eventually, the Satellite Record Shop became a *Billboard* reporting store, meaning every week Axton listed her best-selling records, which *Billboard* then used, along with similar reports from other stores around the country, to compile their rhythm and blues charts. Not surprisingly, Estelle routinely boosted the position of records released by Stax. Being extremely enterprising, Estelle also did local promotion for other record companies in exchange for free product that she would then sell in the store. She also bought and sold the free goods that local disc jockeys regularly received in exchange for radio play from other record companies.

All of Satellite's releases up to this point were distributed by Buster Williams's Memphis-based Music Sales. In addition to his distribution company, Williams owned a local record-pressing facility, Plastic Products, where Stewart had all of Satellite's pressing done. Williams's companies also pressed and distributed Atlantic Records product for the mid-South region.

The record industry at the time functioned much like the food chain. Larger independent record companies often picked up the distribution of a potential hit from smaller, more local concerns. Atlantic proved to be especially assiduous at discovering small labels to distribute. When "Cause I Love You" had sold about five thousand copies in the

Contract signing: *(standing)* Estelle Axton, Jim Stewart, Steve Cropper, *(seated)* Rufus Thomas, Carla Thomas. COURTESY API PHOTOGRAPHERS INC.

Memphis area (and according to Estelle another five thousand in Nashville and Atlanta), either Buster Williams, or his employee Norman Reuben, picked up the phone and hipped Jerry Wexler to the record.[19] Wexler was impressed ("I liked everything about it that bespoke Memphis") and, in turn, sent one of Atlantic's promotion men into Memphis to talk to Jim about the possibility of leasing the master. As Satellite was in no position to even begin to afford to market the record nationally, Jim was more than interested. Soon after, Wexler himself called Jim Stewart, the net result being that—for what Jim remembers as a $5,000 advance—Atlantic got a master lease agreement for all future Rufus and Carla Thomas discs. "Cause I Love You" was re-pressed on Atlantic's pop-oriented subsidiary Atco Records (Atco 6177).[20]

The original signed contract with Atlantic covered only Rufus and Carla Thomas records. A couple of months later, via a handshake deal, Atlantic acquired first refusal rights on the distribution of any subsequent Satellite and later Stax release.[21] "It was a good working relationship," muses Stewart. "It was good for me because the label was in its early stage and I didn't have the staff to do the promotion and marketing. I was

19. Wexler thinks it was Williams, while Stewart thinks that it was Reuben.

20. Estelle remembers the advance being $1,000. In retrospect, it may be hard to understand how close Stewart and Axton were to bankruptcy. According to Jim, they were having problems even paying musicians for sessions, let alone making the monthly rent. Whatever the actual dollar amount, the Atlantic money was like gold. In Estelle's words, "That was the biggest thousand dollars I ever saw. It was like today somebody laid a million dollars in your lap. We were struggling."

21. Although a handshake deal might seem unorthodox, according to Wexler, a precedent already existed in Atlantic's 1955 deal with songwriters/producers Jerry Leiber and Mike Stoller. The Stax deal was the first complete label deal Atlantic had ever made, and was to be the precedent for later deals with Fame, Dial, Capricorn, and Alston. The Satellite (later Stax)/Atlantic distribution relationship, formalized with a written contract in

more concerned with the creative aspect of the business. I had to be developing artists and the publishing." "The essence of the deal," recalls Wexler, "was that they delivered the master tapes at no cost. They paid for the sessions and handed us the tape, and we took the expense from there on—mastering, pressing, labels, jackets, distribution, promotion. It was a low royalty rate, I'll give you that.[22] I made the best deal I could, [but] there were never any charges against them."

Atlantic had very little input into the creative side of the business. "It was very autonomous artistically at Stax," says Wexler. "They did what they needed to do." Jim Stewart concurs. "Atlantic had no input whatsoever. We cut the stuff and sent it to them. They really didn't try to restrict us, nor did they control the timing of our releases."

The Satellite/Atlantic relationship paid immediate dividends for all concerned. Now channeled through Atlantic's distribution, "Cause I Love You" went on to sell another thirty or forty thousand copies, being especially strong in the Oakland area. To paraphrase Peter Guralnick, "the little label that could" was off and running.

1965, remained until May 1968 when Atlantic was purchased by what became known as Warner Communications (now Time-Warner). The deal with Atlantic gave the New York company the option to distribute each Stax release, but if it felt a record did not have national potential, Atlantic could elect not to pick it up. In the first few years Atlantic declined its option on about thirty individual releases by artists such as Prince Conley, Barbara Stephens, the Canes, the Astors, the Tonettes, Deanie Parker, the Drapels, and so on. In total, though, the vast majority of Stax releases were picked up for distribution by Atlantic, although, of those, about 10 percent were initially tested in Memphis to see what sort of interest existed before it was deemed worth the investment for Atlantic to distribute the record on a national basis.

22. It was customary at the time for royalties to be paid on 90, rather than 100, percent of all records sold. This was an antiquated holdover from the days of 78s, when it was assumed that approximately 10 percent of all records shipped would break. In the late 1990s, a number of record companies still maintain this practice.

Gee Whiz: 1960–1961

Flush with the sweet feelings of success and the Atlantic advance money, Jim, Estelle, and Chips quickly recorded and released two more 45s. The first was Charles Heinz's solitary followup to his previous year's local hit, "Prove Your Love." Issued in September 1960, "Suddenly" b/w "Nobody Cares" simply didn't have the necessary legs, and Heinz gradually receded into local legend.[1] Satellite's very next release, Carla Thomas's "Gee Whiz (Look at His Eyes)," broke things wide open for the fledgling company.

Born December 21, 1942, into the musically inclined Thomas family, Carla was the middle of three children, all of whom went on to enjoy careers in music.[2] Along with many of her contemporaries from the first period at Stax, Carla was part of the last generation of black Americans to come of age in the era of segregation. That, of course, had many ramifications, most of them decidedly negative. One of the ironies, though, of such an ugly system was the consequent quality of black schoolteachers and the black school system. Denied access to most high-paying, professional jobs, many of the most gifted minds in the black community became teachers. Respected and venerated, many of these educators had inordinately large influences within their community.

In the late 1950s and early 1960s there were seven black high schools in Memphis: Booker T. Washington, Hamilton, Manassas, Douglas, Melrose, Carver, and Lester. The first three were located relatively close to Stax in South Memphis, and consequently the majority of Memphians who found their way into the Stax family were graduates of those schools. Booker T. Washington, in particular, produced an unbelievable amount of talent, including Rufus Thomas, Booker T. Jones, William Bell, David Porter, Gilbert Caple, Maurice White, the Bar-Kays, Andrew Love, the Mad Lads, Homer Banks, J. Blackfoot, and Carl Hampton. The majority of these musicians never fail to mention their high-school music teachers when discussing the development of their skills. In a community where the money for an instrument and/or private lessons was usually out of the question, the skill, drive, encouragement, and largesse of a music teacher could, and often did, make all the difference.

Carla was no exception. A student at Hamilton High School, she received exceptional training in gospel and opera, learning arias from classical works such as *Il Trovatore* in the

1. The operatically trained Heinz was apparently somewhat reminiscent of teen idol Jimmy Clanton. According to Jim Dickinson, local iconoclast and leader of Mud Boy and the Neutrons, Heinz was a dynamite performer: "You can't imagine how good he was. His hair was sculpted up in a pompadour so high, he would lean it over and flop it down!"

2. Marvell Thomas became an accomplished piano player, writer, and producer whose skills graced countless Stax sessions, while the youngest Thomas sibling, Vanese, sang backup on a number of Carla's recordings and in the 1980s and 1990s did session work in New York, wrote songs for the likes of Freddie Jackson, and enjoyed a moderately successful solo career on Geffen Records.

process. Carla also benefited from being a member of WDIA announcer A. C. Williams's Teen-Town Singers. Williams had started the Teen-Town Singers while still a biology teacher at Manassas High School. When hired by WDIA, at the recommendation of Nat D. Williams (no relation) in 1949, A. C. expanded the Teen-Town concept to include "the best talent from [all] the local high schools." Carla was selected to be a Teen-Towner in 1952 at age ten. Still in grade school, she was four years younger than the specified Teen-Town minimum age.

Being a Teen-Town Singer meant rehearsals every Wednesday and Friday after school at the Abe Scharff branch of the YMCA at Linden and Lauderdale. Each week the choir prepared for a thirty-minute performance at 10 A.M. on Saturday on WDIA. The choir sang blues, gospel, jazz, and pop, and whenever WDIA was promoting a concert, the Teen-Towners would learn all the headlining artists' material and feature it on their Saturday morning shows for three or four weeks in anticipation of the concert. The Teen-Towners also provided backup vocals for all the national artists who performed at WDIA's annual Starlight and Goodwill charity revue programs.[3]

Every year a female and male Teen-Towner were selected out of the main choir and designated that year's "pop" singers. These teenagers were deemed able to handle the most difficult pieces in the repertoire and, in effect, were the stars of the ensemble. One year the female "pop" singer was Barbara Griffin, the future wife of MG's drummer Al Jackson. The next year it was Carla. It was as the "pop" singer of the year that Carla first sang two songs that she later recorded at Stax and issued on Atlantic, "The Masquerade Is Over" and the A. C. Williams composition "All I Want for Christmas." Both had been earlier features for Barbara Jackson.[4]

Mandatory retirement for a Teen-Towner was effectively age eighteen, which meant Carla had literally stepped down from the group just weeks before her father walked through the front door of Satellite Records. As much as Carla learned in school and with the Teen-Towners, being Rufus Thomas's daughter did not hurt when it came to becoming musically educated in the panorama of American vernacular music. As a youngster in the Foote Homes Housing Project, Carla remembers her father teaching all the neighborhood kids the hambone and hand jive, reciting nursery rhymes in proto-rap rhythms, and doing a little tap dancing. At the same time, Carla's mother, Lorene, loved both country and western and Perry Como. The whole family listened to Red Foley's "Breakfast Club" radio show in the morning, and Saturday night's broadcast of the "Grand Ole Opry" was simply not to be missed. Carla and her brother Marvell both became expert at singing Brenda Lee's "I'm Sorry" and yodeling in harmony à la Eddy Arnold.[5] Carla also adored Elvis Presley. "We loved Elvis Presley," exclaims the dean of Stax artists. "We made a big deal over Elvis in the house. We'd be imitating him."

Between her mother's tastes and her own inclinations, Carla was a fair sight more pop-oriented than her rhythm-and-blues-shouting father. That partially explains the thirty-two-bar AABA Tin Pan Alley pop structure and idealized-in-the-extreme love lyric of "Gee Whiz." At the time that she wrote it, Carla was only sixteen years old, and her main modes

---

3. Held in July and December each year, these revues featured R&B stars from all over the country. Each artist performed for expenses only, with all profits being deployed for charity work within Memphis's black community.

4. Other Teen-Towners who eventually figured into the Stax story included future Mad Lads John Gary Williams and Julius Green, future Soul Children member Anita Louis, Betty Brown of Barbara and the Browns, O. B. McClinton, and Carla's brother, Marvell. It was a sad day when WDIA chose to discontinue the program in the mid-1960s.

5. Marvell actually won a few local yodeling contests.

of expression were writing short stories and poems. "Gee Whiz" was an exception in that it truly was written as a song. Carla thinks that the inspiration probably stemmed from her brother Marvell who, forever seated at the family piano, would occasionally show his younger sister a few chords. The Thomases owned a reel-to-reel tape recorder, so Rufus and Carla had the relative luxury of putting their creations down on tape, performing both on their own and together. Unbeknownst to Carla, shortly after she had committed "Gee Whiz" to tape in the fall of 1958, her father had decided to try and market the song.

Every Christmas season Rufus would visit a former Memphis tap-dancing friend, James Gary, in Chicago. This had become a ritual that Rufus describes as his then-annual Christmas present to himself. During the Christmas 1958 visit, Rufus took time out to head down to the office of one of the leading black independents of the day, Chicago's Vee Jay Records, to drop off Carla's tape. When he didn't hear anything from Vee Jay over the next twelve months, Rufus simply stopped by the Chicago company during his Christmas visit in 1959 and asked for the tape back. When Rufus first journeyed down to Satellite to meet with Jim Stewart in the summer of 1960, this was among the tapes he had tucked under his arm.

Hindsight is usually slightly better than twenty/twenty. According to Jim, "Even at the time I was putting out 'Cause I Love You' I had heard Carla sing and I knew that [while] Rufus and Carla [were] fine, the real artist was Carla. I had talked to Rufus about recording her right from the beginning as a solo artist. The first day she came into the studio she sat down at the piano and sang 'Gee Whiz' and it was that magic that we all talk about in the record business. When I heard it, I felt, This is it! This is the record."

Despite having just recorded his first hit, "Cause I Love You," in his own studio, Jim decided to cut "Gee Whiz" over at Hi's Royal Recording Studio, just around the corner from Stax on Lauderdale. "Our studio still was having sound problems," explains Jim. "I wasn't happy with what I was getting. We didn't have the equipment. Hi had already had some success with Charlie Rich and two or three other artists and they were a factor in the local record business. So I hired the musicians and went over to the Hi studios and cut the record."

Chips Moman hastens to add that as "Gee Whiz" was recorded with strings, it was the first Satellite session where Jim had to pay the musicians union scale. This was a major factor in Jim's decision to use the Hi studio. With the basic cost of cutting the song going way beyond anything he had ever attempted before, he wanted the session to run as smoothly and quickly as possible.[6] Because—in Chips's words—the Satellite studio had barely been "turned on," Jim felt that using the tried-and-true Hi studio was the safer route. Ostensibly a reasonable concept, it didn't work. Finished tape in hand, Stewart spent a couple of days pondering the results before deciding this version of "Gee Whiz" was too fast and needed to be recut at McLemore.[7] "I hated it," demurs Moman. "It just didn't sound good. We didn't like the sound we got out of that studio."

This time Stewart was intent on going whole hog, hiring Bob Talley to write a string arrangement to dress up what Stewart was betting would finally be his meal ticket. The strings Jim hired were a trio led by the Memphis Symphony's first violinist, Noel Gilbert, whom Jim had studied under. At his best Jim can be a nervous sort. The "Gee Whiz" session nearly sent him to an early grave. Recording was scheduled for two o'clock

Carla Thomas and Jim Stewart circa "Gee Whiz."
COURTESY FANTASY, INC.

6. In 1997 Jim Stewart suggested that it is quite possible that the Hi version had no strings on it.

7. For the record it should be noted that Carla does not remember ever going over to Hi!

on a hot, sticky August afternoon. A couple of minutes before two, the string players arrived, began to tune up, and then the clock started running. The only problem was that Bob Talley was nowhere to be found. When he still hadn't arrived by 2:30, Stewart got on the phone, but there was no answer at Talley's house. Hopping into his car, he drove like a fiend to Talley's place, banged on the door, and woke the pianist up. When Talley finally stumbled to the door he explained that he had worked a gig the night before that hadn't finished until the early morning hours. The long and short of it was he had completely forgotten to write the arrangement.

"I was going out of my skull," relates Stewart. "I drove as fast as I could back to the studio. This must have been three o'clock. I got my fiddle out and said to Noel, 'Here's the basics. Just play doughnuts [whole notes].' And I showed him the real simple string lines. I got to the bridge and I said, 'Something needs to happen. Noel, when you get to the bridge, doodle by yourself.'" By the time recording actually began, the original session was already past its allotted three hours, and the string players were making union scale plus overtime. "I wound up paying them fifty dollars [for the regular session] and eighty-six dollars in overtime," Jim recalls, laughing. "But somebody was looking out for me because when we hit that first take, it was magic."

As was the case with virtually everything recorded at Stax through late 1967, the session was done "live." While Carla sang the finished vocal, the strings, rhythm section, and background vocals simultaneously performed their parts. The latter were courtesy of the Veltones, all of whom were sharing Carla's microphone, because, between the bass, drums, piano, and three violins, Jim had only one microphone input to spare on the company's Ampex recorder.[8]

Shortly after the recording session, Carla moved to Nashville to attend Tennessee A & I. Her tuition had been paid for via a Teen-Town scholarship. With "Gee Whiz" released toward the end of her first term in November 1960 as Satellite 104, before her freshman year was out, Carla Thomas was a national star.

The record was not an instant smash, but Jim had faith. "I'll tell you one thing," emphasizes Chips, "Ain't nobody in the world ever believed in a record as much as Jim did [in 'Gee Whiz']. He wouldn't give up on that record. Carla was his real pet. That was who he believed in more than anybody." It would take three months before the record made its debut appearance in *Billboard*. Eventually, though, the 45 peaked at number 5 on the rhythm-and-blues charts and number 10 on the pop charts, selling, according to Stewart, about 500,000 copies. As the single slowly began to make its initial impression in Memphis, Carla's first performance as a solo artist was scheduled for the December 1960 WDIA Goodwill Revue. Four months earlier she had been a Teen-Town Singer, helping to provide background for such an event; now she was one of the headliners on break from her freshman year in college.

As Carla geared up for the concert, Jim received a rather rude shock. By his own admission, at the time he was pretty naive when it came to contracts. Having signed the rights to Rufus and Carla over to Atlantic for a five-year period, Jim assumed that Carla Thomas by herself was a wholly separate matter—hence, the initial release of "Gee Whiz" on Satellite. Meanwhile, Atlantic co-owner Jerry Wexler, disappointed with the final sales figures of "Cause I Love You," was so busy with the usual day-to-day matters of running Atlantic in New York that he wasn't even aware of the record's existence. "When 'Gee Whiz' came out," laughs Wexler, "I didn't even know that we owned it.

---

8.   William Bell has always claimed that the Del-Rios sang background on "Gee Whiz," while the Veltones and Jim Stewart have consistently insisted it was the Veltones.

Neither did Jim. Of all people, Hy Weiss [owner of Old Town Records] called me and in his usual blustery, pseudo–tough guy role said, 'Hey motherfucker, you got a record down here, but 'cause it's you, I ain't gonna interfere with it.' He was telling me that I owned the record, and that he was doing me a favor by laying off. I got the message. Sure enough it checked out, and we had the rights."

Hy Weiss owned Old Town Records but made his mortgage payments through a job with Jerry Blaine's Cosnat Distributing, which just happened to distribute Atlantic Records. That December Weiss was in Chicago promoting an Old Town blues release by Bob Gaddy called "Operator." While Weiss was visiting Leonard Chess, a truck pulled up to Chess Records unloading singles pressed in Memphis by Buster Williams's Plastic Products. Weiss was operating on a shoestring and suggested to the driver that if he would let him ride down to Memphis, Hy would do his share of the driving. On the trip down South, Hy heard "Gee Whiz" on the radio. Convinced that it was a hit record, upon checking into the Chisca Hotel in Memphis, he called up Jim Stewart.

"I said, 'Jim, I'd like to distribute your label and I can do a helluva job.' He says to me, 'Okay, we'll sit down, we'll make a deal.' I said, 'Let me look at your papers.' I looked at the papers and realized Atlantic had an option. I called Jerry [Wexler] at home in Great Neck. I said, 'Jerry, my friend, did you ever hear of a record called "Gee Whiz"?' He said, 'No.' I said, 'Jerry, this is a fucking smash record. I think you oughta make a deal [i.e., exercise your option] with these guys but quick.' Any other label but Chess or Atlantic and I would have grabbed that thing and they never would have seen the light of day. I liked everybody at Atlantic and I made a living through them [via his job at Cosnat Distributing]. Anyone who helped me, I never forgot."

The next day Jim received a call from Wexler. He said, "Hey man, I hear my record's doing good," and "Gee Whiz" was immediately transferred to Atlantic 2086. In an odd coincidence, just as Carla's record began its inexorable climb up the charts, a California pop trio called the Innocents released a different song that was also titled "Gee Whiz." Hence Carla's addition of "(Look at His Eyes)" to the title of her song. Satellite/Atlantic ads in the trades stressed that Carla's paean to teen love should not be confused with the other record. They needn't have worried, as the Innocents' disc died a quick and quiet death.

As "Gee Whiz" broke into the top ten of both charts, Jerry Wexler decided to pay a visit to Memphis. While in town he wished to take Jim, Rufus, Carla, and Carla's mother to dinner. Given the reality and attitude about racial segregation at that time in the mid-South, Jerry thought it best if they ordered room service and dined in his room. Thinking this through in advance, he had taken a suite rather than a regular room at Memphis's most luxurious hotel, the Peabody. However, in Memphis at that time, blacks were not even allowed into the lobby of a hotel like the Peabody. "Rather than using the front door," recalls Wexler, "we wound up going into the service entrance into the back of the hotel in an alley lined with garbage cans. It was humiliating and embarrassing to me and even more so to Rufus and the family. I remember on the way up Rufus said, 'Same old story, back walking through the garbage.'"

Once safely ensconced in Wexler's suite, everyone had a wonderful dinner, talked about Carla's and, to a lesser extent, Rufus's career, and then the Thomas family and Jim headed back to their respective homes. A little while later Wexler went to bed, having nearly forgotten about the earlier unpleasantness.

As Wexler tells the story, his encounter with the racial bugaboo of early sixties Memphis was not quite over. "Some time in the middle of the night, long after they were gone, comes this furious knocking at my door—'MEMPHIS POLICE—VICE SQUAD—OPEN UP!' Of course, I didn't open up. I said, 'What's your problem?' They said, 'You got a woman in there.' Well, suppose I did. That's what hotels are for I would presume. Apparently, there had been some misconstruction [*sic*] about my guest list for the evening. The word *miscegenation* was still in the public vocabulary in the South in those days. The inference was I was entertaining a black female in my room, most probably a professional."

Well aware of stories of disappearing civil rights workers and the like, before Wexler would let them in, he insisted that the hotel manager be summoned. In the meantime, he wrote a quick note to his partner in New York, Ahmet Ertegun. When the Memphis police, with the hotel manager in tow, escorted Wexler down to the lobby, he quickly dropped the note in the hotel's mail box. "Maybe I was being super paranoid," Wexler says with a shrug. "But I had notions of winding up in the trunk of a car and being dumped someplace in Mississippi or Arkansas."

These types of ugly realities were not lost on anyone at Stax. According to most Stax personnel, white Memphis tended to be blissfully unaware of their existence until the ascendancy to superstardom of Isaac Hayes in the late sixties and early seventies. When there was some acknowledgment of the goings on at 926 E. McLemore, most would agree with artist, songwriter, and eventual head of publicity Deanie Parker that it tended to be negative.

"I think that most of them thought that we were a bunch of freaks, just into all kind of perverted action and what have you because there were blacks and whites together. 'Oh, you know what they're doing over there. Why else would they be over there?'" Parker says. Musicians, songwriters, office staff, and owners alike were forced to negotiate such racial absurdities on a day-to-day basis when they interacted with Memphis society at large. In many respects the company functioned as a world completely removed from the vicissitudes of the society in which it resided. Although there was no forethought to any of it, Jim Stewart and Estelle Axton's steadily growing mom-and-pop operation provided a case study of how black and white could intersect and interact. And although it might seem disingenuous, I believe Estelle when she asserts, "We never saw color, we saw talent. That was what was so great about being over there."

Such a stance in the Memphis of the early 1960s was ipso facto political, irrespective of whether or not it was intended as such. In the case of Satellite, everything from the word go was accidental. If Jim and Estelle had found another empty movie theater available at the right price in a different neighborhood, maybe the emphasis would have remained on the pop and country product with which they began. Certainly the inventory and clientele of the Satellite Record Shop would have been substantially different, which, in turn, would probably have meant that the likes of Booker T. Jones, Gilbert Caple, Bob Talley, and David Porter wouldn't have been hanging out there. Given how important the shop was as a conduit for Jim and Estelle to make connections with singers, instrumentalists, and songwriters, I believe that the grand accident that was Stax simply wouldn't have happened.

Once it was established in what was fast becoming a ghetto, the process by which the company became integrated is fascinating. Aside from the string players on "Gee Whiz," the musicians on the Carla and Rufus recording and Carla's solo outing had been all black. Similarly, the session musicians were all black on the company's next R&B release by the Chips, January 1961's "You Make Me Feel So Good" b/w "As You Can See" (Satellite 105), but they were all white on Jimmy and the Spartans' April 1961 bid for immortality, the execrable Milquetoast pop confection "You're My Girl" b/w "Why Doesn't She Notice Me" (Satellite 106). All of this changed dramatically with Satellite 107, "Last Night" by the Mar-Keys. Perhaps not so coincidentally, this was also the record on which what became known as the Stax sound began to crystallize.

The Mar-Keys' history is both long and byzantine. The genesis of the group centers around guitarist Steve Cropper. Born in 1941 and raised on a little farm just outside Dora, Missouri (population c. 200), Cropper arrived in Memphis just shy of his tenth birthday after his dad was recruited to be a special agent on the railroad. While growing up in Dora, Steve heard lots of the "Grand Ole Opry" and little else. It was in Memphis that he would first hear black gospel music and fall in love with the rock and roll and rhythm and blues of Hank Ballard and the Midnighters, Bo Diddley, Chuck Berry, and Elvis Presley. "When I came to Memphis and finally had my own radio, I used to listen to WDIA and at midnight they would play gospel music. That really turned me around. I mean I grew up in the church and heard a lot of a cappella music and stuff but I had never really heard black gospel and it just blew me away. This was when I was in probably about the sixth grade."

His first guitar, an eighteen-dollar flat-top acoustic sunburst, was ordered from the Sears catalogue when he was fourteen years old. Pretty soon the budding musician hooked up with a fellow student at Messick High School, Charlie Freeman. By this point, Freeman had been playing guitar for a while and was studying with local jazz luminary Lynn Vernon. Steve managed to horn in on the lessons. "I would meet Charlie over at his house after he would get back from his guitar lessons and he would teach me [what he had just learned]. I don't know if he looked at the fact that I was getting something for nothing, but I think he enjoyed having a buddy to play with." Cropper eventually spent about three months taking lessons from Vernon directly, but he got bored pretty quickly, having little interest in learning how to read music.

In the meantime, Cropper and Freeman continued jamming together, slowly mastering the odd Elvis Presley tune such as "(Won't You Be My) Teddy Bear." Eventually a friend talked them into going down to disc jockey Keith Sherriff's show on WHHM to show off their wares. That same friend had already pulled Sherriff's coat to the fact that the two kids could play. In a story very reminiscent of Elvis Presley's first interview, Sherriff put them in a room and said he wanted to see what they could do. Unbeknownst to either of them, the disc jockey had opened the microphone and put them on air. Audience response was immediate and positive, and Sherriff offered to let them play his sock hops if they got a drummer. Coincidentally, it was in this same time period that Jim Stewart was attempting to record and release the Fred Byler record.

It took a while for a suitable drummer to be found, but eventually Messick High student Terry Johnson was tabbed to fill the bill. Shortly after the newly constituted threesome played their first sock hop, Donald "Duck" Dunn entered the picture. Duck lived at the end of Cropper's block, and he and Steve had grown up together, riding bicycles and playing baseball and football. They both also had shared interests in music and dancing, Duck being good enough in the latter department that he won several dance contests. Duck had already tried to emulate Steve's passion for guitar playing, but somehow found the six strings just a little too much to master. Never one to give up easily, he went out and got a Kay bass. With the addition of Duck, the neophyte quartet spent the summer of 1957 playing a lot of CYO (Catholic Youth Organization) gigs, church functions, and the occasional dance at a place called the Casino.

"The better we got," relates Steve, "the more money we made and the more guys we added to the group. We played a lot of private parties, we played a lot of proms. By the time we graduated in 1959, we were a pretty well-known group around town." Eventually the original quartet was expanded to include Jerry "Smoochy" Smith on keyboards, former Regent Ronnie Angel as featured singer, and a horn section comprised of tenor saxophonist Charles "Packy" Axton, baritone saxophonist Don Nix, and trumpeter Wayne Jackson. All but Smith, Jackson, and Angel had been students at Messick High.

According to Steve, the addition of horns was purely a matter of pragmatism. Packy Axton's mother, Estelle, and uncle, Jim, owned a recording studio and record label. "That's definitely why Packy was in the band. He came up one day out of nowhere at school and says, 'Hey, I hear you guys got a hot group.' I said, 'Well, we hadn't thought about adding any horns to the group. How long have you been playing?' He says, 'I don't know, about three or four weeks.' He was honking and squeaking. 'But my mother and my uncle own a recording studio.' 'Oh, that's different. You're in the band, I don't care how well you play. See you Saturday.' As best as I can remember, that's as true as it gets, with all due respect to Charles 'Packy' Axton. He turned out to be a great tenor player."

Packy has become somewhat legendary within white Memphis. "Wasn't anybody wilder than Packy," asserts Wayne Jackson. "He was as hip as they came." A rebel and an outsider from the start, Packy Axton is described by many as the "blackest white man" they have ever known. "Packy hung out with blacks when it wasn't cool," continues Jackson matter-of-factly. "Packy had a black roommate and he went with black chicks. But Packy wasn't doing it out of love. He was doing it because he was rejecting the white race [with] his fucked-up James Dean attitude. He would do anything to embarrass his mother or his father, as in go out with black people, hang out with black people, stay with black people all the time."

Although Packy may have taken that particular fantasy further than any of the others, in Cropper's circle everyone was infatuated with the black rhythm and blues of groups like the Five Royales, Hank Ballard and the Midnighters, and Bill Doggett. Lowman Pauling, the guitarist and songwriter with the Five Royales, in particular had an enormous influence on what became the sound of Stax. "Lowman was just phenomenal to me," sighs Cropper. "I had already been listening to the records and [then] the Five Royales came to Memphis and did a performance out at the Beverly Ballroom. I got to see them play and I couldn't believe this guy. He had his guitar way below Chuck Berry's, he had it down damn near below his knees, almost to his ankles. It almost dragged the floor. It was the damnedest thing I'd ever seen! He had to play all the funky licks down in the first fret area because there was no way he could reach [any higher]. But, when it came time to take a solo up high, he would pick the guitar up and, of course, the strap would just kind of fall loose and he would hold it and play his high stuff and then he'd drop it back down and go into his rhythm. It just fascinated me. He played between the legs and behind the head. This was the first guy I ever saw do that. He just danced with the guitar. He was all over the place. He was real influential.

"A lot of guitar players play more like piano players. They play the whole picture all the way. Then they'd throw in a riff here and there. Lowman mainly just noodled rhythm and then, when there was a hole, man he'd just come out loud and just give you this big slingshot. I think that really influenced me. I think that's probably what developed my style in doing sessions: listening for holes in the singer so the licks I play are as important to the melody as the melody is to the licks I play, where one flows into the other rather than me sitting there trying to play guitar and stepping all over the singer."

When a group like the Five Royales would play Memphis, more than likely the Veltones would open up. If the gig was at a white all-ages establishment such as the Beverly Ballroom or Clearpool, it was easy for white teenagers to go see them. Three of the hippest rhythm-and-blues clubs, though, were located just across the Mississippi River in West Memphis. Of these, the Plantation Inn was the most popular. According to Jim Dickinson, actually getting into the PI was not always possible or plausible for the younger white set but, fortunately, the club was built in such a fashion that the music could be heard quite clearly in the parking lot. It wasn't uncommon for would-be hipster white teenagers to spend the evening lying down inside a car grooving to the sounds pumping out non-stop from the club.

Duck Dunn and Steve Cropper appeared to have had an easier time of it. "There seemed to be no age limit," laughs Duck, "'cause Steve and I really looked young. Even when we were fifteen, we looked twelve, and they didn't care. I guess they were paying the law off. We never asked any questions, we just got in." Steve picks up the conversation: "Just walked up and said we wanted to go in. All you had to do was pay your two bucks at the door. We'd all take in a little bottle of sloe gin or whatever it was and sip it with Coke, but the main interest was the music. A lot of people would go there and dance. We'd just go over there and listen to the music."

The Memphis clubs were a little stricter. "On this side of the bridge," continues Steve, "we weren't allowed to get in the clubs. But guys like Clifford Curry [owner of Curry's Club Tropicana] knew we were serious about it. We were there to hear the music and were just really enthralled by the whole deal. He would let us stand right there at the door. At the Handy Club behind the bandstand there was a big mirror where you could see the band's reflection. [Owner Sunbeam Mitchell] would tell us, 'If you see the cops, you guys get outta here 'cause it will get me in trouble.' He couldn't let us come in and we couldn't have a beer but we did get to hear the music. That's where I got to see Ben Branch and people like that." A lot of the local black bands such as Willie Mitchell's and Ben Branch's also played Catholic Youth Organization dances on Sunday, providing yet one more avenue for budding musicians such as Cropper and Dunn to soak up the hard-hitting sounds of Memphis rhythm and blues.

WHBQ deejay Dewey Phillips also had an inordinate influence on every white kid who was even the least bit interested in black music in Memphis in the mid- and late 1950s. Phillips was a renegade in every sense of the word, talking trash faster and blacker than his birthright should have allowed for, while spinning some of the hippest records ever cut. "Duck and I kinda grew up on Dewey Phillips' 'Red Hot and Blue' show," affirms Steve. "He played a lot of R-and-B records. We were highly influenced by that."

At some point, Cropper, Freeman, and the rest of the group began playing under the moniker the Royal Spades. In 1959 the Royal Spades (minus Wayne Jackson and keyboard player Smoochy Smith, who had yet to join) landed a residency at Neil's Hideaway out by the Millington Naval Base on Thomas Street where for nine months they ground out the toughest black rhythm and blues and rock and roll that a white band from Memphis could possibly muster.[9] The Royal Spades spent their Sundays journeying out to Brunswick, rehearsing and trying to cut something that was good enough to be released on Satellite. According to Cropper, Jim Stewart tolerated them only because of the fact that Packy was Estelle's son, but ultimately he did not seem to have much faith in their abilities. "Jim Stewart said, 'These guys will never make it.' I think he really thought we were just horrible. It was his sister's son's group so to speak and he let us get by with it somehow."

Shortly after Jim and Estelle moved out of Brunswick, Wayne Jackson was inaugurated as a Royal Spade. Terry Johnson and Duck Dunn had discovered Jackson while the trumpeter was doing a little work with Charles Heinz. When the two Spades dropped by a Heinz rehearsal they were knocked out by what they heard and quite quickly made Jackson an offer to join the Royal Spades that he couldn't refuse. While

---

9. They were not totally unique in tackling this musical style. For quite some time it had been a southern tradition for white frats to hire black bands to play their parties. Gradually a few white bands evolved that could play passable versions of this material themselves, the frats serving as their main outlets. Down in Jackson, Mississippi, Tim Whitsett and the Imperials were stomping down on such a black-imbued repertoire, as were the Del-Rays over in the Muscle Shoals/Florence/Sheffield area of Alabama. Members of both bands would figure in the Stax story in the 1970s.

their efforts in the studio kept coming up empty, on stage, replete with their gray coats with black felt spade on the pocket, they were dynamos. According to Jim Dickinson, baritone saxophonist Don Nix and Wayne Jackson were the visual ones. "They had a Mutt and Jeff comedy routine that was as funny as anything you've ever seen white people do. Wayne was hysterical."

The *Last Night* album is a fair indication of the range of their material in this period. While the Spades may have been infatuated with the sounds of black rhythm and blues, they were also able to play convincing versions of jazz classics such as "Night in Tunisia" and "One O'clock Jump" as well as lighter, pop-oriented affaire. "We had to play a lot of those military gigs," explains Cropper, "and these old colonels would come in and they've got their wives. They want 'Cherry Pink Apple Blossom White.' They want 'Stardust,' 'Misty,' 'Moonlight in Vermont.' We had to learn to play all those things or we didn't get paid. *Then* we got to play our Ray Charles [numbers]."

The group also managed to come up with a handful of originals, including one sort of half-jazz, half-funky instrumental with the memorable title "Bouncing Off the Wall." It was usually the originals that they worked on when they could get studio time, because cutting a record was still their focus. Although the Royal Spades had not been successful in getting a 45 released while Satellite was out in Brunswick, they had not given up. In the spring of 1961, they finally got their first chance to record at McLemore. As Jim Stewart had little faith in the group, Chips Moman was in charge of the session.

By this point, the band had been reduced to a single guitarist because Charlie Freeman had left to go on tour with the Joe Lee Orchestra. It was while playing a gig with Joe Lee in Chicago that Freeman first heard his former group's debut record, "Last Night," on the radio. On Estelle's recommendation, the Royal Spades changed their name. Don Nix had originally suggested the "Marquis" in the grand tradition of group monikers such as the Counts, the Viscounts, etc. Cropper pointed out that "People around here don't read French," so someone else suggested that they could create a pun on the keys of a piano if they modified the spelling to Mar-Keys.[10]

The genesis of "Last Night" came about when Chips Moman and a country keyboard player named Jerry "Smoochy" Smith were fooling around at the piano during a break at a gig they were playing together at the Hi-Hat Club. Intoxicated with a little riff they had stumbled upon, according to Chips they began trying to work it up into a song at Satellite the very next day. Steve Cropper recalls that he and Packy suggested the horn blasts on beat one and its following offbeat. "It was a group effort," asserts Wayne Jackson. "A lot of people claim this and claim that but the truth is it was a spontaneous effort by all of us. It went on for days after we finally worked out what it was gonna be like. We cut that record for a week, day in and day out until we finally got a piece of tape that was from front to back okay."

There is quite a bit of dissension as to how the riff was eventually transformed into the record "Last Night" by the Mar-Keys. Chips, Smoochy, and baritone saxophonist Floyd Newman claim that when the song was cut it wasn't even conceived of as a Mar-Keys session. Naturally most of the Mar-Keys vehemently disagree.[11] Chips says the recording was completed in a day; Steve says that a day or two was spent working it up and then one day was spent cutting it; Smoochy says it took a month to nail the song; Terry Johnson says

---

10. Contrary to what has commonly been claimed, initially it was not a pun on Satellite's theater marquee.

11. It should be noted that the B-side of the original 45, "Night Before," was recorded by the actual Mar-Keys rhythm section—Steve Cropper, Duck Dunn, Terry Johnson—plus an integrated horn ensemble and copyrighted by Wayne Jackson, Duck Dunn, Terry Johnson, Steve Cropper, and Packy Axton.

two to three weeks; Duck Dunn says three weeks; and Wayne Jackson says it was attempted on several days with slightly different feels and tempos.[12]

The road version of the Mar-Keys: (*left to right*) Don Nix, Steve Cropper, Packy Axton, Duck Dunn, Terry Johnson, Ronnie Angel (a.k.a. Stoots), Wayne Jackson. COURTESY DEANIE PARKER.

Probably there were several different attempts made at recording the song on several different days. This is partially supported by the fact that several people remember working on the song at different times with different drummers. Mar-Keys drummer Terry Johnson, who was a year younger than the rest of the band and consequently still finishing high school, recalls coming down to the studio one day after school got out. When Terry walked in he encountered Smoochy, Chips, and some of the members of the band already working on the song. This was probably the first day that Smoochy and Chips brought the

12. Bass player Lewie Steinberg claims it was at one point attempted as a waltz!

riff in. Terry claims he played drums on several early attempts at the song, eventually giving way to black session musician Curtis Green. Duck Dunn also insists that he played on several early versions of the song before he, unfortunately, missed the day the master was cut while out fishing with his dad in Mississippi.

Johnson's and Dunn's accounts jibe with black tenor saxophonist Gilbert Caple's memory; Caple was the one who suggested replacing Johnson on the record with Curtis Green, and it was Caple who brought bassist Lewie[13] Steinberg in to sub for the AWOL Dunn. Caple lived about three blocks from the studio on McLemore Street. A decade older than the members of the Mar-Keys, he was already making his living teaching high-school band in West Memphis. Curtis Green had been a student of his who also was playing at the Plantation Inn. Caple had originally come by Stax on the suggestion of David Porter, who worked across the street from the studio at Jones' Big D Grocery and knew Caple on a casual basis due to their mutual interest in music. Porter, in partnership with Isaac Hayes, a few years later would become one of the most important songwriters in soul music. In early 1961, he was still attempting to get in the door.

Cropper remembers seeing Curtis Green play at the Plantation Inn a number of times. "He used to play with his hands," smiles the lanky guitarist, "and play all these kind of Latin-African kind of percussion things. I'd seen him play a dozen times with the Veltones. I said, 'You're always making these big turns with the toms.' That wound up being the intro to 'Last Night.'"

"No one at Stax really believed in the band [as far] as being real professional musicians," relates Steve. "but they really liked the song 'Last Night.' The funny thing was we were probably the hottest band in Memphis, Tennessee. Every school wanted us for their proms and every club was trying to hire us to be a regular band." Chips Moman was one of those who didn't really believe in the band, which partially explains why the finished record included only Packy Axton and Wayne Jackson from the Mar-Keys. The rest of the group on the actual record was Smoochy Smith (who immediately became a member of the Mar-Keys), Curtis Green, Gilbert Caple, baritone saxophonist Floyd Newman, and bassist Lewie Steinberg. Much to Steve Cropper's chagrin, Moman also decided that "Last Night" didn't need a guitar and hence he does not appear on the record.[14]

As was the case with most of the black session musicians, Floyd Newman had come into Stax by way of the Satellite Record Shop. A native Memphian, Newman had long been an accomplished musician working the road with a Sam Cooke package tour that included Johnnie Taylor, Jerry Butler, and Dee Clark while he was still in college. He had also done some studio work with Jackie Brenston. A couple of years prior to the "Last Night" sessions, Newman had relocated to Detroit. Back in Memphis for a few days to visit his parents, who lived just a block away from Stax on College, he ran into a number of musicians he knew hanging out at the record shop. One thing led to another and Newman soon found himself playing sessions at Satellite by night while teaching high-school band in Mississippi by day. It is Newman who provides the spoken "last night" interpolations on the actual record.

Also supporting the notion that the song was recorded over several different days is the fact that—according to Jerry Wexler, Smoochy Smith, Duck Dunn, and Estelle Axton— early versions of the song did not have the tenor sax solo featured on the released 45.

---

13. Not Louis as has been commonly printed. This has been a matter that has irked Steinberg since day one.

14. It has been written that Cropper played organ on one part while Smith played piano. This is not borne out by listening to the record. In 1996, Cropper confirmed that this might have been on one of the earlier, unused takes.

Supposedly Wexler heard an early take and suggested that a sax solo be added.[15] Chips Moman flatly denies this. In any event, when a solo was deemed necessary, Gilbert Caple was given the job. This was the first solo he had ever recorded and consequently Caple was somewhat scared. "We worked so long that night that everybody got disgusted," sighs Caple. According to the saxophonist, the solo that is heard on the record was actually pieced together from several different attempts.

As convoluted as all this is, the net result was a popping twelve-bar blues-based instrumental. What is significant is that this relatively simple recording featured a racially integrated group sporting a hard-hitting drum sound, an emphasis on the low end of the pitch spectrum, organ (a Farfisa in this instance), and exceedingly prominent horns, all contributing to an enticing, swinging groove that was purely southern. All of these ingredients became essential to the sound of Memphis soul in the 1960s.

Released in June 1961 as Satellite 107 by the Mar-Keys, the record eventually hit number 2 on *Billboard*'s rhythm-and-blues charts and number 3 on the pop charts. According to Jim Stewart, it sold about one million copies. Ironically, neither Jim nor Chips Moman was all that enthralled with the recording; Jim in particular was unhappy with the fluctuations in tempo. If Estelle Axton's son had not been part of the group, the odds are good it would never have come out.

"The boys had put down this little instrumental," Estelle recalls, smiling. "Of course, Chips and my brother weren't too interested because 'Gee Whiz' had taken off and they were doing an album on Carla. So they didn't have time to worry about that instrumental. But, at that time instrumentals were doing pretty good because Bill Black had just come off a biggie with 'Smokie' [on Memphis's Hi Records]. My brother had gone far enough to get a dub made from the tape of ['Last Night']. He took it down to radio station WLOK. The first time that thing was played, customers were coming in and asking for it. They were saying, 'I don't know what it is but in it, it says "last night."' I thought, 'Oh my God, that's our record and it's only on tape.' Of course, I didn't tell the customer that. I wanted him to believe it was a record in the marketplace. The radio station began to get calls for it, 'Play it again.' This went on for three or four weeks. It was driving me nuts knowing that we had a hit back there and nothing was being done about it. It just upset me to no end."

As this scenario unfolded, Jim and Chips were up in Nashville, recording Carla's *Gee Whiz* album, with sessions scheduled around the college freshman's classes. By the time they returned to Memphis, the demand for the record had grown significantly. "Each day more and more people were calling for it," continued Estelle. "WLOK was just playing it and playing it and playing it. The more calls they got, the more they played it. Every time people would hear it, they'd be driving down the street and they'd stop and ask to get the record."

One night Estelle had all she could take. When her husband Everett came to pick her up at the end of the day, she informed him he would have to wait as she had some business to take care of. She headed back into the studio, where she cornered Jim and Chips. At first she tried to reason with them. When that didn't work, she turned on the tears, but that also was to no avail. Finally, she started swearing. "I don't do that very often and my brother had never heard me say a bad word, but I said some *ugly* words. It shocked him. It shocked him into putting the record out. I was trying in every way I could to get this to happen. In the end I got what I wanted. He said, 'I'll bet you a hundred dollars, it won't

---

15. Dunn thought that the song was originally recorded with just a rhythm section, and that Wexler had suggested that a horn section be added to the song.

hit.' Chips was sitting there so smug and he said, 'I'll take half of that.' I want you to know they never paid off that debt!"

Once the go-ahead was given to release the record, to everyone's horror it was discovered that the master tape was missing about sixteen bars off the front end. Apparently, the tape had been sent up to Nashville to be processed with what Smoochy Smith termed "German echo." Unbeknownst to anyone at Satellite, the Nashville cats had accidentally erased part of the tape. As improbable as it seems, Chips, Jim, and Wayne Jackson all recall digging through the trash basket at the studio for "Last Night" outtakes. "The guys dug in the garbage can," Wayne remembers, laughing, "and pulled out pieces of tape and played them until they found one that was really similar in feel and spliced them together!" Fortunately for Satellite, they were still so small that no one was designated to put out the trash on a regular basis. To this day Estelle insists she can still hear that splice.

Steve Cropper claims, "'Last Night' made it strictly for one reason: it was the first instrumental record that you could dance the twist to. It had that Hank Ballard twist beat. That's exactly why it was so popular. It was absolute perfect timing. Everybody was twisting to that song." In fact, Cropper remembers playing Dick Clark's "American Bandstand" television show in Philadelphia and watching the audience twist while the Mar-Keys mimed to the record.

Wayne Jackson points out another element that helped break the record. "The disc jockeys used to love that record. We left a hole in it with nothing. They got to say it ['last night']. It was a great gimmick." One such disc jockey was Memphis's Dewey Phillips, famed for being the first to play Elvis Presley on his "Red, Hot and Blue" show on Memphis station WHBQ. While WLOK may have broken the record for black Memphians, WHBQ did the honors for the white populace. Jackson claims, "Phillips made 'Last Night' happen. He played that record over and over. We sold three thousand records in Memphis, which was total saturation of the market. On the two-bar break Dewey could be heard hollering 'Open your Budweiser and pour it in. Freeze it and eat it.'"

Memphis had already established a bit of an instrumental tradition through Bill Justis's "Raunchy" on Sun in 1957, the Bill Black Combo's "Smokie" in 1960 on Hi, as well as with the repertoires of the leading local rhythm-and-blues bands of the time, such as those of Al Jackson, Sr., Ben Branch, and Willie Mitchell. "Last Night" was to be the first of a long line of hard-edged instrumental recordings by a number of Stax artists, including the Triumphs, the Barracudas, Sir Isaac and the Do-Dads, most significantly Booker T. and the MG's, and eventually the Bar-Kays.

Although Jim and Estelle had already recorded two hits, "Last Night" was the first big hit to have its chart run on Satellite Records. "Gee Whiz" was successful on a national level on Atlantic and the less-successful "Cause I Love You" had sold the majority of its copies on Atco. With such newfound national prominence for their name and logo, Jim and Estelle were to hear from a California organization that was already using the name Satellite Records.

"They wrote us and indicated that they'd be willing to sell the name to us for a lot of money," Jim Stewart recalls, laughing. "I didn't bother to respond. Satellite Records was always a name that I never really liked, but it was the only one we [could come up with] at the time." Jim was more than happy to give up using "Satellite." Luckily he and Estelle already had both a new name and logo in the works. They had originally conceived of "Stax" (the name was Jim's wife's idea: "St" from Stewart; "Ax" from Axton) as a subsidiary of Satellite. Now it became their main imprint, and "Last Night" was hastily reissued as the first record on the new label. To keep some continuity, its catalogue number, 107, was retained, meaning there were never records issued as Stax 100 through 106. The

Mar-Keys' lead singer, Ronnie Stoots (stage name Ronnie Angel), designed the now-famous Stax logo of a stack of dancing records.

The same month that "Last Night" was unleashed on an unsuspecting world, Rufus and Carla Thomas released their second duet, "I Didn't Believe." Oddly enough it was issued on Atco under the rather mysterious sobriquet "Rufus and Friend." A pleasant enough blues, it failed to make any waves. It was at Jerry Wexler's insistence that Carla appeared on Atlantic and Rufus on Atco. This irked Jim Stewart, who naturally wanted records by his two certified stars to be issued on his own labels. After "I Didn't Believe," a compromise was reached whereby Rufus's subsequent recordings would appear on Stax whereas Carla's would be released on Atlantic. This arrangement was to be maintained until the spring of 1965, when Atlantic and Stax finally negotiated a formal written contract. Beginning in May 1965 Carla Thomas's releases would appear under the Stax imprimatur as well.

In the meantime, before the California-based Satellite Records became aware of Jim Stewart's operation via the success of "Last Night," four other records had appeared on Satellite by Prince Conley, Nick Charles, Hoyt Johnson, and Barbara Stephens. Charles was a prominent Memphis pop disc jockey. In the words of Wayne Jackson, his records were strictly "a matter of payola." Johnson, whom Stewart had hooked up with through Erwin Ellis, was the last country artist Jim Stewart ever cut, while Prince Conley and Barbara Stephens both made records that continued Satellite's R&B direction. Produced by Chips Moman, the Conley record, "I'm Going Home," in particular, is a gem. Auspiciously, the Conley session was the first time Steve Cropper was hired as a session musician at Stax, while the Stephens' 45, "The Life I Live," features the songwriting debut at Stax of David Porter and Marvell Thomas.

You Don't Miss Your Water: 1961–1963

With "Last Night" tearing up the charts, a group was needed to go on the road and work the record. Although the piece had been recorded by a hybrid ensemble composed of the all-white Mar-Keys, Smoochy Smith, and black session musicians, it was the Mar-Keys' name that graced the record's label, the Mar-Keys' image, replete with new member Smoochy Smith, that was featured in all the company's promotional materials, and it was the Mar-Keys who were dispatched to fill the demand for gigs.

"We all got new suits out of the deal," says Wayne Jackson, "and a Chevrolet Greenbriar [van]. We were in the music business and I was in a hit band. I didn't know how little I knew about it at that time. I thought that was the way it was supposed to be. You go into the studio and do a song and it's supposed to sell records and you get money. I didn't know there was a back side to it. We didn't come up the hard way. I walked right in the front door."

Baritone saxophonist Floyd Newman, for one, resented the fact that the musicians who played on the record didn't reap the relatively lucrative money to be made out on the road. "Whoever made the decision, I don't know. All I know is that when they started traveling and making money, Gilbert Caple and I knew nothing about it. They didn't even mention it. They didn't even tell us that they were going to do none of this. That's the way it went down."

Newman also claims that Estelle's husband, Everett, took him aside prior to the record's release and told him that someone was trying to prevent him from getting a writer's royalty on "Last Night." Evidently "Lady A," as Estelle was commonly referred to,[1] took care of that problem, and the writing credit on the record ultimately read Smoochy Smith, Chips Moman, Packy Axton, Gilbert Caple, and Floyd Newman.

Most of the musicians on the scene then point out that in 1961 racial attitudes all but precluded the possibility of working the road as an integrated ensemble. Gilbert Caple recalls wondering how the company planned to promote the record given that both black and white musicians were involved. Terry Johnson simply states flat out, "Given the tenor of the times it had to either be a white band or a black band. It couldn't be a mixed band going out and playing in public." Consequently, although over half the former Royal Spades were replaced on the record by black session musicians, it probably never occurred to the band or the company that anyone besides the original all-white group plus Smoochy Smith should play the gigs.

---

1. Satellite Record Shop employee, engineer, and songwriter James Cross came up with Estelle's nickname. According to future Stax gadfly Johnny Keyes, "They said they did that because she's such a good detective, you couldn't put anything off on her."

Ironically, the same racial insanity that fed that sort of mind-set also created a certain amount of difficulty for the all-white road version of the Mar-Keys. Wayne Jackson explains, "We went over great in black clubs as soon as they found out that we were actually the Mar-Keys. [But] nobody believed we were the Mar-Keys when we'd [first show up] because we were all white. It was real strange, but once we started playing, it broke the barriers. Everybody loved it. We were a rhythm-and-blues, ass-kicking band."

Well, at least the majority of the group were. Smoochy Smith was much more at home with country music. "I wasn't accepted too well as part of the Mar-Keys," recalls Smith, "because they were city and I was country. Wayne and them looked at me as a countrified redneck. They didn't care for country music." "Smoochy was far beneath us in our minds," confirms Jackson. "He was real country and we were real slick. We had Beatle boots and we were real cool guys." Jackson goes on to add that Smith did have one endearing quality. A few years older than the rest of the gang, "he was the only one that could actually walk in a liquor store and buy whiskey. That was an asset!" Smith lasted only nine months with the group before permanently casting his fate in the world of Memphis country and western.

The Mar-Keys' first gig was in Birmingham, where Duke Rumour on WVOK had spun their record all the way to the number 1 spot for three consecutive weeks. All told the Mar-Keys would play three times for Rumour, but this first time was an eye-opener. "We tore them up, man," states Jackson, still shaking his head. "It was like the Beatles. We'd leave the stage at the back through the alley and there would be hundreds of black kids back there hollering and screaming and the cops were standing there. It was a thrill for a kid from Arkansas, let me tell you. Outrageous!"

Both Jim and Estelle were along for the ride, so a total of nine people were packed into one Chevrolet Greenbriar. "Jim would take nerve pills," continues Wayne, "and we would drink whiskey! Jim was an accountant and an introvert at heart. Estelle was like all of ours mama and we were just a bunch of heathens. There was no reason to have any discipline." Estelle concurs, "I traveled with those guys some and I'm telling you, they'd drive you crazy. That bunch did anything."

After Birmingham, it was on to Detroit, then the Dick Clark show in Philadelphia, followed by a week-long gig at the Regal in Chicago. The latter was Chicago's equivalent of New York's famed Apollo Theater. Second billed to LaVern Baker, for a bunch of white guys in love with black music, this was simply la-la land. Life just didn't get any better.

By and large the Mar-Keys were living out their fantasies, having a wild and crazy time, but it wasn't all pie in the sky. Steve Cropper quite quickly had enough. "Yeah, I got pissed at the way they were doing business. I couldn't handle it. With all due respect to all of them, they were just like a bunch of monkeys out there. Jesus Christ! It was the first time on the road and these guys just went berserk." Everything came to a head at the Showbar in Bossier City, Louisiana. "It all came out of a little fight onstage," continues Cropper. "[Packy] got to cussing onstage and people were sitting around. It was kind of rude. So I pulled him into the bathroom and I said, 'Well, you've been wanting the band anyway, it's yours. You want it that bad, you got it. I'll see you later.'"

Steve and Packy had been jockeying for position for some time now, and Steve had begun to feel he wasn't getting complete support from all the band members. Wayne Jackson suggests that there wasn't a consensus among the Mar-Keys as to who was actually the leader. "Steve did think it was his band but it really was Packy's," opines Jackson. "Because of Miss Axton we got a break. Packy's mama got us in the recording studio and we made a record. Damn right he was the bandleader! Packy was also pretty drunk and irresponsible. There was a syndrome that was going on back then, sort of like 'Who gives a shit anyway,' and Packy was right into it. Packy was the type that would say, 'Ah, fuck it,' and walk off. And we needed a bandleader so Steve *would* call some shots but Packy was still considered to be the ringleader."

The Mar-Keys quickly summoned Charlie Freeman to fill in for Cropper. Freeman immediately joined the group for gigs in Texas and Florida while Steve headed home and began working full-time for Estelle in the Satellite Record Shop. Although he was no longer playing in the band on the road, he continued to participate in most of their recordings.

Back at Stax, records were being issued at a fast and furious pace. The Mar-Keys released followups to "Last Night" in September, October, and November. The November release, "Foxy," was just one of six 45s issued by the company that month. This is pretty astounding, since there were only two previous occasions when there had been more than one release in a given month.

Two of November's releases were notable, the first of which was issued on a new label. With the Stax name firmly in place as the company's primary designation, Jim and Estelle had decided that a second name and logo were needed for a subsidiary label. This was a standard move within the record industry.[2] One of the Satellite Record Shop's employees suggested the name Volt for the new label, and came up with a red and black lightning design. The first release on Volt was an instrumental effort written and engineered by Chips Moman. Sometime in late summer 1961 Chips had begun playing around town in an interracial instrumental group called the Triumphs. Membership was somewhat fluid, some gigs including a horn section comprised of Floyd Newman and Gilbert Caple, other gigs being done with a stripped-down format of bass, drums, guitar, and keyboards with Chips taking care of all the guitar work. Named after Moman's red TR-3 Triumph automobile, the Triumphs were the first interracial group in Memphis that anyone can remember. "I caught a lot of heat from it," recalls Chips. "But, hey, I didn't see anything wrong with it. To me a musician's a musician."

Needless to say, bookings were not plentiful, although, after a while, the Tiki Club on Summer proved reasonably hospitable. When the Triumphs recorded Volt 100, "Burnt Biscuits" backed with "Raw Dough," Howard Grimes (later of the Hi Rhythm Section) was the drummer, Marvell Thomas held down the piano chair, Booker T. Jones played organ, and Lewie Steinberg was featured on bass. Moman played guitar on the B-side only because, given the fact that everything was recorded and mixed live in one take, it was virtually impossible for him to engineer and play on the same session.

Released in November 1961, "Burnt Biscuits" did well in both Memphis and New Orleans, selling about thirty thousand copies in the latter city alone. Although this proved enough to get the record charted in *Record World,* elsewhere it died a quick death, and the Triumphs as such never attempted a followup. As an interracial instrumental ensemble, however, in many respects the Triumphs were the forerunners of what became known as Booker T. and the MG's.

The same month the Triumphs' record fell upon an impassive public, Moman engineered the debut release by William Bell, a seminal 12/8 country-soul ballad entitled "You Don't Miss Your Water." Born in 1939, Bell had grown up in Memphis infatuated by Nat King Cole and Sam Cooke. At the age of sixteen he entered and won a talent contest at Memphis's annual Mid-South fair. First prize was five hundred dollars (big money in the early 1950s) and a trip to Chicago to sing at Club Delisa for a weekend with the Red

---

2. The reasoning behind it was that a given radio station might be willing to play one Stax record as well as one release under a different label name at the same time, whereas it would be unlikely to play two Stax releases simultaneously. To deal with this situation Motown had the Tamla, Gordy, and Soul labels; Atlantic used the name Atco for its subsidiary; Chess Records had three subsidiaries in Checker, Cadet, and Argo; and so on.

Saunders Band. Saunders, in turn, recommended the child prodigy to Phineas Newborn, Sr., with whom William gigged on and off for the next five years, the first several years with his group the Del-Rios, the final year as a solo act. For two of those summers, Newborn's band found itself in the unlikely circumstance of touring with the Paul Miller Circus, with William singing material such as "A Pretty Girl Is Like a Melody" to accompany the trapeze artist routines!

The Del-Rios were one of the hottest vocal groups in Memphis, rivaling the Veltones in local popularity. Bell's 1955 talent-contest triumph entitled the group to an audition for Les Bihari's Meteor label, resulting in a solitary 78 release. Bell wrote both "Alone on a Rainy Night" and its flip side, "Lizzie," accompaniment being provided by Rufus Thomas's Bear Cats. Seven years later, in June 1962, the Del-Rios' second release, "Just Across the Street" b/w "There's a Love," appeared on Stax. At the time of their Stax release, the group consisted of Louis Williams, who was later the lead singer in the Ovations, Johnny Jackson, Harrison Austin, and William Bell.[3]

Both the Del-Rios and William Bell signed with Stax on Moman's recommendation. The initial contact came via the Satellite Record Shop, where Bell was a regular customer ("It was like a teen hangout"). In the waning days of the summer of 1960, Chips heard the Del-Rios sing at the Flamingo Club, where the group had a residency with Gene "Bowlegs" Miller's band. Moman was impressed and suggested that Bell record something on his own. Surprisingly, Bell didn't jump at the opportunity. In fact, he wavered for over a year while debating the pluses and minuses of a career in music versus being a doctor. Before coming to a final decision, he went to New York to play what was supposed to be a six-week gig with Phineas Newborn's Orchestra. The gig was extended to three months, and Bell, feeling somewhat homesick, penned "You Don't Miss Your Water."

Upon his return to Memphis, Bell informed Moman that he was ready to record, and a session was slated at 926 E. McLemore for what the singer thought was to be a demo recording of his new song. The band consisted of what was, in essence, the Triumphs: Marvell Thomas (piano), Booker T. Jones (organ),[4] Lewie Steinberg (bass), and Ron Capone (drums). The "demo" completed, Moman decided to press it. Ironically, when first released the rather ordinary pop-sounding "Formula of Love" was designated the A-side. Once deejays began flipping the record, "You Don't Miss Your Water" broke first in New Orleans, then Pensacola, Florida, and finally in Memphis. It never reached *Billboard*'s national R&B charts, but that is somewhat misleading because, at the time, *Billboard* was paying only cursory attention to southern radio and retail outlets. Curiously, the 45 did manage to struggle its way up to number 95 on the pop charts, and it eventually sold about 200,000 copies.

When the Triumphs and William Bell singles were cut, Chips Moman was engineering as Jim Stewart was mired at his desk in the trust department of the First National Bank. Moman's job was basically to open the studio each day, audition any prospective talent, work up new material, and record demos. Things at Stax were pretty loose at the time. On any given day jazz great Phineas Newborn, Jr., would drop by, sit down at the piano in the studio and play for hours. Moman would just sit back and soak it all up. Future songwriting great David Porter was also a regular visitor. Porter was working across the street bag-

---

3. Later Soul Children member Norman West joined shortly after the record was issued.

4. Not Spooky Butler as has been previously printed. One has to surmise that if Chips Moman and Jim Stewart had not had a falling out in the spring of 1962 and Chips had continued to serve as de facto A&R and production assistant at Stax, this lineup, with Howard Grimes instead of Capone on drums, would probably have evolved into the Stax house band. There is no denying that this would have been a fine studio ensemble, but it is hard to imagine Stax or soul music without Steve Cropper, Duck Dunn, and Al Jackson.

ging groceries at Jones' Big D. When his shift was over, it was straight across the street, where he tried to impress his singing and songwriting talents on anyone who would listen. Both Steve Cropper and Chips Moman vividly recall Porter attempting to cut "The Old Grey Mare" on several occasions. "He wanted to be Jerry Butler worse than Jerry Butler did," offers Moman. The beauty of Stax was that while "The Old Grey Mare" never did get released, Porter could come back day in and day out, honing his skills to the point where he would eventually cowrite classics such as "Soul Man" and "When Something Is Wrong with My Baby."

In early 1962, as William Bell worked the road in support of "You Don't Miss Your Water," the Mar-Keys became the first Stax artists to have an LP released. Naturally, the album was called *Last Night* (Atlantic 8055) and contained their first three singles, "Last Night," "The Morning After," and "About Noon." The rest of the album was comprised of material from their stage show, including instrumental versions of Paul Anka's "Diana," Errol Garner's "Misty," Ray Charles's "Sticks and Stones," Roy Hamilton's "Ebb Tide," Cannonball Adderley's "Sack O Woe," and Bill Doggett's "Hold It," along with a couple of originals entitled "Night Before" and "One Degree North." "Sack O Woe," with the

spelling changed to "Sack-O-Woe," would be released as a single in October 1962.

Within a few weeks of the Mar-Keys' debut LP, Carla Thomas also issued her first full-length album. Entitled *Gee Whiz* (Atlantic 8057), the album included both of her first two singles along with originals by Chips Moman and Carla and Rufus Thomas, covers of records by the Drifters and the Five Satins, and a handful of Tin Pan Alley standards such as "A Lovely Way to Spend an Evening" and her featured number as a WDIA Teen-Towner, "The Masquerade Is Over."

The Carla Thomas album appeared on Atlantic rather than Stax due to the agreement reached between Stewart and Wexler, but it seems curious that the Mar-Keys' LP would also appear on Atlantic rather than Stax. Jim Stewart explains:

Carla Thomas proudly displaying her first LP in the Satellite Record Shop. COURTESY MARK STANSBURY.

"Jerry Wexler was doing a good sales job on me. I was still a little country boy down here in Memphis, Tennessee, and hadn't been schooled in the ways of the record industry. Jerry said the Atlantic label had identification out in the marketplace and in order to sell albums you need that and blah, blah, blah. He said, 'If you put it on Stax, it's not going to mean anything. It's all right to put out a single on Stax, but these albums should go on Atlantic.'" More than a quarter century later, Wexler stands by the concept: "We wanted to get the best shot from our distributors with label familiarity." He also insists that this is why he wanted the Carla Thomas singles to come out on Atlantic. In the early 1960s full-length albums were relatively unimportant in both R&B and rock and roll. *Last Night,* the Mar-Keys' followup LP, *Do the Pop-Eye* (Atlantic 8062), and Thomas's *Gee Whiz* all failed to chart. "You couldn't sell black LPs much anyway," Stewart says with a shrug.[5]

Not too long after the *Last Night* and *Gee Whiz* albums were issued, Chips Moman left the company. His departure is surrounded by recrimination and hearsay. Estelle suggested to Peter Guralnick that Chips misappropriated both funds and credits, while she told me that the major problem was that Chips wanted to run the whole company. Jim told me that it was obvious that Chips and Estelle could not work together and that one or the other simply had to go. Chips told me that, as far as he was concerned, he and Jim had a verbal agreement to share in the label's ownership. "We were partners," the retired producer states emphatically. "I was going to have twenty-five percent of that company." Chips further claims that he thought Jim would have sole ownership of the remaining 75 percent. "I didn't know that the rest of it was him *and* Estelle! After we changed the name from Satellite to Stax, which was for <u>St</u>ewart/<u>Ax</u>ton, I knew that things wasn't right for me." Estelle vehemently denies that Chips was ever promised any equity. Jim Stewart simply says that at this late date he cannot remember.

"I had gone to Jim, and he said that he's fucking me out of it," insists Moman. "[So] I walked out." By happenstance, Wayne Jackson was curled up on a couch just outside the studio door, unbeknownst to both Jim and Chips, and consequently he heard the whole deal go down. "I was there when Jim Stewart told Chips, 'I fucked you and if you can prove it fine and if you can't . . . I'm the bookkeeper and I've got the money.' Chips said, 'Well, fuck you. If you need it that bad, keep it' and walked out the door. That's when Chips stormed out of the studio. That's the last time he ever went in there. I was sitting on the couch looking up with my mouth open. This was when the money started coming in. Chips didn't get what he thought he should have got and Jim said, 'Fuck you.' I don't know who was in the wrong or exactly what precipitated that conversation."

Eventually Chips hired Seymour Rosenberg, a lawyer by day and music-biz raconteur by night, and ended up with a $3,000 settlement. "I think a deal was cut myself," muses Moman. "The fact is who would settle for that?" Moman went through some very rough times in the ensuing couple of years, eventually being foreclosed on by the bank and losing his house on Mink Road. Ironically he would then form a partnership with Rosenberg and resurrect himself as co-owner of the American Studio and the Youngstown and Penthouse labels. By the end of 1963 he had recorded the debut release of Isaac Hayes. During the course of the 1960s both Moman and Rosenberg would again figure into the Stax story.

With Chips gone, Steve Cropper started spending every moment he could in the studio. For quite some time he had been hankering for Moman's job and was already something of a recording veteran, having played sessions for Sun, Pepper-Tanner, and Duke-Peacock. Reliable to a fault and obsessed with learning everything there was to know about the studio, Cropper had the personality, temperament, inclination, and musical skill for the position. On a daily basis Cropper maintained the equipment, ran the board for demo sessions, and auditioned prospective talent, but Jim Stewart seemed to be in no great hurry to hire him. "Estelle was why I was there," stresses Steve. "She's the one that hired me. She literally put her foot down and said [to Jim], 'You're gonna start paying him. He's in the studio more than he is in the record shop. I'm not gonna pay him anymore.

---

5. Further demonstrating how relatively unimportant LPs were to Stax in the 1960s, neither Carla Thomas nor the Mar-Keys would have subsequent LPs issued until May 1966. Only 42 albums were released by Stax during the first nine years of the label's existence; in contrast, between June 1968 and the end of 1975, 205 albums appeared on Stax and its associated labels. That said, *Billboard* did note in the November 27, 1961, issue "the growing importance of hit singles in the album field," citing the Mar-Keys' *Last Night* as an example.

You're gonna start paying him.' I started getting fifty dollars a week from Jim Stewart instead of Estelle [after that conversation]."

Most of the next nine years of Cropper's life were devoted to Stax Records. Keys to the studio in hand, he would open up 926 E. McLemore each morning while Jim still reported to work at the bank. Part of Cropper's duties soon involved running a jingle business that was an offshoot of the record label. With a guy named Bowman hustling up clients, the Stax studio was regularly used to record commercials and station IDs for several local radio stations on a small Sony seven-and-a-half ips tape recorder. While bringing in some badly needed funds to the company, this little operation afforded Cropper the opportunity to hone his engineering and tape-editing skills.

According to Wayne Jackson, it was when Cropper took over from Moman that Stax Records "became more rhythm and blues" oriented.

Part of Steve's job was running Saturday morning auditions. "People would call during the week and say, 'I've got a song I want you to hear.' Rather than say, 'No, we don't solicit material' or 'We don't have time,' we would say, 'Okay.' It was almost like an appointment thing. 'Come down Saturday between the hours of dah-dah and dah-dah and we'll try to see what you got.' A lot of it was so obviously amateurish that nothing could be done and then every once in a while there was something we'd try to do something with."

No major artists ever came out of these sessions and, over time, they became more songwriting than artist auditions. One notable composition that found its way to Otis Redding via this process was Roosevelt Jamison's "That's How Strong My Love Is." By late 1964, this custom had pretty well petered out, but while they lasted the Saturday morning auditions were one more means by which Stax, in its earliest days, stayed close to the local community.

Stax sessions were generally held either in the late afternoon and early evening, after Jim Stewart got off work at the bank, or on the weekend. A weekend session for rockabilly dynamo Billy Lee Riley, scheduled for a particularly hot Sunday in mid-summer 1962, gave birth to one of Stax's most enduring and important acts, Booker T and the MG's. Stewart booked Cropper, bassist Lewie Steinberg, keyboardist Booker T. Jones, and drummer Al Jackson to provide Riley's accompaniment. Jones had previously contributed his baritone sax skills to Rufus and Carla's "Cause I Love You" while playing organ on the Triumphs and William Bell releases. It was Floyd Newman who had pulled Jim's coat to Booker's keyboard abilities. It was a fortuitous suggestion.

Booker was born November 12, 1944, and raised in Memphis, attending the same church as William Bell, Mount Olive Cathedral at Linden and Lauderdale. His father was a science teacher at Booker T. Washington High School, and consequently Booker grew up in a relatively stable, lower-middle-class milieu. A multi-instrumentalist, Booker's parents initially bought him a little tin drum, then a ukulele, a baritone ukulele, and, when he was ten, a clarinet. In school he learned to play bass, oboe, saxophone, and trombone, and eventually gravitated to piano, finally picking up organ at church. A child prodigy, while still a teenager Booker was hired initially on baritone sax and then later to play bass in Willie Mitchell's band at the Flamingo Room. The drummer in Mitchell's band was Al Jackson, Jr. Booker went on to play bass in Bowlegs Miller's band. Simultaneously he formed a combo with fellow Booker T. Washington students Maurice White (later to form Earth, Wind and Fire) and David Porter to play places like the Elks Club on Beale Street. Known informally as the Booker T. Washington Combo, the group specialized in doo-wop with Jones playing guitar.

At the time of the Riley session, Booker had literally just graduated from high school. Previously, his daily routine consisted of going to school, delivering his paper route, and finally heading down to Stax to play sessions until about nine o'clock. Not surprisingly, at his school convocation ceremony, the high school bands of Memphis gave him a trophy. He would become a mainstay at Stax through 1969. "I liked Booker's style," offers Stewart, "and I liked his attitude. He was very businesslike, and I like dependable people. Even when I'm in the studio, the business side of me is still down there, and I don't want a lot of crap, [such as] external problems with personalities, conflicts, whatever. I want people around me who are serious about what we're doing."

Lewie Steinberg and Al Jackson were both a bit older than Jones and Cropper. Seasoned players, their roots ran deep in the Memphis black music scene. Both were progeny of musical families. Steinberg's father had long held down the piano chair at famed Pee Wee's Saloon on Beale Street. While Steinberg was becoming proficient on first upright and then electric bass, his brother Luther became a professional trumpeter with jazz vibist Lionel Hampton; brother Morris played alto sax with Hampton and later with B. B. King and Bobby Bland; sister Nan left Memphis in the 1930s to work the road as a vocalist with both Fats Waller and Andy Kirk; and another brother, Wilbur, also played bass professionally and, in fact, had played on Carla and Rufus's "Cause I Love You." Steinberg played his first professional gigs with Ike Piron and violinist Uncle Dick Ross. He later joined Willie Mitchell's and Phineas Newborn's bands and made his first recording session with Joe Dobbins in the mid-fifties for Home of the Blues. Steinberg continued to play a number of local studio dates, most notably on Ace Cannon's monster early 1962 instrumental release on Hi, "Tuff," and Willie Cobb's influential "You Don't Love Me" issued on Home of the Blues. He was brought to Stax by tenor saxophonist Gilbert Caple during the "Last Night" sessions.

Both Booker T. and Steinberg had played alongside drummer extraordinaire Al Jackson in Willie Mitchell's band and were anxious to get him into Stax. As fate would have it, what became the first MG's session was also Jackson's debut at the label. Destined at birth to be a musician, Jackson was the son of Al Jackson, Sr., who for years had led one of Memphis's most distinguished black orchestras. Inclined toward big bands under his father's influence, Al Junior's idol was Sonny Payne, who held down the drum chair in the Count Basie Orchestra; he also admired Art Blakey and Philly Joe Jones. Jackson's initial playing experience was in his father's band.[6] Personnel in Memphis's four or five major black ensembles tended to be somewhat fluid, and Jackson went on to play in both Willie Mitchell's and Ben Branch's bands alongside Booker T. Apparently he was a tough taskmaster. "He yelled at me a lot as a teenager," related Booker. "I got a job in Bowlegs' band playing bass with Al and I'd be standing right in front of him. He'd be right behind me onstage and he could yell. 'You little young **** can't you get on the beat!' I mean he was really adamant about that stuff. He'd fuss at me after."

It was Booker who suggested he be brought into Stax. "I said, 'You guys need to know about Al.' He was the best drummer in town, I had been trying to steal him for a good while. So, we got him to come over to Stax for a session." It didn't take much to convince the crew at Stax. Steve and Duck had both heard him play with Willie Mitchell. "Al Jackson almost caused a divorce for me," recounts Duck. "I'd play at this little old all-white hillbilly club after I'd work at King Records. Al played at the Manhattan Club with Willie and on the way home I'd stop in there and he'd just mesmerize you. I'd get off at one o'clock and they got off at four and I'd come dragging in at about five in the morning being accused of being out with other women and all this kind of stuff. All I was doing was sitting there watching Al. He was that good!" "One session with Al," continues Steve,

---

6. When Booker was ten years old, he heard Al playing in this band at Lincoln Park.

"and we knew that we had to have that drummer. Booker was the one that went and begged him and offered him everything to get him to come over."

Al was loath to commit to anyone other than Willie Mitchell, reasoning that he would always make more money playing live than he would in the studio. Consequently, he wouldn't even consider working sessions at Stax without a guaranteed regular salary. "We weren't used to that," exclaims Steve. "I mean, we worked there. It was sort of like an honorary system. We got paid for work but nobody was salaried. I was salaried through the record shop, not through the studio. I think Al was probably the first guy that was actually hired on a weekly salary."

Over the years various people have suggested that Billy Lee Riley didn't show up for the session, others have claimed he was either drunk or did not have adequate material. Cropper is sure that they actually did cut two or three tracks with Riley that day. "We were sitting around waiting after the last cut," recalls Steve, "to find out if we were gonna do another take. Billy and Jim decided that was it, that was good enough for what Billy wanted, and when Jim went to hit the talkback to tell us, 'Hey guys, that's it, go home' we were just jamming on this blues thing."

Jim liked what he heard, grabbed another piece of tape, hit the record button, and caught the tail end of the first take. He then informed the session players that he wanted them to take it from the top and proceeded to record the second complete run-through of the song. "We didn't even know he was recording it," continues Cropper.

The slow blues Booker, Al, Steve, and Lewie were working on was a tune that Booker and Al had played many a night down at the Flamingo Room on Hernando just off Beale Street. Stewart was impressed and immediately deemed it releasable. What was now needed was a B-side. A couple of weeks earlier Booker had been fooling around with a riff in the studio that had caught Steve's fancy. When no one else had any other suggestions, Cropper said to Booker, "Hey, you remember that riff you were playing a couple of weeks ago?" About thirty minutes later, after a couple of run-throughs and two takes on tape, the group had cut what we now know as "Green Onions." The slashing chords that Cropper plays in the intro were originally positioned in the second half of his solo. It was Jim Stewart who suggested they be moved to the intro and that Cropper play a variation of them on the solo. On both sides of the record as well as on Stax recordings for the next couple of years, Booker was playing a used Hammond M-1 spinet organ that Jim had bought privately out of an older woman's living room. The M-1 had an octave and a half worth of plastic foot pedals and an eight-inch speaker by the knee rather than the large separate Leslie speaker that is the hallmark of Booker's eventual organ of choice, the Hammond B-3.

"I knew when we cut 'Green Onions,'" exclaims Cropper. "I said, 'Shit, this is the best damn instrumental I've heard in I don't know when.' I knew we had a winner there." Jim wasn't so sure; to his mind, the slow blues was the meal ticket. In any event, he thought that Cropper should get some dubs made of both sides. On Monday Steve scooted over to the Phillips recording studio, where he had former Elvis Presley guitarist Scotty Moore make two acetates of both cuts.

"I came back to the record shop that afternoon," Cropper recalls, "and we started listening to it and realized that 'Green Onions' was incredible. It was so danceable. Jim Stewart was still working at the bank at that time so he wasn't around for that conversation. I left one dub there for Jim to hear that night. The next morning I got up and I was at the radio station [WLOK] at seven o'clock in the morning. [Disc jockey] Reuben Washington was on the drive time. We were very good friends and I had brought stuff down to him before. I said, 'You got to hear something.' He was playing another record and he went over to his other turntable and he listened to the intro and maybe four bars of it. He said, 'Wait a minute,' stopped the other record that he was playing, started at the top, and hit it. He played it over and over for about half an hour and the phones just lit up. They *literally* lit up. When I got back to the record shop about nine o'clock and opened up, the phones were ringing off the wall. People were wanting to know where they could get this new record that they had just heard on 'LOK. That's how we broke the record."[7]

A hit record on their hands, titles were needed for both tunes, and a name was needed for the group. Interestingly, when they were trying to come up with titles for the songs, they initially decided to call the blues "Onions." (Steinberg says the title was actually "Funky Onions.") "We were trying to think of something that was as funky as possible," laughs Cropper. "I think Lewie Steinberg was the one that said, 'Well, the funkiest thing I ever heard of was onions.' To him they were funky because they were stinky."

After the testing of the market via WLOK, it was clear that the faster tune should be the A-side. The "Onions" tag was then switched from the blues to the dance tune, with Steve suggesting it actually be called "Green Onions." "I said 'Green Onions' is a much funkier title. People like eating green onions but how many people can stand wild onions in their front yard because they are stinky. I just thought 'onions' [by itself] was a little negative." Steinberg thought that it was Estelle who had suggested "Green." Apparently she regularly suggested titles. In the case of the slow blues side Estelle recalls saying, "That sounds like somebody making love and the lady says to the man, 'behave yourself!' Thus was born the title of what became the B-side, "Behave Yourself."

A year previous, "Burnt Biscuits" by the Triumphs had made quite a bit of noise locally and in New Orleans. With another food title for this release, it seemed logical to use another car name for the group; hence; the MG's. Unfortunately, when Atlantic's legal department attempted to clear the name, the MG company vociferously stated that in no way, shape, or form did they want to be associated with popular music. The group elected to use the name anyway, stating in a brief profile in *Billboard* that September that the name stood for "Memphis Group."

Originally issued as Volt 102, "Green Onions" began to sell like hotcakes. Cropper immediately jumped in his car and proceeded to stop at every radio station within a two-hundred-mile radius of Memphis, promoting the record in towns such as Little Rock, Jackson, Tennessee, Brownsville, Jackson, Mississippi, and Tupelo by handing out promo copies and talking up the disc. His efforts paid off, and within two or three weeks Jerry Wexler phoned from Atlantic and said, "Hey guys, this looks like it could really be a big one. You oughta put it on Stax Records and get it off Volt." Wexler's logic was that Volt was a young unknown label that didn't really matter. Stax had some momentum with "Last Night" and "You Don't Miss Your Water" and could use a further boost.

To facilitate the transfer to Stax, Cropper had to cut new parts and rush them down to the pressing plant at Plastic Products and get new stampers pressed up. The turnover took all of three days. By this point, Stax and Atlantic had enough faith in the record that they took a display ad upon its rerelease as Stax 127 in the August 4, 1962, issue of *Billboard*. The same issue mentioned "Green Onions" in a list of singles with "strong sales poten-

---

7. Stax always maintained a very close relationship with a variety of jocks on WLOK. WDIA was a little more difficult to work with as it maintained stricter policies with regard to what records could be played on a given show. Reuben Washington would continue to actively support Stax after he left WLOK for a station in Texas.

tial." "Green Onions" would go on to become a number 1 rhythm-and-blues record and a number 3 pop hit, selling about 700,000 copies over the next few months. As the record ascended the charts, Stax decided to record a full album by Booker T. and the MG's. Also titled *Green Onions* (Stax 701), it was the first album released on the Stax label itself. Whereas neither the first two Mar-Keys LP's nor Carla Thomas's debut long player had charted, *Green Onions* peaked at number 33 on *Billboard*'s "Top LP" chart. In addition to the title cut, the LP included the B-side, "Behave Yourself," and a subsequent single, "Mo' Onions" (Stax 142), as well as a number of covers of popular R&B songs.

Somewhere in this period, Jim Stewart was visited by leaders of the Memphis chapter of the NAACP. "They wanted to know who I was," recounts Stewart, "and what I was all about. They probably were suspicious and had every right to be, as to what my intentions were and if the black people would be treated as they should in the company. Beyond just being a writer or a singer, would they ever be in a capacity of management and have any real power in the company. Of course, obviously, [that happened]. But they had no way of knowing that [in the early days]."

Meanwhile, as "Green Onions" scampered up the charts, Stax lucked into one of the greatest soul singers of all time. Otis Redding was born in Dawson, Georgia, September 9, 1941. Three years later, Otis's family moved to Macon, where his father doubled as a part-time preacher while earning his living at the local Air Force base. Otis Senior soon became too ill to work regularly, leaving Otis, his mother Fanny, his four sisters, and one brother to eke out a living as best they could. By the tenth grade, Otis had left school, helping to support the family as a well digger, gas station attendant, and sometimes as a working musician.

Otis had started playing drums in school, and he could be found every Sunday morning at the studio of Macon radio station WIBB playing behind a series of gospel groups, earning six dollars for each morning's work. He also sang in a gospel quartet as a teenager, developing rudimentary guitar and piano skills along the way. In 1958 Otis went on the road as a vocalist with the Upsetters, fellow Maconite Little Richard's former band. That same year Otis entered local deejay Hamp Swain's Teenage Party contest at Macon's Douglas Theatre.[8] Winning several weeks in a row (often singing Elvis Presley songs), Otis met two key figures in his life: his future wife, Zelma; and guitarist and showman extraordinaire Johnny Jenkins. Subsequent to teaming up with Jenkins, Otis met the guitarist's unlikely young manager, Phil Walden, a white teenager enthralled with the R&B scene then busting loose in Macon. At that point, all the factors crucial to Otis's development, save for a record contract, were in place.

In mid-1960 Otis spent time in Los Angeles, staying with his sister, washing cars, and in July cutting four songs, "She's Alright," "Tuff Enuff," "I'm Gettin' Hip," and "Gamma Lamma."[9] Back in Macon in late April 1962, Redding recorded a second single, this time for Bobby Smith's Confederate label, coupling a rewrite of "Gamma Lamma," titled "Shout Bamalama," with "Fat Girl." Both sides were cut in Athens, Georgia, at the local PBS station with white R&B eccentric Wayne Cochran on bass. "Shout Bamalama" found allies in legendary southern deejay John R., who played it extensively on Nashville's

---

8. Such amateur shows were staple fare within black urban communities well into the 1960s, providing one of the few avenues by which black talent could develop seasoning and be discovered. Rufus Thomas hosted the Memphis version at the Palace Theatre on Beale Street.

9. The first two were released in 1960 on Trans World 6908; the other songs would be issued in early 1968 shortly after Redding's death.

WLAC, and locally in Hamp Swain, who featured it on his "Night Ride" show on WIBB. Elsewhere, however, it was a dud, and by the summer of 1962 it was history.[10]

By spring 1962 Otis had become a permanent member of Johnny Jenkins's band, the Pinetoppers. Although Otis handled the majority of the group's vocals, Jenkins was without a doubt the group's star. Playing guitar left-handed and upside down, his acrobatics caused pandemonium nightly. When James Newton—a banker who also owned a small Atlanta-based label, Tifco Records—heard the Pinetoppers, he was strictly interested in recording the star on an instrumental record. The resulting record, "Love Twist" backed with a rocking B-side, "Pinetop," was badly recorded, but a high level of enthusiasm comes through loud and clear. It captured local attention courtesy of Macon deejay Frank Clark of radio station WNEX. Atlantic Records' southern promotion rep Joe Galkin then picked up the record for his own Gerald label, eventually moving twenty-five thousand copies in the Southeast before leasing the master to Atlantic in September 1961.

"Love Twist" did not sell well enough to entice Atlantic to pick up Jenkins's option. Galkin then went to Jim Stewart and suggested that, given Stax's recent success with instrumental records, Stax would be the perfect label to release a followup. The session proved momentous for all concerned with the ironic exception of Johnny Jenkins. The oft-repeated legend is that Otis was Johnny Jenkins's chauffeur and/or valet at this time. When things didn't work out for Jenkins at the session and forty minutes remained on the clock, Otis asked if he could have a chance at recording a song. This has always seemed dubious because Otis, by this time, had been a regular performing member with the Pinetoppers for nearly four years. Phil Walden explains: "The plan was to make this followup for Johnny Jenkins but also to give Otis a chance to sing. That was my understanding with Joe Galkin. I said, 'Otis, if you get a shot, you got to do it just as fast as you can 'cause you probably won't have much time.' Of course, they didn't know [that this was the plan] and thank God Joe was there 'cause it probably wouldn't have happened if he hadn't been." In other words, Otis's "chance" was very carefully arranged by Phil Walden in cahoots with Joe Galkin, a far cry from the romantic intercession of fate it was always purported to be. For the record, Otis was behind the wheel on the drive from Macon to Memphis because Jenkins didn't have a driver's license.

Things did not go very well with the new Johnny Jenkins material, though two songs, "Spunky" b/w "Bashful Guitar," were released on Volt Records two years later. When everybody finally gave up on Jenkins, Otis did get his shot, although Joe Galkin had to give Stax co-owner Jim Stewart half the publishing on Otis's songs as an inducement to make the record.[11] By this point, keyboard player Booker T. Jones had already left the session, leaving guitarist Steve Cropper to play piano while Jenkins handled the guitar.

The first song Otis cut was an unabashed Little Richard cop, "Hey Hey Baby." At that point Jim Stewart looked at Galkin and suggested that the world didn't really need another Little Richard. Galkin responded by assuring Jim that Otis had a ballad that he had written two years earlier that would knock him out. Entitled "These Arms of Mine," it turned out to be the first in a series of increasingly stunning 6/8 ballads that Otis would record over the next five years. This first time out, Otis sounded nervous and somewhat tentative, his early trademark vocal quaver clearly evident. The cut ended with Otis semi-talking his way

---

10. Sometime during this period, Otis also worked with a phony set of Drifters. Apparently, he could sound uncannily like Clyde McPhatter and, with Johnny Jenkins, often performed Clyde's Drifters standard, "Money Honey."

11. While Galkin gave Stewart half of the publishing on Otis's compositions, he made Stewart give him half of Stax's share of the royalties Atlantic paid out on Otis's record sales.

Otis Redding circa 1966. COURTESY DEANIE PARKER.

through a dramatic ad lib that turns an otherwise good, but routine, ballad into a memorable performance. "It was different," recalls Stewart. "But I don't think anybody really jumped up and down and said we've discovered a superstar. We were all tired and bummed out [by the lack of success with Jenkins]. We simply said, 'Okay, it's good' and the session was over, just like that."

When the record was first released, outside of a small buzz in San Francisco, it received little attention. Two or three months later, John R. at WLAC in Nashville phoned Stewart to inform him that "These Arms of Mine" was a smash. When Jim expressed disbelief, John R. stated that he believed in the record and intended to play it until it was a hit. To ensure his continued support, Jim Stewart gave his share of the publishing to the Nashville deejay. With John R. leading the way, over a period of several months, the record eventually reached number 20 R&B and number 85 pop.

By the time John R. informed Jim that "These Arms of Mine" was going to be a hit, Jim had already engineered Stax's next chart record. Rufus Thomas began his career as a tap dancer, so it's not surprising that he would become best known for a string of dance hits that spanned a decade beginning in early 1963. The first of these was Stax 130, "The Dog," which was soon followed by "Walking the Dog" (Stax 140), "Can Your Monkey Do the Dog" (Stax 144), and "Somebody Stole My Dog" (Stax 149). At the time that Rufus wrote the songs, a dance called "the dog" already existed. The original song was written on the bandstand while Rufus played a dance in Millington, Tennessee.

"There was a tall beautiful black girl," says Rufus, smiling, eyes closed and basking in the memory. "Had a long waistline, and she was wearing a black leather skirt, very alluring, sleek and slick. We were playing a rhythm at the time. There is nothing in my head about this song. When she started doing it, I was just telling her 'do the dog.' I changed the rhythm pattern. I was putting it together as we went along. I couldn't think of but three dogs—bull dog, bird dog, hound dog. Then I got to the part where [I said] 'just do any kind of dog, just do the dog.' We had three choruses and then just played the rhythm. I told everyone, 'You all just start barking like a dog,' and, if you notice, on the record you hear the barking on one chorus, and I was the lead dog with that bark way up there."

According to Rufus, the bass line was adapted from Willie Mitchell's 1962 Hi recording "The Crawl." Released in January 1963, "The Dog" climbed to numbers 22 and 87 on the R&B and pop charts, but, surprisingly, only sold about 200,000 records. Its followup, September's "Walking the Dog," did substantially better, peaking at number 5 R&B and number 10 pop.

Atlantic's chief engineer, Tom Dowd, was responsible for recording this latter hit. In midsummer 1963, Atlantic was anxiously awaiting a new Carla Thomas release. "Jerry Wexler kept on calling," relates Dowd, "and they were saying, 'Well, the equipment is down. We can't do this, we can't do that.' Jerry Wexler got impatient and called me one afternoon and said, 'Hey, Dowd, when can you get to Memphis? I think they're giving us a shuck and jive story.' He was cynical about it. I was a smart-ass. I picked up the phone and called the airlines and I called him back a few minutes later and said, 'Hey, if I leave now I can take a five-thirty, I'll be there by seven and I'll tell you what's happening.' He says, 'Go!'"

Dowd blitzed into Memphis and was picked up at the airport by Jim Stewart early that Friday evening. After checking into his hotel and having a quick dinner, he and Stewart headed over to the studio to see what was wrong with the equipment. He was in for instant culture shock. As his eyes gradually took in the cavernous converted movie theater with the sloping floor, he slowly moved toward the rather funky control room. Dowd first noticed that one complete wall of the control room was taken up by an unbelievably huge playback speaker—part of the sound system of the old movie theater and positioned on what had been the theater's stage—the likes of which he had never seen in a studio. Beneath that and slightly to the right he saw two four-channel Ampex portable mixers that were bridged together, going into an Ampex 350-tube mono tape recorder. All eight knobs on the mixers were permanently marked "echo," "bass," "horns," and so on. Because no one else used the Stax studio and the microphones, drum equipment, and keyboards were never moved, this suited Stax's purposes just fine. To a New Yorker like Dowd, this was insanely primitive. At the Atlantic studio he had been recording in eight-track since 1958.[12] Turning on the tape recorder, Dowd instantly determined that there was a brake band broken on one of the reels. He also noticed that Stax had never replaced basic parts that Atlantic would change every six months. In this age of studio equipment, regular maintenance was absolutely necessary, because the heat given off by the tubes would change the values of various elements within the tape recorder.

The time was about 8:30 at night in Memphis, 9:30 in New York. Dowd picked up the phone and called his assistant, Phil Iehle, who was still working at the Atlantic studios. "I said, 'Phil, do me a favor, tomorrow morning go by Harvey Radio, get me brake

---

12. In Stax's defense, it should be noted that, largely because of Dowd, Atlantic was way ahead of its time. In 1967, the Beatles were still recording in four-track.

bands for a 350, get me a couple of 68K resistors, a couple of 25 micro mikes for the cathode bypass on the 6SJ7's, and so on. Get there early in the morning and then boogie over to La Guardia, grab an American or a Delta stewardess. Give her twenty-five dollars and tell her to deliver the damn parts to Memphis.' There was no package service [such as Federal Express] then. I said, 'Let me know in the morning what flight it's on and I'll meet her at the airport. She can page me and I'll give her another twenty-five dollars.'"

Jim Stewart was skeptical, but nonetheless, he chauffeured Dowd to the airport. Parts in hand, on the way back Dowd casually asked Stewart if there were tools at the studio. Informed that there were a couple of screwdrivers handy, Dowd suggested a detour where he bought a pen-type soldering iron, a set of Hex wrenches, nut drivers, and the like. When Stewart and Dowd finally got back to the studio, Booker T. and the MG's were busy at work rehearsing some new material. After introductions all around, Dowd put the new brake band on and then did a quick-and-dirty maintenance job on the whole unit. When finished, he flipped the tape deck back over and asked for an alignment tape, but no one at Stax had ever heard of such a thing! Dowd did his best to make sure the zenith and azimuth were as good as they could possibly be under the circumstances and proceeded to announce that the machine was fixed. The MG's and Stewart looked at Dowd as if he were a magician.

With everyone a little worried that somehow all this repair work might have altered the sound of the unit, Dowd recorded a couple of minutes of the MG's jamming. Upon hearing the playback, everyone was more than satisfied with the newly repaired tape machine and were then further amazed when Dowd noticed that someone had played a bad note in the jam and decided to edit it out. "Steve was very smart and a quick-to-learn human being," muses Dowd. "He grasped what I did right away." Dowd then hipped Cropper to a number of tape manipulation possibilities, such as what happened when something was slowed down, how one sound could be overlaid over another, and so on. They became fast friends, and Steve still credits Dowd with teaching him how to edit. Packy Axton had watched the whole proceedings somewhat in disbelief before he finally proclaimed "school's out."

The MG's asked Dowd to come by on Sunday morning because they wanted to work on a couple of things. While they were all ensconced in the studio hard at work, Rufus Thomas drove by the building on this way home from church. Noticing all the cars in the parking lot, he decided to stop in, hollering, "What's going on, the equipment ain't working?" "That's when Rufus and I met for the first time," Dowd recalls. "He said, 'You fixed it?' I said, 'Yeah.' He said, 'I got this little ditty I want you to do. I wrote it and I've been wanting to do it but we haven't had the equipment working.'" Dowd threw a tape on the machine, and two or three passes later, they had cut "Walking the Dog."

"I take this tape with me back up to New York," continues Dowd. "I walk into the studio in New York and I said, 'Hey Wexie, they're putting Carla in either tonight or tomorrow. Everything is fixed. Oh, by the way, I made this.' I played him 'Walking the Dog.' He said, 'Master the goddamn thing.'"

When "Walking the Dog" was released, Jim Stewart couldn't believe its success: "I remember our first order out of Chicago. I was in New York in Jerry Wexler's office at the time and Paul Glass, who was our distributor in Chicago, called in an order for sixty-five thousand records. I said to Jerry, 'Do you mean sixty-five hundred?' And he said, 'Hell no, he wants sixty-five thousand.' That was the first order! He believed in the record so much that we ended up selling about two hundred thousand in Chicago alone."[13]

13. This is probably a slight exaggeration. In total "Walking the Dog" sold about 420,000 copies.

Atlantic Records took out a small one-inch ad in the October 5, 1963, issue of *Billboard* in support of the record. Within a year, the Rolling Stones would release a cover of the song on their first full-length album. In January and March 1964, Rufus would chart yet again with "Can Your Monkey Do the Dog" and "Somebody Stole My Dog."[14] The dog craze finally came to a close in 1966 with the Mar-Keys' hit recording of "Philly Dog" (Stax 185).

Dowd would make many subsequent trips to engineer sessions in Memphis. The Stax studio musicians loved working with him. While Jim Stewart undeniably was capable of recording great tracks, he tended to be a pretty uninspiring presence in the studio. Whenever a take didn't meet his approval, his typical response was simply to say, "Nah, let's do it again" while never indicating what exactly the problem was.

"Jim has never been a musician," states Wayne Jackson. "He's a fiddle player, a little wimp fiddle player and that's all. He was involved in the production only to stand there and holler, 'Isn't there one creative prick in the house?' He'd say, 'Someone be creative' and that would be his production input. I love Jim and that's not a put-down but that's what his input was, to stir you up a little bit and make you work harder."

Hearing comments like that all day long without any constructive suggestions could get a little discouraging. Dowd, on the other hand, had played violin, piano, string bass, and sousaphone, could read music and transpose. More than capable and willing to offer specific comments and suggestions, he would commonly suggest changing the structure this way or that, revoicing a chord, and so on. To the MG's, he was an inspiring breath of fresh air.

Three albums were issued on Stax in 1963, Gus Cannon's *Walk Right In* (Stax 702), a various artists anthology entitled *Treasured Hits from the South* (also numbered Stax 702!), and Rufus Thomas's *Walking the Dog* (Stax 704). The first two are oddities in the Stax story, whereas the Thomas LP was an attempt to capitalize on his recent successes.

Gus Cannon was a black banjo player who had recorded in the late 1920s and early 1930s for Paramount, Victor, and Brunswick with his group Cannon's Jug Stompers. One of the songs that he had recorded in 1929 for Victor, "Walk Right In," became a number 1 pop hit in 1963 for a white "folk" group, the Rooftop Singers. Cannon's Stax album was obviously recorded in the hopes that copies might sell on the strength of the Rooftop Singers' hit. No one remembers much about how Cannon came to record for the company, although Estelle recalls that he lived in the neighborhood and was a frequent visitor to her Satellite Record Shop. Jim thought that, all told, only five hundred copies of the album were pressed because Atlantic did not pick up the distribution rights.[15] Cannon was seventy-eight years old when the record was made, yet appears to have been in remarkable shape. In addition to the musical performances, the LP features Cannon speaking at length about his music and his life. Stewart recalls that, despite the quality of the finished product, it was not an easy LP to record: "It was really difficult to work with him. He wasn't really all there because of his age." Although having little to do with the direction Stax would go in, the LP is an important document of one of the last surviving bluesmen from the 1920s.

Treasured Hits from the South was billed as being "presented by Nick Charles," a hot local deejay at WMPS who had earlier recorded three execrable pop singles for Satellite and Stax in 1961 and 1962, would cowrite and produce one Mar-Keys single, "Whot's [sic] Happenin'," and would later have his short-lived Arch label distributed by Stax.

---

14. Two other dog songs, Rufus's own "Can't Get Away from This Dog" and Sam Cooke's "Stop Kicking My Dog Around," were recorded by Thomas at the time but remained unreleased until 1991 when Ace Records compiled them on a CD of outtakes appropriately titled *Can't Get Away from This Dog* (Ace CDSXD 038).

15. However, I recently found a copy in Memphis with Atlantic's address on the back; perhaps it was pressed before Atlantic passed on distributing the album.

Treasured Hits from the South comprised six Stax recordings, four recordings made earlier by Sun Records, one issued by Fernwood Records, and a solo single by Charles himself doing a forgettable cover of Carla Thomas's "For You." The latter was originally issued on Philadelphia's Jamie-Guyden group of labels. The Stax recordings included all of the label's hits up to the beginning of 1963 with the exception of "Cause I Love You." The album was presented with somewhat inaccurate liner notes by *Memphis Press–Scimitar* writer Robert Johnson that attempted to extol the virtues of Memphis music.

Neither the Cannon album nor *Treasured Hits from the South* achieved notable commercial success. Rufus Thomas's *Walking the Dog* LP did a little better, coasting to the number 138 spot on *Billboard*'s Top LP chart in December 1963. The LP included Thomas's two recent hits, "The Dog" and "Walking the Dog," as well as his next single, "Can Your Monkey Do the Dog." As was common practice at the time, the rest of the LP was filled out by B-sides and covers of recent R&B hits, including Nat Kendricks and the Swans's "Mashed Potatoes," John Lee Hooker's "Boom Boom," Lee Dorsey's "Ya Ya," and Chris Kenner's "Land of 1,000 Dances."

One further album, Otis Redding's *Pain in My Heart* (Atco 33-161), was prepared at this time, although it was not issued until January 1, 1964. In the meantime, Redding's second and third Volt singles were recorded and released. With Otis's debut single, "These Arms of Mine," taking many months to reach its chart peak, his second Stax session did not take place until late spring 1963. Two tracks were cut, "That's What My Heart Needs" and "Mary's Little Lamb." Phil Walden recalls, "He had a lot more confidence that second time, having been out on the road some. He wasn't necessarily that much more sophisticated but he had a grasp of what was happening outside of the small college circuit and the black tin-roof clubs of the South." The session was unique in a couple of ways. On both songs Otis sings with a harsh, impassioned gospel voice reminiscent of Archie Brownlee of the Five Blind Boys of Mississippi (the closest secular equivalent is the early James Brown of "Please Please Please"). Listening to the improvised ending of "That's What My Heart Needs," one can only conclude that Otis would have made a superb gospel singer had he chosen to record in that idiom.

Otis's third single, "Pain in My Heart" b/w "Something Is Worrying Me," cut a few months later, exhibits still further growth. With "Pain in My Heart," Otis's dynamic control is front and center as he uses his voice as a horn, swelling and decreasing in volume, swallowing syllables and worrying the word "heart." With a much fuller backdrop in the horns and Steve Cropper playing sweet fills in and around Otis's vocal, his classic ballad style moved that much closer to perfection.[16] It was Otis's most successful effort to date, commercially and aesthetically.

For both the "That's What My Heart Needs" and "Pain in My Heart" sessions, Otis journeyed to Memphis with three members of his revue in tow, guitarist/harmonica player Eddie Kirkland and vocalists Bobby Marchan (a female impersonator from New Orleans who had begun his career as a member of Huey "Piano" Smith and the Clowns) and Oscar Mack. Jim Stewart agreed to record all three artists, each of whom had two singles issued on Volt or Stax. The Kirkland (released as by "Eddie Kirk") and Marchan efforts were very fine, but unfortunately none of these artists' releases on Volt achieved any success.[17]

16. When it was originally issued in September 1963, the writing credit for the song was given as "Redding." Shortly thereafter Otis and Stax were hit with a lawsuit from Allen Toussaint who, under the pseudonym Naomi Neville (his mother's maiden name), had written "Ruler of My Heart" for the queen of New Orleans R&B, Irma Thomas. The songs were too close for comfort and, after an out-of-court settlement, the credit was changed to "Neville."

17. According to Kirkland, Mack died of an overdose in Detroit in the late 1980s. Kirkland and Marchan continue to perform to this day.

As with the Mar-Keys and Carla Thomas debut efforts, Otis's *Pain in My Heart* album was issued by Atlantic, in this case on their Atco subsidiary. The LP comprised both sides of Redding's first and third Volt singles, as well as the A-side of his second release, "That's What My Heart Needs," plus the usual melange of covers, including songs by his two idols, Sam Cooke ("You Send Me") and Little Richard ("Lucille"). *Pain in My Heart* peaked at the 103rd spot on the Top LP chart in the spring of 1964.

The year 1963 was also significant in that it marked the arrival to the company of Deanie Parker. Having grown up in southern Ohio, Deanie moved to Memphis in 1961 at the beginning of her junior year in high school. At Hamilton High she had joined a glee club and formed a group called the Valadors who entered a talent contest at the Old Daisy Theatre on Beale Street. The first prize was an audition at Stax. Deanie recalls the audition well: "Jim Stewart said, 'You do somebody else's material okay, but if you're interested in a recording contract, you have to have your own material.' I said, 'Okay, that's no big deal.' I had never written a song before in my life. I went home, sat down at the piano, wrote 'My Imaginary Guy' (Volt 105), called the guys over, rehearsed and rehearsed."

Neither "My Imaginary Guy" nor its successor, January 1964's "Each Step I Take" (Volt 115), had much more than regional success, Atlantic declining distribution in both cases. Nonetheless Parker was hooked. She spent most of her senior year working in the Satellite Record Shop. After graduating from high school, she worked for a year as a disc jockey on WLOK before returning to Stax in 1964 to do publicity. While developing Stax's publicity department, which she headed through early summer 1975, Deanie continued to successfully write songs for a variety of Stax artists including Carla Thomas, the Mad Lads, William Bell, and Albert King.

When Deanie started full-time work as Stax's publicity officer in 1964, she was one of two company office employees, the other being secretary Linda Andrews. Stewart was always very frugal and continued to make sure that the company's overhead was kept as low as possible. Jim felt that Deanie was one of the key ingredients in the company's success. "I always felt that women are responsible for eighty to ninety percent of records that are bought. I learned that working behind the record counter. . . . If they're influencing [record sales], why not have them in key positions in the company?" Later on Marlene Powell and Sandy Meadors would be prominent women in key executive positions at Stax.

Without any previous training and as Stax's first publicist, Deanie not only learned on the job but had to look outside of the company for guidance. In fact, Stax hired on a retainer basis a number of freelance publicists in various markets. "The reason for that," explains Parker, "was because our location geographically did not contribute to our ability to touch the elements that we needed to have at our disposal for good exposure for the artists in New York and on the West Coast. . . . So, the only way to be there was to retain somebody in those markets that could touch Dick Clark and the others and know where there was an opening here or a possibility there. It was really critical.

"I learned firsthand the art of being a publicist from Al Abrams, who was a freelance publicist who we had on retainer for a while. He was in Detroit, and by mail and by telephone I communicated to him items of interest that needed publicizing, and we would discuss what made valuable news items. From Al I built my first list of media contacts. Then we soon outgrew Al and we were doing all the in-house publicity on our own, but we still felt the need . . . to retain the services of even greater experts in other parts of the country, such as New York, Los Angeles, or Chicago. For me it was a hell of an opportunity to learn so much from some really great guys like Dick Gersch and Associates out of New York and Rogers, Cowan and Brenner off of the West Coast." Besides employing high-profile publicists on a continuing basis, Stax would also hire specific individual publicists on a project-by-project basis. As the label could not afford to have its entire roster listed with outside publicists at any one time, they would rotate which artists would receive independent publicity efforts.

Deanie also tried hard to prepare artists for meeting the press. "I never felt that we did one hundred percent of what should have been done to groom artists," admits Parker, "because we didn't have the manpower. We didn't always have the funds that we felt we could pump into that artist. Then, some artists just weren't that tameable. It was just their personality. That was one of the things that we looked at [with respect to the publicists we had on retainer]: 'In addition to exposure and contact, how can you help us to prepare this artist for the big time?' We would take full advantage of that as well. We were trying to refine our artists, but we were not trying to distort what they were really all about."

In contrast, at Motown in Detroit, Berry Gordy was more than happy to put each one of his artists through an in-house charm school, with the goal being that each artist could fit into middle-class white America's image of respectable deportment, style, and grace. Jim Stewart was not as ruthlessly ambitious as Gordy. Nor did he have the vision to build the type of vertically integrated empire that Motown became. He stresses, "We were, number one, a record company and our business was to sell records on the artist. [The artist's] management was pretty much a decision he had to make. He had to handle his own career." Some artists felt that they could have substantially profited from a lot more guidance than they received from Stax. Several groups tell stories of heading off to the Apollo in New York or the Uptown in Philadelphia for their initial road work after their first hit having virtually no knowledge of stage outfits, musical charts, and the like.

As 1963 came to a close, Stax was still very much a mom-and-pop operation, releasing a couple of singles each month and an album every three months. The office staff consisted of Deanie, Linda Andrews, and, after banking hours, Jim Stewart, while Estelle ran the record shop and Steve Cropper was in charge of the studio during the day. The next plateau was a couple of years away.

Respect: 1964–1965

All told, 1964 was a fairly quiet year at Stax. Although thirty-two 45s were issued by the company on Atlantic, Volt, and Stax, twelve of these were by the label's proven artists: Rufus and Carla Thomas, Booker T. and the MG's, and Otis Redding. Surprisingly, no one at the company was able to achieve anything remotely close to a substantial hit on the level of "Gee Whiz," "Green Onions," or "These Arms of Mine." While the lack of a mega-hit obviously disappointed Stax's brain trust, the company remained in relatively good health. With the exception of the MG's, virtually every release by each of its main artists charted.[1] The bottom line is that sales were steady but unspectacular, the majority of records being sold to a black clientele through inner-city America's numerous mom-and-pop record outlets.

While Stax was struggling, its northern counterpart, Motown Records, was in its ascendancy, with the Supremes, Mary Wells, the Miracles, the Temptations, and Stevie Wonder all regularly tearing up the pop charts. The sign outside Motown proudly proclaimed the company "Hitsville U.S.A."; the marquee outside the Stax studio, on the other hand, was adorned with the words "Soulsville U.S.A." These slogans perfectly sum up the diametrically opposed aesthetic and operating philosophies of the two companies.

Motown president Berry Gordy, Jr., was a product of the urban industrial North. Relentlessly driven, ruthlessly ambitious, and autocratic to the bone, Gordy ran his operation very much from a master plan. Utilizing sound business practices such as vertical integration, Gordy maximized both his control and ultimate profitability by operating a management company, booking agency, and record company under one roof. Jim Stewart, on the other hand, was a product of the rural, fraternal South. Although he wanted to make money, he could easily be content with what might seem to be a modicum of success, not caring a whit about making further profits via management or booking activities. In what has to be one of the great ironies of the Stax story, Stewart was always loudly championing keeping the company's sound as "black" as possible. While various black writers and later co-owner Al Bell were interested in crossover success, Stewart seemingly wasn't the least bit interested if crossing over meant compromising what he was gradually coming to understand as the "Stax sound."

"We could never grab that little thing Motown had," shrugs Stewart. "Of course, they couldn't [grab] ours either. We envied them being able to cross over to the pop market back then when we couldn't, but it just wasn't us. When we tried to do something like that, we would fall flat on our butt. We had to do what we knew best." In general, Stewart

---

1. However, in a year in which *Billboard* suspended publication of its R&B charts, it's hard to precisely measure each record's impact. Suffice it to say that none of the company's releases that year managed to dent the pop Top 40.

was much less authoritarian and much more egalitarian than Gordy. Within a few years, Stax would effectively engage in profit sharing, an unthinkable occurrence at Motown. Finally, Stewart certainly did not operate from a master blueprint; at Stax, things tended to occur by happenstance.

A key contributor to Stax's secure financial position was Estelle Axton's activities at the Satellite Record Shop. By now Lady A had developed into what Jim described as "the damnest salesman I ever saw." Shortly after commencing operation, she had instituted a program whereby, with every ten records purchased, customers would get one free. This little gimmick allowed Estelle to keep a file card on each customer; she not only kept track of the number of records purchased, she also wrote down the titles. The minute a customer would ask for a record, Estelle would pull his or her card and at a glance could see what they had been buying.

"I could see what type of music he'd like," Estelle chortles. "If I'd gotten any records since he'd [last] been in, I played everything that was in that vein and I got nineteen of his twenty dollars. Don't ever let a customer show me twenty dollars 'cause I'll get nineteen of it. I'll leave him money to get home 'cause I'll sell him more records [when he returns]. They wouldn't go anywhere else to buy their records. They'd say, 'If Satellite don't have it, it's not in town.'" Employee William Brown proudly asserts, "We got so good in that shop till you could hum the line and we could go get the record!"

If Estelle ran low on a popular record over the weekend, she would simply go across town to her major competition, Pop Tunes. She would then hit on an unwitting employee and buy, at a wholesale rate, Pop Tunes' complete stock of the title. Of course, that would mean that Pop Tunes wouldn't have the record anymore, and both their customers and Satellite's would have to come over to East McLemore to get their sonic fix.

While sales of Stax and Volt product were less than spectacular in 1964, the company did issue a number of superb singles. One was an instrumental recorded and released under baritone saxophonist Floyd Newman's name that slipped out of the gate just before the first of the year. According to Floyd his lone solo 45, "Frog Stomp" backed with "Sassy," came about directly as a result of intensive lobbying by Estelle. As was the case with most of the Stax session musicians, Newman earned a substantial part of his living playing gigs in and around Memphis. When he got the opportunity to record his own record, he elected to use his own band, including Joe Woods on guitar, Howard Grimes on bass, and Isaac Hayes on piano. Hayes had cowritten "Frog Stomp" with Newman, although he was not credited when the original record came out.

The Newman session was not the first time that Isaac Hayes had headed down to Stax. A couple of years earlier he had auditioned for the company as part of a doo-wop ensemble that went by the name of the Ambassadors, and he had also auditioned as a member of the blues band Calvin and the Swing Cats. To his disappointment, both groups were turned down.

Hayes's story is one of epic proportions. Beginning in 1969, with the release of *Hot Buttered Soul*, he would become the biggest artist Stax ever produced and one of the most important artists in the history of rhythm and blues. In the first few years of the 1970s he single-handedly redefined the sonic possibilities for black music, in the process opening up the album market as a commercially viable medium for black artists such as Marvin Gaye, Stevie Wonder, Funkadelic, and Curtis Mayfield. Earlier, Hayes, alongside partner David Porter, helped shape the sound of soul music in the 1960s with such definitive compositions as "Hold On! I'm Comin'," "Soul Man," "When Something Is Wrong with My Baby," "B-A-B-Y," and "I Thank You." The fact that one artist could be responsible for such disparate but equally great and influential music as Hayes produced in the 1960s and 1970s simply boggles the imagination.

Born August 20, 1942, in Covington, Tennessee, by the time Hayes was eighteen months old his mother had passed away in a mental institution; because his father had disappeared sometime before her death, Isaac was subsequently raised by his grandparents. To sharecroppers such as Hayes's grandparents, radio was their major contact with the rest of the world. For the first several years of Isaac's life this meant a steady diet of what was then called "hillbilly music," with Saturday night's "Grand Ole Opry" broadcast being of particular importance.[2] Hayes's musical imagination was also fired by the gospel music he heard on the radio performed by the Golden Gate Quartet (singing on the "Amos and Andy Show") and the Wings Over Jordan Choir, and he fondly remembers touring gospel groups such as the Spirit of Memphis Quartet putting on programs at the local churches in Covington.

A pivotal moment in Isaac's life occurred in June 1949, when he caught Nat D. Williams's "Sepia Swing" show for the first time on Memphis's WDIA. "That was the first black person I heard as a radio announcer," relates Hayes. "I listened to it and said, 'Wow, a black man on radio!'" That same month Isaac's grandparents moved into Memphis. Urban living was a bit of a shock for the seven-year-old Hayes. Out in the country all of the sharecroppers were equally impoverished but, because they grew their own food and there was relatively little to buy, the burden of poverty was light when compared with being poor in the city. In Memphis, you had to buy your food, and there were plenty of other products that were alluring but only attainable if you had the requisite income. A young Isaac Hayes started to understand that all men are not created equal.

"I used to dream," recalled Isaac, speaking with Phyl Garland in 1970, "just dream about being able to have a warm bed to sleep in and a nice square meal and some decent clothes to wear. But what really tore me up was when we had to split up. We didn't have a place to go, so my grandparents moved in with an uncle, my sister had to go live with an aunt, and I had to go live with a guy who was a friend of the family."

After his grandfather died, when he was eleven, Isaac, his sister and grandmother, together and separately, lived all over North Memphis. At one point the three of them were on welfare living in one room over a storefront church. When they were cut off of welfare, they could no longer afford to pay the gas bill, so they used the wood from their outhouse to burn for heat. Consequently, they had no bathroom. Then the family's utilities were cut off so they had no lights and had to borrow water from a neighbor. The next year, the family ran out of food and Isaac's grandmother and sister got sick from hunger.

"I lived in so many different places," Isaac told me many years later. "You can't imagine, man. We lived in the back of appliance stores, lived in people's backyards. One time I moved in with this guy who was an alcoholic. He got arrested and I didn't have anywhere to stay, so I slept in junk cars at a garage."

To help make ends meet, Isaac worked at the Savoy Theatre, distributed flyers, delivered groceries in a borrowed wagon, hauled wood, and shined shoes down on Beale Street. Despite his efforts, Isaac remained as poor as they came. By the time he reached the ninth grade, he became conscious of both the opposite sex and how ragged his clothes were. Putting two and two together, Isaac noticed that the guys with fine clothes did much better in terms of making time with the girls. Embarrassed by the holes in his shoes and the general state of disrepair of his wardrobe, Isaac dropped out of school.

---

2. This is a familiar trope in the lives of many of the first-period Stax artists. Due to the relative lack of black programming available on American airwaves until the late 1940s, a couple of generations of black musicians grew up imbued with the sounds of country music.

Forced to return by his grandmother, Isaac attended Manassas High School (at the time, it covered grades one through twelve), where he took vocal music, and began fooling around every chance he got with the school piano. Although he liked music, his stated ambition was to become a doctor.

On many a school day, right after his grandmother walked him to the front doors at Manassas, Isaac bolted out the side entrance. Much of the time he would go to the fields and pick cotton for a black farmer named Armstrong. Buses would come into town early in the morning to take black field hands out to the country. If they missed the bus, they had to try to make it over the Arkansas River bridge and hitch a ride out to the fields. Over time Isaac developed a heavy-duty crush on Armstrong's daughter. Attempting to impress her, he decided to enter the school talent contest, where he sang Nat King Cole's 1958 hit "Looking Back."

Several years earlier, while still in grade four, he and his sister, Willette, had performed in another talent contest, working over Perry Como and Tony Bennett songs. At that time, his voice was light and airy, so his schoolmates nicknamed him the "Swoon Crooner" while teasing him about sounding like a girl. His grade-nine performance was a little bit different, because Isaac's voice had already dropped a couple of octaves. "I was scared to death," Hayes remembers, wincing. "They got an auditorium full of people [but] I sang the song and I fell on my knees and the girls just screamed and everything. I got to the bridge of the song, the climax, and that's when I went down to my knees and they just freaked. I mean the whole house came down. After that I was an instant celebrity on campus and I lost my passion for medicine. I found a new thing. Here's a poor kid, dressed in rags, holes in his shoes. All of a sudden beautiful girls in the twelfth grade are asking, 'Ooh, give me your autograph.' I wanted to make a career of music then because of all the attention and everything."

By the time Isaac was fifteen, he was singing in the Morning Stars, a gospel quartet that performed weekly at Pleasant Green Baptist Church on Sunday morning. The church's services were broadcast on radio station WHHN every Sunday night. A short while later, Isaac began singing doo-wop with the Teen Tones, who were proudly decked out in sweaters emblazoned with the letter *T,* emulating Frankie Lymon and the Teenagers' sense of fashion. For a short period Isaac sang with both groups.

The Teen Tones worked out stage routines that they'd use at their infrequent performances at high-school functions and at amateur night at the Palace Theatre on Beale. The emcee at these amateur nights was none other than future Stax star Rufus Thomas, working alongside his comic partner, Bones, and radio announcer Nat D. Williams. The Teen Tones were often in competition with William Bell's Del-Rios and David Porter's Marquettes, their repertoire consisting of material such as the Five Royales' "Tell the Truth" and "Dedicated to the One I Love," Hank Ballard and the Midnighters' "Let's Go, Let's Go, Let's Go," and the Spaniels' "You're Gonna Cry." "We'd get five or six dollars when we'd win and then we'd go buy doughnuts or a hot dog at the Harlem House on Beale and walk back home," Hayes says, smiling as he warmly cherishes the memory.

The Teen Tones made it into a recording studio where they sang backup in ersatz Jordinaires style for a white artist named Jimmy McCracklin, who recorded under the pseudonym Johnny Rebel.[3] While all of this was going down, Isaac also sang for a short while with schoolmate Sidney Kirk in another doo-wop group dubbed the Ambassadors;

---

3. According to Isaac, one side of Johnny Rebel's 45 was called "What Can You Give in Return," and it was released on Pepper Records. Unfortunately, I have been unable to find any trace of it.

this group auditioned for Stax, perhaps Isaac's first trip to the East McLemore studio, but they were turned down.

Back at school in the wake of the talent contest, Isaac was singing in the church choir and took a year of band. He had wanted to play alto saxophone but, because school instruments were limited, he ended up playing the baritone. Alto saxophonist Lucian Coleman, brother of jazz great George Coleman, lived in the neighborhood and in 1959 took Isaac under his wing, teaching him about jazz greats such as Charlie Parker, Dizzy Gillespie, Art Pepper, and Memphis luminaries Frank Strozier and Booker Little. Soon thereafter, Isaac moved in with Coleman. The older musician was kind enough to lend Isaac his alto sax so that Isaac could play alto instead of baritone in the school band.

Getting hooked further by the music bug, Isaac started hanging outside Mitchell's Hotel on Beale Street and Curry's Club Tropicana on Thomas Street. Too young to get in, he would stand on garbage cans, peeking in the windows, and pressing his ear to the walls, trying to take in as much as he possibly could. Every Sunday afternoon, Curry's hosted a jazz jam. On one Sunday in 1961, James Moody was booked to play that evening and stopped by early to take part in the jam. When Isaac finally built up the nerve to say he wanted to come in and sing, Memphis sax great Fred Ford, a.k.a. Daddy Goodlow, smoothed the way for Isaac with the doorman. Isaac eventually summoned up the nerve to get onstage, where he sang Arthur Prysock's "The Very Thought of You" backed by the house band led by Ben Branch. "When I finished," Isaac recalls, "Mrs. Curry came over to me and said, 'Young man, do you want a job?'"

Elated, for the next two years Isaac enjoyed his first professional job, singing one or two songs every Monday, Saturday, and Sunday night with Ben Branch. At the time Branch's band included Floyd Newman, Herbert Thomas on trumpet, Clarence Nelson on guitar, Big Bell James on drums, and Larry Brown on bass. Brown, along with future Stax producer Allen Jones and Lewie Steinberg, was one of the first electric bass players in Memphis. He was to have an inordinate influence on MG bassist Duck Dunn, and, in an interesting twist of fate, Dunn would eventually replace Brown in Ben Branch's band.

A short while after Isaac began working with Branch, Lucian Coleman started playing with Calvin and the Swing Cats, a blues band that included Willie Chase on drums, Sidney Kirk on piano, Mickey Gregory on trumpet, and leader Calvin Valentine on guitar.[4] Through Coleman's intercession, Isaac began singing with the group, often working out-of-town gigs, taking the vocal lead on tunes such as "One Room Country Shack" and "Baby, Please Don't Go." Some of the gigs out in the country apparently got pretty rough; Isaac recalls many a night diving behind the piano to avoid flying bullets. Isaac's second trip to Stax was as a member of Calvin and the Swing Cats; unfortunately, for all concerned, they failed their audition.

During Isaac's senior year in high school, he briefly formed one other combo, the Missiles, giving him the chance to play sax. The Missiles included one Elmo Harris who, as Eddie Harrison, would sing in the Premiers and record one Stax 45 in September 1965, the haunting "Make It Me," which coincidentally was one of Hayes and David Porter's earliest compositions and production efforts. Harrison would later lead the Short Kuts, who recorded a series of 45s for Pepper Records, some cuts of which were written and/or produced by Hayes and Porter.[5]

While all this professional gigging was occurring, Isaac was finally finishing high school, starring in the Manassas annual show three years in a row. Upon graduating in 1962, he

---

4. Kirk and Gregory would later spend time with the Isaac Hayes Movement.

5. The Hayes-Porter productions were credited to U. G. Lee.

was offered seven different vocal scholarships by the likes of Jackson State, Tennessee State, Florida A & M, Lane College, and Rust College. Unfortunately he was now married and an expectant father, so college was out of the question. Prophetically, a number of Manassas students wrote in his high school yearbook sayings like, "See you on television when you're famous." Isaac initially supported his wife and child by working at a meat-packing plant. When gigs were getting scarce in late 1962, Sidney Kirk happened to mention that a new studio had opened at Chelsea and Thomas. Hayes and Kirk walked down to American Sound Studios, met Chips Moman, and asked to audition. Moman was suitably impressed, and Isaac Hayes ended up recording one of the very first releases for Moman and Seymour Rosenberg's Youngstown label. The A-side, "Laura, We're on Our Last Go-Round," was written by a local writer named Patty Ferguson, while the B-side was a cover of Merle Travis and Cliffie Stone's "Sweet Temptations."[6] Future Stax head engineer Ronnie Capone played drums, Tommy Cogbill played bass, and Sidney Kirk took care of the piano chores. Isaac strictly sang, double-tracking his own harmony part.

According to Moman, for quite a while Isaac came by American just about every day after working at the slaughterhouse, hanging out, writing, and learning about the recording studio. Meanwhile, when the record flopped, Sidney Kirk went into the air force, which, ironically, turned Isaac into a piano player. As Isaac tells it, one day Kirk's sister, Fanny, called him up saying that Jeb Stuart had just telephoned, desperately in need of a piano player for a New Year's Eve gig at the Southern Club. She wondered if Isaac wanted to try to fit the bill. Desperate for money, he said yes. The only problem was he hardly knew how to play piano.

"After I accepted it, I broke into a cold sweat," laughs Isaac. "I was scared to death. I said, 'What am I doing? I don't know how to play piano. They're gonna kill me.' But, I needed the money. I got there before anybody, just trying to practice on little things that I did know. I started off playing with two fingers and then I added a few more fingers. Being New Year's Eve the crowd was full of spirits. Had we played 'Three Blind Mice' nobody would have given a shit! The club owner came up and said, 'You know you boys sound pretty good. Y'all want a regular job?' What put me at ease [was that] none of the other guys could play worth a shit, either. So, I was in good company. That's how I got started messing around with piano. We took that gig, built a crowd and got a hell of a following."[7]

Becoming more proficient on keyboards with each gig, Isaac next joined Floyd Newman's band at the Plantation Inn, staying onboard as the group's pianist for some five or six months. He also began writing songs under the pseudonyms Ed Lee and Anthony Mitchell, and played on a couple of Goldwax sessions in Muscle Shoals with Bowlegs Miller behind Spencer Wiggins and James Carr. All of which brings the story back to his playing piano on and cowriting the A-side of Floyd Newman's "Frog Stomp." Newman picks up the story. "That's the first time that Jim Stewart had ever heard him [play piano]. Isaac had an unbelievable ear. He was playing things that he didn't even know he was playing. But, he heard them and he would play them." With Booker T. Jones off at college, Isaac Hayes slowly became a regular Stax session musician. As he gained confidence, he slowly began to make suggestions about the arrangements of material. Eventually, he started writing

6. Many years later the record was rereleased with "C.C. Rider" substituted for "Sweet Temptations" as the B-side.

7. Jeb Stuart was a journeyman R&B singer who over time would record for a host of Memphis labels including Phillips, Bingo, and Youngstown. He kept this particular band together for quite a while, working the Southern Club for three or four months before moving over to the Continental Club and then to the TG Club. Hayes played on and helped arrange one of Stuart's Phillips singles.

songs with David Porter, inalterably changing the face of Stax Records forever.

Another important addition to the Stax family, Andrew Love, replaced Gilbert Caple at around the same time Newman cut "Frog Stomp." A graduate of Booker T.

A rare shot of Isaac Hayes (*back row on the far right*), before he began shaving his head, at the WDIA Big Star Show (named after the show's sponsor, the Big Star grocery). COURTESY THE STAX HISTORICAL PRESERVATION COMMISSION.

Washington, Love had been playing in Memphis nightclubs with the likes of Bowlegs Miller since he was in the tenth grade. Awarded a band scholarship, Love spent two years at Langston University in Oklahoma before heading back to Memphis to make his living as a player. He immediately was hired for sessions at Hi, playing on hit records such as Willie Mitchell's "20-75" and Gene Simmons's "Haunted House." Unable to afford a phone, he eventually moved right across the street from the studio so Willie Mitchell could simply knock on his door whenever he needed him for a session. Al Jackson recommended Love for work at Stax when Gilbert Caple said he was headed to Houston to work in the house band at Duke-Peacock Records.[8]

Isaac Hayes' first paid session as a piano player was for Otis Redding. "I was frightened," relates Hayes, some twenty-two years after the fact. "Here I am in this place I've always wanted to be and all these giants have been through there." At this late date it is

8. Over the next few years, Caple was in and out of Memphis and, on a number of occasions, played on additional Stax sessions.

impossible to ascertain which of Otis's 1964 releases featured Hayes for the first time.[9] My best guess would be February's "Come to Me" or April's "Security."

"Come to Me" was the top side of Otis's fourth Volt single. Cowritten by Phil Walden, it's in Otis's patented 6/8 ballad mode featuring the ubiquitous piano triplets, this time with the addition of church-derived organ. Curiously, it's one of only two tracks recorded and released after Redding's debut Volt session not to feature horns. Peaking at number 69 pop, it undoubtedly would have been a Top 30 R&B hit if *Billboard* had published an R&B chart that year. The lively self-penned "Security," unjustly, had next to no chart action. Today, it is regarded as a watershed release in Otis's early career, featuring for the first time his trademark offbeat horn punctuations dueling with both Cropper's metallic guitar responses and Otis's voice following the horn break. The net result is absolutely sublime.

Otis closed the year with "Chained and Bound" in September and "Mr. Pitiful" in December. The latter, in many ways, was a turning point for Otis and Stax. It was the first record to include another of Otis's distinctive horn patterns, a series of eighths with the offbeats accented. It was also Otis's first full collaboration as a writer with MG guitarist Steve Cropper, and his first Top 10 R&B and Top 50 pop chart entry. Cropper recalls, "There was a disc jockey here named Moohah [WDIA's A. C. Williams]. He started calling Otis 'Mr. Pitiful' 'cause he sounded so pitiful singing his ballads. So I said, 'Great idea for a song!' I got the idea for writing about it in the shower. I was on my way down to pick up Otis. I got down there and I was humming it in the car. I said, 'Hey, what do you think about this?' We just wrote the song on the way to the studio, just slapping our hands on our legs. We wrote it in about ten minutes, went in, showed it to the guys, he hummed a horn line, boom—we had it. When Jim Stewart walked in we had it all worked up. Two or three cuts later, there it was."

By the time "Mr. Pitiful" was recorded Jim Stewart finally felt secure enough that he left First National Bank and began to devote his energies full-time to Stax. Shortly thereafter, Tom Dowd convinced him and Steve to let Dowd install a two-track recorder. "They said, 'You're not gonna lose our sound?'" laughs Dowd. "I said, 'I'll tell you what I'll do. We'll put in the two-track machine and we'll put the mono in the end of it so you can do both at the same time. If you like the mono better fine, but just don't erase the two-track.'" Each track was fed by one of the four-input Ampex mixers that Jim had been using since the studio in Brunswick. This meant that any given instrument would be either in one channel or the other, leading to the bizarre situation where the vocals and echo would be in one channel only. This, of course, only affected LP releases. The majority of the company's business was still conducted in singles which, at the time, were still issued exclusively in mono.

The B-side of "Mr. Pitiful," Roosevelt Jamison's and Steve Cropper's "That's How Strong My Love Is," is one of the pluperfect R&B ballads of all time. Jamison had originally taken it to a Stax Saturday morning audition, where Cropper had helped to refashion the lyrics. Nothing happened immediately though, and Jamison took it to another Memphis R&B label, Goldwax Records, where he cut it with O. V. Wright. In the meantime, Cropper recorded the song with Otis. Wright's and Redding's versions were released within days of each other and the Rolling Stones recorded it shortly thereafter, the combined impact of their versions making it an instant soul classic.

Both tracks were recorded as fall turned to winter. At Stax that meant coats and gloves for the horn players. The studio was equipped with a single heater that was positioned right next to Al Jackson's drum booth. "That one heater was going," laughs Wayne Jackson, "and Al Jackson would be in a T-shirt sweating. We'd be across the room in our overcoats and gloves it was so cold in there!"

9. Unfortunately, the Memphis Musicians Union has virtually no sessions sheets for sessions held before 1966. Curiously enough, Fantasy Records, which bought Stax in 1977, also has no sessions sheets pre-1966.

By year's end, Otis had cut his second LP, most of the tracks featuring Isaac Hayes on piano or organ. *The Great Otis Redding Sings Soul Ballads* (Volt 711) was issued in March 1965, and has the distinction of being the first album to be released on Volt.[10] As *Soul Ballads* was beginning its run up the charts, Stax was readying the release of Otis's seventh Volt single, "I've Been Loving You Too Long." Cowritten with Jerry Butler in a Buffalo hotel room, it represented Redding's greatest commercial success until "(Sittin' On) The Dock of the Bay." Its success was very nearly duplicated in August by "Respect," one of Otis's finest up-tempo romps. Fueled by Duck Dunn's imaginative pulsing bass figure and Al Jackson's flat-sounding four-on-the-floor snare pattern (replete with machine-gun blasts), the track is transcendent. The second voice on the "hey hey hey" hook is that of label compadre William Bell.

Both singles were recut in stereo during the July 1965 sessions for the *Otis Blue* album. The only noticeable difference on "Respect" was that Otis's longtime friend and road manager Earl "Speedo" Sims sings the "hey hey hey" line. "I've Been Loving You Too Long," on the other hand, underwent substantial change. Otis had performed it regularly onstage and had gained a much better feel for the song. With a slowed-down tempo, doubly dramatic stop-time pauses, increased use of dynamics, much more potent horns, and an achingly impassioned vocal, it's one of the finest Otis Redding recordings ever.

For Wayne Jackson, the horn lines served the function of background vocals. "The horn is like a voice," explains the trumpeter, "but you're limited as to what you can do. You don't have syllables so you have to use dynamics tastefully. That's the one way you have of getting across your breath without having a syllable to say. 'I've Been Loving You Too Long' has great horn parts. You can almost hear the horns saying the words in that record. They're also used like a rhythm instrument on the stop line—definite punctuation."

Otis worked extremely quickly. *Otis Blue* was recorded in one amazing adrenaline-charged twenty-four-hour period. With Tom Dowd coming down from New York Thursday night to work the board, the session began at ten the next morning. Around eight o'clock that night the festivities came to a halt as several of the session musicians had to head off to their nightly gigs. Everyone reconvened at two in the morning after the clubs closed and went straight through the night until ten the next morning, and then Otis flew out for a gig the next day.[11]

The story of how the Rolling Stones' "Satisfaction" came to be included on this album provides fascinating insight into the creative process at Stax. Apparently Otis took a brief break from the sessions to have a physical for insurance purposes. Scrounging for material to round out the album, Steve Cropper had a brainstorm: "It was my idea to do it. I went up to the front of the record shop, got a copy of the [Stones] record, played it for the band and wrote down the lyrics. You notice on 'Satisfaction' that Otis said 'fashion,' not 'faction.' I love it. That's what made him so unique. He'd just barrel right through that stuff unaware of anything. He just didn't know the song. He hadn't heard it as far as I know." Phil Walden concurs: "Otis kind of read the lyrics through about once or twice and

10. Including "Come to Me," "Chained and Bound," "Your One and Only Man," "Mr. Pitiful," and "That's How Strong My Love Is," a handful of newly recorded originals, and covers, *Soul Ballads* did not do as well as *Pain in My Heart* on the Top LP charts, only reaching the number 147 position. It did, though, make an appearance on *Billboard*'s new R&B LP chart, first appearing April 10 and seven weeks later peaking at number 3, staying on the chart for a total of fourteen weeks.

11. To the best of Duck Dunn's recollection, "I've Been Loving You Too Long," Sam Cooke's "A Change Is Gonna Come," a cover of William Bell's "You Don't Miss Your Water," and Otis's searing version of B. B. King's "Rock Me Baby" were cut during the second shift while Cooke's "Shake" and "Wonderful World," Solomon Burke's "Down in the Valley," the Temptations' "My Girl," the Rolling Stones' "Satisfaction," and Redding's own "Ole Man Trouble" and "Respect" were cut in the daytime.

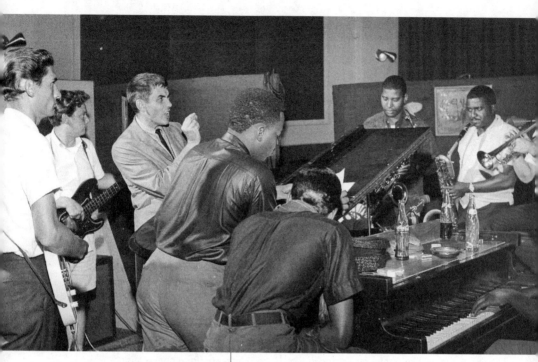

In the Stax studio: (*left to right*) Steve Cropper, Duck Dunn, Tom Dowd, David Porter, Julius Green of the Mad Lads (*seated with his back to the camera*), Andrew Love, Floyd Newman, Wayne Jackson, Isaac Hayes. COURTESY API PHOTOGRAPHERS INC.

then just really jumped right into the thing. That was a real spontaneous record. He had never heard the Rolling Stones version."

Released in September 1965, *Otis Blue* represented a quantum leap for both Otis Redding and the Stax house band of Booker T. and the MG's, Isaac Hayes, and the Mar-Key horns (at this point consisting of Wayne Jackson, Andrew Love, and Floyd Newman, with Bowlegs Miller guesting on second trumpet). Whereas on many of Otis's earlier recordings he sounded tentative, feeling his way through a song, on *Otis Blue* he roars like a locomotive. From this point on in Otis's career, extremes become more apparent: tempos become either faster or slower and the parts hit harder or are treated in a gentler fashion.

A good example is provided by Otis's cover of Sam Cooke's swansong, "A Change Is Gonna Come." It's hard to imagine anyone cutting Cooke on his own song, but Otis and the Stax house band do just that. The triplet and two eighths rhythmic interjection is merely a whisper in Cooke's original; on *Otis Blue* it sounds like a sledgehammer. Otis is at his elliptical best with words, sometimes syllables, bursting from his vocal chords one moment, being swallowed and garbled the next. Emotion is the governing aesthetic throughout.

"I think he was more sophisticated and aware of who he was," suggests manager Phil Walden. "He was successful and he liked that lifestyle, being a star and having people like him. He was into being Otis Redding and I think it reflects in his music. He was a real star finally, not something we tried to fabricate. We could turn to album sales, which was fairly unique for black artists in those days." Wayne Jackson agrees with Walden: "As he gained in stature as an artist with worldwide fame, his confidence level went up. He didn't change as a performer, I think he just got better."

Walden had just returned from a two-year hitch in the army and was both ecstatic and astonished by the session. "Everything was so up. He was finally feeling like a star. You could sense it. Everything happened right, just knocking out songs like this [snaps fingers]. Of course, I didn't know that everybody didn't do it this way, and Tom Dowd's going, 'Phew, this damn guy is a genius.' I said, 'Really?' I knew Dowd had worked with everybody and he said, 'I've only been in the studio with two other people that are in this category, Bobby Darin and Ray Charles.' I said, 'You're kidding me, my Otis?'" Dowd remembers the conversation well. "I said, 'Man, this guy's in charge like Bobby Darin was. He knows what the hell he wants. Otis was a very strong individual. He did not have the acumen or the experience musically to be able to say, 'More like this or more like that.' He'd just say, 'That ain't right' and he'd sing a part to you."

Upon its release in September 1965, *Otis Blue* stayed on the pop LP charts for thirty-four weeks, peaking at number 75, and reached the number 1 spot on the Top R&B LP chart. In addition to achieving these peaks, the album stayed on the charts for several months. Redding had become what is known as a "catalogue" artist. His records tended to sell steadily over long periods of time, reaching sales ranging anywhere from 200,000 to 250,000 copies, rather than selling in massive numbers immediately upon release and then cooling off equally quickly.

Shortly after *Otis Blue* was recorded, Otis, in partnership with Joe Galkin and Phil and Alan Walden, formed a production company, Jotis Records (the name being derived by putting the *J* from Joe Galkin's name in front of *Otis*), and a publishing arm, Redwal Music (*Red*ding and *Wal*den). Jotis lasted for only four releases, two by Arthur Conley, and one each by Billy Young (an army acquaintance of Phil Walden's) and Loretta Williams (a singer with Otis's road band). In 1966, Otis produced two further singles by Conley on Fame, before switching him over to Atco and hitting it big with "Sweet Soul Music" in the spring of 1967. Based on Sam Cooke's "Yeah Man," and with a horn intro variously attributed to a riff taken from either a Maxwell House coffee or a Marlboro cigarettes commercial, "Sweet Soul Music" soared to number 2 on both the pop and R&B charts.

Several months earlier, in May 1965, just after "I've Been Loving You Too Long" entered the *Billboard* charts, Stax and Atlantic finally formalized their distribution agreement, setting down in a legal contract what had existed for years as a handshake deal. Atlantic's owners had begun discussing the possibility of selling the company, and Jerry Wexler suggested to Jim Stewart that a written contract could protect Stewart. Stewart was worried that Atlantic could possibly be sold to a corporation that was not interested in or did not understand Stax's recordings or its market. He insisted on a clause in the thirteen-page document that would allow him to sever the distribution deal with Atlantic immediately should the company ever be sold and Jerry Wexler not remain a stockholder or employee, and within 180 days if the company should be sold and Wexler remained an employee but not a stockholder.

The contract gave Atlantic the exclusive right, but not obligation, to "distribute" any master Stax produced or otherwise acquired. Until Atlantic exercised that right on a given record, Stax could release "such master recordings in your local market, in order to test the salability thereof." Stax had to produce and offer a minimum of six master recordings (e.g., three singles) during a given year.[12] In return, Stax was to be paid by Atlantic fifteen cents for single records and 10 percent of the retail list price of LPs, less taxes, duties, and costs of packaging, for 90 percent of all items sold and paid for in the United States.[13] Stax

12. In actuality Stax delivered 29 singles in 1965, 35 in 1966, and 49 in 1967, plus several dozen LP tracks.

13. As was, and still is among some companies, standard practice in the record industry. See footnote 22 on page 13 for more details.

was to receive 50 percent of these amounts for records sold through record clubs, and 50 percent of whatever Atlantic received for records sold outside the United States. Stax was obligated to pay mechanical royalties for all singles sold, while Atlantic assumed this obligation for LPs. Stax was also obligated to pay all moneys owed to recording artists.

While it wasn't overly generous, there was nothing particularly onerous or untoward about this agreement, with one very major exception. From the beginning of the contract, it spoke of Atlantic's right "to purchase master recordings" from Stax. Paragraph 6C, page 7, was even more specific:

> You hereby sell, assign and transfer to us, our successors or assigns, absolutely and forever and without any limitations or restrictions whatever, not specifically set forth herein, the entire right, title and interest in and to each of such masters and to each of the performances embodied thereon.

Jerry Wexler has always maintained that Atlantic's lawyers slipped this clause in, and that he was entirely unaware of it. However, if Wexler had perused the contract, it would have been clear that this was a legal instrument that gave Atlantic full ownership of Stax productions. In other words, this was not a master *lease* or distribution contract as understood by Jim Stewart, it was a master *purchase* contract.[14] Even more devastating, paragraph 12 on page 11 gave Atlantic the same rights to all Stax productions they had distributed *prior* to May 17, 1965. In one stroke of the pen, for one dollar, Jim Stewart and Estelle Axton lost the rights to their entire catalogue.

It is easy to think that, if Jim Stewart signed it, that's his problem. But it is important to understand that Jim Stewart was every inch a product of the fraternal, personalized South: a person's handshake and word were more important than any contract. Stewart trusted Wexler implicitly; he didn't read the contract or consult a lawyer, or feel the need to do so. His friend, and to some degree mentor and trusted adviser, Wexler had assured him that the contract was a mere formality that would protect him, as he had desired, if Atlantic should ever be sold.

By the summer of 1965, the notion of "The Memphis Sound" was being discussed in the industry's trade magazines. In the June 12th issue of *Billboard*, Elton Whisenhunt wrote a piece headlined "Memphis Sound: A Southern View." Whisenhunt conducted brief interviews with Memphis record label owners Joe Cuoghi, Sam Phillips, Stan Kesler, and Jim Stewart. Stewart described "the Memphis Sound" this way:

> It goes back to the colored influence in the early blues and folk lore [*sic*] music of the South. Our music is still influenced by that.
>
> All our artists at Stax are Negroes. Naturally, our sound is directly oriented in that direction. The sound is hard to describe. It has a heavy back beat. We accent the beat and rhythm in our recordings. It is very dominant. New York recordings wouldn't bring out the drums or beat as we do.
>
> But that beat—a hard rhythm section—is an integral part of our sound. The combination of horns, instead of a smooth sound, produces a rough, growly, rasping sound, which carries into the melody. To add flavor and color there is topping with the piano and fills with the guitar or vocal group.[15]

14. The inscription on Stax Records that read "Distributed by Atlantic Recording Company" was, in essence, fraudulent.

15. Elton Whisenhunt, "Memphis Sound: A Southern View," *Billboard* (June 12, 1965): 6.

Stewart told me in 1986: "That title ['the Memphis sound'] came from outside. We didn't give it to ourselves. It sort of drifted back to us that there was a sound. We really weren't thinking about it. We came to work every day, we did what we had to do, and we went our separate ways. It was a job, but it was fun. It was just an identification thing simply because the same people were doing it day after day—seven people that were doing God knows how many releases a year." "You're going to obviously have an identifiable sound, especially if it's coming out of the same studio," affirms Booker.

Deanie Parker remembers that once the company became cognizant of the outside world's perception, Stax actively promoted "the Memphis Sound." "We were promoting the Memphis sound as a whole and trying to give a definition of a Stax sound. We focused on that to a large degree. I think that partially that happened because the question was asked so often, 'What is [the Memphis Sound]?' So we were given an opportunity to tag what it was that we felt we were creating." When Al Bell came to the company later that year, he insisted that "The Memphis Sound" be inscribed on virtually every piece of paper that emanated from the company.

Five days before the new Stax-Atlantic distribution agreement was signed, Jerry Wexler brought Wilson Pickett down to Memphis. Born in Prattville, Alabama, in 1941, Pickett was possessed of one of the harshest voices in soul music. Moving to Detroit in his early teens, he started out singing gospel with Chess recording artists the Violinaires. When he was eighteen he elected to go the secular route and signed on with the Falcons, whose membership included future Stax songwriters and vocalists Eddie Floyd and Mack Rice. With the Falcons, Pickett sang lead on the hit "I Found a Love." Egos being what they are, he quickly became a solo artist, signing on with Double L. Three chart singles later, Wexler wooed him to Atlantic. His first Atlantic single was recorded in New York at the company's studios but, when no one was happy with the results, Wexler hit on the bright idea of taking him down to Stax.

"I couldn't get over [the way they recorded in Memphis]," explains Wexler. "Coming to Stax literally changed my life. I took Wilson Pickett down there because entropy was setting in in New York . . . I lost interest in recording with the same arrangers who were out of ideas. The musicians were out of licks [and] the songwriters didn't have any songs. It got so I dreaded to go into the studio to make a record with the foreboding that I was gonna come out with the same dreadful piece of crap that we did last time with no fire in it, no originality and, worst of all, no hit potential. . . . When I went down to Stax and saw how they made records, it was really inspirational. The idea of coming to a place [like Stax] where four guys come to work like four cabinetmakers or four plumbers and hang up their coats and start playing music in the morning, and then the beautifully crafted records that came out of this! God, can I get some of this, 'cause this is the way to go. I've never changed since then. That was it. That was the way to make records."

Wexler and Pickett made three trips down to Memphis in May, September, and December 1965. Altogether nine songs were recorded, the first session producing "In the Midnight Hour" and "Don't Fight It," the last giving birth to "634-5789 (Soulsville U.S.A.)" and "Ninety-Nine and a Half (Won't Do)." Booker was away attending university during all three sessions, so Joe Hall played piano in May, and Isaac Hayes in September and December. Pickett was so happy with the success of the first session that he personally sent a $100 bonus to each member of the Stax house band, a virtually unheard-of gesture.

It was during the May sessions that the Stax rhythmic conception of a minutely delayed beat two and four was developed, inspired by Wexler's dancing of the then-new northern fad, the Jerk. This rhythm can be heard on all subsequent 1960s up-tempo Stax recordings, including "Hold On! I'm Comin'," "Respect," "Knock on Wood," and "Soul Man," and remains one of the essential defining features of the Stax sound. To some degree, the Stax rhythm section had always slightly delayed the beat, but with "Midnight Hour" it was to become that much more pronounced. "I credit it to the fact that we didn't play with headphones and we were in a big room," reasons Steve Cropper. "There was a lot of delay between the singer and us. When you put headphones on, everybody just sort of tightens up. We learned to overcome [not wearing headphones]. I had to learn basically to play watching Al [Jackson]'s left hand rather than by going by what I heard in my head. I started anticipating. When he was coming down, I'd come down with him. Rather than wait for the sound to get over to me, I'd go with his hands. . . . Obviously, everything would have fallen apart if we had just followed the delay time, but we learned how to catch up and get the downbeat on.

"The Jerk was a delayed backbeat thing. The first time that Al [Jackson] and I became aware of it, we found it in Detroit. It was the way the kids were dancing. When Jerry Wexler was down there helping to produce 'Midnight Hour,' he made a whole thing about this move, this delayed backbeat thing. We started being more conscious of putting the kick drumbeat dead on and delaying the 'two, four,' which became an actual physical thing, not room delay at that point. We worked on that. That was not something that was accidental. So, we started overemphasizing that and made it a whole way of life because it seemed to work all the time. It was never behind the beat, it's just delayed. It's like if you put it in a little time cube and you turned the switch and then you only play the delay part, rather than the accent. That's what came out."

Cropper takes great pains to point out that after a drum fill at the end of a section, they would very deliberately play the second beat dead on to synchronize the groove again before resuming delaying the backbeat on each subsequent bar.

Vocalists at Stax also tended to phrase in a slightly delayed manner. This was a natural result of standing some fifteen feet from the drummer behind a tall baffle, without wearing headphones. "They had to hear what came over the top, and bounced off the ceiling," explains Steve, "so there was definitely a delay in the room which always kept the singer just a little back so it never ran away. That's why I think the Stax stuff always felt so good."

"In the Midnight Hour," cowritten by Pickett and Steve Cropper, became a massive radio hit, topping the R&B charts at number 1 while also scaling the pop charts to number 21. Surprisingly, according to Jim Stewart, it only sold about 300,000 copies. "634-5789 (Soulsville U.S.A.)," written by Cropper and Eddie Floyd, did a little better, resting at the top of the R&B charts for a full seven weeks while peaking at number 13 on the pop charts. "Don't Fight It" and "Ninety-Nine and a Half (Won't Do)," both coauthored by Pickett and Cropper, also charted.[16]

Buoyed by the success of the first Pickett session, at the end of June Atlantic brought Don Covay down to Memphis to record with the MG's and to avail himself of the Stax songwriters. Four songs, "See-Saw," "I Never Get Enough of Your Love," "Sookie Sookie," and "Iron Out the Rough Spots," were recorded; the first three were cowritten by Covay and Steve Cropper, while Cropper, Booker T. Jones, and David Porter cowrote the last. "See-Saw" was the only hit, reaching number 5 on the R&B charts and number 44 on the pop charts. "Sookie Sookie" was later covered by the rock group Steppenwolf.

16. "Don't Fight It" reached the number 4 and number 53 spots on the R&B and pop charts, while "Ninety-Nine and a Half (Won't Do)," based on a gospel song by Dorothy Love Coates and the Gospel Harmonettes, reached the number 13 and number 53 spots respectively.

According to Steve Cropper, the Covay sessions at times got a little rocky. "I remember that Jim Stewart called Jerry Wexler and said, 'Get Don Covay out of here. He's driving us nuts.' Don Covay was a little bit on the weird side. I loved Don to death. We get along great but I don't think Jim and them understood Don. He thinks in different areas and he was kind of driving people bananas. . . . He's kind of frantic when he makes decisions. He jumps from this place to that. You never know what he's gonna do next." Covay's high energy level and extreme unpredictability were the antithesis of Jim Stewart's banker personality.

In exchange for the use of the Stax studio and musicians, Stax split with Atlantic the publishing and received an override from all sales of Atlantic product recorded at Stax. Given the success of the Pickett and Covay sessions, one would have expected Atlantic to bring a host of artists down to Memphis to record with the MG's at Stax's 926 E. McLemore studio. According to Jim Stewart, such a possibility was unfortunately precluded by Wilson Pickett's irascible personality. "It got to the point," explains Stewart, "where the guys felt they were being used, so I stopped it. They weren't getting much money for that stuff. Another thing was a personal relationship. Pickett got to be an asshole. They told me, 'Forget it, man, get his ass out of here.' The guys didn't want to work with him, and I wouldn't ask them to do it."

Both Steve and Duck deny any ill feelings toward Pickett. While both agree the singer could be difficult, Cropper stresses that that was only when he drank, and at Stax in the mid-sixties, no one, including Pickett, drank or did drugs at daytime sessions. "I don't know if there was a joint ever lit up in that place," Steve recalls, laughing. "Pretty weird, isn't it? Mainly daytime recording, mainly everybody was sober. There was a thing in those days: you drink at night and you sobered up in the morning. Guys didn't drink during the daytime. [If you did] you were considered a bum and an alcoholic."[17]

Cropper also takes pains to point out that he was making a lot of money off the songwriting on the Pickett sessions, and would have loved that situation to continue. Duck, while not sharing in the songwriting, stresses that Pickett was one of the greatest singers he ever worked with and, consequently, he loved those sessions. Jim simply told Wexler and Atlantic that the Stax studio was too busy to accommodate outside sessions and consequently would no longer be able to do them. Steve, Duck, and Jerry Wexler felt that the real reason why Stax closed its doors to outside sessions was that Jim Stewart was not happy "giving away" the Stax sound.

"[Jim] was vague," recalls Wexler. "I knew that Pickett had irritated him. Pickett was always bum-rapping Steve Cropper, claiming that Steve had stolen the song ['In the Midnight Hour'], but I never could get any exact reason. I got a feeling after a while that the real reason was that Jim had some feeling about hits coming out of the studio that were not on Stax [yet were recorded] with his band and his facilities. They really didn't want anybody else there 'cause they didn't want hits coming out of there with their imprimatur that they didn't get the full benefit of."

Al Bell, who arrived at the company just a few months before the final Pickett session, echoes Wexler's suspicions: "We had that policy to preserve the sound that we had developed. That was our identity, our trademark, our trade secret, and we preserved it in that fashion. The other thing was there really wasn't that much time, because the studio was constantly being used. When it wasn't being used, it was supposed to be available for in-house producers and writers, because what made Stax tick was that freedom, the ability to go in that studio whenever a guy had an idea and get it with no restrictions, no clock to watch, none of that. Just to be able to record and record until you got it. If it took all day or it took all week, we had that freedom to do it."[18]

A couple of months prior to the first Pickett session, Atlantic had made a rather unique arrangement with Stax. Wexler offered to loan Sam and Dave to Stax for as long as Atlantic distributed the Memphis company. Sam and Dave, in essence, would be full-fledged Stax artists, with Stax being paid the same money for every Sam and Dave record sold as they were for records by their other artists (minus Sam and Dave's royalty and an override to Henry Stone). The only difference was that Wexler insisted that Stax split the publishing with Atlantic on any songs written by Stax staff songwriters for Sam and Dave. This latter proviso would turn out to be a wise move on Wexler's part.

17. Jerry Wexler also stresses that Stax was an anomaly in that he never saw drugs or alcohol being consumed on the premises at daytime sessions. It was simply understood that Jim Stewart forbade such activity. Various musicians point out that when Jim Stewart wasn't at the studio late at night, it was a different story, and before Jim quit his day job at the bank, it wasn't that uncommon for a quart or two of beer to be consumed in the studio. In general, though, in the 1960s, Stax was a pretty sober environment and consequently Pickett didn't get out of hand.

18. In many ways, it is a shame that this policy was ever instituted. With Atlantic barred from the Stax studio, it turned to both Muscle Shoals and Chips Moman's American Sound Studio. While undeniably great records were cut by Atlantic at both locations, it boggles the mind to imagine the MG's working with Atlantic artists such as Aretha Franklin, King Curtis, and Clarence Carter.

Born in 1935 in Miami, Florida, Sam Moore was the son of a church deacon; his mother sang in the church choir, and his grandfather was a minister. In addition, the Moore family was related to the gospel legends Albertina Walker and Ruth Davis and the Davis Sisters. Singing his first solo in church at the age of nine ("I wasn't nervous. I was a big show-off"), Sam did not develop an interest in secular music, initially doo-wop, until a little bit later, and somewhat against his parents' wishes. "Oh yes, they didn't like to hear the Chuck Berrys, the Fats Dominos, and James Browns," Sam recalls. "So, I would sneak out if I wanted to stand on the street corners and sing with the guys. Never could I bring a rock 'n' roll record in the house."[19]

One aggregation of Sam's street-corner pals that centered around his high school eventually coalesced as a quartet called the Majestics. They were together for two-and-a-half years, working with a similar repertoire as the Royal Spades in Memphis, covering tunes by R&B stars of the day such as Hank Ballard and the Midnighters, the Five Royales, and the Coasters. Playing high-school hops, they eventually became good enough to attract the attention of Henry Stone, the godfather of the Miami record scene, who owned and operated a distributorship (Tone), a studio (Federal), and several labels (Marlin, Alston, and Shot). The group recorded one single for Marlin, a prototypical talking doo-wop, "Nitey Nite" (sic) backed with "Cave Man Rock." Released in late 1954, the record generated a little local notoriety but not much else. By 1957, the Majestics had changed their name to the Gales (after the nationally popular Sensational Nightingales), left the secular world behind, and embarked upon a gospel career.

When the Gales folded two years later, Sam joined another local quartet, the Melionaires. One hot night the Melionaires found themselves opening up for Sam Cooke and the Soul Stirrers. This coincidence eventually led to Sam Moore being offered the almost impossible job of replacing Cooke when the latter decided to leave the gospel world. At the last moment Sam backed out, deciding the gospel life was not for him. "I got chicken," demurs Sam. "The night before I was to go with the Soul Stirrers I went to a show to see Jackie Wilson. I saw the electrification, the excitement. Oh God, he was a hell of a showman. I said, 'That's what I want to do.' [The next day the Soul Stirrers] looked for me. I just disappeared." Ironically, Sam's later Stax-mate, Johnnie Taylor, then of the Highway QCs, ended up taking the job.

Realizing his true calling belonged in the world of secular ecstasy, Sam left the Melionaires soon after and took to the amateur circuit, imitating his heroes. "When I started out I knew nothing about the business," confesses Sam. "The only thing I knew was to stand behind a microphone and sing. I enjoyed singing songs by Jackie Wilson, Little Willie John, and Sam Cooke. I'm a gospel man." The latter comment is telling. Even more than these three role models, Sam was never able to shake his gospel background, always incorporating the melismas, playful voicedness, and sheer intensity that has forever been the essence of black church singing. In the spring of 1961, it was dropping tentatively to his knees—a trick he learned from mentor Jackie Wilson—while singing tunes such as "Danny Boy" that won Moore first prize in a local amateur show, twenty-five dollars, and a job as amateur-night emcee of a local bastion of Miami black nightlife, the King of Hearts club. Sam worked Monday, Wednesday, Friday, and Saturday and when he wasn't emceeing, in his own words, he fulfilled the role of a lounge singer.

On one of those amateur nights in December 1961, who should walk in but Dave Prater, Jr. Prater originally hailed from the tiny town of Ocilla, Georgia (pop. c. 3,000),

---

19. Sam sang second tenor in most of these street-corner groups. Quite surprisingly, he didn't sing lead until his late twenties, just a little before he met Dave Prater.

about five hundred miles north of Miami. Born May 9, 1937, Dave waited twenty-two years before heading to the city, wooed by his brother, bass singer J.T. Prater, to join J.T.'s gospel group, the Sensational Hummingbirds, as lead singer. The Hummingbirds pounded the gospel circuit and recorded one 45 over a period of two years while Dave worked in the daytime, first as a cashier and later as a short-order cook. Dave had known Sam through their respective gospel quartets, and now Dave also intended to test the secular waters via the traditional route of the amateur show. He had planned to sing Sam Cooke's "Wonderful World," but the house band at the King of Hearts did not know the song. The band suggested Jackie Wilson's "Doggin' Around" as an alternative, but Dave didn't know all the words. "But I knew the words," remembers Sam. "So I said to him, 'Look, if you start singing I'll pipe the words to you from the back 'cause I'm going to be up onstage.' So he started, and when he got to the verse part I would just say [the words] and he would sing them.

"When it got to the part where Jackie Wilson would drop to his knees, Dave tripped. I was responsible for all the instruments and microphones that got broken and I didn't want to pay for something that I didn't do, so he and I both went down together and I caught the mike. The audience thought that was the act. It wasn't, but they went crazy." What Sam fails to mentions is that, not only did he catch the mike, he also came up singing, something that would also become a hallmark of Sam and Dave shows for years to come. That night, with the glowing approval of owner John Lomello, Sam and Dave started working the club as a duo.

At this point Henry Stone reentered the picture, recording Sam and Dave locally for both his Alston and Marlin labels. Two singles appeared, "Never Never" b/w "Lotta Lovin'" and "My Love Belongs to You" b/w "No More Pain,"[20] both produced by Steve Alaimo (of "Everyday I Have to Cry" fame) and distributed only in southern Florida by Stone's Tone Distributors. Stone next engineered a deal for the duo with Morris Levy's Roulette label. Five 45s appeared sporadically on Roulette through 1962–63.[21]

Produced by either Roulette A&R man Henry Glover or Steve Alaimo, the records echo the sounds of Sam Cooke, the Soul Stirrers, Ray Charles, and Jackie Wilson. One of the songs, "She's Alright," was actually written by Wilson, and the astute listener can pick out Jackie singing background harmony. Another side, the sweet ballad "It Was So Nice While It Lasted," was written by Johnny Nash under the name "Billy Nash." Sam and Dave themselves cowrote two songs, "My Love Belongs to You" and "I Need Love." The Roulette records are radically different from the better-known Stax recordings.[22] At Stax, Sam assumed the role of lead dynamo with Dave functioning as his foil. At Roulette, Dave was featured much more. Even more pertinent, the writing and playing on the Roulette recordings is largely imitative with some songs, such as Steve Alaimo's "No More Pain," being literal cops of other recordings (in this case the Soul Stirrers' "I'll Build a Fence").

The Roulette singles and Sam and Dave's local notoriety at the King of Hearts served to spread their name nationally to those in the know, including Atlantic Records co-owner Jerry Wexler. In town for a disc jockey convention in Miami Beach in late summer 1964, after a hectic day of glad-handing, Wexler stopped by the King of Hearts. "It was 165

20. "Never Never" appeared on the ultra-rare Alston 777 while "My Love Belongs to You" was released on Marlin 6104.

21. All five plus the Marlin single were later issued by Roulette on LP to capitalize on the duo's success at Stax.

22. It seems odd that the dynamic duo did not continue writing. According to Sam, at Roulette, Stax, and Atlantic, "We were just pawns. They knew what was good for us. The only thing we were allowed to do was sing. There was no sense in telling them that I could write 'cause who would have listened? We didn't have no power or clout."

degrees in the middle of summer," recalls Wexler. "It was unbelievable. It was hot and they were hot. Henry Stone was the one who steered me there. It was wall-to-wall people. We were the only Caucasians in there. Ahmet [Ertegun, Wexler's partner at Atlantic] and I are out there boogalooing like fools, sweating and just having a ball. It was so exciting. I don't know if we were trying to impress Sam and Dave, Henry Stone, or just knock our own selves out, but we really got into the spirit of things. When I heard them there that night, that's all she wrote. I signed them up immediately.

"I thought it would be great to have Stax produce them. So I went to Jim Stewart and said, 'I want you to produce these guys and in consideration it can be released on Stax and we'll pay you the regular Stax royalty. You pay them just as though they're your artists but always with the understanding that this is on loan from us. We have the master contract.'"

It was an ingenious and inspired move on Wexler's part. Ironically, the reaction at Stax to the arrival of Sam and Dave was largely one of indifference. "There was no one interested in Sam and Dave," remarks songwriter David Porter. "It was like a throwaway kind of situation [to] see if anything could happen with them . . . so I developed a relationship with Sam Moore and Dave Prater which involved me trying to come up with material for them. No one else at the time was even thinking about it."

A native Memphian, Porter had been trying to work his way into a music career for quite some time. While in high school at Booker T. Washington, Porter had formed a quartet he dubbed the Marquettes that regularly competed in the Wednesday evening talent shows at Beale Street's Palace Theatre. Under the watchful eye of MC Rufus Thomas, the Marquettes often competed with Isaac Hayes's group, the Teen Tones, the Marquettes' specialty being a version of the Dell-Vikings' "Come Go with Me." "When I first met Isaac during that time," laughs Porter, "I wasn't too fond of him because he was beating me out of the five dollars [prize money]. He felt likewise. We knew each other but we were not running buddies."

When not entering talent shows, the Marquettes were busy auditioning for every record label in town that would listen to them. Jim Stewart was impressed enough to attempt to record a single. At Stewart's suggestion they worked on "The Old Grey Mare," but were never able to cut a version that was deemed releasable. After the initial attempts, Porter, commonly referred to as the local Sam Cooke, opted to record the song without the Marquettes, eventually bringing in the Del-Rios to sing background. But, alas, success was still not forthcoming.

Undaunted, Porter, while working across the street at Jones' Big D Grocery and selling insurance to support his wife and child, struck up a songwriting relationship with Chips Moman. Moman and Porter penned a number of songs with such unpromising titles as "Treasured Moments" and "Woe Is Me" before Moman's acrimonious split with Stewart and Axton curtailed their activity. Porter next started writing with Rufus Thomas's son, Marvell. The pair's debut effort, "The Life I Live," was waxed by Barbara Stephens and released on Satellite in October 1961.

It would be a few years before Porter's name would next appear on a Stax-related release. "They were trying to get me to stop hanging around there," Porter exclaims. "Jim Stewart didn't think I had any talent." Fortunately for David, Estelle Axton thought differently. "She believed in me all the time," continues Porter. "He was trying to get rid of me. She was trying to keep me around. There was a great amount of discussion about me because I was a pest! I wanted to be in the music business. I had no idea how to contact anybody exterior of Memphis. I'm a poor kid. I don't know anything about calling anybody in New York.

"Jim was not a great motivator for me, but his sister was. She was saying, 'Study these records.' I would go in the Satellite Record Shop and play records and scratch them up. She was such a beautiful lady. She would say, 'Well, okay. Just go and study that and see what they're doing. You've got to see what everybody else is doing so you'll know what to do.'"

Not one to give up, Porter kept working on his writing skills while continuing to make the rounds to see if anyone was interested in recording him as an artist. In mid-1962 he recorded a Clyde McPhatter–influenced outing for the Golden Eagle label, "Farewell" b/w "Chivalry." Despite being a bit of a regional breakout, "Farewell" ultimately made few waves. Later that year Porter recorded another 45, this time for Hi Records, under the name Kenny Cain. Hi co-owner Ray Harris told Porter that he wanted to develop a black artist who sounded white. Produced by Willie Mitchell, "Practice Makes Perfect" b/w "Words Can Never Say" was released just before the close of 1962. Porter also made a session for Savoy Records under the auspices of Fred Mendelssohn, "So Long" b/w "Home Is Where You Come," which was released under the nom de disque of Little David, because Porter assumed he was still under contract to Golden Eagle. None of these records achieved significant radio play or sales and, consequently, Porter continued to plug away at Stax, hoping to record and/or write songs. For a short time he dabbled in writing with Steve Cropper, "but our chemistry just wasn't quite right for it." He did, though, serve as the vocalist with the MG's on many of their weekend gigs that required a singer.

Sometime in 1964, not too long after Isaac Hayes began playing sessions at Stax, Porter suggested they write songs together. Hayes, who had gradually begun to contribute arrangement ideas on Stax sessions and had been harboring ambitions as a writer, was more than interested. Hayes and Porter's first efforts to be released on Stax were Porter's lone Stax solo single in the 1960s, "Can't See You When I Want To" (Stax 163) and Carla Thomas's "How Do You Quit (Someone You Love)" (Atlantic 2272), released in January and February 1965, respectively. The Thomas release attained a modicum of success, rising to number 39 on the pop charts. On both 45s, Hayes wrote under the pseudonym Ed Lee to avoid breaking a previous publishing commitment.

At some point, most likely in the summer or fall of 1965, Hayes and Porter, frustrated with their progress at Stax, visited their old friend Chips Moman at American Sound Studio. They formed the Genie label, jointly owned by Hayes, Porter, Moman, and Harold Atkins. The sole release on Genie was a single by future Stax songwriter Homer Banks. Porter knew Banks from Booker T. Washington High School and, with Hayes, wrote both sides of the single, "Little Lady of Stone" b/w "Sweetie Pie." The record failed to create any waves, few of the five hundred copies pressed actually being purchased. When Jim Stewart finally offered Porter a songwriting contract with a weekly draw, Genie was laid to rest.[23] As was the case with Steve Cropper, it was Estelle Axton who forced Jim to put David Porter on salary. "Jim Stewart gave me six months to make it or get out," rues Porter a quarter-century later. "Estelle Axton believed in me and he didn't. But, he was nice enough to give me the chance. Estelle had mortgaged the house so he couldn't refuse her and she was my biggest supporter."

Estelle vividly recalls the day Porter came into the record shop with the lyrics for "Can't See You When I Want To." "He had about three sheets of lyrics. So I sat down and I read his song. I saw he had a good idea but then I began to work on him. I said, 'David, there

23. The above account of "Little Lady Stone" was pieced together via interviews with Chips Moman, Isaac Hayes, David Porter, and Homer Banks. Although 1965 appears to be an accurate date for the record's issue, the song itself was not registered with BMI until 1967.

is no way possible that you could put this many lyrics in a song. You'd run ten minutes.'"
Estelle had a happy knack for simultaneously critiquing and encouraging. Buoyed by her
comments, David would go away, rewrite the song, and then bring it back. Estelle would
then discuss the changes David had made, play some more records for him by way of illus-
tration, and send him off again. She continued to work with David in this fashion for several months. Porter's weekly draw amounted to fifty dollars a week, which he shared with
Isaac Hayes, who was still working in the meat-packing plant. Nonetheless, his foot was
finally in the door. Sam and Dave would be the vehicle by which Porter and Hayes would
get the key to the castle.

Sam and Dave's first single for Stax, "Goodnight Baby" b/w "A Place Nobody Can
Find," coupled a Porter-Cropper composition with a rare example of a David Porter
solo composition.[24] Released in March 1965, both sides of the single featured Dave
Prater singing lead, in marked contrast to Sam and Dave's later Stax recordings. On
"Goodnight Baby" David Porter lovingly juxtaposed organ and vibes, the latter being a
direct influence of Holland-Dozier-Holland's work at Motown with the Supremes.
"Part of what eventually evolved into the magic of Hayes and Porter's writing was my
study of the Motown catalogue and what Holland-Dozier-Holland were doing," Porter
emphasizes. "That was an ongoing process. I was a novice. To be quite honest I was
learning. So [the vibes] was a thought and we tried it." On top of the arrangement, Sam
and Dave are singing in glorious harmony, wringing Porter's lyric for all it's worth. One
can readily hear how close their three-and-a-half years together had brought them. They
answer, echo, and finish each other's lines, join in and drop out of the arrangement,
individually and together, with a grace and ease that is mesmerizing. The whole is
brought to a climax with an ad-lib ending that is pure ecstasy, both singers emoting in
overdrive against the horns and rhythm section.

Despite the obvious strength of this initial effort, the single's success was somewhat
underwhelming, and four months passed before Sam and Dave reentered the Stax studio to cut a followup. For the duo's second Stax release, Hayes and Porter wrote and produced both "I Take What I Want" and "Sweet Home." Future Hi session guitarist Teenie
Hodges shares in the credit on the A-side. According to Porter, Teenie was like a little
brother who often hung around the Stax studio. On this particular day Porter hummed
the guitar line to Teenie, who then played it on the record. To encourage him to write,
Porter and Hayes also gave him a songwriting credit. "I Take What I Want" is an up-
tempo romp that, although it didn't chart, set the tone for the majority of Sam and
Dave's Stax singles. Next time out, Sam, Dave, Hayes, Porter, and everyone else at Stax
would be celebrating.

24. In this period Hayes, as Ed Lee, also wrote by himself the A-side of a Mar-Keys single, "Banana Juice" (Stax
166).

5

Don't Have to Shop Around: 1965

I n 1965, despite its many successes, Stax was still the "little label that could." Only eight of the just over one hundred 45s that had been released on the Stax label, its Volt subsidiary, or Atlantic had entered the Top 10 of *Billboard*'s R&B charts. Only one of these, Booker T. and the MG's 1962 instrumental, "Green Onions," had climbed all the way to the vaunted number 1 position. Even more telling is the fact that only four of the company's releases—"Green Onions," the Mar-Keys' "Last Night," Carla Thomas's "Gee Whiz," and Rufus Thomas's "Walking the Dog"—had been able to break into the pop Top 10.

Even though Stax/Volt issued consistently great records, most of which sported a unique, readily identifiable sound that found favor among black Americans in the South and pockets of the North and Midwest, in mid-1965 white America barely knew the label existed, and among black Americans in Los Angeles and New York, in general, the label's releases fell far behind those of Motown, Atlantic, Chess, and Vee Jay in sales and radio play. This was partially a product of Stax's development of a rootsy, heavily gospel-influenced "black" sound. Within a couple of years this conception of soul music would achieve much greater chart success on Stax and Volt and via Stax-influenced releases on Atlantic, but in 1965 large-scale success was still a dream and a lot of sweat somewhere down the road.

Part of the reason for the label's lack of visibility in mid-1965 was its rudimentary promotion efforts. In 1996, Booker T. described the label's early dearth of promotional skills when discussing the success of "Green Onions": "Stax had no marketing acumen. 'Green Onions' was a phenomena. Stax was just figuring how to get records out and how to collect for them when they did 'Green Onions.' Stax was not at all a priority for Atlantic. There were no promotion men to work 'Green Onions.' There was only Jim and Cropper. There wasn't anybody there to do it. They probably could have sold a couple of million had they been established." Not all that much had changed by the summer of 1965.

Ostensibly to create a greater profile for the individual artists and the label as a whole on the West Coast, Estelle Axton took a Stax Revue—including Booker T. and the MG's, Rufus and Carla Thomas, Wilson Pickett, William Bell, the Mad Lads, and the Astors—to Los Angeles during the first week of August 1965. The climax of the week was performances by all the artists on Saturday and Sunday at the 5/4 Ballroom in Watts, promoted by the disc jockey Magnificent Montague. Most of the artists came straight from Memphis to Los Angeles, while the Astors flew in from Washington, where they had just completed a month of gigs supporting their recent chart hit "Candy."

"Candy" was the quintessential hit in the Astors' career. Initially recording on Satellite as the Chips in 1961, under their new name the Astors had released a second record on Stax proper in July 1963 before finally hitting paydirt in the spring of 1965. Coauthored by MG guitarist Steve Cropper and Isaac Hayes, "Candy" was a hook-laden, up-tempo confection that still sounds fresh over thirty years after its initial release. Ironically, it nearly wasn't recorded. According to lead singer Curtis Johnson, Jim Stewart had lost faith in the group and had no plans to record them again. When Stewart was out of town on business, the group essentially sneaked into the studio to wax "Candy" and member Elihue Stanback's "I Found Out." The latter featured Stanback replacing Johnson on lead vocals. Packy Axton produced both sides.

The first version of "Candy" was recut after a dub was played for customers in the Satellite Record Shop. Apparently, one of problems with the initial recording was that it sounded a little too close to the Impressions for comfort.[1] On their second time through, the Astors smoked both songs. "Candy" strutted its way to number 12 R&B and number 63 pop on the *Billboard* charts. The record was especially popular in Philadelphia, where WDAS deejay Jimmy Bishop plugged it incessantly in exchange for similar consideration in Memphis for Barbara Mason's "Yes, I'm Ready," which Bishop had produced on his own Arctic label. On the strength of Bishop's efforts, Philadelphia's Uptown Theater hosted the Astors' first major out-of-town gig, and the City of Brotherly Love would remain the strongest market for the group throughout their career. Despite two more superb 45s, "Candy" would be the group's only nationally charted recording.

The other Stax vocal group to make the trip out West was the Mad Lads. John Gary Williams, William Brown, Julius Green, and Harold Thomas (no relation to Rufus, Carla, or Marvell) met in the tenth grade at Booker T. Washington High School. Brown lived at 1063 College, just down the street from the Capitol Theater. He clearly remembers seeing the last country-and-western show at the theater before it was converted into a recording studio. By the time the Mad Lads came together, Brown was already an employee at the Satellite Record Shop.

"I was the first black person in Stax, period," asserts William proudly. "Nobody ever walked in that building before me. I went in there when Jim Stewart and Chips Moman were fanning the cobwebs out of the Capitol Theater. I said, 'What y'all doing?' [Jim] said, 'We're gonna have a record company.' I said, 'Well, I can sing.' He said, 'Come back when you get good.' I didn't leave. I stayed there and he never said nothing else. He never said, 'Get away.' Jim was one of them hardcore guys—horn-rimmed glasses, pumped hair. When we see shit like that—ooh, look out! But, he wasn't like that. He was a businessperson minding his own business."

At that point the record store wasn't quite open. As soon as it was, William went after a job, becoming, at age fourteen, the first part-time employee at Satellite. His sister, Norma, also eventually helped out in the store. William also began shining shoes at King's Barbershop next door to the record store, and pretty soon began contributing the occasional background vocal in the studio.

The Mad Lads came together as the Emeralds in the study hall at Booker T. Washington. According to Brown, John Gary Williams, who was then a new student at Booker T., began singing one day in the study hall, and one by one Julius, William, and Harold joined in. The four already were aware of each other because they all had competed in various guises at local talent shows, with Green and Brown regularly singing together. Williams, Thomas, and Green were also former members of the Teen Town Singers. Collectively their influences ranged from Sam Cooke to Shep and the Limelites

---

1. Estelle regularly test-marketed Stax recordings in the record store, and a number of records were consequently redone or scrapped as a result. She also regularly invited local disc jockeys from WDIA and WLOK down to the shop, playing them recent Stax recordings and asking their opinions.

although, overall, their sound tended toward the Northeast doo-wop style. After seven or eight months of woodshedding, Brown approached Miss Axton (to this day many of the Stax artists and employees refer to Estelle in this manner) about recording his group.

"Miss Axton said, 'If you can learn "I'm on the Outside (Looking In)" by Little Anthony and the Imperials [then a Top 20 pop hit], I'll sign a group that could sing that.' We learned that song that night! The next day we walked in and Miss Axton said, 'We're gonna cut you boys.'"

William is probably exaggerating a little bit, but the Emeralds' rendition of the Imperials tune did pique Estelle's interest enough that she went down to Ellis Auditorium in late spring to see them perform at an annual high-school concert that was known in Memphis as a ballet or Jubilet. The Emeralds were headlining that year, and a young John Colbert, later known as J. Blackfoot (lead singer of the Soul Children), performed a solo act. The Emeralds' version of "Sunday Kind of Love" turned out the show that year, and Estelle was convinced to sign them.

It took about four or five months for the group to cut their first single, "The Sidewalk Surf" (Stax 160). On the day of the session, Harold Thomas was replaced by Robert Phillips as Thomas's father forced him to do his paper route rather than go down to the studio. At that point, after a routine name check, it was discovered that someone else already had the rights to the name the Emeralds. Deanie Parker was the one who suggested that the Mad Lads would be an appropriate substitute, partially as a tip-of-the-hat to local deejay Reuben "Mad Lad" Washington (the man who first played "Green Onions" on the radio) and partially due to the crazed behavior of the group. John Gary Williams remembers, "We were pranksters. We brought that high-school thing, that young thing into the company. It was like a family. We were sort of like the kids in the family." "That's why we were called the Mad Lads," echoes William Brown, "because we acted the damn fool." At the time, it was not uncommon to drive down McLemore and see the group acting crazed, performing in the bay window of the Satellite Record Shop.

"The Sidewalk Surf" was written by Marvell Thomas, Isaac Hayes (under the pseudonym Ed Lee), and Carl Cunningham. Cunningham was the first of several drummers in his family.[2] Trained by William Brown to shine shoes at King's Barbershop (which had now moved around the corner on College Street), in between customers Cunningham would hang out at Stax learning everything he could from Al Jackson. Between sessions, he would practice on Jackson's drums. If someone was recording, he would simply sit at the foot of Jackson's drum kit watching the master drummer's every move. Steve Cropper remembers Cunningham regularly being summoned to go back across the street when a customer was in need of a shoe shine. When the national television show "Route 66" came through Memphis to shoot, both Cunningham and Brown made appearances shining shoes.[3] Within a few years Cunningham would be the drummer in the Bar-Kays, with whom the Mad Lads would maintain a close relationship.

Estelle Axton came up with the idea for "The Sidewalk Surf." No one in the group could stand the song. Julius Green simply sighs, "It was nothing like us," while John Gary Williams states, "I couldn't get into it. There was no feeling there." William Brown is more emphatic: "I hate that record. Miss Axton believed in nostalgia." The idea was that the

2. Roy Cunningham would end up drumming for the second edition of the Bar-Kays, and Blair Cunningham would find success in the 1980s with British group Haircut One Hundred and in 1993 would join Paul McCartney's band.

3. If anyone reading this has a video copy of the Memphis episode of "Route 66," please write this author (see Preface for the address).

song would be a skateboard tune. A dance was even made up to go along with it (William's sister, Norma, demonstrated the dance the first two or three times the Mad Lads performed the song at local high schools) but, when released in November 1964, the disc received local airplay only.

Just a couple of weeks before the West Coast trip, Stax released the second Mad Lads single, "Don't Have to Shop Around," this time on the company's Volt subsidiary. It took until October for the 45 to enter the charts, but when it finally did, it sailed all the way to number 11 R&B while settling for number 93 pop. The song was written by bassist Allen Jones, tenor saxophonist Andrew Love, and pianist Richard Shan. Love had just recently become a regular Stax session musician, replacing Gilbert Caple, who had left Memphis to work in the house band at Houston's Duke-Peacock Records. Jones and Shan, both native Memphians, were still trying to work their way into the company. Shan was never too successful, but Jones would soon get hired to audition demo tapes, eventually becoming a staff songwriter and producer before going on to manage the Bar-Kays. The tune he had concocted for the Mad Lads was a gossamer, shimmering ballad that beautifully juxtaposed Isaac Hayes's organ and Booker T.'s piano with a vibraphone. Apparently the song had already been cut by a local white Memphis group (no one recalls who they were anymore). The Mad Lads remember learning the song in the attic above the studio with Shan playing the piano. A few hours and two takes later they had a hit. As was the case with the Astors, the Mad Lads were especially popular in the Philadelphia area.

While the Astors were enjoying their solitary hit and the Mad Lads were perched on the precipice of their first chart record, Booker T. and the MG's were just coming off their first Top 10 R&B hit since "Green Onions." Auspiciously, "Boot-Leg" was the debut as an MG of Duck Dunn, who had just replaced Lewie Steinberg in the group.

"Lewie was sometimes hard to work with," explains Steve Cropper. "He was a little difficult to deal with on the road. He was a real strong individual. I probably influenced it more than anything. I really wanted Duck [Dunn] in the band. I wanted to be with my old buddy and I was in a position to have an influence in those days. It's sort of like Cropper got his way. I didn't want to hurt Lewie or put Lewie out of anything, even though consequently it turned out that way because he didn't do as many sessions after Duck came in." After recovering from the disappointing news, Steinberg went on to join the Club Handy band led by sax wunderkind Bill Harvey.

Duck Dunn was the logical choice to fill the newly vacant position. Dunn, born November 24, 1941, and Cropper had grown up just down the street from each other, riding bikes, playing football, and going to school together. When Cropper formed the Royal Spades, Duck was already a failed guitarist. Not wishing to be left out of the new group, Dunn bought a bass so that he could be part of this activity, too. As the Spades metamorphosed into the Mar-Keys, Duck and his brother, Bobby, began distributing the King Record label in the Memphis area. Duck left the Mar-Keys in late summer 1962, shortly thereafter becoming the only white member of Ben Branch's band. Five months later, Duck began playing gigs at Hernando's Hideaway and the Rebel Room with a band that included pianist Robert Talley, Mar-Key drummer Terry Johnson, Stax session tenor saxophonist Gene Parker, and Mar-Key trumpeter Wayne Jackson. A version of this group, with the addition of Al Jackson and Steve Cropper, went into the Stax studio toward the end of 1963 and recorded a Booker T. and the MG's-ish instrumental interpretation of Roosevelt Sykes's "The Honeydripper" backed with an original entitled "Slumber Party." The single was issued in January 1964 under the moniker the Van-Dells. In Steve Cropper's words, "It was sort of doing Duck Dunn a favor. Everybody wanted their shot at having a record."

In essence, the Van-Dells were a vehicle that Dunn hoped would turn into a hit-making machine like Booker T. and the MG's. Hope as he might, the Van-Dells record died a quick death and a followup was never contemplated. When Cropper dropped by to ask if Dunn might want to join the MG's, Duck did not have to be asked twice. From the beginning the MG's had been an integrated band. With the arrival of Duck Dunn, they became literally half-white and half-black. While such collaborations were not uncommon in the studio, they were still relatively rare for a publicly performing band and, hence, ultimately political.

Ironically, Duck's first recording with his new group, "Boot-Leg," did not even include Booker T. Jones! With Booker away working on a music degree at Indiana University, Isaac Hayes sat in on keyboards; also augmenting the group were horn players Packy Axton, Gene Parker, and Wayne Jackson. In Cropper's words, "Boot-Leg" "was a Mar-Keys record that we decided to put out as Booker T. and the MG's 'cause we thought we'd get a better shot."

That reasoning turned out to be right on the money. With a writing credit split between Packy Axton, Isaac Hayes, Duck Dunn, and Al Jackson, "Boot-Leg" stormed its way to the tenth spot on the R&B charts while peaking at number 58 on the pop charts. Partially modeled on Jr. Walker's "Shotgun," which had been released just a couple of months earlier, its success was deserved. From start to finish the record is one unrelenting stomp, the highlights being Isaac Hayes's funkified organ lines and Packy Axton's unbelievably sensuous workout on tenor sax. Sales clocked in at approximately 125,000 units.[4]

Carla Thomas was also enjoying a minor hit when the Stax Revue went to Los Angeles. Her first release on Stax proper (as opposed to Atlantic), "Stop! Look What You're Doing" b/w "Every Ounce of Strength," entered the charts in late June, where it stayed until mid-August, peaking at a disappointing number 30. Adding to the plethora of chart records Stax was currently responsible for, Wilson Pickett's recording of "In the Midnight Hour" entered the R&B charts the same week as the Carla Thomas single, not stopping until it hit number 1. The final revue members, William Bell and Rufus Thomas, were the odd men out in the chart sweepstakes. Bell had just been demobbed from the army and had recently issued his first postduty single, and Rufus, despite releasing a series of superb singles, hadn't had a chart hit since "Jump Back" in late 1964.

Despite the absence of Bell and Thomas from the charts, with the simultaneous chart records of the Astors, the Mad Lads, Booker T. and the MG's, Wilson Pickett, Carla Thomas, and Otis Redding (who did not go to L.A. on this trip), Stax was enjoying unprecedented success. The time was clearly right to try to capitalize on it. The company had rarely put revue shows together, despite the obvious benefits that had accrued to Motown through this gambit. William Brown remembers a solitary show in Topeka, Kansas, that included the Mad Lads, the Astors, Carla Thomas, William Bell, and Booker T. and the MG's; Deanie Parker sang with a Stax Revue in 1963 in Redding's hometown of Macon, Georgia, that featured Bobby Marchan, Otis Redding, Carla Thomas, Rufus Thomas, and Booker T. and the MG's. There had also been a revue gig in Memphis at Club Paradise a short while before the West Coast venture that Jim Stewart had record-

---

4. This was not the last time Isaac Hayes would be an MG. On a couple of occasions, Hayes replaced Booker on the weekend gigs the MG's played two or three times each month, either because of Booker's college commitments or, on occasion, when two Booker T. and the MG's gigs were booked on the same night. In the latter case, Booker would play one gig with a different drummer, bass player, and guitarist while the rest of the MG's would play with Isaac! Singer David Porter was also a familiar participant in a lot of the MG's gigs through 1967, as were saxophonists Bob Snyder and Charlie Chalmers.

ed with Stax's Scully two-track portable recorder for a potential live album.[5] Other than these one-shot events and a few random local Memphis shows, Stax had never attempted anything like a revue before. Oddly enough, with the exception of a solitary show at the Apollo in New York, the Europe 1967 tour, a charity gig at Fort Polk, Louisiana, in 1969, and Wattstax in 1972, the company would also eschew group shows in the future.[6]

Once the caravan arrived in Los Angeles, they had a few days to do radio interviews, press, television, and other live appearances before the 5/4 Ballroom shows. Memories are not precise or detailed, but William Bell and the Astors remember doing the "Hollywood A-Go-Go" show. The Astors also appeared on "Where the Action Is" with Paul Revere and the Raiders, and some of the other artists did "Shindig." In addition, the Astors recall performing somewhere on the Strip, sharing a bill with Booker T. and the MG's and Billy Preston. Carla Thomas recalls being irked that she was too busy doing Stax-related work to get to the beach! While the artists were kept busy in this fashion, Estelle was visiting distributors and deejays, trying to drum up business and raise the label's West Coast visibility. As things went in the first half of the 1960s, this was Stax promotion in overdrive. It was so effective that *Billboard* did a small article on the week's events, incorrectly stating that the gigs were to occur at the Shrine Auditorium.

All of this activity during the week preceding the gig had certainly raised Stax's profile in Los Angeles, setting the stage for the weekend at the 5/4 Ballroom. The 5/4 acquired its name due to its being situated at the intersection of 54th Street and Broadway deep in the heart of the south-central L.A. area known as Watts. It was an older club that held about seven hundred people, located one flight up a set of old wooden stairs. In Carla Thomas's words, "There was just one way in and one way out." Both nights of the gig were packed, and there is some debate as to whether there were one or two shows each evening.

The show's promoter, Magnificent Montague, was currently holding down the morning slot, and in the process upping the ratings, of Los Angeles's leading R&B station, KGFJ. As with many "personality" deejays in the 1950s and 1960s, the success of Montague's show was based on a highly charged level of maniacal intensity. Charismatic while manifesting continuous high energy, his calling card was shrieking "burn, baby, burn" before, during, and after his favorite records. Montague had been doing this for a number of years in both Chicago and New York before deciding to head west to Los Angeles. In L.A. he infused his show with a new twist, inviting listeners to call in, identify themselves, and then scream "burn, baby, burn." For black Los Angelenos at the time, "burn, baby, burn" was *the* hip catchphrase.

It had been Estelle's idea to do the show for Montague. "The objective," explains Estelle, "is to get your records played, exposed, and eventually sell them. That's really what you think about and you're at the mercy of a disc jockey. If they like you, they'll play your records. If they don't, they won't. [Los Angeles] was a big market and to get exposed in a large market like that, that can kick off sales across the country. That was what I was thinking about.

"[Montague] was real good about playing all of our records and so we thought we'd take these artists out there and put on a show for him. You just have to reciprocate—you do something for them if they do something for you. That always was my philoso-

---

5. For one reason or another the recording was scrapped, and other than the MG's set, no tapes of this gig have been found in the Stax archives.

6. The Fort Polk gig featured Isaac Hayes, Eddie Floyd, Booker T. and the MG's, the Soul Children, and the Bar-Kays. The other "revue" gigs are discussed elsewhere.

phy. . . . Montague was just a big mouth. He always got attention. That basically was the reason we did the show with him." As was the case with most independent R&B companies at the time, Stax commonly provided one or another of its artists for expense-money-only for shows promoted by important deejays. In essence, this was a subtle form of payola that Stax, like everybody else, was forced to engage in as a matter of course in conducting their business.[7]

Carla Thomas has a slightly different version of the genesis of the Stax Revue at the 5/4 Ballroom. "We had done another gig with Montague," Carla explained in 1991. "I was in college. He was supposed to pay Booker and left owing everybody. He ran out the door with the money. Booker had sat there and played behind every artist because the band didn't show up. This was in New York. [The 5/4] was supposed to be a makeup so Booker could get paid. That was what we were led to believe when we went out. Booker would never have done this ever again after being ripped off. This was to try and settle some things that Montague had done." Carla is not the only one to cast aspersions on Montague's character and integrity. According to William Brown, "Montague was an asshole. Miss Axton was the only one who could get along with him." It is quite conceivable that Estelle's and Carla's stories are both accurate.

All of the artists appeared sometime during the week on Montague's radio show. Curtis Johnson remembers the first thing the Astors did upon hitting town was to go down to KGFJ and answer phones, saying "burn, baby, burn." "[Montague] was the thing out there. Every time one of the four of us would hang up a phone, all the lines would be hot again. You'd just pick up and say 'burn, baby, burn.' He had kids so hyped, when you'd walk down the street 'burn, baby, burn' was like 'what's happening.' It was like a greeting. Everybody was hyped on that 'burn, baby, burn' thing."

Montague told writer Bob Baker of the *Los Angeles Times* in 1985 that "'Burn, baby, burn' meant that when I'm playing the record and I am snapping my fingers and I'm talking my talk, I have reached the epitome, the height—there is no more you can do! Everything is up, up, up! And that's when you 'burn, baby, burn.' It is like the high five. You know you've hit your home run. There's no more to say. . . . And when I hit that record and I say, 'Darling I love you,' or 'Put your hand on the radio and touch my heart, bop-bop-bop, burn, baby, burn'—there was no more to say! That was the epitome! That was it!"

The shows themselves were big hits. One of the shows appears to have been broadcast on KGFJ and was simultaneously taped.[8] Everyone is in peak form and, in true revue fashion, the MG's play vamps between each artist's one- or two-song set. Montague is emceeing the whole affair, at various points launching into "burn, baby, burn" tirades. The audience was obviously keyed in, with various audience members shouting out variations on the catchphrase. As the tapes make manifest, the shows were stunning.

Rufus and Carla Thomas and the MG's Duck Dunn returned to Memphis on Monday evening. Most of the other artists and Estelle were planning to leave a little later in the week. They were in for a surprise. On Wednesday, August 11, the tensions that had been brewing in many American inner cities exploded in the 5/4 Ballroom's very neighborhood. What became known as the Watts riots lasted for several days, shocking much of the world and leaving a lasting impression on the Stax artists still in Los Angeles.

---

7. Estelle also admits to an ulterior motive for wanting to visit Los Angeles. Her son, saxophonist and original Mar-Key Packy Axton, had recently left Memphis and relocated to L.A. in pursuit of the proverbial fresh start in life. In addition to visiting with his mother that week, Packy was to rejoin the Mar-Key horn section for the 5/4 gig.

8. These tapes were released on CD by Ace in England and Fantasy in the United States in 1991.

Of those who remained, the Astors got off relatively easy. "We were aware that there was something going on," says Curtis Johnson, "and we had heard that it was a possibility that our flight would be canceled. We actually didn't have any problems but we could see the smoke [of the burning buildings in Watts] as we flew out. We didn't realize what was going on at the time. It was after we got back to Memphis and found out what had really happened [that] all of a sudden the reality of the whole situation dawned on us. It was like, 'Wow, we got out of there just in time.'"

Estelle Axton missed her original flight and couldn't get out of the city for three or four days. "I like to never got a plane out of there," shudders Lady A. "Everybody was trying to leave town. I remember I was staying up in the Continental Hotel up on kind of a hill and I could look down across over there to Watts and just see that fire coming up. It looked like the whole town was on fire." William Bell echoes her thoughts: "It took forever to put those fires out. . . . The whole situation was eerie because we were in the thick of things, and yet not. We weren't a part of it but in looking at the news we'd say, 'Jeez, we were just in that area.'"

For many, the Watts riots and Montague's "burn, baby, burn" are inextricably connected. With the fires blazing, it is an undeniable fact that many of the rioters chanted the popular deejay's catchphrase over and over and, in the midst of the melee, the phrase could be found scrawled on many walls. Montague has always denied the connection and, in all fairness, it is doubtful if Montague's repetition of this phrase incited the riots. Even so, the station management at KGFJ put pressure on Montague to dump the slogan. Montague was not happy about it, but within a couple of weeks his new buzzwords were "Have mercy baby."

Booker T. Jones, Steve Cropper, and Al Jackson stayed in Los Angeles after the gig at Atlantic's request to accompany a big-band Bobby Darin session at Sunset Sound. Cropper was one of two or three guitarists, and Jackson played a second set of drums alongside Hal Blaine on "Something in the Park" and one other tune. The Blossoms contributed the backing vocals. It was while they were doing the Darin session that the riots broke out.

"I called my sister to come and pick me up after the session," shudders Booker. "She says, 'I'm sorry, I can't come pick you up.' 'What do you mean you can't come?' She says, 'Don't you know what's going on?' So I walk outside the studio and there are National Guardsmen on the corner. It happened so quickly and it was so devastating. We ended up feeling very protective about [Steve and the other white guys on the session]. I remember the feeling of having to get these guys out of there with us somehow. We got them to Hollywood and then everything was okay."

Because the three MG's were still in town, Montague, who also dabbled in the record business, talked them into going into the studio and cutting a couple of demos. In addition to Booker on piano, Al on drums, and Steve on guitar, Packy Axton played sax, Leon Haywood played organ, most likely Earl Grant played bass, and Montague played congas.

"Montague was always the bongo man, the conga drummer man," laughs longtime Montague compadre Johnny Keyes. "He loved it. That was his prop. He would have his bongos in the studio. It would be amazing. At six o'clock in the morning he'd play an instrumental and he'd point to the engineer which meant he'd take a solo. Montague would be in there just playing conga drums, sweating and everything on the radio like there was an audience there. He would sweat and he'd take a solo and he'd point back. He played those Mongo Santamaria records. He liked that shit."

Montague's idea was to construct a track similar in feel to Ramsey Lewis's just-released "The In Crowd." Once the track was finished, he paid everyone for a demo session, brought Packy Axton and Leon Haywood back into the studio to cut a B-side, and then without any notice overdubbed some party sounds and issued the record on the Pure Soul label as being by the "Packers."

The A-side was a groovalicious, conga-dominated number that Cropper, Jones, and Jackson had worked up entitled "Hole in the Wall." When the record was released in October on Pure Soul, Montague had added his own pen name, Nathan, to the composing credits. Neither the MG's nor Jim Stewart were very happy about the record's release, especially when it ended up giving Montague a number 5 R&B and number 43 pop hit. None of the MG's were ever paid royalties. "Montague just took advantage of the boys," declares Estelle, "plain used them. Montague had such a charm. He could charm the guys into doing anything he wanted them to do. That's what it was. He railroaded them in there."

While the MG's might have been fooled, it would appear that Packy Axton was in league with Montague right from the start. Packy's move to Los Angeles had been occasioned by a changing climate at Stax. Although he was part of the Stax family from the beginning, and part-author of one of the label's biggest hits, the Mar-Keys' "Last Night," Packy and his uncle, Jim Stewart, had never seen eye to eye. It is no secret that as the years progressed Packy felt increasingly relegated to the sidelines by Stewart. With the Mar-Keys unable to follow up their blockbuster hit, for quite some time Packy had felt shunned and alienated at Stax. Jim Stewart had never been enamored of Packy's bohemian ways and, despite his talents as a horn player, very rarely used him on sessions.

All of this was exacerbated by Jim's relationship with Packy's father, Everett Axton. Everett was an alcoholic who worked at Kimberly-Clark. Every day like clockwork, after finishing his shift at the factory he would head down to the Satellite Record Shop to drink three or four quarts of beer until he was drunk. "Which always pissed Jim off," offers Wayne Jackson. "There was always a big fight going on between Everett and Jim with Ms. Axton between them. That was her husband. His house was the one that got hocked so Jim could buy the equipment and no one ever thanked him. So he was always a little pissed off about everything. He had a little chip on his shoulder. He was trying to get his ego plugged back in." Apparently this would commonly manifest itself with Everett leering at Jim, occasionally getting outright nasty. "Packy had the same chip that his Dad had," continues Jackson. "Packy's purpose in life was to drive Jim crazy. He loved it."

It was quite clear to everybody that if Packy had not been Estelle's son, he would have been banned from the studio several years earlier. With the Mar-Keys' career as a steady working band history by late 1963, there wasn't much left for Packy to do at Stax other than produce the occasional secret session by the likes of the Astors, who, not so coincidentally, Jim also did not like.

Both Booker T. Jones and Johnny Keyes believe that Estelle Axton partially financed the Packers single and the Pure Soul label. According to Johnny Keyes, this was Estelle's first attempt at gaining revenge on Jim for the way that he treated her son. Estelle denies that she financed the label but affirms that it was an attempt at revenge. In any event, Montague and Packy stayed in touch after the 5/4 gig and the Packers were obviously named after him. After the record hit, Montague needed a group to work the record on the road. When Montague had been based in Chicago, doo-wop singers Johnny Keyes and Reggie Gordon had worked numerous record projects for the deejay. In 1965 Gordon was working for an airline and while in Los Angeles happened to give Montague a call. When he got back to Chicago, he immediately phoned Johnny Keyes.

As Keyes recalls: "Reggie said, 'Here's what's happening. Montague's got this white boy out there that's from Memphis, this country cat, he drinks a lot.' I called Montague and

Montague told me that Packy was out there and was drinking. He needed a Packers group on the road because there was no Packers group. The record was done by a studio group."

Keyes immediately flew to Los Angeles, and was met at the airport by Montague and Packy. From that day on, the Packers became Packy Axton, Johnny Keyes, and various and sundry other partners in crime. Keyes played the conga part on stage, earning him the sobriquet "Congo Johnny" from Leon Haywood. A little while later, when Keyes began hanging out at Stax, Al Jackson changed his newly won sobriquet to "Conga Lou." "When he asked me to come out and be part of the band," laughs Keyes, "I said, 'What the devil, I'm not a musician.' He said, 'You can play congas! How hard can that be? All you're doing is keeping time.'"

The road version of the Packers ended up spending a couple of months on the road in early 1966, opening a bill that included in reverse order Pigmeat Markham, Derek Martin, Jackie Ross, Wilson Pickett, and Joe Tex. After the package tour's show in Memphis, Estelle suggested that Packy and Johnny do some further recording. "She wanted to prove something to Jim with Packy," suggests Keyes. "He was very wild and Jim was very straight. [Jim] couldn't understand orgies in the recording studio at midnight."

Following his mother's advice, Packy headed over to the Hi Records studio ("We couldn't use Stax because this was revenge for Jim," adds Keyes), and with Bar-Kays members James Alexander on bass, Jimmie King on guitar, and Carl Cunningham on drums and Hi Records co-owner Ray Harris running the board, proceeded to cut "Stone Fox" (the title was Estelle's) b/w "Dig It." At the time Keyes was working for Memphis Delta Distributors. One of the labels Memphis Delta handled was Nashville's Starday Records. Through this connection Keyes was tight with Starday promotion man Charlie Dick (former husband of Patsy Cline) and Starday general manager Colonel Jim Wilson. Keyes made a deal with Wilson and Dick to issue "Stone Fox" as being by the Pac-Keys on the Starday Records subsidiary Hollywood Records (Hollywood 1108).[9]

Despite Estelle's best intentions, the record died a quick death. Johnny Keyes and Packy recorded one further single, "Greasy Pumpkin" b/w "Hip Pocket" (Hollywood 1118), as the Pac-Keys; two singles as L. H. and the Memphis Sounds,[10] "Double Up" b/w "House Full of Rooms" (Hollywood 1112), and "Out of Control" b/w "I'm a Fool (in Love)" (Hollywood 1122);[11] and two singles as the Martinis, "Hung Over" b/w "Late Late Party" and "Holiday Cheer" b/w "Bullseye." The latter was released on U.S.A. Records while "Hung Over" was issued on BAR Records. BAR was a Memphis concern whose name derived from the first letter of the co-owners' last names: future Stax promo man Eddie Braddock, Estelle Axton, and future Stax sales executive Ewell Roussell. Braddock and Roussell at the time were both employed by Delta Distributing. Further cementing their relationships with Axton and Keyes, Braddock had grown up wanting to play tenor sax because of Packy, and Roussell was currently managing L. H. and the Memphis Sounds.

The Martinis' BAR recording is hysterical. According to Johnny Keyes, "When Packy got enraged, in a fit he'd let loose this yell—'Arghhh'—We did an instrumental and when it came to the break, he did the yell." Everyone, except Estelle, laughed about it afterward,

9. Hollywood had originally been a Los Angeles R&B label owned by John Dolphin. Starday had purchased the label a year or two prior to the Pac-Keys' deal.

10. L. H. White was the singer. Apparently he was a dead ringer for the Temptations' Eddie Kendricks.

11. Although Packy was always on the scene, the only L. H. and the Memphis Sounds recording that he actually plays on is "Double Up."

saying it sounded like he was throwing up, hence the title "Hung Over."[12] Estelle hated the yell, thinking it uncouth, and argued incessantly to leave it off the record. This was one battle she lost. Accompanying Packy was Teenie Hodges on guitar, Leroy Hodges on bass, Andrew Mitchell on organ, and Carl Cunningham on drums. "Hung Over" received a bit of airplay in Memphis and one other market before petering out. All of Packy Axton's records are superb, quirky examples of Memphis soul and are well worth seeking out.

Unfortunately that is the extent of Packy Axton's discography. There were no further opportunities for Packy to record after 1967. From mid-1968 through mid-1969 he ostensibly managed the Satellite Record Shop, and in the year or so before his death he engineered country demos at Fretone Records.[13] Gigs were few and far between, largely being limited to the odd job as a sideman with the likes of Charlie Rich. In 1971 Packy died of cirrhosis of the liver. "What a jive thing to do," laments Johnny Keyes. "We had so many plans. Why would he do that shit? I guess he couldn't help it. It was a self-destructive thing. Heartbroken is what it was. If there's such a thing as dying of a broken heart, that's essentially what it was. He just went on and committed slow suicide."

While Montague was preparing the Packers' record for release, plans were being made to bring Washington, D.C.– based deejay Al Bell into Stax, as the company's first full-time promotion man. This would prove to be a decisive moment in Stax's history. Up to this time virtually all Stax-related promotion was done by Atlantic, Estelle, Jim, or Deanie Parker.[14] Although hired as Stax's first promotion man, Bell proved to be much more. From the start he helped in the writing of songs, he brought a number of artists to the label, and within a few years he would be vice president and co-owner of the company. In October 1972 he purchased Stax outright.

Bell was born Alvertis Isbell in Brinkley, Arkansas, in 1940, one of eight children. Moving with his family to North Little Rock in 1945, Bell eventually received a degree in political science from Philander Smith College in Little Rock. He also prepared for the ministry by attending Oakwood College Bible School in Huntingwood, Alabama. Both the political science and ministerial backgrounds would play large roles in his tenure at Stax.

While in his senior year of high school, Bell was student council president and president of the National Honor Society on campus. That same year, while still just seventeen, Bell landed a radio show on Little Rock radio station KOKY. After entering Philander Smith College, Bell continued doing gospel, jazz, and eventually morning—and afternoon—drive-time rhythm-and-blues shows on KOKY. This hectic schedule would continue throughout his college years. He was also busy hosting record hops and promoting concerts. Al Bell's ubiquitous energy was already well in evidence.

In 1959 Bell dropped out of college, quit KOKY, and left Little Rock to work in Midway, Georgia, with Dr. Martin Luther King's Southern Christian Leadership Con-

12. Despite what has been written elsewhere, Packy did not vomit during the session. As much of an alcoholic as Packy was, the yell in "Hung Over" was simply the product of an inspired idea.

13. When Estelle was bought out of Stax in 1969, she had to agree not to participate in the music industry for a period of five years. Secretly, she masterminded the construction and operation of the Fretone Records studio. When her five-year period was up, she publicly announced her co-ownership of the venture and eventually hit paydirt with Rick Dees's "Disco Duck."

14. In fact, other than a secretary and Steve Cropper, Deanie was the only full-time employee the company had. Randle Catron also did a bit of promotion for the company, taking records to Chicago, Detroit, Cleveland, and Milwaukee. According to Catron, he was not paid for his efforts; he was simply trying to get his foot in the door. The deal he had with Jim Stewart was that if he got a record on the air at a given station he would then be compensated. Never all that successful, he received little more than gas money. Catron also did a bit of janitorial work at Stax on a casual basis. Later—usually in tandem with Deanie Parker—he wrote material that was recorded by Otis Redding, Carla Thomas, Sam and Dave, Johnnie Taylor, the Mad Lads, and the Pattersonaires.

ference (SCLC) workshops. Bell led workshops at Midway and participated in a number of marches, but after about a year elected to leave due to philosophical differences between himself and Dr. King. "I left Dr. King," explains Bell, "and went back into the music business because I was not about passive resistance. I was about economic development, economic empowerment."

At loose ends, Bell phoned various contacts he had within radio, and in 1961 he was hired by Dick "Cane" Cole to host the 6:00 to 10:00 A.M. morning show at WLOK in Memphis.[15] According to Randle Catron, Bell brought a different style to town and in the process galvanized 'LOK and Memphis black radio in general. While most of the local black jocks typified the then-standard frenetic high energy of personality deejays, Bell presented a calm, commanding demeanor on the air, studiously avoiding the high-level rant-shuck-and-jive that was typical of disc jockeys of the era and steadfastly refusing to talk over the beginnings and endings of the records. But when he came on and said "This is Al Bell," in his big, booming deep voice replete with the ringing of a bell, according to Catron, "he had all the ladies listening." From the beginning, Bell was an ardent booster of local music, constantly providing much-appreciated exposure to virtually any Memphis R&B 45. Not too surprisingly, most Memphis record labels and their artists quickly held Bell in high regard. With Bell leading the way, WLOK's ratings improved significantly and the station changed from a dawn-to-dusk operation to a twenty-four-hour R&B powerhouse rivaling WDIA in influence.

While at WLOK Bell developed close ties with Stax,[16] spending a lot of time at the Satellite Record Shop to keep his finger on the listening tastes of Memphis's black populace. "That was one of my yardsticks for determining what to play on the air as a disc jockey," relates Bell. Within two years Bell had left WLOK for a higher-paying job in a bigger market at WUST in Washington, D.C., where he continued his ardent support of all things Memphis.

"I went into Washington," says Bell, smiling, "and did something contrary to everything that was being done programming-wise [there]. They were busy with all that East Coast doo-wop. I went in [playing] Stax Records. [At the time] Stax product was basically selling [only] in the South. In no time at all I established Otis, Carla, and Rufus [in the Washington area]. Booker T. and the MG's [were already] getting some play in that area. On the weekends I would go by bus into Baltimore and Philadelphia and promote the product myself at my own expense,[17] which really got the ball rolling and aided [for example] Otis getting into the Howard Theatre. My southern romanticism integrated into that great music made me one of the top disc jockeys in Washington."

Bell quickly rose to the point where, for all intents and purposes, he functioned as assistant station manager at WUST. He also got further involved in the record business. While at KOKY, Bell had started his own label with songwriter Red Matthews.[18] Hiply titled De'voice Records, the label released only one record, the Acklin Brothers' atmospheric "I Want My

---

15. Up to this point at WLOK, whoever hosted the morning show was always known as Hunki Dori. This was a common practice with white-owned southern black radio stations. As the station owned the name, this meant that the individual disc jockey could (1) not develop a name for him or herself, and (2) was therefore that much more easily replaced. Bell broke this chain, refusing to be known by any name other than Al Bell.

16. Jim Stewart remembers that at the time "Al was a very aggressive young man and very different from everyone else that I had met."

17. In Baltimore Bell would usually visit Paul "Fat Daddy" Johnson, while in Philadelphia he worked on Georgie Woods and Jimmie Bishop.

18. Matthews's main claim to fame was penning "White Silver Sands," which charted in 1957 in versions by Don Rondo, the Owen Bradley Quintet, and Dave Gardner, and in 1960 by Bill Black's Combo.

Al Bell on the air at WLOK. COURTESY DEANIE PARKER.

Baby" b/w the humorous "Junior's Angle" (De'voice 780).[19] In Washington, with the help of former Falcon Eddie Floyd and former Moonglow Chester Simmons, Bell produced, under the supervision of Milt Gabler, three 45s by Grover Mitchell, "Midnight Tears" b/w "Loving You" (Decca 31714), the jaunty if somewhat corny "Someone's Knockin' at My Door" b/w "I Will Always Have Faith in You" (Decca 31747), and "There's Only One Way" b/w "Take Your Time and Love Me" (Decca 32015). Later Stax star Eddie Floyd wrote "Midnight Tears," "I Will Always Have Faith in You," and "Take Your Time and Love Me."[20] The accompaniment for the first two

19. The Acklins were former schoolmates of Bell's. De'voice was partially funded by a couple of doctors and/or dentists.

20. The actual production credits on all three 45s read "Produced by Simmons-Floyd and Isbell Productions, Inc."

singles was provided by the Don Dial Orchestra, which doubled as the Howard Theatre's house band.[21] Excited by the results, Bell then teamed up with Simmons and Floyd to start the Safice label, which was distributed by Atlantic under similar terms as Stax. Safice released a total of five records, three by Eddie Floyd, one by Roy Arlington, and one by Betty and Roy. By the end of Safice's short life, Bell was traveling to Memphis to cut his records at Stax with Booker T. and the MG's.

In the summer of 1965, Stax had grown to the point where the company had a number of artists capable of generating chart hits but next to no resources to promote these artists. Ostensibly Atlantic was obligated to promote Stax product, but Atlantic had also grown and, with only two full-time promotion men, Joe Galkin and Henry Allen, was quite clearly not able or necessarily interested in giving Stax releases the kind of close personal attention that was needed to achieve maximum radio exposure and sales. It is unclear as to who suggested that Al Bell be hired, but one way or another eventually Jim, Estelle, and Steve Cropper all thought it was a good idea.

According to Cropper, Jim initially fought the idea because he didn't want to spring for Bell's salary. "Estelle and I said, 'Hey, we need somebody that can liaison between the disc jockeys and he's the man to do it. Atlantic's going into a radio station with six Atlantic records and one Stax record. We're not getting our due.' We knew that. We needed more promotion and he had all the pull with all those disc jockeys. He knew E. Rodney Jones and all the big cats, the Montagues and so on. He knew every one of them."

Jerry Wexler agreed that Stax had become profitable and productive enough that they needed more focused attention than Atlantic's staff could possibly provide and consequently offered to pay half of Bell's $100-a-week salary, sealing the deal in the process. For Bell it was a pay cut, but he was both in love with the sound of Stax Records and intrigued by the challenge of his new job. In addition, Bell was promised that eventually he would be given equity in the company.

Prior to this, Jim Stewart had done his best to augment Atlantic's PR work by personally phoning both distributors and radio stations, but in this regard he was not the equal of Al Bell. After arriving in Memphis in late September or early October 1965, Bell approached his new job with nearly unfathomable and indefatigable relish. Initially taken around the country and shown the tricks of the trade by Atlantic promotion man and longtime friend Joe Medlin, Bell quickly established close ties with a number of key disc jockeys. Virtually everyone around Stax at the time tells stories of Al Bell on the phone from early morning to late in the evening, talking about the latest Stax releases to important deejays across the country. He would start with the morning jocks on the East Coast and then proceed across the country following the time zones, by midnight discussing records with the evening deejays in California. With his background as a disc jockey, he was tailor-made for the job, having already developed a number of relationships over the years as well as an understanding of the language and psychology of black disc jockeys in the 1960s.

Legendary black disc jockey and program manager of WVON in Chicago E. Rodney Jones affirms the above: "He was definitely different. You're talking about a man that had tremendous radio experience. He knew the needs of the people in radio and how best Stax could serve them as well as how they could serve Stax. It made a hell of a difference. Some of the radio stations then, man, didn't even have a damn water fountain. In those little towns in the South, it was really ridiculous. It was atrocious. But Stax Records

---

21. The Howard was Washington's equivalent of New York's Apollo or Chicago's Regal theaters. At the time of the first Mitchell recording, Bell's wife, Lydia, was in labor with their first son. Milt Gabler ended up as the child's godfather.

through Al Bell's ingenuity and know-how came to the aid of so many stations it was unbelievable." Needless to say, Bell and Stax's sensitivity and generosity were not forgotten when it came time to play Stax product.

According to William Brown, Stax didn't really start until Al Bell got there. Up to that point there had been oodles of talent but no marketing. Steve Cropper agrees, stating that before Al Bell very few Stax releases really got heard outside of the mid-South.

In the fall of 1965 Stax was still very much a small cottage industry. "We had one telephone and one desk," says Bell. "Jim sat on one side of the desk and I sat on the other side of the desk. He'd use the phone awhile and then I'd use the phone awhile."

Quite quickly, Bell became the de facto sales manager. "I came in and drew a huge thermometer," chuckles Bell, "and scaled it where there would be different levels of sales as opposed to temperatures all the way up the thermometer. And then at the top of the thermometer it exploded into an area that we called heaven. I set that right in the lobby so when anybody'd come through the door, it was [right] there. I plugged in three and a half million units at the top to get us in a real profitable position. Each week as we got our sales report, we'd go in and in red mark on this thermometer the increase in sales. I think it was in a period of about nine months that we reached the peak in the thermometer, exploded into heaven, and reached our objective."[22]

Steve Cropper vividly remembers the thermometer, adding that the Big 6—the four members of Booker T. and the MG's plus Isaac Hayes and David Porter—were promised a bonus when they reached that goal. "We wanted to bust that bubble!" exclaims Cropper. "It would not have been the same without Al Bell. He put Stax on the map. He knew what he was talking about, he knew the marketplace. So, he really started making a lot of decisions for us. He made a lot of history out of that thing. He gave it the lift or the charge that it needed to be as big as it wound up being."

"I think there were some references to him as God," adds Duck Dunn. "He was that powerful."

"He had energy like Otis Redding," concludes Booker. "Except he wasn't a singer. He had the same type of energy. He'd come in the room, pull up his shoulders and that energy would start. He would start talking about the music business or what was going on and he energized everywhere he was. He was our Otis for promotion. It was the same type of energy [and] charisma."

Organized down to the last detail, Bell would have made a great politician. Whenever the MG's were on tour, he would phone them in each city and ask them to go stop by so-and-so's store and say "Hello" or phone up so-and-so who worked for the distributor and invite them out to dinner or go see this disc jockey and so on. Everyone at Stax is convinced that these personal touches paid handsome dividends over time.

Given his background as a disc jockey, Bell had contacts with promotion people at virtually every company that was attempting to market black music. He used his contacts at Motown in a particularly efficacious manner, gaining information on the timing of their releases. He would then look at what Stax had already out in the marketplace or ready for release that was analogous. Knowing that the Motown release would bring the black customer into the stores, Bell would then turn his considerable energies to hyping the counter people at important stores in various mid-Atlantic, southern, northeastern, and midwestern cities about the Stax release. His logic was that while the customer would come in

22. Bell had originally projected three and a half million sales over twelve months based on the numbers Atlantic was able to achieve with Pickett and Covay, whose sales figures were readily available to Stax, because the label received royalties on the 45s cut by these two artists at McLemore.

requesting the new Marvin Gaye record, the clerk could also play them the Stax release, enabling Stax to piggyback at least to a small degree on the marketing efforts of its more powerful northern rival.

Bell also quickly developed the phrase "The soul label for your swinging turntable" and put it on the bottom of the company's letterhead. In addition, he started writing "The Memphis Sound" on every piece of paper that left the company.

One of Bell's promotion objectives was to establish Chicago as the company's "break-out" market. "My attitude," recounts Bell, "was to take the middle and force New York and Los Angeles [to play our records]. I felt that I had to do that 'cause I wasn't based in a major metropolitan area. I had to have strength so that when I walked into those markets I would have respect. I wouldn't have to speak in soprano; I could speak in bass."

Bell felt that Chicago and Memphis were connected by what he termed "Mississippi River Culture." "My approach to marketing," Bell continues, "was and still is looking from a sociological standpoint. Even though I employ some of the techniques of the industrial scientist in marketing, it is more social science. If you appreciate the cultures and what the rivers represent to the cultures in this country and the kind of music that Stax was coming up with, it would just be logical to look for exposure along the Mississippi River, because it was Mississippi River Culture as far as music is concerned. The people from Mississippi and New Orleans traveled along the waterways from the Gulf up the Mississippi River. That caused us to work the product that was born in Memphis, Tennessee, that was indigenous to the mid-South area, in Chicago, St. Louis, and Kansas City and even Detroit, Michigan. For most of the people in Detroit were people that had left Mississippi, Alabama, or Georgia and had gone to Detroit for jobs in the automotive industry. So, what you really had in those particular cities was Southerners. Chicago may as well have been in the suburbs of Mississippi. By and large, the majority of the African-American population in Chicago was from Mississippi or you could trace their roots back to Mississippi." Once a record began to take hold in Chicago or Detroit, Bell could then piggyback on that success and work the product on both the East and West coasts.

Bell's techniques and near-superhuman efforts paid immediate dividends. Within weeks of his arrival at Stax, Sam and Dave hit the charts with "You Don't Know Like I Know," quickly followed by Otis Redding's blistering "I Can't Turn You Loose." Things only got better in the new year, with the company signing in quick succession Johnnie Taylor, Eddie Floyd, Albert King, and Mable John, all four artists immediately enjoying chart hits. Before summertime, Sam and Dave had charted again with "Hold On! I'm Comin'," Carla Thomas had hit with "Let Me Be Good to You," a reconstituted Mar-Keys had their second chart record in "Philly Dog," and Otis had hit the Top 10 twice with "Satisfaction" and "My Lover's Prayer." Bell came to be viewed as a man who could accomplish miracles.

"You have to understand," explains Randle Catron, "Al's degree was in theology. [He conveyed the notion] that 'We're gonna have a family and this is the nucleus and I'm the promotion man. I'm Daddy. I'm gonna go out there and make it happen.' By him having the connections across the country as a jock, it was just a perfect marriage for the artists at Stax. When he started making records happen, everybody looked at him as the godfather. He was the king!

"Al listened to everybody. You didn't have a record or tune of any kind that Al didn't take the time to stop and listen to. Jim was the owner, but Al had the ear of every musician, every artist, every songwriter. . . . He became daddy to everybody. Instead of going to Jim with anything, everybody came to Al with it. That's what caused him to get a piece of the company. Everybody was coming to Al and they would just say that Jim was not the man. Al had the personality. He could just win you over. He always had something kind to say to you walking through the halls of Stax. He was just a country boy from Little Rock, Arkansas, that came to Memphis, got with Jim Stewart, and made it happen for everybody. Then when everybody started making money, who did they attribute it to? Al could pick up the phone and get your record played."

Al Bell not only could get your record played, he was a man with a vision. Expansion-oriented from the start, one of the first things he did was launch a gospel label, Chalice. Bell, of course, was more than conversant with gospel music, having studied for the ministry and hosted gospel radio shows at KOKY and WLOK. Stax issued eight 45s on Chalice beginning in late 1965 and lasting through 1967. Seven of the 45s were recorded by local groups: the Christian Harmonizers, the Jubilee Hummingbirds, and most notably the Pattersonaires and the Dixie Nightingales. One other release was recorded by the Stars of Virginia, who had previously recorded for Vivid in Chicago and would later cut full LPs for King and Atlantic. Although Al Bell signed the Stars of Virginia, he cannot remember any of the circumstances surrounding the event. Most likely he knew them from his days in Washington at WUST. Most of the Chalice recordings were engineered by James Cross in the evening, because rhythm and blues had priority at the studio during the day.

Born in 1940, Cross originally came to Stax to audition as part of a group called the Persians (whose members included Eddie Harrison, who would later sing lead in the Premiers and the Short Kuts). The Persians were turned down, but Cross came back a few days later anyway just to look around and soak up the vibe. At the time he was working at WLOK. Intoxicated by what was going on at Stax, he began to accompany WLOK jocks Perry Allen and Dick "Cane" Cole whenever they needed to visit the record label. One thing led to another, and Cross worked his way into the Satellite Record Shop, where he was employed from 1963 through 1968.

In the earlier days, Cross would keenly study Jim Stewart whenever Stewart was engineering a session. Eventually he and Deanie Parker were put in charge of cutting radio spots for the record store. "You talking about fun!" Cross says with a smile. "Two, three o'clock in the morning we'd be back there in the studio cutting spots. We had the freedom to do it any kind of way we wanted, with music or without music. We usually did a little dramatic bit on them. People would come into the record shop to see who were those people making those commercials. We'd act like we were drunk on them—always ending up going to Satellite Records to buy our records. It brought the people in." It was while recording the radio spots that Cross acquired his engineering chops.

In addition to the radio spots, Deanie commonly stayed at the studio late into the night writing songs. Cross often stayed with her, getting down whatever Deanie came up with on tape. According to Cross, it was not uncommon for Packy Axton to also stay and work with Deanie, playing drums, bass, piano, and/or saxophone. Cross came up with the "Chalice" name for the gospel subsidiary, and the label design was created by a local freelance commercial artist, A. B. Adams. Cross also personally auditioned both the Christian Harmonizers and the Pattersonaires (the latter group as well as the Dixie Nightingales were referred to Stax by Randle Catron) and eventually cowrote "Fate" for Carla Thomas and "If the Washing Don't Get You, the Rinsing Will" for Albert King, before marrying one of the great unknown Stax singers, Wendy Rene (née Mary Frierson). Being close to Packy Axton, Cross was consequently never a favorite of Jim Stewart's, which effectively prevented him from working his way into an engineering or songwriting position at the company. Apparently Stewart would often get angry at Wendy Rene for hanging out with James and Packy.

Most of the Chalice recordings featured various combinations of Stax session musicians. Booker T. and the MG's, with Carl Cunningham subbing for Al Jackson, played behind at least one Chalice Recording, the Dixie Nightingales' haunting "The Assassination" (Chalice

102), while Isaac Hayes and Carl Cunningham appear on the label's first release, the Christian Harmonizers' "Don't Need No Doctor." None of these records made much of a commercial impact and, in the words of Willie Gordon of the Pattersonaires, Chalice seemed to be little more than an "experiment." In 1967 the Dixie Nightingales would change their name to Ollie and the Nightingales and embark on a secular career at Stax, scaling the charts with "I've Got a Sure Thing" (Stax 245) in April 1968.

6

Knock on Wood: 1966

Within weeks of Al Bell's arrival at Stax, Isaac Hayes and David Porter crafted what proved to be the breakthrough record for Sam and Dave. With "You Don't Know Like I Know," for the first time in ten releases spanning Alston, Marlin, Roulette, and Stax, Sam and Dave charted, hitting a giddy number 7 on the R&B charts while scraping the lower reaches of the pop listings at number 90. Oddly enough, Sam Moore hated the song.

"Fifty percent of the songs that were presented to me at Stax I didn't like," exclaims Sam. "I remember saying to myself, 'Oh my God, what is this? I don't like this kind of singing.' It's hard singing. I wanted to do stuff like Sam [Cooke] and Willie [John] and Jackie [Wilson]." One of the things that Sam most disliked was that Hayes and Porter always forced him to sing up high in his range. "They always said, 'You sing up there' because they would say that's where my strength was. I would get angry but that's what I would do."

When Hayes and Porter wrote and initially rehearsed the songs with Sam and Dave, the melodies would be set in a comfortable, lower key. But when it came time to record, Hayes and Porter would intentionally raise the key. "I had the main thrust as far as getting him to project," Porter admits, laughing. "Sam used to hate me for that. I would stand in front of the mike and push him in the direction that I wanted him to go for the effect of the song. I always kept him reaching. That was part of the magic. It was high for him but he had some of the greatest pipes that I ever knew. Oftentimes when I would push him I would be amazed at what he was doing.

"I felt if you were right above where you could be [comfortably], then the anxiety and the frustrations and the soul of what I thought needed to be captured out of those songs would come through. I always noticed with the Motown records, the singers were so comfortable, the melodies were so comfortable. I wanted us to have a little different kind of edge and I thought that gave us that. . . . Struggling for you to get there would only enhance you to get the soul. Even though they would get pissed at me pushing them like that, they would attempt to do it and it would work. I didn't think you were really doing the record with any soul unless there was sweat."

Whether Sam liked it or not, "You Don't Know Like I Know" was instantly infectious, opening with unison guitar and popping bass while Al Jackson taps his drum sticks together. The horns, drums, and piano, playing a line that just won't quit, come in on bars three and four, followed by Sam and Dave in unison on the chorus. Dave sings the first verse with the exception of the last smoldering "alright," which is emoted by Sam. On the second verse, they trade lines with Dave on the first and third, Sam on the second, and both on the fourth. They both inject pleading cries during the subsequent horn interlude, and the record ends with a repeat of the first verse followed by a strutting, ad-lib, call-and-

response section. The seed for the song came from Isaac Hayes, who simply adapted the melody, chords, and the first four lines from a gospel song. "A lot of ideas and

David Porter with Sam Moore and Dave Prater.
COURTESY DEANIE PARKER.

titles came from the church," relates Isaac. "This title itself came from a gospel tune, 'You Don't Know Like I Know What the Lord Has Done for Me.' There's different versions in different churches. I thought if the Lord can make you feel good and do things for you, why can't a woman do the same things too. So, 'You don't know like I know what this woman has done for me.'"

One of the record's hooks is the horn interlude that takes the place of what would have been a solo on most recordings. These prearranged horn ensemble sections were an integral part of the classic Stax sound in the mid-sixties, heard to good advantage on other Stax recordings such as "In the Midnight Hour" and "Knock on Wood." According to Wayne Jackson, "Otis called them 'ensambos.' 'Put one of them ensambos in there.' I think we got [the idea of horn ensemble sections] from Otis and we just carried it over to other artists because it worked so well and it involved all of us. We enjoyed doing it."

In the preceding months, Hayes and Porter had been busy. Having quickly established themselves as a viable songwriting team, they had begun to be solicited by any artist in need of material. In the summer of 1965 alone they wrote and, in essence, produced "Willy Nilly" for Rufus Thomas, "When You Move You Lose" for Rufus and Carla, "Make It Me" for newcomers the Premiers, and "In the Twilight Zone" for the Astors.

Isaac had also made a few moves toward becoming an artist himself. The same week that "You Don't Know Like I Know" was issued, "Sir Isaac and the Do-Dads" released their solitary single, "Blue Groove" b/w "The Big Dipper."[1] Flush with his nascent songwriting success, Isaac thought it would be fun to cut an instrumental record. Atlantic Records wasn't all that impressed, and the Do-Dads 45 was the last Stax/Volt release that Atlantic declined to distribute, with the exception of a 1968 charity record by the Memphis Nomads. Hayes had also recorded an instrumental 45 a year earlier as part of a studio group called the Barracudas. The punningly named "Yank Me (Doodle)" (another title conceived by Estelle Axton) was one of those late-night sessions (i.e., cut when nobody cared) that James Cross engineered. For all intents and purposes, the 45 was Packy Axton's last-ditch effort to get something going for himself at Stax. Along with Axton and Hayes, the single featured ex–Mar-Key Charlie Freeman on guitar, Samuel Evans on bass, and Verne Harrell and Andrew Love on saxophones. Evans and Harrell would later play with Axton and Johnny Keyes in the road version of the Packers.

Hayes and Porter continued to be hot in the first few months of 1966, penning Johnnie Taylor's Stax debut, February's "I Had a Dream," followed by three powerful releases in March, the criminally underknown Ruby Johnson's "I'll Run Your Hurt Away," Carla Thomas's "Let Me Be Good to You," and Sam and Dave's incendiary "Hold On! I'm Comin'."

In a couple of years Johnnie Taylor would become one of Stax's mainstays, enjoying an incredible run of hit singles for the label from October 1968 through September 1975 under the production auspices of Don Davis. For his first two years in Memphis, he was produced initially by Hayes-Porter and then by MG drummer Al Jackson. Both opted to work with him in a blues vein.

Born in Crawfordsville, Arkansas, in 1938, Taylor had sung gospel with the Melody Masters,[2] R&B with the Five Echoes (who recorded for both Chance and Vee Jay), and gospel again with the Highway QC's and the Soul Stirrers, before recording a number of secular numbers for Sam Cooke's Sar/Derby labels. After Cooke's death in 1964, Taylor found himself label shopping.

"I was living in Kansas City," Taylor reminisces. "I got to St. Louis and I decided I'd toss up a dime. I said, 'Should I go towards Detroit for Motown or should I take the southern route to Stax?' Stax won out."

For Taylor's Stax debut, Hayes and Porter wrote one of their rare blues songs, the melancholy "I Had a Dream." "That was a song that I originally shopped with Duke Records and Don Robey for Bobby 'Blue' Bland," recalls Porter. "I called Don Robey, who at the time didn't know anything about David Porter or Isaac Hayes. I was trying to find out if we could get the song on Bobby Bland because at that time Bobby Bland was much stronger than Johnnie Taylor. Don Robey called me back and offered me three hundred dollars for the song. I didn't know what he meant. I thought he was offering three hundred dollars and then he'd pay us royalties. He was offering three hundred dol-

1. Sir Isaac and the Do-Dads had been the backing band a few years earlier for Jeb Stuart.
2. Not Melody Makers as has been printed elsewhere.

lars to buy the song totally. I thought, you got to be kidding. So I just said, 'Thank you Mr. Robey' and hung up the phone and never spoke to him again." Taylor's version climbed the rhythm-and-blues charts to the number 19 spot.

Fresh from their success with Taylor, Hayes and Porter went to work on Sam and Dave's followup to "You Don't Know Like I Know." "After 'You Don't Know Like I Know' hit," testifies David Porter, "then it became fun. The [lyric] formula was down and we were not going to miss."

The songwriting formula was one that Porter gleaned from a Motown recording, the Temptations' "Don't Look Back," written by Smokey Robinson and Ronnie White and released in October 1965. Porter figured out the lyric structure for "Don't Look Back" and applied it to a number of Motown hits. He deduced that they all had an opening that laid out the scenario, followed that with a bit of action, and then some sort of denouement. All were in the first person, and none of them ended with a complete resolution. "All of the songs followed that formula," smiles Porter. "I knew right then. I said, 'Hey, we're gonna be some bad dudes in this music industry.' That's when the thought processes really started working and an identity started taking place."

The first song the formula was applied to at Stax was one of the all-time soul classics, "Hold On! I'm Comin'," released in March 1966. Topping the R&B charts, the single also significantly permeated the pop listings, peaking at number 21.[3] The inspiration for the song came about while Porter was in the washroom inside the Stax studio. Hayes, getting impatient, hollered at Porter to hurry up. Porter's response was: "Hold on, man, I'm coming." The lyrics written, the famous opening ascending horn line was lifted from a session that occurred a few days earlier. The drum lick on the verses was a quicker version of one heard on Lee Dorsey's recently released "Get Out of My Life Woman," while Steve Cropper's rhythm guitar part sounds very James Brown influenced. This was as funky as Stax was to get in the sixties.

For the first time, Sam Moore was given the lead vocal from the start, and he comes through with one of his all-time masterful performances.[4] Moore is ably supported by Al Jackson's cannonlike snare and Wayne Jackson's pinched, muted trumpet response on the chorus over ever-so-rich droning saxophones. When Sam and Dave immediately repeat the chorus the second time around, Wayne Jackson is caught by surprise and misses his first response. A second mistake occurs right after the vocal comes in when the tempo slows down.

At Stax it was not uncommon for several songs to be cut in one day. Typically the rhythm section would work the song out while the horn players got something to eat or hung out outside of the studio. Once the rhythm section had it down, the horn players would work out their part and then everyone would cut the record live. Everyone used what Wayne Jackson refers to as "slate memory": each player would remember his part and the arrangement of the tune as a whole for just as long as it took to record it. They would then, in effect, wipe the slate clean and start work on the next tune. Although the Stax house band was a pretty amazing ensemble, small-scale mistakes such as Jackson makes on "Hold On! I'm Comin'" were not uncommon. In today's world of nonstop overdubs such mistakes would be immediately rectified. At Stax it was of little consequence. If a given take had that gospel-infused sanctified feeling, it was a keeper.

---

3. Not counting Wilson Pickett's recordings released on Atlantic, this was the first time a Stax single entered the pop charts in three years.

4. At the time of the session, Sam and Dave had just gotten off the road. With their voices in less-than-ideal condition, it took three days and dozens of takes to nail "Hold On! I'm Comin'."

By now, Hayes and Porter had worked out an unofficial, "stock" arrangement for Sam and Dave: Sam's higher and stronger voice would be given the first verse; Dave's thinner, lower, and rougher timbre took the second; and the third would either be split between the two or be Sam's alone. If there was a bridge, it was most often given to Dave, and the first verse was often reprised at the end with Sam singing lead. Behind each other's solo vocals, the other partner would inject cries and shouts of urging and affirmation. Sam was especially effective at this. Connections would be seamless and the choruses would be in unison. The ending would most often be a call-and-response ad lib. Instrumental solos were rare, although often a four- or eight-bar instrumental interlude such as found on "You Don't Know Like I Know" and/or a reprise of the intro would be included at the two-thirds mark.

"Hold On! I'm Comin'" was coupled with the earlier singles, "I Take What I Want" and "You Don't Know Like I Know" and nine other Stax originals, most courtesy of Hayes and Porter, for Sam and Dave's debut LP, *Hold On, [sic] I'm Comin'*. Released in April 1966, the album did not enter the pop charts until August, eventually reaching the number 45 slot on *Billboard*'s Top LP charts. While it may have enjoyed only middling pop success, it topped the R&B LP charts during its lengthy nineteen-week run.

Hold On, I'm Comin' is significant for a couple of reasons. It is the first Stax LP to be made up entirely of original compositions, breaking away from what had been standard practice at Stax and within the rhythm-and-blues industry in general: the pairing of a couple of hits with any number of covers of hits by other artists. Along with Otis Redding's *The Soul Album,* also released that April, it was the first LP on which Stax, instead of Atlantic, took care of the album artwork and liner notes. Ronnie Stoots, former lead singer of the Mar-Keys and designer of the Stax label, did the artwork, while Deanie Parker took care of the liner notes. Stoots and Parker would share these duties for virtually all the subsequent albums released by Stax or Volt while the two labels were being distributed by Atlantic.

Al Bell was responsible for making the move to keep the artwork and liner notes in-house. Bell was also the catalyst for the increased activity at the company. In 1965 Stax and Volt had released twenty-nine singles. In 1966 that number would only increase to thirty-five (not including gospel releases on Chalice or pop releases on Hip) but, significantly, Stax and Volt issued twelve albums in 1966 compared with only two in 1965. While the times were a-changing in R&B at large with labels such as Atlantic and Motown also increasing their album output, such a large increase in recordings and releases at Stax was directly the product of Bell's energy, vision, and increasing influence.

A couple of months after the release of the *Hold On, I'm Comin'* LP, Al Bell dispatched a Stax Revue to the Apollo Theater in New York to play a show copromoted by disc jockeys Rocky G. and Frankie Crocker. The star-studded bill included Sam and Dave, Otis Redding, Carla Thomas, Rufus Thomas, the Mad Lads, and Johnnie Taylor. With the MG's busy in the studio in Memphis, backing was provided by the Apollo's house band, the Reuben Phillips Orchestra. The weeklong show opened on June 17, 1966, and was billed as "Rocky G's Boogaloo Spectacular." In addition to the featured artists, on Saturday the package included a fashion show "with teenage boys and girls modeling the latest boogaloo clothes." The advance hype also promised that the performers would be teaching the boogaloo! "That's how we broke New York," smiles Bell.

Shortly after Al Bell came to Stax, he brought his former partner and Safice artist Eddie Floyd to Memphis. Although Floyd would go on to become one of Stax's mainstays as an artist, releasing records right up to the bitter end, initially Jim Stewart was interested in him only as a songwriter. Floyd already knew most of the Stax personnel, having come down to Memphis with Bell when they began using the Stax studios for Safice recordings in the early part of 1965. On one of Floyd's first trips, in cahoots with Bell, he penned "Stop! Look What You're Doing" for Carla Thomas. In the late fall, before he was signed as a writer to Stax's publishing arm, East Memphis Music, Floyd wrote "Comfort Me," with Bell and Steve Cropper, for Carla. He had also written a couple of songs for the Mad Lads that the group was eager to cut.

"Jim said, 'Ah, I don't like them,'" rues Floyd. "I said, 'Well, the group likes them. They seem to be right off into the groove of what they can do.' I made a statement. 'You seem to be going in one direction. Why not a variety of things? Hell, you'll suddenly wake up the next morning and that style be done changed and what'll you do after that?' I was asked to leave the room."

After a meeting with Al Bell and the members of Booker T. and the MG's in which Jim asked everyone what they thought of Floyd, Stewart finally relented and offered "Green Tree" (as Floyd was commonly known) a writing contract, suggesting that maybe he could come down to Memphis every other month. This was not the first, nor the last time that Jim resisted something different from what had developed into the core Stax sound. Jim's attitude would prove to be grating to many of the more developed players at Stax, including Booker T. Jones, Isaac Hayes, and Marvell Thomas. According to Isaac and Marvell, for years it was nearly impossible to play minor chords on a Stax session!

"We'd play a chord in a session," recalls a bemused Isaac Hayes, "and Jim would say, 'I don't want to hear that chord.' Jim's ears were just tuned into one, four, and five. I mean, just simple changes. He said they were the breadwinners. He didn't like minor chords. Marvell and I always would try to put that pretty stuff in there. Jim didn't like that. We'd bump heads about that stuff. Me and Marvell fought all the time [about] that. Booker wanted change as well. As time progressed, I was able to sneak a few in."

Floyd was born in Montgomery, Alabama, on June 25, 1935, but within six weeks of his birth his family made the journey north to Detroit. Shuttling back and forth, Floyd spent half his time up North and half down South. In Montgomery he did a bit of singing in the church, but it was in Detroit in the late 1950s that he formed the legendary Falcons who recorded for Floyd's uncle, Robert West's, label, Lupine. In its earliest days the group was half white and half black, but by the time they recorded their first big hit, "You're So Fine," the group was all black and featured the talents of future Stax artist and songwriter Mack Rice, Willie Schofield, and future Contour Joe Stubbs. A little while later Wilson Pickett joined, singing lead on the Falcons' other major hit, "I Found a Love." In 1961, Floyd quit the Falcons and embarked on a solo career, eventually moving to Washington, where he hooked up with Chester Simmons. When Al Bell moved to Washington to work at WUST it was only a matter of time before he met Simmons and Floyd, which led to the Grover Mitchell singles and the Safice label.[5]

It was Jim Stewart's idea, once Floyd was under contract to East Memphis, to pair him with Steve Cropper. It was an inspired decision; two of the first songs that the newly constituted team came up with were "634-5789 (Soulsville U.S.A.)" and "Ninety-Nine and a Half (Won't Do)" for Wilson Pickett's final session at Stax.[6] Pickett and Floyd, of course, had a long history together in the Falcons. Apparently, it was not uncommon for the two

---

5. See Chapter 5.

6. Tom Dowd had some interesting comments with regard to the writing of "634-5789 (Soulsville U.S.A.):" "I remember Steve was saying to me one day in the control room, 'How come all our records are r&b records and Motown has pop records? Why don't we have pop records?' I said, 'Gee Steve, the difference in writing is the

singers to argue to the point of coming to blows, occasionally while onstage. True to form, when Pickett was first presented with "634-5789" and suggested it was "a piece of shit," he and Floyd started swinging at each other in front of a somewhat incredulous Steve Cropper. "That was just a natural for us," laughs Floyd. "He was always so headstrong and so am I."

Jim Stewart liked the song and proceeded to call Jerry Wexler who, in turn, spoke with Pickett, who agreed to listen to the song again and then relented and recorded it. Steve Cropper and Al Jackson flew to New York a couple of weeks later to record some over-dubs on "634-5789." While up in the Big Apple, they also played on a Tarheel Slim and Little Ann session.

By that point, Eddie Floyd had released his first Stax single as an artist. Floyd cowrote "Things Get Better" with Steve Cropper and Wayne Jackson at the Lorraine Motel. The Lorraine, of course, would become infamous in April 1968 as the site at which Martin Luther King was assassinated. In the mid- and late 1960s, it was a hangout for the Stax family. Many of the company's out-of-town artists, such as Mable John, Wilson Pickett, Sam and Dave, and Jeanne and the Darlings would stay at the Lorraine when they came into town to record. The Stax studio crew regularly would break during the heat of the day and retire to the hotel. The McLemore studio did not have air conditioning. Consequently, when the sweat count got more than anyone could bear, it was off to the Lorraine, where session musicians, songwriters, and singers would swim, eat fried chicken specially provided by the Lorraine's proprietor, Mr. Bailey, and drink Cherry Kijofa wine. The Lorraine was also a regular site for late-night/early-morning songwriting sessions.

According to Floyd, "Things Get Better" was no more than a demo. The lyric idea came from the Coca-Cola ad "Things go better with Coke." The record failed to click in the United States, but it did provide Floyd with his third UK hit when it was issued in England a year and a half later.

As Pickett's recording of "634-5789 (Soulsville U.S.A.)" was zooming to the top of the charts and Floyd's debut Stax song was released, Jim Stewart was drawing up a contract for Stax's first blues artist since Prince Conley. Blues guitarist Albert King had recorded for the Parrot, Bobbin, King, and Coun-tree labels going back to 1953. Estelle Axton takes credit for getting King signed to Stax. A writer from Indiana named Sandy Jones had brought in a blues song called "Laundromat Blues" that he hoped the label would use.[7] "I had a time convincing Jim and them to do any blues," Axton says, shaking her head. "They didn't think blues would sell. I tried to convince them by showing how many records I sold on these different artists like Little Milton, Bobby 'Blue' Bland, and Junior Parker."

Estelle had the song for two or three months before Albert King walked into her Satellite Record Shop. She knew that the blues guitarist was popular through selling his records in the store. The two of them discussed the possibility of King signing with Stax. "I said, 'Well, it's gonna take a lot of convincing,'" laughs Axton, "'because we're doing R and B. We're not doing blues. But the first thing they're gonna tell you is, if you've got a song they'll listen to you. It just so happens I've got one.' So I let him hear 'Laundromat Blues.'"

---

thing that's germane because all the doggone Motown songs are like nursery rhymes, every syllable is on a beat. They have a great formula for doing that and they have a gift for writing lyrics that sound intelligent doing it that way. When you write a song, or Otis or William Bell writes a song, they are not sensitive to the command of the language, having everything on the beat. They are more concerned with expression. Where they're short on lyric, that's where they fill it with the "ohs" and the "ahs."' We talked about that. A couple of weeks later, Jerry Wexler went down to record with them and Steve called me up and said, 'Wait till you hear the one I just wrote. Jerry's coming back up with it. Listen to it.' That was '634-5789,' every syllable on the beat. Steve could switch hats. He could write the expression song or he could write the vertical song."

7. In 1972 another Jones composition, "Walking the Back Streets and Crying," became a hit for Stax's other blues guitarist of note, Little Milton.

Axton wrote out the words for King, not realizing that the veteran guitarist could not read. Used to doing everything from memory, King retained most of the song but, according to Axton, he forgot the last verse, which, of course, happened to be the best one. Fueled by King's liquid guitar lead and the rock-solid accompaniment of the Stax house musicians, in March 1966 "Laundromat Blues" provided King with his second chart record ever, the first since 1961, reaching number 29 on the R&B charts.

A month later, Mable John debuted on Stax. The sister of 1950s star Little Willie John, Mable had been the first female artist signed and produced by Berry Gordy. Four 45s were issued by John on the Motown subsidiary Tamla before she concluded that she might have better luck elsewhere. "I discovered that Motown was not going to be the record company that would cater to my type of singing," emphasizes John. "I'm not really a pop singer." Her manager, Chicago deejay Lucky Cordell, took her to Al Bell, who immediately signed her to Stax. When she first came into the studio and was paired with Hayes and Porter, she told them the story that became the basis for "Your Good Thing (Is About to End)."

"I enjoyed the song," sighs Mable. "I enjoyed the relief it gave me because I was in bondage. I really felt that my first husband had given me a raw deal and I was carrying around a lot of bitterness that no one knew about. That song relieved that bitterness to a degree. It was like getting something off my chest." Hayes and Porter crafted a plaintive, aching ballad for the singer. Eddie Harrison, formerly of the Premiers, provided the backing vocal. Released in May 1966, the record provided John with her only national chart success. A number 6 rhythm-and-blues and number 95 pop hit, "Your Good Thing (Is About to End)" was covered two years later by Lou Rawls, who did even better with it, reaching number 3 and number 18, respectively.

That same month Otis Redding effortlessly glided to number 10 R&B and number 61 pop with one of his trademark ballads, "My Lover's Prayer." Otis was on a roll, having closed 1965 with a number 11 and number 85 hit with the up-tempo strut "I Can't Turn You Loose," and in February 1966 his version of "Satisfaction" had been pulled from *Otis Blue*, providing him with a number 4 R&B and number 31 pop hit. As was typical for Otis in his recording and writing, "I Can't Turn You Loose" was largely written in the studio. He went into the session with only the idea for the horn line, the tempo, the lyric "hip shakin' mama I love you," and the title. With Steve Cropper's help, the rest was worked out on the floor. Cropper's name was inadvertently left off the original release. When he attempted to rectify the situation, Redding's manager, Phil Walden, told Stax to give him a credit only on the Redding single, meaning that Cropper receives no royalties on any of the numerous covers of the song. To this day he is still irked.

"I Can't Turn You Loose" was also significant because it was one of the first sessions on which Joe Arnold replaced Gene Parker as part of the Mar-Key horns. Parker had been at Stax for about a year and a half. A brilliant player, unfortunately, he was mentally unstable. According to Arnold, Parker lost it totally when he came home one day and found his wife in bed with another woman. For about four months Arnold had been playing at Lil Abner's Rebel Room in a band that included Parker, Duck Dunn, Ronnie Stoots, Robert Talley, and Wayne Jackson. It was Dunn who brought him down to his first Stax session.

A month before "My Lover's Prayer" was released, Redding headed out to Los Angeles to play three days at the Whiskey A-Go-Go, where he attempted to record a live album officially under the supervision of Atlantic's Nesuhi Ertegun.[8] For the Whiskey recording,

8. It would appear that Al Jackson did the actual production work.

Otis was forced to use his road band because the MG's were too busy in the Stax studio to spend several days away in Los Angeles. Otis worked his butt off, rehearsing the band from 2 A.M. until 10 in the morning; letting everyone sleep until 4, and then rehearsing again until showtime. Although the feel of the engagement was magical with the Los Angeles music and film industry cognoscenti turning out to see the King of Soul Music night after night, the resulting tapes were simply not up to snuff. Redding's band was as ragged as can be, with the horns being painfully out of tune on virtually every song.[9]

While Otis was out in Los Angeles, Booker T. Jones was writing his final exams in his fourth and final year at Indiana University's music program.[10] Within a few weeks, Jones would be back at Stax full-time. Over the next few years, he would strike up writing partnerships with both Eddie Floyd and William Bell, composing some of the most beautiful music Stax would ever release.

With Al Bell marshaling the disc jockeys and distributors, Jim Stewart working the board, Hayes and Porter coming into their own as the premier soul songwriting team, and Booker T. Jones back from college, the excitement level at Stax was at an all-time high. When Brian Epstein came to town in March 1966 to inquire about the possibility of the Beatles recording their next album at Stax, it was nearly too much to bear.

According to Estelle, Epstein initially contacted Atlantic, which then notified Stax. Tom Dowd was immediately dispatched to Memphis to check over the equipment. In the meantime, Estelle, who was always the company's emissary, was sent to the airport to meet Brian Epstein, check him into his hotel, and then bring him to 926 E. McLemore. After giving Epstein a quick tour of the studio, Steve Cropper and Jim Stewart headed off for Florida for a couple of days of much-needed rest and relaxation. Estelle stayed on, playing host to the Beatles' manager, chauffeuring him to and fro from his suite at the Rivermont Hotel to the Stax studio, local restaurants, and an estate out on Walnut Grove that one of the primary stockholders of the First National Bank had offered for Epstein's use.

Shortly after Epstein left Memphis, the news media converged on the McLemore studio, that evening's television news reporting that the Beatles were planning to record at Stax before their upcoming summer tour. The Stax studio was immediately besieged as young Memphians, fraught with Beatlemania, mindlessly gathered at the studio. When Jim Stewart saw it on the news in Florida he was furious, phoning Estelle thinking that she had leaked the story. Estelle has always thought that the women at the front desk of the Rivermont recognized her and Epstein and, putting two and two together, tipped members of the local news media.

In actuality, the news could have leaked out through a variety of sources. Johnny Keyes recalls walking into the studio and encountering Jim's secretary, Linda Andrews, in a very agitated state. "Linda says, 'I know a secret, I know a secret. I can't tell you, I can't tell you. You'll tell somebody. I've got a secret. Oh, I'm about to bust open. Deanie, Deanie, can we tell him?' I replied, 'Hey, either tell me or don't. Don't go through these gyrations.' So they said, 'The Beatles are coming!'" So much for the well-guarded secret!

---

9. Despite the obviously low quality, after Redding died, Atlantic opted to cull a single album from the tapes entitled *Otis Redding in Person at the Whiskey A-Go-Go.* A stomping, if ragged, cover of James Brown's "Papa's Got a Brand New Bag" was edited from the tapes and released as a single in December 1968, penetrating the R&B Top 10 while stalling at number 21 pop. In 1982, a further album, *Otis Redding Live,* was issued by Atlantic of previously unissued material recorded at the Whiskey. Eleven years later this recording was reissued on CD by Fantasy Records with still more previously unissued material.

10. One course short, he didn't actually receive his degree until the spring of 1967. The missing credit was completed at Memphis State University.

Before all hell broke out, Estelle had told several of the Stax songwriters that they needed to get material together as the Beatles were intending to cover some contemporary
rhythm and blues. It seems doubtful that the Beatles had this in mind; at this point in their
career they had stopped recording covers. What probably happened was that Estelle,
being the enterprising person that she was, simply thought that here was an opportunity
to at least try to pitch songs to the Beatles, and so everyone should be prepared. Johnny
Keyes and Ronnie Gordon wrote "Out of Control," which eventually was recorded by L.
H. and the Memphis Sounds. Cropper was hopeful that the Beatles would want to use
him as an engineer and that perhaps some of the Stax session musicians would be asked
to contribute a lick or two.

Deanie Parker doesn't remember writing any songs for the event. She had other things
on her mind. "I was so overwhelmed at the excitement that the Beatles had created with
the mere fact that they might visit the studio that I decided immediately after they left that
the carpet was coming up. I was going to cut it into little pieces and sell them. With the
money I made from that I could replace the carpet and still have a large profit left over!"

Alas, the Beatles never came to Stax to record. According to Steve, from what he was
told, Epstein concluded that there was not enough security in Memphis and consequently decided the Beatles should record at Atlantic in New York. Cropper still hoped to be
involved. "By the time Epstein got back," recalls Steve, "he called me and said, 'Well, I
guess we're gonna have to do it on the next project because they've already got almost all
of the album recorded.'"

Curiously enough, as far as I can tell, this incident is not well known and is not mentioned in any Beatles book,[11] despite the fact that Memphis deejay George Klein vividly
recalls asking the Beatles about it at their Memphis press conference before their August
19 shows at the Mid-South Coliseum.[12] Either George or Paul affirmed that they had been
discussing the possibility of recording at Stax and mentioned how much they admired the
records coming out of the Stax studio. In later years, Steve Cropper played on the original, still unreleased sessions for John Lennon's *Rock and Roll* album. Typical of Lennon's
verbal wit, he referred to Booker T. and the MG's as "Book a table and the maitre D's."
He told Cropper that he listened to Booker T. and the MG's records over and over and
that he had always wanted to write an instrumental for the MG's. The album that the
Beatles might have partially recorded at Stax was *Revolver.* It is intriguing to imagine the
horns on a track such as "Got to Get You into My Life" or "Good Day Sunshine" being
played by Wayne Jackson and Andrew Love.

By this point, Wayne and Andrew had revived the Mar-Keys name and began working
gigs in the mid-South area. In January 1966, the resurrected "new" Mar-Keys cut an
instrumental based around Rufus Thomas's "Dog" rhythm. The resultant recording,
"Philly Dog," rose to number 19 R&B, while stalling at number 89 pop. The single was
soon followed by the first album issued under the Mar-Keys name since 1962's *Do the Pop-
Eye.* Released in April 1966, *The Great Memphis Sound* failed to chart.

As exciting as the spring had been, the summer and fall of 1966 were even better as
Stax became a serious player in the R&B sweepstakes. In July, Eddie Floyd and Carla
Thomas scaled the charts with "Knock on Wood" and "B-A-B-Y," followed a month later

11. Although a news article did appear in the March 31, 1966, edition of the *Memphis Press–Scimitar*. According to
the *Press–Scimitar* piece, the Beatles were scheduled to arrive at Stax on April 9 and were slated to stay two
weeks recording one LP and one single. Estelle was quoted as saying she had been looking for a house that
would be suitable for the Beatles to stay in.

12. The second show was attended by Carla Thomas and her sister Vaneese; in her own words, they were among
the very few African-Americans at the show.

by Sam and Dave with "Said I Wasn't Gonna Tell Nobody." Otis hit the charts in September with "Fa-Fa-Fa-Fa-Fa (Sad Song)" and again in November with "Try a Little Tenderness." The latter month also witnessed hits by Albert King and Sam and Dave with "Crosscut Saw" and "You Got Me Hummin'."

Of course, all of these hits served to drive the thermometer that Al Bell had set up in the entranceway of Stax closer and closer to the metaphorical heaven at the top. Sometime in this period, a producers' pool and regular Monday morning board meetings were initiated.[13] The producers' pool consisted of what was nominally referred to as the "Big 6": the four members of Booker T. and the MG's plus Isaac Hayes and David Porter. Up to this point, individual production credits at Stax had been few and far between, limited for all intents and purposes to work by outside producers.[14] Albums simply listed Jim Stewart as recording supervisor. After some intense lobbying from Al Bell, Jim Stewart finally agreed that the records should be credited as being "Produced by staff" with the producer's royalty being split between the six individuals most responsible for the company's success. For all intents and purposes this was a profit-sharing scheme.

"What actually happened," stresses Steve, "is that Jim Stewart and Al Bell realized that these guys playing on these records were not just sidemen. They were not hired musicians. These guys were in there writing and contributing to the making of these records and that's what made them so great. It was a decision on their part to start sharing some of that return with the guys that made the music.

"We were all pretty instrumental in the production of the records," continues Steve. "We [each] had our own ideas about the way things should go and everybody sort of got their shot. If you came up with some statement that everybody agreed upon, then that's the way it went. If you didn't, then you got ruled out and you did it somebody else's way."

Wayne Jackson concurs: "The production at Stax was always a group effort. No one person ever said, 'Do it this way.' There was too much talent there. Everybody was having a great time bursting at the seams with energy and talent. The records at Stax were a result of spontaneous combustion, not a directed effort by one person. We were all close friends."

Not close enough, evidently, for the horn players to be included in the pool, which still irritates Wayne Jackson and Andrew Love. As integral as the horns were to the sound of Stax, the horn players were always treated as somewhat lesser contributors by Jim Stewart. By his own admission, if he could have found good enough background vocalists, horns would never have become so important to the label's sound. Not only were they omitted from the producers' pool, they would also not be put on salary until well after the rhythm section had been accorded this status.

Groove was paramount at Stax and more often than not, when it came to questions of tempo or groove, Steve and Al Jackson were in charge. "He and I [would go] into a corner," Steve recalls with a smile, "and say, 'You know this song should go this way. It should be this tempo with this groove.' We would sort of force that on them. We'd let them try it [their] way until they were almost beating a dead horse to death. Then we'd try it our way and within a couple of cuts we'd usually have it."

The board meetings were less exclusive than the producers' pool and had started sometime earlier. Largely concerned with A&R matters, much to Steve Cropper's disgust, the

---

13. The board meetings lasted until the latter part of 1969.

14. For example, the Mar-Keys' single "Whots (sic) Happenin'!" has a credit that reads "Produced by Nick Charles."

meetings were open to anyone associated with the company. "That's when I started sneaking out the door," says Cropper caustically. "'I'll see y'all later.' It was kind of weird. Some of it was a farce, just a waste of time. We didn't need twenty people telling us to put out 'I've Been Loving You Too Long.' It was just obvious it was a good record."

After their success with "634-5789 (Soulsville U.S.A.)" and "Ninety-Nine and a Half (Won't Do)," Eddie Floyd and Steve Cropper continued to write together regularly, Floyd writing the words and the melody and Cropper taking care of the chord changes. Floyd's next single, "Knock on Wood," was one of Cropper and his greatest successes. Although he didn't receive a songwriting credit on the record, Isaac Hayes came up with the distinctive horn part on the bridge.

According to Floyd, the song was originally written with Otis Redding in mind but Jim Stewart didn't like the idea (Cropper, though, doesn't remember it this way).[15] Floyd explains how the lyric idea came about: "I was thinking about rabbit foots and stuff like that, the whole superstitious thing, not knowing that there is another 'Knock on Wood' in the film *Casablanca*."

Steve and Eddie wrote the song at the Lorraine, finishing up at about 1:30 in the morning. Pumped by what they had come up with, Cropper phoned Wayne Jackson, who was playing at one of the clubs in West Memphis, and asked if Wayne wanted to come by the hotel after the last set at the club to work on a horn line for the new song. Wayne complied, and the next day at 11 A.M. everyone was in the studio working on "Knock on Wood."

"Jim Stewart walks in," recalls Steve, "listens to it and starts putting it down. He calls me in [to the control booth] and says, 'Nah, it's too close to "In the Midnight Hour." This is no good.' Boy, I just got mad. I couldn't stand it."[16]

That night Steve and Jim went to dinner. Steve strongly conveyed his belief in the song to Jim, imploring the company owner for permission to cut it. Jim gave in and "Knock on Wood" was cut the next day. Jim was still not impressed and the song sat in the can for several months. Eventually, Estelle, Al Bell, and Steve Cropper forced the issue. "Finally he said, 'Well, okay, I wash my hands of it. If you want to put it out, put it out,'" relays Steve. "We had said, 'The record's got to go out.' Al Bell said, 'I'll spend my own money if I have to.' That's how it came out."

At Al Bell's behest, a few copies of Floyd's demo were pressed and distributed in Memphis and in Bell and Floyd's former hometown, Washington. Jerry Wexler was sure it was a hit as was his partner, Ahmet Ertegun ("That's when all of a sudden the push went on," laughs Cropper), and Atlantic soon picked it up and distributed it nationally. Although it entered the charts in late August, its climb to the number 1 rhythm-and-blues spot and number 28 pop took some time, with sales eventually peaking at around 735,000 copies. It was only Stax's third number 1 rhythm-and-blues record.

Typical of how Stax functioned at this stage of the game, David Porter contributed a second voice on top on the chorus, simply because he poked his head into the studio while Floyd was cutting the song. Floyd said that he might have added some more voices except he thought he was just cutting a demo. Al Jackson contributed the idea for the "knocking" drum hook that follows Floyd's evocation "You gotta knock . . ." "He thought about Steppin Fetchit [doing] 'Open the Door Richard,'" explains Floyd. The rhythm of the intro was inspired by Floyd thinking of Native American tom-tom drumming.

15. Redding did eventually record the song as a duet with Carla Thomas for the *King and Queen* album.

16. Jim wasn't altogether wrong. The chord pattern of the intro of "Knock on Wood" is that of the intro of Wilson Pickett's "In the Midnight Hour," but in reverse.

Eddie Floyd. COURTESY RON CAPONE.

While Floyd was enjoying the fruits of "Knock on Wood," Isaac Hayes and David Porter were hitting with Johnnie Taylor's "I Got to Love Somebody's Baby," Carla Thomas's "B-A-B-Y," and Sam and Dave's "Said I Wasn't Gonna Tell Nobody" and "You Got Me Hummin'." Despite "B-A-B-Y" soaring to number 3 R&B and number 14 pop, Carla hated the song. Hayes and Porter had also been writing for her father, who likewise was none too enamored of the material they were writing for him. Carla felt that "B-A-B-Y" was essentially a Sam and Dave outtake.

" 'B-A-B-Y' was taking close to four hours to cut," moans Carla, "because it was sounding like 'Soul Man.' That was the structure of the song. [The rhythm was Sam and Dave.] I said, 'I cannot sing that.' I went home and went to bed. I was so frustrated. They kept making me stand there and sing and I'm frustrated and tired." The next day when Carla came back to the studio, the song had been substantially modified by Booker T. Jones.

Carla Thomas and MG drummer Al Jackson.
COURTESY DEANIE PARKER.

"That whole thing was Booker's," asserts Carla. "When I came back, it was totally softened up and had the organ."

Whatever the initial conception, the new arrangement was superb, bouncing rhythmic piano against a quirky organ sound and Carla's breathy, seductive vocal. Her sister, Vanese, alongside David Porter, contributed the backing vocals because, in Porter's words, "she had that youthful sound." It was Porter's idea to use the initials in the lyrics, although he credits Hayes with writing the lion's share of the song.

Capitalizing on the success of "B-A-B-Y," Stax issued the *Carla* LP in September 1966. The album also included the earlier "Let Me Be Good to You" as well as the usual requisite array of cover tunes. Interestingly, two of Carla's favorite country songs from her youth, Patsy Cline's "I Fall to Pieces" and Hank Williams's "I'm So Lonesome I Could Cry," were included. *Carla* fared similarly to *Comfort Me*, reaching the number 130 position on the Top LP charts and the number 8 position on the rhythm-and-blues LP charts.

Hayes and Porter based Sam and Dave's "Said I Wasn't Gonna Tell Nobody" on another traditional church song, "Said I Wasn't Gonna Tell Nobody But I Couldn't Keep It to Myself." The song had been attempted a number of times over the previous twelve months, but it seems that they could never quite get it right. To this day neither Sam Moore nor David Porter is satisfied with it.

The recording as it stands is somewhat muddy, but the song is exciting nonetheless. Basically a driving three-way exchange between Al Jackson's tom-toms, Duck Dunn's and Steve Cropper's doubled bass and guitar, and the Memphis Horns, replete with flashy organ flourishes, it builds to a frenzy where someone loses it, gets "happy," and starts clapping for a couple of beats at the end of the second verse.

It might be David Porter clapping. Whenever Hayes and Porter were producing an artist, David would work with the vocalists while Hayes would largely take care of the

Stax studio control room: (*left to right*) Sam Moore, Isaac Hayes, Booker T. Jones (*forehead and eye only*), Andrew Love, Wayne Jackson, Dave Prater, Jim Stewart (*seated with his back to the camera*), Steve Cropper. COURTESY DEANIE PARKER.

instrumentalists. Porter would remain on the studio floor with the vocalists, conducting, cajoling, and basically trying to inspire a superior take. Sweating profusely, Porter tended to be very physical and would get so involved that he can be heard singing or clapping on the master recording at times. Again, at Stax that was of no consequence if the rest of the performance caught a magical moment. If anything, the fact that someone got "happy" on a track was evidence that the holy ghost had descended on the studio and consequently reason to celebrate.

"That was really the kind of [high energy] aura we were trying to create with Sam and Dave," affirms David Porter. "We just developed that feel out of the church mode in our songs. The spirit of what Sam and Dave were like as artists was something developed early on through the religious concept that we had. We would often come up with good lines on tunes but it wouldn't feel soulful, something you could have church on. If it didn't do that to us we dropped it." "Said I Wasn't Gonna Tell Nobody" broke the R&B Top 10, although it only reached number 64 on the pop charts. It was followed in November with "You Got Me Hummin'."

"We were so sure of what we were doing," relates Porter. "'You Got Me Hummin'' was a joke. You know ego is a funny thing. When things are happening you start to feel real good about what you're doing and you feel you can't miss. We were going to see if we could get a good song out of something that didn't make any sense. We were just playing, teasing [Porter moans] like we were screwing. When we wrote the song we had it sensuous, but when Sam and Dave sung it they didn't know how to be sensuous. Dave sounds like he's in the bathroom. We had so much fun cutting it but it was created as a lark. We were just surprised that it ended up being a forty-five."

Another slab of burning up-tempo soul, the song opens with the bass doubled with the left hand of the piano. Over the top of this, Isaac plays four of the oddest notes possible in the high end of the piano's range. But, as usual with Isaac's experiments, it works perfectly. Sam and Dave moan their way into the first verse singing in unison. Testimony to the fun they are having is the absurd way they roll their *r*s on the words *through me.*

Another Top 10 R&B hit, "You Got Me Hummin'" only reached number 77 on the pop charts, although a few years later it was covered by Lydia Pense and Cold Blood, charting twenty-five notches higher. The Cold Blood version was the first of what was to be a continuing series of white covers of Hayes and Porter's creations of Sam and Dave material. The most prominent examples include the Blues Brothers' version of "Soul Man," Z Z Top's cover of "I Thank You," and the Fabulous Thunderbirds' take on "Wrap It Up."

Otis Redding had a great year in 1966. In September he toured Europe for the first time.[17] In the United States, his newest release, "Fa-Fa-Fa-Fa-Fa (Sad Song)," continued his string of hits, climbing to the number 12 R&B and number 29 pop positions. Cowritten by Steve Cropper, "Fa-Fa-Fa-Fa-Fa (Sad Song)"'s title stemmed from Redding's habit of humming or singing horn lines using vocables. The second voice on the "fa-fa-fa-fa-fa" part is that of Stax songwriter David Porter.

An integral part of the Stax sound from the beginning, Otis played a greater role than anyone in shaping the aesthetic of the label's horn lines. "Otis always had the hardest horn arrangements," Floyd Newman recalls, shaking his head. "They were different and super difficult. . . . He'd always work his things out on the bus when he'd be traveling. He knew every line and every hole in every place. He knew where he was going on every song, what beats he wanted the lines to fall on. He could walk right in and sing it. There's not a lot of words on Otis's records, but there are a lot of horn lines. James Brown did the same thing, but Otis's horn lines were entirely different from what James was doing. They were more difficult—rhythmically and harmonically. Otis always did things in keys like E, A, and F sharp, the keys that nobody was playing in. The sharp keys are brilliant keys, but people just don't mess around with them much. It gave his songs a lot of punch and drive and made you want to pop your fingers. He would always say, 'Floyd, if you listen to the song and your shoulders don't move, there's no groove to it.'"[18]

Tenor saxophonist Andrew Love continues: "Otis Redding had a lot to do with the Stax horn sound because he hummed a lot of horn lines to us. We took it from there and they

---

17. Sam and Dave would shortly follow him.

18. With groove the be-all and end-all at Stax, Duck Dunn took the same basic approach as Otis: "I was one of those people, if you couldn't dance to it or it didn't make you hug a girl, it wasn't worth a shit. I could almost shut my eyes and see a bunch of warriors around a campfire with warpaint and shit."

turned out to be Memphis Horn lines. He would put the horns in some funny places too. Sometimes it would be hard to feel them where he'd sing them. We'd come in sometimes and we hadn't heard the song before but he would have been sitting up all night working on it and he would feel the horns in a certain place. We'd say, 'Now wait a minute,' but after you played it through, it all came together. It was right. Sometimes we'd be on a funny beat just to stay off the voice. We did it so much, it started being a certain style. It sounded funny at first, but then it started being identifiable. We tried to fill up the holes, stay off the voice, kick the punch parts, emphasize the hook line, and on the fadeout try to get exciting to take them on out."

Wayne Jackson echoes Love's sentiments: "Otis was a good teacher. He taught us a lot about rhythm. He loved the horns. He'd be shaking his fist at you and be singing those parts and it was just electrifying." Cropper eventually developed his basic conception of horn lines from working with Otis. "He got me going," admits the guitarist, "He taught me everything I've ever learned about horns. It was such an interesting thing to do so I wound up later doing a lot of the horn lines while he was concentrating on the songs." Oddly enough, nobody really knows where Otis's conception of horn lines came from. No one can cite his influences nor can anyone remember Otis talking about other people's horn arrangements.

According to Wayne Jackson, Otis in the studio was a very physical person. "Man, you better believe it. He had to have two cans of Right Guard to keep him down. I mean the man was physical. Emotional and physical. Otis was an unusual person. He would have been unusual had he been a fighter, a football player, a singer, or a preacher. He had that kind of energetic ego, drive thing. We all loved him. God, we really did! [Wayne sings the horn line to 'Fa-Fa-Fa-Fa-Fa'] He sang all that stuff to us just as natural as anything. That was how they came about. He loved the horns. He would run from his vocal mike down to where the horns were and go [sings the horn line from 'I Can't Turn You Loose'], shake his fist at you, and be singing those parts, and it was just electrifying. He'd just get right in front of you with that big fist up in the air and strut and sing that stuff at you until you were just foaming at the mouth. He'd just have you so excited. We had to calm him down sometimes. That was pretty much the way he went about inspiring us. We just played exactly what he was singing and that would be the horn line for the song. We were strictly painting a picture for him to dance in."

"Otis gave ten thousand percent," adds Al Bell. "He lost pounds in the studio. He'd come into the studio and strip down to his waist 'cause it was hot in that old studio and, man, just sing until water was coming off him like someone was pouring it out of a bucket."

No matter how intense the sessions got, Otis was always able to create a positive atmosphere among the musicians at Stax. Floyd Newman remembers, "Some artists are so intense about what they're doing that they make everybody feel kind of negative, but when Otis came in he brought happiness and smiles. He was laughing the whole time he was playing and, if you missed a lick, he didn't get upset over it. He'd laugh and say, 'You'll get it.' And, if we were slow in catching on, he would get on his guitar and play. It was happy moments, happy moments." Jim Stewart perhaps sums it up best: "Otis Redding was like a magic potion. When he walked into the studio, the studio lit up and all the worries and problems just sort of vanished. You knew something good was going to happen. He brought that excitement with him. Otis was totally creative, totally positive. Everybody wanted to be there when Otis walked in. It was like magic."

In this period, there was a certain magic to Stax itself. "For me it was like going to church every day," testifies Cropper. "You walked in those doors at Stax, you left everything out there behind you. It was just like going into church. I'd work sometimes eighteen hours a day and never even thought about being tired. I just wanted to be there all the time."

Otis closed out the year with what might be his greatest recording, "Try a Little Tenderness." It is certainly Jim Stewart's favorite. "Of all the things he ever did from the standpoint of the production, everything, the way it's laid out from the bottom to the top, it's the best thing he ever did," asserts Stewart. "The drum part always killed me because [Al] Jackson was like a metronome, how he changed the tempo. I defy any drummer to do that exactly the same. It's one of my favorite Stax records of all time. From beginning to end, it's like the history of Stax is wrapped up in it."

Written by Englishmen Reg Connelly and James Campbell and American Harry Woods, the song has a long life. White clarinetist and bandleader Ted Lewis was the first to record a hit version of "Try a Little Tenderness." In February 1933 Lewis's Columbia recording entered the pop charts, peaking at number 6. A month later Broadway torch singer Ruth Etting entered the charts with a version recorded for Melotone that settled at the number 16 spot. Bing Crosby recorded it in January for Brunswick, but his version failed to chart; Frank Sinatra recorded yet another pop version of the song in the mid-forties.

In 1962 Aretha Franklin recorded the first well-known version of the song by a black artist for her second Columbia LP, *The Tender, the Moving, the Swinging Aretha Franklin,* while Sam Cooke recorded it as part of a medley with another Tin Pan Alley standard, "For Sentimental Reasons," and his own hit "You Send Me," on his 1964 *At the Copa* live album. Columbia Records was attempting to market Franklin as a pop singer and consequently recorded her singing any number of Tin Pan Alley standards replete with pop string arrangements. These records were a far cry from her later Atlantic rhythm and blues hits in terms of instrumentation, arrangement, and performance style. That said, Franklin cannot and does not completely shed her gospel background and consequently, at least to a small degree, transforms the song when compared to the Crosby and Sinatra recordings. Sam Cooke chose to perform the song at the Copa, a New York City "society" nightclub, for reasons similar to those that motivated Columbia to suggest that Franklin record it. In playing the Copa and in modifying his repertoire for the occasion, Cooke was attempting to appeal to an older white, middle- and upper-class audience.[19]

Otis Redding recorded "Try a Little Tenderness" in 1966 originally for his *The Otis Redding Dictionary of Soul: Complete and Unbelievable* LP. As with virtually everything recorded at Stax in the 1960s, accompanying Redding was the label's house band, Booker T. and the MG's, augmented by Isaac Hayes and the Mar-Key horns. MG guitarist Steve Cropper recalls Redding and the session musicians listening to both the Cooke and Franklin versions prior to recording.

As with many of the songs Redding covered, he completely deconstructed and reconstructed the work, in the process redefining the very possibilities and ultimately the meaning of the song. Redding's manager, Phil Walden, had been on Otis for quite some time to record "Try a Little Tenderness" but he hadn't bargained for this version. "Otis had an unbelievable capacity to turn something totally around," states Walden, still in wonderment. "A good example is 'Try a Little Tenderness.' This was when we were talking about

19. A comparison of the Copa LP with Cooke's *Live at the Harlem Square Club* LP, recorded in 1963 in a black club in Miami, reveals just how different his repertoire and performing style would be depending on the context in which he was performing. This is not to suggest that Cooke was not comfortable, competent, and interested in performing in both styles. It simply is indicative that he had an understanding of a palpable difference in what type of repertoire and performance style would have meaning for the two different demographics that would make up the respective audiences at the Copa and Harlem Square Club.

career songs where he could be on the Ed Sullivan Show or playing the Copa. These things were terribly, terribly important. They were a sign of success. I remember he called me late at night [I hadn't gone to that session] and he said, 'You know that song you've been on my ass about recording, "Try a Little Tenderness"?' I said, 'Yeah.' He said, 'I cut that motherfucker. It's a brand-new song.' He could just turn things around, he could hear it in such a different way."[20]

The arrangement was atypical of Stax, rhythm and blues, and pop. Isaac Hayes was responsible for much of it, including the three-part, contrapuntal horn line in the intro (inspired by the strings on Sam Cooke's "A Change Is Gonna Come") and the cymbal break in the climax (which Hayes later reused on "Theme from *Shaft*"). The idea of having Al Jackson lay out during the first verse and then come in on the second verse of the song simply tapping quarter-beats on the rim of the snare came about accidentally when the drummer idly tapped along while Redding was running down the tune. Jackson suggested that he actually hold off from using his full kit until two-thirds of the way through the song.

"Al came up with the idea of breaking up the rhythm," recalls Booker T. "And Otis just took that and ran with it. He really got excited once he found out what Al was going to do on the drums. He realized how he could finish the song. That he could start it like a ballad and finish it full of emotion. That's how a lot of our arrangements would come together. Somebody would come up with something totally outrageous."

Booker contributed the descending piano line bridging bars eight and nine of the verses, and Gilbert Caple played the saxophone commentaries.[21] All four members of Booker T. and the MG's plus Isaac Hayes on organ and the Mar-Key horns are at their absolute finest. As with many Redding recordings, the highlight is the ad-lib section that takes up the final sixty seconds of the song. Most of Otis's ad libs would go on and on with Jim Stewart eventually fading the track out at the board.[22] Wayne Jackson notes to what degree they were planned out in advance: "They weren't worked out as to exactly what he would do. He was just born to do that. You can't practice to be that good. We didn't worry a song to death, at least not with Otis there. We might worry with a track or to get the feel right but when he started singing, man, we nailed it. He was an absolute master, very consistent, very professional."

Otis rarely needed more than two takes, but when he did, as might be expected, the ad libs were quite different. Jim Stewart emphasizes that you had to get a master take early on because with each repeat the ad lib would become increasingly florid, to the point of being overwrought.

All told, "Try a Little Tenderness" took three takes. The net result was a number 4 record on the R&B charts that stopped at number 25 pop. Atlantic dutifully took out the obligatory full-page *Billboard* ad in the January 7, 1967, issue, proclaiming it "his biggest hit ever . . . from his biggest album ever."

Stax released two albums by Otis in 1966: *The Soul Album* in April and *Dictionary of Soul: Complete and Unbelievable* in October. The former, with only one hit single, was his

---

20. For the record, Steve Cropper is emphatic that Otis Redding did not speak in that manner and would never have used the word *motherfucker*.

21. Although Andrew Love replaced him in 1964 when Caple headed to Houston to work in the Duke-Peacock house band, Caple continued to play on the odd Stax session whenever he was back in Memphis.

22. With Stax recordings still largely being cut "live" on the floor with everyone playing simultaneously, part of Jim Stewart's job as engineer was to constantly ride the faders (volume controls), boosting certain instruments at appropriate moments and compensating for different levels of volume being generated by individual players.

greatest success to date, reaching number 54 on the Top LP charts and number 3 on the R&B LP charts, remaining on the latter chart for twenty-eight weeks. *Dictionary of Soul,* despite the inclusion of "Fa-Fa-Fa-Fa-Fa (Sad Song)" and "Try a Little Tenderness," stalled at number 73 on the Top LP charts and number 5 on the R&B LP charts.[23] As satisfying as 1966 must have seemed to Otis, the following year would be when he'd finally become a superstar.

23. It is worth noting that, à la Carla Thomas, Otis chose to cut a country number, Patti Page's "Tennessee Waltz," on the latter album. Before he died, Otis had talked about cutting an album entirely composed of country material.

7

Soul Man: 1967

With the Chalice gospel label up and running for about a year, a greatly expanded catalogue of LP releases, and a passel of significant hit singles under his belt, Al Bell opted to further diversify the Stax operation. The November 26, 1966, issue of *Billboard* announced that Stax was starting a pop subsidiary named Hip. English singer Sharon Tandy (who would take Carla Thomas's place on the majority of the Stax/Volt Europe tour shows in the spring of 1967) and Memphis group Tommy Burk and the Counts were listed as the first acts to be signed.[1]

Between the fall of 1966 and the split from Atlantic in May 1968, twelve records were issued on Hip; all but one were by white pop groups.[2] After the split from Atlantic, twenty-two more singles were issued on Hip through late 1969. Of these, all but two—the Goodees' "Condition Red" (Hip 8005) and Southwest F.O.B.'s "Smell of Incense" (Hip 9002)—were abject failures. The Goodees were a Memphis-based ensemble whose sound harkened back to the early 1960s girl groups such as the Angels and the Shangri-Las. Their one glimpse at the limelight peaked at number 46 on the pop charts in the early weeks of 1969. Southwest F.O.B. hailed from Dallas and featured England Dan Seals and John Ford Coley, who, under their own names, would have a number of pop hits in the late 1970s. "Smell of Incense," their one hit at Stax, was licensed from a Texas label, GPC, and climbed to the number 56 spot on the pop charts.

Most of the pop acts signed to Hip came to the label through the auspices of Ardent Recording Studio president John Fry, entertainment lawyer Seymour Rosenberg, or Al Bell. The vast majority were not recorded at Stax. In Jim Stewart's words: "It was rare that we got [rhythm and blues] records played on white stations, because [they were] 'too black' as they used to tell us, so [Hip] was a sorry effort to try and see if we could [get pop airplay with white artists]."

Rosenberg is perhaps best described as a cigar-chomping, somewhat portly musician/lawyer with a well-developed sense of humor. Many years earlier he had played trumpet with Jim Stewart as part of Sleepy Eyed John's band at the Eagle's Nest. A full-time lawyer, he also managed a number of musicians on the side, the most famous being Charlie Rich, whom Rosenberg represented from 1961 to 1976. For a brief while Rosenberg co-owned the American Sound Studio and Youngstown and Penthouse labels with Chips Moman. At the time Isaac Hayes recorded for Youngstown, Rosenberg also managed him. Rosenberg represented most of the disc jockeys and program directors in the Memphis area and consequently had considerable influence when it came time to get

---

1. Hip never issued a release by Tandy, although Atlantic did a little while later.

2. The one exception was Hip 108 by C. L. Blast: "Glad to Do It" b/w "Double Up."

a record played. He brought Tommy Burk and the Counts, the Poor Little Rich Kids, Johnny Dark, David Hollis, and Lonnie Duval to Hip. In all cases these were finished masters that had nothing to do with the Stax studio, session musicians, or songwriters. Few of these artists were heard outside of the mid-South area.

"Stax already had a successful label," explains Rosenberg, "and it's an ego thing to get into the white area. Basically, I'd bring them these things I'd cut and it didn't cost much to press up records and put them out locally. All I wanted was some exposure at the time [for the artists]. Any way you get started is a good way. As a result [of their Hip 45] the Counts went from $150 a night to $500 or $1000. . . . They had some sort of fame, if just local around the mid-South. Stax didn't care much about Hip. They were doing well with R and B. It was an experimental thing. If something sold, fine, if it didn't. . . ." Before 1967 was over, Seymour Rosenberg became the first legal counsel Stax had ever retained.

Tellingly, neither Jim Stewart, Steve Cropper, nor John Fry remembers anyone at Stax being specifically in charge of Hip. "They just sort of had this label," shrugs Fry, "that they would put anything on that came their way. But in terms of anybody trying to chart a course or direction from an A&R point of view, there was no function of that kind that I can remember."

Just how far Stax was out of touch when it came to their pop efforts is best summed up by the man in charge of marketing Stax singles from 1968 to 1971, Ewell Roussell. "We were cutting the Goodees when there were groups like Led Zeppelin out there. We were trying to cut hit singles when pop music was all in albums. I just don't think we had a caliber act."

Although Hip was rightly put to bed before the end of 1969, Bell would make several other attempts to achieve success with pop and rock artists, mostly via the Enterprise label. All would fail abysmally both aesthetically and commercially, with the exception of Big Star's two albums on Ardent. Even these failed to generate any sales when originally released in 1972 and 1973, but over the course of the next two decades both *Radio City* and *Number One Record* have had an inordinate influence on a host of latter-day rock bands including the Replacements and R.E.M.

Just as Stax was starting up Hip, Jerry Wexler approached Jim Stewart with an offer. Aretha Franklin had recently left Columbia Records and had signed with Atlantic. Wexler offered to lend Aretha to Stax on the same terms as he was currently lending them Sam and Dave.

"Aretha, coming from a gospel background with her equipment and ability," related Wexler to French film director Phil Priestley, "was an ideal candidate for Stax Records' production [team]. I could visualize her in the studio with Steve Cropper and Booker T. making incredible rhythm tracks."[3]

Unfortunately, there was one proviso that had not been part of the Sam and Dave deal. Wexler wanted Stax to pay to Atlantic the $25,000 advance Atlantic had paid Franklin upon signing. By Wexler's own admission, in 1967 $25,000 was "important money." Stewart felt the price was more than he could afford.

"Twenty-five thousand dollars cash that was nonrecoupable to a man who was just starting to sell records and thought five thousand dollars was a lot of money" is how Stewart succinctly explained his decision in 1986. Stewart turned Gladys Knight down as well in 1967 for the same reason. He simply felt she was too expensive for his company at that par-

---

3. Priestly's interview with Wexler was conducted for the documentary film *The Soul of Stax*. All other interviews for that film were conducted by the author.

Carla Thomas and Otis Redding present a plaque to Tennessee senator Howard Baker, who wrote the liner notes for Thomas and Redding's *King and Queen* album. COURTESY FANTASY, INC.

ticular point in time.[4] Stewart's sense of thrift in the 1960s would stand in sharp contrast to Al Bell's management in the 1970s. You can bet that, for better or worse, Al would have signed both artists, consequences be damned.

As 1966 was drawing to a close, Jim's own Queen of Soul Music, Carla Thomas, was preparing to record an album of duets with Otis Redding. Ultimately titled *King and Queen,* the album would be released in March 1967. At the time album concepts were in vogue, and it was Jim Stewart's idea to pair his leading vocalists.

"One of my contributions was to put them together," reminisces Jim. "I had to fight to do it. They really didn't jump overboard about the idea, but after it was done they liked it. I thought it would be helpful to both artists' careers. Carla was always sort of special to me because she was my first artist and I felt she needed a boost. I thought the combination of his rawness and her sophistication would work."

Carla Thomas elaborates: "There may have been a little [apprehension] because I said, 'Well, I'm so used to singing those little sweet ballads, I don't know how I'm going to stack up.' So I talked with Otis and he just said, 'Well hey you from Memphis, you from Tennessee, you can hang.' We just ad-libbed and it came off great."

The album was recorded in January 1967 while Carla was home for the Christmas holidays from Washington, where she was studying for her M.A. in English at Howard University. Six of the album's ten tracks were cut with Otis and Carla in the studio at the same time. For the other four, Otis laid down his part first with Carla overdubbing hers a couple of days later, as both had concert commitments at different times during the sessions. "Tramp" was the first song cut as both singers tested the water, and each other, seeing if the combination would work. It was Otis's idea to cover the tune, which had been a number 5 R&B hit for Lowell Fulson in 1966.

4. Early the next year, according to attorney Seymour Rosenberg, Stax turned down Al Green! Al Bell remembers going after Green but, at this point, is uncertain why he was not signed.

"'Tramp' stands out the most," smiles Carla, "because it was the first and because of all the things I was trying to do to think up interesting lines to say to him. He said, 'Call me whatever you want to call me.' I said, 'Oh, my God,' trying to think of something to say. 'Hey you country, you this or you that.' It helped me a lot. It brought out a lot of my hidden talents. I found out I could really talk about somebody if I wanted to. I didn't know that until then."

When issued as a single in April 1967, "Tramp" zoomed to number 2 R&B and number 26 pop. Two further singles were pulled from the album. Otis and Carla's cover of Eddie Floyd's "Knock on Wood" hit the number 8 and number 30 spots on the R&B and pop charts in September 1967, while the duo's remake of the Clovers' 1954 number 2 R&B hit "Lovey Dovey" was released in the winter of 1968, when it climbed to number 21 R&B and number 60 pop.

Carla asserts that there were plans to record a duet LP each subsequent Christmas. In fact, after Otis's brief flurry of dates in early December 1967, had he lived, she said they were going into the studio to cut the followup album. Phil Walden does not remember this, but he does recall talk of Otis doing a duet LP with Aretha Franklin.

Otis had also discussed one other interesting concept for an LP with Walden. He thought of recutting a number of his former recordings rearranged back to front: ballads would be done up-tempo and vice versa. "It was an unbelievable concept he had," marvels Walden. "His version of 'I've Been Loving You (Too Long)' was an ass kicker from front to end. A song like 'I Can't Turn You Loose' was a beautiful ballad."

Much has been made over the years about the existence of a Stax family; the magic that is so evident on the records that were recorded at 926 E. McLemore is undeniably a direct product of this family atmosphere. A number of artists would simply hang out at the studio even when they weren't scheduled to cut. Often they would end up contributing a line or a lick to a song or singing background vocals on a session. Just as often, they would simply pass the day, shooting the shit with other artists, the MG's, the Mar-Key horns, the Satellite Record Shop employees, or Hayes and Porter. The feeling within the company in the sixties was, in general, very close. This would change for a variety of reasons in the 1970s but, even then, it is clear that a family atmosphere prevailed, although in the later period there were two or three clearly distinct families.

In the 1960s, once the family had coalesced it tended to be quite insular and quite difficult for outsiders to penetrate. The open-door policy that had so obviously set the company in motion when Jim and Estelle had first relocated to McLemore had become a thing of the past.

Homer Banks found it particularly difficult to get in. Born the same year as David Porter, Duck Dunn, and Wayne Jackson, Banks had grown up singing gospel, at the age of sixteen forming the Soul Consolators with his lifelong friend, guitarist Raymond Jackson. The Soul Consolators sang at churches throughout the mid-South as well as at talent shows in the Memphis area, concentrating on original material that Banks and Jackson penned.

After serving the requisite military hitch between 1962 and 1964, Banks began to hang out at Stax, letting anyone who would listen know that he was a singer and a songwriter. He went so far as to cut a demo for Stax with Steve Cropper on guitar and Lewie Steinberg on bass that Jim Stewart ultimately rejected. Shortly thereafter, Banks cut a single on the short-lived Genie label written by Hayes and Porter, "Little Lady of Stone" b/w "Sweetie Pie."[5] Jim Stewart was more than a little piqued.

---

5. For more on this single, see Chapter 4. Banks would also record five singles under his own name for Rene Roker at Minit Records. All ten songs released on Minit were cut in Memphis at either Hi or American Sound Studios. Several were written and/or produced by Hayes and Porter. For anyone interested in Memphis R&B, these are well worth searching out.

"When Jim Stewart found out about it," relates Banks, "somehow or another the word got out that I was responsible [for the record]. I lured [Hayes and Porter] into doing it. That closed the door even tighter. For a long time I was barred from the studio. I wasn't allowed to come in there."

In a move that succinctly sums up Jim and Estelle's relationship to each other and to those who wanted to be a part of Stax, Estelle promptly offered Homer Banks a job working in the Satellite Record Shop. "Then I really started getting serious about my writing," says Homer. "I was up there where I could put on albums and see what was hitting, see what people were buying. I think it was a great education working in that record shop because I found the pulse of the public, what they would turn on to and turn off to."

Homer worked at Satellite for three years. Throughout his time there, Estelle continually encouraged him, reassuring him that he had talent and urging him to keep on trying. Primarily a lyricist and melody writer, when his musical collaborator, Raymond Jackson, headed off to the armed services in 1966, Banks began writing with whoever happened to be available, including Johnny Keyes and Allen Jones.

Keyes, Banks, and Packy Axton (all of whom worked in the Satellite Record Shop) came up with a song called "Double Up" that Jim Stewart was interested in recording with Sam and Dave in the early fall of 1966. His initial discussions with the songwriters led everyone to believe that the writers and the company would split the publishing royalties down the middle. With everyone agreed, Booker T. and the MG's worked up the song in anticipation of Sam and Dave coming to town to record the tracks for the *Double Dynamite* LP.

David Porter served as the go-between. According to Keyes, Porter came up to him one day and said, "'The deal is this: we can't give you no publishing.' I said, 'What?' 'We can't give you no publishing but what we can give you is we'll put it on a Sam and Dave album guaranteed. We will also pull it as a single guaranteed.' I said, 'What about it, Packy?' He said, 'Yeah.'"

This was the sort of practice that a number of record labels had engaged in for years. Rather than splitting the publishing so that the songwriter would get both writer and publishing royalties for every sale and performance of the song, the idea was to simply keep all the publishing royalties within the company. This was standard practice at Stax but, in most cases, they would sign the writer to their publishing company, at least assuring the writer of a potential outlet for subsequent material. In this particular case, Al and/or Jim appeared to have little faith that Homer would write subsequent material of any quality and were attempting to simply keep for themselves what they thought was a creative accident on his part.

As events would have it, Keyes, Axton, and Banks eventually decided not to give up all the publishing. Keyes picks up the story: "Miss Axton came over to our apartment[6] and this was the first time I had seen this body language of hers. She's got the upper hand and she knows she's got the upper hand. She never got excited. She got cooler, crossed her legs and lit a cigarette. She says, 'Don't give Jim Stewart that song. Make him split the publishing. [If you don't] I'll never back anything y'all do including this apartment.' I thought, 'Oh, oh, she's playing her ace.'"

Before Estelle laid down the law to Packy, Keyes thought he was in line for a hit song with Sam and Dave, which he would hopefully parlay into a songwriting contract at Stax. Disappointed, he told Jim to forget it, and he and Packy headed over to Ardent, where

---

6. Johnny Keyes and Packy Axton were then roommates. Estelle Axton paid at least Packy's share of the rent.

they recorded the song with L. H. White and the Memphis Sounds.[7] Shortly after, Keyes was producing journeyman soul singer Clarence Lewis, a.k.a. C. L. Blast, on Atlantic. After Atlantic let Blast go, Keyes produced "Double Up" with the singer and, ironically, Atlantic promotion man Leroy Little placed the master with Stax. Released in July 1967 on Stax and then rereleased on Hip, the song failed to sell by L. H. White or Blast.

Banks endured a similar situation in partnership with Allen Jones. In 1966, Jones had just recently been hired by Stax, auditioning tapes sent in to the company by "wanna be" artists. Working in Jones's dingy office in the Mitchell Hotel on Beale Street,[8] Jones and Banks crafted a ballad entitled "Ain't That Loving You (For More Reasons Than One)." The aspiring songwriters played it first for Estelle and then for Al Bell. Both were impressed. Although Bell was technically still just the label's promotion man, he was also active on an A&R level and proceeded to offer Banks and Jones a contract to *buy* the song outright. According to Homer, Estelle once again said, "DO NOT SELL YOUR SONG!"

Once again David Porter was the emissary Bell and Stewart dispatched, contract in hand, to Banks and Jones. "I wanted to take the contract home and show it to my wife," recounts Banks, "and say, 'Hey, I'm on my way!' I was happy. But David Porter said, 'No, I need you to sign a contract now.' I said, 'Well, I would like to read the contract and take it home and study over the contract.' David Porter said, 'If you don't want to sign the contract, you can leave.' He went and told Jim Stewart and Jim Stewart came back and said, 'I want you to vacate the premises.' Gilbert Caple said, 'Man, I think this is ridiculous. This is a publishing company, man, and you're gonna put a writer out just because a man wants to read a contract over? Man, this is ridiculous. This is absurd.' Jim Stewart said, 'Man, when David Porter tells you something, it's like I'm telling you. If you won't sign the contract, I want you out.'"

After Homer left feeling depressed and abused, Estelle went back into the office area and, as usual, raised hell with Jim. Eventually she got the contract in her hands, which Homer and Allen duly inspected and signed. The song sat around for a couple of months before it was finally cut by Johnnie Taylor. That's when a real songwriting contract was at last prepared for Homer Banks. A year and a half later, Banks would cowrite the biggest-selling single Stax had to that point. In the interim, however, he was continually frustrated in his attempts to get songs approved by "the board" at the weekly Stax A&R meetings.

"I started going directly to the artist because I couldn't get nothing in through the board," Banks recalls, grimacing. "I said, 'Maybe this would be a better way for me to get my songs in there.' Otis used to come over to the record shop and listen at the gospel records. Sam and Dave [did the same thing]. I used to run to the store for these guys. I became their runner. All this was just to get some attention for my music. After a while they came and started demanding some of my stuff to cut." Banks and Jones were able to get "What Will Later On Be Like" recorded by Jeanne and the Darlings, "Strange Things Happening in My Heart" by Johnnie Taylor, and "I've Seen What Loneliness Can Do" and "I Can't Stand Up for Falling Down" cut by Sam and Dave.

"I Can't Stand Up" was an emotion-wrought non-LP ballad that, interestingly, sounds as if it could have been written by Hayes and Porter. It is very different from what Jones and Banks wrote for other Stax artists. According to the late Allen Jones, the song was tailored to meet the Hayes-Porter formula for Sam and Dave. "They created Sam and Dave," explained Jones. "So when [we] wrote 'I Can't Stand Up for Falling Down,' it was based off of writing a song for a style that had been created by David Porter and Isaac Hayes."

---

7. The musicians on the L.H. and the Memphis Sounds record include Joe Gray on drums, future Stax session musician and songwriter Ronnie Williams on piano, Teenie Hodges on guitar, Charles Hodges on bass, future Isaac Hayes musician Mickey Gregory on trumpet, and Packy Axton and Tommy Lee Williams on saxophones.

8. Jones was the bass player in the house band at the hotel.

Al Bell echoes those thoughts, adding that "Hayes and Porter had the magic. In many instances Sam and Dave were merely an extension of Hayes and Porter." In fact, Hayes and Porter often performed at local clubs doing many of the songs they had written for Sam and Dave. "We'd get out publicly"—Porter grins—"what we'd call flushing our brains, and sing in some of these clubs and people would just nut up."

By this point the sessions for Sam and Dave had begun to take on a pattern. The duo, still living in Miami, would come into Memphis for a week at a time. Once they arrived, Hayes and Porter would spend the first few days writing and then they would teach Sam and Dave their parts around a piano. During the actual sessions, Hayes controlled the rhythm section while Porter coached the vocalists. "The structure of our sessions," affirms Porter, "was such that I would stay [in the studio] on the other side of the mike and direct Sam and Dave on the singing of the songs. I would structure them. I would say down, up, soft, full. I directed them like you would a choir."

Twelve days after Homer Banks celebrated the release of "Ain't That Loving You (For More Reasons Than One)," Stax released Sam and Dave's interpretation of Isaac Hayes and David Porter's "When Something Is Wrong with My Baby." One of the most sublime records in soul music's history, the song's lyrics were crafted by Porter while he was married to a woman whom he had impregnated when they were both still in high school.

"I was quite honestly miserable with her," sighs Porter. "There was no love there. In the early part of my career I would fantasize about a lot of the things that I would come up with for my lyrics. I was in bed one night feeling miserable. Big house and a big car but I'm not in love and I'm not happy. I was fantasizing about what it would really be like to be in love. I got up out of bed and went downstairs and said, 'If I was in love with somebody then the relationship should be such that if something is wrong with her, something is wrong with me.' It was about two o'clock in the morning and I wrote the whole song." Porter called Hayes at nine the next morning, sang it for him over the phone and said, "Man, we got a smash."

Introduced by four ringing guitar chords followed by bass, understated snare, and piano triplets, Sam sings the first two lines in a quivering high voice full of melismas. The second half of the verse is sung by Dave, announced by swelling organ, horns, and fuller guitar and piano. The chorus drips with emotion as the two of them sing one of their odd harmony parts.

"I call them abstract harmony parts," says Porter. "Isaac was excellent at harmonies. Isaac would come up with a note for Dave's harmony and Dave would sing the note that he was used to singing when he and Sam had first started out in the clubs. Somehow or another it would be a distant tone from what Isaac would have given them. It often worked and we wouldn't say anything."

The second verse is sung entirely by Sam, culminating with the gut-wrenching "I know, I know, I got to help her solve them," and the whole thing is brought to a close with repeated horns and drum stops, in the style of Otis's "I've Been Loving You Too Long."

Given that "When Something Is Wrong with My Baby" sailed to number 2 R&B and number 42 pop, it seems odd that Hayes and Porter did not write more ballads for Sam and Dave. David Porter agrees: "I wanted to, but when we got a niche with up-tempo things happening with Sam and Dave we just tried to ride that. [In retrospect] we should have done more ballads."

The MG's experienced similar success with their February 1967 release, "Hip Hug-Her." Their first Top 10 R&B hit since "Boot-Leg" and their first Top 40 pop success since "Green Onions," "Hip Hug-Her" eventually sold close to 400,000 copies. Booker T. credits his studies at Indiana University for some of the record's success. "I can remember I was in college when I wrote 'Hip Hug-Her,'" he recalls, smiling. "I remember the way I was voicing the chords. Knowing for sure what those notes were that I was playing gave me confidence I didn't have when I recorded 'Green Onions.'"

Cropper introduces the song with a great metallic descending guitar lick that is quickly followed by ground-shaking bass, organ, and guitar riffing. "We wrote sounds," adds Booker. "We thought a lot about sounds." On all of the early MG recordings Booker played a Hammond M-1 or M-3 spinet model organ. This is the first MG's single to feature the larger Hammond B-3 organ. Complete with its Leslie speaker with a spinning horn, the B-3 afforded Booker a substantially expanded palette of sounds. "Hip Hug-Her" is also unique in that it is one of the few times Duck used round-wound strings on his bass. The astute listener will notice a slightly different bass timbre.

From "Hip Hug-Her" on, the MG's became major artists at Stax, enjoying a string of superlative releases through their demise in 1971. Booker T. Jones gives part of the credit for their ascendancy to Al Bell. "We weren't viewed as an artist by the company before [Al Bell came]. We weren't even listed in the meetings as artists when we talked about what artists would be cutting. Booker T. and the MG's were not one of the viable artists at Stax. I think [Jim] was afraid of losing the house band. [Al] had the idea of, Why squash Booker T. and the MG's as artists? Let them be an artist and bring in other people to produce and be in the studio as well."

While "When Something Is Wrong with My Baby" and "Hip Hug-Her" worked their way up the charts, a Stax Revue to end all Stax Revues was headed to Europe. Scheduled from mid-March through April 9, 1967, the Stax/Volt tour of Europe turned out to be a watershed event for all concerned. For Booker T. and the MG's, the Mar-Key horns, Carla Thomas, and Eddie Floyd it was their first trip overseas. For Sam and Dave, and especially for Otis Redding, it was validation of their superstar status. For the company as a whole, it was a turning point to be followed by large-scale expansion, as the "little label that could" began to move beyond its regional roots and family-based approach. At one and the same time, the tour was a culminating point beyond most people's wildest dreams and the beginning of the end of the label's Memphis-centered classic period.

For everyone involved in the tour the reception in Europe was simply overwhelming. "I was aghast," recalls a still stunned Steve Cropper. "They treated us like we were the Beatles or something. It pretty much overwhelmed everybody in the band. The only one that knew for a fact what it was gonna be like was Ahmet Ertegun. He was totally aware of the situation. We had no idea. It was absolutely amazing."

"I was shocked when we went to Europe," adds Booker T. "Why would they want us to come over there? I couldn't believe it. People knew my songs in Scotland and France. It was really a surprise."

Cropper told Peter Guralnick, "It was totally a mind-blower. Hell, we were just in Memphis cutting records; we didn't know. Then we got over there, there were hordes of people waiting at the airport, autograph hounds and all that sort of stuff. . . . That was something that happened to Elvis or Ricky Nelson, but it didn't happen to the Stax-Volt band." Mar-Key trumpeter Wayne Jackson put it to me more succinctly: "Europe opened our eyes."

Affectionately dubbed "Hit the Road Stax," the tour was a brainstorm initially hatched by Redding's manager, Phil Walden. Upon returning to the United States after Otis's first trip to England and France in the fall of 1966, he immediately pitched the idea of the tour to Jim Stewart and Al Bell. "The Stax/Volt tour was all mine," asserts Walden. "I financed the tour. If I had been a little more sophisticated in those days, those records would have been my records."

The timing was perfect, as in October Atlantic had announced that Stax was to get its own label identity in Europe in 1967. The first European Stax-labeled releases distributed through Polygram—Eddie Floyd's "Raise Your Hand," Sam and Dave's "Soothe Me," and Otis Redding's cover of the Beatles' "Day Tripper"—came out just as the tour got under way.

The posters for the tour read "Arthur Howes in association with Phil Walden and Stax Records present. . . ." Howes was a British concert promoter at the time. Walden's integral involvement explains why Redding's protégé and non-Stax artist Arthur Conley was on the bill and why in some early ads the tour was touted as "The Otis Redding Show." It might also explain why Otis, for the first time, was plainly treated differently from the rest of the artists and musicians, staying separately from everyone else in his own suite in a better hotel. Needless to say, this caused a bit of head shaking and resentment among those who had known him back in the days when he was just starting out. Howes and Walden would go on to partner other European soul tours, including a fall 1967 venture headlined by Arthur Conley, Sam and Dave, and Percy Sledge.

Back in Memphis there were some bitter feelings about who was chosen to go on the European tour. Rufus Thomas, for one, felt that he deserved the opportunity. Carla Thomas appeared on only a handful of dates because she had to fly back to the States to appear at a civil rights benefit in Chicago, a booking that was made *for* her by Al Bell for his own or the label's benefit and/or to pay back a favor to the benefit's organizers. Carla lost valuable exposure because of this obligation. In her opinion, what would have been good for her career was sacrificed in favor of what was good for someone else. Twenty years after the fact it still rankled.[9]

The artists who were involved were informed about the tour just a couple of weeks in advance. The four members of Booker T. and the MG's and the Mar-Key horns were immediately sent to Lansky Brothers on Beale Street to buy two sets of Continental suits, one in green, one in blue. To be able to make the tour, saxophonist Andrew Love talked Floyd Newman into subbing for him in Bowlegs Miller's band. Duck Dunn, Wayne Jackson, and Joe Arnold weren't so lucky. To their dismay, they were forced to quit their regular six-night-a-week gig at Hernando's Hideaway to go on the trip. Dunn, along with the other three MG's, had been put on salary a little before the European venture.[10] For Jackson and Arnold, though, this was a serious economic decision.

"Charlie Foran [the owner of Hernando's] told me, 'Don't come back if you leave me for a month,'" recalls Wayne Jackson, "'cause we had the place packed out there. I thought I was gonna go to Europe, make my little two thousand dollars, which was a lot of money at the time. My house note was sixty-eight dollars, so two thousand was a lot of money. I thought that would probably be the end of it. The big Stax thing went to Europe and toured and came home and, poof, it was over!"

For the most part, the musicians did not get to rehearse until they got to London. Wayne Jackson laughs: "Everybody assumed that Booker T. and the MG's had played on the records, the Mar-Keys had played on the records, and we knew the stuff—wrong! You use slate memory when you're doing records. You remember something for three minutes over and over and when you start the next song, you erase that. We didn't play those numbers all the time. We had to try to learn a bunch of them, we had to hustle real hard. We

---

9. Taking her place for the other dates on the tour was South African Atco recording artist Sharon Tandy, who a year earlier had been slated to record for Stax's Hip subsidiary.

10. According to Dunn, the fact that Al Jackson was perpetually late for sessions in the mornings indirectly led to the rhythm section being put on salary. "He told Jim, 'If you want us here in the morning, you're going to have to get us out of these clubs at night!'" Dunn remembers that his starting salary was precisely $125 a week.

had to rehearse the day we got there with no sleep and hung over, of course. It was like a ship constantly on the verge of going out of control."

Jackson's compatriots in the Mar-Key horns at the time were tenor saxophonists Andrew Love and Joe Arnold. Arnold recalls the horn players rehearsing stage steps in Memphis prior to the tour, partially inspired by the visually dynamic stage show of label mates the Bar-Kays. Andrew Love concurs: "The Bar-Kays were good at that. They did a lot of stepping and swinging horns and all of that kind of stuff, more so than we did. So we decided we needed to have a little movement up there, add a little excitement to it. We got together in Studio B and practiced, you know, step to the left on beat one [and so on], like we used to do in high school bands." Both Arnold and Love thought that the idea of working on steps came from either Isaac Hayes or Al Jackson.[11]

Although there had been a few one-shot gigs over the years—such as the 5/4 Ballroom shows in 1965, the Apollo gig in 1966, and the odd show in Memphis—this was the first time a Stax Revue had actually gone on the road, playing a series of shows in a variety of cities. The excitement that the tour engendered is permanently etched in everyone's memories. When asked if he was excited, Wayne Jackson responded, "Are you kidding me? I came from West Memphis, Arkansas. I never figured I'd get across the river. I had a camera on both hands—a movie camera and a still camera! We thought this was just one chance in a lifetime. I thought this was just a gift from God. He said, 'Okay, guy, you get a trip.'

"We were exhausted. We couldn't sleep because we knew we were going to miss something. [We thought] this was our only shot at it. I couldn't believe I was in Norway riding down the road passing Viking ships and museums."

Andrew Love echoes Jackson's sentiments. "It was a BIG deal! We tried to do everything and see everything we could, because maybe we'd never get the chance to come back again. We took so many pictures. Man, I was taking pictures of clouds. I wasted so much money. You get those pictures back and all you see are clouds and the propeller of a plane."

Carla Thomas has similar memories of the trek: "That was happy. I mean I was never in my hotel room—ever! Everything you want to see in Paris, I saw it. England too. I was just a real live tourist!" To everyone's chagrin, outside of Paris and London, there was not that much time to sightsee. Wayne Jackson described a typical day's itinerary as getting up at seven o'clock, traveling to the next city by bus or train, arriving mid-afternoon, eating, showering, "running down the street and looking at something," and then playing one or two gigs.

Most of the entourage arrived in London on Monday morning, March 13.[12] The Beatles sent their limos to pick up the band which, in Andrew Love's words, "WAS REALLY A BIG DEAL!" After two days of rehearsal, Carla Thomas played a warmup gig with Booker T. and the MG's at a private London club with restricted admittance called the Bag O'Nails. With a capacity of about three hundred people, this club was a hangout for various stars; Thomas's strongest memory of the evening is meeting Paul McCartney. She and her sister Vaneese had gone to see the Beatles in Memphis the previous August and, of course, she was performing McCartney's "Yesterday" on the Stax/Volt tour.

"We talked with him a minute between sets," Carla fondly recalls, "and then I had to go back. When we finished, he got up to go. I said to Booker, 'Let's follow him.' We leapt

---

11. Arnold recalls that Duck and Steve were also asked to do some choreography but "they weren't into it."

12. Redding had flown in a few days earlier to do an endless round of advance interviews, including an appearance on the "Eamonn Andrews Show," and Sam Moore came in that Monday evening.

up out of the club behind him. I said, 'I'm going to talk some more to him. I'm just not through with this situation.' It wasn't anything much. We were just kind of walking with him. I told him, 'Thanks so much for coming. I'm so honored.'"

The tour officially opened on Friday night, March 17, when the Revue played two gigs at the Finsbury Park Astoria. As with most venues for the tour, the Astoria held between two and three thousand people. Atlantic engineering ace Tom Dowd had flown over for the first few shows, and Frank Fenter, A&R for Polygram (which was distributing both Atlantic and Stax in Europe), suggested that Dowd record the Finsbury Park shows. Scrambling as quickly as he could, the best equipment Dowd could find for portable recording in London were two three-track machines. He used both machines in tandem with a five-minute delay between them so that he didn't miss any of the show when he had to change reels. With only three tracks to work from, all mixing was done on the fly. Dowd recorded both shows at Finsbury Park as well as two shows at the Paris Olympia on the following Tuesday, the twenty-first. In Paris, Dowd was able to locate two four-track recorders.

The touring group then proceeded to play a series of one-nighters in England before heading to the continent for shows in Oslo, Stockholm, Copenhagen, and the Hague before returning to London for a final performance on April 9.

The Finsbury Park and Olympia tapes were made into four albums released that July: *The Stax/Volt Revue Volume One: Live in London; The Stax/Volt Revue Volume Two: Live in Paris; Otis Redding Live in Europe;* and *The Mar-Keys and Booker T. and the MG's: Back to Back.* In addition, two-and-a-half weeks after the tour ended, Volt issued a live version by Otis Redding of Sam Cooke's "Shake" on 45, followed a month later on Stax by a live version of Sam and Dave's cover of the Sims Twins' "Soothe Me." Both live 45s reached number 16 on the R&B charts while stalling in the middle of the pop Hot 100.

It might seem odd to record a tour at the outset, rather than documenting the final climactic shows when any flaws would have been worked out and the band would be operating at red-hot intensity. However, Carla Thomas could only stay in Europe for a week due to her prior commitment to play the Chicago civil rights benefit, so the decision may have been made to record the early shows in order to include her on the records. Joe Arnold, for one, claims that the later shows were much better.

Phil Walden as well felt that the shows kept getting better and better. By his own admission, his days of being a fan were long over; he now attended gigs more out of duty. Europe was an exception. "Every night was more exciting than the previous one. There was never a climax. The thing just kept getting better. You would never know how it could be better than it already was."

That said, what was recorded at those first few shows has an intensity matched by very few live recordings. Booker T. and the MG's and the Mar-Key horns had been a unit in one guise or another for just over five years, backing Carla Thomas, Sam and Dave, Eddie Floyd, and Otis Redding on virtually every recording they had ever made. The empathy and sense of second sight exemplified by all seven musicians is still a revelation some thirty years after the fact.

The first half of the show featured, in order, Booker T. and the MG's, the Mar-Keys, Arthur Conley, and Carla Thomas, while the second half commenced again with the MG's, followed by Eddie Floyd, Sam and Dave, and Otis Redding. The MG's started the evening off in high spirits, ripping through what had been a B-side when it was originally released in late 1965, "Red Beans and Rice." Next up was another B-side, which charted in the summer of 1966, "Booker-loo." The MG's finished their first mini-set with the song that had started everything for them, 1962's "Green Onions." The taut, always-on-the-edge tension of the group was one of the riches of popular music in the twentieth century.

The Mar-Key horns were up next, performing their two biggest charted records, "Last Night" and "Philly Dog." Both songs featured heated tenor sax solos, on the former courtesy of Andrew Love, on the latter by Joe Arnold. Both based their solos on the originals recorded by Gilbert Caple and Gene Parker, respectively.

Booker T. and the MGs live in Europe: (*left to right*) Booker T. Jones, Duck Dunn, Al Jackson, and Steve Cropper. COURTESY FANTASY, INC.

Many commentators have noted an element of freneticism in the European performances captured on the live-in-Europe records. In his excellent *Sweet Soul Music*, Peter Guralnick wrote, "There is a frenetic note that is at odds with the spare classicism of the Stax sound." Empirically it is a fact that the tempos were greatly increased, attacks were sharper and there was, in general, less room for the music to breathe. The question becomes then, was this better or worse than the actual recordings made in the studio in Memphis?

Jim Stewart, for one, felt that it was worse. Phil Walden recalls an enraged Stewart bursting into Otis's dressing room after the first show in Paris. "He stormed into the dressing room: 'Otis, you got to drop those tempos and drop them right now. We're taping this and trying to make a record.' Otis said, 'I'm over here playing a fucking date. I make records in Memphis, Tennessee. Don't tell me about my tempos. I'm out here entertaining these people. They don't know shit about this record we're making and the tempos are gonna stay that way if we're gonna make it 'cause I'm over here playing a date. That's my career out there.' Jim [responded], 'You're a fucking star!'"

In my estimation, the Stax/Volt Revue live had an intensity altogether different from that found on the records. As good as the Stax/Volt artists were on their own, on the very few occasions when they were backed by the MG's and the Mar-Key horns they rose to exceptional heights. Carla Thomas's performances of the at-the-time recently released Isaac Hayes–David Porter composition "Something Good (Is Going to Happen to You)" is a case in point. Collectively the band inspires Thomas to deliver a performance that is hard-hitting in a way that is totally unlike anything else she has ever released.

Also unique in Carla's canon was her cover of the Beatles' "Yesterday." At the Paris shows the song was partially sung in French. It was Thomas's idea to attempt it, learning the first and part of the fourth verse phonetically the day before the show. She finished her mini-set and the first half of the show with the two hit singles that Hayes and Porter had penned for her the previous year, "Let Me Be Good to You" and "B-A-B-Y."

Eddie Floyd's set varied each night. On every show, he would sing three or four songs out of a total of seven or eight that he had rehearsed. "Raise Your Hand" and "Knock on Wood," of course, were always performed. The rest of his set consisted of one or two covers including J. J. Jackson's "But It's Alright," Chris Kenner's "Something You Got," Chuck Jackson's "I Don't Wanna Cry," and the folk group the Weavers' "If I Had a Hammer."

Sam and Dave came on next, generally performing six songs, their five chart hits—"You Don't Know Like I Know," "Hold On! I'm Comin'," "Said I Wasn't Gonna Tell Nobody," "You Got Me Hummin'," and "When Something Is Wrong with My Baby"—plus a cover of the Sims Twins' "Soothe Me." Walden found them intoxicating. "I think Sam and Dave probably will stand the test of time as being the best live act that there ever was. Those guys were absolutely unbelievable. Every night they were awesome."

"Every night you would feel sorry for Otis," adds Wayne Jackson. "Sam and Dave had taken this audience to heaven and back. They'd have to carry them off. They would jump out in the audience and just go crazy like they were having a fit and then jump back onstage and faint. They would have to carry Dave off like he was dead and then they would carry him back on like he was resurrected. By the time that was over with, all the wax on the floor was gone, burnt up. Otis would be standing there in the corner praying."

Eddie Floyd remembers the European audiences as being comparable in their frenzied response to those of the Apollo Theatre. For Wayne Jackson they went beyond that. "Sam and Dave left that stage smoking, and when Otis would come on he had to be up. He had to be at his finest. [The audience] was just frothing at the mouth when [Sam and Dave] left, and then when Otis got through with them it was just total chaos. People were weeping, gnashing their teeth, screaming and jumping up and down.

"They rushed the stage like Elvis. We had guards along the stage on that particular tour who actually had to keep people off the stage. I mean drag crying women away, [people] tearing their clothes. First time I had seen that in person. [It was] scary. They were crazed, their eyes were glassed over, and they were wanting to be involved with [Otis] so bad. They would have run right over me.

"Otis was amazed by it. He loved it. Of course, he egged them on, holding his hand out. He was a master showman."

In Scotland, Redding was actually dragged into the audience, and the cops and security guards had to go out after him and pull him back onstage. Every night he turned in an incendiary set. This was a "new" Otis, demonstrating a level of confidence and bravura a notch above earlier outings. The records bear evidence that he obviously loved the English audience, speaking tongue-in-cheek in London of how "it's good to be back home," referring to London as "the greatest city in the whole world," and dedicating "My Girl" (a UK-only hit from his *Otis Blue* set) to the Astoria audience.

All six songs in Redding's nightly set were stellar, but "Day Tripper," "Fa-Fa-Fa-Fa-Fa (Sad Song)," and "Try a Little Tenderness" stood out.[13] As was his wont, Otis completely redefined the Beatles tune, while "Sad Song" was usually turned into an audience sing-a-long with the MG's, Mar-Keys, Redding, and the audience alchemically melding into one.

"Try a Little Tenderness" was the finale of his set and the whole Stax/Volt Revue. Phil Walden recalls that it had been suggested that Redding close with the New Vaudeville Band's "Winchester Cathedral." "They actually worked on it," says Walden, shaking his head. "It was fucking awful. Otis kept singing '*Westchester* Cathedral.' I think that's the most unsoulful song. . . . Finally, good judgment prevailed and it was not used."

The studio version of "Try a Little Tenderness" increased the tension as the song progressed via accentuated tempo, increased density, additional volume, and Redding's near-inhuman vocal machinations. Live, all those elements were stepped up to the nth degree as over seven minutes each night the song would alchemize into a white-hot rage with Redding leaving the stage and coming back three times, each time raising the temperature, while testing the pumping capacity of everyone's hearts, band and audience alike. Otis would eventually be joined onstage by Sam and Dave, Eddie Floyd, Arthur Conley, and Carla Thomas for the final, climactic, neuron-stopping volley.

As exciting as the shows were, Europe itself was a bit of a culture shock. "Basically," recounts Walden, "I think they felt like they were a group of blacks held captive. They all hated the food. They were all about to basically starve to death."

Tom Dowd recalls having Sunday dinner at a prestigious hotel in London with Jim Stewart, Steve Cropper, Duck Dunn, and Sam and Dave. The waiter, as Dowd describes him, was wearing white cotton socks with buckles on his shoes and a puff by the ear, looking like nothing so much as a character out of a Charles Dickens novel. As the waiter was explaining the specials of the day in his best upper-crust accent, Dowd gets an elbow in his side with one of the party exclaiming, "Say, what language is he talking." Duck Dunn, who was seated right across from Dowd, rolled his eyes at the waiter and said, "Ask him if he's got any fatback cacciatore."

"This man is looking at us as if we're crazy," guffaws Dowd. "I'm thinking I must be three shades of purple. The dialogue was just precious."

The Stax/Volt tour of Europe wasn't all great music and fun and games. At one point a meeting was held with everyone crowded into Al Bell's room, during which, according to Joe Arnold, Bell threatened to leave Stax if certain changes did not occur. Arnold says that the gist of the whole affair was that Bell thought that Steve Cropper had a big head. When all was said and done, Arnold describes Steve as looking like a whipped dog.

Arnold found the whole incident unsettling. He was also a little piqued over the fact that, with Wayne Jackson doing all the interviews for the horns, press coverage of the tour tended to focus on Jackson to the exclusion of Love and Arnold. Additionally, while the rhythm section had been put on salary at Stax, the horn players were still working for session fees. Shortly after landing back in Memphis, Arnold handed in his resignation.

Arnold's departure appears to have been a wake-up call for Jim Stewart and Al Bell; Wayne Jackson and Andrew Love were immediately put on salary, making $250 a week each plus whatever they picked up working sessions at Muscle Shoals and Hi. Who would have ever guessed that life could be this good? "God damn!" exclaims Wayne. "We started [with the extra sessions at the other studios] to make four hundred dollars a week. Andrew

13. The other three songs were "Respect," "My Girl," and Sam Cooke's "Shake."

and I had a house and a new car and the kids were in school and doing good, which is more than we had ever expected out of the deal. It was really for me sort of a fluke!"

Sessions continued apace at Stax and the money was good, but somehow the feeling was slightly different. "When we got back home," recounts Jackson, "we went back to work but it was never the same again. When we saw the audience reaction to us it was unbelievable. [Up to then] we didn't know we were stars. We thought we were kids working at the club to make enough money to pay the rent and making records just getting by. We found out there was a big world out there and that we were a big part of that world. We weren't just playing horns in a nightclub and putting horn parts on other people's records for a fee. We had had an impact. I think we felt that [playing theaters] was what we'd rather do than play at Hernando's [Hideaway in Memphis]. After [Europe] my mentality changed. I knew that I didn't have to play six nights a week and kill myself. At that point we were getting old enough to where it made a difference. You can't take speed all your life every day. We [had been] doing a lot of that to stay up."

For several years, both Jackson and Love had endured quite a grind, playing at the clubs every night into the wee hours in the morning, and then arriving at Stax at 11 A.M., ready to record. Sessions often continued until 8:00 at night, when they'd hurriedly pack up and head for that evening's gig.

"It would be eight or eight-thirty," said Wayne, speaking with London disc jockey Stuart Colman in 1986, "and Duck and I'd still be in blue jeans. At that time you had to put on a suit to go play rhythm and blues in a nightclub. I'd be driving and Duck would be in the backseat changing clothes. Then we'd stop at a red light and switch. We'd walk in the club at one minute to nine P.M."

With the security of a steady income, Jackson and Love decided to play gigs on the weekends only, resurrecting the Mar-Keys' name for these performances. After they quit Stax in late 1969, they would change their name to the Memphis Horns.

The success of the Stax/Volt tour catapulted Otis Redding into a superstar in Europe. At the end of that year, he was named the number 1 male vocalist in *Melody Maker*'s annual readers poll, dethroning Elvis, who had dominated that category for years. It also paved the way for Otis's appearance at the Monterey Pop Festival in June. Monterey was to be the first important rock festival. Held over three days, it boasted an astonishing lineup of established rock artists, including Simon and Garfunkel, the Byrds, the Who, Eric Burdon and the Animals, and Jefferson Airplane, and provided the launching pad for Jimi Hendrix and Big Brother and the Holding Company featuring Janis Joplin—as well as Redding.

The three major black artists approached to play the festival were Hugh Masekala, Lou Rawls, and Otis Redding. When Lou Adler first approached Walden to ask if Redding would be interested in playing the date, he explained that, as was the case with all the artists playing the festival, there would be no fee involved but that the exposure alone would make it worthwhile. After consulting with Jerry Wexler, Walden concluded that Monterey was going to be an important event and a possible stepping-stone for Otis to the emerging rock and roll audience.

However, there was a bit of a problem because Otis was planning to take time off to have some polyps removed from his throat and had consequently broken down his band. The logical alternative would be to get Booker T. and the MG's and the Mar-Key horns to back Redding up. By this point Walden's relationship with Jim Stewart was so bad that he asked Jerry Wexler to call Jim to ask if the Stax house band could take time off from the studio to fly to California to back Otis on the date.

Monterey was a shock for everyone. "It was space travel," exclaims Walden. "This was right when the hippie shit was really just starting to happen. It was all peace, love, and water beds. It was a cultural shock. I had seen a little bit of everything but I had not seen people openly smoking dope and taking acid. I don't think too many people in the world have ever been totally free that way. It was like a spaceship had landed for a few days."

"There were the hippies smoking pot right in public," affirms Wayne Jackson. "It was another planet for us. At that time I thought if you got a marijuana cigarette, the next day you'd be on heroin and then jail was two days later with the FBI. I really did. That's what we were taught when we were kids. I was that naive about it."

"Monterey was a wake-up call," says Booker, "because we'd just come back from Europe and we had acceptance there. We had never had acceptance from [a white] audience in the United States. It was like Monterey should have been in Germany or maybe Holland, *but it was California*. It was our first announcement that something new was happening culturally and musically in the United States. There was a new feeling. The policemen were gone. We were led into the concert by Hell's Angels. They were protecting us! You could walk into a restaurant in Monterey and get a free sandwich. Hotels were opened up to people. It was a completely different feeling. History was changing at that moment and we knew it. I think it affected the way we played that night."

At 55,000 strong, Monterey was the largest audience Otis, as well as the MG's and the Mar-Key horns,[14] had ever faced. The MG's hadn't played with Otis since the European tour some two months previously and had only about an hour and a half to rehearse in a hotel room acoustically without a keyboard. Encountering the counterculture for the first time, everyone was a little nervous as to how they might go over. "Us in our mohair green suits," laughs Duck Dunn. "Everybody else in their flower power!" "Some of them [were] really cool," adds Wayne Jackson. "Here come us, we're energetic and doing organized steps. We thought maybe we're gonna bomb because we were so very different from the rest of these people. The fact is we took it away from everybody else."

Otis was slated to close Saturday night, coming onstage right after the Jefferson Airplane. Wayne Jackson emphatically recalls: "When Otis came on it was over. *Over.* End of story for everyone who had played up to that point. The crowd went absolutely bananas. Andrew and I were just shaking. They were mobbing the stage just wanting to touch Otis. When we got through with them, they were insane."

"The feeling there was really unbelievable," Steve Cropper continues. "It was unmistakably different from any other concert we'd ever done. There was something in the air other than smoke." "The audience was on our side," adds Booker. "It wasn't like they were looking at us to see what we had to play. They were saying, 'We're part of you.'"

Otis referred to the audience from the stage as "the Love Crowd," and love him they did. Phil Walden made the right move. With one masterful performance, white America began to awake to the power and majesty of Otis Redding and the Stax house band. Monterey was the most cataclysmic event in an incredible year for Otis. The festival also helped Booker T. and the MG's. After their triumphant performance there, they were regularly booked on the rock festival circuit[15] and in the psychedelic ballrooms that were beginning to spring up throughout urban North America.

A couple of months earlier, a few days after the conclusion of the Stax/Volt tour of Europe, Stax released the debut single by what was being groomed as their second set of

---

14. At Monterey there were only two horns, Wayne Jackson and Andrew Love. By this point Joe Arnold had quit working at Stax but he was still asked to play the Monterey gig. Unfortunately, he was back working at Hernando's Hideaway and the owner would not let him have the time off.

15. The MG's were actually scheduled to play Woodstock but only got as far as New York because Al Jackson refused to fly in the helicopter that was necessary to get them to the festival site.

studio musicians. The Bar-Kays had been playing around Memphis for a while at this point, having evolved out of a group known as the Imperials. The new name was inspired by a Bacardi Rum billboard at the intersection of Crump and Georgia in Memphis. Trumpeter Ben Cauley recalls that the "Kays" were the first "stepping" band in Memphis. Getting into Stax had not been easy.

"We had auditioned for Stax several times," recounts bassist and bandleader James Alexander. "Each time we auditioned, Steve [Cropper] would turn us down. In his opinion, we didn't have what it took to be a recording artist. Jim [Stewart] had heard about the group and he told us we should come down one day when Steve was not there."

The Bar-Kays did as Jim suggested on March 13, 1967, and ended up cutting a hit record that same afternoon, a stomping instrumental dubbed "Soul Finger."[16] The rhythmic idea for the song occurred to the band while they were onstage backing future Soul Children member Norman West performing J. J. Jackson's October 1966 hit "But It's Alright." "At the end of the song we started jamming a little riff," explains Cauley, "extending the song, ad-libbing and stuff, and we came up with the ['Soul Finger'] rhythm to settle it down."

In the studio the band was working on a version of Phil Upchurch's "You Can't Sit Down," which Jim Stewart felt would be a good first single. At one point during the session he went out to get a Coke. When he came back into the studio, the Bar-Kays were jamming on "Soul Finger."

"Jim walked back in," laughs Cauley. "'What's that y'all are doing?' 'Oh, it's just something we all made up.' 'Do it again, do it again.' So we did it again man, and he just about flipped. 'That's a hit. let's cut it.' So we cut that version, and we said, 'Now there's still something missing here.' We got to thinking and I always would do little comical things on trumpet, so I did 'Mary's Little Lamb' and they said, 'Why don't you put that on the front of it, man.' It started happening from that point on. We cut it in about fifteen minutes."

The title was provided by Hayes and Porter. As well, Porter came up with the idea of bringing in a bunch of local children who were hanging around outside the studio to shout the song's title and to carry on as if there was a party ensuing while the record was being made. "I bought them all Coca-Colas," recalls Porter, "and I said, 'Every time I do this, you all say "Soul Finger."'" Then I instructed [Bar-Kays bassist] James Alexander what he should say into the microphone."

"Soul Finger" clocked in at the number 3 rhythm and blues and number 17 pop positions. The B-side, "Knucklehead," written by Steve Cropper and Booker T. Jones, also charted, reaching number 28 R&B and number 76 pop, with the multitalented Booker T. Jones playing the harmonica part.

A few days after "Soul Finger" was released, *Billboard* announced that Stax was issuing a special promo-only LP entitled *Stay in School* (Stax A-11). U.S. Secretary of Labor Willard Wirtz had approached the label to "carry the message of the 1967 'Stay in School' campaign to the nation." Four thousand copies of the album were pressed, which were then distributed by the Department of Labor in August as a public service to disc jockeys and radio stations across the country. Deanie Parker coordinated putting the album together. Most major Stax artists including Carla Thomas, Eddie Floyd, William Bell, Sam and Dave, and the Mar-Keys contributed brief speaking cameos encouraging children to continue their education. In addition, a number of recently released LP

Early Bar-Kays promotional shot: **(front row)** Phalon Jones, James Alexander, **(back row)** Jimmie King, Carl Cunningham, Ronnie Caldwell, Ben Cauley. COURTESY API PHOTOGRAPHERS INC.

16. "Soul Finger" had been recorded just four days before the first gigs in Europe.

MG drummer Al Jackson and blues guitarist extraordinaire Albert King. COURTESY DEANIE PARKER.

tracks by the various artists were included alongside two new tracks, Sam and Dave's "Reason for Living" and Otis Redding's "Stay in School" song. The latter was improvised on the spot with Otis accompanying himself on acoustic guitar; the Mar-Key horns were overdubbed later on.

Billboard also mentioned that Stax/Volt artists were participating in a U.S. Domestic Peace Corps recruitment campaign, recording a message asking youngsters to enlist in the Corps. The messages were to be coupled with the various artists' current releases, with the government shipping copies of each record to radio stations in the spring to serve as spot announcements for the Corps. It is uncertain if this project ever came to fruition, because no copies of these recordings are known to exist.

Altruistic gestures like the *Stay in School* album garnered a certain amount of free publicity for the label and its artists. Deanie Parker confirmed that Stax was well aware of this potential: "Wherever and whenever we could, we did take advantage of it from the standpoint of artists expounding on their participation in it, and we tried to make certain that the country was aware of the fact that we were participating in a project to keep children in school." For a brief period, the message on the marquee outside of the company's studio was changed from "Soulsville U.S.A." to "Don't Be a Dropout." When neighborhood children greeted the new message with a barrage of rocks one evening, it was quickly changed back.

In May 1967, Stax released Albert King's "Born Under a Bad Sign." Soon thereafter covered by the rock group Cream, over the years the song has taken on classic status. Surprisingly, it only reached number 49 on the rhythm-and-blues charts when originally issued.

Booker T. Jones and William Bell wrote the song. "We needed a blues song for Albert King," recalls Bell. "I had this idea in the back of my mind that I was gonna do myself.

Astrology and all that stuff was pretty big then. I said, 'Hey, we've never had a blues tune done about astrology. I got this idea that might work.'" In addition to the lyrics, Bell had also come up with the song's signature riff while fooling around on guitar. The Albert King recording of "Born Under a Bad Sign," with Booker T. and the MG's providing the accompaniment, remains one of the most smokingly intense blues recordings of the modern era.

Born Under a Bad Sign was also the title of Albert King's first LP. Containing the singles "Laundromat Blues," "Oh, Pretty Woman," "Crosscut Saw,"[17] and the title track, the LP surprisingly failed to chart pop or R&B. One has to keep in mind that the rhythm-and-blues market remained almost totally a 45 market until the early 1970s. Stax, in fact, via Isaac Hayes, would be the first R&B label to sell substantial numbers of albums. In 1967, though, neither Atlantic nor Stax could generate much retail action for their LPs. Compounding this was the fact that a blues artist such as King would invariably sell fewer records than a more mainstream soul singer such as Otis Redding.

"Born Under a Bad Sign" was one of the last Stax singles whose label read "Produced by Staff." Ten days later, Stax 221, "Sophisticated Sissy" by Rufus Thomas, was released with the bold declaration "Produced by David Porter and Isaac Hayes." From this point on, any newly recorded product was released with individual production credits.[18] This small change was the first outward manifestation that some of the company's community spirit had begun to erode. Europe had been an eye-opener. Anyone who had made the trip concluded that Stax was much bigger than they had ever realized. Those who remained in Memphis heard enough about the reaction to the tour to take on the same attitude. Individual production credits were just one manifestation of this trend.

"There was a shared kind of responsibility for a long, long time," recounts Deanie Parker, "until people began to appreciate the value of developing a reputation as a producer. The first person to lead out with that kind of attitude, and it created a little bit of friction, was Steve Cropper. Steve is very aggressive and did not, in my opinion, necessarily support that cooperative idea for as long as maybe the others would have in a passive way."

Despite the changes clearly in process at Stax, the label continued to issue records of astonishing power throughout the rest of the year. With a typical Memphis summer beginning to heat up, Hayes and Porter went into the studio to cut "Soul Man" with Sam and Dave. As was their by-now standard procedure, before the session began they took time out to shoot craps. "The artists would be all on their knees," howls William Brown, who was still working in the record shop. "'Lord have mercy, I done lost my paycheck.' [David Porter would reply] 'That's all right man, we'll cut a hit record. We're gonna have lots of money.' 'Still you ain't gave me my paycheck back!'" Whenever William would play he'd find himself running errands for everyone just to make a little change back.[19]

17. The original version of "Crosscut Saw" was cut by a Memphis group called the Binghampton Blues Boys. Legend has long had it that Albert King's version is a note-for-note copy of their record on XL. All known copies of the original XL pressing were destroyed by label owner Stan Kesler when the Binghampton Blues Boys' manager reneged on what Kesler thought was a done deal. Consequently, no copies of the original recording had surfaced until one turned up in Memphis in 1995. It definitively proved that Albert and the MG's completely redefined the tune; their version is anything but a note-for-note cover.

18. Stax 222, 223, and the A-side of 224 had been recorded earlier and, hence, although having higher catalogue numbers, were issued as "Produced by Staff."

19. According to engineer Ronnie Capone, when he came to Stax in the fall of 1967, Sam and Dave would be shooting dice during the instrumental sections of takes on which they were cutting live vocals!

"Soul Man" turned out to be the most successful Stax single to date, topping the R&B charts and hitting number 2 on the pop listings. Sam and Dave would win a Grammy for the single in the second-ever year of the category "Best Rhythm and Blues Group Performance" during the March 1968 National Academy of Recording Arts and Sciences ceremonies. They had been nominated the previous year for their recording of "Hold On! I'm Comin'," but on that occasion they failed to take the gold home.

"Soul Man"'s title continued where "Soul Finger" left off, in the process helping to provide a handle for a whole genre of music. "That was during the days of civil rights struggles," recounts Isaac Hayes. "We had a lot of riots. I remember in Detroit, I saw the news flash where they were burning [the neighborhoods]. Where the buildings weren't burnt, people would write 'soul' on the buildings. The big thing was 'soul brother.' So I said, 'Why not do something called "Soul Man" and kind of tell a story about one's struggle to rise above his present conditions' It's almost a tune [where it's] kind of like boasting I'm a soul man—a pride thing. 'Soul Man' came out of that whole black identification. We got funkier."

"Soul Man" was an important record, keying in to the then–newly emergent black consciousness that was perhaps best summed up by the phrase "Black is beautiful." In 1967 it became an anthem for black America.

Opening with Steve Cropper's chiming guitar juxtaposed with Isaac's low-register piano and Al Jackson's atmospheric riding on the bell portion of his cymbal, the song is infused with syncopation. Duck Dunn claims that Isaac Hayes was responsible for a lot of the funk rhythms on these records. "All those counterpoint things, those pieces that fit together, that was Isaac. You listen to that record 'Soul Man.' The guitar part and the bass part are basically 'Bo Diddley.' He's got everything moving around. It works. It just knocked me out. When he did it that day, I said, 'Isaac, son of a bitch, he knows what he's doing.'"

One of the most memorable portions of the recording occurs in the chorus, when Sam and Dave exclaim "I'm a soul man" four times in a row. Following the second declamation Steve Cropper plays a slide guitar part that has burned deep into the consciousness of anyone who has ever heard the record. The guitar line was Isaac Hayes's idea. Hayes said, "Give me some Elmore James, man," referring to the great blues slide guitarist. Cropper, not having a proper slide with him, used a cigarette lighter to get the sliding effect. Sam Moore was so knocked out when he heard it that he spontaneously injected "Play it Steve" into the mix. The excitement was so palpable that it was all left in.

"Soul Man" epitomizes the Stax sound as much as any record. The key aesthetic was one of "less is more," applied to all players and across all parameters. Drummer Al Jackson's trademark cannonlike backbeat on the snare is juxtaposed for most of the performance with an eighth-note ride pattern on a closed hi-hat cymbal. Jackson typically opted for the closed hi-hat, as opposed to using suspended crash or ride cymbals, which fill up a much larger portion of the pitch spectrum and continue to ring for some time after they are initially struck, creating a much wider and longer sound. The closed hi-hat reinforced the aesthetic of "less is more." To compliment this aesthetic even further, on many recordings the hi-hat is played so quietly that its presence is nearly subliminal.

"We used to basically try to keep cymbals out of most of the songs," explains Steve Cropper. "We thought cymbals were offensive. Demographically we were told that research [showed] that girls bought probably seventy to eighty percent of the records and, if a guy bought one, it was usually because he was buying it for his girlfriend. We thought that women's ears were a little more sensitive and they didn't like cymbals so much, so we tried to keep them way down in the mix almost all the time."

Jackson used a wooden shell snare drum and, by tuning its top head loosely, achieved very little of the taut, metallic properties that many drummers seek. Instead, he produced a deadened sound using very tight snares to dampen the bottom head of the drum. To deaden the sound even further, Jackson would put his billfold on the top head of his snare drum.[20] At the same time that he was altering the snare's basic timbre, he played very hard, hitting the rim and the skin of the snare at exactly the same moment with the heavy, thicker end of the stick. The net result was a readily identifiable sound that truly packed a wallop.

On records Jackson was a simple drummer, generally avoiding embellishments of all kinds, including drum fills typically found at the ends of sections in much popular music. When he did play fills, they would often occur as part of an interlocked pattern worked out with bass, guitar, and keyboards. The exception to this was on Booker T. and the MG's recordings, where Jackson generally played much more complex and flashy parts, often utilizing added timbres such as a cowbell.

A key ingredient in the conception of the Stax groove was that Jackson had an absolute metronomic sense of time. "He was the best timekeeper I've ever played with," Cropper told writer Bruce Wittet in 1987. "If we made forty takes of a song—if we cut it all day long—you could edit the intro of the first take with the fade-out of the last take, and the tempo would be identical."

Jackson was pretty well in control of setting the tempo for most Stax recordings, often setting them a little slower than some might have preferred. Duck Dunn recalled in conversation with Wittet, "Ninety percent of the time Al was right. I'd get a little irritated sometimes, but I would keep it to myself. His tendency would be to take the tempos slower than I could feel them." Dunn told me basically the same thing but added, "Either you played with Al or you didn't cut it. Either you played Al's feel or there was no feel at all. He communicated to the whole band that way—with his playing and with his eyes."

Stax recordings are groove-oriented, and although Jackson could be absolutely metronomic, he was much more than a glorified human click track, often allowing a performance to "breathe" by changing the groove either without changing the tempo or by deliberate subtle tempo adjustments as the piece moves from one section to another.

Timbre was a crucial component of the Stax aesthetic. Overall, the sound was bass-heavy, with Duck Dunn playing a Fender Precision bass through an Ampeg B-15 amplifier. Dunn was a stickler for using flat wound strings. "As the flat wound strings got older," explains Dunn, "they get more of a thud. They match the kick drum with more of a thud than a tone."

Cropper was just as particular about the sound of his guitar. He would always leave his Fender Telecaster wide open, using his amplifier to set the levels. He steadfastly refused ever to use the bass pickup on his guitar, instead opting for the middle position with both pickups on or just the rear treble pickup activated. This partially accounts for the trebly sound he so obviously preferred. The Fender Telecaster that he used for most of his years at Stax had a rosewood neck, which he felt helped to give him a "real nice, biting sound."

Cropper preferred big, heavy-gauge Gibson Sonomatic strings, generally using ten and eleven or two eleven-gauge strings on the top two strings of his instrument rather than the more typical spread of nine- and twelve-gauge strings used by most of his contemporaries. This was important for the two-note sliding figures he commonly played on his highest strings.

"It sounds better when they're closer matched," Steve explains. "I hate new strings on a guitar. There are guys I love and respect that change strings after every solo. Mine, I

---

20. Cropper says that it was so heavy that Jackson didn't need to tape it down. "It was so thick and so heavy, he couldn't bounce it off the snare if he hit it with a baseball bat!"

change them when they break. I even put Chapstick (lip balm) on my strings when I put them on. I just rub it into the strings. It sort of gives you the effect of two or three days of playing them where you get the grease in there and the dirt."

This grease helped give Cropper his characteristic clipped rhythm sound. "A lot of the clipped sound just comes from my style of playing. I play right over the bridge. A lot of the muting things, a lot of the guys, the only way they can get it is to play it backwards, which is an up stroke. I play it with a down stroke. The mute comes within the fingers 'cause all of a sudden my hand isn't on the bridge anymore. I hit the strings with a pick and the finger at the same time. The mute is coming out of the finger. [With the left hand] I finger the chord but I don't press it down all the way so it rings. I let up just enough where they all have the same amount of deadness.

"When I'm playing 'chinks' like that, I don't play dead in the middle of the fret. I play closer to the fret so it's this bright [sound]. I can almost play a wrong chord and nobody would know the difference. That's how unmelodic it is. It's more percussive."

Much of Cropper's playing is performed on the top four strings of the instrument. In doing so, he achieved a high degree of congruence between his sound and that of the horn section. This level of timbral integration was another key component of the Stax sound.

Floyd Newman tells an interesting story in which Jim Stewart stopped a take because he heard a wrong note. Stewart began to chastise the horns until Newman pointed out that the horns were not even playing, because they had yet to work out their part. Cropper was the guilty party, but as Stewart heard it, it was the horns. In Newman's words, "For some strange reason [Cropper] would blend right on to the horns." The idea of congruence was not lost on Booker T. Jones either. There are a number of examples where the piano blends into, gets lost inside of, or simply seems to become "one" with the guitar. When Jones played organ, he was equally adept at blending with the horns. He generally preferred piano when accompanying a vocalist, while the organ was his instrument of choice on most of Booker T. and the MG's instrumental recordings.

The horn players at Stax were interested in a simple but fat sound. To achieve this goal they often played unison lines such as in the introduction, verses, and refrain of "Soul Man." "If we didn't feel [the sound] was coming out as fat as it should be," explains Joe Arnold, "we would just drop one harmony part and have one tenor and trumpet double [playing the same note] and the other tenor play harmony."

Arnold tells an interesting story that indicates just how sound-conscious the Stax house band was. He had been with the label a few months when Wayne Jackson called him and said that Steve Cropper wanted to talk to the horns at the studio.

"I hadn't been there very long," relates Arnold, "and at that time I was playing with a metal mouthpiece. Gene [Parker], Andrew [Love], and Floyd [Newman] all used a hard rubber mouthpiece. Steve called us into the control room and he played some tapes back of some of the stuff that had been recorded before I was there and some of the stuff that had been recorded after. Some of it didn't sound as full.

"He was trying, in a nice way, to get around to a point. He said, 'It just don't seem like it's as fat as it should be.' I thought I was fixing to lose my job. Wayne said, 'No man, ain't no way, don't worry about that.'

"See, a metal mouthpiece pinpoints the sound. That's the reason people use the metal mouthpiece to get a sharp edge, whereas a hard rubber mouthpiece rounds it out. I said, 'Well, I'll get a hard rubber mouthpiece and we'll start from there.' From then on, no problem. I never heard any more about it."

Booker T. claims that while the Stax house band was sound-conscious in general, they were not particularly conscious of constructing a Stax sound: "No idea, no idea at all. It came from outside. I *heard* about the Memphis sound. I *heard* we were creating the Memphis sound. We didn't consciously generate that. That sound had been created [by the time we] realized we were creating a sound." Conscious or not, the sound the four members of Booker T. and the MG's, Isaac Hayes, and the Mar-Key horns created was original, distinctive, and filled with magic. The house of Stax would have been very different with a different set of players.

It also would have been very different without Al Bell. While "Soul Man" was storming up the charts, Stax announced that Al Bell was being promoted from national promotion director to the newly created position of executive vice president. Bell continued to supervise all aspects of national promotion and publicity, but now he was additionally officially recognized as a consultant to the production department.

Within a month of his promotion, Bell announced a distribution deal with Lenny Ceour's Milwaukee-based Magic Touch label. This would be the first of several such distribution deals Bell would make in which Stax would distribute smaller R&B independents. The new arrangement produced immediate dividends when Harvey Scales and the Seven Sounds released "Get Down" (Magic Touch 2007) in October, reaching the number 32 and number 79 positions on the rhythm and blues and pop charts respectively.

In late November and early December, Otis entered the Stax studios for one monumental three-week bash. Otis was always prolific, but the wealth of material cut in this period was simply phenomenal. It turned out to be enough to fill four posthumous LPs plus both sides of a Christmas single. Steve Cropper explains this unprecedented burst of energy: "There was only one reason and that was because he had his throat operated on. He was singing better than he ever had in his life, it was just obvious. So we went back and listened to the things that had been cut on four-track. Things that he didn't sound all that good on, we recut them; things that probably would never have come out. Some of them were over a year old."

Otis had had polyps removed from his throat and for six weeks he had not been able to speak above a whisper. Obviously anxious about the condition of his voice, upon recovery he was absolutely thrilled with the results. Cropper's assessment is right on the money: Otis had never sung better.

A number of the songs that Otis cut in this extended session were recorded in the middle of the night by what Steve Cropper dubbed the "Midnight Recorders." Both Cropper and new engineer Ronnie Capone loved to drink JB and water. According to Capone, Otis would come back after dinner with a big bottle of JB and the three of them would stay to all hours, Capone playing drums, Cropper guitar and occasionally bass and/or keyboards, and Otis singing and playing acoustic guitar. The next day, Bar-Kays drummer Carl Cunningham would overdub drum fills to round out Capone's rudimentary lines and various members of the MG's and Mar-Key horns would overdub other parts. These were happy creative times for everyone involved.

The key song that Otis would record during these sessions was "(Sittin' On) The Dock of the Bay." Released January 8, 1968, it would provide a stunning coda to Otis's career aesthetically and commercially, becoming a million-selling number 1 R&B and pop hit. The song represented a dramatic change for Redding. He had written it in the summer while staying on a houseboat in Sausalito after the Monterey Pop Festival. Many of his closest associates did not know how to react to it. Jim Stewart remembers his initial response: "To me 'Dock of the Bay,' when I first heard it, was not nearly as strong as 'I've Been Loving You Too Long.' Of course, it was a different kind of record for Otis. I always saw Otis as 'Pain in My Heart,' 'I've Been Loving You Too Long,' and 'Try a Little Tenderness.'"

"Most people had doubts about it," affirms Phil Walden. "It was a drastic change. Listening to it in retrospect now it isn't that much [of a change], but for those times, it sounded like it might have been a little too pop."

With so many people commenting that it might be too pop, Steve Cropper and Otis toyed with the idea of adding background singers. "We thought about it," recalls Steve. "We would make it a little more soulful and a little more R&B if we got the Staple Singers to come in and do backgrounds on it." Otis died before the idea came to pass.[21]

"He was constantly working on material and ideas," continues Walden. "The last night we were together we sat up for hours at a mutual friend's house. He was dissecting the Beatles' *Sgt. Pepper* album, trying to figure out what they were doing. He had just met the Beatles in a club in England.[22] Myself, Jerry Wexler, and Otis were there and they were lined up and each one took turns to sit down and talk to him for a few minutes. He was the king and they were the peons. He really liked what they were doing and thought they were exceptionally clever. He would listen over and over again. I'd get him Bob Dylan albums and stuff like that. For a black, southern, basically a rural singer to be listening to a Jewish folk singer from the Midwest. . . ."

Walden remembers Dylan actually giving Otis an acetate of "Just Like a Woman" in hopes that he would record it. "Otis said, 'It's got too many fucking words. All these pig-tails and bobby tails and all that stuff.' Otis liked it and probably would have done it at some point, but he felt it was due a serious lyric edit. It was an awareness of people like Dylan and pop artists like the Beatles that made him much more conscious of the importance of lyrics. You really notice that with songs like 'Dock of the Bay.' That was a very conscious effort to write a song that had a strong lyric sense to it."

Ironically, though, Steve Cropper recalls that Otis blew the words at the end. "For 'Dock of the Bay' we had worked out this little fadeout rap he was gonna do, an ad-lib thing. He forgot what it was so he started whistling."

It has been written many times that "(Sittin' On) The Dock of the Bay" was recorded on December 6 and 7. As it turns out, it was actually one of the first things cut during this extended session, being recorded the afternoon of November 22. That said, Otis did continue recording other material through December 7. As fate would have it, according to Barbara McCoy of the Charmells, on the seventh virtually everyone connected with Stax seemed to have come down to the studio, ending up in David Porter's office drinking Cherry Kijofa wine and eating chicken. It would be the last time any of them would see Otis alive. The afternoon of December 8, Otis and the Bar-Kays flew to Nashville. Otis had first sung with the Bar-Kays at the Hippodrome, a Beale Street club jointly owned by Jim Stewart, Al Bell, and Al Jackson. In the last few months of his life he employed the group as his regular backup band. This was a pragmatic move because Otis had let his regular road band go before his polyps operation. The Bar-Kays were an already constituted unit that was hungry for work, basically available at the drop of a hat, and, with a hit single under their belt, they added value to the bill. Otis was especially fond of Carl Cunningham's drumming, marveling at how closely it approximated that of Al Jackson.

In Nashville, Otis and the Bar-Kays played the first of three scheduled weekend concerts. On Saturday they headed up to Cleveland, where they appeared on Don Webster's "Upbeat" TV show (Otis dueted on the show with Mitch Ryder on "Knock on Wood"), and then later that evening they played a show at Leo's Casino. On the morning of December 10,

---

21. A year later Cropper produced a Staple Singers version of the song for their debut Stax album, *Soul Folk in Action*.

22. This occurred just prior to the first dates on the Stax/Volt European tour.

Otis called his wife Zelma around 8:30. She told Peter Guralnick, "He was depressed about something. I remember that very well and he talked to little Otis who was just

Otis Redding relaxing on his ranch in the last year of his life. COURTESY FANTASY, INC.

three . . . he said he would call me when he got to Madison." The second call never came, however, as Otis and all but two of the original Bar-Kays died when his twin-engine Beechcraft plunged into Lake Monona, just three minutes away from its destination in Madison, Wisconsin.

Bassist James Alexander was not on the plane,[23] while trumpeter Ben Cauley, ironically the only one on the plane who couldn't swim and wasn't wearing a seat belt, survived the crash. Cauley was asleep with his arms wrapped around his seat cushion. When the plane plunged into the water, he was thrown out of an opening in the fuselage with his arms still around his seat cushion, which, of course, was also a flotation device. While he floated in the water, he could hear his friends and bandmates calling out for help until one by one their cries stopped. It's a great irony that exactly three years earlier, on December 10, 1964, Otis's idol Sam Cooke had been shot to death in a Los Angeles motel.

Otis's funeral was a lavish affair held at the Macon City Auditorium, where his body lay in state from 6:30 A.M. By the beginning of the noontime service, 4,500 people had crowded into the 3,000-seat facility, including a virtual Who's Who of the soul world. Joe Simon

23. Otis's plane could not accommodate all the members of his touring party. Consequently two people flew commercial flights to each destination. James Alexander was simply lucky that it was his turn to fly commercial.

and Johnnie Taylor were pallbearers, the former singing "Jesus Keep Me Near the Cross," the latter "I'll Be Standing By" accompanied by Booker T. on organ. Jerry Wexler delivered the eulogy, closing with the observation that "Respect is something Otis achieved for himself in a way few people do. Otis sang 'Respect when I come home' and Otis had come home."

In an impossibly painful Christmas season of 1967 it was left to Steve Cropper and the rest of the staff at Stax to pick up the pieces and finish "Dock of the Bay." The master take of the song had been recorded on a four-track machine. Inspired by Otis's tongue-in-cheek imitation of a seagull on take one,[24] Cropper went over to Pepper-Tanner and borrowed an album of sound effects.[25] He then made a tape loop of the sound of waves and another loop of the sound of seagulls and mixed them down on a two-track tape. For the final version he hooked up both the two-track and the four-track machines and mixed in the tape loops at the appropriate moments.

At least one version sent from Memphis to Atlantic's offices in New York was rejected as, in Jerry Wexler's opinion, Otis was too deep in the mix (according to Phil Walden this earlier version was also a little heavy-handed in the use of the seagull and wave sound effects). The argument over the mix illustrated a long-standing disagreement among Wexler, Stewart, and Cropper. The Stax sound, as envisioned by the latter two, treated the singers as part of the rhythm section, not above it.

"The only thing I was in constant disagreement with Jim Stewart was on the mixes," shrugs Wexler. "Always the battle of the mixes. They always buried the voices [too much] to my taste. At one time Jim got a little salty with me. He said, 'Well, you've got your New York ears and we've got our Memphis ears. We hear it two different ways.' I said, 'Fair enough, but that's how I hear it.' He always prevailed [except for this one time]. I refused to put out 'Dock of the Bay' the way it was. I sent it back and made them redo it. That's the only one on which I really stood up. Otis was dead. In case of a tie, the artist wins with me, always."

Whatever side of the argument one might fall on, with "Dock of the Bay" the final version is a masterpiece. Nothing in Otis's background even remotely suggests the possibility of such a song. Cropper outdoes himself, decorating Otis's vocal throughout with shimmering fills. Everyone in the Stax house band is restrained, as if not wanting to intrude on a magical moment. Otis arguably never sounded better.

Until his death Otis was the mainstay of the company. His success with black audiences was inspirational, totaling twenty-one R&B chart singles in just over four-and-a-half years while he was alive, with another ten charting in the twenty-four-month period following his death. During the last year of his life, he had also started to make serious headway toward crossing over to a pop audience via the Stax/Volt tour of Europe in March and April, an overwhelming performance at the Monterey Pop Festival in June, and finally, with the recording of "(Sittin' On) The Dock of the Bay" in the last few days of his life.

Redding's death, in many respects, signaled the end of an era. "The day Otis Redding died," reminisces Jim Stewart, "that took a lot out of me. I was never the same person. The company was never the same to me after that. Something was taken out and was never replaced. The man was a walking inspiration. He had that effect on everyone around him."

24. Released in 1992 on a CD of Otis Redding outtakes entitled *Remember Me* in North America on Fantasy Records and *It's Not Just Sentimental* in the United Kingdom on Ace Records.

25. Pepper-Tanner was a local jingle studio that for a short while also had its own label, Pepper Records. Over the years, various people associated with Stax also had dealings with Pepper-Tanner.

"He was an awesome person," echoes Steve Cropper. "He'd walk in a room, the whole place lit up, just like when Elvis used to walk in. The only difference was the color. It was amazing."

Jim and Steve's comments are telling. Most people at Stax at that time had similar feelings. In some intangible way Otis Redding had become the heart and soul of the company. His death left a hole that simply could not be filled.

8

Wrap It Up: 1968 (Part 1)

Ever since the arrival of Al Bell in the fall of 1965, Stax's activity and consequent fortunes had increased exponentially. By October 1967 things had heated up to the point where Jim Stewart could no longer engineer every session at the company. In Steve Cropper's opinion, Ron Capone was the obvious choice for the company's first full-time salaried engineer.

Growing up in Baton Rouge, Capone moved to Memphis in 1959 to work as a drummer at Pepper-Tanner studios. On the weekends, Capone kept himself busy playing in a jazz trio with pianist Larry Mahoberac, who also happened to be in charge of the studio. When Mahoberac finally had enough of Pepper—Tanner's substandard engineer, he enlisted Capone, and for a long while Capone engineered vocal sessions in the daytime[1] while playing drums on the evening sessions. Capone also played drums at other studios, including Stax whenever Al Jackson wasn't available. He specifically remembers playing on Nick Charles's "Sunday Jealous," William Bell's "You Don't Miss Your Water," Carla Thomas's "I'll Bring It On Home," and a number of Rufus Thomas sessions. He also played live with the MG's whenever Jackson was tied up with Willie Mitchell's Band, and played a few latter-day Mar-Key dates with Wayne Jackson and Andrew Love.

When Jim Stewart hired Capone as an engineer in November 1967, Capone felt both the equipment and the approach to recording at Stax were still quite primitive. Although the company had been set up with a Scully four-track recorder and overdubbing capability for over two years, headphones were still not used on Stax sessions. When recording an overdub, the studio speakers were used for monitors, which of course meant the sound coming out of the speakers bled into the microphone. Capone also found that Jim Stewart was not really interested in the stereo mix. Forty-fives were released in mono, and the seven-inch 45 was Stax's bread and butter.

"Jim Stewart wouldn't allow you to listen to the four-track," Capone says, still amazed by the fact nearly thirty years later. "He'd put that Voice of the Theatre speaker in front of you with an eighteen-inch woofer.[2] He put that in front of the mono machine and said, 'Now Ron, I do not want you to listen to that

(*left to right*) **Unidentified person, Henry Bush, and Ron Capone mixing a Stax concert. COURTESY RON CAPONE.**

---

1. Some of the artists that Capone cut at Pepper-Tanner included the Gentrys, Larry Raspberry, Bobby Whitlock, and the Short Kuts.

2. The Altec Voice of the Theatre speaker had originally been used when the building was a movie house. About ten feet high with a big metal horn on top, it was used by Jim Stewart for a playback speaker in the control room. "I would sit right under that thing," says the erstwhile producer. "I would drive it so the decibels you could've heard across the street. You could not break that speaker up. No way. It was built in solid wood—unreal. Of course, it would sound awful by today's standards I suppose but the bass pounded you in the chest. [Although it was a single speaker] it was total stereo because the bass was right in my ear and the high end was way up [near the ceiling]. We had the whole room breathing with that damn thing."

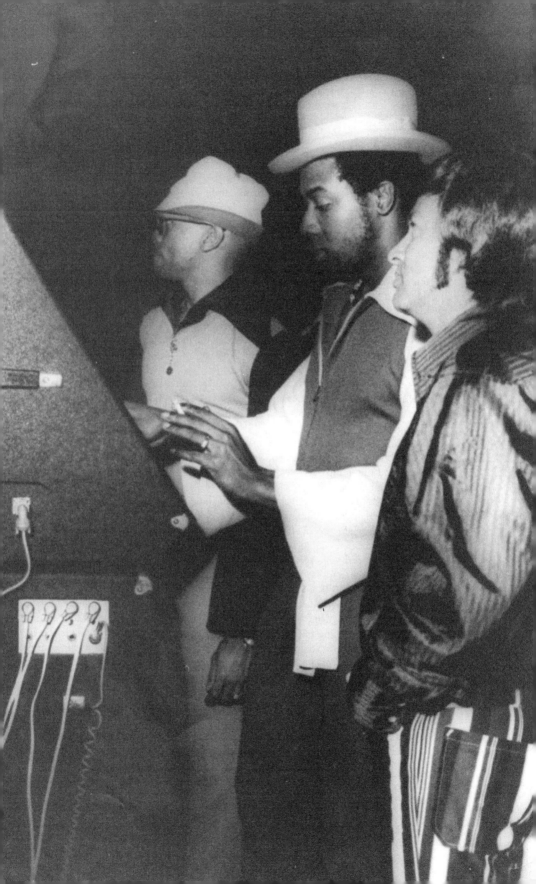

four-track. I don't care what goes to that four-track.' Some of the levels and stuff that
went to that four-track were outrageous."

According to Capone, when Steve Cropper first approached him (at a Crystal ham-
burger joint on Summer) about the engineering job at Stax, Cropper said, "I'm gonna talk
to Jim. We got to have an engineer. Jim is no engineer!"

Welton Jetton had put the board in and, according to Capone, "He padded it down so
that if Jim opened it up wide open and the meters were just cranked, there would be no
way he could get any distortion out of that board."

Maintenance was also not a priority at Stax. The piano was only tuned once a month
and Al Jackson simply refused to tune his drums.[3] For reverb, there were two live chambers at the back of the studio, one of which would constantly get filled with water; there
was also a problem with crickets getting into the chambers. To top it all off, the chambers
were outfitted with the cheapest speakers money could buy.

"You couldn't put a quality speaker in there," laughs Capone, "because in no time the
humidity and the dampness would rust it and the cone would be gone. It wouldn't last a
month. So we put in these little bitty speakers that you had at the drive-in movies."
Apparently the microphone used in the chambers was of a similar quality.

Soon after cutting Otis's final sessions, Capone engineered the Sam and Dave sessions
that produced "I Thank You"[4] backed with "Wrap It Up." Released on January 8, 1968—
the same day as "(Sittin' On) The Dock of the Bay"—"I Thank You" is famous for Sam
Moore's opening invocation, "I want everybody to get up off your seat and get your arms
together and your hands together and give me some of that old soul clapping." Listening
to the way Sam plays with the word "old," one can imagine just what a great preacher he
would have made.

Supporting Sam, Al Jackson lays out an unusual drum pattern, playing straight eighth
notes on the snare with every third one being accented. The concept was David Porter's.
"I said, 'I want the sound of horses,'" recalls Porter. "I was trying to come up with a character for it, and the only thing I could think of when we were in the studio was horses.
When I said that, the cats turned around and looked at me like I was a goddamn fool. But
Al [Jackson] said, 'Okay, I'll try it.' So he counted it off and he just put his sticks over the
rim and that was where it came from. We could take our thoughts and communicate it to
him and he was brazen enough to think that he could do it."

The record in nearly all respects was atypical for Stax. Isaac Hayes for the first time uses
a clavinet and, to match the new keyboard sound, Steve Cropper employs a really dirty,
distorted guitar timbre. It is also the only Sam and Dave record cut at Stax to include
background vocals, provided courtesy of Ollie and the Nightingales. Finally, the lead vocal
for the B-side, "Wrap It Up," was recorded in Paris in the midst of a Sam and Dave tour,
because, once the backing track was finished, Atlantic and Stax, sure they had a hit on
their hands, were anxious to get the record on the market. "I Thank You" turned out to
be the last Sam and Dave 45 issued on Stax and, not so coincidentally, it was to be the last
time Sam and Dave ever entered the R&B Top 10 or the pop Top 40.

The same week that "I Thank You" and "Dock of the Bay" were released, Warner
Brothers bought Atlantic for a reported $17 million. The Stax/Atlantic distribution agree-
ment had been formalized in May 1965 in case of just such an eventuality. The formal
agreement contained a clause that allowed Stax to sever the distribution deal with Atlantic
immediately should the company ever be sold and Jerry Wexler not remain a stockholder

3. It fell to ex-drummer Capone to keep Jackson's drum heads at the proper tension.
4. William Bell thought that "I Thank You" was originally presented to him but "it just didn't fit."

or employee. If Wexler remained an employee but not a stockholder, Stax could terminate the agreement within 180 days. When Warner bought Atlantic, Wexler was retained as an employee, and so Stax now had six months to decide whether or not to remain distributed by Atlantic.

Jim Stewart's initial inclination was to try to work something out with Atlantic or Warner Brothers, because he was leery of going totally independent, feeling that the independent distribution network in the United States was slowly collapsing. Stewart first tried to negotiate with Atlantic so that Warner could buy Stax as part of the Atlantic deal, then attempted to negotiate directly with Atlantic to see if Atlantic would buy Stax itself. Finally, he tried to negotiate a continuance of the distribution deal but with a better percentage. None of these options worked out. In fact, Stewart felt that the offers he was getting back from Warner and Atlantic were little short of insulting. Estelle Axton remembers Atlantic offering $2 million for Stax. By the time that figure was split with first her brother and then the Internal Revenue Service, she would be left with very little for her eight years of effort.

After much thought and discussion, Stewart and Axton elected to sever their relationship with Atlantic. According to Al Bell, the four members of Booker T. and the MG's, Isaac Hayes, David Porter, and Deanie Parker were brought in on the discussions. Bell recalls drummer Al Jackson being particularly vocal in favor of leaving Atlantic.

"The heads definitely thought that Atlantic had shafted us and sent us down the river," comments Steve Cropper. "They weren't being fair with us at all, as is evident when Jim decided to leave that Wexler reneged on his deal with Sam and Dave saying he didn't give them to Stax, he loaned them to Stax. They really did sell us down the river. We kept them in business for quite a long time when none of their artists could buy a hit, let alone get one. That's why they kept bringing people down there. They were definitely using and they knew they were using. They couldn't get out of New York anymore what was really selling at the time."

The Atlantic distribution setup, in most respects, had been nothing more than a production deal that allowed Stax to be able to build a name, logo, and profile. Stax had done none of its own manufacturing or marketing. Once the decision was made to leave Atlantic, Stax could strike out on its own as a full-fledged record label. All parties agreed to terminate the arrangement on May 6, 1968.

In hindsight it is not surprising that neither Atlantic nor Warner Brothers was prepared to pay a high price to buy Stax. The company's most important artist, Otis Redding, had perished that past December; the company's second-most important artist, Sam and Dave, was actually contracted to Atlantic; and the May 1965 agreement was actually a master purchase rather than a distribution agreement, meaning Atlantic already owned everything recorded by Stax that had been distributed by Atlantic up to this point. In addition, in the agreement signed in 1968 upon the termination of the 1965 distribution agreement, Atlantic was given the option for four years to release, distribute, and then retain the rights in perpetuity to any previously unreleased Otis Redding masters. Atlantic would subsequently exercise this option, issuing four Redding albums and over a dozen singles through mid-1970.[5]

The Sam and Dave situation was particularly galling because most of those at Stax had come to accept the dynamic duo as bona fide Stax artists. "When Stax disengaged from us," recalls Wexler, "I had the unpleasant job of reminding Jim Stewart that Sam and Dave belonged to us. He had to get back into the files to realize what the arrangement was."

---

5. The albums were *The Immortal Otis Redding* (June 1968), *Otis Redding in Person at the Whiskey A Go Go* (October 1968), *Love Man* (June 1969), and *Tell the Truth* (July 1970).

In a move that theoretically was in everybody's best interest, it was agreed that Stax would retain exclusive right to continue recording Sam and Dave for up to three singles after the termination of the distribution agreement in May. This could be extended indefinitely if all parties remained in agreement. All told, the first five post-Stax/Atlantic Sam and Dave singles were written, recorded, and produced in Memphis at Stax and all five hit the R&B charts (four also showing some pop action), albeit not matching the duo's earlier successes. Twelve Sam and Dave cuts recorded at Stax, including "I Thank You" and "Wrap It Up," were packaged on an album entitled *I Thank You* released in October 1968. Given the success of "I Thank You" and the fact that the Eddie Floyd–penned "You Don't Know What You Mean to Me" went to the number 20 R&B and number 48 position on the pop charts, it seems odd that the LP is the only Sam and Dave Stax-related album not to enter *Billboard*'s Top LP chart. My guess is that Atlantic, for one reason or another, had decided Sam and Dave were a very low priority.

After running out of Stax material, Wexler took Sam and Dave first to Muscle Shoals, then to A&R studios in New York, and finally to Criteria in Miami. Five more singles were released on Atlantic, not one entering even the bottom rung of a single national chart. All, with the exception perhaps of "Don't Pull Your Love," were markedly inferior to the material cut at Stax.

The failure of Sam and Dave's post-Stax releases on Atlantic has been a source of much conjecture. To Sam it's simple: "We didn't have the same people." That certainly seems a large part of it. Atlantic simply couldn't replace the magic that was 926 E. McLemore, Hayes and Porter, Booker T. and the MG's, and the Memphis Horns.

It was a very frustrating period for all concerned. Sam and Jerry Wexler got increasingly desperate each time out, ending up at each other's throats. Sam wanted to record "Starting All Over Again" (which eventually was recorded by Mel and Tim on Stax in 1972, hitting big on both charts) and "Tennessee Waltz" (which he did record solo a little later). Wexler nixed both ideas, substituting the inept "Knock It Out of the Park" instead.

"Jerry and I fought viciously," frowns Sam, "almost coming to blows about Sam and Dave." Wexler put it succinctly: "We made some shit-ass records with them. I never got into their sensibility as a producer. Never. I always felt that I was talking to a wall of gelatin."

Sam and Dave were having their own problems. Their friendship had pretty well ended by 1968, and in June 1970 they split up for the first time, only to get back together less than a year later. In the interim Sam had recorded three solo singles produced by King Curtis for Atlantic while Dave had one solo release on Alston. Back together, they released one final Atlantic single in the summer of 1971. The duo went on to record a 1976 LP for United Artists called *Back At 'Cha* produced by Steve Cropper and a 1978 single for England's Contempo label (a version of the Beatles' "We Can Work It Out"). In the midseventies their career was at a virtual standstill as disco ruled the Western world's airwaves, but the success of the Blues Brothers' version of "Soul Man" in 1979 led to one final flurry of activity, which included recording a rehash of their hits for Gusto Records. The response was disappointing, and Sam and Dave played their final gig together December 31, 1981. Dave died tragically in a car accident in his home state of Georgia on April 9, 1988. In the late 1990s Sam Moore is still pounding the boards, performing regularly with a voice and a spirit that remain undiminished.

Wexler also got to inform Stewart that he no longer owned his back catalogue due to the agreement Stewart had signed back in May 1965. "Even though they did no financing of Stax whatsoever, the contract stipulated that the masters would be owned by Atlantic Records and not by Stax," Stewart says, grimacing. "It was tough to swallow. It was a serious mistake that I made. They obviously did not have the right or deserve [the masters] because they hadn't paid for them. They never paid for a session. Atlantic Records, I think, had a total investment of five thousand dollars in Stax Records. That was for the purchase of the Rufus and Carla master in 1960. For that they got the distribution rights from 1960 through 1967!"

While the principals at Stax hashed out the situation with Atlantic, the Stax house band continued to write, record, and produce. In the first four months of 1968 (the last four under the Stax/Atlantic agreement), Stax and Volt issued superb records by Ollie and the Nightingales, Eddie Floyd, the Bar-Kays, Johnnie Taylor, William Bell, Mable John, Rufus Thomas, Jeanne and the Darlings, Carla Thomas, the Mad Lads, and Albert King.

The Bell and Floyd records were by-products of the legacy of Otis Redding. When Booker T. Jones finished college and came back to Stax full-time in the spring of 1966, he had struck up writing partnerships first with Hayes and Porter and then with William Bell and, on occasion, Eddie Floyd. Booker had always been a gifted writer but, with the benefit of his music studies at college, he had blossomed into a melodicist of ungodly proportions.

Starting with William Bell's March 1967 release "Everybody Loves a Winner," Bell and Jones created sublime record after sublime record including Albert King's "Born Under a Bad Sign," Ollie and the Nightingales' February 1968 hit "I Got a Sure Thing," the Astors' final single, September 1967's "Daddy Didn't Tell Me," and Bell's own "Eloise (Hang On in There)." One of their most moving compositions was the lovingly tender Otis Redding remembrance, "A Tribute to a King." The song was written a few days after Redding's death and was immediately recorded with Bell handling the lead vocal chores. In the meantime a number of Redding tributes were released by a variety of non-Stax artists. Bell, not wanting to cash in on the tragedy, decided to just send his recording to Otis's widow, Zelma, in his words, "Just as a memento or keepsake. She loved it. So she called back and asked Jim [Stewart] if he would release it. So when Jim asked me and Booker, we hassled back and forth 'cause I was really adamant against putting it out."

Bell eventually agreed to issue it as the B-side of "Everyman Oughta Have a Woman." A number of disc jockeys flipped the record and, whether Bell liked it or not, "A Tribute to a King" became a number 16 R&B and number 86 pop hit. Set in an absolutely gorgeous arrangement complete with strings, the song is sung by Bell with a voice full of equal helpings of love and sadness. What could have been corny and clichéd comes across as an incredibly moving and fitting testimony to the memory of Otis Redding.[6]

Booker T. was also involved with another record connected, at least peripherally, to Otis's death. When Redding's plane crashed, Eddie Floyd was in England on tour. "The day of the funeral was the end of my tour," says Floyd, shuddering at the memory. "I had a flight booked to leave to go to New York and then to Atlanta. We got out of the airport and we got on the plane. The plane taxis out and it looks like it's ready to take off. We went down the runway and suddenly it puts on the brakes, throwing folks everywhere. Something happened to one of the motors on that big jet. They took us back to the airport and we were there for five or six hours. That's where I wrote that song, 'Get on up big bird.'"

Floyd ended up missing the funeral. When he got back to the States, he went straight to Memphis and finished what he refers to as his "rock and roll" record with Booker T.

6. There was some talk at Stax of writing and recording a complete tribute album to Otis Redding, but the idea was eventually discarded as potentially appearing to outsiders as an attempt to cash in on Redding's tragic death.

"Big Bird" is certainly outside of the typical Stax idea of soul. As was becoming increasingly common on records he produced, Jones plays virtually all the instruments including the winding dual guitar parts. Incredibly, on initial release, the song died a quick death. Today, soul aficionados nearly without exception take its greatness for granted.

While Booker T. and the rest of the Stax house band continued working in the studio, Jim Stewart and Estelle Axton continued to try to sell Stax. Al Bell enlisted the aid of Clarence Avant, whom he had met through the National Association of Television and Radio Announcers (NATRA). Avant had been organist Jimmy Smith's manager and was just then embarking upon a career as a "deal" maker.[7] "Clarence knew his way around New York City," stresses Bell. "He knew the decision makers in the music business. I didn't. So I needed to relate to someone who knew their way around the turf."

After a series of unfruitful discussions with MCA, MGM, and ABC, in the early months of 1968 Avant successfully arranged for Stax to be sold to Gulf and Western effective May 29th, twenty-three days after the date the Atlantic/Stax distribution deal was to conclude. Gulf and Western already owned Dot Records, Famous Music, and Paramount Pictures. Acquiring Stax was simply another piece in the puzzle as the Los Angeles–based corporation continued to diversify its holdings.

Gulf and Western agreed to pay the principals at Stax approximately $4.3 million: $1.3 million was to be paid up front in the form of Gulf and Western common stock; the rest was to be paid in the form of an earn-out formula based on a percentage of whatever Stax's net income was. This percentage was then to be converted into common stock on an annual basis until the original purchase price had been met. As a kicker, however high Gulf and Western stock went, until the original purchase price had been met through the earn-out formula, stock was to be converted at $44

(left to right) **Al Bell, Chester Higgins (the writer from *Jet* magazine who popularized the concept of Isaac Hayes as *Black Moses*), and deal maker Clarence Avant.** COURTESY FANTASY, INC.

a share, the price it was selling for when the initial deal was made. For his efforts Clarence Avant was given 10 percent of all debentures. With Gulf and Western predicting that by the end of the year their stock would be valued at over $100 a share, to virtually all concerned, it appeared to be a great deal.[8] Stax's attorney, Seymour Rosenberg, was the only one to express cynicism about the earn-out structure: "Gulf and Western, in essence, bought [Stax] with their own money."

---

7. He was also shortly to launch Sussex Records, whose main artist was Bill Withers.

8. At the time of the deal Gulf and Western was on a roll. It was one of the first corporations to actively start buying up smaller companies. Unfortunately for Estelle, Jim, Al Bell, and Steve Cropper, the company's fortunes subsequently faltered and the stock never reached such lofty heights.

The sale to Gulf and Western allowed Stewart and Axton to effectively "cash in their chips." Moreover, it provided the financing needed to underwrite the establishment of a freestanding independent record company. Under the Atlantic umbrella, Stax had built a name and profile as the premier southern soul label; now the company could put together a sales and marketing staff and, with a new set of logos, expand into a wider range of musics. G&W's Paramount Pictures subsidiary would also provide a logical vehicle through which Stax artists could get involved in movie soundtracks.

At the point of the sale of Stax to Gulf and Western, Al Bell was given 10 percent ownership in the company. According to Bell this was the fulfillment of a promise made by Stewart and Axton back in 1965 when Bell was enticed to leave his position as a disc jockey on WUST in Washington. "The understanding that I originally had with Jim Stewart and Estelle Axton when I left Washington, D.C., and came to Stax and dumped all of my assets into Stax was that I would participate in Stax from an equity standpoint," asserts Bell. Bell, in fact, had been expecting a full, equal, one-third share of the company. "That didn't bother me. What was more important to me at that point in time was that Jim was living up to what he said he would do."

According to Bell, there had been some question as to whether Jim and Estelle would fulfill what Bell saw as their obligations to him. An informal meeting occurred during a picnic on Al's boat on a sandbar in the middle of the Mississippi River. As Memphis, Tennessee, was still very much a segregated community, although race relations were very good within the walls of Stax, black and white employees tended to go their separate ways after work.[9] Consequently, on this particular picnic, only the key black employees of the company were present: David Porter, Isaac Hayes, Booker T. Jones, Deanie Parker, and Al Jackson. A subsequent meeting was held inside the company which, infers Bell, forced Jim's hand *if* it needed to be forced.[10]

Future engineer, session guitarist, and songwriter Bobby Manuel points out, "Jim had no choice because of what was happening racially there. That company never could have survived if Jim had not taken in Al Bell. If he had made another white man his partner . . . it just wouldn't have happened with King and all. We were having to carry guns in there. It was crazy. Jim made a smart move as far as business, how to survive. But I'm sure that killed Steve because Steve was a power broker."

Sometime earlier, probably in late 1967, Steve Cropper had been given 10 percent of Stax's publishing arm, East Memphis Music. When word of this leaked out to other members of the Big Six, there were some hard feelings. Some of the session musicians suggest that this was one of many factors that led to Booker T. Jones leaving the company in the summer of 1969.

While Stax was in the process of ironing out the details with G&W, Memphis and black/white relations in the United States were about to go through profound changes from which they still have yet to fully recover. Dr. Martin Luther King was in town lending support to about one thousand Memphis City Sanitation workers who had been on strike for nearly two months. Just after 6:00 P.M. on Thursday, April 4, Dr. King was gunned down on the balcony outside his room at the Lorraine Motel. The assassin was allegedly James Earl Ray, who fired on King from either a flophouse on Main Street or the tower of a Memphis city firehouse. Most black Memphians don't believe Ray was

---

9. The Lorraine Motel was one of the few locales in Memphis where black and white employees of the company could feel comfortable hanging out together.

10. For the record, Clarence Avant insists that "I made sure before the [G&W] deal was made that Al Bell had ownership in Stax Records."

acting on his own, and to this day much remains unexplained and unknown about exactly what happened that afternoon. What is known is that Memphis and many other urban centers across the United States were immediately set on fire as riots broke out throughout black neighborhoods.

At McLemore and College, logical targets were white-owned businesses, most of which, according to Steve Cropper, were set on fire. It speaks volumes for Stax's role in the community that neither Stax nor the Satellite Record Shop was touched.[11] Not too long afterward, most of the white merchants sold their interests in the neighborhood. Stax would be affected in ways that no one could then predict.

"When we heard that Dr. King was assassinated, it was a shock," Estelle remembers, "and we knew there would be some problems. The only thing we could think of at that particular time was to be safe. We didn't know whether the building would be burned, somebody would break in, or what would happen because there were riots all over the city. So, Jim and two or three others loaded up the tapes we had in the back because that was a lot of investment. They put them in the trunk of the car and we closed our business. We were very fortunate. We were protected."

While the offices were closed for four or five days, on the night King was assassinated the studio remained in operation. Isaac Hayes was very nearly at the Lorraine when Dr. King was killed. Sam and Dave's baritone player was staying there and needed a ride to the studio for the evening session. Isaac had planned to pick him up but at the last moment Isaac's wife needed the car, so Isaac phoned him and told him to take a taxi to the studio. Hearing of the assassination in his own cab on the way to the session, Isaac arrived at Stax utterly devastated.

"It affected me for a whole year," Hayes concedes. "I could not create properly. I was so bitter and so angry. I thought, What can I do? Well, I can't do a thing about it so let me become successful and powerful enough where I can have a voice to make a difference. So I went back to work and started writing again."

After Dr. King was pronounced dead, a curfew was immediately imposed in Memphis between 7:00 P.M. and 5:00 A.M. Those working at Stax phoned downtown and got permission to continue working. The National Guard troops patrolling the area were duly informed. Later that evening, Isaac's right-hand man, Benny Mabone, poked his head outside the studio. The National Guard had changed shift and no one had bothered to inform the new shift that people were still in Stax hard at work. One of the guards, half-scared out of his mind, almost shot Mabone dead on the spot.

Wayne Jackson and Andrew Love were doing a session at Sam Phillips Recording Studio when they heard that Dr. King was killed. "When that happened," relates Wayne, "I packed my horn and said, 'I gotta go.' Andrew also had to go. We went! I went home and got my shotgun out of the closet and sat in my living room with a loaded gun that evening. I was worried something might happen to Andrew and I'm sure he was worried about what would happen to me."

Stax had not been officially involved in supporting the sanitation workers' strike. "The black presence in the executive role at Stax at that time did not have that kind of author-

11. The actual events in the area of College and McLemore could not be verified because the newspaper coverage at the time concentrated on the much worse rioting that occurred downtown. The Memphis Fire Department does not keep records that go that far back, but two senior firemen don't remember that much activity in the College and McLemore area. Both of them recalled that whatever did occur could hardly compare to the devastation that occurred downtown. One of them did remember that Jones' Big D Grocery across the street from Stax was definitely set on fire. Ron Capone says that a Molotov cocktail was found in the echo chamber at the back of the Stax building, which fortunately was filled with water. He feels that someone tried to torch the building. Estelle thought that a bullet hole was found in one of the windows at the front of the building.

ity," laments Isaac Hayes. "Jim Stewart, at that time, was the absolute spokesperson for the company. Had it been years later, [the company] probably would have taken a role, but at that time, no."

A number of the company's black employees, including Isaac Hayes, did march with Dr. King. For their efforts they ended up facing tear gas and attack dogs when Memphis police got out of control and started rioting.

9

Soul Limbo: 1968 (Part 2)

The death of Dr. Martin Luther King wrought long and permanent changes in the firmament of Stax Records. "It had a tremendous impact," attests Jim Stewart. "It kind of put a wedge, or at least opened up that suspicious element, [within] the company. Although we tried to bond together and continue to work together, from that point on it changed considerably. There wasn't that happy feeling of creating together. There was something missing. You couldn't quite put your finger on it, but you knew things had changed and there's no way you could go back. Everybody started withdrawing, pulling back from that openness and close relationship that we felt we had. . . . While we were in the studio I don't think that was ever affected, but once we were through, everybody went their separate ways. There wasn't that mixing and melting together like we had before."

"It heightened internally the racial sensitivity amongst those of us at Stax," affirms Al Bell. "Up to that point in time I don't think we focused in on that much. Dr. King's death had a tremendous impact at Stax. We were there in the middle of the black community and here we were an integrated organization existing in a city where integration was an issue. Dr. King's death caused [some] African-American people in the community to react negatively toward the white people that worked for Stax Records. Immediately after [King's] death we had to protect some of the white people who worked at Stax."

Stax was located right across the street from Jones' Big D grocery. For years, most of the Stax employees parked their cars at the Big D and walked across the street to the studio. In the wake of Dr. King's death, Steve Cropper and Duck Dunn, in particular, found that they were being routinely hassled by a couple of street-corner toughs named Sam Armour and Chicken.

"There were pressures outside the studio," confirms Steve, "in terms of gang-related situations in the neighborhood. Feelings were heating up. People were being influenced by what they were seeing in the news and reading in the paper. They had made the decision that they were gonna stand up to this and crusade behind it. I think just the fact that the public thought that Stax was a solely white-owned company had a lot to do with the feelings in the neighborhood. But they didn't have all their facts together because it wasn't solely a white-owned record company, Al Bell was part-owner of the company."

"As you'd get out of your car," recalls Duck, "two or three guys would kinda circle in and say, 'How 'bout ten dollars for the coloreds today?' You'd always get hit up for ten bucks or something. Al Bell saw that once and he called me in his office and gave me five hundred dollars. Right over in West Memphis there was a Sportsman's One-Stop. He sent me over there. I bought five pistols. I got one, Al got one, who he distributed the rest to I don't know. They never were used."

On one particular day, Chicken put a knife to Cropper's back and asked for a lot more than ten dollars. "They got on me one day," fumes Cropper, "and accused me of slapping this little kid who used to run errands for me. It never happened. They made the stupid story up just trying to harass me and get money out of me. They all of a sudden made it a black and white thing, and we had been everybody's friend there for years. They stuck a knife in my back and made all kinds of threats. Somehow I talked them out of it, got into the studio, and told Al to call them and have a meeting because we couldn't handle this anymore."

Sam Armour and Chicken[1] were also attempting to shake down Sam and Dave. On one particular evening, they went over to the Holiday Inn on Third Street where Sam and Dave were staying. They visited Dave's room first and apparently pushed him around, demanding money. They next dragged Dave down to Sam's room and demanded Sam cough up a couple of hundred dollars, saying, according to Sam Moore, "'that we're tired of you coming in here and letting all the money go to the white folks down at Stax.' All kind of stuff and they wanted to get paid. It was just after the assassination of Martin so everybody was a little up in the air. It was ugly. I knew Dave was scared because when he came over to my room he was almost ready to pass out."

Sam didn't have the money, but told them that he would try to get it. The FBI was called in and set up a sting operation, but neither Armour nor Chicken called or came back to the hotel. Sam and Dave were both asked to look at mug shots and identify who the perpetrators were. Sam Moore recognized Sam Armour's mug shot but, scared, decided it would be healthier to keep his mouth shut. Dave Prater had no such hesitation and fingered him. A short while later Sam Moore was back in New York and received a long-distance call at his apartment. It was Sam Armour demanding bail bond money. "I said, 'How did you find me, man?'" recalled Sam nearly three decades later. "He said, 'If I can find you on the phone and you don't send me that money, you know I can find you in person.' I'm going, 'Oh shit.' I'm scared. I said, 'Man, what do you need?'" Sam Moore reluctantly wired him two or three hundred dollars and fortunately never heard from him again.

The reason that Sam most likely didn't hear from Armour or Chicken again was because two gentlemen from New York, Johnny Baylor and Dino Woodard, appeared on the scene at Stax. Baylor was thirty-eight years old at the time. Born in Jefferson County, Alabama, Baylor had been in the U.S. Army from 1949 to 1952 as either a PFC or a corporal. Dino Woodard says that Baylor was a Ranger (the Rangers were the predecessors of the Green Berets) during the Korean conflict. According to an IRS report compiled on Stax in the 1970s, a confidential source told the IRS that he had met Baylor in Harlem and that he and Baylor were members of the Black Mafia, both of them earning money pushing dope, gambling, dealing in "hot" merchandise such as stolen jewelry and furs, and by various other means. The source also said that Baylor had been a sparring partner of Sugar Ray Robinson. Dino Woodard disputes several assertions in the IRS report. He states emphatically that there was no such thing as the Black Mafia and that Johnny was never part of a larger gang. He also asserts that neither he nor Johnny Baylor were involved in drug dealing. Finally, according to Woodard, although Baylor helped out as a corner man in Sugar Ray Robinson's camp, he was never Robinson's sparring partner. The IRS report does admit that the accuracy of their source was not determined but concluded, "Every one who knows Baylor, and who was willing to talk, described Baylor as a type of strong-arm man." More than one Stax employee claims that Baylor regularly bragged about killing a couple of people.

---

1. It's possible it was Sam Armour and a guy named Football. It is equally possible that Chicken and Football are one and the same person. Football, supposedly, at one point threatened to torch the Stax building.

Johnny Baylor, Cleotha Staples, and Dino Woodard at the spring 1969 Stax sales meeting.
COURTESY DEANIE PARKER.

Dino Woodard was born in the early 1930s in Memphis, where he attended Booker T. Washington High School. In 1952, soon after graduating, Woodard left Memphis in pursuit of his dreams of becoming a champion professional fighter. Landing in New York City, he met Sugar Ray Robinson's trainer, Harry Wiley, who promptly became Woodard's manager. When Woodard started serving as Sugar Ray's sparring partner, he met Johnny Baylor, who for some time had been a regular around Sugar Ray's camp. In the mid-1950s Baylor and Woodard became close friends. Over a decade later Baylor started a record company whose name, KoKo, had been his nickname ever since childhood.

In Memphis, the situation had escalated with Sam Armour and Chicken. "They were playing off of the riots and all that stuff that happened in Detroit and Los Angeles," recalls Al Bell. "They came by and said, 'You've got to pay us and then put our little symbol on your building. Then your building won't be burned down. You've got to pay us protection.'" The level of harassment had made it necessary to escort Stax's female white employees, such as Sandy Meadors and Marlene Powell, out to their cars each evening.[2] This was too much for Al and Jim.

Although the details vary depending on who is telling the story, as Cropper had requested, Al Bell and Jim Stewart did have a meeting in a nearby park off Waverly Street with Sam Armour and Chicken. In the meantime, Mack Guy, who was a photographer and R&B road manager from New York whom Al Bell had brought down to Memphis to work as his driver, had phoned Johnny Baylor and apprised him of the situation. "Next thing I knew," relates Bell, "Johnny Baylor and Dino were in Memphis, Tennessee."

Dino Woodard thought that he and Johnny had come down to Memphis to talk to Al about distributing the KoKo label[3] and, while they were there, found out about the problem with Sam Armour and Chicken. "That other thing came up when we were there," says Woodard, who is now a minister. "We gotta see that—boom—Al is protected. There was some people that was always around and finally it came to a head where we had to really let them know that, 'Hey, you have to stop it!' We met with them, Johnny and myself, and we resolved that. We met with one of the main guys there and just let him know, 'Hey, you gotta do or die.' We was there with Al and Al had the company going, so they had to leave the people alone. They were let known that either they were gonna die or else we were ready to die for our people. You understand? Like for Al. Hey man, enough is enough. It became too much of an annoyance for everyone. We were there to support Al and protect him and whoever else was involved [with him]. . . . There was no money involved. It was the principle of it. We wanted to support Al, who had been our friend."

Sam Armour and Chicken faded fast, but Johnny Baylor and Dino Woodard stayed around. With that problem taken care of, Bell and Stewart also decided to build a twelve-foot-high cyclone security fence with coiled barbed wire at the top around the parking lot in the back of Stax. Cropper, Dunn, and everyone else also stopped parking at the Big D.

In addition to these problems, Stax faced an enormous hurdle simply returning to the business of making records. Starting all over again was not an easy task. With the loss of their two most commercially successful artists, Otis Redding and Sam and Dave, as well as their entire back catalogue, the empire that Jim Stewart and Estelle Axton had labored so long to build appeared to be tottering upon a precipice.

"It was tough," recalls Jim Stewart, "it really was. But it made me more determined. That's when my nature is to say, 'Okay, that's the way it's going to be.' We called everybody in and told them what was happening. I said, 'Look, here we are; we're starting over and we're going to do it.' Atlantic holding on to the catalogue [actually] pulled us together for a period of time."

Years earlier, Al Bell had left the SCLC workshops being run by Dr. King in Midway, Georgia, due to differences in philosophy. "As opposed to the marches, I felt it was economic empowerment that we needed," explains Bell. "Once we developed an economic base, then we could mainstream ourselves. We would have the wherewithal in this capi-

2. To Al Bell this was absolute insanity. This was the second time he had had to confront racism in front of the marquee that so proudly graced the façade of the Stax building. In the first instance Al and Jim Stewart had been talking with Paul Glass of Chicago's All-State distributors. At that time, a white Memphis cop had pulled up and informed all concerned to the effect that in Memphis they didn't allow niggers to talk to white people on the street. In this case the tables were reversed as a small group of local blacks were hassling Stax's white employees. Bell was not going to stand for it.

3. A couple of years earlier when Bell was a disc jockey on WUST in Washington he had met Baylor when the latter was promoting a record called "Missing You" (KoKo 103). Bell remembered thinking the artist, Luther Ingram, was a hell of a vocalist, and suggested to Baylor that it would be a mutually beneficial relationship if Stax distributed KoKo.

talistic society to perpetuate our culture, our history, educate our children, et cetera. Dr. King's death reinforced that thinking in me and I set out from that point forward to make sure that as an African-American that whatever it was I was doing in this music business that I was going to aid in the development of that economic base. I felt that the music of African-Americans was about the only music that America could claim as its own. It was our natural resource, it was our gold, it was our magnesium, it was our oil, and it was with this natural resource that we would be able to build our economic base."

One of the first things Al did was hire a black secretary, Earlie Biles. Biles was twenty-one at the time and got the job interview through an employment agency. Interestingly, although she had grown up in Memphis and lived there until 1965, at which point she headed off to Los Angeles for college, she was not aware of Stax. When she came in for her interview, she was not overly impressed. "The first person I saw was Isaac Hayes, and he walked up with some floral Bermuda shorts, some thongs, no shirt, and says, 'Hi, you applying for a job here?' I said, 'My God, who are you? Yes I am.' I thought, 'Oh, okay, where am I?' I had on a suit, very conservative."

Biles was interviewed by Jim Stewart because Al Bell was out of town. Stewart gave her shorthand and typing tests that Biles found somewhat laughable. "I made some comments about the test they gave 'cause it wasn't well written. They were trying to give me a test on something [and] they didn't know what they were doing. I was just letting them know for future candidates. But they liked that. I really wasn't sure I wanted to work there."

Once her initial reluctance was overcome, Biles took the job and became Bell's secretary. As the company grew and Al Bell increasingly ran the whole operation, Biles, who was promoted to be his administrative assistant, would wield a substantial amount of power. She quite quickly became protective of Al Bell and the mission he had before him. That mission was immense.

As the sun rose in Memphis on May 6, 1968, Stax had been effectively gutted. For all intents and purposes it was a new record company poised to issue its first few records. Three singles were released in May, one more in June, and a further three in July. Of those seven releases on either Stax or Volt, three—Booker T. and the MG's "Soul Limbo," Eddie Floyd's "I've Never Found a Girl (To Love Me Like You Do)," and William Bell and Judy Clay's duet on "Private Number"—were bona fide chart hits. It was an auspicious beginning. All were cut on the company's newly acquired Scully eight-track recorder.

So as not to confuse distributors, Stax and Atlantic had agreed that Stax would use a new numbering system, logo, and color of paper for their labels. Jack Levy at Gulf and Western designed the now-famous finger-snapping logo that first appeared on Stax 0001, Booker T. and the MG's hit recording "Soul Limbo."

"We heard reggae and calypso for the first time," recalls Booker T. "Al Jackson was trying to imitate some of that music and he came up with that beat. He played that beat for two or three days before we came up with the melody and the bass line. It was a sixties attempt at playing some Jamaican-type music."

Al Bell remembers hearing the tape and, in his own words, thought it was a "smash on the MG's but we got work to do on it." For some time now Steve Cropper had been taking Stax material over to John Fry's Ardent Recording Studios for what Ardent engineer Terry Manning describes as "adding colors" and giving shape to the final sound. Following Al Bell's advice, Cropper took the basic track for "Soul Limbo" over to Ardent.[4]

---

4. Manning thought at the time that "Soul Limbo" was being called "Island Girl" or some variation thereof. In an article in the June 29th issue of the *Tri-State Defender,* the song is referred to as "Limbo Rock." At this stage of the game it is impossible to know if this is a mistake on the writer's part or if this was at some point the song's actual title.

"There was something missing," remembers Manning. "We had tried two or three things to put in there . . . that would color it and it wasn't doing what [Cropper] really wanted." Cropper recalls at one point beating spoons on glasses attempting to achieve the desired effect. That proved unsatisfactory, but then he and Manning noticed a marimba sitting in the corner of the studio that was left over from an earlier jingle session.

"Steve and I at the same time," continues Manning, "saw each other looking at it and we thought 'Island,' you know, that sort of feel. This could be a sort of steel drum kind of thing. We had talked about steel drums. So he said 'Go out and mess with it.' I just started mess-ing with it and I think during the second take, it just sort of flowed." Manning's marimba part meshed perfectly with Isaac Hayes, who was doing double duty, playing piano and an overdubbed cowbell figure. The combination drove "Soul Limbo" all the way to number 7 R&B, number 17 pop, and number 32 on the easy-listening chart, selling approximately 470,000 copies in the process. Stax Mark II was off and running in a big way. The funny thing was that Manning had never played marimba before, but after the record went Top Ten, he began to receive calls to play the instrument on many other people's sessions.

"Soul Limbo" in many respects signaled a new beginning for Stax and the MG's. Once the company was sold to Gulf and Western, it hired additional promotion and sales person-nel. The effect was felt immediately. "We didn't really get the airplay we deserved until 'Soul Limbo,'" Steve Cropper asserts. "Instrumentals had a tough way to go anyway. There was a period of time when it was sort of fashionable to do it [but in general] we had trouble get-ting airplay because disc jockeys did not like playing songs without vocals on them. It got worse and worse and worse until they finally pushed every instrumental band in the country out of business." Every instrumental band, that is, except Booker T. and the MG's. For the remaining three years of the group's original career, they would enjoy success after success.

The same week that "Soul Limbo" entered the rhythm-and-blues charts, Stax 0002, Eddie Floyd's "I've Never Found a Girl (To Love Me Like You Do)," also made its chart debut. The song was a three-way collaboration between Floyd, Booker T. Jones, and Al Bell. Floyd and Bell wrote the basic idea with Jones helping to finish it off. The song was completed at 2 A.M. "We called Al Jackson up at two in the morning," Floyd recalls, laugh-ing. "I said, 'Man, get up, c'mon, you've got to.'" A somewhat sleepy Al Jackson arrived at the studio, drumsticks in hand, and, with the multitalented Booker T. laying down bass, guitar, and keyboard tracks, the song was completed by morning.

Strings had been used at Stax as early as 1961 on some of Carla Thomas's records, beginning with her Top 10 hit "Gee Whiz (Look at His Eyes)." In general, though, the readily identifiable sound that the company had developed was predicated on the notion that "less is more." Consequently, on the vast body of material released by Stax in the six-ties, strings were not to be found. Background vocals were also used sparingly, with horns often supplying the support that background singers would give to pop and R&B records made for other companies.

Starting in 1967, Jones began experimenting with strings on some of William Bell's recordings. Isaac Hayes and David Porter did likewise with Sam and Dave in early 1968. "I've Never Found a Girl" marks the point where strings began to become a regular com-ponent of the Stax sound as it manifested itself in the last few years of the 1960s.

Heavy use of strings would become commonplace in most black music in the 1970s, particularly at Stax in the work of Isaac Hayes and the productions of the Detroit-based Don Davis. In 1968 and early 1969, Booker took care of most of the company's string writing, using a much lighter, at times nearly transparent touch.

"I was the person best suited for that," explains Jones. "That was sort of my position, if there was something about music that had to be put on paper or intellectualized at all, then they would get me. My string arrangements were a basic concept springing out of what I had learned about theory. I would just find what I thought was the optimum range for the strings according to where the vocal was, and then just write pretty much basic, quiet arrangements. We were restricted by money. If we hired cellos, it was one; if we hired violas, it was one." According to Isaac Hayes, strings had not been used more often in the past because of "budgets and Jim's restrictions. He wanted to keep that raw, funky sound."

"The problem we had then was that Stax was viewed as a company that was coming up with that 'Bama music," stresses Al Bell. "We had a problem in getting the product played outside of the South, across the Mason-Dixon line. When you got into the bigger urban centers, they were doing the Motown stuff. Being a jock I knew that and then traveling all over the place, I knew what was happening to us in the record stores and what was happening to us at the radio level and on the street level with our music. I started looking to diversify the company and, at that time, I was talking to everybody in there about broadening the music so we could go into New York, Philadelphia, Boston, Washington, and Baltimore much more formidably.

"The position that I had been trying to influence production to get into was maintaining the roots music that we had, but broadening and diversifying the sound. 'I've Never Found a Girl' was one of the first shots at that. The person that was able to contribute most to that, who thought much broader than the roots music that we had been coming up with, was Booker T. Booker was the learned guy. Booker was the only guy on staff who could write music and he was an arranger. That's why that music at that time."

Jones's work on "I've Never Found a Girl" is exemplary. The song begins with a gorgeous upper-string melody played by violins and violas. Cellos play a subtle countermelody to Floyd's vocal on the verse, beginning with the line "It's like burning fire all shut up in my bones." Booker's most masterful touch, though, is the employment of the violins playing pizzicato during the guitar break. The effect is exquisite. Strings were still novel enough at Stax that Eddie Floyd remembers being all excited when he went to the studio to see Booker record the string track. "I've always been a little fascinated with the guys who direct," Floyd says, chuckling.

The lyric line "It's like burning fire shut up in my bones" is one of the most visceral in soul music. Al Bell "borrowed" it from a gospel record by Cleophus Robinson. Robinson, in turn, had taken the image straight out of the Bible, where it appears in Jeremiah 20:9: "His word was in mine heart as a burning fire shut up in my bones. . . ." Robinson, of course, was talking about the Holy Spirit and the power of God. Eddie Floyd and Al Bell were talking about the power of love. "That was so poignant," relates Bell. "To say, 'like burning fire shut up in my bones' was, to me, the most powerful statement one could make in describing something."

The lyrics, string arrangement, Floyd's aching vocal, and Ollie and the Nightingales' affirmative responses combined to take "I've Never Found a Girl" all the way to number 2 on the R&B charts, but it could only make it to number 40 on the pop charts. Although "Soul Limbo" and "I've Never Found a Girl" were issued in the first weeks of May to maintain some continuity in having a Stax presence in the marketplace, the Gulf and Western purchase of Stax did not occur officially until May 29, 1968. Because neither record entered *Billboard*'s charts until July 13, for all intents and purposes G&W enjoyed the fruits of the success of both releases.

Stax's next chart entry, the William Bell–Judy Clay duet on "Private Number," came about via fortuitous accident. Booker T. Jones and William Bell had been working on the song with Otis Redding and Carla Thomas in mind. "I'd write about life," recounts

William Bell, "either my personal experiences or something that I had observed. I'd been out on tour and when I came home, there was this one young lady that I was seeing. I could not reach her because the number had been changed. I was kicking this around and one night during a writing session with Booker I told him about this idea."

That particular writing session produced the first verse, the basic melody, and the chorus. Shortly thereafter, Jones and Bell happened to be in the studio when a session for Judy Clay was coming to a close. William Bell picks up the story: "She completed the session early and she needed something to record. So we said, 'Give us an hour.' We sat there and completed 'Private Number' in the studio."

Clay had problems learning the song, so Bell recorded what he thought was a demo with which Clay could take her time in learning. Clay recorded her vocal the next day and someone, most likely Booker, thought that parts of Bell's demo should be combined with Clay. "Neither one of us had any idea that it was gonna be a duet," laughs Bell. The net result was a number 17 R&B hit that edged its way to number 75 on the pop charts.

Helping to turn these new releases into hits were the new executives Bell and Stewart had hired as they moved toward being a full-line record company. Bernard Roberson was brought in to help Bell with promotion, while Ewell Roussell came onboard to head up the newly formed sales department.

Roberson had never been involved in the record industry before. A native Memphian, he had been doing promotion of various sorts on an independent basis for a number of Memphis-area bars and stores. Rather than hiring a proven talent from another record label, Bell decided to give Roberson a shot at the big time, personally training him. Such a move was typical of Bell's modus operandi of developing people and capital within the

Bernard Roberson outside the Stax studio at 926 E. McLemore Avenue. Note the Satellite Record Shop attached to the studio on the right. COURTESY FANTASY, INC.

African-American community.[5] Roussell had been working for the Delta Distribution Co. in Memphis,[6] which handled the Stax and Atlantic lines in the mid-South area. In his mid-twenties, he was worried that he was too inexperienced. "Then I found out they'd never had to do it either," laughs Roussell. "It had always been Atlantic doing it. It was just a whole bunch of young people with an awful lot of nerve, man, that just believed in the music and went at it." Roussell's official title was vice president of sales. In reality, for most of his tenure at Stax, he was in charge of 45 sales, as in February 1969 Herb Kole was hired to be in charge of the marketing of LP's.

When Bell and Roberson were on the road doing promotion work, after they visited the radio stations, they would go to the local distributor and take inventory. This would normally be the work of the salespeople. By structuring duties in this manner, Bell freed up Roussell to be more aggressive in his efforts to actually sell the product, receiving feedback on distributor inventories much faster than if he had had to make periodic road trips on his own.

Also brought on-line in this period was Robert Harris. A former IRS agent, Harris became the company's first full-time controller. There were a few other personnel moves as Stax made the transition from being distributed by Atlantic to being owned by Gulf and

5. Roberson would leave Stax for Hi Records in June 1970.

6. Which eventually became Hot Line Distributors.

Western. Estelle Axton pulled out of the record shop to run the company's mail room, where Mike Williams and William Brown joined her. Williams's story is unique and speaks volumes for Bell and Stewart's method of operation. A classmate of the Bar-Kays at Booker T. Washington, Williams's brother-in-law, Benny Mabone, had long been a fixture at Stax, serving at various times as Eddie Floyd's road manager and as Isaac Hayes's personal assistant. In mid-1967, Jim Stewart needed someone to clean up the back alley behind the studio, and Benny recommended Williams. Stewart was impressed with Williams's work and offered him a part-time job as a handyman-cum-gofer, the latter entailing everything from fetching coffee and doughnuts to keeping the studio clean, helping to mail out records, and picking up artists at the airport. In 1968 Williams moved into the mail room, and in 1970 he was made a promotion man. When I interviewed him in 1985 he was comfortably ensconced in a middle-class home in the suburbs of Memphis, working promotion for RCA Records. As he sees it, Stax gave him an opportunity to make something out of himself when no other institution in Memphis, Tennessee, had the slightest inclination to do so. He freely volunteers, "Stax saved my life." Williams was not the only employee to start at Stax in a menial, unskilled position who was eventually promoted and taught a professional skill that he or she could use for the rest of his/her life within the industry.

Although everyone had their clear-cut functions, in mid-1968 Stax was still very much a small, grass-roots company. When it came time to mail out records to disc jockeys, everyone participated: Al, Jim, Estelle, Earlie Biles, Deanie Parker, Isaac Hayes, David Porter, and so on. Both Earlie Biles and William Brown described this activity as loaded with fun and good spirits, records scattered all over the place, everyone on the floor labeling, stuffing, and sealing envelopes. Despite some of the polarization brought on by Dr. King's death and a bit of the big-headedness and petty jealousy that was a natural by-product of success, the family spirit was still very much intact at 926 E. McLemore in mid-1968 as Stax charted its new destiny as a full-fledged record company.

With 10 percent equity in the company and Gulf and Western's money to spend, Al Bell began to implement what in retrospect might seem like a master plan of growth and expansion. By July, Stax had announced that it would be distributing Arch Records. Arch was a label established in St. Louis by Stax's old compadre Nick Charles. Its studio was located in his basement. Although it would appear that only five records were ever issued,[7] Arch was the first of a half-dozen or so distribution deals Bell would make over the next few years. That same month Bell had set up international distribution for the company in Canada, England, and France, with plans afoot to shortly make a deal in New Zealand and Australia. In October, it was announced that Stax would be establishing a New York office to be headed by new promotional coordinator Otis Pollard. White promotion man Eddie Braddock was brought onboard to work pop material, and a Stax press release emphatically declared that Bell and Stewart would be expanding the rosters of all their labels as well as signing new writers to the East Memphis Publishing Co. It was further suggested that in the future Stax would be expanding into easy listening and country.

That summer, Stax purchased its second eight-track, a Spectasonic board which was promptly installed in what had been designated as Studio B. Studio B had been set up a few months earlier, running mainly as a demo studio with the old four-track recorder. Located on the other side of the wall that Jim Stewart and Chips Moman had painstakingly installed some eight years earlier to divide the main theater space, it was about half the size of Studio A.

---

7. By the Del Rays (not the Jimmy Johnson group, but probably the same Del Rays who had a record issued by Stax in 1965), Lindell Hill, the Advarks, Fresh Air, and the Montclairs.

The Staple Singers: Mavis, Pervis (*hunched over a bass guitar*), Cleotha (*with head obscured*), and Pops, with Booker T. Jones (*at the keyboard*) and Steve Cropper (*front right*), at one of the Staples's first Stax sessions, December 20, 1968. Note the studio control room window in the upper left-hand corner. COURTESY DON PAULSEN.

By mid-1968 each member of the Big 6—the four members of Booker T. and the MG's and Isaac Hayes and David Porter—was nominally responsible for the production of specific artists. Steve Cropper manned the controls for newcomers the Staple Singers, as well as old hands Rufus Thomas and Eddie Floyd. Booker T. Jones produced William Bell. Al Jackson ostensibly ran the Mad Lads, Albert King, and Jimmy Hughes sessions, while Hayes and Porter produced the Soul Children, Charmells, and later the Emotions. MG bassist Duck Dunn seemed to have little interest in production, although he did coproduce Delaney and Bonnie with former Mar-Key saxophonist Don Nix.

In the summer of 1968, Steve Cropper was given the task of producing the Staple Singers. The Staples, a family group consisting of father Roebuck "Pops" Staples, son Pervis Staples, and daughters Cleotha and Mavis, had their roots in Mississippi but had been based in Chicago since the mid-1930s. When they signed with Stax on July 25, 1968, Pops was fifty-three, Cleotha thirty-four, Pervis thirty-three, and lead singer Mavis was the youngster at twenty-eight. They had recorded professionally as a family since 1953, starting out singing gospel for United and Vee Jay and then shifting in 1960 to Riverside. Later, at Epic Records, they attempted to broaden their audience by augmenting their religious repertoire with "message" songs such as Bob Dylan's "Blowin' in the Wind" and Stephen Stills's "For What It's Worth." In 1967 the latter reached the lower rungs of the pop charts, as did Pops's "Why? (Am I Treated So Bad)." Even so,

Epic was disappointed with the group's sales and on May 16, 1968, elected to forgo picking up their option.

Epic's loss was Stax's gain. It took a few years, but the Staple Singers would become one of the biggest R&B groups of the first half of the 1970s, hitting hard with such classic records as "Respect Yourself" and "I'll Take You There." The group was signed to Stax by Al Bell, whom they had known since the mid-fifties, when he used to play their records on his gospel radio show out of Little Rock; Bell also occasionally booked the band for a week at a time in the surrounding area.

"Ever since I've been in the record business," muses Bell, "one of my hidden desires was to record the Staple Singers. I was just so in love with their singing style. I used to play their music on the air a lot as a jock when I was in Little Rock. The minute I got to Stax and got an opportunity to reach out for them I did. I always believed that the Staple Singers could be one of the biggest acts in the world."

Cropper initially paired the Staples with a Homer Banks composition, "Long Walk to D.C.," recording them with Pop's heavily reverbed guitar front and center. The record virtually duplicates the approach the group had taken with Epic, singing "protest" material against a "folk rock"–oriented beat.

"The songwriters at Stax knew we were doing protest songs," recounts Mavis. "We had made a transition back there in the sixties with Dr. King. We visited Dr. King's church in Montgomery before the movement actually got started. When we heard Dr. King preach, we went back to the motel and had a meeting. Pops said, 'Now if he can preach this, we can sing it. That could be our way of helping towards this movement.' We put a beat behind the song. We were mainly focusing on the young adults to hear what we were doing. You know if they hear a beat, that would make them listen to the words. So we started singing protest songs. All those guys were writing what we actually wanted them to write. Pops would tell them to just read the headlines and whatever they saw in the morning paper that needed to be heard or known about, [they would] write us a song from that."

Homer Banks had been waiting for just such an opportunity. "At the time I was caught up in the cultural revolution," he emphasizes. "They were a group that was really open for that type of material." Unfortunately, "Long Walk to D.C." did not chart. But, in the Staples' case, massive success would be only two years away.

While Steve Cropper was working on a suitable approach for the Staple Singers, the talented team of Isaac Hayes and David Porter was working on the first Soul Children records. In late 1967 Hayes and Porter were on the lookout for new artists. Having achieved major success with the dynamic duo of Sam and Dave, they naturally kicked around the idea of putting together another pair of vocalists. Porter felt that using two male vocalists would be too obvious a Sam and Dave cop, and he wasn't wild about the idea of a female duo. Putting two and two together, he came up with the ingenious idea of putting a quartet together comprised of two men and two women.

Hayes and Porter had already been trying to record John Colbert, who performed under the moniker "J. Blackfoot." "Foot," as he is commonly referred to, was born in Greenville, Mississippi. Coming to Memphis at the age of four, he had grown up in a pretty rough section of the city. Engaged in any number of petty crimes, he ended up doing time in prison from 1964 to 1967. While in jail he shared a cell with Johnny Bragg of the aptly named Prisonaires. Like Bragg, he was given his first chance to record while cooling his heels behind the jailhouse bars, releasing a single on Nashville's Sure Speed label.

Upon his release Blackfoot headed back to Memphis. There he enticed David Porter to audition him in Payne's Cafe, singing along with a jukebox playing Mickey Murray's cover of Otis Redding's "Shout Bamalama." Porter was knocked out, and for quite a while he and Hayes tried to find the right vehicle for their new solo star. In Porter's words, "We were not as focused as far as the pocket for him as we should have been. The music didn't have that thing to it. We were trying to have just a little bit more pop into him. It should have been pop with soul." It was while they were working with Blackfoot that the idea for a quartet came about.

The next Soul Children recruit was Norman West. West hailed from Monroe, Louisiana. He had come to Memphis in 1963 to join William Bell's old group, the Del-Rios, after Bell had his first solo hit, "You Don't Miss Your Water." West stayed with the Del-Rios for a very short time before Flamingo Room owner Clifford Miller convinced him to go solo. He recorded his first record for Miller's Christy label and then Willie Mitchell hooked him up with Hi Records. West recorded two records for Hi and one for the Hi subsidiary M.O.C. before signing with Smash. In 1967 West had two records released on Smash, at least one of which was coproduced by Curtis Johnson, formerly of the underrated Stax vocal group the Astors.

When Hayes and Porter approached West about joining the Soul Children, he was performing nightly in Memphis's Down Under Club in an integrated band called Colors Incorporated that took R&B tunes and combined them with acid rock. The effect was apparently quite something to behold.

With Blackfoot and West in tow, two women were still needed to complete the Soul Children's lineup. David Porter had heard soprano Anita Louis singing on local black station WDIA as part of the Teen Town Singers. Smitten with the seventeen-year-old's voice, Porter went down to 'DIA to audition her. "I [then] went and met with her mother," says Porter. "She was very religious, and I reassured her that Anita would be watched and [her] integrity would always be considered."

The huskier-voiced Shelbra Bennett simply walked into the Stax studios on McLemore Street and said that she wanted a chance to be heard. "How lucky can you be?" Porter says, laughing. "Shelbra came into the place and had that sound. We thought that was it!" With the four members intact, Hayes and Porter cut two songs with them that the producers had already attempted on Blackfoot solo, the up-tempo "Give 'Em Love" and a ballad, "I'll Understand."

The fast-paced "Give 'Em Love" was atypical for Hayes, Porter and Stax. Previously the company had tended to shy away from up-tempo tunes, concentrating on mid-tempo songs and slow ballads. Porter concedes that they were uneasy about quicker tempos. "To be quite honest we never felt comfortable with it. Motown had a lock on the way they did it. We thought it was more soulful to be toward the pocket we had. When we tried something up there, it would always feel strange to us."

Also slightly different was drummer Al Jackson's four evenly accented quarter-beat approach, and the separation of the horn section on the second verse so that the trumpet and sax played different lines in response to each other. Finally, the song is a little less melodic than was typical of Hayes and Porter compositions. With the lead split between Blackfoot and West, who were paired together, and Louis and Bennett, who answered them, the record managed to dent the R&B charts, reaching the number 40 position.

As was becoming increasingly common at Stax, the Soul Children's followup, November's "I'll Understand," benefited from a Booker T. Jones string arrangement. If "Give 'Em Love" was somewhat tentative, "I'll Understand" was nothing short of brilliant. Hayes and Porter had written one of the greatest cheating songs of all time. Blackfoot took the lead at the beginning, with West,

Jo Bridges and Deanie Parker take a close look at the second issue of Stax Fax. COURTESY DEANIE PARKER.

Louis, and Bennett singing the responses. Anita Louis took over the lead on the second verse. By record's end, all four singers milked the song's tension for everything it was worth. What had not worked with Blackfoot as a solo artist is nearly too much to bear in the hands of the Soul Children.

"That was when we said, 'Well to hell with it.'" explains Porter. "Let's go on and take it all the way down to the floor. That was the reason for saying the Soul Children—take it all the way to church. We just got real with it." "I'll Understand" surpassed the group's debut, reaching number 29 on *Billboard*'s R&B charts.

In the midst of all this frenetic activity, Deanie Parker was launching *Stax Fax* magazine. The first issue came out in early fall 1968; the eleventh and final issue was mailed out just over a year later. During that period, the magazine grew from four to forty pages with a glossy cover. Originally designed as a tool to develop a national fan club for Stax, Stax and *Stax Fax* grew at such a rate that a national fan club quickly became a nonviable proposition.

The first issue was mailed to somewhere between two and three hundred individuals with the addresses obtained from a direct mail house as well as Stax's press list. Invariably, other people would see it and write the company requesting future issues. "I remember the first mailing that we made," relates Deanie. "We did get some hate mail back. People didn't want us mailing this 'communist propaganda' to their homes. It's black, that makes it communist. I remember that very distinctly. That was my first experience with anything like that."

Stax Fax was a mixed bag. While it was obviously designed to promote the company with each issue containing record release information, general artist news, a profile of the artist of the month, and an executive message, *Stax Fax* also contained articles on topics such as black identity and struggle, college students cheating, the National Association of Television and Radio Announcers (NATRA), sex education, racism, smoking, the lack of exposure for R&B artists on television, Reverend C. L. Franklin, black reporters leaving black newspapers for white media jobs, abortion counselors, Operation Breadbasket, and so on. *Stax Fax* even regularly printed articles on other labels' artists.[8] It was clearly a unique publication.

"It had a twofold purpose," explains Deanie. "It was larger than just Stax. We recognized the sensitivity to other great black artists who might not have had an opportunity for exposure. I think that was one of the things that made us unique. We did share, we did give, we were community conscious, socially conscious, civil rights conscious."

Whenever the newest issue of *Stax Fax* was ready to mail, the high school kids who made up the Memphis Stax/Volt fan club would come in each day for a week after school and head toward the company's conference room. "That was a part of another community effort on Stax's part," stresses Deanie. "Most of these children were what I consider to be somewhat underprivileged. In addition to the fact that the fan club gave us an opportunity to help them direct their attention to something positive as opposed to some things that they could have been doing, this vehicle had started growing so fast [that] we needed manpower to get it out, prepare it for the mail. We brought these children and paid them to prepare these things. We created jobs for children here in the community just to get this mailing out. As the mail list grew we allowed them an opportunity to help us build our list, dealing with the mechanics of it."

One of the most significant aspects of the *Stax Fax* adventure was that Deanie Parker

8. Various issues contained articles on non-Stax artists such as Young-Holt Unlimited, James Brown, the Isley Brothers, Aretha Franklin, and Nina Simone.

had absolutely no experience editing, publishing, or distributing a magazine, and neither did anyone else at Stax. It was both Al and Jim's philosophy to allow people to be adventurous, to try things and to learn as they went. "That's one of the things that I am very appreciative of Stax for," beams Deanie. "Giving me an opportunity to take something that I had never done before and to go to that extent. That was my college."[9]

While Deanie Parker was working up the first issue of *Stax Fax*, Al Bell, in what would prove to be a decisive and controversial move, had brought a producer from Detroit, Don Davis, into the Stax family. Bell had been introduced to Davis in 1967 by former Memphian and member of Carla Thomas's graduating class Detroit disc jockey Wash Allen.

"I was talking to Wash about Carla Thomas," asserts Bell. "Carla hadn't had a big hit [in a while] and I was trying to find somebody out of that end of the country that could produce a big hit on Carla because I felt Carla could potentially be like Diana Ross. I thought her appeal was on that level. The term I used at that time was 'cross-fertilization': Memphis and Detroit. . . . To me it seemed if one could come up with a cross-fertilization of Memphis and Detroit, musically you would have *the* thing in the marketplace. You'd have the guts on the bottom with Stax and have the middle and top, the lyrics, and everything else that Motown had."

Davis was a guitarist who had played on some of the very early Motown sessions. He had also co-owned Thelma Records with Berry Gordy's ex-wife and her mother, and he had started his own Groovesville label, as well as working as a guitarist and producer for the Golden World, Wingate, and Revilot labels. In May 1967 he had produced a Top 10 R&B hit for J. J. Barnes on Groovesville entitled "Baby Please Come Back Home."

That same year, Davis coproduced with Al Bell "Pick Up the Pieces" for Carla Thomas. The arrangement was so Detroit that the record could have been issued on Motown and no one would have been the wiser.[10] In November 1967 Stax issued a press release that telegraphed Bell's vision of musical cross-pollinization. Headed "Do Mixed Marriages Work?" it was subtitled "(Carla Thomas Unites Detroit and Memphis)." The press release went on to crow, "This mixed marriage is the first of its kind ever performed because it involves the uniting of the musical sounds dominating the popular music field of today . . . the 'Memphis Sound' and the Detroit Sound. . . . The offspring of this mixed marriage is a record that combines the best of sounds." A number 16 R&B hit, "Pick Up the Pieces" was not the monster record Bell had envisioned, but it did well enough that nearly a year later he called Davis again, having decided to make the Detroit producer an integral part of the company.

Davis came down to Memphis and produced Jeanne and the Darlings' September 1968 release "It's Unbelievable (How You Control My Soul)." The Darlings' single sank without a trace, but Davis's next effort, Johnnie Taylor's "Who's Making Love," would prove to be Stax's biggest record to date, selling 850,000 copies before the end of the year, and two million copies before its chart run was over! It would be the first of eight straight singles Davis would produce with Taylor that would break into the R&B Top 10.

"Who's Making Love" was written by Homer Banks, Bettye Crutcher, and Raymond Jackson. Born in 1939, Crutcher had been trying to break into Stax for a good two years. A nurse and single parent with three boys, Crutcher would leave work at three o'clock, go home, cook dinner for her kids, and then head to the studio where she'd stay until four in the morning. She had originally tried to interest Hi in her writing, but found that pro-

9. At least ten people I interviewed in the course of my Stax research described Stax as their college or university.

10. Davis had earlier cut the song on Detroit vocalists Willie Jones and Steve Mancha.

We Three songwriting team: (*left to right*) Raymond Jackson, Bettye Crutcher, and Homer Banks.
COURTESY DEANIE PARKER.

ducer Willie Mitchell didn't have the time to listen to her songs and Don Bryant, after a cursory listen, didn't think they were anything special. At Stax she was scheduled to audition for Deanie, but when she arrived at the studio Deanie was nowhere to be found so, in her own words, "David Porter got roped into it." Porter told her that her songs were good but they weren't bluesy enough; Crutcher had been mainly listening to singers such as Nancy Wilson and Dionne Warwick. Nothing if not determined, she came back a week later with the extremely bluesy "Somebody's Sleeping in My Bed," which eventually was recorded by Johnnie Taylor in the fall of 1967.

Crutcher was primarily a lyricist, so Booker was assigned to write with her. Unfortunately for Crutcher, he had neither the time nor the interest. "I'm just a new writer and I am a female and the only one in the department," recalls Crutcher. "At first the guys were like most guys, they'd just think, 'Well, this is a new piece of meat on the block and it'll peter out.' But, see, I was not for that. After the guys realized that wasn't going to happen, they got serious. They were not serious in the beginning with me. Booker just thought I was going to be something to play with. They didn't give me any breaks, believe me. They loved me but when it came to the studio, it was like I was still somebody off the street.

"There was no giving you a helping hand. There was nobody saying, 'Hey, c'mon in and sit down and let's see if you can get a song on this session.' None of that. The only way I would get a song on a session, I was just persistent. I mean, I was just there. They were going to listen to me until they got tired of me. They actually didn't have much of a choice but to listen to me!" Crutcher's basic attitude was that she would write with anybody. Over the years at Stax she penned material with Marvell Thomas, Mack Rice, Bobby Manuel, Allen Jones, Homer Banks, and Raymond Jackson.

Raymond Jackson was Homer Banks's old gospel and doo-wop singing partner. After Jackson was discharged from the army in early 1968, Banks immediately resumed writing with him. Their first effort that was recorded at Stax was Johnnie Taylor's February 1968 release, "Next Time." When they wrote "Who's Making Love," Banks and Jackson had just begun to work with Crutcher. The three writers would remain together about a year and a half, by mid-1969 crediting themselves simply as "We Three." "Who's Making Love" got their writing partnership off to a meteoric start.

The initial impetus for the song, according to Homer, was Frank Sinatra. "I heard him on television," Banks remembers, laughing. "He had a song entitled 'Who's Taking Care of the Caretaker's Daughter While the Caretaker's Out Taking Care.' I said, 'Now some kind of way I've got to bring this into the reality where people in rhythm and blues can relate to it more.' Naturally they're going to relate to who's making love—that's the thing. I had funny feelings about it at first because I said, 'Now is this infringement or what?' It's a parallel framework, even the phrasing is the same in the title. But, then again, very few people had ever heard [Sinatra's song]. The melody wasn't the same, no other words were the same, [but] his idea triggered mine."

Banks had presented the song to the producers' pool—the MG's, Isaac Hayes, and David Porter—and been rejected.[11] When Don Davis heard Banks's demo and expressed interest, Banks stretched the truth and said that it had been written specifically for Johnnie Taylor. Davis was already looked upon as an outsider and resented by the Big 6; now he was choosing a song that they had already rejected. In what was already an acrimonious situation, this was just one more gesture that created an unbridgeable chasm between Davis and the producers' pool.

Part of the problem from Bettye Crutcher's vantage point was Davis's attitude. "Don was kind of authoritative," recalls Crutcher. "He came in like a mover and a shaker [although] Don Davis had not done anything so spectacular before. But when he came to Stax, he acted like he was somebody special. Here these guys are already here, they're the real core of this operation, and then Don comes in and it just kind of loosened the glue a little bit."[12]

Many others at Stax agreed with Crutcher's assessment. Perhaps the root of the problem was simply Davis's no-nonsense northern ways: southern diplomacy was not his specialty. Exacerbating the situation was the fact that he was given a powerful position that many felt should have gone to a Memphian who had already put in years of service at the company. Carla Thomas, in particular, was livid that Bell planned to make Davis a vice president in charge of A&R. In her mind, that position should have gone to Booker T.

11. Sam Moore remembers the song and thought that Sam and Dave would have cut it had Atlantic and Stax not severed their relationship.

12. Despite Crutcher's antipathy toward Davis's demeanor, she and Banks were also outsiders and, to some degree, Don Davis represented their salvation. "We didn't have a real outlet for our material," stresses Crutcher, "until Don Davis came. As a result, we got a lot of songs on Johnnie Taylor because, as far as Don Davis was concerned, there was no other place to turn."

Jones; Booker most likely agreed. He never played a session for Davis and, by mid-1969, had left Memphis and Stax sessions altogether.

Many at Stax believed that Davis fundamentally altered the Stax sound. Of course, this is what Al Bell wanted to combat the perception of Stax as producing what Bell termed "that 'Bama music." Ironically, Davis was dying to get close to some of that Stax roots music. In his words, "The records in Detroit were too polished and did not have enough of the real earthly gospel simplicity to them. I was used to hearing rhythm played in a certain way. I had never, ever heard it the way that I heard it in Memphis. This was back to the sanctified church. The music was so powerful that I literally cried. It just filled me with so much feeling and it vibrated me in such a way that it just over-powered all of my emotions. I knew that it was a sound that I had been missing all through my life. In Memphis, there was still that real hardcore approach which meant you sang the song until you got it right."

The two things that Davis admired most about Stax were the MG's and the company's approach to horn lines. "I just never heard horns play like that and act like they acted," Davis says. "When I recorded with the MG's it was just the stuff I always wanted to do. The stuff I did in Detroit was to me just an outlet, [an] escape kind of thing. The things that I was doing in Memphis were gratifying kinds of things.

"The sound in Memphis differed from the sound in Detroit inasmuch as there was a people difference. The people in Memphis, particularly at that time, were more real. The people in Detroit were cosmopolitan, superficial, [they] like saying things in a very super-ficial way. They like saying things in Memphis in a very up-front, in a very real way. The contrast of the real versus the superficial whether it's in the music or the lyrics could read-ily be seen between the Detroit sound and the Memphis sound."

Initially unsure of himself, Davis asked Isaac Hayes to help him with the horn lines on "Who's Making Love." "I said, 'Isaac, just give me a couple of lines 'cause I don't know how these guys work.' He came over to the studio with me and, boy, I just thought I had died and went to heaven. Those guys are so innovative with those horns, so rhyth-mic with them."

Interestingly, Johnnie Taylor hated "Who's Making Love," referring to it as "the boogi-ty boogity song." He thought it was too fast. Davis bullied him into recording it. "Johnnie really bitched about doing the song," explains Davis. "I just kept telling him he wasn't singing the song. I just kept harassing him really. I said, 'I'm just going to give the song to Sam and Dave, you can forget it.' That was a big challenge to his ego."

William Brown likens Davis to a Charles Bronson character, because he would never lose his cool. Psychology appears to have been his forte. Always pushing for one more take, Davis would often take the artist aside, get a cup of coffee and say, "Man, don't you want to be on Johnny Carson? Don't you want to be on Ed Sullivan? Well then, give me one more take." Invariably he'd get it.

Hayes's cohort, David Porter, coached Taylor through his vocal performance as well as coming up with Taylor's unforgettable scream-followed-by-"hear-me-now" introduction. Davis played guitar on the record alongside Steve Cropper and Raymond Jackson, leav-ing engineer Ronnie Capone to run the mixing console. Two million sales later, Taylor had topped the R&B charts and sailed to the number 5 pop slot.

According to engineer Ron Capone, Taylor was uncomfortable with the then-new concept at Stax of wearing headphones and overdubbing the lead vocal on a finished vocal track, claiming that he could never cut a hit record that way. After "Who's Making Love" turned his career inside out, he decided headphones and overdubbing weren't so bad after all.

While Al Bell may have been expansionist-oriented, he still had visions of community. In his mind Don Davis would simply become part of the Stax family, and would automatically be a member of the producers' pool. Such an assumption betrays Bell's surprising lack of awareness of how protective the core of the Stax family felt. The Big 6 were not in the least interested in opening up the production pool. Given the fact that Wayne Jackson and Andrew Love were not even included in that hallowed group, there was no way a total outsider, let alone one who tended to be authoritative, had a fundamentally different approach to recording, and was a Northerner to boot, was going to be welcomed into the club. Neither Bell nor Davis was happy about this. The alternative was to give Davis 100 percent of the production royalty on records that he did produce, rather than split the take among the pool as it was done with the all the MG's and Hayes-Porter productions. This didn't sit well with the MG's.

"All of a sudden he's gonna come down there," exclaims Cropper, "and just start using us and put his name on it? All of a sudden we're not producing anymore? Yet we're doing the same thing we've always done? The only thing different is that he's in the room. Actually, he's somewhere else on the telephone, which really upset us. We cut two or three hits for him and he wasn't even in the room." "We weren't doing anything different," stresses Duck. "We were contributing just as much to his records as we were to anybody else's and then they just shut that off [the production royalty] from us. That's hard to accept." Al Jackson suggested that Davis give the session musicians a percentage of the production royalty. This never came to pass, and the resulting enmity was one more dagger in the heart of the original Stax family. Don Davis would eventually eschew recording in Memphis altogether, cutting all his basic tracks in Muscle Shoals instead.

Bringing Davis in was a brilliant move on Bell's part from a marketing angle. Bell's notion that a cross-fertilization of Memphis and Detroit would be potent in the marketplace was proven correct by the success enjoyed by Taylor and, later, the Dramatics. Unfortunately, Bell hadn't taken into account the reaction of the original Stax players and producers.

There was further fallout surrounding Davis's production of Carla Thomas singing Homer Banks, Raymond Jackson, and Bettye Crutcher's "I Like What You're Doing (To Me)." The first record issued by Stax in January 1969, it started the year off on a positive note, ascending to number 9 on the R&B charts while settling at number 49 on the pop charts. Despite the fact that the record was a hit, tensions between Davis and the Memphis-based Stax contingent were on the rise. Carla was particularly upset by Davis's working methods. By now it was standard practice at Stax for vocalists to record their part after the basic rhythm track was cut.

"When he came back to cut me," complains Thomas, "the whole song was finished. I didn't know it. He just had the rhythm tracks turned up [in Carla's headphones] and I was cutting. After he started turning the horns on, I turned blue. I said, 'This is awful, the horns are awful.' I said, 'This is not Stax!' That could have been a bigger hit record had it not been for his arrangement on the top. If he had let [Mar-Key horns] Andrew and Wayne just cut it. . . . But, you see, it was *his* thing, and Memphis musicians were not good enough. He should have stayed in Detroit!"

Davis, as was his custom, had cut the horns in Detroit. Such practices not only offended the Memphians at the company, they also rang up additional costs that were charged back to the artists against their future royalties.[13] Davis himself played the

---

13. In 1997, royalties earned on Carla Thomas reissues are still going to pay off this kind of debt!

Steve Cropper and Don Davis. COURTESY DEANIE PARKER.

crackling, low-end guitar part while, to Carla's delight, songwriter Homer Banks sang along with Thomas on the word "baby" on the chorus. "That's why [that line has] soul," adds Thomas dryly.

Things got really hot when Bell decided to make Davis vice president in charge of A&R. "I was oblivious," admits Bell. "I really found out [how much Davis was resented] when I brought him inside the company and was beginning to put A and R under him. That's when I started getting the resistance and I realized I had all kinds of political problems. I was still immature at that time and didn't handle all of that quite well, either. I think I came out of that bloodied. I don't think I handled it too well with Don, nor did I handle it well with the people internally. . . . I was somewhat idealistic in terms of how I felt the creative people ought to mesh . . . and move past a lot of politics. I jumped into a hornet's nest and I was getting my butt spanked from both sides. It was a big problem."

The proverbial shit hit the fan when Isaac Hayes found out that Davis was now in charge of A&R. "I led a rebellion," Hayes declares. "We even shut the company down for a day. Told all the secretaries, everybody, 'Y'all go home.' I walked in with my little army, had guns and everything. We shut it down. It couldn't happen like that. We tried to reason. That didn't work so we did what we had to do. I won't say Don was a victim but he walked into a situation and I don't think he knew how volatile it could be. I don't think Al knew [either]. I guess Al thought we'd just roll over and say, 'hey, okay' but no, no, no. You cannot do that, especially when we helped build this company. We had put a lot of work in there. We deserved better than that."

The net effect of Isaac's rebellion was that every member of the Big 6 was made a vice president. Isaac became the senior vice president in charge of production and A&R. Ultimately, though, these vice presidencies seem to have been little more than paper titles.

In October 1968, the same month that "Who's Making Love" was released, "Hang 'Em High" and "Over Easy" were pulled from the *Soul Limbo* LP to comprise Booker T. and the MG's sixteenth 45. The A-side was a cover version of the theme song from the Clint Eastwood movie of the same name. Composer Dominic Frontiere had sent Booker a tape of the movie version which the MG's then proceeded to radically rearrange into a broodingly intense *tour de force*. Steve Cropper and Al Jackson came up with the stop-time idea in the middle of the cut, while it was Booker's idea to change keys as the record progressed.

"It was pushing the envelope a little bit," reflects Booker. "It was out on the edge for 1968. At the time I was learning theory and studying music and it was very interesting for me to play a song in many different keys. It creates some of the tension to modulate up."

Frontiere was quite impressed with the MG's record, and approached Steve Cropper about working with him on three additional movies, including two more spaghetti westerns. The idea was that Cropper would work up the rhythm tracks and Frontiere would write the melodies. To Cropper's chagrin, Stax owner Jim Stewart would not allow him to do work outside of Stax. A year later, Stewart would anger Cropper and the other MG's further when he forbade them from playing on Simon and Garfunkel's "Bridge over Troubled Water."[14]

Curiously, "Hang 'Em High" fared relatively poorly with black audiences, stalling at number 35 R&B, while it made it all the way to number 9 pop! It was also the second MG single to show up on the easy-listening chart, albeit at the rather unimpressive 39th slot. Sales stopped at around the 110,000 mark.

Stax closed the year on December 21 with what was billed as "The Stax/Volt Yuletide Thing" at Memphis's Mid-South Coliseum. Appearing on the bill were a Who's Who of the company's stars including Booker T. and the MG's, Johnnie Taylor, Eddie Floyd, Carla Thomas, the Staple Singers, the newly reformed Bar-Kays, the Mad Lads, Rufus Thomas, Albert King, William Bell, and Judy Clay. To top the show off, Janis Joplin was invited to perform. No one remembers exactly how Janis Joplin came to play the show; Al Bell and Deanie Parker think that Joplin's people might have contacted Stax. In any event, having the current rock queen on the bill attracted members of the rock audience and, more important, rock press to the gig who might otherwise not have gone to an R&B show. This fit in perfectly with Bell's long-range plan to break as many Stax artists as possible to a rock/pop audience and thereby expand Stax's share of the overall market. The immediate benefit was that *Rolling Stone* elected to give the event prime coverage, something it had never done before for anything staged by Stax.

Joplin had originally ascended to fame as the lead singer of Big Brother and the Holding Company. In August of 1968 she decided to leave Big Brother and put together a more soulful band, complete with a horn section modeled after Stax/Volt's. Playing Memphis on a bill such as the "The Stax/Volt Yuletide Thing" was a dream come true for her. It was also an intimidating way of breaking in her new ensemble, the Kozmic Blues

---

14. Apparently Booker had gotten so far as to start working out an arrangement for the legendary song.

Janis Joplin, Deanie Parker, and Rufus Thomas
backstage at the 1968 Stax-Volt Yuletide Thing.
COURTESY DEANIE PARKER.

Band. Unbelievably, the new band's first rehearsal was on Wednesday, December 18, three days before the show. They rehearsed again on Thursday, and then on Friday flew to Memphis, where they checked into the Lorraine Motel. Quickly freshening up, they immediately headed over to the studio, rehearsing in Studio B before heading out to Jim Stewart's sprawling mansion that night for the Stax Christmas party.[15] Ronnie Stoots remembers Joplin's behavior at the party only too well. Drunk on Southern Comfort, the flamboyant singer repeatedly threw her finished cigarettes on the newly laid carpet and then ground them out with her foot. An outraged Evelyn Stewart eventually told her to get out. Joplin's entourage then returned to Stax, where they continued to rehearse throughout the night.

On Saturday, Joplin was slated to perform second from last, followed only by Johnnie Taylor, currently riding the crest of the wave of "Who's Making Love." Joplin was scheduled to play five songs, electing to perform covers of Eddie Floyd's "Raise Your Hand"

---

15. Work on Stewart's home had gone on for the better part of two years and had been completed just a few short months before the Stax party. Set on 63 acres, the property had originally been a farm owned by a relative of Stewart's. When Stewart purchased the lot, the solitary living space was a very small white clapboard farmhouse that was subsequently transformed by a former Mar-Key lead singer Ronnie Stoots into an absolute palace. Evelyn, Jim, and their three children lived in the 10,000-square-foot main house. Out back was a 4,500-square foot guest house, three swimming pools (a regular pool, a high diving pool, and a therapy pool), two tennis courts, two stables, two riding arenas, and a fully stocked 5-acre lake. The house itself had a number of special touches including a 50-square foot sunken living room replete with custom designed furniture and a 25 foot-high fire place taking up 15 feet of one wall. A 100-foot-long and 15-foot-wide hallway split the back portion of the house, serving as a veritable art gallery, each wall lined with priceless masterpieces by reknown Southern artists. The shower in Jim's living quarters was a waterfall running off of Arkansas stone but perhaps the most outlandish touch was the fact that the guest house had been built around two 90-foot pine trees that rose up through the floor and ceiling of the impressive edifice.

and the Bee Gees' "To Love Somebody" followed by a new, unfamiliar song. Misjudging her audience, she then left the stage, planning to encore with her two best-known songs, "Piece of My Heart" and "Ball and Chain." When the audience greeted her departure with tepid applause and a lot of silence, the encore was scrapped and Joplin was crushed. While various members of her entourage tried to comfort her, Johnnie Taylor took the stage and turned the house out. For the record, the show did not sell well, and Stax, in Jim Stewart's words, lost "a ton of money."

10

Time Is Tight: 1969

The principals at Gulf and Western never really understood what they had bought. About six months into the deal, Seymour Rosenberg was sitting in his Memphis office at Chelsea and Fifth when he noticed a big, flashy car pull up outside. "I see this little fat guy and another guy with him," recounts Rosenberg. "I figure they're criminal clients. They kind of looked the part. They come in and I say, 'What can I do for you?' The guy says, 'Don't you know who we are? I'm the president and this is the vice president of Paramount Records. We came here to find out what's going on with Stax Records.' I said, 'Well, you're in the wrong place. I'm just a part-time legal counsel.'"

Rosenberg's visitor was Arnold Burke. Burke had already been over to College and McLemore, but Al Bell was out of town and no one could locate Jim Stewart. "I'm sitting there trying not to laugh," continues Rosenberg. Apparently there was very little relationship between Gulf and Western or their Paramount subsidiary and Stax.

Wayne Jackson also has a story about Burke's visit to Memphis. Jackson and Andrew Love had originally found out about the sale to Gulf and Western through Jim Stewart's secretary, Linda Andrews. "It came as a shock to us. I was shocked that an L.A. company, Mr. Plastic City out there, would purchase a funky R&B label. The corporate guys, the experts from L.A., came in here. These guys sent six guys in blue suits with their notebooks to sit around and digest and to decide what this company was doing that they had purchased. All I remember was the grumbling I heard that these guys didn't know shit about nothing. Here they were from Los Angeles in their suits and we're eating baloney and cheese on the floor in shorts and they didn't understand it, just didn't understand it. They paid all this money and here are these grubby bastards drinking wine!"

According to Jim Stewart, no one at Gulf and Western knew anything about the record business. The head of their music division, Arnold Burke, had come out of the motion picture business. "He was a real nice guy," says Jim, shaking his head, "but he knew absolutely nothing about the record business. They never had any record people [and] they had no idea what a black record was all about. We're talking about Paramount Records and Dot Records [also a G&W subsidiary] and Stax. That's a marriage that's not going to work." Fortunately, Stax kept all operations completely separate from the parent company with the exception of the accounting and art departments, steadfastly refusing to go through G&W's branch distribution system.

While owned by Gulf and Western, Stax issued records on the Stax, Volt, Hip, and Enterprise imprints.[1] The latter label debuted during the final months that Stax was being distributed by Atlantic. The mandate for Enterprise never seems to have been entirely

1. The latter was named after the starship on Bell's favorite TV show, "Star Trek."

clear. Although early Stax press releases variously referred to the label as the company's jazz or jazz-folk outlet, over time far more country, pop, rock, and R&B records than jazz titles were issued under the Enterprise imprimatur.

In the Atlantic period, three albums and four singles were released on the new label. One of the three LPs was Isaac Hayes's debut solo album, *Presenting Isaac Hayes.* The other two were by Maynard Ferguson, *Ridin' High,* and Father Herrera and the Trio ESP, *Jazz Goes to Church.* Two of the 45s were by R&B singer Shirley Walton; one was by Hayes, and the other was by a jazz group, the Eddie Henderson Quintet. After the sale to Gulf and Western, Enterprise lay dormant for several months. In November 1968, Stax announced intentions to revive what a company press release termed "the Enterprise jazz line."[2] Plans included the signing of five new acts and a heavy merchandising and promotion program as Stax intended to have a jazz catalogue in place by the company's first national sales convention, scheduled for May 1969. Plans to open a New York office were also mentioned again (see Chapter 9).

One of the new acts signed to Enterprise was jazz saxophonist Sonny Stitt, who had the privilege of cutting the first record on the newly rejuvenated label. Producers Al Jackson and Ronnie Capone opted to record Stitt on a cover of William Bell and Judy Clay's recent hit, "Private Number." According to Capone, either Al Bell or Al Jackson simply said, "Go get the original session tape for 'Private Number' and we'll let Sonny play over it." To my knowledge it is the only record of its kind in Stitt's canon. The session sheet filed with the American Federation of Musicians lists the four members of Booker T. and the MG's and Sonny Stitt as appearing on the record, because the MG's had played on the original session.

The legal niceties surrounding the Stitt record are symptomatic of how the creative and business aspects of the company did not always mesh. Seymour Rosenberg remembers getting a call from Al Bell requesting a contract be drawn up for Sonny Stitt within the hour. Rosenberg could have quite easily complied using the standard contract forms, but he pointed out to Al that they had no proof that Stitt was not still under contract to his previous label. "I wanted to see where he'd been released from everybody he'd been under contract to for the last five years before you give him any money," stated Rosenberg emphatically. Unfortunately, the record had already been cut.

"You don't negotiate with an artist *after* you've cut a hit record!" exclaims Rosenberg. He eventually washed his hands of the situation, suggesting to Bell that Stax already had copies of the standard contract forms. They could simply fill in the name, advance, and royalty and be done with it. Bell did as instructed, but in February 1969, shortly after the record was released and began to see some action, Stax received a cease-and-desist order. As it turns out, Rosenberg's concerns were well founded: Stitt was already under contract to United Artists Records via Richard Carpenter and Tasty Productions. After achieving sales of eleven thousand copies in its first few weeks and garnering a special merit mention in *Billboard,* Stitt's version of "Private Number" had to be withdrawn.

Stax, via Enterprise, made only a very few other forays into the jazz world. Negotiations were entered into with both Max Roach and Abbey Lincoln, but neither led to a contract. Later in 1969, though, Bell signed legendary vocalist Billy Eckstine, who recorded four albums for Enterprise, the first of which, *Stormy,* was produced by Isaac Hayes.

Expanding into the world of jazz was one more facet of Al Bell's grand vision: "It was the total black music experience [that I was into]," stresses Bell. "Milt Gabler and the old-

---

2. By November 1971, Stax press releases were referring to Enterprise as concentrating on "progressive rock, jazz, folk, and easy listening."

timers told me you've got to build a catalogue that's diverse with blues and jazz and gospel, where that catalogue is generating enough revenue on a monthly basis to take care of your general and administrative costs and your overhead. Then when you have that big hit record, that's where you have the profit."

As Stax was sorting out the Sonny Stitt mess, the label was basking in its best showing yet at the 1968 Grammy Awards (held in February 1969). Both Otis Redding and Johnnie Taylor were nominated in the "Best R&B Male Vocal Performance" category, Sam and Dave were nominated for "I Thank You" in the "Best Performance by an R&B Duo or Group" category, "Long Walk to D.C." by the Staple Singers was nominated in the first year of the "Best Soul Gospel Performance" category, Cropper and Redding were nominated for "(Sittin' on) The Dock of the Bay," and the songwriters We Three were nominated for "Who's Making Love" in the "Best Rhythm and Blues Song" category. Otis Redding's widow, Zelma, took home the Grammy in both the "Best R&B Male Vocal Performance" and "Best Rhythm and Blues Song" category, the latter being shared with Steve Cropper. Sam and Dave lost out to the Temptations and "Cloud Nine," while the Staple Singers were beaten by Dottie Rambo's version of "The Soul of Me."[3]

Part of the rationale behind the sale of Stax to Gulf and Western, and part of Bell's grand vision, was to provide Stax with an opportunity to get involved in movie soundtracks through G&W's Paramount Pictures. The first fruit of this relationship was the Jules Dassin remake of John Ford's 1935 classic *The Informer* with an all-black cast called *Uptight*.[4] Booker T. Jones was brought in sometime after shooting had begun and commissioned to write the entire score. In preparation he spent a week with Quincy Jones learning such basic techniques as how to sync music to a twenty-four-frame-per-second piece of film. "Quincy was complimentary when I came to California," relates Booker. "He felt that we were equals. He really made me feel good about my music, asking me for tips about making stuff funky."

Booker composed the score in Paris and then the MG's flew over to join him and record the actual soundtrack in a movie studio with the film being screened as they played. Because everyone was dissatisfied with the quality of the sound equipment at the film studio, the group elected to rerecord the entire soundtrack for release on record back at Stax's McLemore Avenue studio.

Both "Johnny, I Love You" and "Time Is Tight" were featured on the soundtrack LP. "Johnny, I Love You" is unique in that it contains the one-and-only, full-fledged Booker T. vocal on an MG's record. "That was a song that I thought could be sung by anybody," offers Booker. "I guess I had in mind somebody like Ray Charles but I had always sung when doing my writing and [eventually] I saw it for myself."

Apparently Booker T. had been wanting to add vocals to the group's albums for quite some time. "Before ['Johnny I Love You'] and afterwards," affirms the master musician. "But the emphasis was that it should stay an instrumental group. That's where all the success was. I thought we should expand with me singing and do some more vocal things, but the record company didn't want to do that." As can be deduced from the latter comment, Booker was becoming increasingly dissatisfied with the Stax front office. Before 1969 was over, he would move away from Memphis permanently, and within a year he would refuse to work for Stax.

In February 1969, a month after the LP was released, "Time Is Tight" and "Johnny, I Love You" were issued on 45. "Time Is Tight" just might be Booker T. and the MG's finest

---

3. Only two other Stax recordings would ever win Grammys: Isaac Hayes's 1971 soundtrack for *Shaft;* and Richard Pryor's breakthrough album, 1974's *That Nigger's Crazy.*

4. Dassin had been directing features since the 1940s. Blacklisted during the McCarthy era, he relocated to Europe, where he enjoyed a string of successes in the late 1950s and early 1960s. Perhaps his best-known feature was *Never on Sunday.*

moment. The song had originally been written for a James Coburn film, *Duffy,* but when the producers of the film requested the publishing, Stax refused. On several occasions the MG's had attempted to work it up, but until the *Uptight* soundtrack it remained untitled (engineer Ronnie Capone simply calling out "Action Scene" at the beginning of each take) and in the can. When Booker was working on the soundtrack for *Uptight* he had original-ly wanted to call the song "Uptight" but, because Stevie Wonder already had a hit of the same name, it was decided to settle for "Time Is Tight."

Booker T. was especially proud of the melody. "For so many years all of our melodies had been eight bars or twelve bars. I wanted something that was six bars or ten bars just so the melody changed on a different bar of the sequence. That was what appealed to me about the melody of 'Time Is Tight.'"

Cropper, Dunn, and Jackson supplied the rhythm, concocting a bass line that is extreme-ly close to Otis Redding's 1965 recording "I Can't Turn You Loose." "That just seemed to fit there," says Jones, laughing. "That was the right rhythm for it and it just so happens that it was the right rhythm for Otis Redding, too. Thank God the same guys wrote both of them. We knew we were repeating ourselves but it just seemed right so we didn't care."

The song is written with two large-scale distinct sections, the first being a very slow introductory passage with first organ and then guitar languorously stating a wistful and elegiac melody over an organ drone. From there the tempo goes into overdrive as Steve sets the pace with the "I Can't Turn You Loose" riff. Five different strains unfold in sequence, each somehow seeming more climactic than the preceding one. On record the whole piece eventually winds back down for a reprise of the slow introductory material. As superb as the record is, as is the case with the finest soul music, it ultimately pales com-pared to what the MG's do with the song onstage. To this day it remains the absolute high point in their shows, usually extending into ten-plus minutes of neuron-firing, orgasmic delight. Commercially, "Time Is Tight" was their second most successful single ever, sur-passed only by "Green Onions." It peaked at number 7 on the R&B, number 6 on the pop, and number 9 on the easy-listening charts, with total sales of about 600,000 copies.

Shortly after its release, Al Jackson told *Ebony,* "We have a pact, because we're such close friends as well as close musically. We're hot now, but we hope to retire within five years. Then we'll work only as writers or producers. Booker might go on doing movies, but we'll no longer exist as a group. We'd like to go out cool instead of dying slowly."

As Stax was making forays into the worlds of jazz and movie soundtracks, Estelle Axton's departure from the company she financed and was instrumental in building was barely mentioned. In fact, there was no announcement in either the Memphis papers or the national music industry press.[5] With the sale of Stax to Gulf and Western, Estelle had ceased running the Satellite Record Shop and moved into the company's office. Although her main duties were running the mail room, Estelle was not the type of person to keep her mouth shut and her ideas to herself. As she increasingly gave her opinions on all aspects of the business, she found herself in conflict with Jim Stewart and, to a lesser degree, Al Bell. "I could see the writing on the wall," sighs Estelle. "It wasn't going to work, me being back in their department. I approached them to sell my part and get out of it. I said, 'If I can't have a hand in the decision making, I don't want no part of it.'"

Seymour Rosenberg negotiated the settlement between Estelle, Al, and Jim. "She was bitter," says Rosenberg. "It was so bitter that what I did to make the deal fly, was I rented a two-bedroom suite at the Rivermont. I put Miss Axton and her lawyer in one bedroom,

5. Although I have tried for eleven years, I have been unable to precisely pinpoint the month that Estelle left the company. None of the three principals—Estelle, Jim, and Al—can remember, lawyer Seymour Rosenberg long ago threw out the file on the settlement, there was no mention of this event in the music press, and Fantasy, which presently owns Stax, has no record of it in its files.

Estelle Axton being presented with flowers by David Porter in happier times at the 1966 Stax Christmas party; Steve Cropper (*far left*), Duck Dunn (*partially visible just to the left of Estelle's head*), and Booker T. Jones (*far right*) look on.
COURTESY API PHOTOGRAPHERS INC.

I put Jim and Al in the other one, and the Gulf and Western people with me in the outer thing. The lawyers would come and meet in the living room part and go back to their clients and negotiate some more. I threatened them that we were going to lock them all in 'cause at that time Estelle and Jim weren't getting along too well. She was a little bitter and rightfully so."

The essence of the deal was that Al Bell would buy 40 of the 45 percent interest Estelle maintained in the company, while Jim Stewart would buy the remaining 5 percent, thus making Bell and Stewart equal partners. Of course, since Jim and Estelle had sold the company to G&W for stock and an earn-out position, Bell and Stewart were, in actuality, buying Estelle's stake. G&W agreed to guarantee the payments. Estelle was also awarded $25,000 a year for five years, during which time she was not allowed to engage in any activity related to the recording industry. Interestingly enough, Stax continued to pay her the $25,000 after the five-year period was up in the summer of 1974. Estelle isn't sure whether this was a result of inefficiency at the company or due to guilt on her brother's part.

Estelle bought a thirty-two-unit apartment complex with $720,000 of the settlement she received. She also, under Packy's name, established Fretone Records. Until her five-year waiting period was up, she did not actively participate in this venture. Once able to get back in the record business, she assumed control of Fretone, and in the fall of 1976 had a massive hit in "Disco Duck" with Memphis deejay Rick Dees. While her departure from the company did not make the news, there were many in Stax who were sad to see her go. Always a favorite with the musicians and the artists, according to Steve Cropper,

"She was the heart and soul of that whole place. No doubt about it. She had more ideas and she had more pulse on her finger on what was going on in the community."[6]

The Satellite Record Shop was sold to longtime employee Johnny Keyes for the rather odd figure of $2,176. Keyes paid for it with the proceeds from his first royalty check for his part in cowriting Clarence Carter's hit "Too Weak to Fight."[7] Part of the condition of the sale to Keyes was that he had to change the name of the store. After settling on Record World, Keyes ran the shop for about a year and a half. During this time he was also doing double duty as Isaac Hayes's stage manager and consequently was away from the store a lot of the time. The women he had running things while he was on the road let business slip pretty badly, and by January or February 1971 he had lost the store to the landlord. Shortly thereafter the landlord sold the store to Willie Bean, who changed the name to B+B Satellite, skirting Stax's proprietary interest in the name "Satellite." Bean and then his sister ran the store for about three years before finally closing it down for good.

A few months before the sale of the record store to Keyes, Packy had been forced to move the store across the street to 925 McLemore because Bell and Stewart wanted to take over the whole block that housed the Stax studio and offices. With one stroke Stax took over Slim Jenkins' Joint, the radio repair shop, the record store, Gaddy's Beauty Shop, and Jack's Grocery (formerly the Weona Grocery Store). Gaddy's moved around the corner, while the rest simply went out of business or relocated.

To those working in the office, the physical building seemed always to be undergoing change. "I can remember," says Deanie Parker, "we were growing so fast that they were cutting out a wall every other day and knocking out a door or closing up a window or putting in a new set of stairs or laying some carpet. I used to run around trying to preserve records by pulling them out from under sawdust!" The air-conditioning unit of Slim Jenkins's old joint was converted into echo chambers by the ever-creative Cropper and Capone.[8]

With Estelle out of the picture, renovations complete, and "Time Is Tight" storming up the charts, the MG's and everyone else at Stax were in an absolute frenzy attempting to ready twenty-seven albums for simultaneous release in May. This audacious move was orchestrated by Al Bell with the singular purpose of creating an instantaneous catalogue to replace what had been lost in the termination of the Atlantic distribution deal.[9] To put the size of this release in perspective, the company had issued only forty-three albums in total from inception through the dissolution of the agreement with Atlantic. In February Herb Kole was hired away from Atlantic as vice president of merchandising and marketing to help prepare for the massive release.[10]

---

6. Testimony to the respect the community had for Estelle is the fact that in the eight years that she ran the Satellite Record Shop, she was never robbed. "I found out later why," says Estelle, smiling. "There were some guys that were such good friends of mine, they would not allow anybody to touch me. Black people protected me."

7. According to Keyes, when Packy was supposedly running the record store during the time period that Estelle was working in the mail room, it was actually being managed by Packy's girlfriend, Mary. Although Packy and Mary were not married, she had taken on his last name, opening up a charge account at one of Memphis's major department stores under the name Mary Axton. She had also gotten pregnant by another man, and for nine months strung Packy along telling him the child was his. Estelle, needless to say, was none too fond of Mary. Selling the Satellite Record Shop to Keyes was partially revenge on Mary.

8. Cropper and Capone were inveterate experimenters. In the summer of 1968, they had rigged up a speaker, suspended with rubber bands, that they tried using as a microphone for Al Jackson's drums. This technique was actually used on at least two sessions for Eddie Floyd and for Johnnie Taylor before it was abandoned.

9. Twenty-eight albums and thirty singles had been planned, but Rufus Thomas's *May I Have Your Ticket Please* LP was never completed, much to Thomas's continued chagrin.

10. Kole's main duties would involve the marketing of LPs, although he was also the general head of the sales department with Ewell Roussell and Sandy Meadors reporting to him.

Carla Thomas duets with Sam (*left*) and Dave (*right*) on the "Gettin' It All Together" Stax television special. COURTESY FANTASY, INC.

Tied to this ambitious release schedule were a number of major promotional events, linked by the title "Gettin' It All Together." This title was first used for a Stax television special that aired in selected markets beginning on April 24, 1969. The special was produced by Neal Marshall and directed by Art Fisher[11] for Metromedia stations across the country. Shot before a live audience at WNEW's New York studios, the special was apparently inspired and modeled on Motown's Diana Ross and the Supremes and Temptations' "T.C.B.—Taking Care of Business" special aired the previous December. Animated films were used to introduce each artist, leading a reviewer in *Variety* to state that the "production values were extraordinary." Booker T. Jones served as the show's musical director, wrote the "Gettin' It All Together" theme song, and sang a duet with Carla Thomas on "Yesterday." Thomas also dueted with Sam and Dave on their "Don't Turn Your Heater Down" and with Dave alone on "Tramp" from the *King and Queen* album she cut with Otis Redding. The latter was part of a tribute to Redding that also included Sam Moore singing "Try a Little Tenderness" and Sam and Dave singing "These Arms of Mine." The show's grand finale was a rollicking MG's–Carla Thomas– Sam and Dave version of "I Heard It Through the Grapevine." In addition to its New York airing, "Gettin' It All Together" was broadcast in Washington, Kansas City, Los Angeles, and San Francisco. Curiously, this appears to be the extent of its exposure.[12]

Following the airing of the special, Stax booked the weekends of May 16–18 and 24–25 at the Holiday Inn Rivermont in Memphis to unveil its new "instant" catalogue. The first weekend was designed to introduce the product to the people at Gulf and Western as well

11. Fisher had recently directed the widely acclaimed "James Brown: Man to Man" special.

12. For the record the MG's performed "Hang 'Em High," "Time Is Tight," and "Johnny, I Love You"; Carla sang "B-A-B-Y," her recent Don Davis–produced hit "I Like What You're Doing (To Me)," and "Baby, What You Want Me to Do"; and Sam and Dave dueted on "I Thank You," "Soul Man," "Hold On! I'm Comin'," and "You Don't Know Like I Know." Despite eleven years of searching, I have not been able to find a copy of this special. If anyone reading this has a copy, please write me at the address cited in the Preface.

as to retailers and distributors. The second weekend was a media junket in which Stax flew in Memphis trade paper staff writers, and consumer publication record reviewers and editors. The theme of both weekends followed the television special's title, "Gettin' It All Together."

David Porter and Isaac Hayes in a rare live performance together at the 1969 Stax sales meeting; also shown is Bar-Kays keyboard player Ronnie Gordon. COURTESY DEANIE PARKER.

The two weekends at the Rivermont were fabulous successes, with over two hundred guests attending each occasion. Writers from *Rolling Stone, Time, Jet, Down Beat,* the *New York Times, Jazz and Pop, Hit Parader, Pop Wire,* and *Cavalier,* among others, attended the second weekend. They were treated to a wonderful performance by the Bar-Kays, Staple Singers, Mavis Staples solo, William Bell, Albert King, Carla Thomas, Isaac Hayes and David Porter doing Sam and Dave material(!), Isaac solo, and finally Booker T. and the MG's.[13] All of the artists were then made available to meet the various media in attendance. The net effect on the amount of consumer press Stax releases received was palpable.

13. On the first weekend the same basic lineup performed with Rufus Thomas, Johnnie Taylor, Eddie Floyd, and the pop group Knowbody Else replacing Albert King and Hayes and Porter. The second weekend was taped but due to a faulty vocal microphone, it is not of releasable quality.

As exciting as the media weekend was, the first weekend was perhaps even more impressive. At its conclusion Stax proudly announced that it had racked up sales of over two million dollars on the new product it had introduced. Georgia State Representative Julian Bond spoke at the first weekend, and Jim Stewart used the opportunity to announce that Stax planned to launch a massive education program aimed at the underprivileged to be partially financed through the tax-deductible Stax Association for Everybody's Education (SAFEE). "I envision a trade school and day care centers," stated Stewart, "for pre-school children whose parents cannot afford to send them to kindergarten and to day care centers. . . . The trade school will be designed for those pupils who cannot afford to go on to college or other schools." The day care center was slated to open that summer.

No one who participated in the buildup to the twenty-seven-LP, thirty-single release will ever forget the madness and the work overload that enveloped everyone employed in any capacity at the company. Some people saw the whole scheme as a waste, citing the fact that such a small company could not possibly adequately promote such a large volume of product at one time.

"They did a disservice to themselves," states Jerry Wexler rather smugly, "that they never recovered from. When they left us and they went to Gulf and Western, they came out with a twenty-five- or thirty-album release. Hey, that was dirt in the coffin. They never recovered from that. That's a piece of parochial insanity. That's regional nuthead business. That's where they sit around the office isolated from the world and play 'record industry.' I think that's a blow they never recovered from. Think of the costs, think of the assets they used up to put out twenty-seven albums. It was just a bad move. It's a panic move."

Clarence Avant concurs: "I went to their first presentation of product. I think there were about twenty-five LPs at one time coming out. That would scare the fuck out of me if I had been Gulf and Western. Who the fuck can handle twenty-five LPs at one time unless you're CBS? I wouldn't [even] want [them] to be handling twenty-five LP's at one time. There's certain things that just won't jell."

Al Bell accepts the criticism, admitting that much of what was released simply got lost in the shuffle. Still, he and others ultimately saw those weekends as among the company's proudest moments, as it aggressively asserted its independence and its ability to be a diversified, full-service record company.

In Al Bell's opinion, "If we were not an album company, we would not have any presence with the distributors. We've just gone independent. It's important now to get out here and present ourselves as an album company. It's important to be formidable. It's important to have a sales meeting so they can say, 'Oh, this is an independent company like Atlantic and A&M down here in Memphis, Tennessee.' That's what that was all about—to build a catalogue with albums. Berry Gordy's emphasis was on selling singles. My emphasis was on selling albums."

Up to this point Stax had been a singles-oriented company. A session would be scheduled and two, sometimes three, songs were cut: an A-side, a B-side, and maybe a backup. When two or three of an artist's singles became hits, additional tracks would be quickly recorded so that an album could be issued. In 1969, under Al Bell's directive, most artists at Stax would record ten to twelve tracks for an album. When that was completed, the company would then select what they thought should be a single. This is the way rock artists had been working for the past few years, but for rhythm-and-blues artists it was a wholly new approach. To Steve Cropper and Duck Dunn's way of thinking, this fundamental change in company policy was ultimately a mistake.

Since selling to Gulf and Western, to accommodate the sheer volume of activity in its two studios, Stax had hired four new engineers. First hired, in the spring of 1968, was guitarist and songwriter Bobby Manuel.[14] Henry Bush then worked his way from cleaning up the control room for fifty dollars a week to become an engineer. Gordon Rudd signed on next, and then, in the midst of the twenty-seven-album onslaught, William Brown moved out of the mail room to start working sessions.[15] Ron Capone conducted Saturday morning seminar/workshops that all the new engineers were required to attend. These workshops, in effect, were their trade-school education. They also ensured a relatively consistent approach to engineering that helped preserve the notion of a single, identifiable Stax sound.

Ironically, Al Bell was doing his best to, if not undermine, at least substantially alter, that sound. For a long time he had labored to get Jim Stewart out of the studio. Bringing in Ron Capone was the first major move in this regard. By the time of the twenty-seven-album release program, Stewart had ceased to engineer company sessions.

"When Jim was the engineer," explains Bell, "Jim was locked into that formula. He would not let them move. He *could* not let them move. That would have been like taking his arm off. He was fierce about that. He really felt roots, guts, raw, basic fundamental black music stronger than anybody I've ever seen, period. As long as Jim was behind the console, effectively Jim was producing the product. So I was laboring to get other people behind that console which would then give the musicians and artists more latitude."

For the May sales meetings, every major artist at Stax recorded a new album. In addition three *Rare Stamps* LPs were assembled with vintage material from Eddie Floyd, Johnnie Taylor, and, splitting the third package half and half, J. J. Barnes and Steve Mancha. The Barnes and Mancha release consisted of tapes that Don Davis had cut earlier in Detroit. Further product was generated with a John Lee Hooker album licensed from Henry Stone in Florida and the first solo albums by Steve Cropper and Mavis Staples and the second solo LP by Isaac Hayes. Bell was pulling out all the stops, generating albums in any way he could. A number of the LPs put together in this period tapped into the notion of the "concept album," then in vogue in rock circles. Bell was the architect behind most of them. Albert King recorded an album of Elvis Presley songs, aptly titled *King, Does the King's Thing*. King was also paired with Stax's two other most prominent guitarists—Steve Cropper and Pops Staples—for an interesting, at times superb album called *Jammed Together*. Finally, Bell himself produced a double album entitled *Boy Meets Girl*, which paired a number of the label's male and female vocalists including William Bell, Mavis Staples, her sister Cleotha and brother Pervis, Johnnie Taylor, Carla Thomas, and Eddie Floyd.

"*Boy Meets Girl*," relates Al Bell, "was an attempt to take the entire roster and come up with a unique catalogue album by combining the boy with the girl. I felt that if I could come up with the right album with a couple of hits in there, then I could expose every track in the album and, as a result of that, get all of those artists out there and give all those artists exposure. So, it was a merchandising piece as well as what I believed could ultimately be a great catalogue album. Then I felt that, once it got out there in the marketplace, as those

---

14. Born in 1945, Manuel, who was white, began playing clubs as a professional at age fourteen. While still in high school, he began sitting in with all-black bands at the Plantation Inn and Club Handy and, after college, he became the only white member of the Club Paradise band, where he played alongside Allen Jones and Gilbert Caple. He first recorded behind Homer Banks on Minit and from 1966 to 1967 he served in the house band at Ronnie Stoots's Onyx studio, which, with Manuel, pianist Ronnie Williams, drummer Joe Gray, and bassist Ronnie Moore, was a half-black, half-white rhythm section modeled on Booker T. and the MG's.

15. Brown quickly worked up to 108-hour work weeks, and claims to have been employee of the month at Stax for six straight months!

individual artists became successful, then the catalogue value of the album would contin-ue to appreciate." The reasoning was sound, but the album was met with general disinter-est. Altogether, six singles were released from *Boy Meets Girl,* none of them charting.

Bell was not your typical record company executive. Viewed today by most Stax alum-ni as either God or the Devil incarnate, he was very much "hands on" in virtually all aspects of running the company, including production. He conducted sessions for *Boy Meets Girl,* often in tandem with Isaac Hayes or Don Davis, at Ardent and at Muscle Shoals Sound Studios in Alabama.

In Muscle Shoals, Bell made use for the first time of what became known as the Muscle Shoals Rhythm Section: Jimmy Johnson on rhythm guitar, Barry Beckett on key-boards, David Hood on bass, and Roger Hawkins on drums. That particular rhythm sec-tion would become, over the course of the late sixties and seventies, as prominent as Booker T. and the MG's had been, recording sessions with Clarence Carter, Wilson Pickett, Paul Simon, Aretha Franklin, Bobby Womack, Tina Turner, Millie Jackson, and so on. The Muscle Shoals regulars were augmented over the years by a variety of lead guitarists. Blue-eyed soul wonder Eddie Hinton came down from Nashville to play on most of the Stax sessions. This combination is the lineup that within a year would be heard on virtually every Don Davis and Al Bell production, encompassing a passel of classic records by Johnnie Taylor and the Staple Singers. For some of the *Boy Meets Girl* Muscle Shoals sessions, the Muscle Shoals guys were augmented by Stax session musi-cians Marvell Thomas and Isaac Hayes.

Thomas and Hayes also figured into the sessions held at Ardent, where they played with what became one of the standard rhythm sections for Stax at the turn of the decade: Bar-Kays members Willie Hall, James Alexander, and Michael Toles on drums, bass, and gui-tar, respectively. Part of the idea in signing the original Bar-Kays was that they would be groomed as a second "house band" at the label. Tragically, the plane crash that took the lives of Otis Redding and two-thirds of the group ended the first phase of the band's career. In the summer of 1968, the two surviving members, bassist James Alexander and trumpeter Ben Cauley, with the help of producer and eventual mentor Allen Jones, put together the Bar-Kays Mark II. Toles, Hall, and Alexander were the core of the new group's rhythm section. Although both Toles and Hall would leave the Bar-Kays by mid-1971, along with Alexander they would continue to anchor a large percentage of the ses-sions held at Stax in the 1970s. Even after both players had left the group, Stax commonly printed credits that simply read "Rhythm: the Bar-Kays."[16]

During the Atlantic period, virtually every Stax session had been held at the 926 E. McLemore studio. That, combined with Booker T. and the MG's and the Mar-Key horns playing on almost every record and the vast majority of songs being written by a handful of Stax house writers, gave the company a readily identifiable sound. The use of strings and background vocalists from Detroit had partially eroded that consistency. With the use of outside studios and different rhythm sections, the idea of a readily identifiable sound was beginning to recede into history.

16. While the core of the re-formed Bar-Kays became Stax session stalwarts, the group itself felt like they were always treated as stepchildren by the company's front office. While allowed to spend unbelievable hours in the McLemore studio cutting and recutting the same tracks over and over (their producer, Allen Jones, was nick-named "T.J." for "track jammer"), whether in their pioneering black rock phase or in their later funk years, the Bar-Kays felt that their records were not understood, embraced, or adequately promoted. "I thought our con-tributions to Stax could have been different from what Stax was continuing to build," Jones explained a few years before his death. "[We] were always just a little on the outside. I just thought that there was more [Stax] could have done with Memphis music [but] it was outside of the viewpoint of the people that ran the compa-ny. Therefore it was never taken seriously." After Stax folded, the Bar-Kays signed to Mercury and went on to become one of the most important funk bands in the second half of the 1970s.

Significantly, the most successful of the twenty-seven albums recorded for Bell's instant catalogue, Isaac Hayes's *Hot Buttered Soul*, had nothing whatsoever to do with the "Stax sound." No single album had a greater impact on the direction of black music in the first half of the 1970s. In retrospect, several people would like to claim that they saw Isaac as a viable artist. Foremost among those is Al Bell.

"As a marketer I'd look at Isaac Hayes," recounts Bell, "and I'd see [him] banging on the piano and watched his approach which, in terms of the way he held his hands, was sort of like the kind of stuff I would see those guys playing in the country-and-western bars, what I would see on television. Isaac looked like one of those guys [but] black. When he was working up material with Porter, I'd sit around and watch him writing. To me, he was a unique person. He had the bald head and he would come in with a purple shirt on and some pink pants and some lavender socks and some white shoes. There was this little club where I went one time and Isaac was in there playing on the organ and I decided, wait a minute, I've got to record this guy. I believe we can have us a huge, huge artist."

What Al may not have known is that for years Isaac had held ambitions to rekindle his career as an artist. When Bell suggested they go into the studio to record an album after a company party, Isaac needed little persuasion. With the help of Al Jackson and Duck Dunn, in early 1968 he cut his debut solo LP, *Presenting Isaac Hayes.* Everyone was a little tipsy at the session, nothing was planned in advance, and the whole record was cut in the trio format. It was released to little fanfare and was a disappointment in the marketplace. Isaac vowed never to record another solo LP unless he had complete control.

"When I did *Hot Buttered Soul*," Hayes reflects, "it was a selfish thing on my part. It was something I wanted to do. Al said, 'however you want to do it.' I didn't give a damn if it didn't sell because I was going for the true artistic side, rather than looking at it for monetary value. I had an opportunity to express myself no holds barred, no restrictions, and that's why I did it. I took artistic and creative liberties. I felt what I had to say couldn't be said in two minutes and thirty seconds. So I just stretched [the songs] out and milked them for everything they were worth. I didn't feel any pressure that it had to sell because there were twenty-six other albums out there."

Hayes, Marvell Thomas, Michael Toles, James Alexander, and Willie Hall recorded what became known as *Hot Buttered Soul* at Ardent Studios with Terry Manning engineering;[17] Allen Jones, Marvell Thomas, and Al Bell were credited as coproducers.[18] Only four songs were cut, an eighteen-minute version of Glen Campbell's 1967 hit "By the Time I Get to Phoenix,"[19] a twelve-minute version of Burt Bacharach and Hal David's "Walk On By,"[20] a nine-minute track Al Bell called "Hyperbolicsyllabicsesquedalymistic,"[21]

17. Harold Beane happened to drop by the studio during the sessions and plays the smokingly intense extended lead guitar solo on "Walk On By."
18. According to Marvell, he has never received a production royalty statement for his contribution. Early on in the album's success, he asked Jim for an advance against royalties for a down payment he needed on a house he wanted to buy. Jim had a check cut for $10,000, and that's all Thomas ever got.
19. During the long introductory rap for the song, Willie Hall keeps time marking quarter notes on the bell of his suspended ride cymbal. This went on to the point where his arm started cramping up. Not wanting to wreck what seemed obvious to everyone to be the magic take, Hall signaled with his eyes to Marvell Thomas that he was in trouble. Marvell got up from behind the piano, walked over and took the drumstick from Hall's hand, and continued playing the pattern without missing a beat. Hall massaged his arm for a couple of minutes before resuming his duties, allowing Marvell to get back behind the piano for the song proper. Interestingly, the song was also covered at Stax by both the Mad Lads and William Bell.
20. Allen Jones manipulated the wah-wah pedal for Michael Toles's rhythm guitar part on "Walk On By."
21. It bugs Bell to this day that the final two syllables were supposed to read "nistic," not "mistic."

and a relatively short five-minute take on Memphis songwriters Charlie Chalmers and Sandra Rhodes's "One Woman." The length of the songs, the arrangements, the long rap that preceded "Phoenix," and Hayes's vocal style were all radically different from what was going on in mainstream R&B at the time.

Hayes and his songwriting and producing partner, David Porter, would often sit in at local clubs. The Tiki Club, where the Bar-Kays held down a regular gig, was one of their favorite spots. It was at the Tiki that Hayes first developed the long spoken intro, or rap, that is the hallmark of his version of "By the Time I Get to Phoenix." "I first heard 'Phoenix' on the radio," recalls Hayes. "Glen Campbell was singing it. I stopped and said, 'Damn, that's great.' I bought the record and went back to the studio the next day and told Booker and them, 'Man, I heard a hip song by Glen Campbell named "Phoenix."' Nobody showed any enthusiasm, but I felt there was something in that song.

"The Bar-Kays were playing that night at the Tiki Club so I said, 'I'm going to be down tonight and I'm going to sit in. Why don't y'all learn "Phoenix."' So they learned it and I got down there. Everybody's talking so I said, 'Shit, I've got to get their attention some way.' I said to the guys in the band, 'Y'all kick it off and hang on that first chord, that B-flat eleven.' And then I started rapping. I said, 'I've got to create a situation these folks can relate to,' and I started talking and the conversation began to subside as I was telling the story. By the time I got to the [actual] beginning of the song everybody was quiet. When I finished, man, chicks were crying."

The Tiki Club catered to a predominantly black clientele. Isaac also tried the song out at a white nightspot, Club La Ronde, where the Short Kuts were the resident house band. At the latter nightspot, a white disc jockey, Scott Shannon, suggested to Hayes that he record the song. Isaac was already thinking the same thing.

It surprised many that the man who had cowritten such incendiary pieces of gospel-inspired soul would record an album three-quarters of which he didn't write, and half of which was composed of white pop tunes. It was quite a radical move.

"What it was, was the real me," proclaims Hayes. "I mean, okay, the real me had written those other songs ['Soul Man,' 'Hold On! I'm Comin',' etc.] but they were being written for other people. As for me wanting to express myself as an artist, that's what *Hot Buttered Soul* was. Although I was a songwriter, there were some songs that I loved, that really touched me. Came the opportunity, I wanted to record these tunes. I wanted to do them the way that I wanted to do them. I took them apart, dissected them, and put them back together and made them my personal tunes. I took creative license to do that. By doing them my way, it almost made them like totally different songs all over again.

"I was targeting the black listening audience. Very few black people knew about 'By the Time I Get to Phoenix.' But I broke it down and rearranged it where they could understand it, where they could relate to it. Music is universal [but] sometimes presentation will restrict you or limit your range. Glen Campbell and Jim Webb[22] were targeting the pop audience. But when I did it, I aimed to the black market, but it was so big, it went all over. It sounds radical because it had gone against everything that Stax had represented up to that point. All before then I would ask Jim Stewart to record me and he would say, 'Isaac, your voice is too pretty!' Jim was hardcore Otis Redding, Albert King, that sort of thing."

The basic rhythm tracks were cut for the album in a mere eight hours. Strings and background vocals were added in Detroit. Don Davis had introduced both Bell and Hayes to

---

22. Interestingly, a few years earlier Jim Webb had come to Memphis hoping to be signed to a songwriter's contract at Stax. He was turned down.

two Detroit string arrangers, Johnny Allen and Dale Warren, both of whom had done a little work for Motown. Allen was quite a bit older than Warren. Davis had met him while Allen was playing piano, leading his own trio in Detroit clubs. Davis had known Warren for years as Warren had done numerous sessions for most of the smaller Detroit labels.

"I wanted the remainder of it," stresses Bell, "the horns and the strings, to be a soundtrack to a motion picture and the motion picture was what Isaac was rapping about. I talked to Johnny Allen about adding the European influence. [It was] done in a very creative manner where it all embellished and enhanced the story. The idea was to go and put the package wrapped around him as opposed to taking a package and putting him in the package."

Johnny Allen arranged the strings for "Phoenix," while Dale Warren orchestrated "Walk On By." In both cases, after Al Bell had discussed his concept with the arrangers, Isaac Hayes flew to Detroit and, while playing the rhythm track in his hotel room, hummed to each arranger the ideas he had for the string parts. Both the original tape and Isaac's humming were recorded onto a second tape, which Allen and Warren used to orchestrate the parts. Hayes remembers wanting to use strings all along, but he really didn't know exactly what he wanted to do with them until after the rhythm tracks had been cut.

Al Bell came up with the album's title while flying back from Jamaica and reading an ad for Hot Buttered Rum. He simply stroked out the word "rum" and replaced it with "soul." Christopher Whorf designed the brilliant cover shot of the top of Isaac's bald head. Such a hard, round, bald surface signified for many an in-your-face declaration of blackness. Once witnessed, it's an unforgettable image. Hayes had originally shaven his head in the mid-sixties. "There was a fad going around among black musicians to straighten your hair," Hayes explains, smiling. "It was a pain in the ass to keep up. So I decided I'm gonna cut this stuff off, just grow me a fresh crop of natural hair. So I went into King's barbershop right around the corner from Stax and said, 'Cut it all off.' He cut it off and I went outside—'Wow, there's a breeze out here. It feels great.' I decided to keep it. I already had the beard and people were saying, 'Look at that bald-headed guy with a beard.' I didn't care because I liked being different. So I kept it that way."

No 45s were originally envisioned for *Hot Buttered Soul*, and none was scheduled among the thirty singles that were released at the Stax sales meetings. Al Bell had planned to try to break the record *as an album* in Los Angeles, but to his surprise it was broken in Detroit by Sonny Carter on station WGPR-FM. Carter was general manager of the station and hosted his own jazz-based show. He tells an interesting story. Detroit session singer Pat Lewis had arranged the innovative background vocals on "Walk On By." Lewis had a tape of the album before it was released to the public and, for one reason or another, she needed to copy it. She took it to Carter and asked if he would copy it at the station, making him promise not to play it on the air. Carter loved the eighteen-minute version of "By the Time I Get to Phoenix" and broke his promise. "Overnight, it was like a sensation," laughs Carter. "That was possibly on Friday, and Al called me on Monday and asked me if I would not play it again. We got so many requests for it, by Monday it was just ridiculous."

The reaction to *Hot Buttered Soul* in Detroit was so strong that Bell realized instantly that the record was potentially a gold mine. Within four weeks of its release, Stax took out a full-page ad in *Billboard* citing the record's sales in Detroit, Chicago, Philadelphia, and New York. Isaac claims, "We were getting reports about people in Detroit burglarizing record shops and the only thing they'd take out was *Hot Buttered Soul*. That's making a statement."

Hot Buttered Soul went on to sell over one million copies, an unprecedented showing for what was nominally an R&B album. Equally unprecedented was the fact that the album charted in the upper reaches of all four charts—jazz, pop, R&B, and easy listening—simultaneously, a feat few, if any, artists have ever achieved. Hayes virtually owned the jazz charts for the next few years. *Hot Buttered Soul* flitted back and forth between the number 2 and number 1 spots on *Billboard*'s jazz LP charts for over eight months. A year and a half after it was released, it was still in the jazz Top 10, joined by Hayes's next two albums, *The Isaac Hayes Movement* and *To Be Continued*. This was the kind of across-the-board success that Al Bell had envisioned for Stax. Ron Capone quickly edited both "Phoenix" and "Walk On By" down to single length, giving the Enterprise label a double-sided hit, "Walk On By" rising to numbers 13 and 30 on the R&B and pop charts, "Phoenix" reaching number 37 on both charts. Unfortunately for label mates the Mad Lads, their single of "By the Time I Get to Phoenix," which had been released as part of the May sales blitz, died a quick death once all promotional energy was geared toward Isaac's version.

Up to this point, virtually everyone in the record industry simply assumed that the black audience was neither economically equipped nor aesthetically interested in purchasing LPs in large numbers. Consequently black artists were not afforded the luxuries enjoyed by their white counterparts in crafting extended songs or album concepts. Instead, most black LPs were hurriedly and cheaply recorded to capitalize on a string of hit singles. Little thought, effort, or expense was put into cover art design or marketing. *Hot Buttered Soul* unquestionably proved that black artists could sell LPs, and single-handedly revolutionized the notion of the length and musical palette appropriate for black artists. Stevie Wonder, Marvin Gaye, Curtis Mayfield, and Funkadelic would all follow Hayes's lead and, over the next few years, all four would record a series of utterly brilliant albums.

One of the most intriguing aspects of this whole story is the fact that while Hayes had both songwriting and production contracts with Stax, no one at the company had bothered to sign him to a recording artist contract. When this was discovered in early 1970 (presumably when someone went to calculate the first royalty statement for *Hot Buttered Soul*), Isaac was in a uniquely favorable bargaining position. Although he could have held the company up for ransom, he was reasonable and bargained in good faith. According to an exhibit filed by Hayes when he sued Stax in September 1974, he was partially induced to be reasonable by promises from Al Bell of eventual "equity" in the company and substantial "bonuses." Hayes's exhibit goes on to state that none of these was ever forthcoming.

While Hayes was working on *Hot Buttered Soul*, he and David Porter were also writing and producing for two other artists. The Emotions had come to Stax in January 1969. Like the Staple Singers, they were a family group from Chicago consisting of three children led by their father. Joe Hutchinson had groomed his daughters, Jeanette, Wanda, and Sheila, to be performers from the age of three, four, and five. In 1962, when the youngest, Sheila, was nine, the three girls, using the name the Hutch Stereos, recorded their first single, "Santa Got Stuck in the Chimney," for a small Chicago label appropriately named Local. They also recorded for Vee-Jay subsidiary Tollie as the Sunbeams, and usually performed as the Hutchinson Sunbeams. In 1967, they changed their name to the Emotions and began to actively pursue a secular career, recording four singles for the Chicago independent Brainstorm and its subsidiary, Twin Stacks Records, in 1967 and 1968.

On the Chicago church scene, the Hutchinson Sunbeams often found themselves paired with the Staple Singers, with whom their careers eventually became intertwined. Mavis Staples recalls grooming the three younger Hutchinson girls, helping them with their stage outfits and deportment. Pervis Staples became the group's manager and, naturally, had his eye on bringing them to Stax. According to Sheila Hutchinson, though, it was winning a talent show at Chicago's fabled Regal Theater that gave the group a chance to travel to Stax to record one single. The girls made enough of an impression that what was originally a one-single deal turned into an exclusive recording contract.

Isaac Hayes and David Porter became the group's producers. For the group's first single, released in March 1969, Hayes came up with the rather odd but highly effective high-register organ licks that introduce then-sixteen-year-old Sheila's composition "So I Can Love You."

"'So I Can Love You' was a true story," chuckles Sheila, "about a young girl, myself, going to a dance in high school. It just so happened that the young man that took me to the dance had just broken up with his steady and gave me the ring from around her neck. We're at the party and this young man just brought me to get her goat. He still liked her actually. She's there and she wants the ring. So I told him, 'As long as you brought me to this party, you had better be my date the rest of the night and you can deal with her tomorrow.'"

Sheila may have lost her date, but she and her sisters ended up with a number 3 R&B hit that also reached the number 39 spot on the pop charts. Despite the success of Sheila's composition, Hayes and Porter opted to use their own material for the group's next two singles, July 1969's "The Best Part of a Love Affair" and November's double-charting "Stealing Love" and "When Tomorrow Comes."

Porter loved working with the group. "They were so young that it was amazing," he exclaims. "It was fascinating to try and create for them because, being as young as they were and with their dad there with them, we had to juggle our thoughts as to how to be clean yet suggestive. It was a little tightrope walk trying to figure that out. We went through great pains to be sure that we didn't turn 'mummy and daddy' off with the songs. The songs they initially had were light and we were trying to get them with just a little bit more meat and body to the message, yet not be offensive."

At the same time that Hayes and Porter were working with the Emotions, they were also trying to create hits for the Soul Children. For the latter group's third and fourth releases, the dynamic songwriters outdid themselves, writing and producing "Tighten Up My Thang," released in April 1969, and "The Sweeter He Is," released later that summer. "The Sweeter He Is (Part 1)" is the record that finally broke the Soul Children wide open. By the end of 1969 it had gone to number 7 R&B and number 52 pop. Another tension-laden ballad, the record opens with horn, piano, and rhythm while the two men in the group, Blackfoot and West, sing "oohs" in an unearthly double-tracked falsetto. The part is so high that I had always assumed it was two women singing it.

"That was part of the trick of it," Porter explains, grinning. "I was trying to get Foot and Norman to go as high as they could. I've always been a nut for range. . . . It could have been because I didn't have a great range like I wanted to. In the studio I would feel those things. If I were the one on the floor singing, I would have been scared as hell to even try. But I was real comfortable in motivating other people to try it. I didn't want to hear anybody say, 'Well now I can't do that.' I could talk you around that so quick it would make your head swim even though, inside when it's done, I'd say, 'How in the hell did I get them to do that?'"

While the Emotions, the Soul Children, and others were scaling the charts, *Hot Buttered Soul* single-handedly provided Stax with a level of cash flow that no one but Al Bell had ever dreamed possible. True to form, Bell was ready to use the newly acquired funds to expand. At the beginning of March, Bell inked a deal with Robert Weaver to distribute the Chicago-based Weis (We Is) label. The first package slated for release was a spoken-word album featuring powerful black WVON disc jockey E. Rodney Jones, then president of NATRA (National Association of Television and Radio Announcers). The material for the album was written by two inmates of the Illinois State Prison and was entitled *Might Is Right*. This fit wonderfully into Bell's vision of economic empowerment intertwined with social consciousness. Other Weis artists scheduled for subsequent releases included the Soul Merchants, Jean Plummer, Maurice Jackson, and the Forevers. Another distribution agreement was announced during the second weekend of the company's historic sales meetings. Stax, via Al Bell, agreed to distribute soul singer Jerry Butler's and former Vee-Jay executive Calvin Carter's Fountain label featuring Jackie Ross and the Unifics and Infinity. To deal with all this extra activity, Bell hired his cousin, John Smith, to serve as Stax's statistician and market analyst. Smith came to Stax from a position teaching physical science and history at Carver High School in Lonoke, Arkansas.

Countering all this exciting news was the fact that the summer of 1969 also saw Booker T. Jones move away from the company. "It was 1969 and things had become quite corporate," says Booker. "The company had been sold and the arrangements that were made with us were just unsatisfactory. We were dealt with as a group and it was just not good. I was from Memphis, I didn't know anything about business, but I just knew that it wasn't good business. The management allowed the management to change and the management, I think, should have been done by Isaac Hayes, David Porter, myself, and Steve, Duck, and Al. I think we should have been the executives. There were titles given to [us] but we didn't actually make the decisions. That's what was wrong. I think we knew best how to operate Stax."

Booker was very upset when he found out that Steve had been given 10 percent of the East Memphis Publishing Co. while he had been given nothing. He also for years had felt that Jim Stewart and later Al Bell's real motive was to develop a hit factory at the expense of his or the MG's personal growth. As early as 1962, after "Green Onions" had become a hit, Jim Stewart had tried to talk him out of going to college so that he could work Stax sessions all week long. Booker told me on the first day that I met him that that was when he mentally started leaving Stax. In the late sixties he saw Stax begin to groom the Bar-Kays as a second house band. Rather than freeing up the MG's to concentrate on their own work as artists, Booker believed this was a move to allow Stax to go into twenty-four-hour production: the MG's would work all day until six, the Bar-Kays would take over in the evening, and a third band would work the graveyard shift. "It was supposed to be a hit factory. All the soul was basically taken out of that. The MG's were basically Stax employees. We did the MG's music [only] when there was extra time. It had been that way for seven years. When there was nothing else going on, 'Well, let's work on Booker T. and the MG's.' That was the attitude. That wasn't good either.

"I already saw the sinking ship," Booker continues. "I made a prediction. I'm not proud of this statement and I never will be proud of it, but I remember looking Al Bell and Jim Stewart in the eye and telling them, 'If you're going to keep running the company the way you've been running it, it ain't gonna last. And I got to get out of here.' I was really upset that the family had been broken up so it was just better for me to get out of there. I didn't like the way things were being run and who was making decisions. Here I was vice president of the company and I had no say-so. What am I doing being vice president if I can't make decisions anymore? I've been making them pretty good for nine years. Jim really wanted me to stay and I understand that. But Al Bell said, 'Look, if he's really not going to be happy here, then let him go.' So, I left."[23]

Booker's last actual dates as a Stax session musician in Memphis were spent putting the final touches on a couple of projects in March and April for the company's May sales meetings. In June he moved to Indiana before heading out to California in September. Once in California he continued to work for a brief period with Eddie Floyd and William Bell, cowriting and producing hits such as Floyd's "California Girl," but soon he refused to do even that as long as they were recording for Stax. Booker actively tried to entice the rest of the MG's into leaving Stax, relocating to California, and signing with A&M, reasoning that as long as they remained at Stax, they would always be session musicians first, artists in their own right second. Al, Duck, and Steve remained steadfastly loyal to the company and consequently didn't take Booker up on his offer. The four continued to work together as Booker T. and the MG's through the end of 1970, at which point Booker decided he couldn't even continue to do that as long as the records were being released by Stax. What was probably the greatest house band in R&B history and, without a doubt, the most important instrumental group in soul music ceased to exist.

With Estelle and Booker gone, Stax stopped being the same, spiritually or creatively. "I tell you what I hated most of all," laments Bettye Crutcher, "when Booker left. That was a sad day for me. Booker was part of the glue that held the sound together. [The MG's] were so special as a team but it seemed like when Booker left, none of them ever really did anything really super special, not even Booker. That was the beginning of the downfall of Stax Records. Even though Stax Records lived a long time after Booker left and had a lot of hits, it started to lose the team spirit."

"Booker was my best friend," adds Steve Cropper. "Booker was the guy that inspired me. Even though Marvell [Thomas] was good and Isaac was good, it was not the same without Booker. Just the feeling wasn't the same. I always kept the hope up that Booker was going to come back and it was all going to be back to where it was, but it never happened that way."

As the original core of Stax began to dissipate, the label ironically was enjoying unprecedented success. In late July the company issued two separate press releases, crowing about the results of its May sales meetings. If these releases are accurate, two months after the sales meeting Stax had shipped one million LPs and three-quarters of a million dollars worth of eight-track tape cartridges and cassettes.[24] On July 28 the company announced that in its first year of independence, Stax had sold ten million singles. At the time of the sale to Gulf and Western, it was projected that by the company's third year it would be selling seven-and-a-half million singles annually; Stax had surpassed this projection during its first fiscal year as an independent organization.

The number-one reason that Stax found itself sitting so pretty was *Hot Buttered Soul*. Not even Al Bell could have foreseen its impact on Stax's financial picture in particular

---

23. All the MG's as well as Hayes and Porter had been given vice presidencies. Al Bell's administrative assistant, Earlie Biles, felt that these were just paper titles. "There were certain people who had been there from day one," rues Biles, "who expected to be able to function in executive capacity and they weren't qualified. They were musical people and had their own talents. Some of the people who were musicians and writers were given titles of vice president of this, that, and the other. They were just titles. They were even on salary because they had been around for a long time. I think Bell felt like he had an obligation to take care of them and make them happy. They gave them vice-president titles, big suites of offices, secretaries. It was just an appeasement kind of thing I think because Bell and Stewart did the work. Those people weren't the ones who were in charge of the areas they were vice presidents of."

24. Sales figures are often inflated by record companies to boost interest in their product, as well as to attract media attention, so these figures may be high.

and black popular music in general. By late August, Isaac embarked on his first road dates, beginning at Detroit's Masonic Temple. Despite the fact that the gig had sold out two weeks in advance, by his own admission Isaac was nervous as hell.

Using a basic five-piece ensemble[25] that had rehearsed for all of two days, Isaac came on stage wearing a lavender terry-cloth flop hat. Feeling the heat early on in the show, Isaac took the hat off to wipe his brow. At the sight of his bald head, a substantial portion of the females in the audience shrieked with delight. At that point Isaac began to relax, quickly learning how to work an audience.

There were only a handful of gigs played with this stripped-down ensemble. As soon as it was economically feasible, Isaac began hiring small string sections in each city that would rehearse with his rhythm section during the afternoon of the show. In due time, as momentum picked up, Stax's resident enforcers, Johnny Baylor and Dino Woodard, began working the road with Isaac.

"I was getting ripped off severely by promoters on the road," recounts Isaac. "They were not paying me my money. So Johnny came to me and said, 'Hey, man. You're getting screwed around. I'll help you with your money if you help me with my artist.'" Dino Woodard picks up the story: "We felt that he needed some type of guidance and know-how and protection on the road. He had never been out on the road. We had been in New York City and knew the rounds so we thought that it would be best for us to sort of help him out. Whatever it was, when it came to some money and what not, all I can say is that, hey man, Isaac got his due whenever we played anywhere."

The tradeoff was simple: Isaac would let Luther Ingram open his shows and he would play on and/or arrange material Ingram recorded for Baylor's KoKo label; and Baylor and Woodard would collect the money from the promoters when Isaac went on the road. Early on in their relationship, a promoter in Aurora, Illinois, tried to beat Isaac out of his concert fee. Baylor and Woodard pulled their guns on the promoter and Isaac got paid. "A lot of times they corrected things that I didn't even know about," volunteers Isaac. "We had to do some gangster stuff on the road sometimes [but] I got my money and these guys protected me. They were security. They went just about everywhere with me. A lot of people didn't like it but I think they were necessary."

Among those who didn't like it were Marvell Thomas, Johnny Keyes, David Porter, William Bell, and Wayne Jackson. In Cleveland on one particular tour Johnny Baylor put a gun to Marvell Thomas's head at the afternoon rehearsal in full view of everyone. The rehearsal was not going very well because Hayes's conductor, Dale Warren, was severely inebriated. Baylor strode out on the stage and, as he passed behind Isaac's background singers, pinched Pat Lewis's rear end. Marvell Thomas, the keyboard player, suggested to Baylor that the rehearsal was already a mess and that Baylor was just making things worse with his high school-like antics, and that he "would do everybody a favor by getting his silly ass off of the stage." Baylor promptly pulled a gun on Thomas, which he then trained on Marvell's head. Marvell said, "Look Johnny, either you're going to blow my brains out or you're going to put that silly gun away. Now either do one or the other." Thomas then turned his back and, with his heart in his mouth, continued playing; evidently Baylor put the gun away. A few months later, Marvell was fired after a gig at Brown University in Providence, Rhode Island, for being a "disruptive force." Thomas believes it was Baylor who convinced Hayes to terminate him.

---

25. Isaac on organ, Marvel Thomas on piano, Allen Jones on bass, Bobby Manuel on guitar, and Jerry Norris on drums.

In December 1970, Johnny Baylor and Dino Woodard severely beat up Johnny Keyes. Hayes had agreed to play a benefit at Hunter College in New York City.[26] Everyone in his ensemble was asked to do it for free. Johnny Keyes took exception to this.

"I was saying, 'Well why should that happen?'" explains Keyes. "'Hey, if he wants to donate his money, let him donate his money. But why wouldn't we get paid?'"

Angered by the situation, Keyes decided to run up charges on his hotel room, ordering prime rib and other expensive items. After he and Baylor had some words over the phone, Baylor went to see Isaac. Hayes picks up the story: "They said, 'Moses, what do you want to do?' I said, 'Man, handle it however way you want to handle it.'" A few minutes later with Keyes relaxing in his room with sound man Henry Bush and Hayes's three background vocalists, Baylor and Woodard burst into the room saying they wanted to talk to Keyes.

"I'm saying, 'What's up? What's going on?'" continues Keyes. "I stood up and walked towards them and it came out of nowhere. They pulled their nine millimeters out and both of them hit me with them in the head. They knocked me halfway underneath the bed so most of the beating I didn't absorb. I was kicked a lot and everything but I was naturally trying to get under the bed to keep away from them. But the damage had been done. I got hit in the top of the head and over the left eye."

While all this was going down, everyone else quickly scattered from the room as Benny Mabone stood guard at the door pleading with Baylor and Woodard saying, "Man, please don't kill him, please don't." Once it was all over, Keyes crawled his way to the phone and called some people he knew in Philadelphia. His friends came and got him and, once his eye was healed enough so that he could see properly, he got a plane back to Memphis. Needless to say, Johnny Keyes never worked for Isaac again. Within two months, Keyes ceded his record shop to the landlord and moved back to Chicago.

Johnny Keyes.

COURTESY MISSISSIPPI VALLEY COLLECTION.

Just over a year earlier, in late summer 1969, Baylor reportedly had put a gun to David Porter's head. According to Dino Woodard: "There was something that was going on between Isaac and David Porter [about] money and finances. There were some differences where Isaac was always on the bottom end. It was

26. Keyes remembers it as a "Free Angela Davis" event, while *Billboard* mentions a December 7 benefit at Hunter College for the Soledad Brothers featuring Isaac Hayes, the Last Poets, and Harry Belafonte.

something related to that. I don't know if he put a gun to his head but I know that he did go in and speak with him. They were supposed to have been writing partners and all of a sudden man—boom—Isaac wasn't even respected as his partner. [Johnny] felt that Isaac was the man and so like—boom—he had to be protected. So Johnny spoke [to him] on some issues."

According to David Porter, "Johnny Baylor pulled guns during that time on many people [but] Johnny never pulled a gun with a direct threat to me because I told him if he ever fucked with me, it would be a major problem. There's twelve boys in the Porter family, one of them would get [his] ass. He wouldn't make it out of Memphis." Porter went on to suggest that Dino Woodard didn't bother him because Woodard's and Porter's families had roots going back to Dino and David's childhoods.

William Bell recalls ruefully the day that Baylor and company pulled a gun on him, telling him to stay away from Isaac. Many within Isaac's camp at the time feel that Baylor's ultimate goal was to isolate Isaac from all those who had known him for a long period of time. Ultimately this would give Baylor much more control.[27]

Wayne Jackson and Andrew Love were happy to keep their distance from Isaac's camp. For some time the two horn virtuosos had been getting itchy feet. After the 1967 European tour they had been put on salary at Stax. As was the case with the MG's, Jim Stewart felt that this meant that they should not work for anyone else in their off hours. In the meantime Wayne and Andrew were receiving offers left, right, and center for more money than they were making at Stax. When they asked Jim for a raise, they were turned down. This only exacerbated their longtime feelings that the horns were treated as second-class citizens.

"Andrew and I never did feel like we got the credit we deserved over there," comments Wayne. "The rest of the world was saying the horns sound wonderful, the horns made the records, but nobody down there ever said that. We were not getting cut in on the profits [i.e., as a part of the producers' pool]. We never got anything like that. It became more and more obvious that we weren't ever going to get a rightful piece of the pie. As far as anyone including us in on the production pool, it wasn't gonna happen. No one was going to give us stock. We knew that. They always made us feel like it was a big privilege for us to get to come work there. I always got that from Jim."

Compounding matters was the fact that, ever since the death of Dr. Martin Luther King, things had been changing at Stax. Racial tension had begun to rear its ugly head within the company. According to Wayne Jackson, "white wasn't really cool over there" anymore. Wayne, Duck, and Steve had been around long enough that they had no problems with those who had been part of Stax for any length of time, but newcomers, such as Baylor and Woodard, projected a certain negative attitude toward them. "You'd catch guys from up North who didn't know us very well, you'd feel something from them," laments Jackson.

Ever since Baylor and Woodard had arrived, there had been a few instances of gunplay at the studios. Album cover photographer Fred Toma recalls hearing that Johnny Baylor and Ewell Roussell at one point had guns pointed at each other in what Toma terms a "Mexican standoff." The next day a memo circulated stating that all employees were to check their guns at the front desk. Controller Robert Harris, likewise, remembers Baylor and Woodard attempting to intimidate him. When Wayne and Andrew heard that Baylor had pointed a gun at David Porter, they had had enough.

---

27. Even Isaac Hayes's wife was afraid of Baylor and Woodard. In late spring 1971, when she sued Hayes for divorce, Emily Ruth Watson Hayes was quoted in *The Tri-State Defender* as saying that Isaac had "two constant companions who are armed and would carry out every wish and demand of the defendant."

"We quit Stax because it was insane," Wayne says, wincing. "People were carrying guns and Jim Stewart was saying he didn't want us to play with anybody but him. We said, 'We couldn't do that.' Then one day they put a gun up to David Porter's head and threatened to kill him if he messed with Isaac anymore. We left.

"It was payday. Andrew and I walked through the hallway out through the car through the gambit of people, strange people in overcoats, strange people in suits with briefcases, secretaries that didn't know our names. We walked out into the parking lot and got into his car, pulled out a half-pint of vodka from under the seat, just spun the top off of it, and we both had a big drink of hot vodka and looked at each other and said, 'Are we gonna do this or are we gonna continue with our lives?' The opinion between us was that it was time to move on or get caught in the stagnation. That's the day I walked into Jim's office and said, 'We'd like to be off the payroll!' "

Wayne and Andrew promptly incorporated as the Memphis Horns and doubled their prices. Much to their shock, offers for work only increased. In addition to doing sessions, they had long hankered to record as artists themselves. While Stax had actively discouraged this, Atlantic almost immediately offered an artist contract to them.[28] Love and Jackson continued to do recording sessions at Stax on a per-session basis, but it never felt the same again.

"We didn't enjoy it," continues Wayne. "Andrew and I went over there to make session money. It was like my old high school that had gone to shit. So you go back occasionally for a football game or something and it's not the same thing. They started hiring all these arrangers from out of town and bringing them in. Of course we'd sit there and play their music but it wasn't us. It had nothing to do with us."

Symptomatic of the falling morale in the latter part of the summer of 1969 was the decision to dissolve the producers' pool. Cropper was more than disappointed: "It was on the buddy system. Everybody covered everybody's act. Then all of a sudden, everybody got their egos hurt and they wanted to go on their own. Everybody wanted to do their own things. So, if this guy's a schmuck, he's a schmuck; if I make a million dollars, I make a million dollars. Nobody wanted to share anymore. They didn't want the profit-sharing kind of deal. We tried everything in the world to keep that together because it gave us a unit. It was like a football team."

Nevertheless, in October all six members signed an agreement that read in part: "It is the agreement of the undersigned producers that our producer's pool be discontinued effective with any records released after August 6, 1969. . . . Each of the undersigned desires to be treated as individual producers and we are currently negotiating new production agreements." Cropper went on to say that the pool was dissolved mainly due to the feelings of two of the six members; one has to assume that he was referring to Isaac Hayes and David Porter.

It is ironic that as Stax headed into the autumn of 1969, enjoying unprecedented success, virtually every component that had enabled it to grow to this point was withering away. Jim was no longer engineering; Isaac would very soon stop writing and producing for others as he devoted his energies to his own career; Estelle Axton and the Satellite Record Shop were now ancient history; Booker T. Jones, Wayne Jackson, and Andrew Love were gone; Steve Cropper would leave within a year, and the MG's would break up

---

28. It is also interesting to note that Wayne and Andrew wrote much of the material on the Memphis Horns' LPs, while there were only a couple of records released with their names as writers at Stax. According to Wayne, they were writing while they were at Stax, but it was nearly impossible to get their music recorded because they weren't either artists or members of the producers' pool. Andrew Love told me that they envisioned themselves as becoming a writing team in the manner of Hayes and Porter.

shortly thereafter. Replacing this cadre of talent was Al Bell's team, so to speak: the Bar-Kays rhythm section and the Muscle Shoals Sound Section replaced the MG's as the company's primary session musicians; Don Davis, Al Bell, and soon Tom Nixon became the company's primary producers; Homer Banks, Raymond Jackson, and Bettye Crutcher took over from Hayes and Porter as the company's most important songwriters; and new artists, including Isaac Hayes, the Staple Singers, the Emotions, and the Dramatics, replaced the old. Of the primary holdovers—Eddie Floyd, Carla Thomas, William Bell, the Mad Lads, Albert King, Rufus Thomas, and Johnnie Taylor—only the last two would enjoy substantial success in the 1970s.

While all of these events were occurring, Bill Gavin presented Al Bell with the "Record Executive of the Year" award at the Radio Program Conference, held in Atlanta on December 6, 1969.

11

Do the Funky Chicken: 1970

At the end of September 1969, to deal with the company's increased rate of record releases and sales, Stewart and Bell announced the hiring of six new promotion men. LeRoy Little and Bob Spendlove were hired to work at the national level, while David Ezzell and David "Jo Jo" Samuels were set to work the South, Jack "The Rapper" Gibson the Midwest, and Harold Burnside the East. In November, Gibson, one of the first black disc jockeys in the United States, was promoted to the national level.

That same month, Bell was in Chicago courting the man he would hire as Stax's vice president of advertising and publicity, Larry Shaw. Shaw was an expert on the African-American market who, in addition to his regular job, served as advertising and communications consultant for the Southern Christian Leadership Conference's (SCLC) Operation Breadbasket, headed by Rev. Jesse Jackson. Deanie Parker went to Chicago to work on a special issue of *Stax Fax* that focused on the program[1] and was very impressed by Shaw, who she thought was just as audacious as Al Bell. When she came back to Memphis, she recommended to Bell that he meet Shaw. Soon thereafter Bell called the advertising exec and said that he was going to be in Chicago and would like to meet him.

In Chicago, Shaw had pioneered segmented marketing and advertising with Vince Cullers Advertising, Inc.[2] Focusing on the black consumer, he produced innovative material that would be identified directly with the black populace. With the aid of Operation Breadbasket's lobbying, these ads helped make the Cullers agency the first black advertising group with national account billing.

"We were kind of creating as we went," reflects Shaw. "Our challenge was to use words and pictures and symbols and attitudes and casting for photographs that there were no precedents for. We approached it by respecting the marketplace, as opposed to the condescending approach used by major agencies as they sought some response from the black consumer. That's partially what caught the eye of Al Bell. We created commercials for radio that were so unprecedented that the stations were getting phone calls to have the spots replayed. We tied the social and current-event perceptions of the marketplace into the product. Hence, we put Afro-Sheen, a hair product for the natural, in the number one position in the marketplace because we used Swahili words in our presentation. That was really 'on-time' stuff that we were producing."

---

1. While Larry Shaw insists that Deanie was working on a special issue of *Stax Fax*, no such issue of the magazine was ever published. Deanie says it is quite possible that Shaw is correct but she does not remember precisely. In any event, they both agree that it was Deanie who suggested to Al Bell that he might want to meet Larry Shaw.

2. Shaw was into what is now called "psycho graphics." His marketing sensibility was geared around the attitudes and beliefs of the community he was trying to reach. By this logic, according to Shaw, Chicago and Detroit were southern cities. This was perfectly in tune with Bell's theory of Mississippi River Culture.

According to Al Bell, Shaw's "Wantu Wazuri Beautiful People" ad for the Johnson Product Company's Afro-Sheen took the hair product from marketer George Johnson's basement to a national, multimillion-dollar success. Similarly Shaw's campaign for Newport cigarettes based around the radio commercial "The Bold Soul in the Blue Dashiki" made Newport the dominant cigarette in the black marketplace. With Jesse Jackson constantly trumpeting Shaw's abilities to him, Bell started spending a lot of time with the Chicago executive and quickly came to realize how brilliant Shaw actually was. Bell recognized that this was the kind of approach to advertising that was needed at Stax.

Bell proceeded to make an offer to Shaw that supposedly couldn't be refused, saying, "How would you like to have your own advertising agency and unlimited capital?" Shaw's response was (1) he hadn't been in the business long enough to be so foolish as to think he could run his own agency; and (2) he didn't believe there was any such thing as unlimited capital. He then asked Bell what Bell really wanted.

"I talked to him about how they were keeping our black music in a corner," recalls Bell. "Here was a guy that could lock shoulders with me and help me get rid of [the] 'Bama [stigma that Stax suffered from] and help me get rid of the obvious walls that were out there in the industry as it related to black product and come up with merchandising and marketing programs." In the late 1960s, these types of marketing programs hardly existed for black music. No one did point-of-purchase (POP) material for black product. Shaw and Stax would change this in a big way.

What Bell didn't know was that Shaw had been born in Memphis, his wife had just passed away, and he had three children he was not anxious to raise in the Windy City. He was more than ready to move to Memphis. The two men agreed that Shaw would come down for a year and learn the record business at Stax. Then they would see how to proceed. Shaw ended up staying until the day Stax was padlocked in December 1975. He would eventually be put in charge of Stax Films.

Moving to Stax, Shaw's salary increased substantially: he had a profit-sharing arrangement, a bonus based on the activity of the first wave of albums he worked on, and the company paid his moving expenses. Jim Stewart was a little hesitant to make such a generous offer, while Bell, in Shaw's words, was perhaps "overly enthusiastic."

"He saw I was where he wanted the philosophy of the company to go," explains Shaw, "and had some perceptions that could be applied to the industry. As well, he was very impressed with Martin Luther King, and Jesse Jackson was [Martin's] lieutenant. So the King relationship to Jesse, the Jesse relationship to me, my relationship to the movement, and the movement's relationship to Al made a little combination of sensitivities that proved to be very comfortable for him. He makes decisions like that, so unusual things happened throughout the whole Stax experience. It's almost a magic carpet ride from the challenge of the scientific method over against the visceral sensitivity. It makes for an unusual environment to operate in."

Shaw was brought into the company January 1970, followed in April by new controller Ed Pollack. Pollack had been Motown's chief of finance for six-and-a-half years, but had increasingly become uncomfortable with some of the business practices engaged in by the Detroit-based company. Prior to his arrival at Motown, he had been vice president of the Rolland A. Benge mortgage company. He took Robert Harris's place at Stax. At the same time, Motown's director of promotion, Junius Griffin, was also brought down to Stax for a series of meetings, but he eventually decided that the fact that his wife was white could be a problem in Memphis and consequently opted to stay in Detroit.

Bringing in outside executives like Ed Pollack and Larry Shaw from the North only added to the resentment felt in some circles. Many Stax employees openly wondered why local people couldn't be hired to fill key positions, and why the biggest salaries in the company were being awarded to "outsiders."

"I was looking for *experienced* people," stresses Al Bell, "that could come in and give us what we needed in order to achieve what I saw needed to be achieved in the marketplace based on how we were perceived, and that's back to the 'Bama thing. I constantly faced in the industry from my peers, 'Al, you cannot build an independent record company out of Memphis, Tennessee. You're out of the mainstream, you're in a backwater town. You cannot do it out of there. You're outside of the industry. You're in a no man's land.' In retrospect, you couldn't."

In early December, Bell appointed another outsider, Tom Nixon, as director of production control. Nixon's duties included overseeing all aspects of production, a task formerly handled by Al Bell himself.[3] Little seems to be known about Nixon's background, although it would appear that he had been an engineer, perhaps with Motown, on the West Coast. Al Bell had met him through former Motown producer Mickey Stevenson, who had hired Nixon to build his new studio. Al was extremely impressed, feeling that Nixon was an innovative engineer who was especially attuned to what was happening on the West Coast. Al reasoned that—as he already had Detroit and Memphis covered—Nixon would provide Stax with yet one more flavor of contemporary black music aesthetics. "[Tom Nixon] seemed to me a very important addition to our creative team," attests Bell.

Bell was particularly impressed by Nixon's penchant for using a stopwatch to analyze the current Top 10 records. Nixon believed that a certain tempo range (the number of beats per minute) characterized the Top 10 at any particular time, and he would always make sure that whatever he was working on would fit into that range. This was the first time that Bell had ever seen anyone employ such a technique.

Not everybody was as impressed as Al. Marvell Thomas, for one, resented both Don Davis and Tom Nixon: "There were too many people around there who had skills way beyond either one of those two people that should have been, and could have been, utilized for that purpose and were not, which pissed off a lot of folks. If those people had come in with some real skills and had come in there kicking ass as producers, I don't think anybody would have minded too much. But you're sitting there watching these guys and working with them every day and you say, 'Hey, wait a minute. What's the story with this guy? What's his purpose for being here? He doesn't know anywhere near as much about this as I do.'"

The first single that Nixon was involved in the production of was Rufus Thomas's December 1969 release, "Do the Funky Chicken." In the years just prior to this release, Thomas had felt neglected at Stax. He had not been invited to go on the Stax/Volt tour of Europe in 1967, he was not asked to perform on the label's 1969 television special, and his album, *May I Have Your Ticket Please,* was not finished for the big LP push of spring 1969. He felt that many within the company did not take him seriously as an artist. "Do the Funky Chicken" would change all that. Clocking in at number 5 R&B and number 28 pop, the single was the beginning of his career renaissance. Fifty-three years old when it was released, Thomas would enjoy six more chart singles over the next two years.

Most of Thomas's hits, going all the way back to "The Dog," were centered around a current dance. "Funky Chicken" was no exception, being based on a series of steps that

---

3. Tom Nixon was the only major figure at Stax who over the course of eleven years of research I was unable to locate; anyone knowing his whereabouts is welcome to contact the author through the address listed in the Preface.

Rufus Thomas doing the Funky Chicken July 1970 at the WDIA Starlight Revue. COURTESY MISSISSIPPI VALLEY COLLECTION.

originated in Chicago. Thomas decided to write the song while working a gig at the University of Tennessee with Willie Mitchell's band, his only problem being finding something that rhymed with the word "chicken."

"That weekend I worked at a club called the Crestview in Covington, Tennessee," Thomas remembers, grinning. "I did it in the middle of doing another song just like I did the 'Dog'; and the words just started to come. I don't know how, they just came out of the blue.

"I just separated it, 'You raise your left arm up and your right arm too.' When you're doing the funky chicken you use both arms. You don't just use one. It just happened I separated it. Then I put a little rhythm in between it. The same pattern that you heard on 'The Dog' is here on 'The Funky Chicken' but it is cut in half. That's how it came about."

In the breakdown in the middle of the song, Thomas goes into a shtick that he commonly used as a disc jockey on WDIA, saying "Oh, I'm feeling it now. I feel so unnecessary. This is the kind of stuff that makes you feel like you wanna do something nasty like waste some chicken gravy on your white shirt right down front." "It came from my show," laughs Thomas. "When the blues songs started getting really funky I'd go through all these little things."

Full marks on the record go to the Bar-Kays rhythm section, Marvell Thomas, and the Memphis Horns, the latter augmented on this occasion by Ed Logan and Fred Ford. Guitarist Michael Toles contributes the chicken-picking sounds, completing a track that is absolutely dynamite!

While Rufus Thomas was entering the most rewarding part of his career, David Porter was just about to bottom out. Inspired and perhaps a little intimidated by the success of his former partner, Isaac Hayes, Porter finished his first solo album, *Gritty, Groovy, and Gettin' It,* for a February 1970 release. The highlight of the album was an extended work-out on "Can't See You When I Want To," a song Porter had written with Hayes way back in 1965 when they had first worked together. On the 1965 version, David cut the track with the MG's backing him up, but the resulting single received scant attention and Porter put his performing career on hold. The new version was edited down to single length and issued on Enterprise in April 1970.

The production credit on the album went to Isaac Hayes. Now a superstar, Hayes could only find time to help out with the rhythm tracks that were cut at Ardent with the Bar-Kays' rhythm section. No matter how many times he tried, Porter couldn't get Hayes to make time to cut the lead vocals, do the string and background vocal overdubs, or do the mix. "I didn't put my name down as producer," says Porter, "even though I did most of the work on the album because I wanted clout. I had to plead with him to come and work with me because I needed his name attached to mine in my mind because everybody attached us together."

Porter's anguished vocal, complete with mid-song rap, took the new version of "Can't See You When I Want To" to the number 29 R&B spot, while it bubbled under on the pop charts at number 105. Two years later he would enjoy middling success on the singles charts for the second and last time in a duet with Hayes on a cover of "Ain't That Loving You (For More Reasons Than One)." Unfortunately none of his other solo efforts, totaling four LPs and seven singles, generated much interest.[4]

Porter spent much of the early seventies in a serious depression. He was initially very happy about Hayes's success, despite the fact that it obviously would affect the amount of time that he and Hayes would have to write and produce together. "My attitude was we would work when we were able to work," reasoned Porter. "I thought that based on what I had contributed to our relationship and based on what supposedly we were to each other that he wouldn't just disappear . . . but, he did that to me.

"All of a sudden he connected with Johnny Baylor, which was shocking to me. Then we couldn't even talk which was even further shocking. Whenever we could talk, he would get real with me. But it was difficult to connect because the Johnny Baylor thing was to keep us apart because they felt Isaac would listen to me.

"When it got to where we couldn't communicate at all based on people blocking that, we just drifted further and further apart. It wasn't me wanting to do that. It was him doing that. I internalized all of this and it really caused me a lot of mental anguish. There I was going through hell with an identity crisis."

Compounding Porter's pain at the loss of his partner and friend was the passing of his mother that same year. One of twelve children, David had lost his father when he was two. A tower of strength, his mother dug her heels in and raised her family the best way she knew how. Always having been extremely close to her, David was crushed by her death.

---

4. Highlights of this body of material include an eleven-minute workout on the McCoys' "Hang On Sloopy" from his second LP, *. . . Into a Real Thing*; his conceptual third LP, *Victim of the Joke?—An Opera;* and his invigorating final single, February 1974's "I've Got You and I'm Glad."

The combined impact of losing his mother and his songwriting/producing partner sent Porter into a tailspin. He spent the next three years drinking Asti Spumonti, dealing with his internal demons, and creating very little music.

"I just lost it," agonizes Porter. "Creatively I just lost everything. I couldn't create shit. It started me on an unbelievable period. I lost the ability to focus, to concentrate, to be creative. It was out of that that I started drinking. I was never good at drinking but I started bringing booze into the studio. That was not me, but I was going through emotional trauma. I damn near went crazy."

By default, Porter inherited responsibility for the Soul Children and the Emotions, the two artists that he and Hayes had been concentrating on since Stax split from Atlantic. Both groups would suffer due to the breakup of Hayes and Porter. Once Hayes made it clear that he was no longer prepared to write and produce for other artists with or without David Porter, David went searching for a new partner. He was dismayed to find that no one in the company seemed overly interested in working with him. After much thought, Porter eventually found Ronnie Williams, with whom he wrote and produced until Stax went bankrupt.

Ronnie Williams had been a session musician at another Memphis studio, Onyx, with guitarist/engineer Bobby Manuel. He had been brought to Stax by trumpeter Mickey Gregory, who had been working on the road with Isaac Hayes. Williams was one of two keyboardists in a group dubbed the Soul Spacemen that Porter had put together to back him on live appearances to support *Gritty, Groovy and Gettin' It.* For a short period Porter debated over partnering with Williams or the group's other keyboard player, Lester Snell. Williams won out due to the pervasive gospel influence that ran through his playing.

In retrospect, it was probably not the best choice that Porter could have made. "There I was, lost emotionally," grimaces Porter, "and I ended up grabbing people to work with that had about as much talent as a gnat's got in him. I took Ronnie and tried to make him into something. He damn near worked me to death. He had no sense of rhythm. So a lot of the rhythm pockets on the records [we did] were quite ragged. I started sacrificing the integrity of what I had worked so hard to build in working with a Ronnie Williams. That was just one of those mistakes that when you are going through trauma you can just make."

Porter and Williams wrote and produced for both the Emotions and the Soul Children through the summer of 1971 with little success, before Jim Stewart and Al Jackson stepped in to salvage both groups' careers. By mid-1972 Homer Banks, Carl Hampton, and Raymond Jackson had, in turn, taken over the Emotions from Stewart and Al Jackson. In late 1973, Banks and Hampton would also start working with the Soul Children. Porter and Williams were left to work on one LP by the Sweet Inspirations, one album by gospel singer Rance Allen, Porter's solo albums, and precious little else.

While David Porter anxiously awaited the fate of his first album in the marketplace, Al Bell had determined that, after the bumper year of 1969, Stax was ready for the big time. In the first week of January 1970 he promoted John Smith to the newly created position of administrative assistant to the executive vice president. In February he rented a 6,900-square-foot facility on North Avalon into which he moved Stax's front office. The McLemore building would now be used nearly solely for creative staff, most offices being turned over to songwriters and producers. Deanie Parker was the lone holdout. As director of publicity she simply refused to move over to Avalon, reasoning that without maintaining proximity to the studio she would lose touch with the artists and the creative end of the company.

A month after the Stax front office was shuttled over to Avalon, Booker T. and the MG's released the punningly titled *McLemore Avenue* LP. While Booker was adamant about no longer playing regular sessions for the company, he wasn't as yet refusing to work with the MG's. In fact, it was his idea to cover, virtually in its entirety, the Beatles' *Abbey Road* album for the group's *McLemore Avenue* release.

"I was moved by the Beatles," comments Jones. "I thought they were doing really great things. They started to write these beautiful melodies and this stuff was coming from left field. Their records didn't each sound alike ever. Not very many people were doing that. Their approach, to me, was basically like our approach, real rough, real raw. It made me think that what we were doing was okay for the pop market, not just the R&B market. It really changed my musical concepts quite beautifully.

"I thought *Abbey Road* was their best album. I thought they had the best melodies up to then on that album. . . . That seemed like one unit, so I wanted to copy that one unit instrumentally. I was just completely excited about it. At that point I wasn't thinking about making money or anything. I just wanted to do a tribute to the music. I was reaching a point where I was feeling I was coming to a creative zenith. It was all or nothing for me."

McLemore Avenue represented the first time the MG's did not record all the basic parts at the same time. When Jones originally came up with the idea and flew to Memphis to begin work on the album, Cropper happened to be committed to producing a group called Ambergris up in New York.[5] Consequently Jones, Dunn, and Jackson recorded the album in Memphis at Stax, and a few weeks later Cropper flew to Los Angeles, where he and Jones overdubbed his guitar parts at Wally Heider's studio.

"Booker told me every note to play," relates Steve. "I hadn't even heard the Beatles album. I might have heard a cut on the radio but I had not sat down and listened to the album like they had. He showed me the changes and sat down to teach me the songs. I strictly played to what I heard Booker play. [When I heard] the Beatles' versions of those tunes, I went 'Holy shit!' I was very surprised. I didn't know those songs at all." Between listening intently to a copy of the *Abbey Road* album in the studio and Booker humming some of the parts to him, Cropper proved to be a quick study, the completed album being an absolute masterpiece.

"Something" was taken from the album and released as a single in May 1970, two months after the LP had been issued. The MG's start the single by gently caressing George Harrison's oh-so-fragile melody. They finish it with a barn-burning stomp, an arrangement that Booker thought was suggested by Al Jackson and was influenced by the group's work on the *Uptight* soundtrack. The effect is exhilarating. Inexplicably it failed to dent the R&B charts while only crawling to number 76 on the pop listings.

The B-side of "Something" was a non-LP MG's original entitled "Sunday Sermon." Sporting a bass line that is reminiscent of Donovan's "Season of the Witch," "Sunday Sermon"'s call-and-response melody smacks of church in all the best senses. In the first half, Booker states the infectiously graceful tune on grand piano with Cropper comping on the back beat. In the middle Cropper turns in one of his tasteful-to-the-max, ever-so-sparse solos before handing it back over to Booker. The track fades out with Steve and Booker trading leads one final time.

"I really liked the way I played on that," Booker says, smiling. "That was my most open and creative moment that I can remember right now. It's reflective and it's just really raw. The emotion is really pure." It's hard to understand why a track this strong was relegated

---

5. As part of the Gulf and Western deal, Cropper was obligated to produce Mitch Ryder and Ambergris for another Gulf and Western subsidiary, Dot Records.

to B-side status. "This type of tune wasn't encouraged at Stax then," explains Booker. "It's obviously not a blatant commercial thing like 'Hip Hug-Her,' 'Hang 'Em High,' or 'Green Onions.' Jim Stewart wouldn't have encouraged much work on a song like that. That's just a totally artistic endeavor. No bucks are evident there." Beautiful beyond words, "Sunday Sermon" is one of a myriad of great unknown Stax B-sides.

McLemore Avenue was divided into four tracks. Taking a cue from the extended medley on side two of the Beatles' *Abbey Road* album, three of those tracks are medleys clocking in at seven, ten, and fifteen minutes each. Every *Abbey Road* song except "Maxwell's Silver Hammer," "Octopus' Garden," and "Oh Darling" appears in one or another of the medleys, but the order of the songs in each medley does not necessarily follow the order of the Beatles' album. My favorite is the final track on *McLemore Avenue*, which adroitly combines "Sun King," "Mean Mr. Mustard," "Polythene Pam," "She Came in Through the Bathroom Window," and "I Want You (She's So Heavy)." On the surface, covering a complete album of any group, let alone the Beatles, is quite a risky gambit. The MG's pull it off with aplomb, in the process creating a parallel masterpiece to the quintessential Beatles album.

McLemore Avenue was part of the first series of albums that Larry Shaw began working on and was consequently heavily supported with advertising. Shaw designed and took out full-page ads in both *Billboard* and *Ebony*. The *Billboard* ad pictured a cash register, the slogan "Stax the Sound of Money," and contained pictures of the covers of *McLemore Avenue*, Rufus Thomas's *Funky Chicken* LP, Isaac Hayes's third album, *The Isaac Hayes Movement,* and Rev. Jesse Jackson's *I Am Somebody*. The copy at the bottom of the ad read "This is The Memphis Sound."

"It was a blitz on America," muses Shaw. "Al had set this up to bust the country and the industry open. . . . It stretched my capacity. I didn't know the business. I just knew how to present things to the marketplace."

Shaw immediately took out ads in magazines that previously had been, at best, used sparingly by the music industry. He initiated the use of *Jet* magazine for regular music ads. In Shaw's view, *Jet* was a staple of black American households, providing them with their weekly news. At the same time, Shaw ignored *Sepia*. Although this magazine was connecting with the black consumer, it was not black-owned. Shaw's major problem, in fact, was finding enough *appropriate* places to take out ads.

"Our philosophy was not to support junk. We could not find enough media to play the commercial game. So we had to innovate the entire marketing and promotion process. For instance, *Soul* magazine was a struggling publication. We financed it on many occasions and got out issues based on buying two or three ads because we wanted it [to exist] as a medium to show our stuff. So its publishers and writers became good friends of the family and they became of the family. We helped *Essence.* I would fly to any fledgling magazine that we thought would give us some value, whether locally, regionally, or nationally. We worked with *Rolling Stone.* We were peculiar because no black record company had moved in those annals before, into those publications with any ability to design and produce ads. So we made friends." This was much the same approach Al Bell had taken years earlier with small radio stations in need: help them out and the favor will be returned, often tenfold. It proved to be a good philosophy on both the spiritual and marketing levels.

Shaw decided to take the concept of "The Memphis Sound," which had been noted on every missive emanating from Stax since Al Bell had come to the company, and institutionalize it. To do so he took out full-page ads in *Billboard* and the black version of *Life* magazine, *Ebony*, in the spring of 1970. The *Ebony* ad contained an insert not featured in

Billboard, picturing the new albums by the MG's, Isaac Hayes, Rufus Thomas, and Jesse Jackson, while the major part of both ads boldly proclaimed "The Memphis Sound" in large block letters. At the bottom of the ad, in much smaller type, was printed: "Stax, deep in the fertile soil of the southern United States has cultivated and nurtured an energy that has its roots firmly planted in America and its branches spreading the continents of the world [sic]. The Memphis Sound: Soul Music, an energy with a message that has no regard for political preference, ethnic background or ideologies. Check it out . . . It's the real thing from Memphis U.S.A."

"We attempted to put into all our visual material a combination of things," explains Shaw. "There was a little political [content], a little social and a little cultural all together."

Following that was an alphabetical list of twenty-four Stax artists, including the rock bands Dallas County and Moloch, and the gospel artist Maceo Woods. Dallas County and Moloch came to the company through former Mar-Key Don Nix, who the previous fall, via his Deerwood Music Company, had signed a production deal with Stax. Over the next several years, Nix delivered a series of albums to Stax that, by his own admission, "were less than memorable." Rev. Maceo Woods was a thirty-seven-year-old Chicago preacher who founded the Christian Tabernacle Baptist Church in Chicago. He would record several albums for Stax. His first album, *Hello Sunshine,* recorded with the church's choir, was released on Volt in the fall of 1969. Several months earlier the Edwin Hawkins Singers had shocked the music industry by taking a gospel song, "Oh Happy Day," into the Top 10 on both the pop and R&B charts. Although Stax in 1969 was not active in gospel music, Al Bell felt that "Hello Sunshine" had a chance to replicate the success of "Oh Happy Day" and consequently made a master purchase deal for it.

"The Memphis Sound" ad was the only full-page spread Stax ever placed in the more prestigious black publication *Ebony*. "*Ebony* didn't have as many readers as *Jet*," Shaw explains. "We couldn't afford to sit on the coffee table. We did that ad to render that [idea as] an institution. We wanted to make a point. *Ebony* didn't get thrown away. When you put it in there, you institutionalized it. In the black community, if it's in *Ebony* in a full-page ad, it is what it is. The pages were bigger than average, *Life* magazine size. So it was a bigger deal. We couldn't [afford to] go there a lot and there was no need to go there a lot. When I went to *Jet* I got all the people that listened to our music. An *Ebony* reader is not a Stax music buyer per se. [Our music] was not designed to reach them."

The *Ebony* ad contained one of Shaw's favorite phrases: "Where Everything Is Everything." "This was our attempt to put the Motown sound in perspective," he laughs. "Everything was everything because it was undefinable in essence. That's a line I brought out of Chicago. I had been using it and it had become part of our vernacular. It sort of kept us ethereal and above. I was really fighting concretizing these things.

"We needed to have one definition [of the Memphis Sound] so that everybody could agree that there was a Memphis Sound. It had to be all-encompassing. This was a fusion conception. We had to encompass the European contribution and the African contribution to music, both the country and the city. It had to keep everybody in the deal. I wanted to establish that we were big enough to get our piece of the action, and Elvis could also get his piece of the Memphis Sound. See, we thought more about the city than the city would believe and certainly [more than] they thought of the company. We wanted Memphis to benefit from what we were saying internationally. We knew the PR would be for us as well as Memphis. So, if we made the Memphis Sound encompassing country, R and B, gospel, and whatever Elvis is, we could outdo Nashville. [As well, there was] Stax's interest in country, jazz, pop, R&B. All that was part of the program of having that [concept of the Memphis Sound] realized."

Shaw, in many respects, was the executive who was most in sync with Bell's sense of community, black consciousness, and profit. He took the snapping-fingers logo that had been designed by Gulf & Western, changed the color of the fingers from white to brown (which was a significant change), and added the word "Records" beneath the logo. He also designed new logos for Enterprise and Stax's newest label, Respect.

Respect was founded to issue recordings that in one way or another were politically and socially attuned to the newly emergent black consciousness. To that end, the label's logo contained the slogan "Tell it like it is," and its recordings were distributed through school systems and churches in addition to regular retail record outlets. The first release was a spoken word album by Rev. Jesse Jackson. Taking its title from Jackson's famous declaration, *I Am Somebody,* the album was supposed to be the first of a series of albums by Jackson under the running title "The Country Preacher."

Bell had first encountered Jackson through WVON program director E. Rodney Jones. Jones was director of NATRA for several years in the 1960s, and at a regional NATRA meeting in Detroit he spoke about Jackson to its membership. Jackson was based in Chicago, the same city as WVON, and for quite some time WVON had been carrying Jackson's Operation Breadbasket broadcasts on a weekly basis.[6] In addition to Jackson's fiery rhetoric, these broadcasts commonly contained performances by the Staple Singers, the one-hundred-voice Operation Breadbasket Choir, and the twenty-five-member Operation Breadbasket Band led by former Memphian Ben Branch.

"I introduced [Jesse]," Jones proudly declares. "I was speaking to a whole lot of people who were [at the NATRA meeting] that were in a position to help [Operation Breadbasket] because I knew exactly what it stood for in Chicago. This man within one year solidified more than fifty thousand jobs for blacks. It was unbelievable—the little mini-boycotts they had where white retailers had no black clientele. So, hell, a man like that needed help. I put him out there. I helped him to get the start that he needed."

Of all in attendance that evening, Bell was probably the most smitten. He went up to Jones afterward and said that he would like to meet with Jackson. Jackson already had heard of Bell because the Staple Singers told him about this guy in Memphis who was perfectly in sync with his raison d'être. A little while later, Bell was in Chicago on business and Rodney took him along one Saturday morning to attend an Operation Breadbasket meeting.

"It was like going to a church service," remembers Bell, "but the emphasis was on economic development and civil rights. I got an opportunity to experience that. Reverend Jackson had a litany that he was doing at the time called 'I Am Somebody': 'I may not be educated but I am somebody, I may be from the other side of the track but I am somebody, I may not be this but I am somebody.' I was really moved by that and moved by what I knew that could do to people in terms of motivating them and causing their self-esteem to change, and that was a concern of mine, of course, as it related to African-Americans. I met Reverend Jackson and developed a rapport in subsequent meetings as I would go in and out of Chicago, and decided after hearing this litany over and over again that it needed to be recorded because Reverend Jackson was moving all over the place, but there weren't enough people that were hearing this."[7]

6. Operation Breadbasket was the economic arm of Dr. King's SCLC that first emerged when Dr. King came North during the open housing marches. Breadbasket successfully picketed and boycotted chain stores that refused to stock black products, would not hire black employees even when the stores were located in black neighborhoods, would not allow black advertising in their shared advertising programs, and would not hire black construction companies to build new locations. The organization came together every Saturday morning in meetings that took on spiritual overtones. People came away from these meetings feeling involved with a strong sense of community and purpose.

7. Don Davis was also impressed by Jackson, working his "I Am Somebody" theme into a 1970 Top 10 R&B hit by Johnnie Taylor.

Jesse Jackson, Isaac Hayes, and Al Bell outside the back of the Stax studio and offices at 926 E. McLemore Avenue. COURTESY DEANIE PARKER.

Jackson played several roles in the Stax story. Besides his recordings on Respect, he was one of three hosts at 1972's Wattstax extravaganza, and would attempt to rally support for the label in its dying days. Stax, in turn, supported both Operation Breadbasket and later Jackson's splinter organization, Operation PUSH, in a variety of ways, including "donating" the services of several of its bigger artists at the annual PUSH EXPO, a business and cultural exposition, and donating and lending large sums of money to the organization. When Stax went bankrupt, PUSH owed the record label $100,000.

At the time of the release of *I Am Somebody*, Al Bell was quoted in a company press release as saying that with the Respect label "We are attempting to document with recordings outstanding black people in all fields. We want to preserve history on wax so that young people will be able to hear and feel the words, rather than just read them and not understand the man who uttered them."

Jackson recorded one subsequent album on Respect, 1974's *Pushing On (Holy Day/Memphis, U.S.A.)*.[8] John KaSandra recorded four of the other five albums released on the label. KaSandra was a journeyman artist who had recorded as part of two different

---

8. Recorded in Memphis live at Mason's Temple on the anniversary of Dr. King's death.

doo-wop groups, the Cherokees and the Cuff Links. He had also written Bobby Blue Bland's 1964 hit "Ain't Nothing You Can Do," recorded for Imperial Records, written and produced for Ray Agee and Lou Rawls, and recorded two jazz-tinged albums for Capitol before signing with Stax. With four LPs and three singles to his credit, KaSandra was the most recorded artist on Respect. As was true with everything released on Respect in this period, none of his recordings made much of an impact in the marketplace.

Radical Detroit journalist and broadcaster Jim Ingram recorded the remaining Respect album, *Drumbeat,* released in 1974. Besides writing most of the material on the record, Ingram narrated, sang (exceedingly flat!), and played congas through a mixed bag of instrumentals, politically and socially charged narratives, and the spiritual "Walk Around Heaven." His one Stax release came to the company through a master purchase deal with Detroit deejay Al Perkins.[9]

It is ironic that, while Stax was marketing its first release on Respect, the company was experiencing internal problems with respect, much of the fallout being racially tinged. On March 14, 1970, Jim Stewart addressed a company meeting. The ostensible reason for the meeting was to institute a new corporate structure that included introducing new controller Ed Pollack.

In his five-page prepared speech, Stewart addressed a number of other issues beyond Stax's new corporate structure. After noting that 1969 had been an incredibly successful year for the company in which the number of employees had grown from twenty to sixty, the left-field success of *Hot Buttered Soul* had given the label its first gold album, and studio facilities had been expanded, Stewart declared: "It was a year of many improvements and accomplishments and yet, we failed. We failed to overcome our immaturities, we failed to overcome our jealousies, our prejudice, our mistrusts. You see, there is a disease that has spread in our Company, and it has reached epidemic proportions. It's called STAX-ITIS. That's when the mind is undernourished and the ego is overnourished, resulting in underdeveloped minds and overdeveloped egos."

After suggesting that every faction of the company seemed intent on blaming everyone else for any and every problem, Stewart added, "AND ALL THE WHILE THE RUMORS ROLL ON . . . The M.G.'s were kicked out of the Studio; the Blacks are taking over; the Whites are taking over; Al Bell is getting rid of Jim Stewart; Jim Stewart is taking power away from Al Bell. There's a 'WHITE HOUSE'; there's a 'BLACK HOUSE'; there's 'BLACK POWER'; there's 'WHITE POWER'; it is quite apparent to me the people who are spreading this verbal garbage don't have enough work to keep them busy!! No more. NO MORE!! There is no Black Power. There is no White Power. There is only 'GREEN POWER.' There is no White House or Black House. There is a STAX HOUSE, and I say to you neither Jim Stewart or Al Bell is 'taking over.'"[10]

Part of the tensions within the company emanated from the Isaac Hayes camp. A year and a half earlier Hayes had been instrumental in getting the company to hire its first black secretary. He had also helped pave the way for Mike Williams to move from handy man/janitor to the mail room, and in early 1969 he facilitated the move of Henry Bush from cleaner to sound engineer. "I was rebellious," admits Isaac. "I was militant. When Dr. King was killed I flipped and I just did a lot of reevaluating and I said, 'Wait a minute,

9. In Stax's waning days the Respect label's mandate was broadened to include regular R&B, pop, and country 45 releases. At that time, Stax used the subsidiary label in an attempt to circumvent its distribution arrangement with CBS.

10. All spelling, underlining, punctuation marks, and so on are as they were printed in Stewart's written text.

Jim, this company is selling to predominantly black [people]. You've got to get some [black] people working here.' We spearheaded a lot of that stuff."

Isaac's lobbying didn't stop at balancing the racial makeup of the company's office staff. He also forced Jim to pave the parking lot out back. "Jim didn't want to do it," he recalls. "I passed out a petition and got people to sign it and *made* them pave it. It was gravel. We had to get out trudging in the mud and shit! You know, Jim didn't want to spend no money." Isaac had also fought against the office moving out of McLemore and over to Avalon.

In March 1970 Hayes released the followup to *Hot Buttered Soul*, simply titled *The Isaac Hayes Movement.*[11] The new album was very much modeled on its predecessor, featuring only four songs, three of them extended, heavily orchestrated workouts. Of the extended pieces, "I Just Don't Know What to Do with Myself" was a Burt Bacharach–Hal David song, similar to "Walk On By," that had been a hit for Dionne Warwick just a few years earlier. The other long tracks were covers of the Beatles' "Something"[12] and Jerry Butler's "I Stand Accused." The one shorter piece was another Chalmers-Rhodes original, called "One Big Unhappy Family."

"I Stand Accused" was released as a single in July, and to this day is probably the most requested song whenever Isaac performs. While "By the Time I Get to Phoenix" and "Walk On By" had their roots in white pop, Hayes's version of "I Stand Accused," with its piano arpeggios, ethereal background voices, and Michael Toles's circular guitar figure in the song's second half, was steeped in gospel music. "Well, you know that's my roots," attests Hayes. "In fact, I gave [Michael Toles] that lick to play. That was where I wanted to take it down to, as we call it, First Baptist Church."

Isaac's lead vocal on "I Stand Accused," for my money, is his finest moment as a singer. The interplay with Pat Lewis's background lines and Toles's guitar figure is pure alchemy. Although Hayes was the first soul singer whose primary medium was the LP, the 45 of "I Stand Accused" managed to reach the number 23 R&B and number 42 pop slots, respectively.

The other highlight on the album was Isaac's arrangement of "Something." Guitarist Michael Toles remembers it taking the band three weeks, two sessions a week, to learn the arrangement, because it was so difficult. Isaac concocted the whole thing on the spot in the studio as the band and string players were learning their parts. Nothing was written down. The highlight of the whole piece was an extremely out-there solo violin part played by John Blair. Isaac had met Blair when he was playing a gig in New York. "This guy came up with this karate outfit"—laughs Isaac—"and says, 'Man, I want to sit in with you.' 'Okay, wow, man you cool.' John was a radical."

As radical as he was, Blair was happy to listen to Isaac's innovative arrangement ideas. Life wasn't always so easy with the Memphis string players.

"[For a] session they would walk in," says Isaac, "and they had their nose in the air. They were very snobbish and they looked down on the music. 'We playing this?' 'Yeah, but you're getting *paid* to play!' In order to get the best out of these players, in my arrangements I would feature at one particular point a particular instrument or a particular group of instruments. It was a challenge for them because they had to stay within rhythm. They couldn't play like they played classical music. You've got to get the feel,

---

11. Marvell Thomas had come up with the name for Hayes's backup ensemble, the Isaac Hayes Movement, earlier in the year. He modeled the name on the Jimi Hendrix Experience.

12. In an interesting coincidence, in May Booker T. and the MG's released their version of "Something" as a single from the *McLemore Avenue* album.

you've got to go with the flow, you've got to go with the groove. Dale [Warren—the nota-tor and conductor] would walk in a session with a bottle of gin in his back pocket. We started loosening them up and we would get them in the control room on the playback. I would watch them and when their part would come up, they're listening, and if their part is approved by us saying, 'Yeah, man, that's hip,' they'd smile, but at first they didn't want you to know that they were really getting off on it. They'd come back in the next session, 'Mr. Hayes, would you autograph an album for my son?' It became a hip thing to do. Then they got loose."

The Isaac Hayes Movement first entered *Billboard*'s soul LP charts for the week of April 18, 1970. Its predecessor, *Hot Buttered Soul*, was still comfortably nestled at number 5. Within four weeks, the new album had reached number 1, where it remained for five weeks. After seven subsequent weeks at number 2, the album returned to the number 1 spot for one more week. It remained in the Top 10 until the last week in November. *The Isaac Hayes Movement* also reached number 1 on the jazz LP charts and stayed on the pop LP charts for a total of seventy-five weeks, peaking at number 8.

In the midst of this phenomenal success, Hayes agreed to do a benefit in Chicago being produced by E. Rodney Jones. As was the usual protocol for such events, Jones had asked Isaac in advance what he would need for expense money (i.e., plane tickets, hotel rooms, and per diems for his band and entourage). Isaac had given him the appropriate figure and a short while later flew to Chicago to play the gig. As it happened, the benefit was phenomenally successful.

Marvell Thomas and Johnny Keyes were in the dressing room when Rodney came in to settle up with Isaac. Thomas picks up the story: "Rodney came in the dressing room with a suitcase full of money. He opened up the suitcase, counted out the expense money they had agreed to on the front end, gave it to Isaac, and was on his way out the door. Johnny [Baylor] jumped between Rodney and the door and said, 'Hey, look here. It seems to me that might just not be enough.' He had seen eight thousand times more money in the suit-case. Isaac just kind of sits there and it's like Johnny Baylor was speaking for him. Rodney just kind of smiled this little smirky smile he used to do all the time. Johnny at this point has a nine-millimeter pointed in [Rodney's] immediate direction fairly close to his face. Rodney just looks at him, he looked at Isaac, he looked at everybody around the room and then he just sort of moved the gun out of his face, opened the door and walked out."

Rodney concurs with all details of the story except for the gun. "I don't recall any gun being drawn on me. If that had been the case, Johnny Baylor would have left this world earlier than he did. Johnny tried to demand more money. I just said, 'Hey, there's no more money. This is a benefit. What I was told [would cover expenses] is right here. That's it.'"

At the time Rodney was head of NATRA, and by simply picking up the phone and mak-ing a few key calls, he was able to apprise most of the important jocks at all the major black stations across the United States of what had gone down.

"I had a vendetta against the company," continues the powerful disc jockey, "because having an individual on its staff with that kind of attitude was totally ridiculous to me. You don't need that. I didn't want anything to happen in that respect to any [other deejay] in any other major market so I called them all together. That was something that I could do with just picking up the damn phone."

Rodney let it be known that he wanted to meet with Al Bell about the incident, and Bell hightailed his way to Chicago to sit down with the influential disc jockey.[13] "I explained to

---

13. Al Bell has no recollection of this event, and was deeply puzzled when I relayed what Thomas, Keyes, and Jones had told me.

him my feelings," recounts Rodney, "and the feelings of the guys that I had talked to about that kind of an incident happening. It shouldn't happen. In a company that's as viable as Stax you shouldn't have this kind of reputation. That was the whole gist of the conversation with Al and I. We worked it out. Right is right."

Marvell was sure that Al probably had to make amends by giving Rodney a sizable amount of cash but, according to Rodney, money did not play a part in settling the situation. He just needed Al Bell's word that such an incident would never, ever happen to a disc jockey again.

While Bell was smoothing things over with Rodney, he and Stewart were spending precious little time in the studio. Most of the their time in the first several months of 1970 was taken up either negotiating with Gulf and Western to buy Stax and East Memphis Music back and/or attempting to raise the requisite funds to do so. Both of the principals in Stax were sorely disappointed with the stock performance of G&W. At the time they had sold the company in June 1968, the stock had been valued at forty-four dollars a share. It was expected to go up considerably over the next few years. Instead of this sunny scenario, in the summer of 1970 the stock was worth about half this amount. Bell and Stewart were also aghast at G&W's desire to distribute Stax product through the branch outlets of G&W's other record company, Dot Records. They felt that if this ever occurred, the mom-and-pop record stores in black neighborhoods that were Stax Records's sine qua non would be left out of the loop. Finally, G&W had problems with the deal Al had struck with Isaac Hayes. They thought Hayes was getting paid too high a royalty.

"Al and I said we got to get out of this crap," Jim Stewart remembers. "Their whole music division was going down the tubes and we were going to be sucked down with it because we were making money but the division was losing money. They had no product and all that damn overhead. They were putting out albums out your rear end—just garbage. Where is this shit coming from? The only thing we can do is buy the company back. So we started negotiating with them and, at first, they didn't want to hear about it. We just finally kept on and on and insisted and finally they made a price and I said, 'Fine, we'll do it.'"

Clarence Avant was brought back into the picture to help with both the negotiations and the leveraging of funds. He initially made a deal with Jim Judelson at MGM for MGM to buy Stax from Bell and Stewart for $6.5 million once they, in turn, had bought the company back from G&W. Of that $6.5 million, Ampex was contributing in excess of $1 million for tape rights and EMI was shelling out about $1 million for foreign distribution. The fly in the ointment was the fact that G&W had approval over who could buy Stax because Stax would still owe them money after the deal was done. Unfortunately, MGM executive Mike Curb hit the papers with news of the impending deal in early May and, as all parties had agreed that nothing was to be said publicly until the agreement was officially consummated, G&W nixed the deal.

Avant next spent two days talking with Robert Stigwood. When he found out that Stigwood was financed by Polygram/Deutsche Grammophon, he went directly to the source and eventually obtained a loan from DG in exchange for giving the German corporation the rights to foreign distribution of Stax product through March 31, 1974. At the time the deal was consummated it was reported that in 1969 Stax had grossed $8 million, of which they netted a tidy $2 million profit. It would take a few months to arrange all the financing, but after a loan was obtained from the German-based Deutsche Grammophon company, on July 24, 1970, Stewart and Bell purchased Stax, East Memphis, and Birdees Music Corporation[14] from Famous Music Corp. (G&W) for $4,533,265.

14. Birdees was established by Stax as a second publishing company affiliated with ASCAP.

"It was hell trying to get that company back," sighs Jim Stewart. "We gave them a million dollars profit over and above what they paid for the company just to get it back. We went round and round with those people for almost a year. I spent one summer in New York going back and forth to Lincoln Plaza, and then from there to the West Coast."

The terms were $2,233,265 in cash (the Deutsche Grammophon money) and a $2,300,000 note due $175,000 every quarter with a twelfth-quarter final payment of $375,000. The note was secured by (1) the recording studio and equipment; (2) all present and future copyrights of East Memphis Music and Birdees Music Corp.; and (3) all other assets of East Memphis and Birdees. The cash was obtained by "selling" to DG, operating under the name Music Ventures, 45 percent of Stax stock for $3,500,000. On November 10, 1971, Bell and Stewart repurchased the 45 percent of the shares owned by Music Ventures. For putting the deal together from all sides Clarence Avant was paid $100,000 on August 5, 1970, $3,333.33 on March 16, 1971, and $40,000 on April 14, 1971, June 7, 1972, and July 6, 1973. He was supposed to receive another two $40,000 payments in 1974 and 1975, but due to Stax's impending financial problems the latter two payments were never made. All told Avant received $223,333.33 for helping Jim and Al to buy back what had been their own company.

As early as April, Bell and Stewart began making plans for their upcoming independence from Gulf and Western. One of their first moves was to put Tim Whitsett in charge of their two publishing companies, East Memphis Music and Birdees Music. Whitsett's story is fascinating. Born in Jackson, Mississippi, in 1943, by the time he was seventeen the trumpet-playing teenager had formed a seven-piece R&B show band, Tim Whitsett and the Imperials, that had a nationally released 45 on Imperial Records ("Jive Harp" b/w "Pipe Dreams"—Imperial 5757). Over the course of the 1960s the Whitsett-led Imperials issued over twenty more singles, several on his own Rim Records, and Whitsett was involved in another fifty or sixty recordings as a writer, producer, or publisher. Whitsett was nothing if not astute and had figured out as a teenager that, at a certain level at least, publishing was nothing more than filling out the appropriate paperwork and cashing whatever checks are due to you.

"When I made the first record," Whitsett says, "I gave my publishing to a local guy. [Afterwards] I thought, 'Well, what did he do? He didn't do anything. I can do nothing too!' So I started my own publishing company at seventeen."[15]

The Imperials had started out playing New Orleans rhythm and blues in the late 1950s. As the decade changed and the New Orleans sound began to die out, the group turned to Memphis and the new hip sounds that were emanating from Stax. Already equipped with a Hammond B-3 organ, they could easily work the early hits by the Mar-Keys and Booker T. and the MG's into their repertoire. Over time, the all-white frat band added two black vocalists, Tommy Tate and Dorothy Moore.[16] Touring around Mississippi as an integrated band in the mid-1960s was, on more than one occasion, a hair-raising experience.

As the decade wound to a close, Whitsett sent some newly recorded demos up to Avco-Embassy Records in New York, where Norman Reuben heard them and subsequently played the tape for Don Davis. Within days Whitsett found himself on the receiving end of a call from Davis.

15. Gulf Way Publishing Inc.

16. Tate figured into the Stax story as both a recording artist and as a writer, while Dorothy Moore would go on to fame on the Malaco label with such hits as "Misty Blue," "Funny How Time Slips Away," and "I Believe You" in the mid- and late 1970s.

"Don Davis called me up," recounts Whitsett, "and said, 'Oh, you know I'm working at Stax now. I'm the new vice president there and I want to build a new studio house band. I want you to put it together and I want you to come up here and bring all your guys.'"

Unknown to Davis was the fact that the Imperials had recently fallen apart as their drummer had just enrolled in graduate school to avoid the draft, their saxophonist was already over in Asia in the employ of Uncle Sam, and Whitsett's keyboard-playing brother, Carson, had just headed up to New York City to join Avco-Embassy artist Eric Mercury. That left Tim, vocalist Tommy Tate, and the bassist and guitarist. The latter two decided not to leave Jackson.

"I called old Don up," chuckles Whitsett, "and I said, 'Man, look, I hate to tell you this, but there's only two of us left.' He said, 'Oh, this gives me a headache. Come up here anyway, we'll figure out what to do.'"

A beleaguered Tommy Tate and Tim Whitsett made their way up to Memphis on April 13, 1970. Upon their arrival, Davis suggested that they both should be signed as writers to East Memphis Music.

"So," continues Whitsett, "that first day we sat in there with the other Stax songwriters and we wrote some songs. And that night Don Davis called me aside. He hadn't even heard anything. We'd only been there six hours. He said, 'You had your own publishing company, didn't you?' I said, 'Yeah.' And he said, 'Would you like to run our publishing company? At this moment our publishing company is being run by Famous Music [of Gulf and Western] but we're going to take control of it in a few months. We are going to need someone to run the publishing company and we'd like for you to do it.' I said, 'Fine. Great!' And I became the head honcho of the publishing company!

"They never told me anything. They gave me a big office. There was a carpet you could fall over as you walked [it was so thick]. It was the swankiest-looking place you ever saw. Great fabulous desk, swivel chair with a big throne. This was my second or third day in Memphis! He said, 'Here's your office, go run a publishing company,' and that was it. I sat there for a day. I didn't know what in the hell I was supposed to do."

Whitsett ended up teaching himself the ins and outs of the publishing business, initially by buying every book he could lay his hands on concerning copyright law. He quickly realized that the publishing company was in a pretty disorganized state—to the point where a lot of the Atlantic-era songs hadn't even been copyrighted! To say the least, he had his job cut out for him.

Just to ensure that he never suffered from boredom, Whitsett was also put in charge of auditioning incoming tapes.

"Steve Cropper said to me," says Whitsett, laughing, "'Now think carefully before you say yes: would you like to take over our audition department?' I was really busy with publishing and I said, 'Well, I don't think I'll have time.' He said, 'All right,' and the next day box after box came in and I took over all the auditioning of those tapes from then on. I was listening to all these bloody audition tapes that came in from hillbillies in Tennessee whistling and beating the side of their rocking chairs. I heard everything. I got all the weirdest kind of letters too. I got awful stuff!"

As the details of the buyback from Gulf and Western were being worked out by the lawyers, Whitsett's benefactor, Don Davis, was packing his bags.

"Don only lasted a few months after I got there," recalls Whitsett. "All of a sudden he came into my office one day and said, 'I've been fired and I'm going back to Detroit. You can have it and I hope you have fun.' All of a sudden he wasn't executive vice president anymore. His palace was taken away from him where the projection booth at the theater used to be."

Not surprisingly, given all this activity, relatively few records were released on Stax, Volt, Enterprise, or Respect in June and July. In August, though, Stax was releasing records at full speed again. That same month Al Bell stepped back into the studio, taking over the responsibility for producing the Staple Singers from Steve Cropper.

"I had gone into Chicago to visit Jesse [Jackson]," explains Bell. "He was sick. While there at his home with his family by his bedside, Jesse said to me, 'Mate, you know y'all missin' it with Mavis and them. See, can't nobody cut the Staple Singers but you. You got to understand Mississippi to be able to cut the Staple Singers, you got to understand that harmony that they do, you got to be able to understand the gospel. Now mate, I think you're doing a disservice to Pops and you ain't doin' your company well. If you went into the studio and cut the Staple Singers yourself and devoted the time and attention to them like you're doing to that bald-headed rascal over there, they would be very, very big for you and you'd be getting a good message out here. Culturally, it would be important for us.'

"His argument, on its face, made sense to me," continues Bell. "Jesse was very creative and he understands creative people. [He has] a great ear. I respected what he was saying."

Bell took the group to Muscle Shoals. When asked why he elected not to record them in Memphis at Stax he responded: "[The MG's] would resist me on a lot of stuff, the reason being because I wasn't a musician. That's why I did all my productions outside of Stax. I wasn't respected internally as a producer. I couldn't direct [the session musicians] internally. They had their own thoughts. I needed to deal with somebody that I could direct." For Jim Stewart, Bell's decision to record in Muscle Shoals had larger ramifications: "I quit trying to understand it a long time ago but [Al] never liked the McLemore atmosphere. I always maintained that the minute that studio died and that energy died, the company died. I think history has proven that correct."

The first session at Muscle Shoals in August 1970 produced the double-sided hit "Love Is Plentiful" and "Heavy Makes You Happy (Sha-Na-Boom-Boom)." Al Bell must have had some inkling that both sides might chart, because the record was shipped to radio without a "plug" side.

Bettye Crutcher, having parted ways with Homer Banks and Raymond Jackson, cowrote "Love Is Plentiful" with session guitarist Bobby Manuel. Crutcher remembers: "[The Staples were] artists that nobody wanted to write for. Steve Cropper had produced the Staple Singers before and nothing happened. Al Bell asked for songs for weeks for the Staple Singers. Nobody would write for them! As far as Homer and all of them were concerned, we had already written all these songs for the Staple Singers and [Stax] didn't promote them."

The demo of "Love Is Plentiful" was quite a bit slower than the Staples' recording. To Crutcher's chagrin, Muscle Shoals pianist Barry Beckett and Al Bell decided to speed the song up: "They wanted to put more fire in it and, when they did that, it kind of pushed it out of the range of the Staples as far as I was concerned."

With Bell both producing the Staple Singers and owning the company, promotion was not likely to be a problem. "Love Is Plentiful" became the singing family's first R&B hit, shooting all the way to number 31. The other side, "Heavy Makes You Happy," did even better, breaking the R&B Top 10 before stopping at the number 6 slot and climbing all the way to number 27 pop. The latter song was written by Bobby Bloom of "Montego Bay" fame in tandem with Jeff Barry. Australian impresario Robert Stigwood was about to sign the Staples to management and publishing contracts and had brought Bloom down to meet them.[17] Bloom offered the group the song that to this day commonly opens their shows.

17. In 1971 Stigwood brought Eric Mercury to Stax; he also had signed Mercury to a management contract.

"That song was a happy song," says Mavis Staples. "That's what was so hip." Her excitement is palpable as she opens the track with a scream followed by the declamation, "Good gosh almighty now."

In every way, the Staples had been transformed. The records they cut with Steve Cropper had been superb, but the Muscle Shoals recordings under the guidance of Al Bell are nothing short of ecstatic.

"The Muscle Shoals guys were just a *funk* band," enthuses Mavis. "These guys were so cool. Man, we had some times. We would all do it together. The Muscle Shoals guys were a rhythm section that a singer would just die for. They were bad back then! That's what was happening up in there, magic."

The Muscle Shoals section was great, but so were Booker T. and the MG's. It seems odd that Mavis would have found Muscle Shoals to be so much better. "You know why," counters Mavis. "Booker and them would mostly put the tracks down before we'd be in there. We would all be in the studio together with Barry [Beckett] and them. We were feeding off of each other. That made a difference." That is an interesting observation. The magic of Stax in the sixties was at least partly based on the fact that the rhythm section, horns, and vocalists all recorded together "live." When multitracking became available to them, they gradually abandoned this approach, losing some of the spontaneity in the process.

The Muscle Shoals guys could and did cut tracks without the vocalists as well. That's certainly how they worked on Don Davis's sessions. Al Bell, though, always took the Staples to the studio and recorded the whole thing live. More often than not, the vocal cut in Muscle Shoals would end up being a "scratch" or "dummy" vocal that would be recorded over back in Ardent at a later date. Engineer Terry Manning remembers several of Mavis's vocals being pieced together from a number of different takes. Working this way, the Staples had the best of both worlds: all the advantages of contemporary technology in the drive for perfection as well as the magical kinetic interplay that could be obtained by recording "live."

Hard to believe, given that she had been recording for seventeen years, but Mavis was also growing as a singer. "I was trying more things. I was getting looser, getting more within myself and knowing myself and what I could do. I think I was getting bolder as far as trying things." The Staples' Al Bell/Muscle Shoals recordings are among the greatest soul records ever made.

A few Stax session musicians have expressed considerable reservations about Al Bell as a producer, pointing out that he was not a musician. Ardent engineer Terry Manning, who worked on every Al Bell–Staple Singers recording, strongly disputes this: "Al just had that amazing ability, more than I had ever seen, to know the required emotion, to be able to impart that to people, and for it to come across. People who say he's not a producer don't understand the emotional aspect of recording. Just because he can't come in and [say] 'play a m7+9' does not mean [he's] not a producer. I think that's sour grapes from somebody who is not as talented as Al Bell.

"These albums, to me, just reek of emotion," continues Manning. "Everybody played a part. I played some part, Mavis played a huge part, all the other people played a part, but Al Bell was, to me, the director of emotion. That's a corny-sounding term, but he just knew how to do it."

"Love Is Plentiful" and "Heavy Makes You Happy" were recorded in August but not released on 45 until November 1970. They were both included on *The Staple Swingers* LP. Bell named the album in the hope that it would subtly serve notice that this great gospel group was now singing songs that were more mainstream. If that idea could get across to radio and retail, the Staple Singers would garner substantially more exposure than they had heretofore enjoyed. The idea worked better than anyone ever could have imagined.

Two months earlier, in a move that once and for all signified the changing of the guard at Stax, Steve Cropper had handed in his resignation. Ever since the European tour of 1967, Cropper felt that he had had most of his power taken away from him. The arrival of Don Davis and the diversion of a substantial number of sessions to Muscle Shoals had simply exacerbated the problems. Although he was still the company's primary guitarist and one of Stax's chief producers, he was anything but happy. With Booker no longer being a part of the equation, his heart was pretty well gone from Stax.

While playing a series of weekend gigs with the MG's, Steve discussed how he was feeling with Duck Dunn and Al Jackson. Cropper reasoned that if they all went in to see Jim and Al together, they would get what they wanted, because neither executive would want to lose all three of them. They all agreed that on Monday morning they would go in together to state emphatically that they wanted to be put back in control of making production decisions. However, Duck and Al backed out of the confrontation at the airport in Memphis, suggesting to Steve that he go in and do it himself.

"That's really the first time ever," sighs Steve, "that I was really disappointed in Duck Dunn and Al Jackson. I felt really let down by them. I said, 'Ain't this some shit.' I couldn't even sleep that night. I couldn't believe these guys did this to me. I had a game plan of how we were going to work it. So, I said, 'To hell with it.'"

Around the same time Ronnie Stoots, former lead singer of the Mar-Keys, had talked to Steve about going in with him and Jerry Williams as partners in a new studio they were opening at 1711 Poplar that was going to be called Trans-Maximus Inc. The studio had been built by Jerry Williams and his brother. Stoots helped design the electronics in cooperation with Auditronics and was in charge of advertising, public relations, and the design of all album covers for the proposed TMI label. Stoots felt they needed Cropper for his production skills. Stoots and Cropper were very close and, consequently, Stoots was well aware of how unhappy Steve had become at Stax. In addition to feeling essentially powerless at the company he had been instrumental in building, Cropper bitterly resented the fact that Jim Stewart had blocked him from working with Dominic Frontiere on soundtracks and the MG's from working with Simon and Garfunkel on "Bridge over Troubled Water." Steve told Stoots he would think about it.

"The more I thought about it," explains Steve, "I said, 'This is it. I'm through. I've got a place to go. It's not like I'm going to be kicked out on the street.' So I went in and I sat down with Jim and I said, 'Jim, I want to leave the company. I'm not happy here, I'm not gonna be happy here. There's nothing you can do to make me happy here. It's just reached its end. It can't go any further and I want out.'"

Jim told Steve that he couldn't let him out, as he was worried that Cropper's departure would start a domino effect in which Duck, Al, and perhaps others would also leave.

"I didn't have any luck with Jim," continues Cropper, "so I went to Al Bell and he said, 'Yeah, yeah, yeah.' He kind of hem-hawed me."

Bell's technique of appearing all ears and sympathetic whenever someone brought a problem to him was legendary within the company, but Cropper was having none of it this time. "I used to go to Al with a complaint and I mean it wouldn't be five minutes, he'd be walking out the door patting you on the back and both of you would be laughing. You'd be gone about ten minutes and you'd say, 'Wait a minute.' You'd still have the same problem but you'd have a smile on your face. That's one of his best fortes. I said, 'That ain't gonna work this time, Al.'"

Steve proceeded to get a lawyer and eventually reached a compromise with Stax. He had to give up his 10 percent of East Memphis Music and his earn-out position hanging over from the G&W deal, which was easily worth more than $100,000. He also had to sign an exclusive writer's contract with East Memphis for two years (up to this point he only had a handshake deal), and he had to agree to produce a certain number of records for Stax at Trans-Maximus for one year. Further, news of Cropper's departure could not be made public. Instead, Cropper had to agree to let Stax issue a press release that stated he had been made a vice president. Jim and Al played hardball, but on September 20, 1970, a date indelibly burned into his memory, Steve Cropper had his freedom.

At TMI he would produce successful albums for Jeff Beck, Tower of Power, Jose Feliciano, and Poco, among others. He would also start the TMI label. To satisfy his obligations to Stax, Cropper produced Eddie Floyd's *Down to Earth* and Eric Mercury's *Funky Sounds Nurtured in the Fertile Soul of Memphis That Smell of Rock* in 1971. Other than a solitary session he played for David Porter a little while later, the Floyd and Mercury albums were the last things he ever did related to Stax.

While Cropper's and Stax's lawyers were hashing out the details of the guitarist's departure, Al Bell was giving Tom Nixon and Josephine Bridges their own label, We Produce. Nixon had enjoyed success earlier in the year with his production of Rufus Thomas's "Do the Funky Chicken." Jo Bridges had taught school in the Memphis City School system and ran her own public relations agency. In 1968 while working on a program for a charity, she came into Stax to solicit an ad. She met with Al Bell, who hired Bridges to handle most of the big parties the company staged for various events and to do some work for Stax on special projects related to Memphis teenagers. One such project was the monthly staging of talent shows.

"Because things were not evolving the way I wanted them to with Tom at Stax," explains Bell, "[We Produce] was my way of giving him his outlet creatively so he could do his thing." It also allowed Bell to satisfy Josephine Bridges's desire to produce records.

Bridges and Nixon were also given a publishing company called Red Stripe. They released five albums on We Produce, three by the Temprees, and one each by Lou Bond and Ernie Hines, as well as sixteen singles, twelve by the Temprees and two each by Ernie Hines and Lee Sain. Aside from the doo-wop-oriented Temprees, Nixon and Bridges had absolutely no success with their label and publishing company. The Temprees managed to place three singles on *Billboard*'s R&B charts in 1972 and 1973, the most successful being their rococo cover of the Shirelles' "Dedicated to the One I Love," which reached number 17 in the fall of 1972 while scraping to number 93 pop.

While Nixon did his best to get We Produce off the ground, he continued to enjoy great success with his productions of Rufus Thomas. As 1970 drew to a close, Stax released the Nixon and Al Bell–produced Thomas recording of "Do the Push and Pull (Part 1)." Sporting a backing track that positively sizzles, "Push and Pull" went on to be Thomas's first number 1 R&B hit and, at number 25, his highest-charting pop single ever.

In December Isaac Hayes released *To Be Continued*. For all intents and purposes, the album was the third installment in a trilogy that had started with *Hot Buttered Soul*. As with its predecessors, the LP featured four extended tracks, including a Bacharach-David tune, "The Look of Love" (a hit for Dusty Springfield in 1967 and Sergio Mendes in 1968); a pop cover, the Everly Brothers' "You've Lost That Lovin' Feelin'"; and an R&B cover, Aretha Franklin's "Runnin' Out of Fools." However, instead of a Chalmers-Rhodes original, for *To Be Continued* Hayes recorded a fourth cover, Ruby and the Romantics' 1963 hit "Our Day Will Come." The album jacket actually listed six tracks, but the remaining two cuts, "Ike's Rap 1" and "Ike's Mood 1," were, in the first case, the same type of

Rufus Thomas and Tom Nixon enjoying their success in the early 1970s. COURTESY FANTASY, INC.

extended monologue that he had been using going back to "By the Time I Get to Phoenix," and, in the second case, a long orchestrated introduction to "You've Lost That Lovin' Feelin'." Someone realized that if these sections were titled and copyrighted, songwriting royalties could be made.

In January 1971 Isaac's world-weary take on "The Look of Love" was released in edited form on 45. Surprisingly, the single failed to chart R&B and barely made it to the number 79 spot on the pop charts. Despite the relatively poor showing of the single, as was the case with his previous two albums, *To Be Continued* shot to number 1 on both the soul and jazz LP charts while settling for number 11 on the pop LP charts.

The year ended with the Beverly Hills/Hollywood branch of the NAACP naming Isaac Hayes "Male Vocalist of the Year" and "Producer of the Year" while Stax was named "Record Company of the Year." Even more impressive were the six awards the company received from NATRA: *Hot Buttered Soul* was voted "R&B Album of the Year," Johnnie Taylor was selected as "R&B Vocalist of the Year," Maceo Woods and the

Christian Tabernacle Baptist Choir were chosen "Best Gospel Choir" and their performance of *Hello Sunshine* was named "Best Gospel Record," and the Staple Singers received an award as "Best Folk Gospel Group." The crowning achievement was NATRA's designation of Al Bell as "Man of the Year." "The little company that could" had come an awfully long way.

The Stax team at the 1970 NATRA meeting: (*left to right*) Dino Woodard, Jack "the Rapper" Gibson, Harold Burnside, Al Bell, John Smith, Mack Guy, and Jo Jo Samuels. COURTESY DEANIE PARKER.

12

Shaft: 1971

t the beginning of 1971, Stax, for the first time
since Atlantic picked up the distribution rights
for "Cause I Love You" in the fall of 1960, was
truly a full-fledged record company. Figuratively
and literally, the company had shed a number of skins as it embarked on its own "new beginning." From Al Bell's vantage point and from a sales perspective, 1971 and 1972 were the
climactic years in the company's all-too-brief history. Continuing to expand the company's
operations in a variety of directions and in sheer cumulative size, Bell seemingly could do no
wrong, one success continually following another. If Bell did not have the Midas touch, in
the early 1970s he certainly had his fingers squarely on the pulse of black America.

As is usual in the record industry, January was a relatively quiet month in terms of
record releases. Instead, while consumers were recovering from the annual Christmas
madness, Al Bell and Jim Stewart were reorganizing their promotion department. On
February 18, 1971, the company issued a press release headed "Stax Oust All Promotion
Men." As Stewart and Bell explained it, all promotion men were now being termed "Field
Representatives." In the process, their duties had been greatly expanded. In addition to
servicing radio with Stax product, these employees were now expected to become
involved in merchandising, marketing, advertising, distribution, public relations, and any
other activities that Stax might need carried out in the field.

This expanded marketing department was to be headed by Stax's newest appointee,
Chester Simmons, who was given the broad title of administrative service manager.
Former Moonglow vocalist Simmons had befriended Al Bell when Bell was a disc jockey
in Washington. Together with Eddie Floyd, they had started the Safice label. After Bell
and Floyd headed for Stax in 1965 and 1966, Simmons had become national promotions
director for Chess Records. Assisting Simmons at Stax was Mike Williams, who had started his days at 926 E. McLemore cleaning out the trash behind the building, and had most
recently been in charge of the mail room. Another former Chess employee, Michael
Papale, was appointed national field representative with a mandate to focus heavily on
Stax's pop product. Former disc jockey Jack "The Rapper" Gibson climbed the corporate
ladder from promotion director to director of special services, concentrating on working
Stax product in jazz, contemporary rock, and the college market. Stax's regional field rep-
resentatives remained David Samuels in the South (replaced by Jaye Howard in April),
Hank Talbert (soon aided by Richard Smith) in the Midwest, Harold Burnside on the East
Coast, and Edward Shields (John Smith's brother) on the West Coast. Two months later
Simmons brought a third former Chess promotion man to Stax, Fred Mancuso, who was
hired as market development coordinator for all Stax labels.

One of the first 45s promoted and marketed under this new structure was the final
Booker T. and the MG's single, "Melting Pot." Whereas past singles "Hang 'Em High,"

The greatest instrumental soul group in the world, Booker T. and the MG's: (*clockwise from upper left*) Booker T. Jones, Duck Dunn, Steve Cropper, and Al Jackson, Jr. COURTESY FANTASY, INC.

"Time Is Tight," and "Something" had been slightly edited down from their longer LP masters, "Melting Pot" had to be cut from over eight minutes to just under four to fit radio play limitations. The album from which it was taken, released the previous December and also entitled *Melting Pot*, was all about stretching the limits. Comprised of eight originals, the disc proved to be one of Booker T. and the MG's crowning achievements, befittingly providing a rich swansong for the greatest instrumental soul group ever.

By this point in time Booker refused to record at Stax, and so the group recorded the title track and perhaps one or two other cuts in an afternoon in New York while they were playing gigs in the area. The rest of the album was comprised of tracks that had been cut earlier in Memphis and that previously had been vetoed for release by Jim Stewart. The whole album, including the title track, was very jazzy in its orientation, which was largely why Stewart had been leery about issuing the tracks in the first place.[1] Jones's refusal to return to Memphis to record any new material left Jim with no choice but to use these tracks if he wanted a Booker T. and the MG's album.

Predictably Booker T. was the member pushing for the new direction. "I remember I thought that we really needed to make another change," avers Booker. "Our music was

1. Someone at Stax had actually written the word *jazz* on several of the tape boxes that contained *Melting Pot* material.

beginning to sound the same. So let's become creative again and do something fresh. That was the personification of *Melting Pot* to me.

"I wanted the group to progress. I always thought that our success had to do with the fact that we came up with something people hadn't heard before. So I always wanted to make that the basic criteria for what we were recording. Was it exciting? Is it new? Is it a little bit unique? I think when I went to California I had reached the point where I thought the group was not sounding new.

"I fought hard to get *Melting Pot* recorded. Those were ways we had never played before. It had some totally new musical attitudes on it. I loved that album. I thought this is what we should be doing. We should be charting out new territory. We had set up a legacy. We were Booker T. and the MG's. We had made 'Green Onions'! How could we not do something new is the way I saw it. *Melting Pot* was the right direction but it took a good while to get there.

"I was fighting the company. 'What do you mean you don't want to record in the Stax studio? You recorded all your hits in the Stax studio. It's crazy to go to New York and record. That doesn't sound like Booker T. and the MG's.' The company had grown large by that time. Sometimes new ideas and attitudes are just difficult for established institutions to accept. I really needed *Melting Pot* for myself, to make that record and feel like we were progressing."

Duck confirms Booker's take on the situation. When asked why they recorded "Melting Pot" in New York he replied, "We didn't think our sound was up to date [and] just to get away from that whole environment of other people telling us what to do. Independence!"

"I think the energy on that album," adds Steve Cropper, "shows that we were all having a good time. We really enjoyed doing that up there and being out of the pressures of Stax. Stax had gotten into a situation where all of a sudden it wasn't fun to go to work there anymore."

Ironically, when it was initially released, *Rolling Stone* characterized the album as basically more of the same old MG's sound. "I went livid," exclaims Cropper, "because it was probably the newest, freshest thing we had done in our whole career. Obviously the guy never even listened to the album. I'd like to punch that guy in the nose. You can get over a bad review but, for that, the guy wasn't even there."

The "Melting Pot" 45 achieved a respectable level of success, charting at number 21 R&B and number 45 pop. The LP version is much richer. Written in the style of "Over Easy," running over eight minutes and fifteen seconds, the song became in the hands of Booker, Steve, Duck, and Al a sonic journey of immense proportions. Steve had suggested the song's title, reasoning that it fit the reality of a band with four such disparate personalities ("It was like throwing a bird, a cat, a dog, and a pig all in the same pen," jokes Cropper). "I love the song 'Melting Pot,'" says Steve. "I could listen to that over and over and over. Of the songs that are more musical and more into a jazz rhythm, that's probably my favorite." The longer version of the song remains an integral part of the group's live shows to this day.

Following hot on the heels of "Melting Pot" was one of the biggest hits ever released on Stax, New Orleans native Jean Knight's "Mr. Big Stuff." Knight (real name Jean Caliste) had first entered a recording studio eight years earlier, covering Jackie Wilson's "Doggin' Around" for Huey Meaux's Jetstream label. By the late 1960s she had almost given up on a singing career.

As if in a fairy tale, while on her way to pay a light bill in the summer of 1970, Knight was stopped by someone hollering her name from across the street. A songwriter and casual acquaintance told her that New Orleans producer and writer Wardell Quezerque was looking for her. Quezerque had three or four songs that he thought would work well with Knight. "I really liked the lyrics of 'Mr. Big Stuff,'" says Knight a decade and a half later, "but it was an old-time melody. It was a sassy song but the way they had it sounding, it sounded sad, real sad. It just didn't go. I told them, 'Something's got to be done about this melody.' I knew enough about singing then to know that.

"This other songwriter, Albert Savoy [who was presumably just hanging out at the rehearsal], said, 'Well Jean, everybody know you to be sassy, you'll tell somebody off in a minute.' He said, 'Just get the attitude like you sacking a guy out.' . . . Believe it or not, I just read all the way through the song just like that. It was magic, it really was."

A couple of days later Quezerque returned from Jackson, Mississippi, having cut a very dry and funky reggae-influenced rhythm track at Malaco Studios. After rehearsing her with the rhythm track, Quezerque took Knight to Malaco one Sunday to cut the lead vocal.[2] On the same spring 1970 day that Quezerque was recording Knight's "Mr. Big Stuff," he was also cutting King Floyd on "Groove Me." In exchange for the studio time, Quezerque had cut Malaco into a piece of both records. With Jackson native Tim Whitsett recently ensconced at Stax running the East Memphis and Birdees publishing companies, it was natural for Malaco to take both records as well as several other recently completed tracks up to Memphis.

Tim Whitsett picks up the story: "They came up to Stax, hoping that we would sign someone up, and I took them in to see Don Davis. We played these five, six things they had and Don Davis said, 'Which one did you think, Tim?' I said, 'This one "Groove Me" by [King Floyd] and this one "Mr. Big Stuff" by Jean Knight and this other one by a group [whose name Whitsett couldn't remember].' Don said, 'Hmm, well I don't think so fellas. I'm sorry, I don't think you got it this time.'"

Malaco released "Groove Me" on their own, then very tiny, label. When the 45 started becoming a hit in New Orleans, Atlantic picked it up for national distribution, turning it into one of the monster records of the fall of 1970. In the meantime "Mr. Big Stuff" languished in the can.

"I liked 'Groove Me,'" continues Whitsett, "but my favorite was 'Mr. Big Stuff.' I kept thinking about that record and thinking about it. I [phoned Malaco and] said, 'When are you going to do something with that?' They said, 'Well, Atlantic doesn't like it.' I mulled it over in my mind for a couple of months and I called [Malaco co-owner] Tommy Couch and said, 'Send me "Mr. Big Stuff." Let me take it to somebody else. I think it's a hit.' 'Nuh, it's just a B-side [Couch replied].'

"So he didn't send it. A month later I called [again] and said, 'Send it to me.' 'Oh well, I will, I will.' He didn't. So I was home to see my parents one weekend and it's Sunday and I was about to go to Memphis. I had a whim. I called Tommy up and said, 'Meet me at the studio, give me that tape!'"

Whitsett hustled back to Memphis, and the next Monday morning presented the song to John Smith, who didn't know what to think. "It was different," explains Whitsett. "It was a novelty thing. It wasn't like the Stax stuff and no one quite knew what to do, but because I was jumping up and down about it, they thought, 'Well, maybe we'll give the guy [a shot]. We can always fire him if it flops!'"

Whitsett had nothing to worry about. "Mr. Big Stuff" sold over a million and a half copies on its way to the coveted number 1 spot on the R&B charts, and also crossed over big time, reaching number 2 on the pop listings. Unbelievably the King Floyd record had

2. Background vocals were supplied by three Jackson singers including Dorothy Moore, late of Tim Whitsett and the Imperials and later of "Misty Blue" fame.

done nearly as well, also topping the R&B charts while settling for number 6 pop. In September 1971, the same New Orleans songwriting and production staff came through with the predictable sequel to "Mr. Big Stuff," turning a phrase from the original record's chorus, "You Think You're Hot Stuff," into the new song's title. As is often the case with sequels, the second record enjoyed some success, but was not nearly as successful as the original, only reaching the number 19 and number 57 spots on *Billboard*'s two primary charts. Stax issued three more 45s by Knight through December 1972. Each sold fewer copies than its predecessor, and consequently the label declined to pick up Knight's second option.

Knight's single was one of a slew of master purchase (and very occasionally master lease) deals executed by Al Bell in the early 1970s. An inordinate number of the records acquired through these deals were produced and/or owned by disc jockeys: from New Orleans jock Larry McKinley came Margie Joseph; from Detroit's Al Perkins Stax got Hot Sauce; through Philadelphia's LeBaron Taylor came the Limitations, United Image, and Joni Wilson; blues harmonica player Little Sonny was signed to Stax under the auspices of Detroit disc jockey (and later Stax promotion man) Bill Williams; and St. Louis disc jockey Bernie Hayes engineered a deal for himself. Bell made similar deals with distributors and even jukebox operators: Stax's New Orleans distributor Bob Robin cut master purchase agreements for the Cheques and John Eric; Larry King of Atlanta's Southland Distributors brought Dino and Doc and R. B. Hudmon to Stax; while Baltimore's Colette Kelly came to the company via jukebox operator Sam Ungar. Although Margie Joseph, Little Sonny, Hot Sauce, and R. B. Hudmon achieved a modicum of success, most of these artists enjoyed only one or two releases. From Al Bell's perspective, these deals and the relationships they helped to develop and/or cement with disc jockeys and other industry members paid for themselves in the generated goodwill.

"You had expanded relationships for sure," explains Bell. "The lawyers call it quid pro quo. On the street they say, 'You scratch my back, I'll scratch yours.' We were quickly becoming perceived as the leader in black music. . . . We were the combination of the Vee-Jay, the Duke-Peacock, the Motown, et cetera, of this era. And, we were the company that had the open-door policy. So the people would come. The disc jockeys would come. All of these people would come to Stax and get an opportunity and get a shot where they couldn't even get in the door at other places. We were the company that was the *mecca*. Everybody could come to Mecca. Frankly that was the image and philosophy that I had.

"Jerry Wexler used to tell me, 'Al, listen to every record that comes in your door, pick up and talk on the phone to every producer and writer because you never know where your next million seller is coming from.' That was Jerry's philosophy. It stayed with me. Everybody was associated with somebody that had some degree of influence somewhere out here in this industry. If you're a mecca, you've got to put it out."

Most of this licensed product seemed to get less than full attention from Stax's promotion and marketing personnel. "The Stax-bred product got the first priority whether I directed it or not," confirms Bell. "It was not an easy task to try to bring some of this other product home because of the nature of a close family-type company with everybody in the same city. When you bring in other people it wasn't as easy initially to get them the kind of attention that would get them in *Billboard* and all the other print media."

Media attention was not a problem with regard to Al Bell's next master purchase acquisition, Melvin Van Peebles's *Sweet Sweetback Badasssss Song*. Born in 1932 in Chicago, Van Peebles was nothing if not a maverick. Excited by the first wave of underground cinema while working in San Francisco in the mid-1960s, Van Peebles decided that he was going to be a filmmaker. Going into debt to acquire some equipment, Van Peebles shot his first thirty-minute film on 16mm stock in San Francisco, learning his basic technique from Sergei Eisenstein's *Film Form: Essays in Film Theory.* Completed film in hand, Van Peebles headed to Hollywood, where he was offered jobs as both an elevator operator and a parking lot attendant. So much for breaking into the American cinema.

While Hollywood may not have been interested in a young radical black filmmaker, the Cinematheque in France was. After a showing of his early work in Paris, Van Peebles took up residence there as an expatriate, raising enough money to film a screenplay he had written entitled *Story of a Three Day Pass.* He returned to the States in 1967 as the French delegate to the San Francisco film festival, where he won the Critic's Award. Not surprisingly, Van Peebles now found himself courted by the very same Hollywood industry that had had no time for him just a short while before. In 1970 Columbia Pictures hired him to direct his second feature, *Watermelon Man,* and Van Peebles became, along with Gordon Parks, one of the first black feature directors in Hollywood's modern era. At the same time that Van Peebles was acquiring a name in film circles, he signed a recording contract with A&M, for whom he recorded four off-the-wall albums of semi-spoken verbal declamations that challenged virtually every generally held notion of record making.³

Van Peebles's next feature, *Sweet Sweetback's Badasssss Song,* was shot in Los Angeles in nineteen days and had a profound effect on the entire film industry. The maverick filmmaker had been told in no uncertain terms that a black film had never made any money. His response was simple: Hollywood had never made a black film. Instead, they had occasionally foisted a white fantasy of black culture that they assumed a black audience might want to see. This was the impetus for *Sweetback.* Unable to interest any studio in producing the film, Van Peebles became his own studio. Unable to find any partners, he financed the work himself, largely from his profits from *Watermelon Man.*⁴ "Years later," Van Peebles told *Motorbooty* writers Mike Rubin and Derek Yip, "some little guy asked me, 'Mr. Van Peebles, how did you get to the top?' I told him the truth: 'No one would let me in at the bottom.'"

Van Peebles produced, wrote, directed, composed the soundtrack for, and starred in *Sweetback.* Dedicated to "All the brothers and sisters who had enough of the Man," at the time the film was described in *Ebony* as "the first American film in the black idiom made entirely outside the white power structure's control." At first Van Peebles could only find two theaters in America that would show the film, but after its initial success in Detroit and Atlanta, large numbers of theaters in black neighborhoods picked up on it. *Sweetback* eventually grossed $14 million, putting it on the then-current list of top-grossing movies of all time and kick-starting the blaxploitation genre in the process.

Although Van Peebles was under contract to A&M, the Los Angeles–based label declined to release the film's soundtrack album. "I went to A&M and they felt that the movie was anti-Semitic or something and they didn't want to be associated with it," asserts Van Peebles. "You must understand *Sweetback* was very shocking."

Rejected by the head honchos at A&M, Van Peebles went to "Mecca," where he made a deal with Al Bell. For Bell, the idea was a natural: "A major film with a black director, a black star and a soundtrack by a black composer," stressed Bell in a July 1971 issue of *Billboard,* "is an enormous source of pride to the black community. It's more than just a movie—it's a special event. Box office figures on these films indicate the enthusiastic

---

3. These recordings went on to have a seminal influence on the hip-hop nation of the 1980s and 1990s.

4. When Van Peebles almost had the film completed and was running out of money, Bill Cosby kicked in the final $50,000.

response. Since music is usually such an integral part of these movies, soundtrack albums have a ready-made market if you know how to reach the people."

To accomplish this objective, the album was marketed in an innovative fashion: it was sold in the foyers of a number of the theaters where the film was being shown. Van Peebles and Bell were both into the idea—then novel, now commonplace—that the soundtrack could sell the film and the film could sell the soundtrack. The album was issued in April 1971, and an edited version of the seven-minute title song, "Sweetback's Theme," followed as a single in July. The LP featured Earth, Wind and Fire at the very beginning of their career and used snippets of dialogue from the film to connect each song. A second Van Peebles album, the soundtrack of the Broadway musical *Don't Play Us Cheap* (which was adapted from Van Peebles's novel *La Fête à Harlem*), was issued on Stax on June 13, 1972. In addition to aggressively marketing the double LP, Stax invested $100,000 in the actual Broadway production, which opened May 16, 1972.

At the time that Stax was issuing *Sweetback*, Isaac Hayes was already hard at work on the soundtrack for the mother lode of blaxploitation films, *Shaft*. To aid in the marketing of *Shaft*, Larry Shaw had brought together a consortium of black-owned communications and consulting companies for the most part based in Memphis, Los Angeles, Chicago, and New York into an umbrella organization called Communiplex. With *Sweetback* now on the table and *Shaft* not quite ready for release, Van Peebles's film became Communiplex's first project. Communiplex worked on a number of projects over the next few years, most notably *Shaft* and *Wattstax*. As with most developments at Stax in the 1970s, Communiplex may have been formed out of a desire to increase the company's bottom line, but it was also deployed in the service of the African-American community at large. On several occasions over the years, on a pro bono basis, Communiplex helped successfully market the election campaigns of a number of African-American politicians, large and small.

As the *Sweetback* soundtrack album was being prepared to ship, Ewell Roussell was promoted from national sales manager to vice president of sales. A month later Al Bell inked a deal to distribute Jerry Phillips's and former Stax promotion man Eddie Braddock's Hot Water label, and in June Stax announced a distribution deal with Henry Stone's Dig Records. Nothing of consequence came from either of these deals.

Of substantial consequence was Don Davis's re-signing of Detroit vocal group the Dramatics to his Groovesville concern. When Davis had first come to Stax, he had brought with him a number of artists—including Darrell Banks, J. J. Barnes, Steve Mancha, Roz Ryan, and the Dramatics—that he had signed to production contracts via Groovesville. Although he had ceased to be an official at Stax in mid-1970, Davis was still signed to the Memphis label as a producer through May 1973. Under this latter agreement, he continued to produce Johnnie Taylor's seemingly endless streak of hit singles, as well as an occasional record by one or another Stax artist including the Mad Lads and, in the summer of 1971, newcomer Little Milton. Davis also continued to make distribution deals with Stax for a number of artists he had signed to Groovesville, which is how Major Lance, L. V. Johnson, Roger Hatcher, and Harvey Scales all had records released on Stax or Volt in 1971 and 1972.

The Dramatics had two tenures with both Groovesville and Stax. The first was rather brief. The group had started off as the Sensations at Pershing High School in Detroit. Changing their name to the Dramatics, they had recorded two singles for the Detroit label Wingate in 1966.[5] In 1967, they enjoyed a minor hit with "All Because of You" on the Sport

5. One of the Dramatics' Wingate singles incorrectly listed their name as the Dynamics.

label. Don Davis then signed them to Groovesville and in late 1969 brought them to Stax, where they cut the superb, group-written "Your Love Was Strange." By this point their lineup had stabilized with Ron Banks, Albert Wilkins, William Howard, Larry Demps, and Willie Ford. Howard took the lead on "Your Love Was Strange," projecting a raspy voice that alternately is reminiscent of the Four Tops' Levi Stubbs and the Temptations' David Ruffin. When the record undeservedly died a quick death, Davis was so disappointed that he released the group from their contract, figuring he couldn't do any better with them.

With the group languishing in Detroit, Don Davis suggested to songwriter Tony Hestor that he go check them out and see what he could do. "Tony was actually a genius with the pen," exclaims Ron Banks. "He had his own route with painting the picture of a song. We set up the appointment and went to Tony Hestor's house and went downstairs where the piano was. Tony sat down and we talked for a minute. We let him know our concerns and we said, 'Man, we need a hit record!' When he first started playing things for us, he start-ed playing a song [Banks imitates Hestor singing 'Whatcha See Is Whatcha Get']. We said, 'Oh man, wait a minute.' It was sounding like a carnival song on the piano to us. We said, 'Man, no no no no no. We want a hit record!' Tony came up off the piano. He looked at us and he said, 'But this is a hit record. Let me finish it!' It [turned out to be an] amaz-ing experience."

Hestor's intuitions were right on the money. Once the group had worked it up, he brought the results back to Don Davis. Davis was so impressed that he re-signed the Dramatics but let Hestor handle the production duties. Everybody was the richer for it. "Whatcha See Is Whatcha Get" reached number 3 R&B and number 9 pop. It was the beginning of a run of thirty-three subsequent chart records for the group, the first seven of which were on the Stax subsidiary Volt Records.

Part of the success of the song was due to Hestor's extraordinary arrangement. Various members of the Dramatics alternate singing lead on each lyric line à la Sly and the Family Stone and the Temptations. The slight Latin feel in the groove fit the first wave of disco like a glove, while the use of claves and congas combined with a fuzzed lead guitar line and Johnny Allen's seraphonous strings and horns for a simply irresistible arrangement.[6]

With *Sweetback* and "Whatcha See Is Whatcha Get" generating a steady stream of ready cash flow, Al Bell took Stax in yet another new direction. Stax's first foray into the alien world of country music was via that rarest of artist, the black country singer. O. B. McClinton was born in the Gravel Springs cotton-picking community near Senatobia, Mississippi. Never too interested in cotton farming, from his earliest years he had been lis-tening to and singing country music. When he moved in with his sister in Memphis to attend high school, McClinton entered and won talent contests at both Hamilton High School and WDIA's Teen Talent Time. At the time, his repertoire consisted of covers of Carl Perkins's "Blue Suede Shoes" and Tennessee Ernie Ford's "16 Tons."

"Doing those songs," recalled McClinton, "early on I realized kids looked at me a little different. They had guys out there singing songs by the Platters and all this stuff and they didn't get the response that I got when I came out and did something different. I would always win the talent show. It was just different to see me do it. It wasn't that they liked this music better than the other music, it was just different to see me [sing country]. So, quite naturally, the response was greater. It gave me an incentive to go ahead and pursue that."

Ensconced in Memphis in the early 1960s, McClinton began to try to sell some of his songs. Like a lot of other young black Memphians, he spent an inordinate amount of time

6. The Dramatics were the only artist signed directly to Davis that would be of any consequence in the Stax story. Davis's control of the group combined with his eventual estrangement from Stax would prove to be a sore point a couple of years down the road.

hanging out at Stax, pitching songs at every opportunity. A gifted imitator, one day in late 1964 McClinton managed to catch Estelle Axton's ear by mimicking the way Otis Redding might sing a tune McClinton had written called "Keep Your Arms Around Me." Shortly thereafter Redding recorded the song for his 1965 album *Otis Redding Sings Soul Ballads.*

McClinton continued hustling his songs while he attended Rust College on a choral scholarship. He also pursued a recording career, releasing one single under the pseudonym Oboe on Quinton Claunch's Beale Street label and three subsequent 45s on Claunch and Doc Russell's Goldwax label. One of the tunes McClinton recorded for Goldwax was covered on the same label by deep, deep soul singer James Carr. Carr went on to record a number of McClinton compositions, garnering two Top 20 R&B hits, 1966's "You've Got My Mind Messed Up" and 1968's "A Man Needs a Woman."[7] McClinton also placed songs with Clarence Carter and Arthur Conley in the latter part of the 1960s, and, as late as 1974, the Staple Singers recorded his "Back Road into Town."

Although he was clearly a superior R&B songwriter, McClinton's heart was still very much in country music. It was while he was serving in the armed forces in the late 1960s that he first began to think that it might actually be possible for him to carve out a career as a country singer. While McClinton was stationed in Okinawa writing a slew of country-oriented material, a fellow soldier came back from leave with a Charley Pride album. Like McClinton, Pride was also black and from Mississippi. Arriving in Nashville in 1964, Pride fell under the wing of Jack Clement. As Sam Phillips's former right-hand man, Clement was more than schooled in accepting and marketing the unusual. He persuaded Chet Atkins to release a few singles by Pride on RCA that were accompanied by no photographs or literature mentioning the fact that Pride was black. No one suspected otherwise, and by springtime 1967 Charley Pride was an established country music star, going on to be named the Country Music Association "Entertainer of the Year" in 1971.

O. B. McClinton. COURTESY OF FANTASY, INC.

Being stationed in Okinawa, McClinton was unaware of the story of Charley Pride. "[My friend] played the album for me," McClinton remembered, laughing, "and he hid the cover under his mattress somewhere. I said, 'Boy, that's a country dude.' Then after

---

7. "You've Got My Mind Messed Up" charted again in 1973, when it was recorded by black female group Quiet Elegance on Hi Records.

he finished and I told him how much I liked it, he brought the album out, and it was Charley Pride. I couldn't believe it. I said, 'Man, maybe the time is right.' That's when I made up my mind. [People] had been saying I was country all along and laughing at me. I said, 'Well shoot, if God deals you a lemon, make lemonade.' What I had considered a liability before I went into the service, I turned into an asset."

Stax Records seemed an unlikely place for an aspiring country performer in 1971. While the company had in recent years been diversifying into jazz, blues, pop, and gospel, the label's meat and potatoes remained southern rhythm and blues.

"It was where I felt I could get somebody to listen," explained McClinton. "I had heard the story of Charley Pride and how he got started and I knew that it wasn't easy. I had been around Stax and places enough to know that it wasn't easy to break into any kind of music. I thought that I could get through the door at Stax. I had had some big records as a writer and I knew David Porter and Isaac Hayes at Stax. I got with them and played them some songs and they talked to Al Bell."

Unbeknownst to McClinton, his timing couldn't have been better; Bell had been toying with the idea of venturing into country for a while. McClinton had also gone to see the head of A&R at Chart Records. While Chart was interested, they were not prepared to offer an advance. Bell, on the other hand, was offering McClinton $10,000 to sign on the dotted line. Recently married and just out of the service, McClinton didn't take long to make up his mind.

Upon signing with Stax in January 1971, McClinton was dispatched to Nashville. "That was the first thing they said when they signed me," related McClinton. " 'We'll go to Nashville and we'll find a good producer.' Their philosophy was that they didn't know anything about country music."

Stax's first choice for a producer was Billy Sherrill, but it turned out that he had an exclusive deal with Columbia. They then tried Jerry Kennedy before settling for Jim Malloy, who had just produced the Country Music Association Single of the Year, "Help Me Make It Through the Night," for Sammi Smith. While Malloy may have seemed a logical choice, McClinton ended up none too happy. The crux of his dissatisfaction was that Malloy wanted O.B. to sound as generically white country as humanly possible.

"I couldn't stand to listen to the playback," McClinton recalled, still grimacing. "He thought that the next black country singer had to be even countrier than Charley Pride. He would come down out of the control room and say, 'You sound black on that word!' I'd say, 'Well, look at me 'cause I am!' "

McClinton's first single, "Country Music That's My Thing," was released by Stax's Enterprise subsidiary in June 1971, with an album, simply entitled *O. B. McClinton Country,* following in January 1972. Stax chose to release the album with a cover that depicted O.B. at a distance with his back turned to the camera looking at the Nashville skyline; the casual shopper would not notice that he was black. To Stax's credit, it did include a picture of McClinton on the back. It would appear that the label was not so much interested in fooling the would-be consumer as in making sure that its product could be racked in the country section of record stores in some of the more racist sections of the country.

Three singles were released from the album, none of which generated much action. McClinton wanted to do his second album, 1973's *Obie from Senatobie,* differently. "After [Jim Malloy] cut that album, I went to Al Bell and I said, 'Al, listen to that. That is not me. That is just as phony as a three-dollar bill. I know I've never produced a record but I know me better than Jim Malloy or anybody else will ever know me. I know how to be natural.' "

To the day McClinton passed away in 1987, he remained grateful to Al Bell for giving him a chance to produce himself. The result was the finest of the four albums McClinton cut for Stax. In control of his own destiny, the talented singer chose to record a number of country versions of R&B. McClinton's take on two of these, William Bell's "My Whole World Is Falling Down" and Wilson Pickett's 1971 R&B hit "Don't Let the Green Grass Fool You," broke into the Top 40 on the country charts in 1972 and 1973 respectively.

"I cut a lot of those songs," explained McClinton, "to prove a point to a lot of people at Stax and a lot of other people that a song is not either country or R and B. It's the artist, himself, who sets the mode of the song. Johnny Cash can make a blues song a country song, while Muddy Waters can make a country song a blues."

All told, McClinton placed seven of the 45s he recorded for the Stax subsidiary Enterprise on the country charts. Stax recorded a number of other country acts, all of them white, including Eddie Bond, Connie Eaton, Paul Craft, Roger Hallmark, Paige O'Brien, Dale Yard (a.k.a. Bobby Manuel), Rolan Eaton, and Cliff Cochran, but none of them enjoyed much success. In many ways the company simply wasn't in a position to break into that market, as it had neither the knowledge nor the contacts. Stax eventually hired Nashville veteran Jerry Seaboldt to promote its country product. Being the only one at Stax who knew anything about country, Seaboldt did everything related to country product, from A&R to marketing and promotion, through August 1973.[8] The situation was not a very productive one.

"Nashville giggled at our country," attests Larry Shaw. "We were out of our place because we were rather ambitious. That's part of why we're not there now. We sought entry into everybody's category and thought we had some contribution to make. It's just a matter of politics and business. You can't allow darkies to go too far. They would hit the ceilings in these places. We were threatened in Nashville at the country conventions. [There were] overtones of, 'You boys are in the wrong place don't you think. Things could happen to you in places like this.'"

Despite these problems, McClinton stayed with Stax until the bitter end. "Stax gave me an opportunity," stressed the singer. "And I will forever be grateful because if it hadn't been for Stax, I might never have been in country music. I don't know whether a label like RCA or CBS would have signed an O. B. McClinton. Al Bell really did a great thing. He did something that many executives wouldn't do. [He] let a new artist go into the studio and have control. [Al Bell] permitted me to break into a field that was predominantly white. If you check, over all these years there has been only one black [country] artist signed to a major label, and nobody knew he was black when he was signed."

Part of the Stax philosophy, to quote Larry Shaw, was "everything is everything." That's certainly where Al Bell's head was at. He regularly made decisions based on intuition and social and personal philosophy as opposed to relying exclusively on hardcore business sense. The story of O. B. McClinton is one particularly rich example where Bell's penchant for shooting from the hip paid dividends for all concerned.

Just before the first McClinton single was shipped in June 1971, Johnny Baylor made some startling allegations to Al Bell. "Johnny Baylor said," sighs Bell, "'Dick [that's how Baylor always referred to Bell], let me tell you something. You're losing money, your product is being bootlegged and [some of your employees are] stealing from you.' He called off all the names, told me what they were doing and told me I was crazy if I didn't do something about it because they were robbing me blind and going

---

8. Two months after Seaboldt's departure, Bill Hickman and Carol Stevenson were hired as coordinators of Stax's country product and Merlin Littlefield was brought on board to do country promotion.

to put me out of business. . . . I thought he was being too harsh on them but, he knew what he was talking about."

Bell, a trifle shaken, repeated Baylor's allegations to Jim Stewart, who suggested that they investigate further before taking any action. Bell next spoke to Ron Altman of Stax's New York accounting firm, Weissbarth, Altman and Miller. Altman suggested that Stax hire Norman Jaspen and Associates to conduct an undercover investigation. In early August, Jaspen's investigation commenced.

"Norman Jaspen didn't find out any more than what Johnny Baylor told me," asserts Bell. "They just verified it and it cost me a lot of money [for them to do so]. Johnny Baylor, like any good record person at that time that's out in the field, worked the marketplace thoroughly. If you're learned and intelligent and you work the marketplace correctly, there isn't anything going on that you don't see and understand, particularly the way [Baylor] worked it. . . . [He] knew when [he] walked into a one-stop whether or not there should have been six hundred pieces [of a particular title] on the floor or three hundred pieces on the floor because [he was] that much up on top of the purchases of that one-stop."

Baylor, no longer in the employ of Isaac Hayes, was in the field working his KoKo releases, but at the same time, he was keeping an eye on Stax product because KoKo was being distributed through Stax. Apparently, on more than one occasion he visited a one-stop record distributor and saw several hundred pieces of a given title above and beyond that which had been purchased according to the company's books. (A one-stop handles recordings from all labels, which it then sells to retail outlets too small to deal directly with most labels. In the early 1970s most black record stores could only buy product from one-stops.) Obviously kickbacks were going on.

The prime suspects of the Jaspen investigation were Herb Kole and Ewell Roussell. According to a later IRS investigation of Stax,[9] Kole admitted to Jaspen that he had taken advantage of his position by accepting sizable kickbacks from various sources. For example, Kole received a penny from A&B Duplicators for every cassette tape that Stax had manufactured at their plant; over time, this added up to $5,000. From Globe Albums, Kole received a percentage on all printing bills paid by Stax. The amount cited in the IRS report was $5,500. Similarly, Kole received kickbacks from George Alexander Displays (so much per display), and Monarch Record Pressing (so much per record pressed). Kole also received kickbacks for the shipment of free records from a number of distributors including Paul Glass ($8,000), Hot Line Distributors in Memphis ($450), Double B ($1,300), Slotkin's One-Stop ($2,500), Dean's One-Stop ($2,300), and Bob Robin (no amount listed). The kickbacks came in the form of cash or checks made out to either Kole's brother or wife.

Roussell told Jaspen that he had sent records to various people to reimburse them for "personal business," he had accepted small amounts of cash for records, and he had padded his expense-account reports. He had also, on a number of occasions, sent free product to a number of individuals to take care of personal gambling debts and/or other favors. For example, Bob Robin of Bob Robin Enterprises of New Orleans had been sent fifteen thousand singles over two years free of charge to cover money that Roussell had lost in Las Vegas. Similarly, Jim Crudginton of Hot Line Distributors in Memphis had been sent five hundred LPs and one thousand singles to cover expenses Roussell had incurred during a card game. The list went on. Roussell also admitted that he knew Kole was getting kickbacks. Despite these admissions of wrongdoing, on July 25, 1973, Roussell

9. IRS Report #62730053S.

told the IRS in a sworn statement that "the only reason he was dismissed from Stax was because he did not inform management of the wrong doings of Herb Kole."

A number of other employees in the sales and marketing departments at Stax further incriminated Roussell and Kole. Olivia Smith stated that she had received a check from Roussell to cover a raise that she didn't get; Roussell then charged this back to his expense account. She further stated that she shipped out, under instructions from Roussell, thousands of records that were never invoiced, estimating that Stax lost $100,000 a year due to these practices.

John Smith admitted that he authorized the shipment of free records on several occasions to his mother's House of Hits record store in Fort Smith, Arkansas, and his father's

Herb Kole and Ewell Roussell at the 1969 Stax sales meeting. COURTESY OF DEANIE PARKER.

House of Wax record store in North Little Rock. Smith had several explanations for his dishonesty: he had been given too much freedom and trust; he needed to help his parents; he felt that others less deserving were making more money than he was; and he knew executives such as Kole and Roussell were also making back-door deals. "The environment was very conducive to dishonesty," Smith told Jaspen, "which flowed over to almost everyone with whom I was in contact, including the girls, the mail room, advertising and others." Smith also implicated Roussell, Kole, Mike Williams, Jeanette Parish, Thelma Miller, and Olivia Smith in similar schemes. Adam Oliphant also admitted to expense-account violations, while Jeanette Parish implicated controller Ed Pollack.

The whole scenario was one of petty and not-so-petty levels of dishonesty run rampant throughout the sales and marketing departments at Stax Records. Some executives would have cleaned house. Instead, John Smith was actually promoted in August to corporate manager![10] The only casualties were Kole and Roussell, who were fired by Bell and Stewart in October 1971. On February 25, 1972, the company filed a proof of loss claim with Aetna Life and Casualty for $406,737 "due to the dishonesty of Herbert Kolesky [Herb Kole], Ewell Roussell, and unidentified others." Curiously, Bell and Stewart settled for payments of only $6,750 from Aetna and $40,000 from Kole. Kole told the IRS that his attorney had instructed Stax to either settle or "Aetna would like Kolesky to make his statement," the implication being that there was something that Stax did not want Kole to make public.

According to Al Bell, there were other reasons why Stax settled for such small compensation. Neither Al nor Jim was a ruthless businessman; they also had serious ques-

---

10. Earlie Biles felt that Al Bell was too soft. "He felt that everybody would reform," explains Biles. "If he talked to them, they would change."

tions as to what wrongdoing Ewell Roussell had actually committed, and Jim was concerned that Ewell's daughter had health problems. In addition, Bell admits that they did not pursue this investigation because Stax would need to continue to do business with a number of these distributors, and did not want to publicly say that they had been dishonest.

Irrespective of Bell's claims, the IRS and the federal grand jury situated in Memphis later would take great interest in the fact that Stax so easily settled for $359,987 less than they claimed they had lost.[11] The district attorney would later state that, because Stax did not report this incident to government investigative sources, he felt that Stax, in effect, had conspired with two employees to cover up a kickback scheme.

While such unseemly machinations were occurring in the sales department, new personnel were being brought into the studio as Stax further expanded its complement of engineers. Dave Purple was a white engineer who had started working at Chess Records in October 1967. When company founder and namesake Leonard Chess sold the company to GRT in February 1969, he agreed to stay on for five years as Chess's president and chief executive officer. Unfortunately Chess passed away that same year, and for much of the Chess staff, the whole operation went downhill very quickly.

Dave Purple remained with the GRT-run Chess operation for a year and a half after Leonard Chess died, but by the early part of 1971 Purple found himself becoming increasingly disheartened with the situation. In March, he discussed his concerns with former Chess promotion man Chester Simmons, now happily ensconced at Stax and heading up the marketing department. A month later Simmons invited him to come and speak with head engineer Ronnie Capone. By April, Purple was living in Memphis and working at 926 E. McLemore.

At the time Studio B was still an eight-track facility, but a new sixteen-track recorder and console was on order which would be installed in June. In general, though, all important sessions continued to be carried out in Studio A because none of the engineers at Stax was ever able to get a good sound out of Studio B.

One of the first projects Purple worked on was the soundtrack to *Shaft*. If *Hot Buttered Soul* had been the watershed album for both Hayes and Stax, *Shaft* was Niagara Falls. Isaac had originally recorded the soundtrack in Hollywood at the movie studio in four days at a three-track facility. For the record release, he wanted to get better sound than was possible in a movie studio and consequently rerecorded all the songs at Stax. Rerecording the material also allowed him to stretch out some of the songs beyond the length of time they were allotted in the movie, ultimately making the soundtrack album a more pleasurable and satisfying listening experience.

At the same time Isaac was recutting *Shaft*, he was also working on his followup album, *Black Moses*. Further complicating matters, sessions were continually being interrupted because Isaac would have to leave Memphis and go out on the road for two or three gigs at a time. For the engineers at Stax, it was just sheer madness.

"Some days Isaac would book the studio starting at nine at night," says Dave Purple. "Some nights he wouldn't come in until midnight or so and on some nights you might not press the red button on the tape machine until four in the morning. You'd do one tune, one track, and he'd run it through about four or five times and he'd say, 'Okay, we're ready' and you'd hit the red button. If that was at two o'clock, you got to go home. If that was at eight o'clock, you got to go home. That was real loosely organized."

---

11. The IRS report lists $50,196.33 in kickbacks that it could positively identify. Although this is well short of the $406,737 that Stax claimed with Aetna Life and Casualty, the IRS report very specifically suggests that the Stax figure could indeed be accurate.

Shaft was one of the crowning achievements of Stax's second era. Al Bell had been wanting to move the company into the world of film since at least 1968, when Stax had been sold to Gulf and Western. The label's premiere artist, Isaac Hayes, shared Bell's keen interest. In early 1971 Isaac, Al Bell, the head of MGM, Mike Curb, and possibly Jesse Jackson all got together to discuss Isaac's involvement.

"I always wanted to act," relates Hayes. "The concept [of the film] was okay. Here's a black movie aiming at the black market with a black director, a black lead actor, a black editor and a black composer to score it. I said, 'Okay, I'll do the score if you give me a shot at the lead role.' They agreed. I waited and waited and a couple of weeks passed and I said, 'Hey man.' 'Oh, Mr. Hayes we're sorry but they already casted and they started shooting in New York. They got a fellow named Richard Roundtree.' I was crushed because I wanted a shot."

Shaft was the second Hollywood feature for black director Gordon Parks.[12] It would make his career. Both Parks and producer Joel Freeman were excited about using Hayes, but they were also a little apprehensive given that Stax's resident genius had never worked on a soundtrack before. To test the waters, while shooting was still being completed, they sent Isaac raw footage of three scenes: the opening scene where John Shaft is coming out of the subway; Shaft's walk through Harlem; and his love scene with Ellie. When Isaac sent them back "Theme from *Shaft*," "Soulsville," and "Ellie's Love Theme" they knew they had made the right choice.

The remainder of the score was written in Los Angeles at MGM over a period of about six weeks, in and around the near-continuous dates that the Isaac Hayes Movement was playing every weekend. To aid Isaac in learning the ropes of film scoring, Tom McIntosh was brought in to lend both advice and assistance on technical matters whenever necessary.

The recording of the soundtrack at the MGM studio had its share of cultural clashes. "We walked in," recounts Isaac, "and the engineer says, 'Okay, where is your sheet music?' 'We ain't got no music. We don't use music, we don't write anything. We're just going to do it headwise.' 'Say what?!? You ain't got no music?'"

The engineer's fears were quickly allayed. Isaac had been allotted two days to do the rhythm tracks. He was finished an hour and ten minutes ahead of quitting time on the first day. The next day Isaac recorded the string and horn parts,[13] and on the third day he laid down his vocal tracks, apparently still finishing the lyrics to some of the songs in the back of the limousine on the way to the studio.

As a first soundtrack, Isaac's score was nothing short of ingenious. For a scene in which a cab ride glides through New York City at night, Isaac employed muted trumpets to suggest nightlife. When he needed to create incidental jukebox music for a restaurant scene, Isaac recalled that jazz guitarist Wes Montgomery always had records on the jukebox at the Four-Way Grill in Memphis. Consequently, he wrote "Cafe Regio's" in the style of Wes Montgomery. Similarly inspired was the way Isaac treated John Shaft's two different love scenes. For "Shaft Strikes Again" he used flutes as the main instrument, whereas for "Ellie's Love Theme" vibes are the dominant instrument.

"For 'Shaft Strikes Again,'" explains Isaac, "when he had the girl in the shower, it was a love scene but it didn't matter to him like it did when it was Ellie. It was more a promis-

---

12. Parks's first feature was *The Learning Tree,* which was released in 1969, a year earlier than Melvin Van Peebles's *Watermelon Man.*

13. Jazz trombonist J. J. Johnson in tandem with Isaac orchestrated "Walk from Regio's." Strings and horns for the rest of the album were arranged by Hayes and Johnny Allen.

cuous thing with that girl but [with] Ellie it was warmer with the vibes. I had to differentiate between the two women."

The score to *Shaft* contains numerous highlights, not least among them is the incredibly moving "Soulsville," and the nineteen-plus-minute funk vamp that filled all of side four of the soundtrack album, entitled "Do Your Thing." For most people, though, the film, Isaac Hayes, and the blaxploitation era are inextricably wedded to the title song, "Theme from *Shaft*." Released as a single in September two months after the album was on the market, "Theme from *Shaft*" contains an inordinate number of hooks. The two that are invariably the most indelibly etched into the listener's cranium are the sixteenth-note hi-hat riff and the wah-wah rhythm guitar part that are heard virtually from the beginning to the end on the track. Both licks were recycled endlessly during the disco era.

Hayes had first used the hi-hat lick on the break in the final section of Otis Redding's 1966 recording of "Try a Little Tenderness." The wah-wah part had come about sometime earlier, when Hayes and guitarist Charles "Skip" Pitts were working on a long-forgotten track that for one reason or another was never released.

"It was just one continuous thing that never went anywhere," recalls Hayes. "But I liked the sound and said, 'Okay, we'll tape this. We're gonna put this on file and just use it later.' When it was time to do the 'Theme,' I was told Shaft was a relentless character, always moving all the time, never stopping. I said, 'Hmm, what can we do? The hi-hat could be the underlying thing but I need some other thing.' I went back and pulled that tape out and said, 'Skip, come here a minute. Play this lick.' He played that lick and it fit so perfectly."

Topping it all off were the incredibly dramatic string parts. To integrate the film's main theme with the rest of the soundtrack, Hayes ingeniously added elements heard later in the score: the opening flute line was derived from "Bumpy's Lament," while the French horn part comes from "Ellie's Love Theme."

The *Shaft* album went to number 1 on both the pop and R&B album charts, staying on the pop listings for a staggering sixty weeks. The single, "Theme from *Shaft*," also went number 1 pop, although, oddly enough, it only made it to the number 2 spot on the R&B charts. Stax was obligated to pay a royalty to MGM of $2.54 for each double album and $3.37 for each tape of the soundtrack sold.

"Theme from *Shaft*" won two Grammy Awards that year: Isaac and Johnny Allen won in the "Best Instrumental Arrangement" category; and Dave Purple, Ron Capone, and Henry Bush won in the "Best Engineered Recording" category.[14] Isaac also won a Grammy in the "Best Original Score Written for a Motion Picture" category. Even bigger than the Grammies was the Academy Award Hayes walked away with on April 10, 1972, for the "Best Song" category. It was a night that no one who saw it will ever forget. By Isaac's own admission, he was as nervous as he's ever been. He told *Ebony* in 1973, "I was trembling. I felt an enormous weight on my shoulders. There was a lot riding on that Oscar—not so much for me as for the brothers across the country. I didn't want to let them down." For many African-Americans, Isaac's capturing of an Oscar that night was an event comparable to Joe Louis's knockout of Max Schmeling in 1938. It was a victory for all of black America.

Early on in the broadcast, Isaac had performed "Theme from *Shaft*" in his now-standard suit made of chains. For both black and white North Americans, it was a performance that would not be soon forgotten. "I used to wear a lot of vests," relates Isaac, " 'cause that was during the days of the hippies' influence. I wore bell bottoms with moc-

---

14. William Brown should have also shared in the "Best Engineered Recording" Grammy but he had neglected to properly fill in the session sheets with his name at the time the track was recorded. This was a mistake he would never make again.

Isaac Hayes and his grandmother Rushia Wade proudly display Isaac's Oscar and Golden Globe Awards for his soundtrack to *Shaft* in April 1972. COURTESY MISSISSIPPI VALLEY COLLECTION.

casins and these fringed rawhide vests with a lot of beads that a lady from South America used to do in Los Angeles for me. It was hot [onstage]. There was a guy in Memphis that had a chain necklace and a chain belt. He brought it over to the studio and I said, 'I like that.' I put on some black tights and put that chain necklace on and belt and I said, 'I can't walk out onstage like this.' Somebody said, 'Well, put a cape or something on.' I saw this cape in the window of Saks Fifth Avenue in New York, an Emilio Pucci cape, orange and black and white terry cloth. I bought that cape and I had my wardrobe mistress find me an orange flop hat to match that. I got some orange tights and I came out onstage with that on and I threw that cape off—SHOCK TREATMENT, man! It was an effect. It was dramatic. After that, this guy named Charles Ruben said, 'Hey man, I got an idea to make you some chains.' So he made me all kinds of chain vests, tails, formals."

After the ever-debonair Hayes finished his performance, he changed into a rather hip tux with fur-lined cuffs and lapels and then returned to his seat. The effect, to say the least, was striking. When he beat out Michel Legrand and the "Theme from *The Summer of '42*" in the "Best Song" category and slowly came down the aisle with his grandmother, Rushia Wade, in tow, the entire audience rose to its feet in appreciation. At the podium, Isaac presented the Oscar to the woman, three weeks shy of her eightieth birthday, who had struggled so hard to raise him.

"That was an opportunity I couldn't pass up," remembers Isaac. "I gave it to her and honored her in front of millions of people because here's an old lady who had stuck with me all those years, raised me when my mother died when I was a year-and-a-half. I'd seen this lady do all kind of hard work and stuff so that I would try and make something of myself in life. I wanted to pay her back, but I wanted to do it in that style, where the whole world could see this lady, the source of my success."

Larry Shaw suggested that Isaac should give the Oscar away once more. This time Hayes would symbolically give it "back" to the black community. Upon an invitation by Jessie Jackson, Isaac and his grandmother went to Chicago. Oscar in hand, they spoke at an Operation PUSH meeting and then went around to hospitals and jails "taking the Oscar to the people," letting them see and touch it. "It wasn't a contrivance," reasons Shaw. "The black community was what made him and if he would give that gesture and we could record it and send out publicity on it, put it on the air in Chicago which is a good market, it was appropriate. We just stuck to principles that are just always going to be winners."

The success of Hayes's score for *Shaft* opened up Hollywood to black composers and the record industry to black soundtracks. Soon thereafter Curtis Mayfield, Marvin Gaye, Donny Hathaway, Joe Simon, James Brown, and Bobby Womack were all hired to write the scores for what became an epidemic of blaxploitation flicks. In essence, Isaac Hayes and *Shaft* created the phenomenon of the R&B soundtrack. *Shaft*, and its followup, November's *Black Moses*, were also the first non-live or -greatest-hits double album releases by an R&B artist. It was only two short years earlier that Hayes had demonstrated unequivocally that black Americans would purchase full-length albums in large numbers. He was now demonstrating that they would also buy multidisc sets if the material warranted the expenditure. Double-pocket sets soon followed by Marvin Gaye, Aretha Franklin, and Funkadelic.

At the completion of the *Shaft* sessions a very unhappy Ronnie Capone left Stax to join Steve Cropper over at TMI. Dave Purple replaced Capone as director of engineering. One of the first moves Purple made was to bring in another Chess alumnus, Pete Bishop, in April 1972. "I originally hired Pete as a maintenance man," explains the laconic Purple. "We had eighteen two-track machines to take care of. I was involved in an enormous company that had absolutely no engineering guidance whatsoever until I arrived. I was trying to make some degree of order out of this chaos that existed."

Purple also wanted to improve the sound of Studio A, but he had to devise a way of making changes without Jim Stewart being aware that he was altering the room's acoustics. "It was really very, very poor at first," asserts Purple. "Jim Stewart wanted to improve the appearance of the studio but he didn't want to change the acoustics. He was very superstitious about that. So I said, 'Well, would you mind some black cork with some wainscoting along the edge?' He said, 'No, I suppose that would look real good but I *don't* want you to change the sound.' I said, 'Done, I'm not gonna do that, Jim. Don't worry about that.' So what I had the guys do was to mount some of this cork on what I suppose you'd call brackets where it was freestanding in there and what it did was change the low-frequency absorption in the room because all of a sudden the room was becoming a balloon at the low frequencies so it would give a little bit, whereas it was all hard plaster before and the low-frequency ring in that room was just terrible. It didn't do much to the high end in there but it certainly did have a rather pleasing effect on the low end. Jim really couldn't tell any difference, but it made a difference as far as the acoustic properties of the studio were concerned."

Pete Bishop was also appalled at the state of the equipment at Stax. "It was awful. It was outdated when I got there," he recalled. "They didn't put money into the studio or the equipment at all. They had the original hand-wired Audiotronics console that they cut all of the original hits on back in Studio C, which was the demo room. I had to rebuild it. It was in pretty sad disrepair. All the outboard gear was limited and old. The only thing we eventually got was DBX noise reduction when it first came out. The echo chambers were amazing. They were soggy. They had these plaster echo chambers down in the basement and it was next to a wall that leaked. You could see through one wall. Every time it rained, you'd get three feet of water in the echo chamber! They would just let it sit there and evaporate. [It was] just ridiculous. They had a decay time of maybe a half to one second."

The chambers had been put in what had been the pit for the organ blower when the studio had been a movie theater. A common story in Stax lore involves an Isaac Hayes mixing session that Dave Purple was engineering. On this particular date, the echo chambers were dry enough to use. Partway through the session, Purple and Hayes could hear gun shots shaking the studio speakers. Henry Bush walked in a few seconds later with a .38 that was smoking. Apparently he had been shooting rats outside behind the studio, and he had accidentally hit the echo chamber!

On more than one occasion, Bishop tried to get Jim to allow him to improve all three studios. "We had discussions about it," sighs the former engineer. "We had near fights about it sometimes, but it was the whole Stax philosophy. They wanted as natural a sound as possible and they felt if you got modern equipment, it would make it sound like all the modern tinny records that were out there. They just weren't willing to take a chance. They felt their sound came from what they had. Whereas the 'Stax sound' came from the earlier console, which was now back in the demo room!"

Bishop eventually convinced Jim to let him hire Dan Flickinger to rebuild the amplifiers in the Spectrasonics recording consoles because, to Bishop's ears, the Spectrasonics amps had a tendency to be a little soft in the low end. The only other change made to the studio equipment occurred in the seventies, when Dave Purple changed the playback speakers to Electrovoice 3s. "We kept blowing them out"—Bishop laughs—"because David Porter liked to hear everything at 140 decibels or above. We were wiping out speakers left, right, and center.

"It really was not an engineering or a technically oriented studio," continues Bishop. "The music required a gut feeling more than anything like technical mixing of any sort. Everyone there really felt about the music the same way. The amount of bass present or drums, or guitars, or vocals, was like a tradition. It was just like something that *was*. It was bigger than the parts."

Although Jim Stewart would go to the wall before allowing anyone to mess with the equipment or acoustics in the McLemore studio, in December 1971 he finally acceded to Dave Purple's constant prodding to spend $77,000 and purchase disc-mastering equipment. The genesis for Purple's campaign came when Ronnie Capone, William Brown, and Larry Nix were installing a new stereo system in Jim Stewart's office.

"There were three or four of us installing this thing," recalls Nix. "After we got it installed, we turned on the radio and they were playing Motown. Right after that they played a Stax record and it was like 'Wow!' There was a staggering amount of difference in the overall sound. We started questioning why. Purple got on this campaign to get total control of disc mastering."

Stewart was initially reluctant to spend the money, until Purple informed him that Stax already was spending about $75,000 a year with Mastercraft for disc work. The system would pay for itself in just over a year. Stewart next questioned whether they would be able to find anyone in Memphis capable of operating the equipment. Jim was unaware that Purple had probably cut over twenty-five thousand acetates and installed two disc-mastering systems during his tenure in Chicago. Although the engineer wasn't interested in getting locked into spending all of his time mastering lacquers at Stax, he was happy to install the equipment and train someone to operate it. That someone turned out to be Larry Nix. Larry was Don Nix's brother, and had learned how to engineer while doing some favors for his elder sibling by helping out on a variety of sessions. Nix ended up parlaying that experience into an engineering job at Stax some eight months before the disc-cutting equipment arrived on site. Most of his time had been confined to cutting demos in Studio C.

The new equipment was installed in Steve Cropper's former office, and Purple and Nix were the only employees who had keys to the room. As a matter of principle, artists and producers were not permitted in the disc-recording room. "It was generally treated as some kind of juju—black magic," cracks Purple.

Jim Stewart's mandate was that the singles be mastered as loud as humanly possible. "I used to get mad as hell with the mastering people," asserts Stewart, "because they couldn't get [the volume I wanted] on the record. I'd get them to cut them so hot sometimes they wouldn't track, and they still wouldn't be hot enough for my ears. I fought that for many years."

To get the phenomenal level that Jim Stewart demanded, Stax 45s had little low-end sound, as a rule containing no information below 120 Hz. This was not really a problem because the company's records were generally heard over the tiny transistor-radio speakers or the equally tiny car speaker systems of the day. When they were actually purchased, the odds were the home system they were played on was not that much more sophisticated.

Nix was initially trained by Purple and then, some time later, the company sent him to California so that he could visit a number of disc-mastering facilities and pick up whatever techniques Purple may not have known. Nix developed into a superb disc cutter and, in the late 1990s, he runs his own highly successful disc-cutting company in Memphis. He is one more example of someone with no previous training who was given a chance to develop a lifelong skill while at Stax. For that, he is eternally grateful.

With the *Shaft* album storming up the charts in its third week of release, Al Bell announced his most ambitious marketing campaign to date. Kicking off on August 16, "Stax Sound in Chi-Town" was designed to saturate the country's second-largest record market, Chicago, by using both media (print, television, and radio) and retail display. A bevy of Stax stars descended on the city, putting in personal appearances at various retail outlets and on Chicago radio and television programs.

Bell's plan was to prove that Stax LP product was a viable commodity in mainstream record outlets. As a test, he placed Stax albums in the entire Sears chain in the Chicago area during this promotion. He hoped that, if this proved to be successful in Chicago, the rack jobbers that supplied all the major department stores and other large white-oriented retail outlets countrywide would be willing to buy Stax product. Up to this point, the vast majority of Stax's releases were simply unavailable except in the mom-and-pop stores that traditionally serviced inner-city America. At the end of the campaign Bell had all the statistics from "Stax Sound in Chi-Town" tabulated and printed in a booklet that he then presented as part of a speech he gave to a meeting of the National Association of Record Merchants. In what would have important ramifications for Stax in the future, CBS president Clive Davis was one of those in attendance.

Following close on the "Stax Sound in Chi-Town" campaign was the biggest hit to date for Chicago's own native sons, the Staple Singers. "Respect Yourself" was largely written by Mack Rice, a former member, along with Eddie Floyd and Wilson Pickett, of the Detroit vocal group the Falcons. In 1965 Rice wrote and recorded the soul staple "Mustang Sally" for Mercury subsidiary Blue Rock. A year later Wilson Pickett covered the song, taking it into the R&B Top 10. Soon thereafter Rice briefly recorded for Stax, issuing two fairly unsuccessful singles in the spring and summer of 1967. Rice next record- ed for the Atlantic subsidiary Atco. In late spring 1971, he returned to 926 E. McLemore, this time signed to a writer's contract with East Memphis Music. By July he was enjoying a number 2 hit with Rufus Thomas's recording of the Rice–Thomas–Eddie Floyd–penned "The Breakdown."

"Respect Yourself" resulted from a discussion Rice had with Luther Ingram. At one point Ingram stated emphatically something along the lines of "black folk need to learn to respect themselves." Rice took the idea, and quickly cut a demo of the song with the help of Tommy Tate in Studio C. Bettye Crutcher heard the demo and suggested the song would be perfect for the Staple Singers. "We cut [the demo] in a really sanctified up- tempo type of groove," recalls Rice. "That's what Bettye Crutcher probably heard. I knew it was funky but I didn't hear it [as being appropriate] for them." Al Bell, though, agreed with Crutcher. "I heard that lyric and I heard that melody and I said, 'That's it. This is the song I've been waiting on. I've just got to capture this.'"

Bell remembers Muscle Shoals vets keyboardist Barry Beckett and drummer Roger Hawkins playing a key role in creating the record's rhythmic feel. "Roger would lock into me rhythm-wise," Bell says excitedly. "I kept the time in my shoulders. I was conscious of that. My shoulders became the metronome for them. They'd lock into that. I'd feel them locking in because something would happen to me physically. Once they locked in, my body became a part of whatever they were playing. It became at one with the rhythm. That's when I knew I had it."

Bell had become so enamored of the Muscle Shoals rhythm section that on January 8, 1971, he signed a Musician's Incentive Royalty agreement with Hawkins, Beckett, Hood, and Johnson which gave them 1 percent of 90 percent of the retail selling price for all tracks that they played on that Bell produced. The agreement was retroactive to their first Staple Singers sessions and would continue for any and all future sessions. Part of Bell's rationale was that cutting them into a royalty would cause them to put that much more into the sessions. In the case of "Respect Yourself," he wasn't disappointed.

Bell and the Muscle Shoals crew made a number of substantive changes to Rice's com- position, one of the most important being the slowing down of the tempo of the song. Rice had recorded it at a fairly brisk clip. "The influence was Watts 103rd Street Rhythm Band's 'Express Yourself,'" muses Bell, explaining the tempo change. "That was rhythmically where, in beats per minute, R-and-B radio was at that moment. That was right in the gut of a rhythm that R-and-B radio couldn't deny if you had something on top of it."

Roger Hawkins's drumming is simply marvelous, employing the rim of his snare and a wet-to-dry sound on the hi-hat. Bell and Ardent engineer Terry Manning mixed both sounds up front. They also added an extremely fuzzed guitar line that seems to arise out of the back of the mix in the middle of the track, becoming slightly louder as things fade at the end.

"It was designed to be subliminal," explains Bell. "Terry and I spent a lot of time dis- cussing subliminal seduction at that time as it related to the utilization of music. If you were into fuzz, you could feel it and perhaps even hear it without it being loud. If we had it there subtlely on the front end, then it didn't overshadow the tune. If you [then] build it as it goes along, then the tune is building in intensity and the possibility is you might have a song that might have some rock appeal. That was the idea for putting it on there."

"It was an early power guitar kind of move," Manning recalls. "I just wanted to get something that resembled saxophones like, say, in 'Locomotion' by Little Eva—a fuzzy distorted kind of sound that also resembled a Yardbirdish or English rock kind of heavy guitar. It was a texture. Let's face it, it's great if this crosses over into the white market and gets on AM stations and becomes a big hit, but the bread and butter of all the Stax records was black radio. You can't come in with a totally different sound and blow that. So, I wanted textures. I wanted it to be subtle—subtle fuzz, loud guitar!

"On that particular song," continues Manning, "we made a conscious effort to experiment. It was kind of like all or nothing. We consciously put majors and minors together and rock and blues together. It was a lot of elements trying to fuse together, purposely putting little high tinkly sounds to catch kids' ears, and just seeing if it would work. That was, more than any record I can ever remember working on, a real experiment." It is symptomatic of Bell and Manning's crossover goals that Stax ads for the Staples' *Bealtitude: Respect Yourself* album were headed "The Message That Rock Music is Still Looking For." Not so coincidentally, Mavis, Pops, and Al Bell all began viewing this stage in the Staples' career as moving away from straight "protest" into what they termed "message" material.

Pops sings the first verse in a dignified and evocative manner before Mavis takes over and delivers what just might be her finest vocal performance on record. The highlight is undeniably the point where Mavis explodes on the words "big ole man" as she heads into the chorus at the end of the second verse. Right before the second verse there is an extraordinary hook where Mavis scats for four bars and is then joined by the whole family on a four-bar riff consisting of the vocable "dee" over a bass breakdown. Apparently Mack Rice had sung both of these four-bar sections on his demo. Al Bell was sure that Rice was singing what he envisioned as horn lines, but Mavis and company simply sounded too good doing it themselves.

Rice was aghast at the whole production, especially the change in tempo and rhythmic phrasing. He felt that his song had been destroyed, but gradually changed his mind as the record sailed its way to the second-highest spot on the R&B charts and number 12 on the pop listings.

By the fall of 1971, Booker T. Jones had been gone from Stax for just over two years. Although he had been excited about the MG's work on "Melting Pot" earlier that year, he had finally decided to leave the group as well.[15] After making a number of overtures to the other members to leave Stax and sign with A&M, Booker basically ceased communicating with the rest of the group he had cofounded some nine years earlier. Stax responded by suspending Booker on November 12. Frustrated, Steve, Duck, and Al released one further single in October 1971, "Jamaica, This Morning" that they recorded on their own, backed with "Fuquawi" from the *Melting Pot* album. The A-side was issued under the moniker "the MG's" while the B-side was credited to Booker T. and the MG's. Pleasant enough, the record falls far short of prime Booker T. and the MG's, and by the end of 1971 had died a reasonably quick death. Under pressure from Stax, Steve, Duck, and Al tried to cut some more tracks at Cropper's new studio, TMI, without Booker, but in Steve's words, "Obviously that wasn't going to work." The MG's never officially broke up; they simply stopped recording together.

While there were those within the company who were obviously saddened by the demise of the MG's, there was little time to think about it. In November, Isaac Hayes released his second double album of the year, *Black Moses*.

---

15. *Melting Pot* had created one further sore spot between the MG's and Stax. While on tour with Creedence Clearwater Revival in 1970, the MG's had been hipped to the fact that there was no reason in the world why they shouldn't have their own publishing company. "We were out with Creedence," recalls a still-miffed Duck Dunn, "and we just got to learn a few things. We went in one day and asked for half the publishing. They refused us." The fact that Don Davis controlled his publishing was all the more galling.

It was Dino Woodard who came up with the "Black Moses" tag. "Dino said, 'Man, look at those people out there,'" explains Isaac. "'Do you know what you're bringing into their lives? Look at these guys from Vietnam, man, how they're crying when they see you, how you helped them through when they was out there in the jungle and they stuck to your music. You like a Moses, man. You just like Black Moses, you the modern-day Moses!'

"Somebody got wind of that and when I opened in Philadelphia at the Spectrum, [in front of] eighteen thousand people, Georgie Woods, who was a local radio personality and a promoter, introduced me that night. He said, 'Ladies and gentlemen, I bring to you the Black Moses of the music world—Isaac Hayes,' and the whole place stood, people just screaming and it caught on. A writer for *Jet* magazine named Chester Higgins did an article on me and he used the term Black Moses, and then Larry Shaw had the savvy to capitalize on it and entitle the album *Black Moses*.

"I had nothing to do with it. I was kicking and screaming all the way. But when I saw the relevance and effect that it had on people, it wasn't a negative thing. It was a healing thing, it was an inspiring thing. It raised the level of black consciousness in the States. People were proud to be black. Black men could finally stand up and be men because here's Black Moses, he's the epitome of black masculinity. Chains that once represented bondage and slavery now can be a sign of power and strength and sexuality and virility."

Ever since he had come to Stax, Larry Shaw felt that the company had severely lagged behind in its cover art development. The nadir for Shaw was David Porter's *Gritty, Groovy, and Gettin' It* LP, released in February 1970, where a naked Porter was pictured with an equally naked female partner from the armpits up. Porter has his head turned toward the camera giving off a hard, menacing look that seems totally devoid of any of the tenderness one might associate with lovemaking.

"To me," comments Shaw, "it was just a nasty presentation of an artist humping some chick. The disrespect that the designers of it had for the artist and the music was not necessary. It was their translation of guts. It was not appropriate. I constantly found that the white perspective on the black visceral sensitivity [was to] try to be literal with the darn things that were emotional!"

Stax album artwork had improved tremendously since Shaw, with help from former Bar-Kay Ron Gordon, took over its direction. With *Black Moses* he outdid himself, designing what has to be the most elaborate album package for a black artist up to that point. The two records were encased in a regular cover that portrayed Hayes from the neck up, shrouded in a caftan against a backdrop of endless sky. The cover clearly signified the notion of Hayes as Moses in the Middle East. Enveloping the regular cover was a multi-panel graphic that unfolded into a cross shape four feet high and three feet wide. Here was the same image of Hayes as Moses, but now it was a full body shot with the artist at the edge of a large body of water.

"Once we saw what we classified as a good move," Shaw explains, "we captured that and promoted it. The music in there was of such poor quality, we had to sell the box it came in. We put an inordinate amount of money into that album jacket. It was to capture fully all the things about him that were not in the record. The record *was* the box."

Although Al Bell does not agree with Shaw's assessment of the music, he did tell Shaw that the company needed to spend the extra money on the album packaging because, following on the heels of *Shaft*, it was going to be very difficult for *Black Moses* to get the

attention it deserved. He had recently learned from the rack jobbers that 40 percent of the LPs sold in the market were impulse purchases. Given the importance of Hayes's album sales to the bottom line at Stax, whatever

Black Moses is here!

Black Moses

ISAAC HAYES

Enterprise Records,
Division of Stax Records, Inc.,
North Avalon, Memphis, U.S.A

Enterprise Records,
A Division of Stax Records, Inc.,
98 North Avalon, Memphis, U.S.A

was necessary to actually sell the album was deemed appropriate. "You'll notice," adds Shaw, "that there's a difference in his music from what he produced when he took a bus to the studio as opposed to when he took a limousine to the studio. We saw the literal demise of a genius."

There is no denying that with his ever-increasing success, Isaac's productions and presentations had grown more expansive. Following the general imperative of Western capitalism, the number of musicians on his recording sessions increased, his arrangements often grew more elaborate (some would say excessive), and the associated costs of recording and staging his concerts grew exponentially. The mere expanse of *Black Moses* is evidence of this mind-set. That does not necessarily have to mean, though, that the quality of his recordings deteriorated.

Black Moses is a wondrously crafted, intense evocation of the vagaries of love gone bad. In many ways the LP contains Isaac's most personal work. "I was going through some emotional turmoil," recalls Isaac. "You can tell by the tunes on the album. I was going through a breakup of my marriage. I was heartbroken. I was lamenting. That's the only way I could express myself, cry out through that."[16] Although no one has ever written about it as such, *Black Moses*, in essence, is a concept album. Carefully sequenced, Issac leads the listener through a touching and emotionally bracing roller coaster ride. Over the course of fourteen songs and three extended raps, Hayes chronicles the pain and denial of separation, infidelity, the desperate emotional need for a replacement love, the joys of sex, and the bittersweet memories of what once was and now can never be, concluding with a cover of a Bacharach-David tune that had been a hit for Dionne Warwick a year earlier, "I'll Never Fall in Love Again."

The list of songs that Hayes chose to cover details the emotional terrain of the album: the Jackson 5's "Never Can Say Goodbye," the Bacharach-David–penned Carpenters hit "(They Long to Be) Close to You," Toussaint McCall's 1967 hit "Nothing Takes the Place of You," the Curtis Mayfield–authored Gene Chandler 1963 hit "Man's Temptation," Little Johnny Taylor's (no relation to Stax's Johnnie Taylor) 1963 smash "Part-Time Love," Kenny Gamble and Thom Bell's "A Brand New Me," which would chart for Aretha Franklin in April while Isaac's recording sessions were in full swing, Friends of Distinction's 1969 hit "Going in Circles," Gamble and Leon Huff's "Never Gonna Give You Up," Luther Ingram's "Help Me Love," Curtis Mayfield's "Need to Belong," which had been a hit for both Jerry Butler in 1964 and Laura Lee in 1968, the Whispers' May 1971 hit "Your Love Is So Doggone Good," Kris Kristofferson's "For the Good Times," and finally "I'll Never Fall in Love Again."

Isaac's ability to take other people's material and make it so deeply personal is nothing short of brilliant. The original versions of three of the songs, "Never Can Say Goodbye," "Brand New Me," and "Your Love Is So Doggone Good," were actually on the charts while Isaac was in the studio; it takes a lot of guts to cover current material and pull it off with such aplomb. For my money "Help Me Love," "Need to Belong," Isaac's own composition "Good Love," and "A Brand New Me" rank with his finest recordings ever.

Recording sessions for the album started in March, with the album's opening track, a cover of the Jackson 5's then-current hit "Never Can Say Goodbye," being issued in April. Going head to head against the Jacksons, Isaac's very different version worked its way to number 5 R&B and number 22 pop, while the poppier Motown group went all the way to numbers 1 and 2, respectively, on the two different charts.

---

16. For the recording of one of the album's songs, Isaac asked his secretary to come into the studio so that he could sing to her. "I was at the mike, tears running down my face," sighs Isaac, "and I was singing the song. I needed somebody to just hold on to at the time. That was a painful experience."

As Stax was readying *Black Moses* for release, it issued a press release headed "Stax Record Organization Opens Fight Against Record Piracy." *Shaft* and other recent Stax releases had been extensively counterfeited in various areas of the country. Al Bell was determined to make sure the same thing didn't happen with *Black Moses*. To that end, according to the press release, the release date and shipping information for the album were only known to two Stax executives. The idea was to quickly get the album out in all markets to the point of saturation before it could be bootlegged. The press release claimed that "a team of ex-FBI agents will institute close surveillance tactics at the fabricating plants, pressing operations and known bootlegging operations throughout the U.S. FBI methods will be utilized in detecting and apprehending pirates."[17]

How much these efforts curtailed the counterfeiting that is so often the bane of the regionally based independent label is hard to know.[18] The following February, Stax was still concerned enough about counterfeiting that it issued a press release saying that it was delaying the release of O. B. McClinton's debut album until February 15 in order to give it the protection provided under the provisions of new copyright legislation designed to counteract record piracy.

In one sense, the counterfeiting problem was simply further testimony to Isaac's impact at the time. It is impossible to overestimate how important he was as a symbol to black America at large. Here was a black popular musician who had won both Grammys and Academy Awards, whose recordings repeatedly scaled the heights of the R&B, pop, easy-listening, and jazz charts, who, in essence, went boldly where no popular black musician had ever gone before. Not yet thirty years old, he was truly a larger-than-life cultural icon in a way that perhaps no previous R&B performer had ever been.

Isaac took his role as a leader in the black community seriously. In April he had formed the Isaac Hayes Foundation. In addition to Hayes, the board of directors included Georgia State Representative Julian Bond, Rev. Jesse Jackson, Stax's accountant Ronald Altman, and the president of Memphis's Lemoyne-Owen College, Dr. Odell Horton. Fund-raising was begun at the Mid-South Coliseum in Memphis when Hayes appeared as a guest soloist with the Memphis Symphony Orchestra. All proceeds from that concert went to fund the replacement of a senior citizens' home in Memphis that had been destroyed by fire. The organization had future plans for the construction of two hundred apartments for the elderly with complete medical and recreational facilities. In 1972 the Isaac Hayes Foundation financed through the United States Department of Housing and Urban Development an $8 million, twenty-acre, 250-unit housing complex for low- and moderate-income families in St. Croix, U.S. Virgin Islands. Dubbed the Lorraine Village, in addition to the two-story garden apartment and townhouse units, the complex contained recreational facilities and a mini-park for children.

It was no accident that the first major project of the Isaac Hayes Foundation was placed in the Virgin Islands. Larry Shaw suggested that Stax's advertising department branch out and go after the Virgin Islands public relations tourism account. If successful, this would provide yet one more avenue for marketing Stax product in a new part of the world. "We wanted the Caribbean market," reasoned Shaw. "They needed marketing of their biggest industry, which is tourism." Hence the location of Isaac's housing project. Ultimately, Stax didn't get the Virgin Islands account, and no further outside public relations accounts were pursued.

17. When queried in early 1997 as to whether Stax actually hired ex-FBI personnel, Al Bell said it did, but he also admitted that he may have exaggerated their importance in the publicity designed to capitalize on it.

18. Dave Purple, for one, felt that the counterfeiting could be traced to one or two Stax employees who had keys to the auxiliary duplicate off-site tape storage facility on Highland Street. For obvious reasons, he was unwilling to divulge the names of those whom he suspected.

Lorraine Village was to be the first of several housing projects that Isaac planned to sponsor.[19] Unfortunately Stax's financial troubles in 1974 and 1975 aborted any such additional philanthropic plans for Hayes or anyone else involved with the label.

In October 1971, Isaac demonstrated that his social conscience extended beyond raising money for tax-deductible charities. In mid-month the Memphis police beat a seventeen-year-old black student by the name of Elton Hayes (no relation) to death. The police had originally claimed that Hayes had died in a car accident. When the truth came out, many young black Memphians took to the streets and rioted, throwing bricks at white cars and firebombs at various stores. At least one person was shot and looting also occurred. Mayor Henry Loeb immediately slapped a 7 P.M. to 5 A.M. curfew on the entire city.

Three years earlier, after Dr. Martin Luther King's death, Isaac Hayes and Warren Lewis, a black banker in North Memphis, had formed a group they called the Black Knights. The mandate of the Black Knights was to champion the cause of black people in Memphis especially in regard to job discrimination, improper housing and police brutality. The organization also collected money, produce and canned food goods for needy families. When necessary, they took their grievances to City Hall.

Unbeknownst to Mayor Loeb when he implemented the curfew was the fact that Isaac Hayes and others were scheduled to play a benefit that evening for Eva Clayton. Ms. Clayton was in dire need of a kidney machine and if the benefit did not proceed as planned with the necessary funds being raised, she was likely to die. It was with this in mind that Isaac and several other members of the Black Knights went down to City Hall to meet with the mayor to urge him to lift the curfew.

Isaac picks up the story: "We said, 'Mr. Mayor, we'd like to bring something to your attention. There is a benefit concert on tonight. If the curfew stays in place, we can't do the benefit and to black folks that's gonna seem like another slap in the face and the riots will escalate. You need to lift the curfew so the show can go on and that might quiet this tension that's in town.'"

According to Isaac, Loeb smugly responded, "If you get fifteen responsible black people in the next hour, I'll get you fifteen responsible whites and we'll meet in the chambers here."

Isaac, Lewis, and others rushed out and immediately phoned various doctors, school principals, and Stax artists and executives. Among those who immediately headed down to City Hall were Rufus Thomas, Larry Shaw, Deanie Parker, John Smith, and trumpeter Mickey Gregory. Isaac functioned as the spokesperson for the black delegation.

"[Loeb] was shocked," continues Isaac. "All he had to do was get on his intercom and just have fifteen white people come in. Even the chief of police, Chief Lux, showed up. We laid our case before them and said, 'Y'all got to stop the curfew or else there's gonna be a blood bath.' All the black responsible people took our side on the issue because they knew. Chief Lux was totally against it. It looked like we were at an impasse. The president of City Council's name was Jerry Blanchard. I said, 'Mr. Blanchard, you got property down here. You other gentlemen might have properties. If the riots escalate, your businesses are going up in flames.' That got their attention. They said, 'Well, Henry, they might have a point there.'"

19. In September 1972, it was announced that the Isaac Hayes Foundation was preparing to sponsor a $100 million housing program for low-income families throughout the United States again in partnership with Housing and Urban Development funds. If the project had come to fruition, twenty thousand people would have been living in the program's garden apartment communities within the next five years.

Another vote was taken and it was decided to lift the curfew. A press conference was immediately called with Loeb insisting that Isaac stand beside him. "I didn't want to stand beside this man," recalls Isaac in disgust, "because he had gone on record and said he was a staunch racist. But, just to get the peace, I stood with him and we made the announcement. On behalf of the black community, Isaac pledged that all efforts would be made "to prevent any member of our community from initiating any incidence of violence." Mayor Loeb pledged that, along with Police Chief Henry Lux, he would "see that members of the Memphis Police Department will initiate no such incidents and will use only such force as may be necessary to control lawlessness." Together they "urged everyone to cooperate in carrying out this objective."

Isaac himself took to the streets to try to break up gangs on corners and thereby defuse the situation. Accompanying him was City Council president Jerry Blanchard and a reporter from one of Memphis's two daily newspapers. While Isaac was asking all youth to either go home or accept free tickets that he was offering to the benefit that night at the Mid-South Coliseum for the Eva Clayton Kidney Fund, his entourage observed police TAC (tactical) forces riding three or four deep in a car harassing blacks.

"They were trying to provoke blacks into doing something," spits Isaac, "so they could shoot them like dogs. That's what they were doing!"

Although twelve thousand tickets had been sold for the benefit, most people stayed off the streets, and Hayes and others played to only about three thousand patrons.

The following night there was another meeting at City Hall with Chief Lux wanting to restore the curfew. "I'm saying," states Isaac, shaking his head, "'No, you need to keep it off. It's defusing. Don't do that.' I said, 'Mr. Mayor, you have to somehow restore the faith in your credibility to the black community.' He banged on the desk, 'I ain't got to do nothing!' Well, that pissed me off. I walked out and said, 'Y'all got it, somebody's gonna get killed. This thing is still a powder keg. It ain't over yet. You need to show some good faith or you can forget it!'"

Loeb sent the only black person on City Council, insurance man Fred Davis, after Isaac to bring him back. "I said," recalls Isaac, "'I'm not going back in. I'm not going to be a party to this mess. I totally, on the record, disagree with what's being done in there.' I left."

That night a TAC force car speeding through the black community hit a little kid who ran out onto the street between parked cars and killed him. The riots flared up again.

The following March, Isaac Hayes and label mate Rufus Thomas were honored along with seven other black citizens by the Memphis City Council for "outstanding contributions to the community."

The day after *Black Moses* shipped, Hayes appeared on local Memphis television station WMC-TV in a pilot program dubbed "Rufus Thomas Presents."[20] Although not quite as hot as Hayes, Thomas, the world's oldest teenager, was finishing up the most successful year of his career, placing four records on the *Billboard* R&B charts including the chart-topping "(Do the) Push and Pull" and the number 2 funk workout "The Breakdown." In addition to Hayes, Rufus's guests on the one-hour show were fellow Stax artists Jean Knight, the Bar-Kays, and Carla Thomas. Isaac lip-synched his performances of "Never Can Say Goodbye" and "Never Gonna Give You Up" in their entirety, whereas everyone else sang live vocals to a canned backing track. The highlight was a duet by Rufus and Carla on "The Night Time Is the Right Time." The program was the pilot for what was hoped to be four such specials. High on corn and light on production values, the program had difficulty attracting sponsors, and consequently no subsequent shows were taped.[21]

While all this was happening, Al Bell and Jim Stewart were in the process of borrowing $2.5 million from Union Planters National Bank for the purpose of buying out the 45 percent of Stax stock still owned by Deutsche Grammophon through their American paper company, Music Ventures. The actual cost of buying DG out was $4.8 million. Bell and Stewart paid the remaining $2.3 million in cash. The Union Planters loan was executed November 10, 1971. Stax was so hot at the time that Bell and Stewart paid the complete debt off by June 27, 1972, several months ahead of schedule. It was Stax's ability to pay off such a large loan so quickly that made both Stax and the expansion-oriented Union Planters Bank so eager to negotiate future large-scale loans. Both corporations would end up regretting this decision.

In December 1971, Bell and Stewart established a new subsidiary of Stax Records Inc. Lynn and Associates, Inc., was initially designed as a tax shelter, allowing the company to

---

20. The pilot was also aired in Cincinnati and Kansas City.

21. For anyone interested in licensing footage from the pilot, it is available from Berger Productions, P.O. Box 770297, Memphis, TN 38117.

defer $660,168 worth of income taxes in 1971. Officially Lynn was in the cattle business. To facilitate this activity, in early 1972 Stax approached the Chase Manhattan Bank in New York for a loan to buy cattle feed. At the time, Union Planters had a very aggressive loan policy and was quite disturbed that Stax would go to a New York bank rather than giving them the business. Union Planters eventually approved loans to Lynn on December 5, 1972, December 27, 1972, and January 10, 1973, totaling $888,725. Stax paid these off in their entirety by May 14, 1973, at which point Lynn had sold its cattle stock to Wilhelm Feeds. Lynn was effectively out of the cattle business, although toward the end of 1973 Stax would borrow again under the Lynn umbrella to supply Stax with badly needed operating capital.

In the latter part of 1971, Stax was obviously pulling in money hand over fist.[22] One would think that all would be rosy at the now–completely freestanding company, but according to Tim Whitsett, Larry Nix, and Dave Purple, all was not well in the hallowed house of Stax. Bell and Stewart, happily ensconced in their offices on Avalon, had begun to lose control of the McLemore studios. Dave Purple was the most emphatic: "After they moved their executive offices over to Avalon, they lost all control in the studios."

For most of Stax's history, Studio A had been left set up day and night, ready to cut a session in an instant. With only one or two drummers using the facility, the drum set never had to be changed. Because all records were basically cut with the same instrumentation and, for the longest time, personnel, the microphones could be left set up in the same positions. This began to change in the 1970s. By the fall of 1971, there were a number of outside musicians at various times playing on sessions at McLemore.

"Isaac's group alone was huge," attests Larry Nix. "We didn't know a lot of those people because they were on the road. They'd come in and they'd hang out down there. Some of those [people] were very undesirable to a criminal level. There was a lot of people in there you'd probably want to watch."

Microphones and other pieces of equipment began to regularly go astray. Engineers began to have to set up and tear down for each session, locking all equipment up when the day was done. "As it grew, it changed a lot," bemoans Nix. "The security thing got real involved, and coming to work felt like going to jail sometimes. They came in with the fences and the guard houses, motion devices in the rooms. [For] certain rooms, people had coded electric keys in a little leather case that you would punch in and open the door electrically. It was paranoid."

One of the unanticipated results of hiring Norman Jaspen to investigate Roussell and Kole was a recommendation from the New York firm that Stax take better care of its master tapes. These tapes were the company's primary asset and, as things then stood, there was virtually no security or protection for them. Jaspen felt that Stax's insurance coverage on the tapes should be increased. To obtain such a policy, Stax had to substantially improve its security. To that end, Bell and Stewart hired an employee of Jaspen's, Dick Lafontaine, to expand and then manage Stax's security system. He took his job seriously.[23] According to Al Bell, the system Lafontaine put in place at McLemore "was likened to the security system that the Ford Motor Company had at that time."

22. Gross sales for the year were $16,919,022. Out of that salaries were paid to the chief officers, Bell and Stewart, totaling $170,270, and to the rest of Stax employees totaling $690,321.

23. Too seriously, says Tim Whitsett. "He got himself appointed deputy sheriff or deputy police chief of some invisible town outside of Memphis that had three people in it, proceeded to put badges on his cars and a siren and blue lights and seventeen antennas, carried little beepers and walkie-talkies and guns until somebody made him stop. But, you know, he was from New York and he just loved being down in the South and being a policeman. It was something!"

Everyone was issued an employee card beginning in January 1972. According to Nix, one day Duck Dunn forgot his card and was actually turned away. "I think that's when it wasn't fun for him anymore," adds Nix.

"There was animosity about [the heavy security]," recalls Pete Bishop. "It increased over a period of time, but there were a lot of people stealing equipment. Actually, there were a few people stealing a lot of equipment."

"Going in and out of there was like a Gestapo trip," says Jimmy Johnson. "They had all these guards. It was unbelievable to get in and out of there. You had to have a certain badge to be on a certain floor. If you didn't, it was like a concentration camp almost."

For anyone who had been a part of Stax in the 1960s, the changed level of security at the studio was hard to fathom. "You had to sign in and out," remembers Wayne Jackson. "We had to open our horn cases so they could see if we were bringing in a gun. Some of the people inside were carrying guns. And on the way out [we had to open our cases again] to see that we weren't stealing something because there was a lot of stealing going on then. There were just myriads of people hanging around all the time that had nothing to do with the music, that had nothing to do with the Stax family. The feelings of warmth and love and excitement that we'd always had there were gone. Just like smoke in the wind . . . over."

Jerry Wexler was equally shocked when he visited Stax one final time in the early 1970s. Wexler encountered a bunkerlike atmosphere with the studio and offices being patrolled by armed guards and guard dogs. What really shocked the former owner of Atlantic Records were the remote cameras in the hall. In Wexler's words, there was "a general atmosphere of paranoia and implied terror in the halls."

Perhaps the last word on this state of affairs belongs to Steve Cropper. Like Wexler, he visited Stax only once after his regular work with the label came to an end. In Cropper's case, he came back to play a session for David Porter. "That was in the Dino days, the pistol whippings and the craziness," says the lanky guitarist. "I just said, 'Hey, I don't want any part of this crap. This is ridiculous.' It was like going to prison. It was a really strange, weird feeling. The studio was fine. It was the guard thing, the chain link fence in the parking lot, guards on the front door. The whole air and the whole feeling of everything had changed."

13

I'll Take You There:
1972 (Part 1)

S tax's new high-tech security may have stopped the theft of microphones (while simultaneously introducing high levels of paranoia in the studios), but it didn't take care of every security problem. In 1972 blue-eyed soul singer Stefan Anderson was cutting a single when he decided to take a break and go outside for some air.

"He opened the door to the back of the parking lot which is encircled by a fence," recounts Tim Whitsett. "He's smoking a cigarette. Meanwhile, the neighborhood something-or-other had crawled up onto the roof, gone exploring commando [style], high on something. He peered over the edge of the roof and saw Stefan sitting there and like a panther seeing a prey, pounced. Stefan is rolling around, screaming, kicking and [the security guard] Kelly is asleep in the guard booth with his guard dog. He hears all this and he gets up and ambles on over there to see what's going on. He gets halfway and thinks he better go back and get his dog and the dog won't move! So he goes back and thinks he better get his gun. Stefan has got the PA system on, calling back into the studio, 'Help somebody, somebody help me.' Bobby Manuel comes out there with a music stand, opens the door, sees what's going on and closes the door. It took a lot of work to subdue all that."

The heightened security didn't address another problem: many of the company's employees at McLemore exhibited what can best be described as a laissez-faire attitude in the extreme. Homer Banks thought that, in general, things were too loose. From his perspective, it was only during Don Davis's brief vice presidency that a sense of professionalism was readily manifest. This was a problem that Al and Jim were constantly attempting to rectify.

"Every six months," chuckles Tim Whitsett, "you'd have some eighty-thousand-dollar-a-year guy come in from Los Angeles who was a business expert. They would come in and they would roam through the departments with their clipboards and ask people questions and scare them to death and depart. Bell and them would know things were not going professionally. You'd go into your office in the morning and there'd be one of these guys sitting there—'Come in here. I've got some questions to ask you.' You'd think, 'What am I doing wrong? Did I do something?' They'd ask all these questions, then they'd submit their reports and go away and collect their fees and then there'd be a flourish of activity. 'We're going to get this place together. From now on [blah, blah, blah].' They'd issue policy manuals and all that. We'd have big meetings and everybody would sit there and Bell would pontificate like Jesse Jackson up and down the stage. Bell would [also] post these glorious memos on the walls that were full of quotes from everyone from Kahlil Gibran to the Bible. There would be this rush of activity and then, of course, everything would go right back to the way it was."

Part of the problem was that Stax had outgrown its original facility, structure, and systems, and, with further growth proceeding at an exponential rate, management was simply too busy to attend to the nuts and bolts of running the company. Given the constant success of the company and the resultant cash flow, no one at the top can be blamed for feeling that, despite a few bumps in the road, the good ship Stax was doing just fine.

In the trenches, there were those who thought otherwise. William Bell recalls, "We had so many new people that half the time I only knew one or two of the people in the company. I remember one incident, walking down the hallway with Jim. We were discussing something and we ran into this person in the hallway. This guy was over [in] marketing or something. Jim said, 'Oh, have you met William Bell.' He looked at me kind of blankly and said, 'Oh, you're Stax zero something, something [the catalogue number of Bell's latest release].' I'm going, 'Oh wow, this guy's handling my career?!' You can see then that the family and the caring and all that was becoming a big corporate structure, a number in a computer."

"They started bringing in so many people to work at Stax," agrees Eddie Floyd, "that I was a stranger there myself. That was a little weird. That was definitely a little strange."

Similar stories abound from those who could remember the earliest days of the company. Rufus Thomas opines, "In the beginning of Stax, it was family oriented. It wasn't big business. [It changed] when they really started to make money." In the early days Rufus could simply drop by the office and talk to Jim or Al if he had something on his mind. By 1972 he had to make an appointment and, frankly, he resented it deeply. His frustration boiled over one day in 1973 when he went by the offices to get a copy of one of his LPs and was told he needed a requisition form to get it. That didn't make him happy, but if that was the new system, he would oblige. The problem was, in what has to be an absolutely galling classic case of bureaucratic red tape, in his quest for this elusive requisition form Rufus was passed from one office to another.

"I got real nasty," admits Rufus. "I've never been that nasty before, never in the history of it. 'Don't you pass no buck on me! None of you pass no buck on me because if it wasn't for people like me, none of you son of a bitches would even have a job!'" Smoke coming out of his ears, Rufus simply took his album and stalked out.

From nearly everyone's vantage point, Al Bell had become increasingly remote. With the corporate offices now on Avalon, he rarely set foot in the McLemore building. Tim Whitsett had been in charge of Stax's two publishing companies, working at the McLemore location for eight or nine months before he even met Al Bell. "I didn't know the guy," exclaims Whitsett, with a fair bit of resentment. "His presence was everywhere— the great Al Bell—his pictures were on all the walls, and all the memos were signed 'Al Bell, Chief Executive,' and his name was always in *Billboard*, but I never met him! He was a ghost. When I went over to Avalon it was, 'Mr. Bell is in Washington.' If I ever had to call him to find out anything, 'Mr. Bell is in New York' or 'Mr. Bell is in Paris.'

"Jim Stewart would come in [to the McLemore facility] every now and then and say, 'How are things going? Are things all right? Good, good.' I didn't know whether they were all right or not, and he'd go away. But no Al Bell. Finally after I'd been there about eight or nine months, one day the office door opened and here comes Al Bell with two or three guys, and he says, 'Mr. Whitsett, I want you to meet Mr. So-and-So of Polygram, Holland. Mr. Whitsett's doing an *excellent* job running our publishing company. We're very *proud* to have him. See you later, Mr. Whitsett. Carry on. Good to see you again.' He walked out and I said, 'Who *was* that masked man?' First time I'd ever seen him. It was maybe another year before I had a conversation that lasted more than a few minutes with him. He was completely 'hands off' publishing."

Pete Bishop, who also worked at McLemore, had similar experiences: "Al was seen as either God, who's brilliant, or alternatively as the person who was grabbing control, [who was] money oriented, personal fame oriented. You didn't actually get to meet Al, talk with Al, work with Al. You just didn't see him much, and when you did it was like he was being political, 'hail fellow well met' kind of backslapping and all that. The problem was, you never knew where he was. He'd talk to you one way and he'd talk to someone else and say the exact opposite. He was a real politician. I wouldn't say he was two-faced because that denotes some intention which I don't think he had. But, it's the same ultimate effect, and a lot of people thought he was two-faced because of that. I think he was sincere about trying to build a major force in the music business [but] I don't think he was equipped for it."

For longtime Stax personnel, the change in Al Bell really chafed. "He got political," complains Duck Dunn. "He got corporate and he just lost it. He lost his touch with the common person. He lost his touch with the disc jockeys. He lost his touch with the people who made him. To get to see him for two minutes a week you were lucky. Then he would pat you on the back and say, 'It's going to be all right.' After about six months that shit gets old."

Even Bell's old partner at Safice, Eddie Floyd, had difficulty getting to see him, and often resorted to parking himself outside of Bell's office. If Floyd knew Bell was scheduled to be in at 9:00 A.M., Eddie would be there at 8:30.

Songwriter Bettye Crutcher used the same approach. "There were times when [Al's secretary] Earlie would say, 'Oh, Mr. Bell is so busy, he can't see anyone today. He's not going to have time to see you today.' Honey, I would park outside his office and say, 'He's going to have to pee sometime. He's coming by me. I'm going to be right here until he comes out. He is not going anywhere today without seeing me.'"

"I was the first person they got to before they could get to him," admits Earlie Biles. "I was like the shield. I was the person to blame for all that because Al Bell never refused to see any-

Earlie Biles. COURTESY MISSISSIPPI VALLEY COLLECTION.

body. He would stay up all night, if it took all night, to see someone. But the man was *so* tired! He had so many things to do, his desk would be full of papers to read. So I was to block off time for him so that he would have time to look at things that had to be taken care of by him only.

"So, the artists did, at the end, have to wait longer. They couldn't just walk right in his door. It wasn't an open-door policy. Artists were important too, but some wanted to see him just to say 'Hi,' or just to be like old times. But *it was no longer old times.* You couldn't function like a mom-and-pop shop when you had a multimillion-dollar company to run. You could no longer sit around the fireplace with your shoes off and shoot the breeze. [Al] seemed to be the type of person who people could get to and tell him anything and get what they wanted. I didn't like that because I thought they took advantage of him. A lot of times he would be tired. When you're tired things tend to get by you. So, I would always try and protect him."

Biles hit it on the head when she said "it was no longer old times." The "little label that could" had grown to the point where it had its own little bureaucracy. By August 1972 Stax employed close to two hundred people. Such rapid expansion is never accomplished without growing pains. In Stax's case, those growing pains included the problem of kickbacks in the sales department, the elaborate security system, the relative inaccessibility of Al Bell, and the alienation many of the earlier artists were experiencing. Unfortunately, the goose that had laid the golden egg was beginning to choke.

For Jim Stewart, Stax had simply stopped being fun. The company that he had started on a wing and a prayer so many years earlier had changed drastically. With the demise of Booker T. and the MG's he had ceased feeling comfortable working at the studio. In fact, Stewart had not produced a single session between 1967 and late 1971. At that point he briefly reentered the studio to produce, in tandem with Al Jackson, the Soul Children's *Genesis* LP and the Emotions' "My Honey and Me" single. He found that the sound and aesthetic of Stax that he had helped forge, nurture, and loved so dearly had become a dim memory to most of the company's current personnel.

During an editing session for the Soul Children LP, things came to a head. "Jim Stewart wanted me to cut something out [of one of the songs]," recalls Pete Bishop. "I really liked what we were cutting out. Larry [Nix] was there and he loved it [as well]. We kept arguing with Jim and finally Larry said something about, 'Jim, I promise you, if you do this, you're going to cut out almost all white sales.' Jim looked at him, slapped his heel and said, 'I don't give a good God damn if we never sell another record to a white person.' He stomped out and turned around and said, 'If I hear anything more, you're fired.' It was a pretty dramatic confrontation. I'd never seen Jim so mad. I saw Al Jackson there that afternoon and said to him that Jim cut this thing out and it ruins the record. Al said, 'I agree man, but he's set.' Al wasn't going to argue with him."

Stewart would not enter the studio again until March 1974, to produce Shirley Brown in a vain effort to save a sinking ship.

The sheer size of Stax's operation further limited Stewart's ability to do much production work. His day-to-day routine had increasingly begun to resemble all too closely the monotony of shuffling papers that had defined his life at First Tennessee Bank. In many respects, the problem with Kole and Roussell that arose during the previous summer and fall was the straw that broke the camel's back. It simply took what little enthusiasm Jim Stewart had left.

Carla Thomas volunteered that Jim was at least partially responsible for the situation in which he found himself. "During those days he probably felt very alienated," reasons Carla. "But what he didn't know was he was allowing the alienation. He pulled out of everybody's life. Jim was backing up and staying out of situations."

Sometime in late 1971 a tired and disillusioned Jim Stewart informed Al Bell that he wanted out. "Monetarily it was a successful company," explains Jim, "but I wasn't happy. I had been going at a tremendous pace since 1957, working day jobs in the first years, going to the studio, going to gigs on the weekend. My day was like a twenty-four-hour day. I had been going at this pace for a number of years. I told Al I was tired. We had had a bad situation with Gulf and Western. We had to buy out of there and it cost us a lot of money and almost a year to make it happen. By the time that we had finally resolved that and gotten independent again, there were a lot of problems with independent distribution. By 1972 major record companies had almost entirely devoured or wiped out the independent distribution system and formed branches. There were not enough labels left to support independent distribution. It just got to the point where I said, 'Al, I'm tired of dealing with this. I'd like to just stay in the creative area and sell the company. But this time [I want to] sell it for cash. I don't want any more stock.'"[1]

Although Bell had no desire to sell the company, he acceded to Jim's wishes and, with Clarence Avant's help, began to pound the pavement attempting to find a buyer for Stax. In the meantime, Bell needed to replace his recently fired sales managers, Herb Kole and Ewell Roussell. He turned to a man whom most would have deemed unsuitable for the job: Johnny Baylor. Bell's reasoning was that, because they were now attempting to sell the company, he didn't want to either increase the company's overhead or hire staff only to have those people lose their jobs when the company was sold. "I didn't want to do that to people," Bell insists, "because in order to find the people that I wanted to fill those positions, I was going to have to bring somebody in from someplace other than Memphis, Tennessee."

Bell needed an interim sales and promotion staff for what he assumed would be a very short period during which he would complete a deal for the sale of Stax. Baylor and his crew of Dino Woodard, former recording artist Jamo Thomas, and Ted Storey became Bell's field representatives, while former Old Town Records owner Hy Weiss flew down from New York three or four days a week and manned the sales phone at the Stax offices.[2] None of them charged Al Bell or Stax a penny for services rendered. According to Bell, Weiss was compensated in a quid pro quo deal with a record-pressing company, Viewlex in Great Neck, New York; in exchange for having all Stax records and tapes manufactured by them, Viewlex gave Weiss an override on every unit made. Baylor and his crew would receive their payoff from the proceeds of the eventual sale of Stax. In the meantime, as Baylor and his cronies were already out in the field working the KoKo catalogue, taking care of the Stax line wasn't that much of an additional burden.

"They were like the Green Berets," marvels Bell. "They could go into a marketplace; Teddy would go to the distributor and take inventory, Jamo would hit the retail outlets, and Dino would be at the radio [stations]. Johnny was the field marshal. They would go into a marketplace and hit everything that needed to be hit."

Baylor and Woodard had some rather effective, if novel, ways of promoting a record. "They would get results," says former Stax controller Robert Harris, smiling. "They'd spend four days in town. They'd fly in, go to the hotel and check in, pay four days up front, go to the radio station and let everybody know they were there, leave, and catch

1. Although both Bell and Stewart deny it, Don Davis, Ronnie Stoots, and a few others believe that Stewart was ultimately forced out of the company due to Johnny Baylor's belief that Stax should be solely black-owned. "He was forced to sell it," asserts Stoots bitterly. "He was forced into getting out of there. They didn't want no ofay son of a bitch in there *extorting their people*. The protector [Baylor] became the fucking enemy. You talk about thugs? Jesus Christ! Those people scared the shit out of me. [Jim was] terrified. Of course he will always deny [that he was forced out] because he was told to deny it." Stoots claims that while he was living at Jim Stewart's mansion, on more than one occasion Stewart received phone threats. Even more disturbing, according to a source who wishes to remain anonymous, were the drive-by grenade tossings. Stewart was being extorted for several hundred thousand dollars at a time. The FBI were eventually called in but, as Stoots recalls it, Jim was too scared to press charges. A number of people I interviewed, including Tommy Tate and Luther Ingram, believed that Al Bell might have been the figurehead but ultimately Johnny Baylor was calling the shots at Stax.

2. Storey had been a running partner with Baylor since they were kids in Birmingham. Thomas, who had a brief recording career most notable for his version of "I Spy for the FBI," joined the crew when Baylor, Woodard, and Storey were dispatched to Washington, D.C., to beat him up on behalf of a disc jockey that Thomas had allegedly roughed up. He somehow talked his way out of the beating, and ended up part of the team. In addition to managing Stax's sales office, Weiss also ran Baylor's publishing company, Klondike Music.

a plane and go on to the next town. They wouldn't stay in town but three hours but they got a four-day room. Everyone knew that that [radio station] would play [Stax Records] for four days. They'd call the hotel, 'Well, he's not in right now; he hasn't checked out yet.' They did that across the country and did it quite well. They were effective in their promotion."

"That was one way of letting people know," volunteers Woodard, "that even though Stax was not a major, we felt that we was a major. So, we should be respected the same as the others because our artists were just as good as any of the others. We should have been respected as a top company. That's how I felt about it, that's how Johnny felt about it, and we wanted that respect. We tried to carry ourselves to get that respect. We respected everybody but hey—boom—if they didn't [respect us] and play the records, then we felt that we needed to talk to them."

Woodard would not hesitate to call a radio station ten times a day to request that they play his record. "We were looked upon like some rough dudes," continues Woodard. "The thing about it, in my heart, my mind, and my soul I worked hard. I pushed hard. That was all there was to it. Like, if I had some records on Luther [Ingram], 'Gimme a play, man.' When a record's first released, the audience deserve to hear the product and, if it takes off, great. If it don't, then, hey, after so many plays, so many weeks—boom—hey, it's not gonna go. We know that but, hey, gimme the chance."

The IRS file on Stax includes an unsubstantiated report that alleges that Baylor and his cohorts used whatever methods were necessary to get airplay for Stax product. Such methods, the report continues, included payments to disc jockeys, force, threats, furnishing drugs, and other nefarious means. When made aware of the IRS report, Dino Woodard emphatically denied that he or Johnny Baylor ever furnished drugs to disc jockeys for record play.

In addition to their promotion acumen, Baylor and Woodard also proved handy on a couple of occasions when it came to collecting money from distributors. "We just went around and let them know that we were in need of the money," offers Woodard. ". . . You know, you go in, you sit down, and you talk to people and let them know that you demand your money. It was that way. There was no hate, no animosity or nothing like that. We just let them know that they had to come up with the bills."

Many people at Stax have suggested that Baylor and Woodard often threatened distributors in this situation. "No, not necessarily," chuckles Woodard. "We were sort of known out there and—boom—when Johnny spoke he made sure that people knew that he knew the business and knew what he was talking about." Woodard added that they only had to visit a distributor once for Stax to get paid what it was due.

According to Al Bell, Baylor and/or Woodard had to collect from distributors on only two occasions, one involving All State Distributors in Chicago, the other, Handelman in Detroit.[3] The latter situation resulted from the fallout surrounding the firing of Herb Kole. It seems that the controller at Handelman was a friend of Kole's, and let Bell know in no uncertain terms that he wasn't going to pay Stax because Bell and Stewart had fired Kole.

"I said, 'No, you're going to pay me my money,'" recounts Al Bell rather heatedly, "and I got on a plane [with Dino Woodard, Johnny Baylor, Hy Weiss, and Ed Pollack] and I went to Detroit to get my money. He owed me too much money, mid-six figures. 'You're telling me you're not going to pay? You're gonna put me out of business just because

3. Ted Storey says that they helped collect on three or four occasions, citing two further incidents with Schwartz Bros. in Washington, D.C., and Joe Voynow of BIB Record Distributors in North Carolina. "They see we wasn't playing," offers Storey, "hell, they gonna give it up. You had one or two you had to kinda shake up."

you're gonna sit there and say you're not gonna send me my check? You're crazy. What are you talking about? You gotta be out of your mind!'

"I came in there hollering and screaming and ranting and raving and going on. Mr. Handelman said, 'What's going on, Al?' 'cause it was out of character for me. He said, 'Don't worry about it. I'll take care of it.' And he did. He cut me a check that evening and sent me another check later on for the remainder of the money."

That money was very necessary. On January 20, 1972, Stax entered into a new contractual agreement with Isaac Hayes. The terms of the new deal, to say the least, were rather lavish. As a performer Isaac was to be paid 13 percent of the wholesale price that his records were sold for. As a producer, he was to be paid seven cents for each LP sold and up to three cents for each 45 sold.[4] However, the royalty rates were not that out of line with industry standards and certainly weren't the most striking part of the deal. Much more unusual were the perks included in the contract. Stax agreed to lease for Hayes a $26,000 1972 peacock-blue, *gold plated* Cadillac that Isaac would have the option to purchase outright on July 19, 1977. The car was insured by Lord's [*sic*] of London and sported a refrigerated bar, a television set, and twenty-four-carat gold exterior parts including the windshield wipers and custom-crafted wheels.[5] Stax also agreed to lease a house for Isaac on luxurious Coldwater Canyon Drive in Beverly Hills. The company was further obligated to pay for a gardener, pool maintenance, an exterminator, a maid, electricity, water, and draperies for the Beverly Hills address. Isaac was given a telephone credit card (reserved for the economic elite in those days), although it was stipulated that this was to be used only for Stax business. Stax was also obligated to pay for disability insurance for Hayes.

Finally, Isaac was to be paid a $25,000-a-year salary as a producer (it had been eons since he had last produced anybody but himself at Stax), and his Strange Publishing Company was to be paid $30,000 per year for "management and the administration of production services." These latter payments were part of a plan whereby Hayes would produce a number of acts that would be signed to his production company. First up was supposed to be an instrumental album by the Isaac Hayes Movement. This was to be followed by an album by Hayes's three background vocalists, Hot Buttered Soul, Ltd. In February Stax announced that it had plans to produce a black musical play to be directed by Isaac Hayes. None of these projects ever came to fruition.[6]

Although Isaac's contract was very generous, no one at the company was ever in doubt that he was worth it. As 1972 began, Hayes had just received a *Billboard* Trendsetters Award for achievements in the previous year. His last 45, "Theme from *Shaft*," had sold over a mil-

---

4. The precise terms of Hayes's production contract stated that he would receive no royalties for the first 75,000 copies sold of any given single; for the next 75,000 copies he would be paid a 2 cent royalty, and for any sales above 150,000 copies he would be paid a 3 cent royalty.

5. Over the years much has been made of such ostentatiousness on the part of Hayes. He was particularly stung by an "Open Mike" talk show on WHER radio in Memphis in which many black callers were extremely critical of the car. In this regard, it is worth noting that in 1996 I spoke with a journalist for the *Tri-State Defender* and a Memphis fireman. Both had been kids in the neighborhood when Hayes acquired the gold Caddie and both described it as something they and others in the neighborhood were inordinately proud of. In fact, it was such an event within the community that the first day the car appeared on the Stax lot the journalist's mother picked him up from school in a taxi, whereupon they headed straight down to Stax to see the car themselves. Hayes was also feeling slightly embittered at the time due to the racism that still ran rampant through Memphis. He had wanted to buy a home on Walnut Grove, but the man who had planned to sell it to him was threatened by neighbors and consequently backed out of the deal.

6. Shortly after signing his new contract, Isaac Hayes was on his way to Los Angeles to produce Sammy Davis, Jr., singing a newly written variant on "Theme from *Shaft*" for the Rat Pack member's next MGM single. The Davis recording, retitled "John Shaft" with a full set of words written by Bettye Crutcher, was the brainchild of MGM president Mike Curb, who was trying in vain to give Sammy Davis, Jr., a new contemporary image.

Isaac Hayes proudly showing off his newly minted gold-plated Cadillac in February of 1972.
COURTESY MISSISSIPPI VALLEY COLLECTION.

lion copies.[7] In February, when the annual Grammy Award nominees were announced, Stax artists received ten nominations, seven of those going to Isaac Hayes.

In light of its recent success, Stax began further expansion. In February 1972, the company announced plans to invest in a forthcoming Broadway musical, *The Selling of the President*.[8] A company press release at the time stated that this was to be the first of "numerous moves by this Company into the leisure-time areas." February also marked the release of the first country album by Stax and black singer O. B. McClinton.

At this same time, Stax decided to enter the gospel field again with the establishment of a new label, Gospel Truth. Veteran promotion man Dave Clark was to oversee the new

7. Spurred by the performances of "Theme from *Shaft*" by a number of college marching bands, Stax published a folio of the music from the LP *Shaft* as well as Hayes's followup album, *Black Moses*. The company also released sheet music for a number of hit songs by other artists including Rufus Thomas's "Do the Funky Penguin," the Staple Singers' "Respect Yourself," and the Emotions' "Show Me How."

8. According to Stax publicity at the time, this was the first time a black record and music publishing company was a major investor in a Broadway musical. Based on a best-selling book by Joe McGinnis and directed by Robert Livingston, *The Selling of the President* opened at the Schubert Theatre March 29, 1972. It quickly failed after five performances. On April 17, 1973, Stax was assigned a one-half interest in the music compositions from the play written by Jack O'Brien and Bob James. A soundtrack album was scheduled for release but, when the musical closed, the album was scrapped. Stax lost a total of $176,000 on the Broadway play.

label with assistance coming from the former executive secretary to Larry Shaw, Mary Peak.[9] Clark was somewhat of an R&B legend. Beginning in the mid-1930s as first a musician and then an advance man for the Jimmie Lunceford Orchestra, Clark had singlehandedly pioneered the art of black promotion in the record industry, working first as a "consultant" for Decca Records and, | Al Bell presents legendary black promotion man Dave Clark with a framed copy of the promotional-only album *Dave Clark thru '72* at the Testimonial Dinner for Dave Clark sponsored by Stax May 6, 1972, at the Sheraton Metro Hotel in Detroit. COURTESY DEANIE PARKER.

from 1952, spending just shy of two decades in the employ of Don Robey and Duke-Peacock Records. When Robey informed Clark that he intended to sell Duke-Peacock, Clark leapt at the opportunity to work promotion for Stax in early 1971.[10]

In addition to his promotion duties, Clark had produced much of Duke-Peacock's gospel product, working with such seminal artists as the Mighty Clouds of Joy, the Dixie Hummingbirds, the Five Blind Boys of Mississippi, and the Sensational Nightingales. When Al Bell decided in late 1971 to start the Gospel Truth label, Clark was the obvious

9. According to Shaw, "Peak was ambitious and wanted to be an executive so we found a slot for her in the Gospel Truth area."

10. Larry Shaw was so intrigued by Clark's history that he and Deanie Parker conducted a series of interviews with Clark that were then edited and pressed on a promotion-only LP, *Dave Clark thru '72*. "I had been listening to this guy's story for a year or two," explains Shaw. "I began to hear that it was the history of black music in the commercial sense in America; how it got made and played and promoted on the air. It was so fascinating and incredible how he used to ride the highways looking for radio antennas, how he would have episodes with the police and how they would throw his stuff on the highway; literally how black music got to be a commercial entity in radio in this country. So we just pulled up some chairs and got some microphones and told him to start talking and tried to interview him like writers do when they're trying to get data." The album was distributed to all those in attendance at a Testimonial Dinner for Dave Clark sponsored by Stax on May 6, 1972, at the Sheraton Metro Hotel in Detroit. Entertainment was provided by Rance Allen, the Soul Children, and non-Stax artist Swamp Dogg. Profits from the affair were put into a scholarship fund for Clark's son and grandchildren.

choice to head the operation. Fitting the Stax maverick modus operandi to a tee, Clark attempted to market the Gospel Truth label well beyond the usual avenues, promoting the records directly to church bodies and working especially hard at the conventions various black denominations held around the country.

The first artist Clark signed to Gospel Truth was ebullient Monroe, Michigan, native Rance Allen. A guitarist, singer, and songwriter, Allen headed a trio manned by his two brothers, drummer Tom and bassist Steve.[11] Clark had "discovered" the family group when he was serving as a judge in a gospel contest in Detroit. No doubt he was awestruck by the trio's secret weapon, Rance's stratospheric falsetto, guaranteed to send shivers down one's spine every time it was unleashed. Members of the Church in God in Christ, the three Allen brothers were not in the least reticent about shouting the Lord's praises by whatever means necessary, including the adaptation of secular tunes. The first bio on the group issued by Stax crowed that "the Rance Allen Group has [the] potential of closing the gap between pop and gospel"; it was not an idle boast. Their debut album, simply titled *The Rance Allen Group,* included a soul-destroying (in the best sense of the word) rearrangement of the Temptations' "Just My Imagination." Replete with sacred words and the added subtitle "Just My Salvation," when it was released on January 28, 1972, the track served as the debut Gospel Truth 45. It was a rich beginning indeed.[12]

Following hot on the heels of the Rance Allen Group's debut were seven albums and two singles scheduled for release in May on Gospel Truth. Stax press releases suggested that the new label would be oriented toward the "youth gospel market," recording "gospel rock," which would merge gospel's "truth" lyrics with a "contemporary backup." Aside from the Rance Allen recordings, this mandate is not evident in the fifteen singles and twenty-plus albums issued on Gospel Truth over the next two-and-a-half years. The label never really developed an identity as Clark signed and recorded artists from all areas of the United States in all formats: solo, group, and choir.

Later that year, Stax began marketing a comedy label, Partee Records. By year's end, two albums had been released, Clay Tyson's *Laugh Your Ass Off* and Moms Mabley's *I Like 'Em Young.* The Tyson LP was acquired in a master purchase deal from Washington, D.C., retailer Waxie Maxie, while the seventy-five-year-old legend Moms Mabley was signed directly to Stax. Her sole release on Partee was recorded live in September at the Stax studio in front of an invited audience. Accompaniment was provided by Duck Dunn, Al Jackson, Bobby Manuel, and pianist George Butcher, with emcee duties being taken care of by Randy Stewart.[13] Three more albums would be released on Partee over the next two years, Timmie Rogers's *As Super Soul Brother Clark Dark,* Richard Pryor's breakthrough album, *That Nigger's Crazy,* and Bill Cosby's *At Last Bill Cosby Really Sings.*

In a company press release at the time, Al Bell was quoted as saying, "We are developing a total record company. This does not in any way mean that we are minimizing our

---

11. A fourth brother, percussionist Esau, would become an occasional member of the group a couple of years later.

12. The Rance Allen Group's self-titled debut album also included exquisite versions of Boz Scaggs's "Make My Life Shine" and Canadian group Ocean's pop hit "Put Your Hand in the Hand."

13. Randy Stewart was a minor figure in the Stax story. A member of the doo-wop group the Fiestas, who enjoyed a couple of hits on Old Town in the late 1950s and early 1960s, by his own account he was practically raised by Hy Weiss. A compadre of Johnny Baylor, Stewart wrote a number of songs that eventually found their way to Stax artists, the most notable being the Staple Singers' "When Will We Be Paid" and Rufus Thomas's "6-3-8." With both Weiss and Baylor spending more time at Stax, Stewart relocated to Memphis and began working concessions for Isaac Hayes. Over time he would perform several functions for Hayes including tour manager, road manager, and emcee. Stewart was also responsible for bringing Inez Foxx to the label, and produced both Foxx and the white rock group Round Robin Monopoly. In the last desperate days at Stax, he reunited the Fiestas and recorded one single for the company.

black product; for that is our base and will be expanded. But we will enter new fields which we consider relevant to the concept of a total company."

Stax, indeed, did not minimize their black product. Although January was typically quiet, in February 1972 the company cranked things up with a crowded release schedule, issuing ten 45s, seven of which charted. The big sweepstakes winner was the Detroit vocal group the Dramatics. Their followup to "Whatcha See Is Whatcha Get," "Get Up and Get Down," penetrated the R&B Top 20, but their February release, Tony Hestor's "In the Rain," turned out to be their most successful release ever.

"When we first heard 'In the Rain,'" recounts group leader Ron Banks, "we thought that that would be a real record but we never realized what [Tony] had in his mind with the storm and the rain falling and all of that. We had no imagination about that. When we came back off the road and they played the track for us, we looked at each other and said, 'Whoa, that's a smash,' and for once we were right."

Al Bell had some doubts about the record, and it took Hy Weiss's persistent urging before he agreed to release the song as a single. When it finally was released, "In the Rain" shot all the way to the top of the R&B charts while nestling in at number 5 pop. William "Wee Gee" Howard takes the lead vocal and Dennis Coffey plays the heavily echoplexed guitar, while Johnny Allen crafted the emotionally charged arrangement, juxtaposing unison high strings with painstakingly precise woodwind countermelodies.

The Soul Children started the year off nearly as successfully as the Dramatics with their January 1972 release, "Hearsay," ascending to number 5 R&B and number 44 pop. After their first five Hayes-and-Porter written-and-produced singles had all charted, the Soul Children had languished under the direction of Porter and his new partner, Ronnie Williams. Their first single of 1972 drew upon a new production team consisting of former Booker T. and the MG's drummer Al Jackson in tandem with company president Jim Stewart. "Hearsay" was the first single to be written by group members J. Blackfoot and Norman West. Apparently the two singers had been writing for quite a while but found it difficult to get Stax's producers interested in their material.

As was the standard arrangement for the group, J. Blackfoot takes the lead vocal. Norman West can be heard singing harmony on the turn around, while Anita Louis and Shelbra Bennett sing the title line. Bobby Manuel plays the song's ever-so-funky rhythm guitar pattern, songwriter Raymond Jackson plays the second guitar part, and the keyboards are handled by Rufus Thomas's son, Marvell, and a friend of Al Jackson's named John Keister. Manuel, Jackson, and Thomas were Stax regulars, while this was one of only a handful of sessions that Keister ever played on at Stax.

The record concluded with a rap between Blackfoot and Shelbra Bennett. Apparently Jim Stewart and Al Jackson had suggested an "opera-type thing," and the two singers began to play-act. This finale never failed to bring the house down on live gigs, with Norman West often creating a third role, that of an instigator. Also worth noting is the syncopated horn line dubbed in by the then five-piece Memphis Horns a month after the rhythm track was recorded.

The big surprise among the February 1972 Stax releases was Birmingham, Alabama, singer Frederick Knight's "I've Been Lonely for So Long." Knight had been trying to get into the music business for quite a while. In the late 1960s he had recorded "Have a Little Mercy" for Capitol. WLAC disc jockey John R. had then brought Knight to Nashville producer/entrepreneur Buddy Killen. Killen got Knight a deal with Mercury Records, for which Knight recorded "Throw a Switch." Unfortunately, the record was never released. Knight then tried to take the tape to Stax, but in Memphis he got the runaround from executive John Smith, spending a couple of nights sleeping in the bus station for his trouble. Discouraged, but not yet ready to give up, Knight began serving an apprenticeship at Neil Hemphill's Sounds of Birmingham Studio in the capacity of engineer and would-be drummer. In the meantime he kept writing songs, sending them to Tim Whitsett at East Memphis Music.

"Every time I sent him a tape," recounts Knight, "he said, 'Man, you're real close but I just don't hear that out-of-the-park smash.' I was too far in the mainstream. If you're gonna be an artist you've got to be different. He was saying, 'If this was on the Staple Singers, it would be fine. We could run with it because they're already established but you're trying to break in and it's just not quite there.' So I said, 'Okay, you want different, you'll get different.'"

True to his word, Knight came up with one of the oddest and most intoxicating records of the decade. The germ of the song originated with guitarist Jerry Weaver. Knight had stopped by the Sounds of Birmingham studio to pick up something on the way to taking his wife to work. "Jerry was in the studio," says Knight. "He said, 'Man I want to play you something,' He starts singing, 'I've been lonely for so long.' I fell to the floor, I went out— just that one line. I said, 'By God! What a melody! Don't go nowhere. I'm gonna take my wife to work and I'll be right back.' We started working the song and all the time I had my creative mode from Tim Whitsett. I'm saying, 'Totally different, totally different.'"

At the recording session that evening, Knight sent everyone home but engineer Glen Wood and tenor player Aaron Varnell. Wood played the slide guitar, Jerry Weaver played bass and acoustic guitar, while Varnell substituted for the dismissed drummer by hitting a bar stool with a two-by-four plank that Knight equalized so it sounded as dry as possible. Knight then overdubbed a hi-hat and tambourine and sang the falsetto and bass leads as well as all the harmonies.

"I finished the record that night," continues Knight, "and left the studio about five that morning. I had mixed the record. I had it sitting on the control board and I put a note, 'Here's your smash, I'm at home, don't wake me.' I came in around twelve, and I looked at everybody, and they were, 'Are you serious man, you've been in the cooking sherry or what?' I said, 'Man, it's a smash, send the record off.'"

At the time Knight had signed a production deal with Elijah Walker, who then cut a deal with Sounds of Birmingham owner Neil Hemphill. Hemphill sent the tape to Polydor, Atlantic, and Stax. Atlantic turned it down while Polydor showed some interest but proceeded to play cat-and-mouse with the singer. Stax took a little longer to respond while Tim Whitsett attempted to corner Jim Stewart and play him the tape.

Tim Whitsett remembers well all the tapes Knight had sent him in the past. "Frederick and his manager had been sending me tapes. They were always close but not quite there. I kept the dialogue with them because I thought it was worth it. I don't know whether they got so frustrated that they cut 'I've Been Lonely for So Long' as a joke and sent it to me or whether they cut it on purpose. I thought, this is it! I took it right away to Jim and John Smith and they were flipped out over it."

Released as Stax 0117, "I've Been Lonely for So Long" broke into the R&B Top 10 while settling for number 27 pop. The bass lead at the beginning of the chorus was inspired by Sly Stone. Ironically, two years later Sly bassist Larry Graham plagiarized the tune with a cut he entitled "We've Been Waiting" on the debut LP by Graham Central Station.[14]

14. Label readers will notice that Knight's recording is credited to *Posie* Knight and Jerry Weaver; Posie was Frederick's wife's name. In the early seventies, Frederick was signed to a writer's contract with Rick Hall at Fame. Hall had verbally agreed to release Knight from the deal, but the paperwork had not been completed when the record's labels were printed up. Hence the credit to Posie.

In February, Bell and Stewart formed a separate partnership from Stax, dubbed the McLemore Company. The purpose was to buy the McLemore location and then to "rent" it to Stax.[15] The cost of the building was $85,000. It was purchased via a twenty-five-year mortgage with Union Planters National Bank.

In March, Stax continued the torrid pace of the previous month with the release of the Staple Singers' "I'll Take You There." Cut at the same sessions as their 1971 blockbuster "Respect Yourself," "I'll Take You There" topped both *Billboard* listings. As was by now standard practice for the group, the record was produced by Al Bell, with the rhythm cut in Muscle Shoals and the horn part devised by former Bar-Kay Ben Cauley and the South Memphis Horns.

"I'll Take You There" is striking in virtually every respect, from the opening muted guitar lead played by Jimmy Johnson through Mavis Staples's impossibly sensual groans, Roger Hawkins's busy rim work on the snare, David Hood's absolutely arresting bass breakdown at the two-thirds mark, Eddie Hinton's soulful guitar fills and solo, and Cauley's syncopated horn lines buried way back in the mix. The one-two punch of "Respect Yourself" and "I'll Take You There" are among the finest moments in the careers of the Staples, the Muscle Shoals rhythm section, Al Bell, and all of R&B.

The Muscle Shoals players were in especially fine form. Bassist Hood and drummer Hawkins had just come off the road from touring with the British rock group Traffic. "Our chops were way up," recalls Hood. "We were just kind of very exuberant when we cut those records."

Bob Marley and the Wailers were signed to the same label as Traffic, and every night on the tour a tape of the Wailers' first Island Records LP, *Catch a Fire,* was played over the PA. Hood and Hawkins were impressed. "We kept hearing that," explains Hood. "I thought, 'Wow, this is the greatest, wildest music I've ever heard.'" While the Traffic tour unfolded, Island owner Chris Blackwell had given Jimmy Johnson a paid vacation in Jamaica. Johnson took some time to visit local recording studios and record stores, picking up a slew of current Jamaican records along the way. Upon his return, he distributed the records to all the members of the Muscle Shoals rhythm section. On top of all this, Al Bell had made several trips to Jamaica in the preceding few years.

Everybody recalls the session differently: Al Bell is sure the reggae groove was his idea; Jimmy Johnson takes credit for it; and Roger Hawkins felt that it came from Hood's and his recent infatuation with the then relatively little-known style. David Hood offers yet another version: "The song was really written on the spot. Really and truly there was no song to begin with. They had an idea for this 'I'll Take You There' thing so they put it to us to work out a rhythm pattern that was sort of a Jamaican influence. We were just jamming on different things and they'd say, 'Not that' or 'Try this.' Basically there are no chord changes. So it was kind of a group effort between the rhythm section and Al Bell and Mavis Staples. I feel like we all cowrote it because there was no 'I'll Take You There' until we cut this track. The idea for that was kind of out of the air."

In actuality, the record's introduction, bass line, and general groove were lifted directly from a 1969 Jamaican instrumental recording by the Harry J Allstars entitled "The Liquidator" that, interestingly enough, reached number 9 on the British charts when released by Trojan Records. This was probably one of the records Jimmy Johnson had brought back from Jamaica, or else it was something Al Bell had purchased on one of his many trips there. In any event, the session's participants took the basic groove of

---

15. Stax had been paying $9,780 a year in rent to the original owners. The company now paid $837.10 a month to Bell and Stewart's newly formed McLemore Company.

"The Liquidator" and transformed it into a reggae/soul fusion that is absolutely mind-numbing.[16]

In addition to the differences of opinion regarding the origin of the groove, there is also some dispute as to the writing of the song's lyrics. Al Bell receives credit for it and he clearly remembers writing "I'll Take You There"'s solitary verse in the back of his parents' home in Little Rock while grieving over the recent murder of his brother, Louis Isbell. Mavis Staples is equally insistent that she and Al collectively worked out the song's verse one evening in her Chicago apartment; Bell is quite sure that he was actually teaching Mavis the song that evening.

The Al Bell/Staple Singers/Muscle Shoals sessions quite closely approximated the old Stax working method of the 1960s, in which all the parts were developed collectively and cut live on the floor. The Staples would nearly always cut a scratch vocal live with the rhythm section, and then Al Bell and engineer Terry Manning (who plays the harmonica on this record) rerecorded the vocals back in Memphis at the Ardent Recording Studio. The final vocal often combined several takes cut at Ardent as well as occasionally one or another phrase from the original Muscle Shoals track.

In the case of "I'll Take You There," there is even some disagreement about that. Al Bell and Roger Hawkins are positive that Mavis did not sing the song in Muscle Shoals, while David Hood and Mavis Staples are equally confident that they remember Mavis's ad-lib lines, where she calls out to the musicians as they play their solos, being sung while the track was being cut![17]

Forgetting the vicissitudes of memory over twenty-plus years, "I'll Take You There"'s one written verse, which everyone agrees Al Bell wrote at least half of, the remaining ad-lib vocal lines, which everyone agrees Mavis is responsible for, and the reggae groove and bass line which were lifted from "The Liquidator," combined to produce one of the greatest moments in rhythm-and-blues history.

In what in retrospect was a very prescient move, Stax shot promotional videos for both "Respect Yourself" and "I'll Take You There." After a trip to Mallorca, Spain, where he saw a Philips demonstration of video technology, Bell was convinced that this would be an important medium in the near future.[18] He was also well aware that cable television was on its way and that there was going to be a substantial need for programming. He wanted Stax to be up and running with personnel already experienced in the new medium and with an already well-stocked video library. Because there were no television outlets for video at that time, Stax attempted to get the promotional clips of the Staple Singers into movie theaters in black neighborhoods. Unfortunately the idea was simply too far ahead of its time. The label was unable to garner many showings, and the actual video clips were very expensive to make. Stax's move into video was put on hold. In July, "I'll Take You There" joined "I've Been Lonely for So Long" in the British charts, marking the first time that Stax had ever had two hits in the UK charts simultaneously.

According to Al Bell, the success of "I'll Take You There" is at least partially attributable to the Herculean efforts of Johnny Baylor's team of "field representatives." Baylor was the sort of guy who rarely gave less than 200 percent. If he was on your team, he would do whatever it took to make sure you came out a winner. At this particular moment his sole

16. The fusing of North American and Caribbean black musics fitted nicely into Al Bell's developing philosophy of pan-Africanism. Bell aggressively worked Stax product in Jamaica and had similar plans for Brazil and a number of African countries. Unfortunately, Stax did not survive long enough for him to realize his dreams.

17. According to Hood, at the session Mavis referred to Eddie Hinton during the guitar solo, because Pops Staples did not actually play on it. Mavis remembers changing the line to "Daddy" when the vocals were redone at Ardent for the pragmatic reason that onstage Pops, of course, would be playing the line.

18. MTV debuted a mere six years after Stax went bankrupt.

focus was on the success of Stax Records. By early March, though, Baylor began complaining to Al Bell that while he and his crew were working Stax product, he wasn't having enough time to devote to his own label, KoKo.

"He would tell me," recalls Al Bell, "'Hey Dick, I'm running around taking care of your business, I can't take care of mine.' I said, 'Hey man, I'll take care of you. Don't worry about it. As soon as I sell this thing, Johnny, I'll make sure you're taken care of.'"

Bell, with the assistance of Clarence Avant, came very close to selling Stax to RCA Victor. RCA was prepared to offer $16 million—the only problem being that the offer was in stock. Feeling burned by the Gulf and Western stock deal, Jim Stewart was not interested in anything but cash in hand, and consequently the RCA deal fell through.

Baylor was unhappy with these developments, and insisted that he had to come off the road to produce a new record for Luther Ingram. All of Ingram's previous Stax-distributed releases on KoKo had been cut at Stax's McLemore studios, but this time everyone headed to Muscle Shoals. According to Luther Ingram, the change in venue was due to the falling out Baylor had had with Isaac Hayes sometime after the release of *Shaft*.[19]

A number of people close to the scene believe that Baylor had been taking more than his share of Isaac's concert receipts. These same people suggest that when this was brought to his attention, Hayes was understandably angered and summarily fired Baylor. According to Isaac, "I didn't fire him. We just parted ways. It got so bad. People started being afraid to come around me. They started telling him one thing and started telling me another."

While Isaac was trying to work out what he should do about the situation, Baylor had heard through the grapevine that Isaac was badmouthing him and intended on severing the relationship. Not one to take such an affront lightly, Baylor, Woodard, and their entourage marched into Stax, told the secretaries to go home, and confronted Isaac in his office.

"I was very despondent over my marriage," recounts Isaac, "and Johnny and Dino come in and pulled guns on me. They were going to shoot me. I was so despondent I said, 'I don't care, man. You think I lied on you, then shoot me. Fuck it. Kill me.' Life didn't mean anything at that point. I wasn't scared. I was actually hurt that they thought I would do that. If I was going to say, 'Hey man, I've got to let you guys go,' I would have been a man and come to them 'cause we had that kind of understanding and relationship."

While Baylor and Woodard had guns trained on Isaac, various members of their crew and Isaac's crew were lined up outside the office on opposite walls facing each other guns at the ready. Songwriter Raymond Jackson's brother, Robert, was a security guard at Stax at the time. Thinking quickly, he locked the doors to Studio A, thereby protecting those who happened to be involved in a recording session at that moment. In the meantime, according to Larry Nix, everyone could hear Baylor, Woodard and Isaac screaming at each other from within Hayes's office. "It was just run for cover and stay down till it passed," recalls Nix, still a little shaken.

Robert Jackson's next move was to call the police and then announce to everyone that Memphis's finest were on their way. It was a smart move on Jackson's part because it quickly defused the situation out in the hall with everyone scurrying to hide their guns in Tim Whitsett's inner and outer offices, as Whitsett wasn't there that day and his office happened to be situated nearest to Isaac's. In the meantime, neither Baylor or Woodard were aware that the police had been called and continued to point their guns at Isaac. When the cops knocked on Isaac's outer door, Baylor and Woodard put their guns in the trash can.

---

19. The IRS file on Stax mentions that the Memphis Police Department reported that something happened to cause Hayes to fire Baylor. Another report, cited by the IRS, suggested that Baylor had stolen over $1 million from Isaac. The IRS was unable to confirm this.

Isaac walked to his window and pulled the curtains back to be greeted by Memphis police with their shotguns drawn.

"The cops surrounded the building," continues Isaac. "They knocked on my office door from the outside 'cause I had an entrance out to the street. They said, 'Is everything alright in there?' I said, 'Hey man, we're having a family discussion.'" Seeing through the window that Isaac was fine, the cops left. "When I did that," continues Isaac, "Johnny said, 'Man, he ain't did all that shit. Look what he's doing. He could have given us up. He's covering our ass now. This man couldn't have done that shit, we're barking up the wrong tree.' They left."

Although the situation had been temporarily defused, the relationship between Isaac and Baylor's crew dissolved shortly thereafter.

Tommy Tate was at the time recording for Baylor's KoKo label. When he recounted the story, he just shook his head. "They went back in Ike's office and jacked him up, threatened him—up in Stax during business hours! That was kind of freaky and I was reluctant to go back to New York [with Baylor] then."

From Luther Ingram's vantage point, there was at least one positive outcome from the Baylor-Hayes feud. He had long felt that the musicians at Stax would not listen to him and consequently was very pleased with the decision to cut in Muscle Shoals. "[The guys at Stax] wouldn't do what I needed," insists the veteran singer. "They wanted to do my thing their way. But Barry Beckett [and the rest of the guys at Muscle Shoals] did exactly what I needed. It took us forty-five minutes to cut a platinum record. They would listen to you!"

"(If Loving You Is Wrong) I Don't Want to Be Right" had been written sometime earlier by Homer Banks, Raymond Jackson, and Carl Hampton.[20] By the time Luther Ingram attempted it, the song had already been recorded by both the Emotions and Stax newcomer Veda Brown, but neither version was deemed suitable for release.[21] Having faith in the song, one night while sitting around the office Banks played it for Luther Ingram. Ingram liked the demo but decided to slow it down. He also came up with the high, crying wah-wah guitar part heard throughout the track, singing it to lead guitarist Pete Carr at the session. Carr's wah-wah playing is, without a doubt, a big part of the song's allure, but the ultimate magic lies within Ingram's vocal track.

According to both Luther Ingram and Muscle Shoals guitarist Jimmy Johnson, Ingram produced the backing track, not Johnny Baylor. However, Al Bell insists that Johnny Baylor deserves a lot of credit for the final vocal take. "Johnny had a phenomenal sense of timing," marvels Bell. "It was Johnny standing there directing this man like the boxer that he was. It was unbelievable. Johnny knew better than anybody I had ever seen how to produce and record a vocalist. He knew how to find that pocket on that track and get that sense of timing worked out with that vocalist and pull the beat out of him. It all had to do with timing and it was the timing in his body. He was living the rhythm in that record in his body and in his body language and in his movements and directing Luther's vocal chords with his movements. It impressed me so much, man. They took that song to another level."

"[Baylor] was a ramrod," says Ingram. "He wanted me to learn the right way. He overlooked and oversaw. He was a coach. He taught me. I wouldn't have learned under anybody else but Baylor. Baylor was determined for me to show the world and the industry

20. Banks, Jackson, and Hampton would also write Ingram's followup hit, "I'll Be Your Shelter (in Time of Storm)," which, as with "(If Loving You Is Wrong) I Don't Want to Be Right," was first unsuccessfully attempted by Veda Brown.

21. Veda Brown's version was simply anemic, and Jim Stewart felt that the subject matter of the song was a little too mature for the Emotions. Banks had also taken the song to Don Davis and Isaac Hayes but was turned down in both cases.

and Stax Records and everybody else that I was a great talent. That was his concept of me. He loved me and he wanted to see me do the best that I could possibly do. Everybody else could not agree or get along with him, but he was always looking out for me. Anything that I needed or wanted, he would make sure that I got it. He wanted to live his life through me. That's what it really was."

Released May 3, 1972, "(If Loving You Is Wrong) I Don't Want to Be Right" soared to number 1 R&B and number 3 pop, becoming ubiquitous over the radio waves that summer. One of twenty singles Ingram has placed on the R&B charts, it was, by far, the biggest record of both his and Baylor's careers.

Before the single had scaled such lofty heights, Baylor approached Al Bell asking that, in exchange for the promotion and marketing work he and his staff were doing for Stax, East Memphis Music split the publishing with him on all East Memphis songs, including "(If Loving You Is Wrong) I Don't Want to Be Right," recorded by Ingram.

Bell acceded to Baylor's wish. He also effectively gave Baylor all the proceeds from the sale of KoKo product. Whereas before Stax had distributed KoKo and, of course, made money doing so, now all Stax took out of the wholesale price of KoKo product was the manufacturing costs. Baylor got everything else as if he were doing his own distribution. Stax did not make a single penny on "(If Loving You Is Wrong) I Don't Want to Be Right" (aside from half of the publishing of its own East Memphis copyright), yet it was fronting the manufacturing costs and funneling the record through its distribution channels. In return Baylor and his team continued to aggressively work Stax product in the marketplace.

"It was just that simple," claims Al Bell, "and that was an oral handshake agreement between Johnny and me. We didn't have that on paper.[22] I could have come back and said after the record was a hit, 'Oh no, what I meant was this,' but no. This man was out there breaking his chops for me, keeping my costs down 'cause now I didn't have to increase my G and A [general and administrative] putting on all this staff and dealing with all these people and all these headaches, and I don't have to wonder about what Johnny Baylor is doing. I know what Johnny Baylor is doing in the marketplace. I'm talking to him three times a day and then I don't have to talk to fifteen people. I talk to Johnny Baylor and he tells me what's going on. I talk to Hymie Weiss and he tells me what is going on. So I have a nice little operation that was very cost effective."

Bell had gotten the idea for structuring the KoKo deal with Baylor in such a manner when someone told him that Berry Gordy had made a similar deal at Motown for one of the subsidiary labels. As Bell understood the scenario, Gordy couldn't pay the employee what the employee wanted and ostensibly was worth, so he let the employee build his own label. Gordy covered the costs in the form of a loan that would be returned upon the sale of the records.

"I thought that that was just a brilliant idea," exclaims Bell, "of how you deal with uniquely talented people that are entrepreneurs trying to build their own thing, especially if they're working with you helping you build your thing. That was what was in my mind when I proposed what I proposed to Johnny. All I was doing was, 'Hey, I haven't made this deal with RCA or anyone else at this point in time. You've been out there doing what you've been doing and sacrificing for me and I appreciate that. I'm not in a position to give you any money for that now because I don't have any money to give you. But, what I will do is give you all the money from your label. So, go put your product out. I'll do that for you right now. [Now] go back out here and go to work on my product until I can make a deal.'"

22. Several people remarked that Baylor did not like anything to be on paper, although the original distribution deal for KoKo was drawn up and executed formally on October 15, 1968. Baylor's penchant for oral agreements would later cause considerable troubles for both himself and Stax.

Stax, via Birdees Music Corp., also leased apartment 36-E for Baylor at 45 East 89th Street in New York. The monthly rental was $995, although, according to a memo written by Ronald Altman of Stax's New York City accounting firm, Bell was willing to go as high as $1,800 a month. After the lease was executed on May 22, 1972, Baylor's sister-in-law, Helen Drake, was hired by Birdees to remodel and redecorate the apartment. Another memo from the accounting firm states that Al Bell had said "the sky was the limit" regarding the furnishing of the apartment. From June 6, 1972, through June 19, 1973, Drake received $105,500 to cover the costs of items she purchased for the apartment and her commission. Some of the more interesting furnishings included a king-size fur throw costing $3,100; giraffe, gazelle, zebra, and leopard pillows priced at $581.45; a ritual mask valued at $2,715; two works of art by Ramon Santiago priced at $3,150; and masks, a masui spear, masui shield,[23] and buck horns that combined cost $1,275. The dining area had a mirrored back wall from floor to ceiling.

In April 1972, Stax rented on an ongoing basis a suite at the Holiday Inn Central in Memphis for Baylor and Dino Woodard. In May 1973, in a further example of the level of indebtedness Bell felt to Baylor's crew, Stax transferred ownership of a Memphis residence at 872 W. Shelby Drive to Dino Woodard. When Bell finally consummated a deal with regard to Stax in October 1972, giving CBS distribution rights in exchange for a loan of $6 million, Baylor was paid rather handsomely for his efforts on behalf of Stax.

Baylor's two KoKo artists, Luther Ingram and Tommy Tate, both felt that the relationship between Baylor and Bell was not that simple. "Baylor was the one who really made Stax go," insists Ingram. "He called most of the shots and ramrodded the whole deal through Al Bell and Jim Stewart. He got the six million from Columbia. He just laid back in the background and called the shots. He was a ramrod, a Green Beret." Tate concurs, stating emphatically that Baylor was actually running Stax.

Both artists lived in deep fear of Baylor and, at least in Tate's case, felt as though they were his prisoners. Baylor was a very smooth operator and a control freak. Although it was not uncommon behavior for him to give Tate and Ingram five or six bills each, neither ever had a regular salary. They were always dependent on Baylor's mood and consequent largesse, receiving cash whenever Baylor decided to parcel it out. They were also kept constantly under wraps, with Tate being obligated to travel to every one of Ingram's gigs even if he himself was not performing.

"Wherever Luther went, I went—always," remembers Tate, shivering. "Baylor kept us together. When I discovered what I had hooked up in, it scared the hell out of me. Dino was a pet. As long as he remained in his place, he was cool. A few times Johnny and Dino had some serious, serious words about something Dino had fouled up, and it was done in our presence. Luther and I discovered then that we weren't the only people kept on edge by Johnny's temper tantrums. His thing was always proving something. He was one of those cats—gung ho—the real Rambo. He just lived life hard and fast. He had two German shepherds, furious dogs, dangerous-ass dogs. People say that your animals usually tend to take on your personality. I guess whatever resentments Johnny had built up in him, he passed them on to his dogs. They were just mean-ass dogs—like Johnny. He was mean, but he was kind too. He was thoughtful. It was like, if you needed anything, you got it."

The latter was true as long as you didn't cross Baylor. After being harassed by Woodard for being late for a session at Stax, Tate decided he wanted out. "I finally decided to cut it off," recounts Tate, turning somewhat ashen at the memory. "Johnny called and said, 'Look, I want you to meet me in Atlanta. We have a little session booked.' I told him, 'I

23. *Masui* is the exact wording printed in the IRS report. What this word refers to is unclear.

won't be coming to Atlanta. As a matter of fact, I won't be coming back to New York. As a real matter of fact, I don't even want to be involved with KoKo or Klondike Music.' He told me that he would come to Mississippi and bury me. That was a threat. He was saying, 'I will come there and off you.' He even described how it could be done. [He'd] hire somebody and, when the question comes up, 'Where was Johnny Baylor?,' 'Well, he was in New York with blah, blah, blah. He has witnesses.' Very, very calculating. [He] did not back down from anybody or any situation."[24]

Tim Whitsett was also threatened by Johnny Baylor. "He wouldn't come into my office without his pearl-handled revolver," Whitsett recalls. "He would sit there and say, 'We gonna talk business,' and he would show me that pistol and I'd get real businesslike. [One day] Baylor called me up and said, 'All these songs written by so and so [the East Memphis songs that Luther Ingram had cut], I'm supposed to have half the publishing.' I'd say, 'Well, that's fine but I've got to hear this from Al Bell or Jim Stewart.' So, he would do the pistol act.

"He would imagine things that I had done and not done," continues Whitsett. "He accused me one time of being responsible for Watergate! Me and Al Bell, we were both responsible for Watergate! Furthermore, to stop Watergate, he knew where my parents' house was in Mississippi, he had a shotgun down there and I would be taken care of the next time I went down to Mississippi. . . . He was a *bad* person. He didn't have any redeeming qualities. You know, some gangsters give flowers to the ladies and go buy Girl Guide cookies, but this was not one of those kind of gangsters. He was a *bad* man. He threatened me a few times. That guy was the worst person I ever met. He was bad!"[25]

There is no denying that the presence of Baylor and Woodard struck fear in a great many hearts. A few Stax insiders felt that Baylor, for the most part, was bluffing and that ultimately he was much more than just a streetwise enforcer. "Johnny Baylor and Dino were on the outside tough guys," insists Larry Shaw, "guys who would bang you over the head, shoot you in the leg, or whatever, but who on the inside were loyal and patriotic believers in the rights of humans to have everything they're supposed to have. They adored Martin Luther King and Jesse Jackson. My relationship to Jackson had a lot to do with Johnny Baylor's respect for me and the lack of badgering his pistols in my face.[26] Probably in his years with Stax, he never had to do any of the things he would threaten. His potential was what people feared, but he was a pussycat inside. He was more sensitive than anybody would ever suspect. Much of his behavior was defensive so he could not reveal those tender spots. He *loved* Al and loved the effort. He was *maybe* misguided on a few occasions because of his experiences and [lack of] education, but his insight was that of Socrates."

While Baylor was busy producing Luther Ingram on "(If Loving You Is Wrong) I Don't Want to Be Right," Al Bell and Ardent owner John Fry were announcing the formation of the Ardent Records label. Fry had issued a few singles on Ardent on a local level in the mid-1960s, but this was for all intents and purposes the beginning of the label. With the

---

24. Tate wasn't the only one afraid of Baylor. Sandra Jackson of the Goodees recalls, "One thing he said to us, he would kill to protect us but for the right amount of money, he would kill us. That really freaked me out. I believed every word he said."

25. Baylor's associate Ted Storey admitted that Baylor had a long-running problem with prescription drug addiction, which might account for some of his bizarre behavior. Isaac Hayes recalls: "Sometimes he'd get uptight and full of tension and he'd say, 'Dino, I got to shoot.' He'd say, 'Moses, can I shoot?' I'd say, 'I don't care.' He would shoot up the ceiling and dust and shit that's been up there for thirty years would fall to the floor. In the studio, a 9mm!"

26. Ted Storey says one or another of Baylor's posse regularly provided protection for Jesse Jackson.

Hip subsidiary label being mothballed in November 1969,[27] the Ardent deal was yet another attempt by Bell to capture the white rock/pop market.

Having become quite successful, Fry had moved the Ardent studio into a custom-built, state-of-the-art facility in November 1971. With the able assistance of Terry Manning, he was now prepared to start issuing his own records on a national basis. In March and April, the debut albums by Cargoe, self-titled, and Big Star, *#1 Record,* were issued. Subsequent recordings followed by the over-the-top Scotsman Brian Alexander Robertson, local Memphis group the Hot Dogs, and Big Star, whose sophomore disc, *Radio City,* was issued on Ardent in 1974. At the time they were first released, none of the Ardent product sold very well.[28]

Much more profitable for Stax was a master purchase deal Bell signed around the same time with Muscle Shoals vets Roger Hawkins and Barry Beckett for Mel and Tim. Mel Hardin and Tim McPherson were first cousins from Holly Springs, Mississippi. As teenagers they had begun to dabble in writing songs and singing in a gospel group, the Welcome Travelers. Hoping to hit the gospel circuit big-time, the whole group moved to St. Louis in the mid-sixties. With their dreams slowly evaporating, the Welcome Travelers dissolved, and Mel and Tim began driving buses for a living. After the two singers separately did their requisite tours of duty with Uncle Sam, they decided to leave gospel and give the secular music world a try.

Their first break came when Gene Chandler, of "Duke of Earl" fame, was starting his Bamboo label. Chandler was impressed with a couple of songs that Tim had written, and signed Hardin and McPherson to writing and recording contracts. The sweet-singing duo lucked out immediately, going Top 10 in 1969 with "Backfield in Motion." A year and one chart hit later, Bamboo began to experience financial problems. Mel and Tim asked for their release and, when the company refused, they spent a frustrating two years on the sidelines waiting for their contract to expire. Local disc jockey Charles Johnson befriended the duo and eventually took a tape to Muscle Shoals, where Barry Beckett and Roger Hawkins were trying to get into producing. Beckett and Hawkins signed Mel and Tim to a production contract and then took the tapes of the first session to Stax. A deal was immediately inked and the prophetically titled "Starting All Over Again" returned the group to the R&B Top 10 and the pop Top 20.

"Al Bell had an incredible ear," marvels Muscle Shoals guitarist Jimmy Johnson. "I remember when Barry and Roger played him Mel and Tim's 'Starting All Over Again,' he heard it immediately. I loved record companies back then because Jim [Stewart] and particularly Al could hear a record and like [Jerry] Wexler say, 'I want that record.' And, they wouldn't change on you a week later. If they liked it now, they'd like it a week from now, a month from now. In a very short period the record'd be out and they'd be promoting the hell out of it. You'd see action. Stax was the last, to me, of the great companies."

"Starting All Over Again" had been written a couple of years earlier by Philip "Prince" Mitchell, one of a handful of songwriters contracted to the Muscle Shoals rhythm section's publishing company. Sam and Dave had wanted to release the song on Atlantic, but the powers that be didn't see the song's potential. Sam and Dave's loss turned out to be Mel and Tim's gain.

"When Mel and Tim became available to us," recounts Hawkins, "Barry and I just looked at each other like, 'Oh, oh—we've got a good song for these guys.' We were look-

---

27. The final release being "Feelin' Groovy" by Southwest FOB on November 20, 1969.

28. Over the years Big Star, led by former Box Top Alex Chilton, has achieved a substantial cult following, being cited by a number of alternative rock acts such as the Replacements and R.E.M. as a seminal influence.

ing for different ways to record that song. We did a lot of listening. We came across the Chi-Lites' 'Have You Seen Her' and we thought, 'That's a good-sounding format for 'Starting All Over Again.'" "

The Chi-Lites' record had been a number 1 R&B and number 3 pop hit in the fall of 1971. Beckett and Hawkins borrowed the earlier song's spoken intro, sitar hook, and a good part of its melody for "Starting All Over Again." Tim takes the lead vocal while Mel contributes the high harmonies and falsetto fills. Their ecstasy would be short-lived, because the two would never enjoy this level of success again.

With "(If Loving You Is Wrong) I Don't Want to Be Right" and "Starting All Over Again" storming up the *Billboard* listings—and Stax also enjoying chart records by the Soul Children, the Emotions, the only duet ever recorded by Isaac Hayes and David Porter, Albert King, the Staple Singers, the Temprees, and the Dramatics—the company was preparing to embark on its most ambitious project ever. Several months earlier a West Coast office had been established in Los Angeles. Headed by jazz drummer Chico Hamilton's son, Forest, Stax West was conceived with a mandate that included the promotion and marketing of existing Stax product, the ferreting out of heretofore untapped regional talent,[29] and, perhaps most important from Al Bell's perspective, the establishment of Stax within Hollywood's motion-picture and television circles.

The twenty-six-year-old Hamilton was a concert promoter who had met Al Bell when he had made a pilgrimage to Memphis to talk to the Stax owner about booking some of the company's artists. He was considered arrogant, egotistical, and not very competent by many of the Stax employees in Memphis. Suffice it to say, such feelings did not go very far in engendering goodwill between Memphis and Los Angeles. "The engineers did not like Forest much," confirms Pete Bishop. "We were recording the Bar-Kays [in Los Angeles] and his group [of bodyguards] tried to evict us from the concert, saying, 'We're Stax Records, we're Stax Records.' We said, 'Who are you?' because we hadn't met any of these people, and they ended up being these bodyguards for Forest. Every time we came out [to the West Coast] we had problems. Everybody in Memphis that I can remember thought we were just being totally ripped off by the California people. . . . We had bills that were four hundred dollars for one session for guitar strings. It was just ridiculous."

Eddie Floyd recalls being booked to play at the Roxy in Los Angeles. Forest Hamilton scheduled three days of rehearsal when, in Floyd's words, it only took two hours. Forest also paid an arranger to write out parts for the players that Floyd felt were totally unwarranted. To cap it off, the sheet music was encased in leather books with Floyd's name embossed on the front in gold. "That's how money started moving from Stax," says Floyd, shaking his head.

Earlie Biles felt that both Hamilton and John Smith lied to Al Bell, and she tried to tell Bell this on more than one occasion. "But he's a very religious man," says Biles. "He doesn't work with things like that. He feels like, 'I don't worry about that because God'll take care of that in the long run.' They'd come in with the Bible in their hand to talk to him because they knew that would get to him. When I'd see them coming, I'd just go, 'Please!' But it would get to him. [Al] felt that everybody would reform. If he talked to them, they would change."

Whatever reservations some of the Memphis family had about Hamilton and Stax's West Coast operation, it was directly responsible for the event that served as the climactic moment in Al Bell's career at Stax: August 1972's Wattstax concert. According to John KaSandra it all

---

29. The majority of artists signed by Forest Hamilton, including Stu Gardner, Cix Bits, Carolyn Hurley, Calvin Scott, and Joe Hicks, were abject commercial stiffs. The one major exception was comedian Richard Pryor.

started in March when "I came down [to the L.A. office] with an idea that we'd have a black Woodstock." Seven years earlier, to the chanting of "burn, baby, burn," a sizable section of the Watts community in Los Angeles had been destroyed by flames during the first of the 1960s' so-called race riots. To commemorate the riots and to raise money for a variety of community needs, the Watts Summer Festival had been established. It was Forest Hamilton's brainchild that Stax should be involved in the 1972 Festival for promotional purposes. He remembered KaSandra's "black Woodstock" comment and the concept grew from there.

The initial idea, dubbed "Wattstock," was to feature three acts performing in Will Rogers Park at the Watts Summer Festival site. Over time, this developed into an all-day concert to be staged at the Los Angeles Coliseum on the final day of the Watts Summer Festival featuring virtually every current Stax artist. The artists would give their performances free of charge, Schlitz beer would sponsor the event and thereby offset some of the production costs, and Stax would pick up all other incurred costs. Admission was held to a one-dollar, tax-deductible contribution per person so that virtually anyone in the community could afford to buy a ticket. Even so, several thousand tickets were distributed absolutely free of charge. When it was all over, ticket sales generated a total of $73,363 which was given to the Watts Summer Music Festival, Martin Luther King Hospital, the Sickle Cell Anemia Foundation, and the Watts Labor Community Action Committee.

At the time Larry Shaw summed up Stax's attitude toward Wattstax in a company press release: "Any strong record label could do something like this to support their community. We hope that WATTSTAX '72 will be a model for other companies to put forth similar events. This sort of all-star benefit is not so humanitarian as to be entirely without profit. And, it's a rare opportunity that lets you do something corporately valuable without being guilty of exploitation.

"Sure, Stax could have just given the Watts Festival $100,000. But, this way we have a prototype for something that can be done by many other record companies in many other cities, and it involves the community rather than being a handout. A successful all-star concert like this also focuses pride in a community image."

Fourteen years later Al Bell commented, "It was designed to aid in [increasing] the visibility of black culture, but it was also designed as a PR tool for Stax and its artists. [Thirdly, in filming it], it was my investment in a training program for Stax Films to start preparing us for motion pictures as well as develop the talent base for doing video, because I knew at the time that video was coming."

As with all such productions, the concept continually evolved.[30] By the concert date of August 20, the name had been formally changed to "Wattstax," arrangements had been made with two local radio stations, KGFJ-AM and KMET-FM, to broadcast the complete concert for those unable to attend,[31] David Wolper's film company was hired to visually document the event, and Wally Heider's mobile equipment was brought in to professionally record the music for subsequent release on LP. Out of all of this emerged the Wattstax film, two double albums, and a handful of singles. The Watts Summer Festival would receive a portion of the profits generated from the film and a portion of the producer's royalty from the LPs.

Wattstax itself was a glorious event. The Los Angeles Rams had played a football game the night before, forcing the construction of the stage into the wee hours of the morning. Nonetheless, by midday Sunday all was ready. That morning Isaac Hayes, celebrating his

30. In early June it was planned that each artist would do a fifteen-minute gospel set followed by a fifteen-minute R&B set. The grand finale was to feature Isaac Hayes leading all the artists through a half-hour gospel set.

31. XRPS-AM in Los Angeles ran a taped broadcast of the entire concert on the Labor Day weekend.

thirtieth birthday, was the grand marshal in the Watts Festival Parade, in which several other Stax artists also participated.[32] By the 2:30 showtime, a reported 112,000 people had filled every nook and cranny of the Coliseum's seats (the grass was off-limits to protect the football field). The capacity audience would spend seven

Jesse Jackson and Al Bell give clenched-fist salutes during the singing of the Black National Anthem, "Lift Every Voice and Sing," by Kim Weston at the opening ceremonies of Wattstax August 20, 1972. COURTESY FANTASY, INC.

hours peacefully celebrating all that was embodied in the music of Stax in an environment where the security was conspicuously all-black and equally conspicuously unarmed.[33]

Melvin Van Peebles, John KaSandra, Jesse Jackson, Billy Eckstine, William Bell, and black movie stars Fred Williamson and Richard Roundtree handled the emcee chores. The show began with Dale Warren leading the Wattstax '72 Orchestra through his "Salvation Symphony," written expressly for the event. Shortly before 3:00 P.M., Kim Weston led the audience through "The Star Bangled Banner." The American National Anthem was followed

---

32. Stax paid $3,000 to build the Mafundi Institute's float. The Mafundi Institute was a Watts-based organization that provided workshops in filmmaking, theater, and dance.

33. Every attempt was made to hire black businesses and organizations to provide all services necessary for the staging of the concert. Security was provided by three black organizations: the Watts Festival, the Sons of Watts, and the Watts Rangers.

by a number of brief speeches, including Jesse Jackson's "I Am Somebody" litany that Al Bell had been so taken with upon first hearing it a few short years before. Reverend Jackson then introduced Kim Weston again, who proceeded to perform the Black National Anthem, "Lift Every Voice and Sing." The Staple Singers, minus an ailing Yvonne, took the stage next, performing at two-thirds power. Following the Staples were Jimmy Jones, Louise McCord, Debra Manning (all three performing gospel material), Eric Mercury, Freddie Robinson, Lee Sain, Ernie Hines, Little Sonny, William Bell, the Newcomers, Eddie Floyd, the Temprees, and Frederick Knight, each doing one three- to three-and-a-half-minute song. All of these artists then congregated for a group version of "Give Me That Old Time Religion." At that point the sets got a little longer with the Rance Allen Group, David Porter, the Bar-Kays, Tommy Tate, Carla Thomas, Albert King, Rufus Thomas, and the Soul Children each doing ten- to fifteen-minute performances. After Billy Eckstine sang "If I Can Help Somebody," the concert was brought to a close with Jesse Jackson introducing Isaac Hayes, who performed for a full hour followed by a prayer of thanks from Jackson, and Jimmy Jones and Kim Weston leading the audience through "If I Had a Hammer." The Emotions, Luther Ingram, Johnnie Taylor, Joe Hicks, Mel and Tim, and the Sons of Slum were all scheduled to perform, but with the show running overtime, they were canceled at the last minute, the Emotions being informed of this decision while they were literally standing on the side of the stage waiting to go on. Over twenty years later, they were still rankled by this turn of events.

Aside from those whose performance was canceled, virtually every member of the Stax community whom I have spoken with over the years who was there remembers the event in absolutely glowing terms.

"I got the feeling it was a tremendous community event," reflects Homer Banks, "because of the fact [that I got to] sit in the stands and hear people talk. They set the price so that anybody could come. That automatically sent a signal to the people that here's something being done for us. I really think [that] behind Wattstax, Stax became stronger out that way.

"There were really some interesting things happening. For instance, they had to do two anthems before the start—they did the American national anthem and then they did the black national anthem. You could see some of the militants stand up, holding the fist up.[34] It was a lot of things that you wouldn't normally see. I remember the security people who were there; some of the policemen, they would take their hats off during the national anthem and then put them back on during the black national anthem. Some guy [in the audience would ask them], 'Would you please pull your hat off?' [The policeman would] say, 'No!' It was amazing."

"Wattstax was a wonderful experience," agrees Isaac Hayes. "People brought their kids with picnics in baskets and people got up and danced if they felt like it. They'd yell and scream and whatever they did, there was no violence. It was really, really beautiful."

As Judy Speigelman wrote in *Soul,* Wattstax was "more than just a show . . . the event marked the first all Black entertainment event of its size and scope ever to be completely Black controlled!" The significance of Wattstax was even accorded recognition at various levels of government. Mayor Sam Yorty appropriately declared August 20, 1972, "Wattstax Day" in Los Angeles. Even more impressive was the commendation by Senator Alan Cranston (D-Calif.) that was read in the United States Senate and subsequently inserted into the *Congressional Record* on Friday, October 13, 1972:

> Mr. President, a major American business has made a notable contri-
> bution to the people supporting it, a contribution worthy of recognition.

34. See the picture on page 269, where Al Bell and Jesse Jackson are standing side by side on the stage with their fists clenched in the air.

The Stax Organization, a leading black business in America, and the dedication of its leaders to the basic principles of American citizenship deserves our commendation.

Primarily involved in the production and distribution of musical records, for which they have been known as the 'Memphis Sound,' the Stax Organization, headed by a dynamic man named Al Bell, recognizes that its success depends upon the public. With this in mind, Al Bell and his associates recently began a program of giving back to the people some of the benefits the company has received from them.

A most significant example of this kind of corporate responsibility was displayed on August 20, 1972, in Los Angeles when Stax, a Memphis-based company, organized 'Wattstax '72,' a massive 6-hour musical spectacular that brought some 100,000 black citizens together at the Los Angeles Coliseum. The entire event was a gift from Stax to the community. Stax provided the entire list of top music stars. . . . Stax also provided much of the personnel staffing the event and underwrote most of the expenses.

Admission to 'Wattstax '72' was $1, enabling all members of the community to attend and also giving them the opportunity of contributing to their community. The entire proceeds from the event have been distributed to the Watts summer festival [sic], to enable them to carry out a yearlong program of community support, the sickle cell anemia program, the Martin Luther King Hospital, and the Watts Labor Community Action Committee.

Al Bell and Stax are not planning to stop with the success of 'Wattstax '72.' The company has a plan to continue such events in major black areas throughout the country. Similarly, continuing the spirit of black corporate responsibility, Stax is presently involved in a major anti-drug program in New Haven and intends to put much of its own successful gains into all areas that will aid fellow man. Stax feels this is a mission in life which has had many rewards—human rewards of the highest order.

I commend the Stax Organization and those associated with them in this project. They are, indeed, inspirational examples of good citizenship to all Americans of every race, creed, and national origin.

In 1972, with President Nixon virtually ignoring inner-city America, commendations in the United States Senate for a black business were not exactly everyday events. These were indeed heady days for the "little label that could." What had started by happenstance as an interracial mom-and-pop company in Memphis, Tennessee, had blossomed into a national powerhouse with a decided and fiercely proud black identity. According to Al Bell's vision, Stax had just started to get into the game. Alas, as events would turn out, Wattstax was the pinnacle of everything Al Bell would achieve at the label.

14

(If You're Ready) Come Go with Me: 1972 (Part 2)

I t is telling that neither Jim Stewart nor Don Davis was in attendance at Wattstax. Both had gradually become increasingly estranged from the company. Moving under a full head of steam, Al Bell, Larry Shaw, and Johnny Baylor had transformed Stax into something neither Stewart nor Davis could easily understand. At Stax's Avalon offices there was simply no looking back.

Immediately following Wattstax, the National Association of Television and Radio Announcers (NATRA) named Isaac Hayes's *Shaft* its Album of the Year. Luther Ingram was voted Most Promising Male Vocalist, Rance Allen was cited as being the Best Religious Group, and the Staple Singers were honored as the Best Mixed Vocal Group. A couple of weeks earlier Stax had captured nine of the twenty-six categories at the first annual Soul and Blues Awards held at the Beverly Hills Hilton.[1] In the last week of September, Isaac Hayes, the Staple Singers, Luther Ingram, and Johnnie Taylor gave concert performances (donating their usual fees) at Jesse Jackson's annual PUSH EXPO at Chicago's International Amphitheater, Taylor performing a rare gospel set on the final day.[2] At PUSH EXPO '72, the Stax booth continuously showed excerpts of *Wattstax,* and Stax also donated two thousand dollars for what was dubbed the "Stax Art Award," a competition involving six hundred pieces of art by two hundred black artists from three continents.

Also in September 1972, Mavis Staples released her last solo single on the Stax subsidiary Volt. Back in 1969, when Al Bell was attempting to generate an instant back catalogue, Mavis had been persuaded to record her eponymously titled debut solo album. Bell saw the Staples family as a potential triple threat, reasoning that over time he could achieve secular success for the group, turn Mavis into a solo star, and promote solo recordings by Pops Staples. In a studio for the first time outside of the family context, Mavis, by her own admission, was scared to death. In 1970, with a little more confidence, she recorded her sophomore effort, the Don Davis–produced *Only for the Lonely.* Two singles were originally culled from the album; the first, "I Have Learned to Do Without You," climbed to number 13 R&B and number 87 pop in late summer 1970.

Mavis Staples solo. COURTESY FANTASY, INC.

---

1. Isaac Hayes was cited as Best Male Vocalist and as composer of the Best Musical Score for a Motion Picture; the Staple Singers were named Best Vocal Group; the award for Best Gospel Group went to Maceo Woods and the Christian Tabernacle Choir; Dave Clark was named Best Promotion Man and also received a Special Humanitarian Award for Outstanding Contributions and Achievement to Black Arts and Culture; Al Bell was voted Record Company Executive of the Year, and, capping it all off, Stax was honored as Record Company of the Year.

2. Jackson's annual Black Business and Cultural Exposition had debuted in 1969. In each subsequent year he had received substantial support from Stax Records.

In September 1972, Mavis's cover of Brook Benton's "Endlessly" was pulled from the two-year-old album as a followup single. Benton and longtime compadre Clyde Otis had written the song in the late 1950s one afternoon when Benton was in dire need of an advance from his publisher. A couple of years later, Benton recorded a moderately up-tempo version on Mercury complete with flamenco guitar, hitting number 3 R&B and number 12 pop for his efforts. Both Don Davis and Mavis Staples had long admired Benton's recording, making it a natural choice for the *Only for the Lonely* sessions. Inspired by what she clearly thought was a superb Don Davis production, Mavis carves out a vocal persona that is in decided contrast from what she used with the Staple Singers.

"It was the way the song goes," explains Mavis, "and the way I felt it should have been delivered. I tried to give it a softer sound. It's almost a more jazzy sound. Certain tracks will take you a different place and that's the way I heard it. On my solo things I wanted to sound different to show that Mavis can sing another way." Mavis explained that she was also concerned that she not replicate Benton's original. To my ear, she is the more adventuresome of the two, decorating the melody with carefully wrought ornamentation.

Despite its quality, Mavis's version only climbed to number 30 R&B and number 109 on the pop chart. Davis insists that Stax personnel told him that they were instructed to hold back on promotion of Mavis's solo releases. The poor performance of this single, and Mavis's disenchantment with Stax's refusal to allow her to copublish her own songs, led her to put her solo career on hold.[3]

As disgruntled as Mavis was with Al Bell's decision in regard to giving her copublishing on her songs, she had no intention of letting that affect her family's career at the label. In the first week of October 1972, the Staples journeyed to Muscle Shoals for what would turn into seven days of recordings, beginning October 5 and continuing, with a two-day break, through October 13. Strangely, this extended session would be the last time the group would record backing tracks until after they left Stax in the last months of the label's existence. The sessions were begun with the understanding that the group was going to release a double LP. Some time after the session, that idea was shelved and instead two separate LPs, *Be What You Are* and *City in the Sky,* and seven singles were eventually released from these sessions. Although the rhythm tracks complete with scratch vocals were recorded in this one mammoth stretch that fall, as each song was selected for release over the next two-plus years, the Staples returned to Memphis to cut finished vocal tracks at Ardent. It would be at that point that all horns, strings, and other overdubs were added.

Several Stax writers made the trek to Muscle Shoals for these sessions. The Staples were hot and they were being produced by the company's vice president and co-owner, meaning ample promotion was not going to be a question. A song written for the Staples had a better-than-average chance of making its author some money. The attitude is best described by Carl Hampton: "We said, 'Hey, let's get on this ride, let's get on this train. This is our chance to hit the big time.' We were looking at it like this is Al Bell's group . . . we know the money gonna be behind them."

Hampton had his personal piano trucked down from Memphis and set up in his hotel room. For the first several days, Mack Rice and Bettye Crutcher would be in the studio helping out with the recording of one of their songs while Homer Banks, Raymond Jackson, and

---

3. As was the case with Booker T. and the MG's, Mavis found it particularly difficult to swallow the fact that Stax was unwilling to let her share in the publishing of her own compositions, and yet Don Davis retained all of his publishing through Groovesville Music. Her response was to simply take her first two compositions, "I'm Tired of You Doing Me Wrong" and "You're All I Need," off the *Only for the Lonely* album and refuse to record subsequent solo efforts for Stax.

Carl Hampton were back at the hotel crafting any number of songs that they would pitch to the Staples in the evening, when the day's session had come to a conclusion. There was usually plenty of time to audition new material, because the Muscle Shoals players were all pretty serious family guys and generally refused to schedule sessions after 8:00 P.M.

The first single released from these sessions, "Be What You Are," was one of the songs that was crafted on the spot in the hotel room. Most of the song was written by Banks and Jackson, with Hampton adding a little flavor into the mix. "The idea was taken from biblical scriptures," relates Banks. "It might have been Nicodemus who said, 'Be what you are and live the life.' I was trying to bridge that gap between straight gospel and a social statement. So I adapted that and put it into how people could relate to it in this day and time. 'Don't live outside your means, don't try to be someone you're not. Just be who you are.' That was the intent."

Everyone was excited when the Staples first heard it. "Pops loved our songs," says Hampton. "We wanted Mavis to sing the song, but he said, 'I'm gonna sing this one.' I said, 'Oh Lord, there goes my gold.' It did five hundred thousand records anyway, but I wanted a gold record."

Homer Banks has a dissenting opinion. "Carl was so infatuated with Mavis, but I knew too that Pops was such an instrumental part of that sound with the Staples. With Mavis doing some little ad libs behind Pops, it's traditional Staples. Carl thought that Mavis was the key to it. I think it was the Staples as a whole."

It was always the family's decision whether a given lead would go to Mavis or Pops. "When we would see one that didn't take a lot of gut, that was just straight, we knew it was for Daddy," explains Mavis. "He sings cool and he don't want to sing with no strain at all where he'd have to put some effort. Songs that called for effort he would let me have. We just kinda knew."

Gold record or not, when released as a single in late spring 1973, "Be What You Are" was a hit. Pops is his usual idiosyncratic, folksy, brilliant self, and either Eddie Hinton or Terry Manning plays some mighty crunchy rock-and-roll guitar on the fade. At the end of the year, the track garnered a Grammy nomination to boot. At the time of its release, Al Bell was planning to produce a straight-ahead gospel album for the group, and Stax announced that they would be producing a television documentary on the Staple Singers' life and music. Neither project ever came to fruition.

In the meantime, Stax continued to release material from the massive October 1972 Muscle Shoals sessions. Four more singles—"If You're Ready (Come Go with Me)," "Touch a Hand, Make a Friend," "City in the Sky," and "My Main Man"—charted over the next two-and-a-quarter years. As with "Be What You Are," "If You're Ready (Come Go with Me)" and "Touch a Hand, Make a Friend" were written by what was now Stax's preeminent songwriting team: Homer Banks, Raymond Jackson, and Carl Hampton.

Released in September 1973, "If You're Ready (Come Go with Me)" was another lyrical gem from the pen of Homer Banks. An R&B chart topper that also poked its way into the pop Top 10, for Al Bell, the song was the pinnacle achievement in what had been, and would continue to be, an awesome string of Staple Singers records. "In 'Come Go with Me,'" stresses Bell, "you hear the absolute completeness of what I was trying to pull together production-wise. I had finally gotten the sound that I was trying to get. The key to it was the influence of Raymond Jackson. He became the piece I needed to carry forth. I looked forward to the next sessions because I knew we had a sound that could cut in all directions in the marketplace."

"If You're Ready (Come Go with Me)" was the one song that Banks, Jackson, and Hampton had written in advance of the Staples session. Jackson played guitar on the demo, and was reluctantly coaxed by all concerned to play the lead on the actual recording. On the demo he had played the rhythmic lick heard on the breakdown near the end. At the session, he put individual notes to the rhythm, creating an unforgettable hook in the process. Mavis is the proverbial icing on the cake, scatting along with Raymond, and ultimately taking the song over the top.

The song itself was a deliberate reworking of some of the elements found in "I'll Take You There." "That was easy for me," Hampton says, laughing. "I can write a followup perfectly, come right behind it and pop the charts again. I knew all it needed was a bass line. I think 'I'll Take You There' was more gutsy and more Staxy, but we put a little bit more meaning in 'Come Go with Me.' Homer went deep in his mind. The lyric was real heavy. I'm proud of that song."

Mavis had a few more reservations. "I almost didn't want to do that song because I said, 'It sounds just like "I'll Take You There." We're good enough that we don't have to do that.' Then Daddy said, 'Mavis that's all right, if you find something good, stick with it. A lot of James Brown and Curtis Mayfield stuff sounds the same.' I tried to argue it down but then I looked at the lyric again. The lyrics were so tough!"

Apparently Homer Banks's singing on the demo was also pretty impressive. "Homer would have some bad ad libbing on his demos," continues Mavis. "I used some of Homer's stuff because I knew Homer could phrase. Homer would put down a demo to make you sing better. You better sing, because his demo is gonna be better than what you're doing if you don't get up on it. Homer goes all through me."

While "I'll Take You There" was one long insouciant groove, "If You're Ready" was more of a formally written and structured song. The Muscle Shoals section retained a bit of the reggae flavor from the earlier hit, but the groove and texture of "If You're Ready (Come Go with Me)" comes off altogether differently, at least partially due to Al Bell and Terry Manning's brilliant postproduction work. Manning's carefree but rich acoustic guitar overdub is especially crucial to the final result.

"Touch a Hand, Make a Friend" was issued as a single in January 1974. It also soared up the charts, not stopping until it had reached numbers 3 and 23 on the R&B and pop listings, respectively. Both Hampton and Banks recall structuring "Touch a Hand" around Joe South's "Games People Play." Hampton came up with the idea while noodling on the piano, Jackson immediately jumped on it, and Banks had lyrics written within the hour. Tired of writing tunes that drew upon other people's work, Hampton balked at presenting the song to the Staples. Fortunately, Banks and Jackson carried the day, and the Staples loved it. Everyone involved, from Al Bell and Terry Manning to the Muscle Shoals rhythm section and arranger Johnny Allen, came through with an unbelievably gorgeous track. Barry Beckett's piano part, which quotes from the calypso tune "Down By the Seashore Sifting Sand," is particularly praiseworthy; presumably Beckett's line inspired Terry Manning's marimba overdub.

Although "Touch a Hand, Make a Friend" was not released as a single until January 1974, the Staples' vocals were added to the track a couple of weeks after the multiday rhythm session in Muscle Shoals in early October 1972. Tragically, it would be the only one of the three Staples hits written by Banks, Hampton, and Jackson that Raymond Jackson would hear in finished form.

A few weeks after the Muscle Shoals sessions, Jackson attempted to kill a rat that had burrowed down a tunnel in his backyard. Filling the hole with gasoline and then lighting a match, the songwriter was instantly engulfed in flames. He struggled for his life for two weeks in the hospital before finally succumbing on November 10.

"['Touch a Hand, Make a Friend'] has special significance to me," relates Homer Banks, "because right before Raymond passed he had all the medicine in him and I guess he was hallucinating. When I went up to the hospital to see him he said he saw Jesus Christ and the Staple Singers singing 'Touch a Hand, Make a Friend.' That always has stuck with me. Two days later he passed away." Jackson had just turned thirty-one. Banks had lost a childhood friend; along with Hampton he had also lost a writing and producing partner; and Stax, in general, lost one of its gentlest, most loving souls. It would be a while before all recovered.

Two-and-a-half weeks before Raymond Jackson's death, the fate of Stax Records as a whole was effectively sealed when on October 24 Al Bell signed a distribution deal with CBS that he had been negotiating since June. Given CBS's historic lack of involvement with rhythm and blues, it is not surprising that the New York mega-corporation was literally the last company Bell had spoken with about selling Stax. The fact that a deal was worked out at all shocked a lot of people in the record industry.

Raymond Jackson. COURTESY FANTASY, INC.

"During those days CBS was the larger-than-life white company," points out Bell. "There were a lot of people who were not comfortable with CBS, and I was one of those people. That's why CBS was last. What made me [ultimately] comfortable in dealing with CBS was my dialogue with Clive Davis. When I sat and talked with Clive in a hotel room one evening about the possibility of developing some sort of relationship with CBS, what I heard and felt from Clive made me feel a lot better about dealing with CBS simply because of Clive Davis. I could relate to Clive Davis, I respected Clive Davis as a record man. Even though he was an attorney, he still had a creative mind, and he had a sensitivity to the part of the business that I functioned in. He had an appreciation for our music. He had a genuine appreciation for Albert King. I didn't think that CBS would have had that appreciation."

Bell proposed that CBS simply buy Jim Stewart's half of the company, but CBS's lawyers felt that they would run into trouble with the then-current United States antitrust laws. Instead, an agreement was worked out whereby CBS would lend Al Bell $6 million[4] which Bell would partially use to buy Jim Stewart's half of the company. In return, commencing on October 24, 1972, CBS would distribute all releases on Stax, Volt, and Enterprise for a minimum period of ten years.[5] According to Bell, CBS pledged that it would at least double the sales of Stax's three main labels. The company's

---

4. Taking the RCA stock offer as his benchmark, Bell had originally been asking CBS for $15 million dollars for full ownership of Stax. In the course of the negotiations with Davis, that figure got whittled down to the $6 million Bell ultimately settled for.

5. The actual wording of the deal gave CBS distribution rights until three-and-a-half years after Stax had paid off the $6 million loan or until November 30, 1982, if Stax had paid the loan off by that date. Bell was not very comfortable with such a long-term agreement, but seeing as he had not been able to make a deal with anyone else, he felt he ultimately had no choice.

more specialty-oriented imprints such as Partee, Respect, and Gospel Truth were explicitly left out of the deal.

CBS insisted that Jim Stewart must remain an executive with the company for the following five years, thereby ensuring in their minds continuity and continued success. In the meantime, Stewart was to receive from Stax $2.5 million up front, a promissory note for $1.5 million payable January 3, 1978, and then a further installment promissory note outlining sixty equal monthly payments for the balance (the final payment being due on December 1, 1977),[6] bringing the total sale price of his half of the company up to $7.6 million. Bell also had to remain with Stax and could not enter into any chief executive or management function with any record company in the United States or its territories until Stax had repaid the $6 million loan to CBS. To make the deal fly, Union Planters National Bank, then owed $1.7 million by Stax, had to agree to subordinate this indebtedness to the $6 million CBS loan. Union Planters agreed to do this, understanding that Stax intended to use the CBS cash to expand and theoretically become that much more of a powerhouse within the music industry.[7] All parties agreed that it was not to become public knowledge at either company that Jim Stewart had sold his equity to Al Bell.

"David Porter said to me," offers Bell, "'Man, don't you let these people know what you're doing because if you do, it's going to be a problem. You're gonna have jealousy among the people inside because we all grew up together.' From that point forward my mind went to work. [In addition] I felt like and ultimately experienced that the white community in Memphis would have a problem with a black man sitting there owning that record company. That white-black issue was a serious concern."

Theoretically everyone should have been happy.[8] Over time Stewart would get his money and in five years his peace of mind, and Al Bell would continue to run and now wholly own the company that had become his very lifeblood. Through CBS, Stax would get access to the rack jobbers that largely controlled the record inventories at all major department stores; in the days before the big record store chains came on the scene, these retail operations serviced the majority of white consumers and moved serious numbers of LPs. Bell believed that the CBS deal would facilitate crossover sales of any number of Stax artists, as well as supporting in grand style his desire to expand Stax's efforts in the world of rock, pop, country, and jazz. For CBS, the distribution deal would hopefully force the small mom-and-pop stores that in the main serviced the inner-city black population to come to CBS for Stax product and, while doing so, buy other CBS product such as the wealth of material the company had begun releasing through its *Philadelphia International* imprint, thereby accessing a segment of the music industry that had heretofore generally eluded it.

6. According to controller Ed Pollack's testimony in the Stax bankruptcy trial, Stewart was paid $1,175,000 on December 22, 1972, and $62,500 a month afterward. Payments continued through July or August 1974 when Stax's cash flow made further payments impossible. These payments were recorded on a private ledger so that Stax's bookkeeper, and anyone else for that matter, would not know that Stewart had sold his part of the company to Bell.

7. Among the exhibits in the Stax bankruptcy trial is a note from Al Bell to CBS that states that the purpose of the $6 million loan was "to use portions of the loan proceeds as a down payment against the agreed price for the repurchase of the outstanding shares of our stock currently owned by James Stewart; to acquire a recording studio; to purchase a small independent record label, which we are now distributing; to fund artist signings and for working capital purposes."

8. In addition to the principals, the Big 6 from the company's first period—Steve Cropper, Booker T. Jones, Al Jackson, Duck Dunn, David Porter, and Isaac Hayes—also benefited from the deal. According to Al Bell, there had been a lingering dispute between the six and Jim Stewart with regard to remuneration they felt they were due under the old producers' pool agreement. Bell saw the CBS money as an opportunity to put this lingering problem permanently to rest.

CBS's director of special markets (i.e., black product) Logan Westbrooks recalls: "We were elated. The idea was that some of the methods and procedures that they were using, hopefully we could pick those up with CBS and do some of the same kinds of things. We thought that they were highly successful, that they were a specialized label that knew exactly what they were doing. The idea was, in bringing the might of the CBS distribution network, it would just be unlimited."

Clive Davis, Logan Westbrooks, Jim Stewart, and Al Bell might have been happy, but Clarence Avant was upset. He had spent months negotiating the RCA deal with its then-president Rocco Laginestra. As far as he was concerned an agreement in principle had been made. "[Then] one day I got a telephone call," says Avant. "It says, 'Ain't no more deal. Al Bell's gonna go to CBS.' That was his biggest fuckup he ever made as far as I'm concerned. The RCA deal was a helluva deal, a real big deal."

According to Avant, RCA was offering $16 million in RCA stock for 80 percent of Stax; Bell and Stewart could sell the remaining 20 percent at any time between the first and the fifth year of the deal for up to $5 million more in stock. In the meantime, they would be able to continue to run Stax with total autonomy, and they would be paid annual salaries of $250,000 a year plus bonuses. This was some $160,000 a year before bonuses more than they had ever previously made. "It was unheard of," a still perplexed Avant maintains. "That was more fucking stock in RCA than all the black guys in the world own together probably!" In retrospect, Bell and Stewart both wish they had followed Avant's advice.[9]

Don Davis was also distressed at this turn of events. "The transition of Stax Records to CBS was one that I took very, very hard. To me that was the end of an age. To take this southern company and put it in the hands of CBS was blasphemy as far as I was concerned."

Clive Davis's career at CBS had been nothing short of phenomenal. When he took over as president of Columbia Records in 1967, with the exception of a handful of "folk-rock" artists such as Bob Dylan and Simon and Garfunkel, CBS had yet to establish itself in any meaningful manner within the burgeoning arena of 1960s rock music. Davis was to change this in a big way, quickly signing Donovan, Big Brother and the Holding Company featuring Janis Joplin, Blood, Sweat and Tears, and, a little later, Santana, Johnny Winter and Chicago Transit Authority (known as simply Chicago by the group's second album). In a very short period of time he had transformed Columbia into a rock powerhouse.

In 1971, together with Columbia's vice president of marketing Bruce Lundvall, Davis began to consider how further to expand the activities of the Columbia Records Group. By this point in time, CBS was number one in virtually every field of the industry, including rock, country, easy listening, and jazz. What the company was missing out on was soul music. Although in the sixties the company had briefly flirted with two black-oriented custom labels, Okeh and Date, little of consequence was released through either operation and both had ceased activity. On their main labels, the only artist that appeared on the soul charts with any consistency was Sly and the Family Stone. In addition to Sly, other than Taj Mahal, O. C. Smith, and the Chambers Brothers, none of whom were serious soul chart artists in 1971, CBS had little in the way of an R&B roster.

Davis had ignored this area of the market early on in his career, feeling that it was far too dependent on singles, which were not nearly as profitable as full-length albums. This had all changed with Isaac Hayes's recording of *Hot Buttered Soul*. Davis was also cog-

---

9. After Stax went bankrupt, Avant went to every major label trying to get a production deal for Al Bell. He couldn't get a nibble.

nizant of the blaxploitation phenomenon and the subsequent success of black soundtrack albums such as *Shaft*. In conjunction with Lundvall, he logically concluded that CBS should move aggressively into R&B in the same fashion that Davis had done so success-fully with rock some four years earlier. The first step was to hire someone who knew some-thing about soul music. In late 1971 Logan Westbrooks, a six-year industry veteran most recently employed at Mercury Records as national R&B promotion manager, was appoint-ed as director of special markets (a CBS euphemism for R&B). Westbrooks's mandate, as he articulated it in his 1981 book *The Anatomy of a Record Company: How to Survive the Record Business*, was to "create a black marketing staff to penetrate the black market."

Leaving no angle unexplored, CBS executive Larry Isaacson commissioned his alma mater, the Harvard Business School, to conduct a study and make recommendations as to whether CBS should, and how they might best, become a dominant force in soul music.[10] Submitted to CBS on May 11, 1972, and formally titled "A Study of the Soul Music Environment Prepared for Columbia Records Group," this report has since become known simply as *The Harvard Report*.

It has been alleged for years that the report suggested that CBS should, in the best-case scenario, buy either Stax or Motown, and that Stax was the more likely of the two to be purchased. It has been further alleged that in the event that neither black music concern could be purchased, CBS should distribute one of the two labels instead. Once an ongo-ing relationship was established, CBS could position itself to be able to purchase the com-pany sometime in the future. Despite widespread belief in these allegations, these are not the conclusions drawn in the actual report.

The report estimates that the black music market was then worth $60 million annually in gross sales at the wholesale level. Albums and 45s each accounted for roughly 50 per-cent of that total, representing sales of some twelve million albums and sixty million soul singles each year. It was further estimated that soul music accounted for 7 to 10 percent of all record sales in the United States; Motown and Atlantic each accounted for 20 per-cent of that business, while Stax took 10 percent. The remaining 50 percent of the mar-ket was divided between a host of smaller companies.[11]

The report advised CBS that "The specialized national companies [Motown, Atlantic, and Stax] will provide [CBS with] the most formidable competition. They have an entrenched position and control half of the total market. They have most of the estab-lished Soul artists. Their management and professional staffs have extensive experience in this market, and a deep understanding of its subtleties. They operate through a highly sophisticated personal and informational network which they have built up over a period of many years. Finally, they have a profound understanding of the art form with which they work, and of its commercial possibilities. In fact, they have helped to shape it."

---

10. *The Harvard Report* was not commissioned by Clive Davis as I and several others have erroneously written in the past. Totaling twenty-four pages of text plus another eighteen pages of appendices and a ten-page adden-dum submitted separately by one of the members of the study group, the report cost less than $5,000 and involved six students carrying out research over the course of a half year. The existence of this report first was made public in 1974 when CBS and Stax were suing each other over their distribution agreement. Stax's legal team interpreted the existence of the report as evidence that CBS intended to "buy" the soul market or at least buy out Stax itself. There have been many other theories spread by those who have had secondhand knowledge of the report. However, after a ten-year search, I finally acquired a copy of this legendary document in early 1996; I am now able to correct some of my earlier statements about the report that were based on incorrect, secondhand information.

11. A further indication of the size of the soul music market in the early 1970s comes from a CBS presentation at its annual convention in 1974. During the course of the presentation, it was stated that, whereas in 1964 there were only 30 R&B stations nationwide, in 1974 the number had grown to over 250. Stax had played a large role in this growth.

The report also noted that CBS knew virtually nothing about the soul market and, in fact, had a rather negative image within the soul music industry that would need to be substantially altered: "CRG's [Columbia Records Group] historic neglect of the Soul market has brought upon it some problems in respect to its image in this market. Interviews with people in the Soul music business indicate that CRG is perceived as an ultra-rich, ultra-white giant which has for the most part chosen to snub Blacks in the business. Blacks in the trade feel that CRG has heaped upon them the ultimate insult: that of ignoring their existence. Even when the slight involves seemingly superficial things (CRG fails to invite them to functions; DJ's say they do not get free tickets to shows from CRG as do white DJ's) these are seen as manifestations of a broader pattern. Further, they perceive a degree of arrogance in CRG promotion personnel who try to get airplay for a Soul product viewed by Black radio personnel as sub-standard. That these promotion personnel were almost always white did not help matters."

The conclusion of the report was that soul music constituted a significant market that Columbia Records had heretofore ignored, and that it should immediately begin to aggressively pursue it. The report recommended a long-term strategy that would involve substantial start-up costs and lose money for the first two years. The Harvard MBAs concluded that, if their recommendations were followed, CBS would break even by the third year and that by the end of year five (1978), CBS could make a profit of $1,401,000 on R&B sales and control 10 percent of the market.

The report's recommended strategies to reach these goals included: (1) Expand external sources of product by augmenting present custom-label activity and increasing outside product resources; (2) Develop internal means of soul music product generation; and (3) Establish a semiautonomous soul music product group. The first recommendation could be interpreted to suggest making a distribution agreement with a label such as Stax, but elsewhere in the document it was stressed that the myriad number of indies operating on a scale much smaller than Motown, Atlantic, and Stax potentially provided CBS with readymade sources of talent (artists and producers) and executives with knowledge of this segment of the industry. The implication was that Motown, Atlantic, and Stax would be best left alone. Nowhere is it even remotely suggested that CBS attempt to distribute a company such as Stax with the objective of an ultimate takeover. In fact, *The Harvard Report* explicitly states: "Two alternative sets of recommendations *were* considered. The first was the acquisition of a company presently strong in the Soul music business. *This strategy is not a feasible one for Columbia* for the following reasons: (1) The dominance of the CBS organization in the communications and entertainment industry could possibly precipitate anti-trust action if it were to attempt the acquisition of a major company in the music industry. (2) Of the three companies strong enough to offer Columbia a base from which to operate, Atlantic has been bought out by the Kinney group, Stax was acquired by Gulf and Western, and it is rumored that Motown is not in a position to contemplate an acquisition at this time."

The second alternative considered but ultimately rejected by the Harvard study group was the acquisition of presently established talent. This was viewed negatively due to the high costs of such acquisitions, the risks that the acquired artists might not produce quality material for Columbia, the lack of a base structure to properly promote or market the product, the possibility of inspiring other major labels into a bidding war, and the possibility that payment of large advances to newly signed R&B talent might lead to jealousies among artists presently under contract and lead to consequent escalation of their money demands.

The report specifically recommended that CBS start by building an internal, semiautonomous black-music division and establish a presence in the market initially through starting custom labels in conjunction with noted producers or performers, working toward the signing and development of its own homegrown black talent. The custom label deals CBS made for Philadelphia International with producers Kenny Gamble and Leon Huff and for T-Neck Records with the Isley Brothers were precisely the sort of arrangements the report was recommending.

Taking over Stax or putting the company out of business seems to have been the furthest thing from the minds of the authors of *The Harvard Report*. The addendum submitted by Marnie Tattersall gives the strongest indication that the report's compilers envisioned an independent Stax label continuing to exist as a competitor. Tattersall was an ambitious MBA student who was ultimately hired to work in CBS's Black Music Division by Logan Westbrooks. She recommended a much more aggressive approach whereby after five years CBS would control 15 percent of the R&B market, netting a profit of $2,280,000. The pie chart that accompanies this set of recommendations shows Atlantic controlling 15 percent of the market (down 5 percent from their present position) and Motown retaining its current 20 percent share while Stax was projected to increase its share of the market to 15 percent. CBS's projected 15 percent would not come from either Stax or Motown; it would come partially at the expense of Atlantic and mostly at the expense of the remaining smaller independents. *The Harvard Report* actually envisioned a very healthy, strong, independent Stax five years down the road!

Clive Davis has long maintained that he never actually read the document. In conversation with Logan Westbrooks for the latter's book *The Anatomy of a Record Company: How to Survive the Record Business,* Davis stated that, with regard to his move into black music, "It was not based on any blueprint. . . . I went straight ahead on creative feel, intuitive reasoning and common sense, *not* because I had any study or blueprint. I've never read that study, I've never seen it, and I've certainly never used it as a blueprint. [The study] did not form the basis for any move that I made."

Al Bell does not believe that Davis never read *The Harvard Report* and, in fact, believes that Davis supplied Harvard with some of their most crucial statistics. After the "Stax Sound in Chi-Town" program the previous summer, Bell had compiled a number of statistics generated during the course of the campaign. When asked to speak at NARM (National Association of Record Merchants) later that same year, Bell chose as his subject "Black is beautiful . . . business." The essence of his talk was how much money retailers could accrue if they properly marketed black LPs. He particularly focused on the fact that black LPs could sell through outlets such as Sears supplied through rack jobbers. Alongside his talk, he distributed a booklet titled "Black Is Beautiful" as supporting evidence that contained the results of the "Stax Sound in Chi-Town" campaign. Clive Davis was supposedly among those in attendance.

"I'm told that Clive took that," exclaims Bell, "and that's what he gave to Harvard, the book and all the statistical data that I had in there on the sales that we had realized in the Sears stores during that 'Stax Sound in Chi-Town' campaign."[12]

While *The Harvard Report* did not recommend it, Columbia Records, after Davis left the company in May 1973, very clearly was instrumental in putting Stax out of business, and, if Bell had never made the distribution deal with CBS, it is likely that Stax would still be alive and well. Besides ultimately leading to the disintegration of Stax, Columbia's entry into the soul music marketplace had extensive ramifications for black music in general. As predicted in *The Harvard Report*, other majors followed Columbia's lead. Within

---

12. Marnie Tattersall, who was the most active member of the Harvard study group, does not remember CBS making any booklet or statistics available to them.

a few years virtually every major record label had a black music division. Also, as predicted by the Harvard group, these black music divisions were largely staffed from the ranks of the smaller, independent R&B companies, a number of which found that they simply couldn't compete anymore. CBS lead the charge. By 1980 CBS had over 125 R&B acts under contract, comprising approximately one-third of its total artist roster.

Logan Westbrooks recalls that the way he and other CBS executives found out about the Stax agreement was highly unusual. Usually in a deal of this magnitude, Clive Davis would have consulted with a number of department heads before asking the lawyers to draw up an agreement. In the case of the Stax agreement, Davis put it together entirely by himself. Outside of a few rumors that were mostly discounted, no one at the company had a clue what was going on until early one October morning, when all the department heads were summoned to the CBS conference room. "Basically he dumped the deal in our laps" is how Westbrooks remembers the meeting.

The ultimate responsibility for making the deal work fell on Jim Tyrrell, the vice president of marketing for Epic Records and all custom labels. Tyrrell is a fascinating individual. A bass player active on the New York R&B scene in the 1950s and 1960s, Tyrrell had played sessions for James Brown, the Fiestas, Inez and Charlie Foxx, the Manhattans, and Maxine Brown, among others, and had spent two years in the Apollo Theatre house band before moving over to the business side of the industry in 1965. After stints at International Tape Cartridge and Buddah–Kama Sutra, Tyrrell came to CBS as a product manager in the merchandising department in 1970. When he was promoted to the position of vice president of marketing for Epic Records he was the first black executive at that level in CBS's history.

Tyrrell saw problems with the deal from day one. "It was clear," recalls Tyrrell, "that [Davis and Bell] each had a thought in mind. But it was also clear that each of the individuals' thoughts were never fully reconciled [with each other]. They didn't [actually] do the deal [although] they wanted to do the deal badly. Clive had the notion that Al was going to produce beautiful music and that the relationship would be not unlike as it was with the Gamble-Huff enterprises. Al, on the other hand, had megalomania."

Tyrrell went on to explain that, as he saw it, Bell wanted to build an empire his own way on his own terms and that, in Bell's mind, CBS was simply a conduit that Bell could use to get into the rack jobbers. This is not inconsistent with Al Bell's own comments. It was not, though, stressed Tyrrell, consistent with Clive Davis's concept.

"The visionaries who made the deal," stresses Tyrrell, "never thought it through. As the operations man, I had to make it work. I was in need of reconciliation. For weeks we worked back and forth with Al Bell to try to hammer out an operating plan, if not an operating deal, to find out that what Al was immediately interested in was a large placement of catalogue and that ain't possible."

At a major company like CBS, money is available for the marketing of records in two fashions. When a record is initially released there is a national kickoff promotion program. If the record becomes a hit, additional funds become available for the promotion and support of additional inventory placements. Secondarily there are what is known as distributor and co-op funds that, in essence, are incentive funds to get rack jobbers and/or distributors to take large quantities of product in exchange for advertising support.

"Al had a notion," explains Tyrrell, "that the co-op funds were available to him. I'm a real team player. CBS was my organization and I was not going to put the control of co-op funds, which we use to control our customers, in the hands of Al Bell, or even give him a notion that he could do such a thing. Al just put a full-court press on trying to get a hold of these co-op dollars. That was all that he wanted to know about because he wanted to use that as leverage to place catalogue orders. In other words rack jobbers, whom he knew we had good access to, should take great quantities [of Stax product] and this way, within three or four months, he would have a positive cash flow."

Tyrrell refused to do business in this manner. For his taste, it was too speculative. Forcing the product on the rack jobbers' floor doesn't mean that the product ultimately sells, and it exposes a record company to the possibility of massive returns. Tyrrell wanted net sales, and, from his perspective, Al Bell was simply too impatient. Further compounding the problem according to Tyrrell was that there was an inordinate amount of pre-CBS Stax product glutting the market that needed to be cleared out before it made sense for CBS to place a substantial quantity of new inventory in the racks.

Putting aside the possibility of larger motivations on CBS's part, the business and operations philosophies of Jim Tyrrell and Al Bell were simply too far apart to lead to anything but a fractious relationship. In many respects, it was a classic case of the ill fit between a major corporation's mode of operating and the shoot-from-the-hip way an independent label often works.

Not helping matters was a strategic telephone call placed by Johnny Baylor to Tyrrell. "Johnny calls me up," recounts Tyrrell, "and says, 'You better do whatever we say. You got to put out some goods because if you don't do it, you're gonna have to take a helicopter back and forth to work!' I said, 'Oh, okay.' But I was cool because I was born and raised in Harlem. I've got friends! I called my friends and said, 'I don't know who this guy is but I know some of his people.' I knew Dino and I knew Ted Storey before he went to jail the first time. I went through some folks that knew Ted and they told Ted to back off and Teddy told Johnny, which led to a phone call a month later with Johnny saying, 'Why didn't you tell me?' I said, 'You didn't ask!'"

Troubled days lay ahead.

Within a month of the consummation of the CBS distribution deal, Isaac Hayes was performing in Lake Tahoe, a concert that would be recorded for a double live set that both CBS and Stax were certain would generate large revenues for both corporations. For this performance, the Isaac Hayes Movement included its usual eight-piece rhythm section (nine counting Hayes), an expanded eight-piece horn section, and Hayes's regular four female background vocalists (Pat Lewis, Diane Lewis, Rose Williams, and Barbara McCoy, billed as Hot, Buttered Soul, Ltd.). As was by now his common practice, Isaac augmented the Movement by hiring local orchestral musicians who were now being conducted on the road by Onzie Horn, Sr.

Providing visual support in the form of interpretive dance were seven dancers headed by David Porter's niece, Helen Washington. Four years earlier, Washington had been doing time in the Tennessee State Prison for Women in Nashville for five counts of larceny. On hearing of Washington's plight from David Porter, Hayes wrote to the warden of the prison promising to do everything he could to help Washington if she was released. On that promise, Washington was given her walking papers after serving five years. After a short, frustrating period trying to find work, Washington was signed to an East Memphis songwriting contract and went on the road with Isaac. Little came of her songwriting efforts but, having shaved her head in emulation of Isaac, she provided an intriguing visual aspect to Hayes's performances. Washington became personally involved with Johnny Baylor and consequently signed a management contract with Baylor and an artist contract with KoKo Records, although no recordings by her were ever released.

Isaac was scheduled to perform two shows each night on November 25 and 26 at the Sahara Hotel in Lake Tahoe. On the twenty-first he provided color commentary for the Muhammad Ali–Bob Foster fight staged at the same hotel. Stax chose to record Isaac's

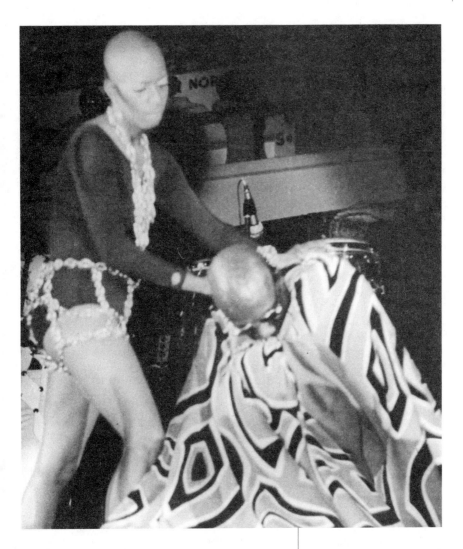

second night and captured a stunning performance. Included are classic Hayes reinterpretations of Jose Feliciano's version of "Light My Fire," Bacharach-David's "The Windows of the World" (which Isaac had

Helen Washington places a cape on Isaac Hayes's shoulders live in concert. COURTESY THE STAX HISTORICAL PRESERVATION COMMISSION.

recently performed in England on a Bacharach-David television special), Bill Withers's "Use Me" and "Ain't No Sunshine," Carole King's "It's Too Late," Roberta Flack's version of Ewan MacColl's "The First Time Ever I Saw Your Face," T-Bone Walker's "Stormy Monday Blues," and Traffic's "Feelin' Alright." Those tracks alone could have been recorded as a new Hayes studio album.

Augmenting this newer material in his repertoire were indelible treatments of three tracks from *Shaft*, plus Hayes's recent singles "Never Can Say Goodbye," "The Look of Love," "The Theme from the *Men*," and its flip side, "Type Thang," a new Hayes composition entitled "The Come On," and an extended treatment of the blues standard

"Rock Me Baby" that Isaac had included on his very first solo album, 1968's *Presenting Isaac Hayes.* When released in the spring of 1973, complete with liner notes by jazz critic Leonard Feather, *Live at the Sahara Tahoe* predictably shot to the number 1 position on *Billboard*'s Soul LP charts and number 14 on the Pop LP charts, selling just over 550,000 copies.

Four days after Isaac closed out at the Sahara, Johnny Baylor set a number of forces in motion that would have considerable consequences for Isaac Hayes and everyone else who was employed by Stax Records.

Of the $6 million CBS lent to Stax, at least $1 million was paid to Johnny Baylor.[13] From Al Bell's perspective, he was simply making good on his promise to compensate Baylor and the KoKo team for working Stax product in the marketplace over the past twelve months without charge. "We made the deal with CBS," claims Bell, "and I had to call Johnny—Johnny Baylor didn't know how much money I even owed him—and tell him how much money I owed him. He said, 'You owe me that much money?' I said, 'Yeah, that's what I owe you man.' 'Well Dick, let me come to Memphis and get my money!'"[14]

Be that as it may, the moneys paid to Johnny Baylor were not accounted for in any normal, straightforward manner, and very shortly would be of considerable interest to the IRS and Union Planters National Bank. According to testimony in the Stax bankruptcy trial given by the company's controller, Ed Pollack (who was granted immunity in exchange for his testimony), Al Bell instructed Pollack, beginning for the royalty period ending June 25, 1972, to pay Baylor's KoKo royalties on gross sales and not take into account returns of KoKo product or free goods! Bell also told Pollack to make the payments to Baylor personally rather than to KoKo, and to more than double the KoKo royalty rate. KoKo had previously been paid 11 cents on every 45 and 49 cents on every LP sold; now Baylor was being paid 26.22 cents per 45 and $1.85 per LP.[15] Baylor was to be paid retroactively under these terms for all KoKo shipments prior to this date, less royalties already paid. Pollack went on to say that no such agreement existed for anyone else at Stax, including Isaac Hayes.

Pollack also testified that he never saw a contract for Baylor. There wasn't one. Both Baylor and Al Bell testified that they had an oral agreement, although Stax lawyer Craig Benson stated—in a deposition read in the lawsuit brought against Baylor several years later by Stax trustee A. J. Calhoun—that Bell asked him in April 1973 to prepare a contract backdated to October 15, 1968, embodying these terms.

For the statements ending June 25, 1972, and December 31, 1972, under these new terms Stax owed Baylor/KoKo $688,917.21 and $881,968.74. Taken together, the royalties and promotional fees totaled $2,710,038.83, with promotional fees being a flat $1 million.[16] This is extraordinarily high compensation, given that Bell and Stewart were only

13. Between the execution of the CBS deal in October 1972 and August 1973, Baylor was paid over $2.6 million by Stax. How much of this came directly from the CBS loan and how much came from subsequent royalty payments by CBS to Stax is a matter of conjecture and, although a lot of time was spent arguing about this at Stax's bankruptcy trial, is ultimately a moot point.

14. For the record, only one KoKo 45 was ever distributed through CBS, Luther Ingram's "I'll Be Your Shelter (in Time of Storm)," which was already in the marketplace at the time the deal was struck. Baylor did not approve of the CBS deal, and consequently all KoKo product continued to go through the independent distribution network alongside Stax's Partee, Respect, and Gospel Truth lines. Due to Baylor's impending IRS difficulties, Koko basically ceased operation in the summer of 1973 for a three-year period. Luther Ingram's career never recovered from this hiatus.

15. To put this in perspective, Isaac Hayes was only being paid 12 cents per 45 and $1.00 per album sold!

16. Untangling the morass of Stax finances so many years after the fact via bits and pieces of information from a number of sources is fraught with difficulty. The figure cited above is derived from concrete knowledge I have

making $90,000 a year, and that the next highest-paid Stax executive was Ed Pollack, who was paid $39,536 in 1972. Not a penny of this was deducted as an ordinary and necessary business expense on Stax's 1972 income tax return.[17] In fact, Ed Pollack was told to write a letter instructing Stax's New York accounting firm, Weissbarth, Altman and Miller, not to file the Baylor payments as an income-tax deduction. After consulting with his attorney, Pollack refused to sign the letter. Weissbarth, Altman and Miller, also upon their lawyer's advice, gave the Stax account up in April 1973 when, after persistent inquiry, they could obtain only vague and evasive explanations regarding the moneys paid to Johnny Baylor.[18] The account was taken over by Laventhol, Krekstein, Horwath and Horwath.

These details came to light in the course of the Stax bankruptcy trial. Union Planters attorney Wynn Smith attempted to prove that most of the $2.6 million paid to Baylor for royalties and promotional work was actually money rightfully belonging to Stax. He believed Al Bell was laundering these funds through Baylor as part of a grand scheme in which Bell would let the company go bankrupt and defraud Union Planters and several other creditors out of moneys they were owed by Stax.[19] In 1974 testimony before a U.S. grand jury investigating Stax for possible tax fraud, Pollack stated that when he asked Al Bell why Johnny Baylor was being paid this amount of money in this fashion, "Bell replied, 'What's the price you put on a man's life?'" The IRS report, from which this quote is taken, goes on to say that Bell informed Pollack that Jim Stewart's life had been threatened by certain people who wanted to take over the company and that Baylor had been called in to prevent it. When I asked Al Bell about this in 1996, he simply said that Pollack's claim was not true.

The house of Stax began to come tumbling down in Birmingham, Alabama, on November 30, 1972, when Johnny Baylor was detained by the FBI after stepping off a plane arriv-

---

that Baylor was paid $500,000 November 30, 1972; $500,000 March 6, 1973; $1,000,000 April 10, 1973; $541,409.54 on July 24, 1973; and $168,629.29 on August 3, 1973. That said, I have also run across a statement in the files of Stax's New York accountant that suggests the total figure is $2,682,323. Ultimately the difference is not significant. Whatever the precise figure, these checks were variously charged as "loans to officers," royalties, and promotional fees.

17. Bell and Stewart wrote in a letter dated September 17, 1973, to their New York City accountants, Laventhol, Krekstein, Horwath & Horwath, "We have instructed you that the following expenses, which were paid or incurred during the year ended December 31, 1972, are not to be claimed as deductions on the tax returns for the year ended December 31, 1972 as prepared by you. (a.) Royalties and promotion fees paid to, or accrued in the name of J. Baylor and/or KoKo Records in the amount of $2,682,323. (b.) Royalties accrued in the name of Dino Woodard in the amount of $88,577." There is a virtually identical letter dated September 16, 1974, with the same instructions re: "(a.) Royalties and advances paid to, or accrued in the names of J. Baylor, D. Woodard, T. Storey, J. Thomas and/or KoKo Records in the amount of $494,028. (b.) Salary paid to T. Storey in the amount of $13,115." Just as curious as Stax's desire not to claim these payments as tax deductions was the fact that Baylor took no tax deductions, aside from attorney's fees, for any expenses incurred in his work: no expenses for traveling, for other employees, or for any other outlays. For the record, for the week ending November 26, 1972, both Dino Woodard and Ted Storey appear on Stax's payroll, Woodard pulling in a $50,000 per year salary, Storey earning $15,500 per year. This is the only time they show up on Stax's books. Controller Ed Pollack told the IRS that Woodard refused to take his checks. "I just felt that—boom—I'd rather have mine in a lump sum," states Woodard, adding cryptically, "We made some agreements."

18. Howard Comart of Weissbarth, Altman and Miller told a U.S. grand jury while testifying under immunity that Bell may have said with regard to the money paid Baylor that "He is worth a million dollars for what he has done."

19. In an affidavit filed in a later court case where Stax trustee A. J. Calhoun was suing Johnny Baylor over these funds, an investigator hired by Union Planters named Roger Shellebarger stated unequivocally with regard to Baylor's royalty payments, "There is nothing in the books, accounts and business records of Stax to justify the unreasonable royalty statements allegedly prepared by Stax for KoKo Records. To the contrary, such royalty payments are illogical, irrational, without fair consideration and without legitimate business purpose, and could not logically have been paid for their stated purpose. In short, these payments and the documents which reflect such payments are a mere sham and pretense for huge payments of Stax moneys to Johnny Baylor without adequate consideration or explanation." Shellebarger went on to make the same claim with regard to the $1 million Baylor was paid for his promotional services.

ing from Memphis. While going through security in Memphis it was discovered that Baylor had $130,000 in cash and a check from Stax for $500,000. This seemed suspicious, and Memphis authorities phoned ahead to the FBI in Birmingham. Three days earlier Al Bell had requested a check written out to himself for $150,000. He then asked Pollack and Dino Woodard (the latter for security purposes) to go to the Union Planters branch at 100 North Main where the loan officer in charge of the Stax account, Joseph Harwell, was based and cash the check in denominations of fifty- and one-hundred-dollar bills. This check was charged to a Stax account labeled "loan to officers," which, according to the IRS, was never paid back. Pollack testified in court that this was extremely unusual. Presumably this is where the cash originated that was being carried by Johnny Baylor on the Memphis–Birmingham flight. Baylor testified in court that he did not remember where all the cash had come from, that he had carried thousands of dollars with him from city to city since the beginning of 1972, and that he had just won $50,000 in three days betting on horse races. On the morning of November 30, Pollack cut a check for Baylor totaling $500,000. This check was originally charged to the Stax "loan to officers" account. It was subsequently charged as a royalty payment before being moved to a promotional fees account.

After the FBI interrogated Baylor, the Internal Revenue Service elected to seize the funds and, at that point, began to investigate Stax Records for possible income-tax fraud, interviewing Stax controller Ed Pollack on the very next day.[20] The IRS subsequently seized several further payments to Baylor totaling over $1,850,000, with one of the net results being that Luther Ingram's career was, in effect, put on ice for the next few years while Baylor fought the IRS. He initially won his fight, convincing the court that the money was legitimately his, and the IRS returned slightly over $600,000 to him (the rest of the money was kept as the income-tax liability on the money he received from Stax).[21]

Despite these problems with the IRS and the FBI, both Bell and Baylor were convinced that Baylor would get his money back and that nothing too serious would result from the investigations. In the meantime, the label had plenty to look forward to. Stax was getting ready to release the *Wattstax* film, two double albums of Wattstax material, and several Wattstax-related singles. The company had moved forcefully into the arenas of gospel, comedy, and country in the past year, and, with the signing of the Ardent deal, would hopefully make significant advances in the world of white rock. Now that Stax was aligned with a rock album powerhouse like CBS, the latter should only be a matter of time. Little did anyone at the company imagine that CBS would be engaging them in economic strangulation within a year-and-a-half, and that, following upon the Baylor airport incident, the IRS, through the U.S. Attorney's Office, would hound Stax until it was bankrupt.

Meanwhile, life for Stax and its artists continued as usual. Isaac Hayes busied himself with his usual Christmastime charity efforts, personally delivering groceries to needy families; and Al Bell basked in the fact that he was awarded a National Pacesetter Award by the U.S. Department of Commerce and the Office of Minority Business Enterprises. The Pacesetters Award honors the accomplishments of minority group members who have

20. In the spring of 1995 I requested under the Freedom of Information Act the FBI files on Johnny Baylor and Stax. On February 12, 1996, the FBI sent me a letter stating that it had "no record responsive to my request" with regard to Johnny Baylor. I immediately appealed this response, citing the IRS file number that I had uncovered in the court proceedings and the fact that the FBI had certainly interviewed Baylor in Birmingham on November 30, 1972. At the time this book was going to press I still had not received a response to my appeal.

21. On January 27, 1977, Baylor was subsequently sued by the receiver at Stax who argued, as had Union Planters in Stax's bankruptcy trial, that the money was fraudulently paid to Baylor as part of a scheme to launder money out of Stax Records. Baylor wasn't so lucky this time, and on October 25, 1978, he was forced to turn over the approximately $800,000 that he had left to what was now a defunct Stax.

established successful business enterprises. Bell was also included in *Ebony*'s list of the "100 Most Influential Blacks" in the United States. Although Stax sales were a little bit off the peak of 1971 (how many years does any record company get a *Shaft?*), the company still grossed $11,798,292.[22] The good ship Stax looked as healthy as ever and, with new albums and singles due from Isaac Hayes, the Staple Singers, and the Dramatics, the label appeared poised for a banner year in 1973.

22. This is the figure that was reported on Stax's 1972 corporate income tax return. Al Bell claimed in an undated speech (most likely 1975) labeled "Corporate Objective" that Stax had grossed $12,226,000 in 1972. The difference in the two figures is not that significant.

15

Rolling Down a Mountainside:
1973

As Stax employees came to work on January 2, 1973, the first task for the public relations department was the preparation of a press release for an exclusive feature in *The Hollywood Reporter*. Its opening paragraph read: "Following a landmark year of achievement for The Stax Organization, the company is entering 1973 anticipating the most significant strides in diversification, sales and community activity in the company's 12-year history."

Positively brimming with optimism, the release highlighted Stax's expansion into the areas of gospel, comedy, country, pop, the Broadway stage, and movies, as well as the recently executed distribution deal with CBS. It also mentioned the company's and Isaac Hayes's numerous philanthropic activities. In 1972 alone, in addition to Wattstax, Hayes and/or other Stax artists had played benefits for Al Bell's alma mater (Philander Smith College in Little Rock, Arkansas), the Memphis Police public relations department, the American Cancer Society, WDIA's annual Starlight and Goodwill Revues (the proceeds of which went to numerous black-focused Memphis charities), and Operation PUSH. Hayes had also donated his services and money to a musical presentation at Memphis State University entitled "An Evening of Soul" and played a free gig at the Overton Park Shell in Memphis, and a number of other Stax artists had played several free concerts at federal and state prisons. The Soul Children were particularly active in this regard, J. Blackfoot not forgetting his experiences in a Nashville prison so many years earlier.

As an organization, in 1972 Stax gave money to the Memphis chapter of the National Business League, the First Offender penal rehabilitation project, contributed the production facilities for the Miss Essence of Tennessee Pageant, and sponsored the third annual Jim Brown golf tournament, the proceeds of which were directed to the Black Economic Union. In June Stax borrowed $178,567 from Union Planters National Bank that it then loaned to a community project for the purpose of buying a church property on Jackson Avenue. Stax planned to retire the debt through a benefit show featuring a number of its artists. Hayes and Al Bell were also, of course, active through the Isaac Hayes Foundation in developing low-income housing projects.

Many more such events and programs were planned for 1973. Al Bell and other Stax executives and artists felt a tremendous responsibility to give back to the community that had supported them in the first place. It's easy to be cynical about such a stance, but many of those who were central to the Stax experience shared a deep-seated pride that their company was doing more than its fair share to make a difference. Isaac Hayes and Al Bell clearly saw themselves as relatively wealthy individuals who had an obligation to simultaneously provide leadership and give back to the community. If things had turned out differently at Stax, one could very well have imagined Bell going into politics.

For the black community in Memphis, Stax was a source of pride and inspiration. Many black Memphians—who were not employed by Stax—speak glowingly of the fact that this company was in their community. It was well known in Memphis that if you were part of a black organization and were canvassing for donations, advertising in a program, or in some other way trying to raise funds, Stax would more than likely support you.[1] Similarly, it was not uncommon for Stax to come to the aid of people in the community who had their utilities turned off or who were in some other desperate strait. Homer Banks and Isaac Hayes recall an incident in which the IRS was padlocking an Afro shop on Park. The black owner went berserk, pulled a gun, made the IRS agents undress in the street, and demanded to speak with Isaac Hayes. Within a few minutes, police had surrounded the area. A number of Stax personnel, including Hayes, went to the store and helped defuse what had been quickly turning into a very ugly situation.

"Black people were really proud of Stax," says Banks, "because Memphis had a heartbeat when Stax was happening. Black people saw something visual that was a real success right in their community. I don't think that most of the white community in Memphis really knew what they had, and if they did know, they really didn't care."

Central to this general feeling that Stax was part of the community was the fact that the McLemore Studios were housed in a residential neighborhood. Most recording studios and record-company offices are located in industrial areas or in downtown office spaces. Stax and Motown are two of the very few significant studios that were actually located in the midst of a community. Local schoolchildren passed Stax on the way to class and dreamed that one day they too could be a part of something as exciting and rewarding. Many adult black Memphians knew various Stax employees and recording artists as schoolmates and/or neighbors. They were extremely proud of local successes such as David Porter, Rufus Thomas, and Isaac Hayes.

The glowing prose encapsulated in that first press release of 1973 accurately reflected the general tenor at the company. At the time, Memphis was the fourth-largest recording center in the world, and the music industry was the third-largest commercial activity in Memphis, generating a dollar volume of some $185 million a year. After two unbelievably stunning years at Stax, the modus operandi for 1973 was onward and upward in multitudinous directions. After the hiring of a new sales manager, Richie Salvador, to replace Johnny Baylor, who was embroiled in his problems with the FBI and IRS,[2] the first major project of the new year for the company was the release of the *Wattstax* film.

Under the guidance of the award-winning director Mel Stuart, the *Wattstax* film remains one of the finest examples of social commentary involving music on celluloid. Stuart, with the aid of assistant director Larry Shaw,[3] shot substantial footage within the Watts community. This material was then cleverly intercut with a Richard Pryor monologue and the concert material itself, the combination dramatizing the reality of contemporary African-American life and the absolutely vital role that music plays within, and as a mirror of, the community.

1. From Earlie Biles's perspective, this was sometimes a problem. "Some took advantage of it," explains Biles. "It was like it's a black company so every black group in Memphis hit on Stax for a contribution. It was almost like, 'You have to give me something because you're a black company.' Stewart did a lot of it himself. It was like they'd put a guilt trip on you all the time."

2. Salvador first came to work on February 12, 1973. He remained a sales manager until January 1974 when he was promoted to the position of vice president in charge of marketing.

3. Shaw was paid $50,000 above and beyond his regular Stax salary for his work on the *Wattstax* film. He would soon head up Stax Films. Forest Hamilton was also paid a cool $50,000 for his work on the film.

"The concept was," Al Bell explains, "black music is a reflection of what goes on in the lives and lifestyles of the people. We were trying to cause that to happen in that film so you could listen to the song and then see visually what was going on. We brought in black [film] crews to make sure that we got on film images from a black perspective, from a black vantage point. We went into Watts and we took the concert itself, went into the community and did candid shots of activities going on in people's lives, and we staged some of the events, but what we did was we made some of the songs live. As you heard the artist sing, you recognized the role of that song in black lifestyle, in black lives and in black culture. . . . It then became, in one sense, a mirror for African-Americans to just look and see themselves and it became a piece that let the rest of the world know what was really happening. . . . We purposely kept that piece in with the guy who said, 'If I can't work and make it, I'm gonna steal and take it,' so that the message would be gotten across because that's what was going on in the lives and lifestyles of those kinds of people that were part of the African-American experience."

The film was jointly produced by the newly formed Stax Films and Wolper Pictures. For its production efforts, Wolper was entitled to recoup the first $400,000 from the net receipts of the film, and thereafter a percentage of net receipts. In addition to the financial details, the Wolper-Stax contract contained some interesting clauses. Wolper maintained "the right to make final decisions on all creative and business matters relating to the Picture"—with one major exception. Stax Films was given "the absolute right of prior approval of film or narration which is included in the Picture which relates to Black relationships and feelings; words or phrases having a special Black connotation; and, if the Picture has a narrator, approval of the narrator and the accuracy of the narration script as to the music contained in the Picture." While Larry Shaw and Al Bell were willing to partner with an established filmmaker such as David Wolper and to cede overall creative direction to someone more experienced than they were, they were not willing to risk the misrepresentation of anything to do with black culture and/or the black experience.

The Stax contract with the Watts Summer Festival gave the festival (and its related charities) 50 percent of all U.S. film profits and 50 percent of all net profits obtained through merchandising. In exchange, Stax maintained the rights to film and record the concerts at the next five Watts Summer Festivals. This latter right was never executed.[4] The Watts Summer Festival was also to get a share of the producer's royalties of the two Wattstax albums issued by Stax.

The marketing effort for the film and double-album sets was incredibly intense. Stax saw the *Wattstax* campaign as, to quote Larry Shaw, "the company's spearhead for the young white market of middle America." In each first-run city, theaters were chosen that were equally central for black and white youth. Album ads referred to the film and motion-picture advertising referred back to the album. Eighteen different radio spots were produced with radio buys being purchased on soul stations, FM underground outlets, and Top 40 radio, in that order of priority. Print advertising was unusually heavy in college newspapers, major metropolitan dailies, and black community publications. Billboards were purchased in top markets, and bus posters were paid for in several other cities. Fifty soul stations were given the four-hour edited tape of the entire concert first broadcast over XRPS-AM in Los Angeles on the Labor Day weekend. In advance of the official world premiere, the film was shown in New York, Chicago, Atlanta, and Los

4. On August 19, 1973, the Watts Summer Festival staged a similar concert. Featured artists included Bobby Womack, the Intruders, Billy Paul, Barbara Mason, Barry White and Love Unlimited, Edwin Starr, Azteca, El Chicano, Thelma Houston, the Infallibles, and Bloodstone. Stax was represented by the Soul Children, the Dramatics, and emcee Richard Pryor.

Angeles for some two hundred deejays and programmers in soul, FM underground, and Top 40 radio, many of whom were flown in to the private screening by Stax. The film was then screened for Welfare Mother organizations to spread the word that the film was given an "R" rating because of the inclusion of blunt language that was common parlance in inner-city America, rather than because of scenes of sex or violence. Subsequent publicity from Stax referred to the "R" rating as standing for "Real."

The world premiere of the *Wattstax* film, held at the Dorothy Chandler Theatre in Los Angeles on February 4, was a brilliant affair. Stax decided to make its Hollywood gala in the grand old lavish tradition, complete with klieg lights, stars, and television. "We spent a lot of money promoting our commercial called *Wattstax*," says Shaw, laughing. "It was a fabulous kind of old Hollywood trip for a black picture by the folks out of Watts. We kind of bent everything out of shape."[5]

The day after the Los Angeles premiere, spirits were somewhat dampened when MGM vice president Doug Netter informed Stax-Wolper Films that he would sue if they didn't remove Isaac Hayes's performance of "Theme from *Shaft*" from the film. The fine print in the Stax/MGM *Shaft* agreement forbade Hayes from performing the music from *Shaft* in any other motion picture for a set period of time. Consequently, Hayes was flown back from Europe where he was currently touring and was filmed on a Hollywood soundstage, which was simulated to look like Wattstax, performing a new song he was planning on releasing as a single, "Rolling Down the Mountainside."

"Rolling Down the Mountainside" was just one of several performances included in the movie and/or on the two double-album *Wattstax* sets that weren't in fact from the Wattstax concert. The Staple Singers' version of Muscle Shoals writer Philip Mitchell's "Oh La De Da" had actually been recorded in Muscle Shoals at the second Al Bell–produced session way back in the fall of 1970. In January 1973, Mavis put a new vocal on the track and Ardent engineer Terry Manning overdubbed audience sounds to simulate the Wattstax environment.

Engineer Dave Purple remembers "Oh La De Da" all too clearly. "The single came out and Al Bell called the disc recording room," he recalls. "I answered the phone and he says, 'I need one hundred disks on the new single.' This is on a Friday afternoon. 'Okay Al, I can probably get those for you by Tuesday or Wednesday.' He says, 'No, no. I need them tonight.' I said, 'You're shitting me.' They were going to have this Learjet come around, servicing all these different cities taking disc jockeys their own personal copy of ['Oh La De Da']. That's the way he was doing business at the time. So I came in on a Saturday and knocked them all out in a six-hour day. Then he flew them around in a Learjet from jockey to jockey. What an amazing waste of money!"

Like "Oh La De Da," Eddie Floyd's "Lay Your Loving On Me" was marketed as being recorded live at Wattstax. Eddie told me it was actually recorded at Montana Studios in Los Angeles four days after the Wattstax concert with a band assembled by arranger Dale Warren. The Floyd and Staples cuts both appeared as singles and on the first double album set, *Wattstax: The Living Word,* released on January 18, 1973. The Isaac Hayes cut was also issued as a single and included on the followup album, *The Living Word: Wattstax 2.* Over half of the latter album, including all of sides three and four, was not actually taken from the Wattstax event. According to Al Bell, this was done consciously to use the overall Wattstax phenomenon as a marketing tool for some of the company's artists who

5. Subsequent openings were held in Chicago at the Oriental Theatre on February 14, New York City on the 15th, Washington on the 23rd, Detroit on the 26th, Memphis March 3, and Atlanta on March 4, with Philadelphia to follow shortly thereafter. In each city the premiere was to be a benefit for a local black charity with a number of Stax stars on hand to publicize the event.

had not actually played the concert. This concept had limited success. While the first *Wattstax* album sold just over 225,000 copies, sales of *The Living Word: Wattstax 2* disappointingly stalled at the 37,000-unit mark.

A couple of tracks, such as Little Milton's "Walking the Back Streets and Crying" and the Emotions' "Peace Be Still," are included in the film but were clearly shot separately from the concert itself. The Emotions had performed "Peace Be Still" in a Los Angeles church in advance of the actual festival. For many viewers, the trio's performance was riveting, providing one of the absolute highlights of the film. However, its inclusion in the film, on the second soundtrack album and on 45 in the place of a secular performance by the group that might have been a hit was a mixed blessing for the group's career, according to group member Sheila Hutchinson. The Emotions were not attempting to build a gospel career; "Peace Be Still" was, at best, a secondary side trip to their goal to achieve mainstream R&B success. Being so deep within the gospel vein, "Peace Be Still" was all but ignored by secular radio, while most gospel deejays wouldn't touch it because it was performed by a well-known secular group! Despite its being a stunning performance, Sheila was probably right in her assessment that it was a poor career move.[6]

Wanda Hutchinson, who sings the ever-so-moving lead, recalls learning "Peace Be Still" as a child. "My father had a James Cleveland record that he used to play every Sunday that had that song on there. We used to sing it at all the family reunions that we would have in Terre Haute, Indiana, every August sixteenth. We would lead the whole family in the singing and they would join in on the chorus. All the grandmothers and aunts would always ask us to sing that. That song is amazing."

As the song builds to its astonishing climax, Sheila, Wanda, and Theresa Davis stretch further and further toward the stratosphere, singing higher than most human voices are able to reach. "That was very touching," agrees Sheila. "When we were the Hutchinson Sunbeams, that used to be what Dad would call our shtick. He'd say, 'If we didn't get 'em on all the rest, we'll do this and just put 'em to rest.' Things like that are part of the crux that we named the group on because we knew how to arouse emotions."

Over time the *Wattstax* film was very successful. On May 10 it was positioned as the opening feature at the prestigious Cannes Film Festival.[7] The Cannes showing was such a hit that Claude Nobs, the director of the Montreux Jazz Festival, requested *Wattstax* be shown at that year's Montreux festival on July 1.[8] Four days after the Montreux showing the film began its regular run of European movie houses. By November 24, 1973, it had grossed $1,300,300.62.[9]

Al Bell was especially proud of the fact that when *Wattstax* opened in Lagos, Nigeria, in September, the demand to see the film was so large that the admission price was increased. For some time now he had been wanting to further put into practice his pan-African philosophy. Stax was well established in Jamaica. He now wanted to move into Brazil and parts of Africa. To that end, he had applied for trademark copyrights in several

---

6. The group was also upset because they were bumped from the actual Wattstax event as the show was too far behind schedule. They had also filmed a club scene at the Summit prior to the Wattstax concert, and had hoped a segment of that would be used in the film; to their disappointment "Peace Be Still" was the only footage of theirs that was shown.

7. It was also the only black feature at that year's film festival.

8. Also appearing at Montreux were Stax artists Little Milton, Albert King, and Chico Hamilton. In September 1974, Stax released a live album that combined the Montreux performances by all three artists.

9. According to documents located within the Stax files, black films at the time grossed 90 percent of their revenues from first-run sales. The document went on to state that 80 percent of the black market was located in only twenty cities.

African countries, including Uganda, Tanzania, Lesotho, Kenya, Ghana, Malawi, and South Africa, and had arranged for licensing agreements for Stax product in Ghana and South Africa. Stax's European licensee, Polydor, was already marketing Stax recordings in a number of African countries including Algeria, Angola, Burundi, the Cape Verde Islands, Dahomey, Egypt, Ethiopia, and French Somalia.

John KaSandra (*with bow tie*), Jesse Jackson (*with PUSH button*), Jesse Jackson's bodyguard, Larry Shaw (*with headset*), and unidentified person at Wattstax on August 20, 1972. COURTESY FANTASY, INC.

Although *Wattstax* proved profitable, according to Larry Shaw, Stax's entry into the world of motion pictures was not an easy ride. "We knew that the film world was against us," stresses Shaw, "and we were just going to make a place for ourselves in it. We were just going to push it on through. We had more money than most of the other pushers. You see, we were very culturally loyal. We pursued the freedoms that the constitution provided, that the Bill of Rights says we are supposed to have. We were sort of brass about it because we could afford it, which has just not been true of many black situations. That's one of the saddest parts of the demise [of Stax] is that we used it as a lever for the entire race. It was very interesting how naughty we must have appeared and dangerous."

"We were a company," adds Al Bell, "that was perceived by and large in the industry as a black company. Unknowingly, we had moved into a fraternity that is closed even more than the phonograph industry, which is the motion-picture industry. [We] financed our own motion pictures and didn't have to get permission, and it was turning into a success. It became evident to me that some people got a little nervous about that because, 'What's next?'

"I had been told that some elements in the power structure had problems when a black man could go into Los Angeles, California, where they're so competitive—entertainment capital of the world—and go into the Los Angeles Coliseum and put 112,000 [people] in there and do it himself. That's too much power. I've been told that I was getting above myself. 'Who do you think you are to have that much audacity? It's all right to do the stuff you [have been] doing but this is not your place.'" Undeterred, Bell and Shaw continued to try to develop Stax Films but, unfortunately, in light of Stax's upcoming economic problems, Shaw was unable to get much more accomplished.

In 1974, Bettye Crutcher, Mack Rice, and Dale Warren were commissioned to write the soundtrack for *The Klansman,* a second-rate melodrama starring Lee Marvin, Richard Burton, Lola Falana, and O. J. Simpson. "I just couldn't stand the movie," says Crutcher. "It was horrid to me. That was one of the things you do for the money. You say, 'Hey, this is an opportunity to make money and that's what I'm in business for,' and so you do it. But when I saw the movie, it was so gross to me that I was really wiped out." According to Crutcher, the deal for the soundtrack was worked out through Forest Hamilton. *The Klansman* was produced by MGM and, as part of the deal, MGM also got the soundtrack rights.[10]

A year later the Newcomers, the Mad Lads, and the Dramatics appeared in another racially tinged but trashy movie with the unpromising title *Darktown Strutter's Ball.*[11] Larry Shaw sums the film up succinctly when he says, "We tried to run away from it after we saw the results. The script, in my perception, was one thing. The perception of the director and the producer was totally different. We had Forest Hamilton covering it, monitoring the success of it. He called up and said, 'This film is crazy. It ain't going nowhere we thought it was going.' So, we dashed out there and tried to find out where it was at. Of course, it was going into very white folks comedy—slapstick, pies in the face, weird Batman sounds, horrible—we don't laugh at that stuff. It was what we call contrivance. We couldn't stand it.

"I tried to get Richard Pryor again, to put him into this picture to salvage it, to kind of thread through it. I remember we had a screening for him. At the screening we're all watching the picture and all of a sudden I didn't see [Richard Pryor's] head anymore. He was on the floor crawling out the door. I dashed out and said, 'What're you doing?' He said, 'Please Shaw, I know I owe you a few favors but don't ask me to do this, Shaw.' So we couldn't save it."

Directed by William Witney and starring Trina Parks, *Darktown Strutter's Ball* was produced by Stax-Netter Films. Doug Netter was a freelance producer who formerly, as a vice president at MGM, had threatened to sue Stax over the use of "Theme from *Shaft*" in the *Wattstax* film. From Shaw's vantage point, Netter was someone who already understood the film world and knew how to make deals in Hollywood. Netter tried to help out with *Darktown Strutter's Ball* but, according to Shaw, "there [simply] was no help for it."

Many Stax employees thought that the company's move into film was largely motivated by Motown's recent success with *Lady Sings the Blues.* Don Davis believes, "Al Bell was out to emulate Berry Gordy. If Berry Gordy can make movies, then Stax should be able to do this too. We spent a lot of money at Stax Records making movies that we weren't

10. For its inital video release, *The Klansman* was retitled *The Burning Cross.* As of spring 1997 it had been reissued on video under its original title. The only Stax vocalists who appear in the film's soundtrack are the Staple Sisters, who perform the Crutcher-Rice authored "The Good Christian People," unavailable anywhere else.

11. *Darktown Strutter's Ball* was retitled *Get Down and Boogie* sometime in the early 1980s. Despite several years of searching for this the author has never been able to view this film. Anyone reading this who has a copy can contact the author at the address included in the Preface.

prepared to make, in my opinion. I think that that was the real downfall of Stax, in the sense that it was pouring money into areas that it had no expertise in. And, it was pouring money into [an] area that had a lot of con men in it, that it was very easy to waste a lot of dollars in. It did that to the point that it eventually got to where it couldn't pay the bills."

Films were not the only area that Bell was looking to expand into. The January 4 press release boasted that "The Stax Organization is moving heavily into the television musical variety field." The initial effort was developed in partnership with Merv Griffin Productions. On December 12, 1972, the first of a planned six sixty-minute shows, *Isaac Hayes and the Stax Organization Presenting the Memphis Sound,* was taped at Caesars Palace in Las Vegas in front of an audience of two thousand. When the program aired in April 1973, American television audiences were treated to performances by Hayes himself, the Emotions, Albert King, Johnnie Taylor, Carla Thomas, Luther Ingram, and the Staple Singers. Isaac, seated at the piano, provided the narration that linked the appearances by each artist. Stax also announced plans for a soundtrack album based on the program. Shortly after the taping Murray Schwartz, the president of Merv Griffin Productions, was quoted in *Billboard* as saying that the relationship between Stax and Griffin Productions was so good that they were considering doing a film together starring Leslie Uggams, whom Griffin represented. Unfortunately, no more TV shows were taped, a soundtrack album was never released, and the film project was never developed.[12] Talk of a series of hour-long radio specials featuring Stax artists was discussed in this same time period but these, as well, never came to fruition.

Meanwhile, the label's primary business of releasing records continued. In February, the Dramatics offered their take on another Tony Hestor gem. "Hey You! Get Off My Mountain" ably sustained the group's hit streak, breaking the R&B Top 10 and the pop Top 50. Hestor envisioned Ron Banks taking a good part of the lead on this song. Up to this point, William "Wee Jee" Howard had been singing virtually all of the group's leads, and was more than a trifle nonplussed by Hestor's new game plan. Eventually cooler heads prevailed and Howard came onboard.

"It was perfect," stresses Banks. "I was the setup man. After Wee Jee opened the song up, I did the soft 'Bring me down' section and the sensual parts for the verses, and Wee Jee'd come in pumping the thing [on the chorus]. Then it became a little battle when we both sang together."

Hestor's masterful arrangement represented all that was fine about sweet soul music in the early seventies. Along with the Soul Children's "It Ain't Always What You Do (It's Who You Let See You Do It)" and the Staple Singers' "Oh La De Da," it gave both CBS and Stax much to be happy with in the first few months of their new distribution agreement. After a minor hit by William Bell, "Lovin' On Borrowed Time," in May the two companies released three more certified hits, Johnnie Taylor's "I Believe in You (You Believe in Me)," newcomer Veda Brown's "Short Stopping," and the Staple Singers' "Be What You Are."

According to Don Davis, CBS was totally unprepared for the success of "I Believe in You." A number 1 R&B and number 11 pop hit, the single sold in excess of one million units. "They just didn't believe that black artists could sell that many copies," relates a still exasperated Davis.

In what was a typical modus operandi for Davis, the track for "I Believe in You" had been cut in Muscle Shoals three years earlier under the working title "Tomorrow." The

---

12. For years I have tried to find a copy of this program and have been unsuccessful. If anyone reading this has a copy, I would be very grateful to hear from you (see the address cited in the Preface).

song was based around a chord structure that Davis had employed in 1960 for a release also titled "Tomorrow" by Emanuel Lasky on the Detroit independent label Thelma. It was one of Davis's favorite songs, but when it was initially released, it did absolutely nothing. So Davis decided to recycle it.

"I Believe in You (You Believe in Me)" was the first record on which Don Davis constructed the track via layered riffs instead of functional chord changes. Davis referred to this as the "monolithic approach." The net result was a more melodic, Sam Cooke–influenced Johnnie Taylor. The song was recorded and mixed with Dolby but, when it came to mastering it, Larry Nix left the Dolby off. This is extremely unorthodox, but to Nix's ear it brightened up the high end and he didn't feel that the added hiss was that consequential given the quality of the pressings. Van Morrison fans will notice that the introduction is nearly identical to that used on Morrison's "Warm Love," released the same year. Because the rhythm track for "I Believe in You" was cut three years earlier, either Morrison copied the Johnnie Taylor record or this is one heck of an interesting coincidence!

With CBS ordering large numbers of LPs and paying promptly sixty days after the receipt of product, Stax was rolling in cash. On March 21, 1973, Stax retired the $1,755,000 debt it owed to Union Planters at the time of the CBS distribution deal. On May 14, 1973, Lynn and Associates made the final payment on the $888,725 the Stax subsidiary had borrowed at the end of 1972. An expansion-hungry Union Planters was, not surprisingly, anxious to do more business with a company able to generate cash as readily as Stax appeared to be. Consequently, in early April, Union Planters approved a $3 million line of credit for Stax's publishing subsidiary East Memphis Music. On April 10 Stax borrowed $1.5 million[13] on this line of credit to supposedly open up a series of retail outlets.[14] Not so coincidentally, on the same day this money was borrowed, a check was made out to Johnny Baylor for $1 million. Stax was never able to pay a penny of this debt off. This and all subsequent Union Planters loans would be made to East Memphis Music and/or Lynn and Associates because all of Stax's assets were encumbered in the $6 million loan from CBS. To secure the $3 million line of credit, Stax gave the bank a collateral pledge agreement that assigned to the bank one hundred shares of common stock of both East Memphis and Birdees Music. Bell and Stewart would regret this when, in the fall of 1974, Union Planters used this stock to take over the day-to-day operation of the two Stax publishing companies.

Meanwhile, CBS was facing problems of its own. In April 1973, following questions raised by the U.S. Attorney's Office in Newark, New Jersey, CBS initiated an internal audit. Both CBS and the U.S. Attorney were particularly concerned with the activities of Clive Davis's righthand man, David Wynshaw. The federal prosecutors in Newark were interested in a range of issues, foremost among them being payola and the consequent ties between the music industry and organized crime. Wynshaw was found to have set up a number of companies in partnership with Patsy Falcone, whom Fredric Dannen describes, in his excellent book Hitman, as "an associate of the Genovese family" crime syndicate. It turns out that Wynshaw and Falcone's "companies" defrauded CBS of tens of thousands of dollars. Davis was asked to fire Wynshaw in April, and eventually Wynshaw faced criminal charges, being sentenced to a year in jail for conspiring with Patsy Falcone to defraud CBS.

---

13. I have found various documentation that suggests that this figure is $1.6 million, but according to a Union Planters schedule of loans to Stax and its related affiliates the figure should be $1.5 million.

14. It would appear that the retail outlet activity, Record World in Chicago, did not actually commence until early 1974.

In addition to this untidy mess, CBS was in a near panic over rumors that a federal grand jury probe, operating under the moniker "Project Sound," suspected that the giant corporation might have been involved in payola with a number of black radio stations. If this proved to be true, CBS's valuable television and radio licenses could be in jeopardy. Leaving no stone unturned, while cleaning out Wynshaw's office, CBS uncovered papers that led them to conclude that Clive Davis had also engaged in unscrupulous activities. On May 29, CBS shocked the music industry by terminating Davis. Wasting no time, company security immediately and unceremoniously escorted Davis first to his office to pick up his personal effects and then out of the building. That same day, Davis was served with a civil complaint alleging $94,000 worth of expense-account violations over the six years that he had been president. On June 24, 1975, Clive Davis was indicted by a grand jury for six counts of tax evasion based on these same expense-account violations. He pleaded guilty to one count and was fined $10,000 in September 1976. Fourteen months later, he privately settled the civil case with CBS.

These events, so far from Memphis, Tennessee, would prove to have dire ramifications for Stax Records. Al Bell had always had reservations about CBS as a corporation. His respect for Clive Davis's "sensitivity" had been the only reason he was willing to do business with such a monolith in the first place.

The Stax/CBS distribution deal was novel in its day. According to Bell, no one but he and Clive Davis truly understood it. Davis and Bell's understanding was that Stax would not be distributed *by* CBS; rather, Stax's product would be distributed *through* CBS's branches. This is an important distinction. The CBS distribution machine would be used by Stax to reach the coveted rack jobbers, but CBS sales and marketing brass, from Bell's perspective possessing little or no knowledge of Stax's product, would not determine marketing, sales, or promotional strategy. Instead, Stax's own people would continue to fulfill these functions, obviously in as close communication as possible with CBS personnel. Stax would also continue to be responsible for all its manufacturing.

"When the deal was made," John Smith explained to Logan Westbrooks, "there . . . [were] a lot of meetings between CBS and Stax, in Memphis. We felt that it was super important to have the meetings in Memphis, where they'd have the opportunity to see our offices. Part of our strategy was to drive home the one key point that we were not a production company; we were a full-service record company, with an advertising department, a publicity department, and so forth. We were highly departmentalized. We didn't just have an A&R department and a promotion department. We did other things.

"We had enjoyed a lot of success and we weren't about to have a company like CBS come down to Memphis and tell us they were the experts in Black music. By our past successes, we felt that we had demonstrated that we were the experts. CBS was trying to get into [black music], but we were already there. They had to respect us, if this deal was going to work."

Despite many meetings, in the seven months that the deal had been in effect prior to Clive Davis's dethronement, an efficient interface between the two companies had yet to be established. No one at Stax, though, had felt any cause for undue alarm. According to Al Bell, Davis had suggested that Stax product initially be sold through the Epic Custom Division for an interim period of orientation. He assumed that over time most, if not all, of the bugs would be worked out. When Davis was fired, Stax's product had not yet been moved out of the Custom Division and put directly through the branches. With Davis's understanding of the deal a moot point after his termination, Stax would remain mired in the Custom Division for as long as CBS continued to distribute its product. According to CBS's Jim Tyrrell, either Al Bell misunderstood Clive Davis or Davis communicated very poorly, because there was no other place in the CBS structure for a distributed label but the Custom Division. Tyrrell also stresses that product was not treated differently in this division, and, to support this, points out that such ultrasuccessful labels as Philadelphia International and T-Neck were also marketed through the Custom Division.

At the time of his dismissal, Clive Davis had been wearing two hats: he was both president of Columbia Records and the head of the CBS group, including Columbia, Epic, and all other labels marketed and distributed by CBS. After Davis was gone, former CBS television executive Irwin Segelstein was brought in to head up the CBS Record Division, while Goddard Lieberson became president of CBS Records Group. According to Al Bell, neither Segelstein, Lieberson, or any of their underlings understood the nuances of the Stax agreement or cared about them. As far as they were concerned, Davis had made a bad deal.

Stax was being paid $2.26 per every $5.98 list LP that was shipped to CBS. In return for "distributing this product *through* their branches," CBS would make in the neighborhood of a 15 percent profit. This was pretty close to the exact opposite of the Atlantic-Stax distribution agreement in the 1960s. In that deal, for LPs Stax had been paid a mere 10 percent royalty, with Atlantic keeping the majority of the money from each sale. The crucial difference was that the Stax/Atlantic arrangement was for what is known as a P&D, production and distribution, deal. Stax was recording the music, but Atlantic was paying all manufacturing as well as most marketing and promotion costs. In the case of the CBS deal, Stax was maintaining responsibility for all of these areas. All CBS was supposed to be doing was *distributing* the product. To put this in perspective, before going with CBS, Stax was selling these same LPs to its network of independent distributors for approximately $2.40 per LP. As Al Bell explains it, Stax was actually taking a slight cut in income per sale in exchange for CBS taking them into the rack jobbers. Theoretically this tradeoff would net substantial increases in sales, and therefore Stax would ultimately profit from the deal.[15]

After assuming Davis's position as head of CBS Records, Segelstein brought in a consultant from Ford to analyze the current situation of the record division. According to Al Bell, one of the first things this expert said was, "he'd never seen anything like [the Stax/CBS deal]. A corporation like CBS doesn't make a deal like that with a corporation like Stax Records! They had a problem with the economics of that deal." To the new brass at CBS, Davis should never have agreed to any of it. If any deal was to be worked out with a company like Stax it should have been a straight P&D deal for a minimal royalty. This difference in business philosophy and consequent understanding of the agreement that Clive Davis and Al Bell had so optimistically worked out would, within a year, bring the once mighty Stax to its knees, and in just over two-and-a-half years force the company into bankruptcy.

John Smith told Logan Westbrooks, "When Clive Davis left CBS, the relationship changed instantly, *that day*. . . . So then, we at Stax developed certain fears about what was going on because the deal really had been made . . . based on the integrity of the man. . . . The spirit of the deal, and the initial working relationship came as a blessing from the top. If Clive Davis says, 'We're going to get behind the deal and support it,' it's going to filter down to his subordinates.

"When Clive Davis left, Goddard Lieberson took over. He was less into the music, I think, than Clive Davis. He was more corporate-oriented, so the relationship changed.

---

15. To further put this in perspective, on a P&D deal CBS typically took 25 percent of the wholesale price as a distribution fee, less manufacturing costs of both the vinyl album and its jackets. Manufacturing costs would be about a dollar, leaving the distributed label with about $1.20 per album sold.

With that, you're dealing with a Black entity in Memphis, Tennessee that was everything but corporate. Stax was very personalized, a family kind of operation. Any relationships that were entered into were based on more things than a person's talent or ability. it was 60 to 70 percent ability, and 30 to 40 percent vibes."

CBS immediately tried to change the agreement to a standard production and distribution deal, but Bell wasn't interested. "I wouldn't do it," says Bell, "and that gave them a problem." In due time, CBS would make it Stax's problem. "After I didn't yield to putting together some sort of P&D type deal," continues Bell, "was when I think we began to have our problems and I think that's when somebody made up their minds that they were going to deep-six [Stax] and put it under."

A further problem besetting Stax was the continuing deterioration of Al Bell's and Don Davis's relationship. Significantly, Davis had not attended Wattstax. For some time, he had felt that Al Bell was shutting him out, basically cutting off all communication. Separately, both Bell and John Smith sent telegrams to Davis in the fall of 1972 requesting the return of Stax masters. On November 6, 1972, Davis wrote a letter to Bell in response to these telegrams. In the course of the letter he stated, "Unsuccessfully, I have tried to reach you as well as John Smith concerning the return of Stax's masters" and "Since our communications are so stagnant, I would like to point out. . . ." The letter went on to query Bell as to discrepancies in the reasons given in the two telegrams with regard to the return of the masters, Davis finally asking "What's the deal?" Davis pointed out that he was presently working on new albums by Johnnie Taylor and the Dramatics as well as singles by Little Milton and Harvey Scales. He obviously couldn't complete his work without retaining possession of the relevant masters.

Reading between the lines, it seems obvious that Bell no longer trusted Davis, and was trying to get back all Stax possessions that Davis might be holding. Fed up with the Stax situation, Davis had begun to find a number of alternative avenues for his productions, producing Bobby "Blue" Bland for Duke-Peacock and then the Dells for Cadet, with whom in early 1973 he enjoyed a Top 5 hit, "Give Your Baby a Standing Ovation." When his production contract expired with Stax on May 15, 1973, he was preparing to take the Dramatics to ABC.

"Al and I had a parting of the ways," reflects Davis a little ruefully. "We had enjoyed a very, very close relationship. There was a very serious fallout with Al Bell and myself which was never verbally expressed. He just sort of disappeared and made himself unavailable. I very painfully got the message. I had not talked to him for about two months. Finally, when I did track him down he told me that he had gotten some information that I was trying to sabotage him or something like that, which was totally untrue. He never said 'end the contract,' but, for me, one of the main reasons why I was down there was because of Al. I enjoyed the relationship more than I enjoyed anything else. When he had no reason to relate to me as we used to relate, then I had no reason to be there.

"I saw the company not being what it used to be and [myself] not being able to play the part I used to play. I had grown and prospered and had other deals that were out there waiting on me. It was like, if it ain't what it used to be, why not go somewhere else. But, my main thing was Al's not wanting to relate for whatever reasons. [That] was the straw that broke the camel's back that made me say, 'Well, get on out of here.'"

In May, when Davis's production contract expired with Stax, he had yet to deliver the Dramatics' second LP, *The Devil Is Dope*. On June 20, 1973, Stax sent a certified letter to Davis demanding repayment of $128,320.51 that they claimed he was overadvanced (above and beyond session costs). When Davis did not respond, Stax sued on July 27, demanding delivery of the masters for *The Devil Is Dope* LP. In addition to the overadvanced funds, the suit claimed Davis had spent $80,000 of Stax's money on the Dramatics' disc and that Davis had "attempted to extort the payment of hundreds of thousands of dollars of additional funds."

The dispute was settled out of court four days later. Davis agreed to finish and turn over the masters for the Dramatics album (which would be retitled *A Dramatic Experience*) as well as several other masters he had in his possession. He further agreed to continue to produce Johnnie Taylor, gave up his half-interest in a number of recordings that he had done earlier for Stax, and agreed to reduce his production royalty from 3 percent of 90 percent of retail price to 2 percent of 90 percent.[16] On its part, Stax *paid* Davis $75,000 in cash and agreed in writing that he was not indebted to the company, and that he could sell the Dramatics contract elsewhere four months hence, although Stax was to be given a chance to negotiate a contract with Davis for the group.[17]

Meanwhile, Stax's problems with its McLemore facility and its employees continued. On June 19, a company memo signed by Jim Stewart and addressed to "All Employees" read, "The use of, carrying, or concealing of any narcotic drug classified as unlawful, including marijuana, by any employee while on company property or on company business, will be grounds for immediate termination. It is our firm decision to deal immediately with any employee so thoughtless as to endanger this firm and every employee's position by carrying or using drugs on company premises or while on company business."[18]

On June 20, John Burton circulated a memo very similar to Stewart's missive on drugs concerning the carrying of weapons on site or while on company business. Unless an employee was properly licensed by a duly constituted law-enforcement agency, this would be grounds for immediate termination. It concluded by stating that "The above policy will be rigidly enforced."

On June 21, Burton wrote yet another memo, this one concerning access to the McLemore studio complex. Two pages in length, the gist of this memo was that no visitors of any sort (including girlfriends) were to be allowed in McLemore unless on official business. Studio tours and unsolicited auditions (two of the various ways Stax had historically made itself part of the community) were forbidden. The memo outlined detailed procedures under which visitors on official business were to be escorted into and out of the building. So much for the laissez-faire, easygoing Stax of the mid-1960s. This was, by necessity, a different time and a different place.

It all seemed so strange to Duck Dunn and Al Jackson who, at the moment this flurry of memorandums was being circulated, were working on an album by a new version of the MG's. Duck Dunn and Stax session guitarist Bobby Manuel had attempted to create a band to play behind a blue-eyed soul artist named Stefan Anderson, whom Stax had recently signed. They called in Tim Whitsett's brother, Carson Whitsett, to play keyboards; Whitsett had some time earlier been writing songs with Stefan. Several rehearsals

---

16. For several decades, it had been standard practice in the record industry to pay royalties based on 90 percent rather than 100 percent of the records sold. This was supposedly to compensate the record company for breakage and defects. While this probably made sense in the days of the highly breakable, shellac 78-rpm record, it made little or no sense with the vinyl LP. Yet, virtually every record company through the 1970s continued to include this provision in their contracts. Many record companies to this day routinely include this in their contracts.

17. In early 1974, Davis took the Dramatics to Chess for a joint album with the Dells, and by the end of 1974 he had signed them to ABC, where they enjoyed a number of R&B hits, including such monster records as "Me and Mrs. Jones," "Be My Girl," and "Shake It Well," through the first part of 1981.

18. That same day Stax's new chief operating officer, John Burton, circulated a memo stating that any inquiries concerning the Stax Organization in connection to the IRS audit should be referred to Deanie Parker or, in her absence, to him.

were held at Duck Dunn's house with a drummer who just wasn't working out. It was decided that Al Jackson would do a better job but, not too soon after, Stefan began to peter out. Neither version of the ensemble actually ever played a gig with the singer.

Carson Whitsett picks up the tale. "We started looking for some other projects that we could get involved in and Al and Duck decided why don't we just start with the MG's and try to get the group back together. I was thrilled to death about it. I couldn't believe it. I actually couldn't believe that I was going to be doing that 'cause I was in such awe of these guys." For much of the previous decade, Carson had played with his brother Tim in a legendary Jackson, Mississippi band they called Tim Whitsett and the Imperials. Each new Booker T. and the MG record became an instant part of their repertoire. Carson states emphatically, "They were our heroes!"

"I learned more about music in that one year—recording, dynamics, expression, everything. Al Jackson taught me more than anybody ever thought about their concept of cutting hit records. Basically, what they were always after was a danceable rhythm. Al envisioned dancers while they played. His style sort of made you feel like you were floating when you were playing with him because it was so free. He would do a roll or a turn right in the middle of a phrase and you'd think he was not gonna come out of this but, bam, [he would be] right on it and you were set to go into the next section of the song. He taught me a lot about simplicity. It wasn't what you played, it was what you didn't play that counted."

When Carson agreed to participate in a new version of the MG's, he had imagined that he wasn't going to have to imitate Booker. He had hoped Al and Duck would want to go in a different direction, but this was not the case. "It seems as though Al and Duck just wanted to take over [from where they had left off] and keep everything the same," laments Carson.

The group cut one album, simply entitled *The MG's,*[19] and two singles. The top side of the debut 45, David Madden's "Sugarcane," was a song that Al Jackson had heard when he was in Jamaica with Al Bell and Eddie Floyd. With its gently swaying melody, the track was very much right up the old MG's alley. The new group cut a creditable version of the song, but radio support was lacking, leading the record to peter out at number 67. This version of the MG's had not long to live, and never actually played a live gig.

In May 1974, the MG's released their second and last single, a non-LP original that they called, in a move that signaled a return to the earlier group's penchant for food titles, "Neckbone." While Al Jackson and Duck Dunn were still intent on continuing the legacy they had established with Booker T. and the MG's, Carson Whitsett and Bobby Manuel were chomping at the bit to move forward into uncharted territory. "Neckbone" was somewhat of a compromise. The introduction is a bit of left-of-center weirdness, but once the song proper kicks in, it returns to standard MG instrumental fare. This was the group's final release. Al Jackson was busy working sessions at Hi Records, and when Stax further tightened its belt, Carson Whitsett was taken off the payroll, sealing the instrumental group's fate.

For five days in late July, the McLemore complex was taken over by Elvis Presley and the Memphis Mafia. The reaction from Stax personnel ranged from awe to disgust and resentment. Presley, as was par for the course, kept his distance, with various members of his entourage calling the shots. As was their custom, they carried themselves as if they owned the place, bending a few noses out of shape in the process. Prior to the first

---

19. Jackson and Dunn were paid a $25,000 bonus each for the LP. A Stax interoffice memo directing this payment stressed that Manuel and Whitsett were not to know about this.

evening, they came through the studio outlining a variety of changes that needed to be made. Jim Stewart followed along, taking notes, and repeatedly saying "No problem." Stewart's desire to let Elvis use the Stax studio at any cost also meant that he asked Isaac Hayes to relinquish studio time that he already had booked. This certainly did not sit well with a number of observers. Making matters worse was Marty Lacker, one of Presley's Memphis Mafia, who constantly kept asking Isaac how soon he would be finishing up.

"The vibe didn't work," says Bobby Manuel. "It was like, 'Who is this guy? So what!' coming in with all this mess and all these clowns around him. It just really wasn't taken well. It wasn't in the spirit that we thought it was gonna be. There was no cooperation."

Stewart was then informed that no Stax personnel were allowed to be in the building while Elvis was cutting, except those absolutely necessary for the sessions. For the first three nights, that basically meant a receptionist and Larry Nix.[20] Nix's presence was necessary because Elvis refused to listen to tapes; instead, Nix had to transfer every song demo that Elvis was contemplating recording, and every completed take that Elvis made, from tape to disc before Elvis would listen to it.

"He would not listen to a tape," says Nix, shaking his head. "I would have to take the demo, transfer it to a disc, carry it in [to Jim Stewart's old office], and they'd put it on a record player, when he could have put a tape on! It was real strange."

Because no "outsiders" were allowed at the sessions, Elvis used his own engineer, Al Pachucki, rather than one of the Stax veterans who was familiar with the room and the equipment. Given his unfamiliarity with the room, Pachucki elected to record everything flat with no EQ, achieving what, to the Stax session musicians, was a rather poor sound.

Elvis recorded on five consecutive nights from July 21 through July 25. For the first three nights, he used a band that was largely comprised of Chips Moman's famous American Sound Studios musicians—Tommy Cogbill, Bobby Woods, Bobby Emmons, and Reggie Young—augmented by Elvis's regular guitarist, James Burton. For the fourth and fifth nights, Stax stalwarts Bobby Manuel, Duck Dunn, and Al Jackson were scheduled to accompany Presley.

Manuel and Dunn were, to say the least, very excited. Elvis had been a big inspiration for both of them as kids. "The reason we were called," recounts Manuel, "we were gonna do Otis songs or we were gonna do some Stax-styled stuff. He was gonna sing some of that. That would have been real killer to get him back to something really natural, to get some raw thing going again, but then they laid out these goofy pop songs. It was just ridiculous. I didn't know what to play. I had no idea what they were looking for. It was just really a strange thing."

Ultimately what they wanted was for Dunn, Jackson, Manuel, and rhythm guitarist Johnny Christopher to replicate as closely as possible what was on the demos for the songs, making the Stax musicians wonder what they were hired for in the first place. No one ever told them why the original idea to cut Stax-related material was scrapped. Al Jackson, for one, was disgusted by the whole vibe and simply refused to come to the next night's session.

For Bobby Manuel, the entire experience was a downer. "I was really awed by him because he was one of my heroes. He was why I [started playing] really and truly. Meeting him was a big, big, big thing, but it was *most* disappointing to me. I really thought it would be something. It's amazing to me what we could have done and what the producer let happen."

---

20. Bobby Manuel also managed to observe those first sessions, most likely because he was going to play on the last two nights.

Seven more nights were booked for Elvis from December 10 through December 16. When it became obvious that the Monday session was going to mean missing "Monday Night Football," Presley had a number of wide-screen state-of-the-art television sets delivered to the studio. When everybody got hungry, William Brown, who had somehow managed to be allowed into this session, piped up that his wife's aunt was a caterer. According to William, Aunt Hazel cooked some three hundred hamburgers that were picked up and transported using the empty boxes that the television sets had been delivered in. The leftover food was given to the neighborhood kids hanging out on the street around the studio. Aunt Hazel ended up catering for Elvis at his last shows at Memphis's Mid-South Coliseum.

The two Presley sessions at Stax produced a number of chart records. From July, two singles were issued, "Raised on Rock" b/w "For Ol' Times Sake" and "I've Got a Thing About You Baby" b/w "Take Good Care of Her." All four songs achieved middling success on the pop charts, with both sides of the latter release making it to number 4 on the country charts. None of these tracks featured the Stax sessions musicians. The December recordings were even more productive. Four chart singles were issued from these sessions. Presley's cover of Chuck Berry's "Promised Land" reached number 14 on the pop charts and both it and its flip side, "It's Midnight," hit number 9 on the country charts; "If You Talk in Your Sleep" managed to penetrate the pop Top 20 while both it and its B-side, "Help Me," sailed all the way to number 6 on the country charts. After hearing Presley's version of "If You Talk in Your Sleep," Stax's blues guitarist Little Milton was inspired to cover it.

"When I first heard that I just flipped," Milton says. "I could hear where it was leading to and all the greatness that the song had in it without him doing it. I said, 'Well, I know we probably won't sell the kind of records that he sells but we can damn sure do this song better than he did it.' And we did!"

Milton was right. Released in April 1975 when Stax was on its last legs, his superb cover, an inspired blend of blues and pop, managed to struggle its way to number 34 R&B.

Two further singles were released by Elvis Presley from his December Stax sessions. "My Boy" broke into both the pop and country Top 20, and two years after his death, "I Got a Feeling in My Body" b/w "There's a Honky Tonk Angel (Who Will Take Me Back In)" went all the way to number 6 on the country charts.

In August 1973, the Dramatics continued what was starting to be quite a respectable run of hits with another Tony Hestor opus, "Fell for You." The 45 marked the debut of new member L. J. Reynolds, who replaced original lead singer William "Wee Jee" Howard. As so often occurs in group situations, Howard had begun to suffer from delusions of grandeur. "Tony Hestor had spoiled Wee Jee," relates Ron Banks, "and Wee Jee went to thinking he was just the Dramatics by himself. Between listening to his friends and maybe even some people in his family, it was the beginning of ruining a great relationship."

The group had met L. J. Reynolds in New York backstage at the Apollo about a year earlier. He had insisted he could sing and, when asked to prove it, delivered a letter-perfect version of "Whatcha See Is Whatcha Get." Wee Jee had missed the entire week at the Apollo, and Banks wisely kept Reynolds's number for future use. As Banks recounts it now, "It was a blessing in disguise." A year later Reynolds was a Dramatic.

"Fell for You" had been originally taped during sessions for the group's second LP with Wee Jee and Banks splitting the lead. After Wee Jee quit the group, Reynolds recut his parts. Ascending to number 12 R&B and number 45 pop, "Fell for You" represented a successful debut for the new singer. Elbert Wilkins shortly thereafter followed in Wee Jee's footsteps, and was replaced by Lenny Mayes. Because Wilkins only sang background parts, his vocals were not replaced.

Johnnie Taylor's September single, a Mack Rice composition, "Cheaper to Keep Her," was pulled from the *Taylored in Silk* album. The track had been recorded a year and some months earlier at the company's McLemore studios, the first time Don Davis had cut a Johnnie Taylor session in Memphis since 1969's "Love Bones." Taylor wanted to be more involved in his sessions, so Davis returned to Memphis, figuring Taylor would be more at home there than in Muscle Shoals.

The jazzified "Cheaper to Keep Her" was a bit of a novelty for Stax, Davis, and Taylor. The groove was based around a Jazz Messengers record called "Killer Joe."[21] "I really liked what [songwriter] Mack Rice had, but I hated the groove [on the demo]. I thought we had enough going with Johnnie to stretch his base and do a 'Killer Joe' jazz thing. So we took 'Killer Joe' and we put 'Cheaper to Keep Her' on top of it. It was something that was really fresh and it worked. The message was right on. It hit the community dead where it needed to hit it." "Cheaper to Keep Her" was fresh enough that it sailed to the number 2 spot on the R&B listings while reaching number 15 pop. September also saw Stax enjoying the fruits of the Staple Singers' hit "If You're Ready (Come Go with Me)."

While there had been plenty of tension between Stax and CBS after Clive Davis's untimely departure, Stax was still evidently more than capable of producing hit records. With that in mind, Al Bell was set on expanding Stax in several different directions. When Detroit disc jockey and Little Sonny producer Bill Williams was fired from WCHB in March, Bell approached him in regard to a new product manager position Bell was contemplating creating. Bell asked Williams to write a one-page report on how he envisioned this position would be of benefit to the company. Williams wrote twelve pages and was hired in the early fall. Bell's idea was to enlist a number of product managers; each would have a handful of artists assigned to him/her, and would be responsible for following the releases by those artists from conception to the marketplace. Williams was the only product manager hired, because the department never really got off the ground due to Stax's ensuing financial difficulties.[22]

On the suggestion of the recently arrived John Burton, Stax investigated the possibility of buying radio stations in Detroit and St. Louis. Nothing came of this but, upon Burton's recommendation, Stax entered into both the retail and one-stop parts of the record business through Record World and Ernie's One-Stop in Chicago, both in partnership with record industry vet Ernie Leaner. Burton reasoned that expanding into these areas would give Stax another means to market and break its product.

The original Ernie's One-Stop in Chicago was purchased in October 1973. A short while later, Bell opened up a Memphis division of the company,[23] hiring J. Leonard Smith to oversee it. A real disciplinarian with a military background ("Military mind, military attitude," laughs Bell), Smith was brought in from Houston. Part of the motivation for the purchase of Ernie's One-Stop was to preserve what was at that point the only independent black wholesaler in the United States. In early 1974, the initial Record World retail outlet was opened in Chicago. Three more Chicago-area stores were slated to open in the next few months, with Leaner telling *Billboard* that the long-range plans included build-

---

21. Guitarist Bobby Manuel admitted that he appropriated his guitar part from jazz guitarist Howard Roberts's "Color Me Funky."

22. In February 1974, Williams's job title was changed to national sales manager. In that capacity, along with Sandy Meadors, he worked under the vice president of sales, Richie Salvador.

23. Ernie's One-Stop in Memphis was located at 1209 Terminal Street before moving to Main Street in July 1975. There had been plans to open a third Ernie's One-Stop in New Orleans, but Stax's financial problems precluded it.

ing a national chain with up to two hundred outlets.[24] Both Ernie's One-Stop and the Record World stores were set up as subsidiaries of East Memphis Music to avoid any encumbrance on these operations by the CBS loan to Stax.

In a very short period John Burton had become Al Bell's righthand man. An accomplished pianist, Burton's main gig for many years was as an attorney for Chess Records in Chicago. Bell had first spoken with him on the advice of Phil Chess. Recalls Bell, "I was just delighted, overwhelmed, and awed at what I heard [from John Burton]. I recognized that I had run upon what obviously was a brilliant lawyer and one of the finest entertainment minds that I'd ever encountered in this business. I got that in my first meeting with [Burton]. Every word that came out of his mouth was wisdom and jewels. I really said to myself, 'Where have you been all my life?' It caused me to appreciate what Phil and Leonard Chess had in John Burton." Burton began to work as the chief operating officer of Stax on January 8, 1973. From his first day he held an inordinate amount of influence with Bell.

Unbelievably, these latest expansion plans were in full swing while, for several months, Stax had been experiencing cash-flow problems. Ed Pollack testified in court that cash flow first became an issue in May 1973. By the first week of July, Stax had depleted the full $3 million line of credit extended by Union Planters in April, and had gone into an overdraft situation. The cash-flow crisis stemmed from a few related problems. The large payments to Johnny Baylor were, of course, a significant part of the drain on the company's line of credit.[25] Stax was also burdened with a massive overhead that now included two hundred employees housed in two separate facilities at McLemore and Avalon. It had an inordinately large roster of artists, and was manufacturing albums in greater quantities than before to meet CBS's orders for product that was supposedly being put into the marketplace. The expansion into film, television, and wholesale and retailing was also putting a large burden on the company's coffers.

On August 27, Stax, through East Memphis Music, borrowed another $530,000 so that it could purchase larger office space. The company's new digs, located at 2693 Union Avenue Extended, were purchased from the First Evangelical Church.[26] Bell elected to keep the chapel, which became the site for a few of the more interesting company meetings, and then proceeded to add an additional wing. Stax's management staff moved out of 98 Avalon to their new, more spacious abode in late September.

Not everyone in the company was happy about the move to Union Avenue Extended. As director of publicity, Deanie Parker had refused to move to Avalon, reasoning that it was imperative that she stay close to the studio where the writers, producers, and artists that she was publicizing worked. Similarly, Tim Whitsett, the head of East Memphis and Birdees Music, also preferred staying at McLemore, where he could regularly interact with the writers. Neither Parker nor Whitsett had a choice this time around. When Whitsett was finally forced to move to the Union Avenue office, it turned out that there was no room in the main structure for his group, so the publishing division was assigned a small house adjacent to the main building. He was not amused, feeling embarrassed to have out-of-town people come to the office.[27]

24. Al Bell thought that only one or two Record World locations actually came to fruition.

25. $1 million of that line of credit had been paid to Johnny Baylor on April 10; Baylor received a further $541,409.54 on July 24, 1973, and $168,629.29 on August 3, 1973.

26. While the purchase price was indeed $530,000, the amount that Stax borrowed toward this purchase may have been only $400,000.

27. For some time Jim Stewart had been talking about building a brand new complex that would include studios and office space and effectively reintegrate the whole company; this would never happen.

Before the year was out, through Lynn and Associates, Stax took out further loans from Union Planters for $750,000 on October 24 and $1.6 million on December 6. These latter two loans were made with an understanding that they would be repaid from the proceeds of a $12 million contract that Bell anticipated signing with Polydor early in the new year for foreign-licensing rights. Polydor's current agreement with Stax was expiring March 31, 1974. Unfortunately, the Polydor deal was never consummated, and Stax eventually made a deal with Pye Records for the United Kingdom for only a relatively small advance. Stax was never able to pay off either loan. In the meantime, the company's wage base had grown from a total of $903,989 in 1972 to a whopping $1,472,328.[28]

Although no one yet realized it, Stax was headed down the road to destruction. The staggering volume of product that was being manufactured and shipped to CBS had a lot to do with the problem. Who was responsible for these overly ambitious numbers is an interesting question. Because CBS was merely distributing Stax *through* its branches, it was up to Stax to "sell" them new titles, meaning that Stax would attempt to hype CBS on the viability of a new release, and then CBS would determine how many units they thought they could sell and put together an order. This was not essentially different from the process by which any label sells product into an independent distributor. It would seem that from Stax's vantage point, the bigger the order the better. That's certainly how it proceeded to do business.

The problems that ensued from this ordering system were threefold. According to trial testimony given by Ed Pollack, CBS commonly gave verbal indications that they were going to order a certain number of pieces. Stax would then manufacture product based on that verbal commitment, but, when the order was received, it was for substantially less product, meaning that Stax had incurred voluminous and unnecessary manufacturing costs. Problems number two and three are interrelated. CBS was not placing as much product into the marketplace as Stax anticipated. This, in turn, led to huge returns of unsold product from CBS to Stax, which were credited against the money CBS had already paid to Stax.[29] Anticipated income was not forthcoming, while costs continued to grow. In 1974, the combined weight of these three factors would begin to economically strangle Stax.

Not surprisingly, CBS's Jim Tyrrell has a different perspective on this chain of events. While he agrees that CBS was not getting as much product into the marketplace as Stax might prefer, he feels Stax bore some responsibility for the failure of the product to move. There was no continuity or coordinated effort put into the marketing of Stax product, in Tyrrell's opinion. "When you talk with Stax, anybody at Stax," claims Tyrrell, "it's never a plan. It's always, 'How many records are you gonna *put* out?' which is a phrase that's used in independent distribution, but not at CBS when I can turn an inventory around in a week. We were not responsible for their promotion, so whatever happened there, we could only be responsive to. You don't get it on radio, I don't put inventory in place in any significant quantities."[30]

28. Bell and Stewart's salaries increased by only $1,000 apiece to $91,000, but Ed Pollack's salary leapt from $39,536 to 49,000; John Smith enjoyed a similar increase from $34,236 to $41,506 (in 1969 Smith's salary was $7,800—not a bad increase for a five-year employee!); Isaac Hayes's salary (outside of royalties) went from $25,000 to $34,000, and David Porter's salary (outside of royalties) jumped from $13,000 to $32,000. New to the company's payroll was John Burton, who at $60,000 made more than anyone except Bell and Stewart; attorney Craig Benson, who was paid $21,000 for about eight months' work; and Ernie Leaner, who had only been with the company for the last quarter of 1973, but still pulled in $18,000. Larry Shaw's wage stayed relatively stable, increasing only one thousand dollars to $34,000.

29. The return percentages on various Stax products were staggering. Many items had up to 80 percent returns on CBS's books. Fifty percent was not uncommon.

30. Tyrrell claims that, although Stax had a number of chart hits in this period, many of these were not what he would call sales hits. In other words, however they got on the charts, the consumer demand was not commensurate with the chart numbers.

In the independent record world, the goal was to put as much inventory on a distributor's floor as possible. This would then obligate that distributor to a big payable, and thereby motivate him to work his buns off to sell your product. CBS's modus operandi was the exact opposite. They had no desire to place large quantities of inventory in the marketplace. Their philosophy, instead, was to reduce inventory and replace it as needed based on the drawdown in the marketplace, because inventory represented immobile capital, precluding the use of these funds in potentially more lucrative ways.

"Al Bell was singular in his thinking that you *placed* inventory," continues Tyrrell, "and that what CBS was gonna do was to *place* inventory at the rack jobbers. The rack jobbers themselves were working with inventory management schemes and [CBS] as a distributing and sales entity was working with inventory management schemes, and these were scientifically coordinated in that you just didn't consider inventory and the replenishment of inventory in a vacuum, because in the equation is as well the financial condition of the customer and your ability to produce inventory virtually overnight for replenishment. This meant in your asset schedule, you could reserve for less capital liquidity to support accounts receivable. Al Bell didn't understand that inside his own company. You don't staff up if your revenue stream isn't uptrending."

As far as Tyrrell was concerned, of even more consequence was the fact that Stax was undermining the marketing of its own product by selling records into the marketplace behind CBS's back. "There were other records on the street from other sources," swears the CBS executive. "My salesmen were reckoning with it out there. I had to send memorand[a] having to do with taking no returns on Stax product. When I know that there is other inventory on the street, I'm not going to take responsibility for that.

"Let's assume that my guys caught the fever [on a given Stax release] and went out there with some ad dollars in support of additional inventory placement. What kind of reconciliation would we be faced with six months from now? Whose product do they send back? Do they send back Al Bell's product that didn't sell or do they send back my product? I don't want to sell into that [marketplace] except with great caution!

"I'm in charge of the net numbers, so I don't want anybody to affect my year-end revenue projections. So I don't put out goods when I know I have problems in the field. And I don't put money out there to relieve that either."[31]

CBS's perception that Stax was subverting their deal by putting its product in the marketplace by other means led to a substantial deterioration in the relationship between the two companies, which aided and abetted what were obviously significant differences in business styles.

John Fry, the president of Ardent Records, felt that there was never a meeting of minds between the two different corporate cultures. "I think there were a few encounters with some of the Stax people toward the outset that were kind of unpleasant," Fry opines. "You had some guys associated with Stax [i.e., Baylor] that had a temper and were prone to tell just anybody exactly what they wanted and how it was gonna be done and what was gonna happen if it wasn't. Some of the people in CBS in New York were not really used to being approached in that manner. You just don't become real agitated with people and talk to them abusively. That's not the way to get a positive response. There was a little of that which tended to turn off some of the CBS people, or at least make them wonder what they had gotten into here."

31. According to CBS's records, they accepted returns on a number of Stax catalogue items that were greater than the total number of units that they had initially shipped. Some of these returns probably were product that had been sold by Stax prior to the CBS deal. In any event, this was a problem.

Al Bell and John Fry outside Ardent's new location at 2000 Madison in 1972. COURTESY DEANIE PARKER.

According to Fry, most Stax personnel didn't bother to try to understand how an organization like CBS worked, and simply persisted in communicating directly to the people in the field. "All of a sudden," continues Fry, "you have people [at Stax] who are used to being able to call up Old Joe who is the field promotion man for the distributor in New Orleans. That guy wasn't there anymore. Now it's an entirely new organization and one that generally speaking is a more structured organization. Now they had CBS with a strong central authority, then regional organization, then branch, then individuals who work in the field who aren't supposed to communicate directly with you. They certainly aren't going to take orders from you. They work for CBS!"

In general, it was hard to generate enthusiasm from the staff at CBS or overcome their perception that Memphis was some sort of God-forsaken hinterland. "They'd seen it all," Fry relates. "There was a certain cynicism or hardness—prove it to me. [From their perspective we had] bare feet and outdoor plumbing and dirt floors. The chauvinism can be [immense]. With the exception of a few people in the higher levels of the CBS organization at that time, it was very difficult to get enthusiasm or interest in the artist or the product." In June 1974 Fry requested and CBS agreed that Ardent no longer be distributed through the CBS/Stax deal. Two months later, Fry ended his record label and concentrated his efforts on Ardent Studios.

Bill Williams recalls that another problem was that too many functions were duplicated between the two companies. "There was always that friction with CBS because CBS was interested in handling the whole thing. They wanted to handle the promotion, they want-ed to handle everything. The Stax guys and the CBS guys would clash sometimes in the streets. They'd wind up at the radio stations together both hauling Stax product, the Stax guy saying this is the priority, the CBS guy saying something else was the priority. It just became a lot of friction. . . . Al was the type of individual who just refused to turn over all of his operation to anybody. I admired him for that, but CBS with their money, their power, and their people, is a hard company to fight."

In general, CBS seems to have been effective selling only the Stax artists that crossed over and achieved significant pop sales, such as the Staple Singers, Isaac Hayes, and Johnnie Taylor. CBS's structure simply did not accommodate the label's meat-and-potatoes artists who could consistently and profitably sell a couple hundred thousand singles through the mom-and-pop record stores in the inner city. The majority of personnel at CBS simply didn't know about, understand, or care about that market or that size of sale. "The R&B product that really didn't cross over pop, or wasn't likely to, was just immensely strange to CBS," rea-sons John Fry. "They were not geared up for that aspect of Stax's business."

Jim Tyrrell concurs that CBS was not really set up to work with the mom-and-pop stores. "You don't make money on singles," reasons Tyrrell. "We had built an organization that thrived on the quick turnaround with the album. Yes, they [the mom-and-pop stores] can sell records, but the kinds of numbers that we are burdened with, with the size of the [CBS] organization, we can't be content to put out single after single on a Johnnie Taylor. We need a hit single and then pump the album big-time, and, after the album is out there and the hit single begins to flag, we come with the second and the third single. That's how we get the numbers from the white acts, that's how we get the numbers from the country acts, and that's how we get the numbers from the black acts!"

Further impeding the marketing of Stax 45s was the fact that CBS tended to act on a national level, whereas Stax product often sold regionally in relatively small, localized bursts of activity. When stores in New Orleans might be desperate for product by the Soul Children, the Temprees would be hot in Washington and Little Milton would be creating a buzz in New York. Two months later, the Soul Children record might have finished its run in New Orleans while just beginning to catch fire in Washington. CBS was unable, nor were the numbers sufficient for it to be worth their while, to chase such isolated activity on 45s.

"CBS couldn't target very well," opines Ardent owner John Fry. "To do some of the things that needed to be done for some of our artists and to respond to some of the places where there was airplay or pockets of interest, you needed to be more like the Israelis making a commando raid than like the United States attacking with nuclear weapons. It was a different kind of response that was called for in order to build up on that grassroots interest and finally make something out of it. It was something that CBS was just not set up for and not very good at."

No matter what understanding Clive Davis and Al Bell had regarding the marketing of Stax product, for those doing the day-to-day work at CBS, the Stax approach to market-ing made little sense, and certainly didn't fit in with the way CBS was able to function. The net result was that Stax began to lose a huge portion of its sales base.

In what turned out to be a portent, there was not a single Stax-affiliated winner at the second annual Soul and Blues Awards held in August 1973. Only one year earlier Stax had dominated the event, capturing nine of the twenty-six awards, including Record Company of the Year.

Problems for the label continued to multiply. On February 9, 1973, Stax had been informed that it was under investigation by the U.S. Attorney's Office and the IRS in

Memphis in regards to Johnny Baylor's association with the company. In August, Stax found itself the subject of another investigation. A Newark grand jury looking into payola and underworld influence in the record industry requested that Stax executives appear before it. At the same time, District Court Judge Frederick Lacey required Stax to turn over data to the U.S. Attorney's Office relating to the 1971 $406,737 Herb Kole/Ewell Roussell kickback scheme. Lacey was openly censorious toward Stax for not informing the proper authorities of Kole's and Roussell's activities, suggesting that the record company's main concern was to "conceal as much as it could from the public."

In November, Stax declined to have any company personnel appear before the Newark grand jury on payola unless an indictment was returned against it. Paul Wolff, Stax's Washington-based attorney, explained to the grand jury subcommittee staff in writing that "it would be inappropriate for Stax to answer payola questions at this time. At least three grand juries are conducting investigations, and when Stax is cleared, the company will in all diligence respond to your questions." No indictment ever came forth, and Stax never answered any questions about payola.

If the executives had been indicted, there would have been problems. The Newark grand jury was not the only government agency looking into the question of payola as it pertained to Stax Records. The IRS investigation of the company, touched off by the apprehension of Johnny Baylor at the Birmingham airport in November 1972, had also been looking into this area as another possible source of income-tax fraud. The IRS investigators were not disappointed by what they found out.

After being granted immunity in April 1974, Ed Pollack outlined in detail how payola worked at the company.[32] In early 1973, as Stax's controller, he was given $13,744 in cash that came from the sale of records marked for in-store promotion through Stan Lewis in Shreveport ($12,174) and RonDel Distributors in Philadelphia ($1,600). Pollack kept the money in a file cabinet and distributed it at different times to Stax employees John Smith, Mike Williams, and Jack Shields. On another occasion, Pollack says he was given $14,700 in cash that was disbursed in a similar manner. Pollack then produced documents that disclosed the names of disc jockeys and the amounts of money they received in this fashion from various Stax employees.

The IRS next visited all the jocks Pollack had named. Six of them admitted to receiving cash payments from employees of Stax Records going as far back, in the case of Everett "Dee Dee" Dudley, to the days of Bernard Roberson, right after Stax had severed its relationship with Atlantic in the spring of 1968. The amounts of cash were generally quite small, ranging from fifty to two hundred dollars at a time. Cash was not the only form payola took. Memphis deejay Robert Thomas admitted that Al Bell had paid his son's college tuition. Two hundred other disc jockeys listed on Pollack's receipts denied ever receiving such payments.

The IRS also visited a number of former Stax promotion men, including Pete Tyler, who worked promotion for Stax from 1970 to 1972, and James Brooks, who was employed briefly in 1972. Tyler's wife told the IRS that Tyler had told her he had to give disc jockeys money in order to get them to play records. His normal method was to ship them free records which they could then turn into cash. James Brooks told the IRS that, in addition to free records and cash, payola was also administered in the form of gifts, hotel bills, and airplane tickets. Finally Richie Salvador, now a vice president in charge of marketing at Stax, told the IRS that although payola was illegal, it was an American way of life.

32. IRS Report #62730053S includes the following information obtained from Pollack.

Salvador's statement sums up the extent of payola in the music business. What the IRS turned up at Stax is ultimately not surprising. They would have been able to find exactly the same kinds of activities going on if they had chosen to investigate any other record company actively pursuing hit records. In fact, if they had pursued a company more active with pop radio, the figures would have been dramatically higher. It is impossible to operate in the business of popular music without engaging in payola.[33] Stax was simply unlucky in that Johnny Baylor was foolish and/or arrogant enough to carry $130,000 in cash through an airport checkpoint, thereby triggering an IRS investigation.

Al Bell likes to refer to Stax's activities in this areas as "prideola." He stresses that for the most part Stax did not give cash for play. Instead, recognizing that black disc jockeys were horribly underpaid, Stax tended to supply tangible goods. One of Bell's favorite stories involves Pete Tyler going into a small Louisiana town. Rather than going to the radio station and visiting the jocks, Tyler would phone their wives and take them grocery shopping. He then would leave town, having helped out the men who were spinning Stax releases without having to push money in their face. As Bell saw it, this type of activity fitted in perfectly with the company's general policy of economic empowerment and was consistent with other company gestures, such as the no-strings-attached improvement of facilities at a number of backwoods radio stations and the placement of ads in a variety of small publications simply to enable the magazines to keep publishing.

One bit of good financial news came Stax's way in September 1973, when an audit that the company had initiated some months prior revealed that Atlantic had been seriously underpaying the Stax royalty account on the pre–May 1968 Stax product that Atlantic continued to have the rights to market. A settlement was entered into on the last day of the month, with Atlantic remitting a check to Stax for $550,000 as full settlement through December 31, 1972.

While the executives struggled with all of these problems, the McLemore staff still endeavored to continue the business of making hit records. With Jim Stewart increasingly removing himself from the company, the Soul Children were on the lookout for a new producer. Former Mad Lad John Gary Williams and Al Jackson teamed up to produce the group's summer release, a cover of Lou Rawls's "Love's a Hurtin' Thing." For their next sessions, which would eventually lead to the superb *Friction* album, the Soul Children approached Homer Banks and Carl Hampton about taking over the producer's chair. Banks and Hampton had been writing and producing as a twosome ever since Raymond Jackson's tragic death in November 1972. Accepting the Soul Children's offer, Banks wanted to take the group in a slightly different direction.

"Blackfoot had been the traditional lead singer for the Soul Children," explains Banks. "I said, 'This group is full of lead singers, what if we explored other territories.' It could broaden their market if we let the other people sing some of it."

Banks was specifically thinking of giving the lead on the group's next single to Shelbra Bennett, believing that, configured in this fashion, the Soul Children could replicate the recent success of Gladys Knight and the Pips. With that concept in mind, he proceeded to write a lyric that required a female lead, the exquisite and moving "I'll Be the Other Woman." Trying to reason out the best way to present the idea to the Soul Children without creating problems, Banks first approached the group's official spokesperson, Norman West, and suggested that West bring Shelbra down to the studio by herself. After the lead vocal was completed, the remaining Soul Children were brought in to create the backgrounds.

---

33. Anyone in doubt should read Fredric Dannen's *Hitmen: Power Brokers and Fast Money Inside the Music Business* and William Knoedelseder's *Stiffed: A True Story of MCA, the Music Business, and the Mafia.*

The result was a stunning record that bore little relationship to earlier Soul Children creations. Banks notes: "Hayes and Porter [who had previously produced the group] had them more like Sam and Dave because they were so successful in that vein. Their output was tremendous high energy. They're so churchy. The Sam and Dave format just came from the emotional cut of Hayes and Porter. But my emotional cut was different. I heard them differently."

There was some concern as to whether Shelbra would be up to delivering the song. According to both West and Banks, she tended to hold back in the studio, never quite producing what she was capable of. That was part of the reason why Banks elected to record her solo without the other group members present. "I said, 'I think I can talk to her, psyche her out, pump her up until where I could get it. But, it has to be a one-on-one situation.' Having known Shelbra since she was growing up, I just studied her voice formation and that type of song seemed to lend itself to her personality as I saw it through my eyes." It worked: Shelbra delivered the vocal of her life, and the rest of the Soul Children capture the Pips' sound so closely it is scary.

Cowriter Carl Hampton thought that "I'll Be the Other Woman" was inspired by Luther Ingram's monster hit "(If Loving You Is Wrong) I Don't Want to Be Right," that Hampton, Banks, and the late Raymond Jackson had written over a year earlier. However, Banks felt that there was no intentional reference to the earlier song. Whatever the case, "I'll Be the Other Woman" ranks as one of Banks's finest lyrics, articulating with extraordinary depth the dignified demands of one in love with a partner who is already married. Peaking at number 3 R&B and number 36 pop, "I'll Be the Other Woman" was the commercial high point of the Soul Children's extraordinary career.

Following hot on the heels of the Soul Children's effort was the latest Isaac Hayes single, "Joy." In the summer of 1973, the television news show *The Reasoner Report* did a feature on the music industry. They approached Isaac Hayes about walking them through a record from its inception to the point where a promotion man takes the actual disc into a radio station.

"I was going to do a mockup of that," volunteers Hayes, "and [arranger] Johnny Allen just happened to be in my office when the guys came. He said, 'Why don't you write something?' I said, 'Man, I don't want to write.' He said, 'You can do it. C'mon.' I had my keyboard right there in my office so the guys set up the equipment and I started writing 'Joy.' We went into the studio, they filmed me putting the rhythm together, filmed me laying down my vocal, filmed me and Johnny getting the horns and strings together. Went back in and filmed me putting the backup singers on, then filmed me putting the strings and horns on, filmed me mixing it. Then we got on a plane, I went to Madison Square Garden to play a gig. They filmed the rehearsal and filmed me debuting the song in front of over twenty thousand people. [It was] well received. That's how 'Joy' came about."

The kicker is that the clip was never aired. Isaac, though, did come away from the experience with his first major hit in over a year. When all was said and done, "Joy" settled at number 7 R&B and number 30 pop. It would be Isaac Hayes's last Top 10 R&B hit until "Ike's Rap" in 1986.

As Stax was readying the release of the Soul Children and Isaac Hayes singles, on November 6 federal judge Bailey Brown ordered Stax to submit virtually all of its financial records for the past two years to the clerk's office of the Memphis Federal Grand Jury.

Simultaneously, Union Planters branch manager Joseph Harwell, in partnership with Paul Gibson—former saxophonist with Sam the Sham and the Pharaohs and a former Union Planters officer—were incorporating a company they would call Action for Ideas. Harwell had first come into contact with Stax Records in 1966, when he had started work at Union Planters' Bellevue Branch just a few blocks down McLemore from Stax. Ever since Stax had moved to McLemore in 1960, Jim Stewart had done all his banking at this branch. When Harwell came to the branch, he immediately made himself well known at Stax, soliciting additional business from any and all employees and recording artists. As Stax developed into a major financial concern, Harwell continued to court company officials and became, in effect, Stax's personal banker. When he was transferred to the bank's North Memphis branch in April 1972, he took the Stax account with him.

It is important to understand the context in which Harwell was lending money to Stax. Through the late 1960s the American economy had been in generally good shape, and Union Planters maintained a very positive loss record in its loans department. In the spirit of the times, the bank was aggressively seeking additional loans in the early 1970s. The several million dollars in loans that Stax had borrowed and paid back under its own name or those of its affiliates, East Memphis and Lynn, had all been made under the auspices of Harwell. Stax had become one of the bank's major customers, making Harwell's bosses look upon the young executive with extraordinary favor. It was not uncommon for the bank's president, James Merkle, and other top executives to be seen wining and dining Al Bell. Union Planters' readiness to continue to lend Stax's subsidiaries money and to allow extraordinarily large overdrafts through 1973 and early 1974 took place with the full knowledge and approval of key bank executives, including the top of the bank's chain of command. The motivation was profit, pure and simple.

After incorporating Action for Ideas, Harwell requested a six-month leave of absence from the bank. His stated purpose was to make a documentary on the Memphis music industry. It does not appear that he ever made much headway on this project. His newly formed company was designed to be a loan broker between various members of the music industry and the banking community. Stax Records was his first customer. Al Bell wanted Harwell to put together up to $12 million of funds for Stax. Half of the money Bell wanted to borrow was to be used to pay back the CBS loan and thereby free Stax from a debtor-creditor relationship with the New York conglomerate. The other half was to be used for expansion and desperately needed operating capital, the latter necessitated by the problems Stax was having with CBS. For its services, Action for Ideas was to get 5 percent of whatever funds were ultimately obtained. In the meantime, it was obvious that to put together a package of this scope, Harwell would need to travel to other areas of the country, necessitating a reasonable chunk of startup capital. Bell agreed to lend Action for Ideas $100,000 for this purpose, at 10 percent interest, both principal and interest to be deducted from the earnings Action for Ideas would be due upon getting Stax the funds the company so desperately needed.

The $100,000 Bell lent to Harwell's new company came from the December 5, 1973 $1.6 million loan Stax received from Union Planters via its Lynn and Associates subsidiary. This most recent Stax loan was necessary to cover Stax's expenses through December 1973 and January 1974 as CBS was planning on returning a large volume of unsold product that would seriously cut into Stax's receivables for those two months.

The odd thing about this $100,000 loan was that, instead of Stax simply cutting a check payable to Harwell's new company, Al Bell *personally* borrowed the money from Stax and then *personally* lent the money to Action for Ideas. This might seem to be a small point, but when Al Bell was indicted along with Joseph Harwell in September 1975 on fourteen counts of fraud, this maneuver would be interpreted by both Union Planters and the U.S. government as evidence that Bell was giving Harwell a kickback for various favors and/or fraudulent activities Harwell allegedly did for Stax to get the company the loans it needed to deal with its increasingly intense cash-flow problems.

Part of Harwell's leave of absence agreement with Union Planters was that he would continue to serve as the bank's principal contact with Stax until he returned to full-time active duty on July 1. In return for doing this, the bank accorded Harwell a number of perks, such as uninterrupted pension contributions and seniority status. Harwell's leave began January 1, 1974. He would never return to active duty at the bank.

16

I'll Play the Blues for You:
1974

I n 1974, *Black Enterprise* magazine listed Stax as the fifth-largest black business in the United States, behind Motown, Johnson Publishing (publishers of *Ebony* and *Jet*), Fedco Food Corp., and Johnson Products.[1] Little did they know that the financial position at Stax had become so severe that on January 8, 1974, Bell and Stewart sent the following letter to all Stax executives: "As an Executive of the Stax Organization, you are cognizant of the problems we have faced in the last fourteen months and you are also aware of the difficulties we are faced with at the present time.

"To help the Stax Organization weather the storm, management is requesting your cooperation in accepting a pay reduction of 50 percent. It is our hope and intention to reinstate this reduction when conditions permit.

"We believe that with your assistance and cooperation this will be soon."

While the Stax executives were swallowing this 50 percent pay cut, and a further eleven recently terminated employees were in search of work,[2] Isaac Hayes was putting the finishing touches on a renegotiation of his 1972 artist and producer contracts. The negotiations had been long, arduous, and not without enmity. On October 19, 1973, Isaac wrote a terse letter to Al Bell, nominally for the purpose of investing Onzie Horne, Jr., Hayes's administrative assistant, with the authority to represent Isaac in the negotiations. The body of the letter referred to "pending serious matters of concern to both Stax and myself" and concluded somewhat acidly with "I most sincerely hope that neither Mr. Horne nor I will be subjected to the usual 'run-around' so characteristic of some of our past activities."

On November 26, 1973, Ed Pollack sent a memo to John Burton, who was now officially designated as the "Assistant to the Executive Vice-President, Al Bell." At Burton's request, Pollack had computed the gross profit Stax made on 45s, LPs, and tapes for the purpose of trying to get a handle on just how much of a royalty Stax could give to Hayes and still make money. Pollack concluded that if Hayes was paid a 15 percent of suggested retail price royalty as both artist and producer, he would be netting half of the gross profits on every unit sold. Pollack pointed out, though, that in actuality, an 11 percent artist and producer royalty would give Hayes 50 percent of the gross profits if the following annual expenditures (which Stax was presently paying and not charging back to Isaac's

---

1. For the record it should be mentioned that Al Bell objected to Stax being listed as a *black* company. In his mind, Stax was still very much an integrated organization. Consequently, he refused to give *Black Enterprise* the statistics that they had requested in regard to Stax's number of employees and gross sales. According to Bell, the magazine simply estimated the company's financial position and ranked it accordingly. Stax's income tax returns verify that *Black Enterprise* was estimating its numbers.

2. Over forty employees had either left on their own accord or been terminated in the latter half of 1973.

royalties) were taken into account: Hayes's $50,000 salary; his nonrecoupable royalty advance ($105,000 for 1973); $104,832 for Isaac's guard service; $11,000 for Isaac's secretary; approximately $25,000 for Hayes's Los Angeles home; and the $6,000 maximum Isaac was allowed to charge on his Stax American Express card: a grand total of $301,832 per year. This figure does not include Isaac's company telephone card, free use of the Stax studio, or the two cars that Stax had purchased for his use.

The renegotiated agreement, signed January 20, 1974, totaled thirty-five pages, and covered Hayes as an exclusive recording artist while also engaging his services as a nonexclusive producer, in both cases for a period of three-and-a-half years ending July 20, 1977. Isaac was obligated to produce his own recordings for Stax (forty-eight masters per year) but he could also produce any other artist he so desired for any other company he might want to. This provision was included because Isaac was intending to purchase his own Hot Buttered Soul recording studio in the near future and to start up his own Hot Buttered Soul recording label, the recordings of which he could now license wherever he pleased.

The new contract obligated Stax to pay Isaac $1,890,000 in seven equal payments of $270,000 at six-month intervals. After January 1975, the company had the right to recoup $472,500 of this amount against Isaac's royalties; the rest was Hayes's to keep. The royalty agreement was somewhat unique in that it did not specify percentages but instead listed actual amounts to be paid to Hayes for the sale of his recordings at a variety of different suggested retail prices. For example, Isaac was to be paid 10 cents on every $1.00 record (obviously this covered 45s); 69 cents on every $5.00 record, and 10 cents more for every increase of $1.00 in the suggested retail price. In essence this meant his royalty on 45s was 10 percent, whereas his royalty on LPs fluctuated from just under 14 percent on a $5.00 album to just under 13 percent on a $7.00 album. In addition, he was to be paid a supplemental royalty equal to 20 percent of the gross royalties he was to receive on LP sales, which meant that he would be actually making just under 17 percent on a $5.00 LP! For tape sales, although there was no such supplemental royalty, he was to receive a sliding scale starting at 83 cents for a $5.00 tape (16.6 percent).

In addition to the guaranteed advances and royalty payments, Stax was obligated to cover all of Isaac's recording costs (including paying the musicians, arrangers, orchestrators, and copyists); maintain disability insurance for Isaac ($100,000 a year for a period of five years) and a whole life/disability insurance policy in the amount of $4 million (if Hayes died his beneficiaries would receive $2.5 million and Stax would receive $1.5 million; if he was permanently disabled he would receive $1,250,000 and Stax would receive $750,000). Stax was also to transfer into Isaac's name the green Eldorado Cadillac with gold trim and a silver Jaguar V-12 that he was already using, and to make available to Isaac and his staff the 2881 Coldwater Canyon Drive, Beverly Hills, home that was now referred to as the "Stax staff living quarters." In its day and age this contract was pretty well unprecedented.

When asked why he had agreed to renegotiate Isaac's 1972 agreement three years before it expired, Al Bell took a long breath, sighed, and then finally replied, "Because he wanted it and he even wanted more than that. For some reason or another Isaac had begun to think that his participation in the revenue generated through the company should be greater and he wanted more. He just wanted more than the [1972] contract afforded. So, in order to try to keep the peace and settle that down a bit, I agreed to renegotiate his contract and give him the majority of the earnings from the agreement. I made that deal at that point in time [because] publicly as a company I didn't need to get involved in any kind of whatever with Isaac Hayes. So, I acquiesced. It seemed as though if I didn't give him some sort of 'lavish deal' like that I was going to have some problems. I'd be better served doing that so I could go on and continue to try to grow the company."

Bell's reasoning is sound. Isaac Hayes was so hot at the time that even a minority share of the net profits from his recordings would benefit the company more than losing any and all interest in them. Given Stax's current troubles with CBS, the adverse publicity and consequent ill will that a public dispute with a star of Isaac's stature would most likely generate would be devastating. It was just not worth trying to hold Isaac to a contract he wasn't happy with. Unfortunately, in the not-too-distant future all parties would suffer due to the fallout from this contract.

On February 13, 1974, Ed Pollack cut Isaac the first $270,000 check due under this new agreement. Nine days earlier, Al Bell was doing his best to keep Union Planters National Bank placated in the face of Stax's inability to meet its loan obligations. Bell assured bank officials that a $10 million deal[3] with Polydor for European distribution rights was imminent. This agreement, Bell explained, had been delayed because CBS had the right of first refusal for Stax product in Europe once the current Polydor agreement expired on March 30. Bell also informed the bank that CBS was withholding sums in the amount of $600,000 and $700,000 due Stax.

By this point, Stax overdrafts totaled $1,678,567.50. Union Planters wanted to consolidate them all into one loan with additional collateral. To meet the latter condition, Jim Stewart agreed to personally guarantee this loan, as well as all other Stax indebtedness to the bank, assigning to Union Planters his notes from Stax for the $4.3 million he was still owed on the sale of his half of the company. Stewart also elected to inject $400,000 of his own money into Stax to help cover operating costs. These moves would end up costing the former banker and country fiddler his house and personal fortune. "I reacted with my heart instead of my head," says Stewart, "and so I suffered the consequences as a result of it. I should have realized that I couldn't have saved it. It was an emotional [decision], not a prudent sensible one."

Despite these problems, Bell was still set on expanding the company. By March, Stax's wage base had climbed to a staggering $567,000 per quarter ($2,268,000 per year). Several new employees were brought onboard specifically to work pop and country product, the sales of which Bell expected to increase dramatically through CBS's direct pipeline to the white LP buyer. At this point, Bell was still reasonably confident that the problems with CBS could be worked out.

In the meantime, John Burton set about overseeing large-scale administrative restructuring. On March 4, he sent an ominous memo to all McLemore personnel that, in part, read: "Presently, most Departments on Union have been reorganized and now are functioning according to such changes. As we must study very *thoroughly* changes which must be dealt with on McLemore, you are being advised of the following: All activities on McLemore are to be temporarily terminated immediately.

"This will not result in the discharge of any personnel and your salaries will continue while you enjoy a few days rest.

"You will be notified by telephone or by letter of the date when you will report back to work. We trust that upon your return you will be able to resume your normal duties in a creative atmosphere which all of us can appreciate."

A day after Burton's memo, Joseph Harwell's company, Action for Ideas, arranged for a $500,000 loan for East Memphis Music from the First American National Bank in

---

3. Down from the $12 million figure Bell had bandied about two months earlier while securing the most recent loans for Lynn and Associates.

Nashville. This would be the only installment on the $12 million that Bell had requested Harwell to raise. On April 30, Harwell, in the midst of his six-month leave, abruptly resigned his position with Union Planters.

That same month Stax issued the soundtrack to the blaxploitation flick *Three Tough Guys,* the first piece of product recorded under the terms of Isaac Hayes's new contract. The film had premiered in Chicago in March and was noteworthy for Isaac's first stint as an actor on the silver screen. As had been the case with *Shaft,* Isaac recorded the soundtrack for the actual film in Los Angeles, and then rerecorded the score for release on album at Stax eight days after signing his new contract. A typically action-packed, innovative, and complex Hayes recording, the "Title Theme" was released on 45 but disappointingly petered out at number 72 on the R&B charts.

A month before the release of *Three Tough Guys,* Isaac recorded yet another blaxploitation soundtrack for the film *Truck Turner.* In May he rerecorded the score for album release at his newly purchased Hot Buttered Soul Recording Studio at 247 Chelsea in Memphis.[4] This time, Isaac had a leading role in the film, a late-summer release. Although both *Three Tough Guys* and *Truck Turner* have their moments, neither score is anywhere near the standard of *Shaft* and both fared miserably at the box office, *Three Tough Guys* moving 161,835 copies while *Truck Turner* could only manage 114,199 sales. Ironically, at the point in time that Stax desperately needed hit albums, Isaac was unable to deliver the goods.

In April, CBS began to withhold 40 percent of the money due to Stax as a reserve against records already paid for that had not sold. The immediate result was that Stax began to experience cash-flow problems, severely cramping their day-to-day operations. They responded by laying off twenty more employees. CBS had started engaging the smaller company in what was, effectively, economic strangulation.

With the noose tightening around Stax's neck, the bank that had heretofore been propping the company up was in deep trouble itself. From the early 1950s, Union Planters National Bank had been the dominant financial institution in the mid-South. In the mid- and late 1960s, the bank was saddled with numerous problem loans due to what bank historian John Pepin[5] refers to as "unsound credit decisions and loose controls which resulted from the frenetic effort to keep ahead of other banks" in the area. The bank's marketing strategy, fallacious as it was, essentially boiled down to "Pursue growth at all costs, and ultimately profits will result." Through 1971, this philosophy appeared to be actually working.[6]

In the early 1970s, the United States was experiencing widespread inflation. To combat this undesirable trend, the federal government took steps to slow the economy down that ultimately resulted in a tight money market, driving up the cost of acquiring funds for all financial institutions. Normally an increase in the cost of funds would simply be passed off to the consumer through higher interest rates. In Tennessee, however, there was a law that forbade banks from charging more than 10 percent interest on loans. This meant that,

---

4. Hayes's new recording complex was formerly the Mark IV studio. In October 1974 Isaac purchased a second Memphis studio, TMI, from Steve Cropper and Jerry Williams, which he intended to use for the recording of film scores.

5. In John Pepin, *The Turnaround* (Oklahoma City: Western Heritage Books, 1980).

6. At the time, the bank was engaged in large-scale branch expansion and branch remodeling; the value of the bank's premises and equipment more than doubled that year; for the first time in the bank's 102-year history, its assets exceeded one billion dollars; and several new employees had been hired, increasing the bank's wage base by 12.6 percent. The year 1971, seemingly, had simply been one more in what was a series of record growth years for UP.

with funds costing the bank more, its profit margin was squeezed. The only way to keep profits up was to increase loan volume. The problem with that strategy was that the general state of the economy produced a largely conservative business climate that naturally led to a reduction in the demand on banks for consumer loans. To combat the reduction in consumer demand for funds, Union Planters went after real-estate loans with a vengeance. The reckless pursuit of these loans ultimately proved to be disastrous, many of the loans floundering due to what Pepin describes as inadequate analysis of the projects by the bank's loan officers.

In 1973 the proverbial chickens came home to roost in what proved to be a catastrophic year for the bank. With interest rates continuing to climb and money supplies tightening, Union Planters suffered a million-dollar loss in its bond-trading account and unusually high losses in the installment credit department (particularly disastrous were a host of automobile loans that simply should never have been made), and found itself under investigation by the Securities and Exchange Commission. By November, it was obvious internally that the bank was in serious trouble. James Merkle, president of both the bank and Union Planters Corporation, the bank's holding company, resigned.

In the four years that Merkle had headed the bank, deposits had increased by 52 percent, and the bank's loan portfolio had grown even more spectacularly, from $377.5 million to $735.15 million. In 1973 alone, the loans average increased 38 percent over 1972 figures. The only problem was that the provision for loan losses had increased at a rate even faster than the loan portfolio, from $2,873,318 in 1972 to a staggering $7,045,358 in 1973, largely due to bad automobile loans. In the meantime salaries at the bank increased by 28 percent, but pretax and net securities gains profits fell from $6,117,952 to a shockingly low $120,771, a net decrease of 98 percent in one year! Union Planters was a bank that was totally out of control, a ship without a rudder that was verging on capsize. By September 1974 the United States comptroller of the currency was threatening to issue the bank a cease-and-desist order.

The bank's "savior" turned out to be William M. Matthews, Jr. Brought in from Atlanta, Bill Matthews was a twenty-eight-year veteran of commercial banking who had spent most of his career at the First National Bank of Atlanta. By 1972 Matthews had risen through the ranks to become president of the Atlanta bank's holding company. When he assumed his new position as president of Union Planters Corporation on May 13, 1974, he had no idea just how perilous a state it was really in. He would later confide that if he had known how bad things actually were, he never would have accepted the position. Matthews's first priority was to get the bank's balance sheet under control. He quickly recognized that Union Planters was losing too much money through customer overdrafts and that the bank's loan control system was wholly inadequate.

The problems with the bank's loan activities were many and various. According to Pepin, there was an unstated policy at Union Planters that "any loan officer could commit the bank's legal loan limit." This was obviously driven by the bank's insane quest for growth at all costs. Worse, the bank's liability ledger did not show how one loan related to another. This, in effect, meant that no one at the bank outside of Joseph Harwell realized the extent of Stax's total indebtedness through the loans and overdrafts to the East Memphis, Lynn, and Stax accounts. In fact, Union Planters' loan situation was so preposterously out of hand that, according to Pepin, not only was it impossible to determine if dangerous concentrations of credit existed, but no employee knew what the bank's total loan exposure actually was.

Faced with such an absurd situation, Matthews ordered that no further overdrafts be permitted. He then established a Loan Administration Division headed by Rudy Holmes which quickly concluded that a full 15 percent of Union Planters' entire loan portfolio was concentrated with eight customers and their related interests. This select group included Stax Records.

In the meantime, the U.S. Attorney's office in Memphis and the grand jury began to investigate all large customers of Union Planters who were in default on their loans. This, naturally, led back to Stax, a company that the IRS and the grand jury were already interested in due to the cash found on Johnny Baylor at the Birmingham airport back in November 1972.

On top of all this, according to testimony by United States District Attorney Thomas Turley, there was yet one other series of events that motivated the U.S. Attorney's office to take a hard look at the activities and behaviors of Stax Records. In the summer of 1972 Turley's office was conducting an investigation of Arthur Brown, a pivot in Memphis drug trafficking. In the course of their investigation, they came upon a musician (unfortunately unnamed) who had substantial royalties coming in but was continually broke, spending all his money to support a drug habit. According to Turley, the question then arose as to whether the recording industry was tied in to women[7] and drug dealing. Shortly thereafter Johnny Baylor, whom Turley referred to as a "courier," was intercepted at the Birmingham airport with all that cold hard cash in his briefcase and the Stax check for $500,000. In Turley's mind this reinforced the notion that the record industry was tied into drugs. "In other words," Turley testified, "money was being funneled out of it [meaning Stax] into illegitimate purposes."

In another coincidence, the grand jury in Newark began to look into payola at CBS Records, which happened to distribute Stax. All of these factors led the Memphis grand jury to look into Stax's finances. They also led the U.S. Attorney's office to subpoena Union Planters' records with regard to Stax. "Back down the line," stated Turley, "we found a very remarkable thing in Union Planters' records that we subpoenaed for the grand jury, and that was that there were at different times over two million dollars in overdrafts [to Stax]."

As Stax was fighting off the beginnings of economic strangulation by CBS Records, they found themselves also dealing with government investigations on several different fronts at once. In the meantime, Stax was having to stall a bank that was becoming increasingly concerned, partially due to its own rather immense problems, with the record company's level of indebtedness.

Joe Harwell's replacement as manager of the North Memphis branch of Union Planters was Lee McGinnis. A twenty-seven-year veteran of the bank, McGinnis first met with Al Bell on May 20, 1974. On May 28 he wrote a memo to Rudy Malone, retail divisional manager at the bank, reporting on his day-long conversation with Bell. The Stax owner outlined for McGinnis a number of activities that would bring substantial revenue to the beleaguered record company. Bell stressed that he had immediate plans to hire a European manager for the label that would lead to the licensing of Stax product in England, Italy, France, the Netherlands, Germany, Canada, South Africa, and Japan. He expected to enter into a three- to five-year contract with companies in each country, estimating that Stax would receive $200,000 per year minimum from the deal in each country, 50 percent of which would be payable in advance.[8] Bell also told McGinnis that he was

7. The reference to women in light of the rest of the investigation was not explained.
8. It would appear that Stax was only able to negotiate a deal for England. On July 24, 1974, the company issued a press release stating that John Burton and Pye Records Group chairman Louis Benjamin had just signed a long-term licensing contract for Stax product in the United Kingdom. Burton stressed that Stax had gone to

meeting with the New York Times Publishing Company to negotiate the management rights for the East Memphis Music catalogue. When consummated, this deal was expected to net anywhere from $500,000 to $1,500,000 in advance money.[9] Finally, Bell assured McGinnis that he was presently talking to CBS about taking Stax out of the New York company's custom division and placing it alongside mainstream CBS product. He concluded that Stax would be able to cover its overdraft situation in two to four weeks with the advance money from the *New York Times* deal and the weekly remittances of CBS. After the overdrafts were taken care of, Bell stressed that he wanted to start reducing Stax's overall indebtedness to the bank, and to that end he would meet with McGinnis each week until they were in the black. Unfortunately, the *New York Times* deal never came to fruition and, five weeks after this meeting, CBS ceased to remit any funds at all to Stax, claiming the Memphis company was overadvanced long beyond the sales potential of its current releases.

Bell also had high hopes for two new albums Stax had on the market. Two years earlier, Richard Pryor had been hired to perform short satirical bits on black life that served as the overriding thread of the *Wattstax* film. With both parties more than happy with the relationship, it was only natural that Pryor would be signed to Partee Records, the Stax comedy label. His one and only Partee release, April 1974's *That Nigger's Crazy,* proved to be a breakthrough album for both Pryor and African-American comedy in general. Although Partee was specifically excluded from the CBS distribution deal, Stax was anxious to get this album in the hands of young "hip" white consumers and consequently offered it to CBS for distribution. The New York monolith recoiled at the very suggestion.

"CBS was concerned with its image at the time," recalled John Smith in conversation with Logan Westbrooks. "They flatly refused [the] Richard Pryor project because they didn't understand the dollar impact, the dollars that could be generated for them on this comedy was always kept underneath the counter. They were afraid of it, and once they listened to it they were absolutely certain that they didn't want to be a part of it. So they missed an album that was super-super big in the interests of image. We went through independent distributors with it."

That Nigger's Crazy ended up going gold and winning the Grammy Award for Best Comedy Album of the year. It was the culminating recording in what had been a three-year, 360-degree turnaround for Pryor, as the comic genius moved from what Mel Watkins, in his superb book *On the Real Side,* has described as "the whitewashed, 'respectable' comedy that had initially made [Pryor] successful" to "the candid presentation of character-based comedy derived from aspects of black culture, language, and humor." It was a "startling transformation" which influenced black comedy to the same degree that *Hot Buttered Soul* and *Shaft* revolutionized black popular music in the 1970s. Sadly, Stax was unable to realize the full benefits from the brilliant record. On September 23, the company returned to Pryor his master tapes in lieu of $200,000 in royalties it simply couldn't pay while facing the continuing "assaults" from CBS, the U.S. government, and Union Planters National Bank. Within a year Pryor licensed the album to Warner Brothers.

Pye for the British company's distribution ability but that Stax intended to do its own promotions in the UK with its own promotion men. He reiterated Bell's earlier assertion that Stax intended to use England as its base for European operations. It is likely that Stax was unable to conclude similar agreements in other countries due to the gradual slowdown of product the label was generating as it found itself being slowly choked by CBS.

9. According to an unsigned Union Planters memorandum, on June 4 Bell had told bank officials that Stax was expecting $1,200,000 in advance payments from distribution rights for Stax product in various foreign countries, and that the New York Times Publishing Company had offered $3 million for management rights to the East Memphis catalogue and $8 to $9 million for the outright purchase of East Memphis.

Ten-year-old Scottish singer Lena Zavaroni was another kettle of fish altogether. Zavaroni was a pop sensation in the United Kingdom who had originally come to the public's attention through a TV talent show called "Opportunity Knocks." She was also a regular feature on the UK's "Junior Showtime" television program. Astonishingly mature for her age, and with a set of pipes to die for, Zavaroni possessed across-the-board appeal, selling equally well to teens and grandmas. When Stax inked its deal for Zavaroni, according to the company's publicity the young artist had already sold over one million albums in Europe. The repertoire included on her *Ma! He's Making Eyes at Me* album reflected Zavaroni's diversity. The title cut, a Top 10 smash in the UK, was originally a music-hall ditty dating back to 1921. It was programmed with other throwbacks such as "Rock-a-Bye Your Baby with a Dixie Melody" and "My Happiness," alongside such contemporary material as "River Deep, Mountain High," "Take Me Home Country Roads," and "Help Me Make It Through the Night."

John Burton was the official at Stax who was most excited by Zavaroni, and it was he who flew over to the United Kingdom to outbid a number of United States record companies including Capitol, RCA, and (ironically) CBS for the North American rights to the album. From the Stax perspective, this was a coup and a major step in the company's ongoing program to diversify and expand the label's activities. Al Bell was also excited because Philip Solomon, who managed Zavaroni, was also in a position to license to Stax the soundtrack for *The Warrior* from a South African stage production called *Ipi'n Tombia*. "I saw the opportunity," relates Bell excitedly, "to get into South Africa."

Released in September 1974, *Ipi'n Tombia*'s marketing was part of Al Bell's larger pan-African agenda. His long-range vision included aggressively marketing Stax product in Africa while promoting and selling African recordings in the States. If Stax had survived to enjoy the world-music phenomenon of the 1980s and 1990s, Bell would have been hailed as a genius. In 1974, *Ipi'n Tombia* sold just under five thousand copies.

As things stood in 1974, the Zavaroni deal looked quite foolish. Despite making her debut American appearances on the Johnny Carson and Mike Douglas shows, substantial promotion on the part of Stax, and the shipping of some 670,000 copies of the album on the first day,[10] Zavaroni didn't translate well for American audiences. Her "Ma! He's Making Eyes at Me" 45 struggled its way to the 91st slot on the *Billboard* pop charts. The album was a total stiff, stalling at just under 115,000 units.[11] Part of the problem, according to those at Stax, was that CBS was not getting Zavaroni or any other Stax product into the marketplace.

Bill Williams, for one, was particularly frustrated. He felt that CBS was deliberately ordering large numbers of Stax product and then simply warehousing the material. "I had that feeling," says Williams, still evidencing anger, "[but] I couldn't prove it. People would write me from areas like Utah and up in the Dakotas wanting to know why they couldn't get her record, which was already released. To me it looked like there was some kind of deliberate attempt to keep the product out of the stores. . . . Why [couldn't] these people buy our record? It just doesn't make sense. It appeared to me, from a personal standpoint, that they were trying to suppress Lena in terms of getting her out there.

10. In the May 15, 1974 issue of *Billboard*, Stax took out a brilliant, full-page ad for the Zavaroni album. Headlined "She went 9 years without a hit record," the ad compared the Scottish thrush to Judy Garland and Bette Midler before closing with copy that read "Lena Zavaroni, the 10 year old with so much talent she probably could have been a star years ago."

11. Zavaroni's career also fizzled pretty quickly in the United Kingdom. After the success of "Ma! He's Making Eyes at Me" in late winter, she enjoyed just one more charting single, June's "Personality," which only reached a rather anemic number 33 on the British pop charts.

"I saw some little things that gave me the idea that they weren't really, really stretching out in our best interests. To nail it on the head remains a little bit impossible because if they were doing it, they set it up that way so that you were not able to really know. It's hard to prove but I saw some things that just didn't look kosher to me.

"It was very frustrating because you know you have artists here with great sales potential, with great talent, and you know that they can sell records and you're sitting in that office and you're wondering, 'Why? Why aren't the records moving? What's going on out there? You know they're getting played so what's wrong, what is wrong.' It would drive me up the wall."

By January 1974, the Stax front office realized there were serious problems with CBS's distribution of their product. When CBS had earlier denied that Stax releases were not getting into stores, in June 1973 Al Bell had his brother Paul Isbell head up a seven-person retail relations department to canvas several hundred stores across the country asking if they had a demand for Stax product and if they were able to satisfy that demand. A few examples from Isbell's report confirm Stax's claims of underrepresentation. On February 28, 1974, the head buyer of Shoppers World Records in New Orleans complained that he had been trying to get stock of the Soul Children's *Genesis* LP from CBS for the past six weeks without success. Similarly, the buyer from the One-Stop Record House in Atlanta stated that he had been trying to no avail for three weeks to get the most recent Temprees release, while Rainbow Records on 125th Street in Harlem said that they had been trying for four weeks to get Little Milton's "Walking the Back Streets and Crying" in stock.

Several stores complained that it took from ten to fifteen days to get stock from Columbia. So much for turning inventory around overnight! Another common complaint was that, in general, CBS salesmen seemed to have very little interest in Stax product, making little or no effort to avail retail outlets of in-store promotional material in support of it. The general attitude toward CBS by the stores Stax canvassed is perhaps best reflected by the buyer for the Bradford Record Shop in Newark, New Jersey: "Columbia feels it is too big to be dealing with the Record Shops individually and because of this, acquisition of Stax product is a hell of a problem." According to Stax's research, CBS was ordering substantial quantities of Stax product but, for one reason or another, most of it was staying in the larger corporation's branch warehouses.

In response, CBS argued that: (1) Isbell's research was erroneous, and Stax product was widely available; and (2) where product was not in stores, it was due to a lack of demand. Further, CBS declared, truckloads of Stax material was being returned and consequently the label was grossly overadvanced.

Up to this point, by his own admission, Al Bell had been giving CBS the benefit of the doubt. However, John Burton finally convinced him that something more sinister was occurring in the CBS-Stax relationship. "Burton had been telling me," recounts Bell, "'Man, these people are trying to put you out of business and you just don't see it.' I had never experienced anything like that before. I'm from Arkansas and Tennessee. I hadn't been in that big business world. All I knew to do was make music. I didn't know how you took over corporations."

Bell would quickly learn. Threatened with its very life, Stax began to seriously consider ways of working around the CBS distribution agreement. In March the company announced the formation of Truth Records. Because the distribution agreement with CBS specifically included only those records issued on Stax, Volt, and Enterprise, to circumvent CBS, Al Bell and John Burton decided to release R&B product by new artists on this new imprint. This certainly flies in the face of the spirit, if not the letter, of the distribution agreement, but it appears that CBS didn't care. In fact, according to an affidavit that

Al Bell filed in support of Stax's October antitrust suit against CBS, officials of the New York company suggested that Stax place on Truth the Volt, Stax, and Enterprise artists that the CBS officials derisively (and with racist overtones) termed "cotton patch artists," thereby relieving CBS of the burden of trying to sell records by them.

Jim Tyrrell recalls that at the marketing level at CBS there was no extensive conversation about the Truth label. The relationship between CBS and Stax had soured to the point that the record people at CBS were just as happy not to be bothered by more Stax product. "You don't even want to step into that relationship," volunteers Tyrrell, "for fear that you might be facing the same kind of subverted consequences as you were before. That's really heart and soul of what's happening here. There's so much subversion [meaning Stax placing product on the marketplace behind CBS's back, competing with the placement of the same product by CBS]. After you get whipped once or twice, do you ask for more? 'Whip me again, give me a third label that's all screwed up out there!' At CBS our aim is always to control the flow of goods. If we can't control the flow of goods, then our ability to collect for what we put out there is undermined."

The debut Truth release was "Wounded Woman" by Sandra Wright. Released in March as Truth 3201, it appears that the record was quickly re-pressed in May as Stax 0212.[12]

In late April, a short article appeared in *Billboard* stating that Stax was exploring the possibility of returning its full line of labels to independent distributors. The source of the article was definitely not a Stax press release. Apparently, someone at *Billboard* was tipped off by one or another of the distributors that Stax had approached. The article mentioned that Stewart and Bell were reportedly asking for "big money out front if the lines [were to] comeback" to the indies, and that neither Al Bell nor Jim Stewart was available for comment. Unfortunately Stax wouldn't be in a legal position to follow through on this until the following February. By then, the fate of the company was all but sealed.

The problems at Stax ran deeper than the distribution situation with CBS. From Jim Tyrrell's perspective, Stax was delivering a lot of substandard recordings, an absurd amount of them falling outside the company's R&B base. Jim Stewart tends to agree: "Stax was in trouble really at the time I sold it. It had overexpanded tremendously. The overhead was exorbitant [and] one thing was missing and that was the product; 1972 was the last year that we really had [quality] product. In getting the company set up to go into Columbia with its new distribution system there was just no effort put into putting together some good product like we had done back in 1969 when we went into a major change [the sale to Gulf and Western]. That wasn't done this time because by then all our creative people were gone. . . . The McLemore situation was gone and the studio was vacant much of the time. I'm not saying that Columbia is totally blameless but I have to be honest with myself. Back then, it was an emotional thing and I couldn't really judge it from a prudent, practical sense. I could not be objective about it because I was fighting for my life, my baby's life, even though it wasn't even mine anymore. If we'd had blockbuster records, then we would have been sitting in the driver's seat. I don't feel that Columbia was the cause of the demise of Stax. That's only a partial truth. I have to really say that Stax caused its own demise [through] sheer overhead, waste, excess baggage."

There is no denying that Stax's overhead had grown dramatically over the course of the 1970s. Some of that growth, of course, was a necessary component of the success that Stax was experiencing. Such quick, large-scale growth also meant that there were a lot of people at the company who never really understood the Stax family atmosphere.

---

12. The paperwork on this record is extremely confusing. It is equally possible that it was initially designated to be released on Stax and then reassigned to Truth in June!

"There were a lot of these folks," testifies John Fry, "that were just redundant. [With the CBS deal] there was an opportunity to make a change there but, golly, Al was not gonna [let people go if he could help it]. He regarded this as a family sort of thing. With a lot of people unfortunately that feeling was not reciprocated. There were a lot of these people who were opportunists, who were there for whatever they could get out of the situation for as long as they could. Al allowed himself to be taken advantage of in many of these cases."

"It was a status thing," reasons Wayne Jackson, "for a black guy to be at Stax with a silk suit and a briefcase—there might be nothing in it! Nobody had any qualifications at all. There were street hustlers over there with a desk and a secretary. How they got their jobs, I don't know."

"Al thought that everybody thought the same way he did," adds Fry, "that everybody had the same visions of what this thing was gonna be and that everybody had the same dedication and so forth. His generosity toward other people was based on certain feelings of idealism that I think a great many of the people who were around, particularly some of the people who came later on, just didn't share those feelings. They were there to get whatever they could and their dedication went just as far as the check went.

"I told him this many times [but] the only cutbacks on staff or expenses were those that were really forced. The idea of letting people go was not in his way of thinking. I think it's because he's softhearted. 'People are dependent on this, this is their livelihood and their sustenance.' Which are, of course, noble feelings, but if it kills the organization in the end. . . . The way I have to think about it is that the surgeon who spares the knife is not helping the patient. I don't think you can underrate his idealism and his tendency to personal generosity as a factor in the thing."

"It was turmoil, confusion, chaos," says Stewart. "A few of the older creative people could not work in that kind of environment, although there weren't that many creative people left at that point 'cause so much outside work was being done that McLemore was nothing but a shell at that time."

Duck Dunn was one of those old-timers who simply couldn't relate to the current climate. More than one Stax engineer commented that it became obvious that Duck no longer cared to be there. Although he still showed up for sessions every couple of weeks and still collected his salary, his heart had long ago gone out of a company that he barely recognized.

Al Jackson largely extricated himself from the company, producing a very limited number of records and playing on an equally small number of sessions. Increasingly his time and energies were spent elsewhere. Way back in 1970 he had begun working with Willie Mitchell again over at Hi Records, writing and playing on most of Al Green's seminal hits in the first half of the decade.[13] Further signalling his disaffection with Stax, in October 1971 he formed his own publishing company, South Memphis Music, among whose copyrights was included "Breaking Up Somebody's Home," a hit for Ann Peebles on Hi in late winter 1972, and subsequently covered by Albert King on Stax, charting again in winter 1973.

At the very moment that Stax was starting to seriously explore ways of getting around CBS's stranglehold on its product and consequently its cash flow, the company had been

13. Jackson's "moonlighting" upset Jim Stewart to no end. When he first learned about it, he called the drummer into the office, gave him a big raise, and asked him to stop working outside of Stax. Jackson apparently thanked Jim for the raise but said that with Al Green getting hot, he could not stop participating in at least Green's sessions. Fuming, Stewart slapped his heel and pulled on his beard, but there was absolutely nothing he could do about it.

actively negotiating to purchase the Memphis Tams ABA basketball team from flamboyant sports owner Charles O. Finley. As was the case with so many of the company's non-record activities in the last few years of its existence, the idea was John Burton's brainchild. Burton felt that ownership of the Tams would be an efficacious way of working Stax deeper into the mainstream of the Memphis community, thereby setting up the company in an advantageous position to attract investment for expansion. In June, with the company's cash flow slowing down to a trickle, Stax had to back out of the deal.

In the meantime, upon taking over his new position at Union Planters, Bill Matthews took an immediate and sustained interest in the affairs of Stax Records. Matthews's attitude toward, and relationship with, Stax would ultimately turn ugly, but at first glance he appeared to be supportive. In fact, shortly after his arrival in Memphis he began publicly discussing the logistics of building the local music industry's position within the community at large. According to Al Bell, Matthews spoke with him about the role that Matthews and/or the bank was going to play in moving Stax into a key position in this effort.

Suitably impressed with the newly arrived banker, Bell and Larry Shaw worked on a speech that Bell was planning to deliver on Memphis's WMC television station. The title of the speech, "Who Will Own America?" was modeled on a "Rebuild America" campaign then being mounted in Washington.[14]

Calling on all the oratorical powers instilled in him from his training in the ministry, Bell began the speech by saying that he found himself in the precarious position of being either a victim of "shrewd manipulation" or the receiver of a "mystical blessing in disguise." From there he began to talk about the notion of "Who will own America?" deftly weaving into this theme a discussion of politics, economics, culture, and the media while insisting on the constitutional right and freedom to entertain and inform people. After referring to Stax as "a recent victim," Bell stated, "We're compelled to say to those who have not yet felt an assault on their assets that we have evidenced that those noble principles of the people's government are in jeopardy."

This introduction was followed by a brief history of Stax, crediting the company for pioneering before it was fashionable an integrated work environment while stressing the degree to which Stax had exercised its corporate responsibility in Memphis "wherever the need was found to be the greatest." He also mentioned Stax's efforts to raise the standard of business acumen within disenfranchised minorities.

Bell next recounted the basic facts of the three government investigations Stax was currently undergoing, describing the large amount of time that was being taken up by these investigations, time which could have been better and more profitably spent making and selling records. He also wrote of how difficult it was to operate an organization as complex as Stax when all of its past records were in the custody of the government.

Bell next stressed the economic impact that Stax had on the city of Memphis, asserting that Stax alone cycled over a quarter of a billion dollars annually through the Memphis economy. "We have been one of the largest customers of the South Central Bell Telephone Company. For years the Stax Organization and its employees spent directly over $750,000 per year with the telephone company. We also spend, or cause to be spent, millions of dollars in retail sales, general merchandise, apparel, home furnishing, in automotive stores,

---

14. Although the speech was ultimately never delivered, a former employee of Stax kept a copy that is marked "Confidential—Rough Draft." Its contents give some sense of the governmental pressures presently being brought to bear on Stax. Running some twenty-two pages, the majority of the speech seems to be addressing the IRS investigation of Stax, the payola investigation in Newark, and Judge Frederick Lacey's demand that Stax turn over data to the U.S. Attorney's Office relating to the 1971 $400,000-plus Herb Kole/Ewell Roussell kickback scheme.

service stations, and passenger cars only to have our corporate image, integrity, and banking confidences regarding the cashing of checks embarrassed through postings as were found in Kroger [a Memphis grocery store] and other food stores. . . . These are some examples of an ungrateful, short-sighted community."

While criticizing the lack of support Stax was experiencing from various sectors of the Memphis community, Bell took great pains to exempt Union Planters from castigation. "I wish to publicly give credit and thanks to the stockholders, directors, and officers of the Union Planters National Bank for their union, faith, and trust in another southern planter, Stax Records. Bill Matthews . . . has pledged complete and continued support to help make and keep the Stax Organization posture to fight for the ability to control its own destiny. He is standing on the square behind us. This clearly indicates that Union Planters National Bank, of the people, intends to win with Stax for the people with the people's money, which is Serious Business—Big Business."

Evidently, at this time Matthews had yet to reveal his stripes. Two decades later Bell isn't sure whether or not the new bank president deliberately misrepresented his ideas for developing the Memphis music industry, but one way or another, Matthews's grandiose plans never actually materialized. "Somewhere shortly after that," rues Bell, "[the bank's relationship with Stax] started going in another direction."

In early summer, though, Union Planters was still on Stax's side. On July 3, 1974, Rudy Malone sent a memo to bank executive Jesse Barr mentioning that Portman Guaranty Ltd. of London had agreed to handle Stax's foreign contracts. Gerald Truman, chairman of the board of Portman, was scheduled to be in Memphis on July 8–9. "It is very possible," wrote Malone, "that Portman will advance funds for Stax to pay their CBS debts in full." Malone's memo also mentioned Stax's "newest star" Lena Zavaroni, claiming that her record sales were steadily increasing. On July 17 Malone sent a memo to two other UP executives, Crawford Irvine and Tim Cook, which concluded that although all loans to Stax, East Memphis, and Lynn were "off program . . . we do not believe there will be any loss on these loans and feel they should be classified as standard."

Truman's visit to Memphis really opened Bell's eyes to CBS's role in undermining Stax. "He said," recalls Bell, " 'You don't get it, Al. . . . You understand South Africa [but] you don't understand what they're saying to you at CBS. They're saying [Bell knocks the rhythm of the following words on his desk and then says] "Hey big chief, hold them down, keep them down." Unless you understand that, then you're gonna continue to have a problem with these people.' "

Despite similar statements from John Burton, Bell had been skeptical until now. "That one hit home," continues the charismatic record company owner. "It was the first time it had been brought to me where I could see it from an international perspective. I had been offered this money [by CBS] to make this deal and to really just front Stax off and take a little override and become a corporate VP [of CBS]. I would have had the job that LeBaron Taylor has today [senior vice president of corporate affairs]. When I refused this deal is when they really started raising hell. That's when they started squeezing my vital organs.

"They wanted [Stax]. They would have paid the artists, paid the producer and given me an override. I'd have become a corporate VP, fly all over the place and speak on behalf of CBS and tell folk how great CBS was. They wanted me whenever they got ready to negotiate with these artists, as these terms and conditions were whispered to me, to come in on those negotiating sessions and explain to these artists that CBS would be good to them and they shouldn't be in there asking CBS for all of these ridiculous amounts of money and things. I should help them negotiate on behalf of CBS and let [the artist] know they should be grateful and all that kind of good stuff. That was gonna be my role. I'd be the house nigger. I would have the full support of their television network and everything else to support me in my continued evolvement as a leader.

"I would have been the biggest nigger in America. That's what Gerald Truman was telling me. He saw me not reading what was going on. . . . He banged that away as he stood on my desk beating the drum—'Hey big chief, hold them down, keep them down.'"

Jim Tyrrell affirms Bell's claim that CBS offered him a corporate vice presidency but, typically, has a somewhat different interpretation of the events. "CBS was very supportive of Al Bell the person. If Clive is gone and they say to him, 'Hey, we're going to look out for you. We understand that you're the deal guy and you're the one that we're close to. Now, here are the ways that we can protect you and here are the ways that we can cover this other thing and make it nice-nice for everyone,' that doesn't sound to me like a breakdown in the relationship. Yes, it is a takeover but what would you do if it wasn't working well for your company?"

The corporate vice president job Bell was offered came with a guaranteed salary most likely in the range of a half million dollars a year. "At that point that was a big salary," continues Tyrrell. "[Al Bell] was seen by the executives at the company to be a mover and shaker in the industry. Plus, he was a big black face. Remember, we're talking the seventies here. Every major corporation needed a big black face. Al would have been *the prototypical* big black face—so articulate, so handsome, so prepossessing and charismatic and coming with roots! No question about it."

With Al Bell's eyes slowly opening up to the situation Stax faced with regard to CBS, he worked into the conclusion of the "Who Will Own America?" speech a veiled reference to the New York company's activities. After quoting John F. Kennedy, Bell wrote: "To echo the current president, another business man who is attempting to manage the world's most complex organization, in his battle plan presented to the Joint Session of Congress, I too ask Congress to grant prompt authority to increase maximum penalties for anti-trust violations. And I call upon the President to promptly and aggressively pursue enforcement of the anti-trust laws regarding enterprise so that the people in the land remain free and the brave can own their home in America."

On July 20, the company's second $270,000 installment due Isaac Hayes under the terms of his renegotiated contract was due. Stax duly cut a check, but when Isaac deposited it in his bank account it was returned NSF [nonsufficient funds]; he was not amused. Unable to contact Al Bell either by phone or at Stax's Union Avenue offices, on July 29 Isaac formally notified Stax that they were in default of his contract. Eleven days later he served written notice of his termination of the agreement. Stax had asked Union Planters to extend it sufficient credit to meet its obligations to Hayes, but according to an affidavit later filed in court by Al Bell, the bank informed Bell that it could not lend Stax any more money because it would exceed its legal loan limit.

Despite their refusal to lend further funds to the label, Union Planters executives attempted to help Stax sort out its situation with CBS. In July, a number of Union Planters executives, including Rudy Malone, Crawford Irvine, and attorney William Solmson, went to New York to talk to officials of CBS. Representing CBS in these discussions were Ray Schwartz, vice president of finance and planning for the CBS Records Group, and attorney Anthony Caterino. The meetings lasted for two weeks, with Al Bell and John Burton flying up from Memphis during the second week.

In exchange for CBS sharing with the bank an interest in the CBS lien on the assets of Stax, UP offered to share with CBS some of UP's lien on the assets of East Memphis Music. UP represented to CBS that Stax was presently in debt over $10 million to Union

Planters, which was $2.5 million greater than UP's legal loan limit. The bank then suggested that CBS lend Stax a further $3 million to reduce Stax's indebtedness to the bank and get it below the legal limit.

CBS at first was adamant about not putting up any further funds. However, after a few days of discussion, it seemed a deal could be made, but then CBS backed off again.[15] UP also attempted to get CBS to release the money it was withholding from Stax as a reserve against returns, but CBS declined. According to Crawford Irvine, while CBS claimed that approximately $250,000 was at that moment in the mail to Stax, its basic position was "Why are we meeting with you?"

In the last few days of meetings a businessman from the United Kingdom joined the discussions. "He was a real estate banker," recalled UP attorney Solmson, "who was going to be the knight in shining armor, who was bringing all the money from Jolly Ole England to bail the deal out. Ended up the knight in shining armor was as broke as Stax was."[16]

There were at least two other occasions when officials from Union Planters spoke with executives at CBS's New York offices. In October, Solmson and UP consultant Roger Shellebarger met with Schwartz, Caterino, and the "head of marketing for the Record Division,"[17] and soon thereafter, Bill Matthews and Solmson met with Irwin Segelstein and other CBS representatives. It would appear that nothing of consequence was accomplished at any of these meetings. In Solmson's words, "The meetings got less and less friendly, as you might expect." At the final meeting in October, the UP representatives were asked to leave the building before they were physically escorted out.

In July, CBS ceased remitting funds to Stax altogether, contending that the Memphis company was ludicrously overadvanced. Bell and Burton didn't know it at the time, but they would never see another penny from the New York company. In the meantime, they continued to downsize, laying off twenty-three employees that month.

Although UP was attempting to help Stax with its problems with CBS, Al Bell was growing increasingly wary of Bill Matthews. His suspicions were born out one summer's evening when Matthews asked Bell to meet him after hours at the bank's headquarters. "We were sitting there," remembers Bell. "He says, 'Listen, I have to get some cash flow into this bank.' Something had been done where some kind of music foundation thing had been set up there [the Beale Street Development Foundation], and the bank was going to be the repository for the funds. He wanted me to put together a blues album and bring it to him. I got excited. I said, 'Oh yeah, and we can do this and that, a television special [and so on].' I went on with this whole Beale Street thing. He said, 'Nah, nah, nah, just get some master tapes, put them together and bring that down to me.' He was going to give me 'x' amount of dollars and he wanted me to put '1x' in the bank and take '1x' and get it back to him. I said, 'What are you talking about, man? I can't do any mess like that. That's illegal!' He said, 'Nigger, I didn't ask you to do it, I told you to do it!' I just wasn't going to be what he wanted me to be. He wanted me to be his boy. I think somewhere in there he actually said that."

A short while later Bell and Matthews met for breakfast at Shoney's Restaurant. "He

15. According to a deposition taken from UP's William Solmson on August 17, 1976.

16. From the same deposition of August 17, 1976.

17. This is the phrase that Solmson used in his deposition, but there was no such title at CBS. There were several vice presidents of marketing for different divisions within the record group. Jim Tyrrell, the vice president of marketing of the custom division, through which Stax was distributed, does not recall ever meeting with representatives from Union Planters.

says," continues Bell, "'I want to let you know that the things that I want you to do, I want you to do because I want you to be my man. But you just know I don't have no problem busting a black company.'" From Al Bell's vantage point, this was a direct threat, the import of which was not lost on him.

By August 30, most of Stax's accounts at the bank were seriously overdrawn. The level of overdraft indebtedness, exclusive of loans, was as follows: Stax owed $1,992,608.81; Stax Films was overdrawn a further $204,288.59; East Memphis was $186,071.13 in the red; Lynn and Associates was behind $98,010.75, and Al Bell, personally, was overdrawn $36,680.31, totaling a whopping $2,517,659.49 above and beyond the company's ongoing loans with UP. Union Planters began to force the record company's hand.

As August turned into September, while Stax press releases were busy crowing about the establishment of a new department called "Stax Country,"[18] Union Planters requested/demanded that Roger M. Shellebarger set up offices at Stax. Matthews brought Shellebarger in from Atlanta, where Shellebarger and Burton Leman co-owned a recently formed company dubiously named Crisis Management Incorporated. Prior to incorporating Crisis Management, Leman and Shellebarger had worked together for a firm called Management Science America. Leman eventually joined Shellebarger at Stax's Union Avenue Extended address.

Shellebarger, Leman, and Bruce Hathaway, a CPA from Columbus, Ohio, spent four weeks at Stax, the purpose of which was, according to court testimony submitted by Shellebarger, to "make a thorough going review of the operations and financial conditions of the company." Ostensibly this was to help the bank and Stax ascertain exactly where Stax stood financially and what was the best course of action to rectify the situation. Shellebarger was consequently given the complete run of the company, and was given access to any and every document he so desired. Over four weeks he interviewed a large number of employees,[19] examined the cost accounting and cost structure within the company, its contract with CBS, and its sales and financial history for a number of years through September 1974. He would later testify, "It was my conclusion at that point in time that Stax Record Company was by all reasonable standards that I would impose, a bankrupt company." He also stated that he encouraged Al Bell to avail himself of Chapter 11 bankruptcy proceedings.[20]

While Shellebarger was investigating Stax's business and financial affairs, on September 9, the federal comptroller of the currency officially required Union Planters to make "monthly reports to the comptroller with regard to the status of the bank's loans to Stax and its related entities." A day later, Isaac Hayes filed a civil suit against Stax requesting $5.3 million in damages. Among other claims, Hayes asserted that he was owed over $1 million in producer's royalties for *Hot Buttered Soul*, "which royalties Bell diverted to himself and others with deliberate intent to defraud Hayes of the benefit thereof." Isaac also contended that for many years he had been led to believe that he would be given "equity in the company."

---

18. In September and October 1973, Bill Hickman and Carol Stevenson had been hired as the coordinators of this renewed effort to establish a beachhead in the country music business. Merlin Littlefield was also brought onboard that autumn to be Stax Country's "man on the road."

19. After interviewing Al Bell for a few hours, Shellebarger apparently thought he understood all there was to know about the record business. "After we finished talking for three hours," relates Bell, "he said, 'You know, this record business is real simple. After sitting here talking to you for just these few hours, I can run this company myself.'"

20. Chapter 11 is, in essence, voluntary bankruptcy, in which the troubled company or individual files a plan with the court for reorganization so that while being protected from its creditors, it can take the necessary steps to get back on its feet and retire its indebtedness.

In addition to Isaac, Stax was having difficulty meeting its financial commitments to a number of artists. On September 11, Ed Pollack wrote to blues star Little Milton that "due to the poor cash flow situation prevalent throughout the country and at Stax Records, Inc., we [are] unable to issue your quarterly check, which was due September 1, 1974." However, Pollack's letter assured Milton that said check would be forthcoming on October 1.

The Hayes suit was settled out of court within a week, largely through the intercession of Union Planters. Sometime earlier, Rudy Malone had approached Bell with a proposed agreement for Stax to release Isaac from his contract. According to an affidavit filed in court by Al Bell, Malone told him that Hayes was supposed to obtain approximately $7.5 million from another recording company for a new contract (most likely ABC, with whom Isaac signed in early 1975): from this advance, $3 million was to be paid to Union Planters and applied to the debts of East Memphis, and another $2 to $2.5 million against Hayes's personal debt. Hayes, in turn, would receive an assignment from the bank of all assets pledged by Stax to Union Planters! John Burton advised Bell not to sign the agreement. A few days later, Crawford Irvine met with John Burton to present the Malone proposal one more time, but again the label refused to agree to it.

Having failed to get Bell to agree to release Hayes, on Friday evening, September 13, Union Planters called a meeting of Bell, John Burton, Onzie Horne, Bill Matthews, Union Planters' lawyers, and Isaac Hayes's lawyer, McDonald Yawn. Bell and Burton were sequestered in one room, and Horne and Yawn in another, with Union Planters' attorneys and Bill Matthews going back and forth between the two rooms. Bell stated under oath in the Stax bankruptcy trial that John Burton had been told in advance that if Stax did not go along with Union Planters' demands to release Hayes, the bank would foreclose its Stax-related loans. Feeling he had absolutely no choice, at 4:30 A.M. on Saturday morning, September 14, Bell gave in. By Monday, Union Planters' attorney William Solmson had drawn up an agreement to be signed by all parties.

As Bell stated in his affidavit, "The bank knew that the release of Hayes would cripple Stax and seriously impair any future ability for me or Stax to repay the bank." Losing its premiere artist in this fashion was a decisive nail in Stax's coffin. Despite the money that Hayes was to receive by signing a new contract with another record company, one has to wonder at Union Planters' logic and motivation. Surely it had a better chance ultimately of collecting on the complete Stax and Hayes debts if Hayes continued to record for Stax, thereby generating income for both himself and Stax that could be used to retire the indebtedness of both parties.

The terms of the settlement were as follows: Stax agreed to release Isaac Hayes from his recording and production contract. The company further agreed to pay Hayes $270,000 immediately (which was lent to Stax by Union Planters despite the bank's previous protestations that it could not lend Stax this money when the check to Isaac was originally drawn in July), and a further $100,000 upon Isaac's recording of one more LP for Stax. Hayes agreed to accept a royalty of 50 percent of the rate agreed to in his January 20, 1974 contract for this final album. Stax, subject to the approval of CBS, also agreed to deliver to Hayes the master tapes for all the material he had recorded under the new agreement, the soundtracks for *Truck Turner, Three Tough Guys,* and the Top 20 R&B single "Wonderful," as well as all existing inventory for these recordings. Hayes was to pay in cash for this inventory the price equal to the aggregate sum of Stax's expenses for the pressing, jackets, and musicians' union fees related to the product. Stax further agreed to deliver to Isaac all unreleased (completed or otherwise) tapes.

Not so coincidentally, on the same day that Bell signed the agreement releasing Isaac from his contracts with Stax, Hayes entered into a Trustee Agreement with Union Planters whereby the bank would collect all moneys earned by Hayes until his debt position with the bank was retired. Isaac's debts to UP were never cleared up, however, and in December 1977 Isaac Hayes was declared bankrupt. UP, claiming that Hayes owed them $1,508,680.81, acquired much of Hayes's personal property, professional equipment, and, most damaging of all, Isaac's contract rights and accounts receivable, including all royalties Isaac was currently owed and *would ever receive* from all material that he had written, produced, and/or recorded up to this point.[21]

Losing Isaac Hayes was a devastating blow to Stax. A short seven days later, the company was also forced to cut loose its most recent best-seller, Richard Pryor, due to its inability to pay Pryor some $200,000 in royalties. Losses such as these were not only crippling in the immediate sense that potential revenue was lost. The attendant publicity surrounding the settlements with both artists made many of the current roster anxious to jump ship, and drove away potential new signings.

Union Planters' hard-line negotiations with both Stax and Hayes may have been influenced by the bank's discovery that its former employee Joe Harwell had defrauded UP via the execution of a number of loans to fictitious individuals, many of whom were listed as employees of Stax Records.[22] Several of these loans were supposedly guaranteed by Al Bell and Jim Stewart. This came to light when Harwell's successor as manager of UP's North Memphis branch, Lee McGinnis, was forced to answer a grand jury subpoena about unrelated auto installment loans and bond records. When McGinnis could not find addresses or other pertinent information for a number of individuals and companies, he began to get suspicious. On August 16 he sent a memo to Rudy Malone outlining the details of these suspicious debits. An internal investigation was immediately launched.

The bank hired Earl Davenport, a handwriting expert, to analyze the documents in question. On September 2, Davenport filed his report concluding that Harwell had faked both the signatures of several fictitious borrowers as well as, on several occasions, the signatures of the guarantors of those loans. The forged guarantor signatures included those of Jim Stewart, Hi Records star Al Green, and Al Bell. On Sunday morning, September 8, Harwell was called down to the bank, where he confessed to everything. According to a memo written by Rudy Malone to UP attorney Wynn Smith, Harwell gave the names of four car dealerships who gave kickbacks to UP officers and nine bank officers who had defrauded the bank. He also explained that for a fee an individual with a bad credit record could have the report changed. With regard to a suspicion that Harwell had misrepresented Stax's financial situation, Malone wrote, "Harwell stated until recently he had always felt that the company [Stax] was viable and had a great future. He admitted this feeling was verified by memos and personal presentations by himself to the bank. He stated that he now feels that he was overwhelmed by Al Bell."

Eight days later—the same day that Al Bell signed the UP-devised annulment of Isaac Hayes's contracts with Stax—Harwell confessed to FBI agent Cyril Busch, who, in a series of *astonishing* coincidences, had recently visited the Stax offices to ostensibly investigate the bootleg record industry, and would later, according to Al Bell, work full-time for Union Planters![23]

---

21. To this day, Isaac Hayes receives no royalties on any of the songs that he wrote and produced for Stax artists such as Sam and Dave, the Soul Children, and the Emotions, and for any of his own recordings on Stax. Whatever the legal niceties, this is ultimately ethically untenable.

22. For example, Carl Karob was listed as both a chief technical engineer and East Coast promotions director for Stax, while R. E. Robinson's occupation was given as production supervisor at Stax. Neither of these individuals in fact existed. Both their names and occupations were created by Harwell.

23. To this day Al Bell does not know if there is any connection among Busch's activities, but he and others have often wondered about the possibility.

On September 25, attorney Wynn Smith took a sworn statement from Harwell. Harwell told Smith that on up to twelve occasions Al Bell had signed as a guarantor on loans for individuals that Harwell represented as his friends. He said that Bell did so because he and Harwell had such a close relationship.

Although the bank assured Al Bell that he was not under investigation, they requested his cooperation in their investigation of Harwell. To that end, Bell agreed to give a sworn statement on September 26. When Bell was confronted by Wynn Smith with guarantees that he had actually signed for loans to people who didn't exist, he explained under oath, "I trusted Joe Harwell above and beyond a shadow of a doubt, and Joe Harwell was handling our business as far as the bank was concerned. When Joe Harwell brought me a document to sign, I didn't bother to read it or whatever. I signed it." Bell's version of the story was eventually accepted in court.

On September 27, Union Planters filed a Proof of Loss claim with its bonding company, Fidelity & Deposit Company of Maryland, asserting that: (1) Harwell was guilty of making loans to fictitious individuals totaling over $200,000 and then retaining the funds for his own use; and (2) Harwell had extended credit to Stax, Al Bell, and others totaling over $5 million while fully informed that the person or company to whom credit was extended was financially unable to meet existing financial commitments. The total value of the claim was $5,899,621.47. Under this ruse, Union Planters hoped to collect much of the outstanding Stax loans from its bonding company. If it worked, it would be a very expeditious move to try to correct a serious imbalance in UP's provision for loan losses. Nowhere in the bank's claim filed at this date was there any mention that Bell and Harwell had acted in conspiracy. At this point in time, UP was hanging its hopes on proving that Harwell was crooked all by himself. Nine months later, Roger Shellebarger would suggest that a different approach be taken.

On December 12, 1974, Joseph Harwell was indicted by a federal grand jury. He was eventually convicted for the loans he made to fictitious individuals and served a prison term as a result.

After Harwell had confessed to the FBI, his company, Action for Ideas, was unlikely to be of any further assistance in obtaining funds to extradite Stax from its steadily mounting crisis. Consequently, Bell turned to other potential finance brokers. On September 20, Bell wrote a letter to Charles Call, Jr., of Morristown, New Jersey, requesting that Call help raise funds to retire Stax's UP and CBS debts. For his efforts, Bell assigned to Call $100,000 "due to us from Polydor International as evidenced by their letter dated August 23, 1974 and do hereby agree to pay you an additional One Hundred Thousand ($100,000) Dollars upon completion of arrangement of the aforementioned financing." As far as is known, Charles Call never raised any of the needed funds. Bell and Stewart would continue to personally exhaust every possibility to try to raise the capital to buy CBS out.

In the midst of all these financial and legal problems, there was one bright moment for the label. In May, Jim Stewart signed Shirley Brown, a singer with a set of vocal chords that could challenge Aretha Franklin. It was Stewart's first active signing of an artist to the company in several years, part of Jim's general renewed level of activity occasioned by his decision in February 1974 to personally guarantee Stax's debts to UP.

Born in West Memphis, Shirley Brown moved to St. Louis at the age of nine. As a young adult, she sang with most of the bigger names on the St. Louis R&B scene, including Oliver Sain, Little Milton, and Albert King. Through Sain, Brown released a record on A-Bet, a subsidiary of Nashville's Nashboro label. After that flopped, King brought her to Stax. Jim Stewart was so impressed by her version of Lorraine Ellison's "Stay with Me" that he not only signed her to a contract but decided to produce her himself. It was the first time he had been in the studio in a couple of years.

"I went back into the studio," Stewart says, smiling wanly, "hopefully to start some sort of a revival of the company as a small-scale kind of situation. It worked pretty good but, of course, the bank had other things in mind and was not going to allow us to regroup and do that. So, they [eventually] shut us down."

The first song Brown recorded at Stax was a James Banks–Henderson Thigpen–Eddie Marion composition that had already been rejected by Inez Foxx.[24] "Woman to Woman" has a beautifully plaintive melody that Brown's larger-than-life pipes imbue with power and grace. The song's lyrics are written from the viewpoint of a wife who has found the telephone number of another woman in her husband's pockets. Before the first verse Brown has a long spoken rap:

"Hello, may I speak to Barbara. Barbara, this is Shirley. You might not know who I am but the reason I'm calling you is because I was going through my old man's pockets this morning and I just happened to find your name and number. So woman to woman I don't think it's being any more than fair than to call you and let you know where I'm coming from."

Television soap operas have nothing on this! The monologue was James Banks's brainstorm, inspired by Isaac Hayes's recent work. "Isaac was a male singer talking to the woman," explains Banks. "So I thought it would be a unique idea if we had a female coming off real bold saying that, 'Hey, this man is mine. I spend my money on him, you can't mess with this guy.' I thought that would be very slick. It was kind of a chance because we didn't know whether the public would eat it up or not."

According to Banks and Thigpen, the demo they cut was even better than the record. Thigpen was particularly disappointed that Stewart and coproducer Al Jackson chose not to have a phone ringing on the track. They were pleased, though, with Shirley's performance. Stewart allowed them to coach Brown through every nuance of the rap. After a half day of working with her, the vocal was done in one take. Released in August on Truth, "Woman to Woman" entered the charts in the last week of September and was Stax's first number 1 R&B record in a long time. It also managed to make number 22 pop, providing Stewart and Bell with a tiny bit of hope that their company just might pull through.

"Woman to Woman" eventually sparked two hit answer versions, Barbara Mason's "From His Woman to You" and Lonnie Youngblood's "Man to Woman." The former, featuring a new set of lyrics over an exact replication of the original melody, climbed to number 3 on the R&B charts in the final month of the year. Brown's version of the song was nominated for a Grammy for Best R&B Performance by a woman, and, before all was said and done, her record had sold over one million copies. Alas, as Jim Stewart so ruefully put it, "our financial problems were far greater than that. It was just a drop in the bucket compared to the expenses, but it gave me some enthusiasm." One of only four Top 10 R&B records that Stax could generate in 1974,[25] it would be the label's last hit of any significance.

As "Woman to Woman" was working its way up the charts, Union Planters hired yet another acquaintance of Matthews, William Dick, to look after the Stax situation. Dick was an eleven-year veteran of Georgia banking, having worked with Matthews at the First

24. Banks, Thigpen, and Marion were relative newcomers to the company. Although a few of their songs had been recorded by the Bar-Kays, "Woman to Woman" would be their first hit. Banks and Thigpen would later pen a couple of the Bar-Kays' biggest post-Stax hits such as "Cozy" and "Spellbound."

25. The other three were the Staple Singers' "Touch a Hand, Make a Friend" and "City in the Sky" and Johnnie Taylor's "We're Getting Careless with Our Love."

National Bank of Atlanta. He most recently had served as president of a small Savannah bank. According to a deposition he later filed in court, in the fall of 1974 Union Planters desperately wanted to keep Stax operating. "We determined," stated Dick under oath, "very early that the only possibility of recouping the substantial dollars that were out was to keep the company alive."

During Dick's first meeting with Al Bell, the Stax owner stressed that they had to dissolve Stax because the CBS contract was strangling them. Union Planters encouraged Al Bell to launch an antitrust suit against CBS.[26] Bell felt that that was unnecessary, and instead he and John Burton went to New York in one more attempt to try to solve the problems with CBS. Over several days, Bell hammered away at CBS's poor performance in selling Stax product, and asked that their distribution deal be terminated.

"I was raising hell," admits Bell, "but I wasn't adversarial or antagonistic at this point. I was still trying to work it out and figured it could be worked out. But they had *no intentions* of working it out! It was one way or the other. The one way was you do like we tell you or the other was we'll bust it out."

On Thursday, October 3, after reaching an impasse at the end of a particularly heated day of discussions, Bell and Burton returned to their hotel rooms and waited until the beginning of the next week for CBS to call to resume their talks. In the meantime they called Bill Wood in the sales department at Stax and told him not to accept any orders from CBS until further notice. When the phone eventually rang on Tuesday, it was Jim Stewart calling to inform his two colleagues that Stax had been served with an injunction and restraining order that effectively prevented them from circumventing the CBS distribution agreement. After Bill Wood did as instructed and refused to take an order from CBS for Stax product on Friday afternoon, October 4, the New York company's attorneys began preparing to make a move in court, drawing up a restraining order that they filed before a judge in Memphis on October 8.

CBS claimed its injunction was made due to Al Bell giving verbal notice on October 2 and 3 that Stax would "no longer abide by, honor or perform its Distribution Agreement and would instead deal with other distributors." However, Bell denied having verbally canceled the contract. CBS also charged that when Stax released Isaac Hayes from his contract it had violated Paragraph 7 [e] of their agreement, which stated that Stax could not assign, terminate, or dispose of any of its artist's or producer's agreements. To Bell, this injunction finally confirmed his belief that CBS was attempting to take over Stax.

Stax countered on October 25 with a $67 million antitrust suit which, in effect, charged CBS with attempting a hostile takeover. Stax's countercomplaint and a supporting affidavit from Al Bell stated that CBS had violated the distribution agreement on a number of occasions in a number of ways. According to Bell, in late winter or early spring in a meeting with Irwin Segelstein, Goddard Lieberson, Ron Alexenburg, and Bruce Lundvall, CBS had insisted that Stax "reduce the number of recording artists and record producers then under contract to Stax to those recording artists and record producers who had achieved so-called 'national acclaim' and release, transfer, and assign certain recording artists ('cotton patch artists') and record producers to the new 'Truth' label."[27]

26. In another interesting attempted maneuver by the bank, at one point shortly after Isaac Hayes had left Stax, Union Planters officials visited Bell's house on East Parkway and suggested that he turn the company over to them and that they would install Isaac Hayes as the president.

27. Al Bell remembers quite clearly CBS president Arthur Taylor telling him "that they were not really interested in these artists because he called them 'cotton patch' artists. He didn't want those cotton patch artists coming through CBS." As Bell understood it, any black artist that didn't cross over was a "cotton patch" artist in Arthur Taylor's worldview.

Bell's affidavit further contended that, in late July or early August 1974, he met with Ron Alexenburg and Walter Dean (executive vice president of the CBS Records Division) in Los Angeles. At that meeting Alexenburg "insisted that Stax reduce its full-service record company to a 'label' or production company." At another meeting, Bell continued, Walter Dean stated that CBS desired to terminate the distribution deal and urged Bell to meet with Martin Pompadur of ABC to negotiate a new distribution deal. Bell also stated that, at one point, Dean insisted that Bell change the deal to a standard P&D contract and "that only then would CBS put its full muscle behind Stax."

Of more consequence were the funds that CBS had begun to withhold in April. Bell's affidavit and the countercomplaint charged that it was due to this course of action by CBS that Stax had been unable to meet its obligations to Isaac Hayes and had consequently been forced to release Hayes from his contract. Bell feared that the label would lose more artists in the near future if CBS was not forced to remit these funds. By CBS's own admission, by December 1974, the New York conglomerate had withheld $6,321,698 due Stax for records sold by CBS.

Bell next cited "the failure and refusal of CBS to coordinate and key its distribution and sales force into the promotional merchandising and national advertising programs of Stax. CBS had inadequately positioned product in the market place to satisfy consumer demand for Stax products and has failed to have items promoted by Stax available at the consumer level, all of which actions have damaged the reputation and business of James Stewart, Stax, and myself as a full-service record company. The policies of CBS, if allowed to continue, create a danger of reducing Stax to a mere 'label' or production company, completely under the domination and control of CBS."

The result of these actions, continued the affidavit, was that Stax had been forced to downsize by terminating "valuable and irreplaceable artistic and business personnel." CBS further added to Stax's financial stress in early 1974 by instituting a policy of accepting only 18 percent returns on CBS-owned labels while at the same time it was accepting over 40 percent returns on Stax product, thereby "wrongfully and maliciously increasing return demands from CBS to Stax."[28]

The countercomplaint as filed by Stax further alleged that CBS had deliberately overordered Stax product; that CBS had refused, contrary to the terms of the distribution agreement, to allow Ed Pollack or Stax's sales manager, Richard Salvador, to inspect both the books and inventory records with respect to Stax product; and, again in direct contradiction of the terms of the distribution contract, CBS categorically refused in October 1973 to negotiate an increase in the selling price of Stax product to CBS based on increases in manufacturing charges.

Putting all this together, Bell and Stax were charging CBS with attempting a hostile takeover. In the course of pretrial discovery proceedings, Stax learned of *The Harvard Report*. In their eyes this was just more grist for the mill, ultimately proving what they had contended all along, that CBS was systematically attempting to gain control of Stax Records as a way to secure a significant part of the black music market.[29] In an affidavit filed October 21, 1974, and during the Stax bankruptcy trials on November 26, 1976, Ed Pollack testified that, in a conversation he had with the head of Epic Records, Ron Alexenburg, on August

28. According to Ed Pollack, before going through CBS, Stax returns were on average 22 percent for 45s, 18 percent for LPs, and 5 percent for tapes. These were much lower than industry averages.

29. See the discussion of *The Harvard Report* in Chapter 14. Although I conclude that CBS did not follow this report and was not using it as a blueprint to take over Stax, this does not mean that CBS was not attempting a hostile takeover of Stax. It is simply to say *The Harvard Report* did not recommend that CBS do this. Bell's charge was never actually resolved in court because CBS and Stax reached an out-of-court settlement in late February 1975.

18, 1973, he came to the conclusion that CBS was out to destroy Stax.

Pollack's affidavit reads as follows: "I was in New York for a meeting with several of the executives of CBS. Mr. Ronald Alexenburg, a Vice President of CBS, offered to take me to the airport when I was leaving and I accepted. Our conversation in the car naturally concerned CBS and Stax business. Mr. Alexenburg claimed that CBS was not making money on our account and I told him that he was wrong, that CBS had a good deal. CBS was grossing a profit of 26% to 28% and did not have to worry about returns. Mr. Alexenburg stated that it was not enough and then said, 'You know we can take your company over at any time. All we have to do is stop selling your product—you wouldn't be able to repay our loan and we'll call the note—you belong to us.' I made no reply to this as I felt any reply would lead to an argument."

For the record, when interviewed in 1997, Ron Alexenburg denied that he had ever said any such thing.

The same day that Stax filed its $67 million antitrust suit against CBS, Al Bell received a rather distressing mailgram from Pops Staples. It read: "Dear Al: Under present circumstances we have determined that Stax Records, Inc. is unable to serve the Staple Singers as agreed to. We will agree to complete two (2) LP'S and then respectfully request a cancellation of our agreement. More details will follow in a letter by counsel. I am personally making this request to avoid litigation."

Al Bell was incensed. Since the mid-1950s, he had had a professional and personal relationship with the Staple Singers, and it had been his vision of the Staples that was central to the transformation of the family from gospel warriors to soul superstars. Further, he had personally produced every substantial hit the group ever had. If there was any artist that he expected to be loyal in his time of trouble, it was the Staples. A few weeks earlier Stax had remitted $250,000 to the Staples, thereby executing the option clause extending the group's contract for another year.[30] Just nine days earlier, Bell had met with the family in Chicago at Pervis Staples's club, Perv's Place. He thought that he had come away from the discussion with the family's full, unwavering support.

Upon reading the mailgram from Pops, Bell fired off a rather acid-tinged response replete with various words and phrases underlined and/or in capital letters: "It distresses me to know that you are taking this position, knowing that Stax and I PERSONALLY have gone above and beyond the contractual commitment between us. Not only have we fulfilled our obligations under that contract 'but through recorded music we have built the Staple Singers into one of the most valuable and respected recording artists in the recording industry.' Inherent in that is your responsibility of leadership. We have also supported and aided in financing the group's and your personal business ventures in an attempt to aid you in reaching the financial heights that you are reaching for. AFTER ALL THAT'S WHAT FRIENDS ARE FOR. (I SEE YOU.)

"Your mailgram raises one question in my mind: IS IT REALLY A FAMILY AFFAIR? Only you can answer that! I believe in being a friend in DEEDS and not a friend in NEEDS. 'Inasmuch as ye have done it unto one of the least of these brethren, ye have done it unto me.'"[31]

---

30. In one of the weirder moments in the Stax saga, after the label's first check to the Staples was returned NSF, a company named the River City Music Corporation lent Stax $100,000 to cover the shortfall. Union Planters had originally been approached about a loan. When they refused, Roger Shellebarger formed River City Music Corporation, which borrowed the money from Union Planters and then turned around and lent the money to Stax. Given that Shellebarger was UP's point man with regard to Stax, this makes no sense at all. If the company was worth the risk of a loan in Shellebarger's estimation, why did UP not simply lend the money itself? I have been unable to deduce the reasons for these machinations.

31. Religious imagery and rhetoric had become so integral a part of Al Bell's persona at this point that Isaac Hayes, picking up on the Black Moses moniker, began referring to Bell behind his back as "Black Jesus."

The Staple Singers would never record for Stax again. On April 15, 1975, they were officially released. The walls were seemingly closing in from all sides.

Meanwhile, Bill Matthews at Union Planters had his own concerns about Stax. Frightened that CBS's claims against Stax would ultimately lead to the New York behemoth seizing the label's assets leaving UP holding the bag regarding its own considerable stake in Stax, Matthews decided that immediate action was necessary. On a number of occasions he suggested to Al Bell that UP take over Stax's antitrust suit. Much to Matthews's chagrin, Bell was having none of it. So, in the first week of November 1974, Union Planters further tightened the noose around Stax's neck. Due to Stax's inability to meet the payment requirements on its East Memphis loans, the bank acquired the right to vote the one hundred shares of East Memphis stock that they held as collateral on those loans. Pursuant to that right, Union Planters elected Shellebarger as chairman of the board of the publishing company. In plain English, the

bank took over East Memphis, subject to a repurchase agreement whereby Stax could regain control of it if it paid off its complete debts to UP. As it was now transparently obvious that Union Planters was the enemy, in December UP ceased to be the main depository for Stax's money, and Ed Pollack opened up a number of accounts at the Commercial and Industrial Bank branch located next door to Stax's Union Avenue offices.

Bell began to believe that it had been Matthews and Shellebarger's goal all along to take over Stax; acquiring East Memphis was simply their first step in a much more sweeping plan.

Shellebarger kept most of the East Memphis staff in place,[32] offering everyone a raise and appointing

Tim Whitsett. COURTESY TIM WHITSETT.

Tim Whitsett officially to the position of president of the publishing company. It was Stax in-house attorney Craig Benson who first informed Whitsett that Roger Shellebarger was taking over East Memphis. Whitsett remembers his first reaction being "'Roger *what?* What kind of a name is *that?* Is he a communist?' Shellebarger spent the whole day with Craig and then Craig brought him in to meet me. I thought at first glance that Shellebarger looked a lot like Spiro Agnew."

"He seemed so nervous," adds Whitsett. "He seemed scared of everybody and he would try to establish a rapport or loosen things up by telling jokes with a lot of bad language in them. I wasn't any prude but I sort of resented this guy that looked like a digni-

---

32. In addition to Tim Whitsett, the staff of East Memphis at the time included Craig Benson, Bernard Denimal, Janice Harper (later Whitsett's wife), Jackie Styles, Joyce Gordon, former Goodee Sandra Jackson, Phil Rawls, and songwriter Joe Shamwell, the latter two being largely responsible for plugging the company's songs.

fied businessman telling these things. I was very sarcastic with my approach to him because I was resenting all of this. I should have been fired, should have been kicked right out on my butt. I was unhappy at Stax with all the things that had gone on in the past year, especially since we had moved over to Union Avenue. And now, here comes the bank and they're sending this idiot named Shellebarger in here and nobody will tell me anything. But I was wrong about Shellebarger. He came across as a bummer to a lot of people. He would frustrate a lot of people but I [ended up liking] him. In his own roundabout way, he was pretty good."

Whatever his thoughts about Shellebarger, life changed for Whitsett instantaneously. "We had people from Stax who thought that we had become the enemies overnight," recalls Whitsett, shaking his head in wonderment. "Our job was basically to keep the publishing company intact, keep the writers working, keep the company valuable."

The publishing company became a target for Stax's frustration with the bank. At one point, East Memphis's main song plugger Joe Shamwell was threatened with castration. Justifiably freaked, he immediately got a permit to carry a weapon. Tim Whitsett received any number of harassing, obscene calls. Rumors were spread that Whitsett's secretary Janice Harper was sleeping with Roger Shellebarger. "They were trying to discredit everyone right and left," Whitsett summarizes. At its worst point, Whitsett had his life threatened. "One of the songwriters came up and demanded his copyrights back," Whitsett remembers. "I got up to give them to him because he was pretty high-strung. When I got up, he said, 'You better watch how you move.' I said, 'I was just getting your copyrights.'"

John Gary Williams, the songwriter in question, held his hand inside his coat pocket, pointing at Whitsett as if he had a gun. "I never knew if he had a gun or not," continues Whitsett, "but he had been known to [carry] a gun and I wasn't going to ask. He told me in front of our attorney, our two secretaries, Janice and a lady from the telephone company, 'I'm not going to kill you right here and now but you're going to be dead within a couple of months. I got friends. I'm not going to do it personally.' He said this very seriously and very loudly, everyone heard it and I felt pretty awful." That night Homer Banks and Carl Hampton phoned Whitsett to reassure him that Williams had simply lost his head, and within a day or two Williams himself called and apologized. Mack Rice immediately nicknamed Williams "Kung Fu."

At one point John Burton and Jim Stewart called Harper and wanted her to spy on Shellebarger and report back to Stax on his activities. According to Whitsett, Harper was more than a trifle indignant over the whole episode.

Needless to say, it was a trying time for all concerned. "We didn't want to work for the bank," emphasizes Whitsett. "We came to work for a music company. The bank said, 'Don't worry. All this is just a maneuver. We're holding [East Memphis] for the record company. We want to help the record company get back on their feet. As soon as it is, we want to be able to hand the publishing company back over to it intact.' We believed that. [The bank said], 'We're protecting the publishing company from the creditors. Don't you worry.'"

On a cool and foggy November 18, East Memphis's offices were moved to the Old Shrine Building at Monroe and Main, right next door to Union Planters' main office.

Shellebarger would spend the next year of his life obsessed with Stax Records. Along the way he came up with a number of bizarre stories. He claimed to have found checks payable to Stax bearing the signatures of Latin American generals. He told Tim Whitsett that he had sent a team of investigators to Chicago who reported back that Ernie's One-Stop was a bookmaking joint. Shellebarger also found on a personal financial statement submitted to the bank under Al Bell's name a radio station listed as an asset worth

$200,000. When he investigated, the radio station did not exist. Its call letters, KMVV, had been assigned briefly in 1946 through 1949 to a ship operating in the Chesapeake Bay. What he neglected to detect in his "investigation" was that it was Joe Harwell, not Bell or anyone at Stax, who had listed the fake radio station as an asset.[33]

On November 13, Union Planters launched a suit of its own, listing CBS, Stax, Al Bell, and Jim Stewart as defendants and claiming that CBS's $6 million loan back in October of 1972 to facilitate the buyout of Jim Stewart was illegal, and that CBS's "primary purpose . . . in entering into the arrangement with Stax . . . was to gain control of a substantial portion of the 'soul' music market and used said arrangement as part of a course of conduct intentionally and willfully calculated to gain control, dominion, and beneficial ownership of Stax for said purpose to the detriment of Stax and its creditors." The complaint also accused CBS of deliberately overordering Stax product which could then be credited as returns as part of its master plan to gain control of Stax by "controlling and limiting the cash flow derived by Stax from the sale of its products to an extent to render Stax unable to meet operating expenses and fixed obligations to creditors, particularly the Plaintiff."

In its complaint, UP alleged that Stax and its affiliates currently owed the bank $10,493,220.06. They requested that the court find in their favor and: (1) null and void the loan and security agreement between Stax and CBS; (2) null and void the distribution agreement between Stax and CBS; and (3) null and void the subordination agreement UP had executed that made its claim on Stax secondary to that of CBS. UP also, of course, wanted the $10 million plus that it claimed Stax owed together with interest and costs, the latter including the bank's attorney's fees.

On January 24, 1975, CBS filed an answer and counterclaim against UP, denying all of UP's allegations, accusing the bank and Stax of conspiring to undermine their distribution agreement with Stax, and suing both parties for the $6 million owed by Stax plus various and sundry damages. The opening volleys had been fired in what would be several years' worth of an increasingly ugly legal war over first the lifeblood of Stax Records and then the spoils to be derived from the carnage.

As the curtain began to come down on what had been an extraordinarily depressing year at Stax, Al Bell was trying to do everything he could to find cash and rally the troops. In November, he signed June Hunt, daughter of Texas billionaire H. L. Hunt, to the Gospel Truth label. Many people viewed this as simply another attempt to find potential revenue. Bell states emphatically that this was not the case. He was enamored of Hunt's songwriting message and, in any event, as he remembers it, she was not in a position to leverage any of the family's money even if this had been Bell's goal.

On November 27, the day before the Thanksgiving holiday, Bell sent a memo to all company employees headed "Creative Ideas–Constructive Criticism." In this memo, Bell optimistically called for their input, "because with our organization at its lowest ever (financially, functionally, attitudinally), NOW is the time to sweep, mop, dust and polish up the organization in an effort to start putting it together right." Bell requested that every employee jot down his or her ideas and criticisms and drop them in the "W.I.N. WITH STAX" box located across the hall from John Burton's office. It was stressed that these missives needn't be signed, and that Al was the only person with a key to the box.

Bell went on to state, "It is important to me to know HOW YOU FEEL, WHAT YOU THINK, AND WHY YOU FEEL AND THINK AS YOU DO about The Stax Organization and its practices in total.

33. The details of this came out in court.

"I will spend my Thanksgiving Holiday *very seriously* sorting, studying, and absorbing those items which you carefully prepared to aid me in our endeavors.

"YOUR VOICE NEEDS TO BE HEARD—AND YOU WILL BE HEARD!

"You could be sitting on a million dollar idea or an idea that could help boost moral [sic] and better your company. Please let me know about it no matter how simple or trite it may seem to you.

"*INFLATION* exit [sic] and RECESSION is RAMPANT in this COUNTRY and in our COMPANY!

"From my posture and overview, I can tell you Stax is beginning to WIN our WAR on inflation, recession, and depression. YOU can *help* us become VICTORIOUS. The *objective* is to *secure* the company—so can we *insure* our jobs. To do this requires *TEAM EFFORT.*

"'He that is without fault—let him cast the first stone.'

"I can't (smile).

"We do have a lot to be *thankful* for this Thanksgiving—*let us count our blessings.*"

Just how desperate the situation was is made manifest by Eddie Floyd's tales of his November release, "I Got a Reason to Smile (Cause I Got You)." "The song went to number one on three stations in only one place in the whole world—Columbus, Georgia," Floyd claims, "because we didn't have any distribution by that time. I just had a pressed record and I sent it to people in Columbus, Georgia, that I knew. They started playing it and they even got it on the pop stations. By that time Stax was [almost] gone." Floyd thinks it may have sold a meager total of two or three thousand copies.

The song itself was inspired by Stax's plight. Floyd elaborates: "That was during that doggone time when the man might take our old beat-up Cadillac. They might cut off our lights tonight but that's all right, I got a reason to smile 'cause I got you. It's sort of like the company getting ready to go out."

By this point, Stax could not use any of its regular pressing plants, because the company was unable to pay off its accounts since CBS had not been paying Stax. To circumvent this very serious hurdle, a month after "I Got a Reason to Smile (Cause I Got You)," Al Bell and John Burton approached Union Planters about borrowing $210,000 to buy a funky old pressing plant, Rimrock Manufacturing Company, located in northeast Arkansas, which was currently owned by former country-boogie star Wayne Raney and Loys Raney. One small pressing plant filled with outdated equipment could hardly fulfill the needs of a company like Stax; unfortunately, they had no alternative. Very few copies of any given Stax release were being pressed at this point in time.

The actual cost of purchasing Rimrock was $150,000, the balance of the requested loan being for operating expenses. The two Stax executives had hatched an elaborate scheme in which they would establish a separate company called East Memphis Productions, Inc. They proposed that the whole indebtedness of Stax, East Memphis, and Lynn be transferred to this new company, and that Union Planters then return East Memphis Publishing to Stax with the bank once again holding a stock collateral pledge. It would appear that in one form or another this idea came very close to being consummated, but the bank eventually got cold feet and said no.

Stax eventually purchased the Rimrock facility with other funds, and to celebrate and ingratiate themselves into the close-knit community of Concord, Arkansas, where Rimrock was located, they bought the town an old fire engine. From engineer Pete Bishop's perspective, the hill people up in Concord were pretty special. "They were really good people," Bishop recalls. "They were salt-of-the-earth kind of people and they really put out for Stax. Everybody around there helped work to get the pressing plant going and most of the people in the town worked at the pressing plant."

By spring 1975 when Shirley Brown had a minor hit with "It Ain't No Fun," Stax owed money to virtually every independent pressing plant going. With no one willing to press their records, according to Bishop, every copy of Shirley Brown's hit was manufactured at Rimrock. To meet the demand, the facility went to three shifts, with copies of "It Ain't No Fun" being manufactured around the clock.

"That was one of the reasons they bought the fire truck," continues Bishop. "If a fire [had] ever happened there it couldn't have been put out. So, in one sense it was self-centered but, these people really put out. These were people that were not used to working twenty-four-hour days [so Stax] bought this fire truck and they had a big celebration with a *wrestling bear!* It was wild!"

Back in Memphis, there were fewer people celebrating. By the time 1974 had ground to a halt, with Bell and Stewart trying desperately to keep their company afloat, a total of eighty-five Stax employees had been given their pink slips.

17

Walking the Back Streets
and Crying: 1975

While Al Bell and John Burton were desperately trying to acquire a facility to press their records, the financial crisis enveloping Stax was growing progressively worse. On January 8, Viewlex, Inc., one of the record industry's largest record-pressing and tape-duplicating facilities, filed suit against Stax alleging the record company had failed to remit over $400,000 in pressing costs.

Even more troubling was that, for the first time, the "little label that could" was unable to meet the employee payroll. Stax employees were paid every second Friday, and the first check in January 1975 was somewhat smaller than usual. "When the check came it was for one week, instead of two," recalls Larry Nix, "and that had never happened before. They said, 'That's all right, next week you'll get the rest.' Well, the next week we did and we thought, 'Well, fine.' Then the following week [we] were supposed to get another one. 'Well, we're going to wait and pay you next week.' The thing kind of got away to where you almost didn't know what they owed you and what they didn't. That's why, to this day, I don't really know what they went out owing me."

In the midst of these problems, Stax put on a brave face and announced that promo man Buddy King had just been named "national disco representative."

While these disturbing developments were unfolding at Stax, Union Planters National Bank was undergoing its own state of crisis. On November 22, 1974, six days after Union Planters had filed its lawsuit against CBS and Stax, the U.S. comptroller of the currency requested a meeting with Union Planters' board of directors to discuss issuing a "cease and desist" order against the bank. According to bank historian John Pepin, "Such an order publicly requires a bank's directors and management to cease engaging in illegal and/or unsound banking practices." If such an order were given, the ensuing publicity would have created a groundswell of panic in the community, with Union Planters probably losing its large corporate deposit base as well as many of its individual clients. Most likely the bank would then have been declared insolvent, would have been forced to close, and its board members would have potentially faced the possibility of sustaining large personal liability. In the meantime, Union Planters stock had already begun a free fall, plummeting by September to seven dollars a share; eight months earlier it had been worth nearly triple that amount.

The Union Planters board immediately hired a bevy of lawyers in Washington who worked feverishly to stall the order. Bill Matthews drafted a letter to the comptroller of the currency arguing, according to Pepin, that a "cease and desist order was both unnecessary and counter-productive. The Comptroller's office responded by stating, in effect, that it did not believe Union Planters would make it, but would give Matthews a chance."

At the end of 1974, Union Planters reported a net loss of $16,753,220, and an asset structure that had shrunk $187 million over the course of one year. The provision for loan losses had leapt from $7 million the previous year to a whopping $25.6 million, and the bank's capital had been reduced nearly $19 million. Of the remaining $59.7 million, $10 million only existed on the bank's balance sheet as an asset described as a "bond claims receivable."[1] This was the figure that the bank felt it would eventually collect from its bond company, out of a total $16.5 million claimed, based on the fraudulent actions of a number of employees, including Joe Harwell.[2] A sizable portion of this figure represented Stax Records' debts that UP hoped would be covered by their bonding company, because the loans were made by Joe Harwell when, according to UP, he was fully aware that Stax would not be able to pay the money back. The $10 million so listed was vital to the bank's solvency. If the bank's capital fell below $52 million, Union Planters would have been legally insolvent. Collecting on the bank's bond claims was clearly central to UP's survival. Pepin compares Union Planters' crisis at the time to the bank panics of 1907, 1914, and the Great Depression. Among Union Planters' directors were some of the most prominent and powerful financial and political players in Memphis. It is testimony to the political clout of this select group that the bonds claim receivable figure was deemed an acceptable entry and that the bank wasn't forced into immediate legal insolvency by the government.

With the board of directors potentially susceptible to substantial personal liability, the word went out in Memphis power-broker circles that the bank was to be saved at any and all costs. According to Al Bell, one of the local power barons confidentially explained to him why no local businessman was willing or able to help Stax. Matthews's mandate, according to what had been relayed to Bell, was to "save the bank and it doesn't matter who he has to step on, kill or destroy to do it. That was Shellebarger and Leman's role. They were the 'hit men.'"

With $60 million worth of problem loans, Matthews adopted an aggressive approach. Union Planters embarked on a series of foreclosures of both businesses and personal property that ran through most of 1975 and 1976. As UP both sued and was countersued by a number of its loan customers, the bank became embroiled in litigation that totaled one-quarter of a billion dollars by the end of 1975. To deal with this legal morass, in February 1975 Matthews instituted a special support unit that was responsible for major litigation and the pursuit of the bank's $16.5 million bond claims. Dubbed "Financial Affairs," this new department was headed by James Cook. Over the next ten months, Financial Affairs grew in size to fourteen employees and developed what bank historian John Pepin terms a "professional working relationship" with the U.S. Attorney's Office. This latter relationship would have severe ramifications for Al Bell.

As it stood, Stax was Union Planters' single greatest problem. On February 5 Shellebarger met with Jim Stewart. He subsequently described the events of the meeting in a memo to the bank's new liaison with Stax, William Dick. Stewart informed Shellebarger that Stax and CBS were close to reaching a settlement that would free Stax to distribute its records independently. With that in mind, Stax had been creating a high

1. This was so unusual that the bank's auditor, Peat, Marwick, Mitchell & Co., withheld unqualified approval of the bank's financial statement.

2. Dishonesty was rife at Union Planters. By the fall of 1975 Bill Matthews had accused twelve former employees, including eight officers, of "misconduct, dishonesty and infidelity." By October, according to *Business Week,* three former employees, including Harwell, had been sentenced to jail, another had been indicted by a federal grand jury, and four others had been named as nonindicted co-conspirators in a fraud case. Six businessmen outside the bank, including Al Bell, had either been indicted or convicted of committing fraudulent acts with employees of the bank. More indictments were expected. Matthews also fired a number of employees who were accused of thefts of $250 or less. UP was so out of control that the latter transgressions included "rifling the pantyhose machine in the women's rest room" and swiping "tires and batteries from repossessed cars."

volume of new product by its better-known artists to be ready for release as soon as Stax was free from the distribution clutches of CBS.

Shellebarger was comforted by the fact that Stewart "seems to have assumed—or reassumed a position of control and authority over Stax. . . . He was knowledgeable of Stax's excessive overhead situation—dead wood; poor financial planning; and over extension—indicated he was moving to cure these problems. . . . He spoke often of cutting off and out the extraneous activities and wasting of resources on non-record business endeavors and of 'getting back to running a record company.'"

The content of Shellebarger's memo reflects an increasing level of frustration the bank had been experiencing in their dealings with Al Bell. "One of the things that we concluded fairly early on," stated William Dick in a deposition filed in July 1979, "was that Al Bell was an exceedingly popular guy in the industry, unquestionably a good promoter, but probably a pretty poor businessman, and it was our feeling that Jim Stewart might bring a little more business responsibility to the affairs by getting back involved."

Shellebarger informed Stewart of the bank's position with regard to Bell and Stax's continual default on various interim agreements to resolve its credit problems. He also pointed out that in the absence of any forward movement on the part of Stax, very shortly the bank could find it necessary to take whatever legal remedy was available to it, including: (1) foreclosing on and selling the studio; (2) foreclosing on and selling the Union Avenue Extended offices; and (3) moving to collect on Stewart's and Bell's personal guarantees.

Shellebarger concluded his memo by stating that "Stewart is sincere and honest, however, he may not have [an] adequate grasp of the reality of the situation. The debt structure and current payables may be of a magnitude beyond Stax's capabilities to handle outside [of] bankruptcy."

On February 26, 1975, William Dick met with Al Bell for the last time. Bell told Dick that the settlement with CBS would be concluded within days, and that all inventory currently in the possession of CBS would be transferred back to Stax. He then outlined a variety of ways for generating income to begin to retire Stax's debt and return to a sound financial basis. The first step in Bell's plans was to dump much of the CBS-held inventory in South Africa and Australia where he had lined up potential sales totaling some $6 million.

On the domestic front, Bell was planning to sell all Stax, Volt, and Enterprise product directly to the dealer market at one-stop prices. This would give Stax the one-stop markup in addition to its normal profit, and all sales would be made on a C.O.D. basis. Although this was an audacious move, Bell felt Stax could get away with it as long as the company produced hits. The other four Stax labels, Truth, Gospel Truth, Respect, and Partee, would continue to be sold through the twenty independent distributors that were currently handling those lines. Bell also unveiled plans to produce four "Best of" LPs drawn from the back catalogue of Isaac Hayes, the Staple Singers, the Dramatics, and Johnnie Taylor that would be initially test-marketed for TV marketing through the William Tanner Company in Atlanta and Chicago, then extended to other major markets, and eventually brought into normal distribution channels. Dick wrote that Bell had "diligently guarded against their release throughout the problems with CBS." At the conclusion of their meeting, Bell proposed to Dick five requests for additional credit "which were categorically denied."

Dick never bothered to meet with Bell again, stating: "There were an endless number of plans that never came to fruition. It always seemed the discussion was for more money and that there was nothing ever really positive from the other side." John Burton replaced

Bell as Stax's main contact person for Union Planters at this juncture, Dick meeting with Burton in May, June, July, and August. Frustrated by his lack of progress in settling the account, in the early fall Dick turned it over to Parnell Lewis. At the same time, Union Planters closed its Bellevue Branch, claiming it had not made a profit since it first opened in 1965. Located just a few short blocks down McLemore from Stax, this had been the branch from which Joe Harwell had initially courted the business of both Stax and Al Bell. It was in all likelihood the Union Planters branch with the largest African-American customer base.

On February 28, Stax reached an out-of-court settlement with CBS. Needless to say, with the New York conglomerate maintaining an absolute lock on Stax's ability to generate income, the settlement heavily favored CBS's interests. "Ultimately they had me," admits Al Bell. "I settled a lawsuit under duress. I didn't work anything out. I just settled it under duress. I had no alternative. The only way that I was going to get out of that situation and keep from dying at that point in time was to settle it with them and take the beating. The only reason they were willing to do anything at that point in time was because the press was going against them. They were getting bad press.

"Arthur Taylor said to me, 'We won't argue with you about the merits of your antitrust suit, Al. We just have more time than you and more money than you.' That's the head of a major corporation making that statement! They were very careful with how they dealt with this situation. A lot of this stuff was oral. It was over dinner, walking down a street."

CBS agreed to relinquish its rights to distribute Stax product if Stax repaid its debt to CBS by August 31, 1976. The debt currently included the original $6 million loan CBS had made to Stax in 1972 plus $326,797.68 in unpaid interest dating back to September 1974. CBS agreed to cut the loan in half if Stax repaid it by the agreed-upon deadline. Stax, in turn, agreed to let CBS keep $4,255,038 worth of record inventory that was currently stored in CBS's warehouses and dispose of it in any way it saw fit. If CBS realized gross receipts in excess of the cost of this inventory, such receipts were to be credited against Stax's total indebtedness to CBS. If there was a shortfall, it was to be added to the Stax debt.[3] Finally, if Stax failed to pay the debt by the agreed-upon date, CBS could once again decide to exercise the right to distribute Stax product, although they were not obligated to do so.

Although Stax was clear of its distribution problem with CBS, it was still in rather desperate straits. In the words of a June 1975 Al Bell memo, "the battle was over but . . . the war had just begun." The company owed several million dollars to both CBS and Union Planters National Bank. It had lost, or was about to lose, its contract with virtually all of its key artists including Isaac Hayes, the Dramatics, the Staple Singers (released April 15, 1975), the Emotions (released in May), and comedian Richard Pryor due to its economic problems in the latter half of 1974. In some ways, ironically, the label was, for a third time, starting from ground zero. This time, though, Stax was saddled with back-breaking debts and did not have the financial resources of a Gulf and Western to use as startup capital. The odds of survival were not great but Al Bell, Jim Stewart, and several others soldiered on.

At the time, an unnamed Stax official put forward a brave face, saying to Memphis writer Walter Dawson, "We're getting into picking up the same kind of tempo we had before things went downhill. Stax has regained its ability to determine its own destiny and

---

3. The size and subsequent cost of this inventory was to ultimately include all returns on Stax product that CBS accepted from January 1 through June 30, 1975. The shortfall ended up reaching $5,194,099. With interest on this and the original $6 million loan, Stax owed CBS as of December 31, 1975, a staggering $12,255,006.

can now go about the business of selling records and making money for all of us in the Southern tradition of independence."

With so many of the company's mainstays headed off for greener pastures, Stax was forced to set its hopes for renewed success on a combination of second-tier artists and a number of new acts. In its final year, one-off 45s were issued by several of these new acts, including Barbara & Joe, the Green Brothers, the Dynamic Soul Machine, Freddie Waters, the Fiestas, former Emotion Theresa Davis, and R. B. Hudmon. Despite the obvious quality of most of these releases, Stax was unable to realize substantive income from any of them. Nonetheless, records trickled onto the market, two singles appearing in January (including the final Volt 45, Hot Sauce's "I Can't Let You Go"), two more in February, and one in March. The latter was the Temprees' cover of Redbone's "Come and Get Your Love," which turned out to be the very last record issued on We Produce.

Releasing product was a necessary corollary of attempting to get back in the game, but—given Stax's then-limited ability to press records, promote them, and ultimately get them into the marketplace—the company was in need of a much longer financial rope than Union Planters was even remotely interested in extending to them. Consequently, Bell, Stewart, and John Burton continued foraging for capital, ideally hoping to find a benefactor who could provide the necessary funds for Stax to pay off both CBS and Union Planters. Then, and only then, could Stax really go about the business of rebuilding its artist roster.

Leaving no stone unturned, they came very close in March to connecting with a very unlikely sugardaddy, Saudi Arabia's King Faisal. Working through intermediaries, Bell and Burton had initiated dialogue with representatives of the king, and a tentative agreement had been reached whereby Faisal would make available to Stax an astronomical amount of money.[4] King Faisal's motivation was his interest in supporting African-American economic empowerment in the most general sense. In the third week of March, John Burton boarded a plane heading to Beirut.

"All it required at that time," sighs Bell, "was just an eyeball meeting and the deal would have been done. I remember talking to him from Beirut while we could hear gunfire on the outside." But Burton never met the king, because—in an incredible twist of fate, as far as Stax was concerned—Faisal was assassinated by his nephew on March 25. Back in Memphis at 2693 Union Avenue Extended, the disappointment was so thick that it could have been cut with a knife.

Stax was also in debt to several key radio stations, having failed to be able to pay for advertisements. Despite Stax's indebtedness to these stations, it was crucial that the label maintain its ability to get its records played on the air, and thus it needed the stations' goodwill. In early April, Paul Isbell, now Stax's director of promotion, sent out a letter to these stations, requesting their patience and invoking the biblical Job's rather legendary proclivities in this area. He promised that Stax was making every effort to fulfill its financial obligations in the shortest time period possible.

As was the common modus operandi at this point in time, the tone of Isbell's letters placed Stax's problems in the context of struggle, portraying Stax as the underdog, fighting the good fight. The parallel to David and Goliath could not be missed. The general attitude was that "the little label that could" would survive each and every calamity if everyone rallied around and did the right thing. Isbell's letter concluded, "We cannot and will not ever forget the patience that you showed toward us as we struggled to survive."

4. Al Bell does not remember what the specific amount of money involved was but he thought it might have been in the area of $100 million.

While Isbell was attempting to placate various radio stations, John Burton was drafting a plan to raise $25 million through the private placement of what he termed "Senior notes" with a fifteen-year maturity. Unfortunately, nothing came of this plan.

Meanwhile, Stax owed East Memphis Music approximately $4.5 million for mechanical royalties for copyrighted songs that had been used on Stax albums. UP's Roger Shellebarger put pressure on Tim Whitsett to go through the motions of attempting to collect this money from Stax as East Memphis was obligated to pay 50 percent of these royalties to its writers. Although the bank knew that Stax would not be able to pay East Memphis the money that it owed, East Memphis still had to attempt to collect these royalties or face possible lawsuits for negligence by its songwriters. Whitsett duly drafted a letter that in rather formal terms listed the total debt and demanded payment forthwith.

A day or two after Whitsett's letter was sent, Stax announced a company-wide meeting that all the publishing employees were requested to attend. As it happened, Whitsett already had an important meeting scheduled for that evening, and figured that his staff could fill him in on what transpired at Stax. However, midway through the day of the meeting, Earlie Biles called East Memphis and said that it was imperative that Whitsett be at the meeting. Unwilling to take "No" for an answer, she eventually got Whitsett on the line personally and informed him that Mr. Bell requested his presence at the meeting. Whitsett apologized, but said he had to take care of his other commitment. Five minutes later, Al Bell himself called Whitsett and repeatedly stressed how important it was that Whitsett attend. Bell finally got Whitsett to agree to try to get out of his commitment, and Roger Shellebarger ended up covering for Whitsett at the non-Stax meeting.

That evening, every Stax and East Memphis employee gathered at the chapel at the Union Avenue Extended office. On the stage sat Earlie Biles, John Burton, Jim Stewart, and Al Bell who, one by one, got up and gave a pep talk. Al Bell then produced a letter on East Memphis stationery that he proceeded to hold up for everyone to see, explaining that "We have just received this letter from Mr. Whitsett." Bell paused and Whitsett felt all eyes riveted in his direction. "Now Mr. Whitsett," continued Bell, "I don't know if he actually wrote this letter himself or just allowed it to go out over his signature as a dupe." The letter was then read in its entirety in a very sarcastic tone.

"I had never been so furious in my life," fumed Whitsett, still angry some twenty-two years later. "I was speechless. I was so furious. He would stop and look at me. 'Did you write this letter yourself, Mr. Whitsett?' All I could do was look the sharpest daggers in the world at him. I beamed my eyes like a laser on him and thought, 'If looks could kill, you're dead, son!' I have never been so furious since."

Whitsett left the meeting feeling he had been a patsy. The whole rigmarole to get him to come to the meeting had been solely to conduct a public witch hunt. "[Al] set me up," affirms the former publisher. "The meeting was to get me. That was the whole point. I was the prime example of showing them that there was an enemy out there they all had to fight." This siege mentality would increasingly work its way into the Stax psyche: a religious war was upon them.

Walking out to his car, somewhat fearful for his safety, Whitsett was surprised when Stax's two star songwriters Homer Banks and Carl Hampton appeared on either side of him. "They were saying," says Whitsett, "'Man, we just want to tell you, we're with you one hundred percent of the way.' I said, 'Really?' They said, 'You're right, you stuck up for us, the writers. We appreciate that and we appreciated the way you handled yourself in there. You were a man.'" Whitsett received similar commendations over the phone from Eddie Floyd, Larry Nix, and others, and the next day was given a standing ovation when he showed up for work at East Memphis. The battle lines were certainly drawn, but not every employee was on Stax's side.[5]

In April, Stax pressed on, issuing six 45s, including Shirley Brown's reading of the Frederick Knight–penned "It Ain't No Fun." It became a hit, albeit a modest one, settling at number 32 R&B while scraping the lower reaches of the pop Hot 100 at number 94. "That song was written specifically for her," sighs Knight. "I wrote it in an Aretha Franklin vein and I just gave it to her. It's like how can you tailor a song and imagine all of the things that Aretha would do with it? You don't have that kind of imagination. All you can do is try to write a good song and put it in a vein that you think [she] could do justice to. Over and above that you have to leave it to [her] creativity, which you automatically have to factor in when you write. You might not know exactly the runs and the licks that they're gonna put on it, but you know it's gonna be there. Shirley has so much to give in a song. The problem you have is trying to get her to hold back a little bit. She can really, really go some different ways in her performance."

Knight is not exaggerating. Shirley Brown had one of the most brilliant voices to ever grace the recorded medium. On "It Ain't No Fun," she is ably supported by two of the original MG's house band members, Duck Dunn and Al Jackson, plus longtime Stax session musicians Marvell Thomas, Lester Snell, and Bobby Manuel. Manuel's work is especially engaging, juxtaposed against Thomas and Snell's church-informed organ and piano lines. In a curious sort of way, especially considering that Jim Stewart was producing, Shirley Brown's recordings in this period come closest in tone, intent, and execution to what the label was doing in the mid-sixties. Also worth noting is the spoken monologue in the middle of "It Ain't No Fun," which playfully alludes to Brown's earlier hit, "Woman to Woman." Although it wasn't as big of a hit, "It Ain't No Fun" is probably the better of the two records.

Another of the company's April releases was a new tune written and sung by Eddie Floyd entitled "Talk to the Man." As was the case with many of Stax's earliest artists, Floyd remained loyal to the bitter end. In late June he told a reporter from the mid-South's leading black newspaper, *The Tri-State Defender,* "I came to Stax with Al Bell. He brought me here and unless he puts me out, I'll be here 'till he takes me from here himself.

"I am not running, Really none of us who care are running. I have had hard times before, but hard times come and they go. In the past, when they came, Stax stuck by me—so now I am sticking with Stax.

"It's more than a record company, but it's not a family either. Stax is a business organization and when one of their associates is in trouble the people at Stax invest. They invest money sometimes—or contact—or time—or favor—they help. And in the end they get that back.

"Now there are people here in Memphis, in New York, out in California, all over—who are helping Stax because Stax has helped them. Al Bell and Jim Stewart built this company by investing in people—and now they are collecting the interest. A lot of these people are glad they have a way to pay back now that it's needed."

With reference to his latest release, Floyd prayed that it would be a hit "not just for me, it's always important to me, but I want a hit for what it can do to help the company right

---

5. Al Bell does not remember this incident at all. While he admits that a similar event may have occurred, he denies that it took place in the chapel. Bell takes great pains to emphasize that the chapel at the Union Avenue office was literally and figuratively sacred as far as he was concerned. "There is no way under God's sun," emphasizes Bell, "that I would have gone into that chapel with any negativity in me. It would have been the exact opposite. There is no way I would have stood up in that chapel and done anything to demean Tim Whitsett or anybody else." It is plausible that what Whitsett describes did indeed happen but that Al Bell's intentions and Tim Whitsett's perceptions regarding the event are directly at odds.

now. There is no other company I could say that for or sing this song for, for the song has a deep personal meaning for me. I am sorry for the problems the company has had but I've never been sorry for a minute that I came here with Al, and like I said, I ain't leaving unless he puts me out." The level of compassion for Al and Jim that many of their artists and employees exhibited is testimony to what Stax had meant in the lives of these people.

A further two 45s, including former Mad Lad John Gary Williams's second solo single, the gorgeous "Come What May," were released in May.[6] That same month, as a Stax press release claimed that the company's "momentum is positive, increasing and upward," long-time Stax stalwart William Bell's contract expired, and he elected not to renew it. The Emotions also were released from their contractual obligations to Stax in May. A month later, in what surely added insult to injury, the Soul Children signed with CBS, where Don Davis was scheduled to produce them. The Emotions and Johnnie Taylor would also, not so coincidentally, sign with CBS over the next few months.

As Stax's artist roster continued to unravel, Roger Shellebarger began to theorize that Al Bell had acted in cahoots with Joe Harwell in defrauding Union Planters. Shellebarger hypothesized that Bell guaranteed a number of the loans that Harwell had admitted extending to fictitious individuals. In return, Harwell continued to loan Stax money that he knew it couldn't pay back and, to justify these loans, knowingly accepted false representations with regard to Stax's financial situation. Further cementing Harwell and Bell's nefarious scheme, according to Shellebarger, were a series of kickbacks Harwell received from Bell.

In another of those amazing coincidences that seemed to occur in the onslaught that Stax was experiencing from all sides, on May 29 Union Planters received a letter from the U.S. Attorney's Office pointing out the bank's duty to report suspected criminal activities to government authorities. The U.S. Attorney's office sent this letter to all federally connected banks in western Tennessee, but it was later admitted in court that the letter was partially motivated by the investigations into the affairs of Stax Records then being conducted by the U.S. Attorney's Office and the grand jury. According to U.S. Attorney John Mulrooney, beginning in December 1974 that investigation had begun to focus on Al Bell.

On June 5, James Cook, the head of the financial affairs unit at Union Planters, wrote U.S. Attorney Thomas Turley, outlining the bank's belief that Bell and Harwell had conspired together to commit criminal acts and defraud Union Planters National Bank. One of the key pieces of evidence that Cook deployed in support of this argument was the $100,000 check Al Bell had written to Harwell's Action for Ideas company in the fall of 1973. This was interpreted by UP as a kickback for Harwell's approving a $1.6 million loan to the Stax subsidiary Lynn and Associates.

Cook's letter, in part, read: "The Bank now has evidence in its possession which proves that Harwell entered into a criminal conspiracy with Isbell [Bell's legal last name] to defraud the Bank in this particular instance of $1,600,000. It is the Bank's belief that this was only one act of many in which Harwell and Isbell together conspired to defraud the Bank and thus achieve their own dishonest and illegal ends."[7]

On July 23, Cook filed an amended claim with the bank's bonding company, the Fidelity Bank and Deposit Company of Maryland. The bank's first bonding claim charged that Harwell had made improper loans in that he concealed true information from the bank with regard to Stax's financial condition. However, the potential problem

---

6. A few weeks earlier Williams had been terminated by East Memphis as the cash-strapped publishing firm began to cut back.

7. On July 24, Cook sent supplementary information to the government.

with this claim was that, if Harwell had believed false financial information supplied by Bell and/or Stax and had simply used bad judgment in granting the Stax loans, the bank could not collect this money on its employee fidelity bond. All it would be able to collect would be the money lost through Harwell's loans to fictitious individuals, which were penny ante when compared with the Stax debt. Desperate to stave off its impending insolvency, the bank's amended claim charged that Bell and Harwell were in conspiracy. Not surprisingly, the amended claim conveniently failed to make any mention of the fact that Harwell had admitted to forging Bell's signature on a number of the fictitious loans. It did, however, luridly denigrate Al Bell's management of Stax, stating that in early 1973 the record company "began to evidence the results of over expansion, poor business planning, and gross mismanagement in the form of staggering operating losses, which resulted in insufficient cash flow necessary to meet the then current cash operating requirements." In yet one more curious coincidence, there is an amazing similarity in the wording of Union Planters' amended bond claim and the U.S. Attorney's Office indictment of Al Bell on September 8.

All of this activity was unknown to Al Bell, Jim Stewart, or anyone else at Stax. They were trying to rekindle the ashes of their once-glorious record company. Squeezed virtually to the limit, they managed to issue at least three, and perhaps as many as six, 45s in the month of June, including Johnnie Taylor's final chart record for Stax, the Don Davis–penned "Try Me Tonight." The record could only crawl its way to number 51 R&B but, in the middle of 1975, that was a small victory for Stax. Whatever elation might have been experienced by those still believing in "the little label that could," it was more than tempered when, acceding to Taylor's demands, on August 15 Stax agreed to tender his contract to CBS.[8]

Two other 45s were definitely released by Stax in June: the Fiestas' "I Can't Shake Your Love (Can't Shake You Loose)" and Frederick Knight's "I Wanna Play with You." Hailing from Newark, New Jersey, the Fiestas started out singing doo-wop on street corners in the mid-fifties. With Hy Weiss's Old Town Records, they had scored chart hits twice, in 1959 with "So Fine" and again in 1962 with "Broken Heart." When the hits stopped coming, the Fiestas continued to work, playing shows in Europe, Japan, the United States, and Canada while their membership slowly mutated. By the time they were signed to Stax in February 1975, only one original member, Eddie Morris, remained. The Fiestas came to Stax under the auspices of Johnny Baylor crony Randy Stewart, who years earlier had been a member of the group; more recently Stewart had been serving as road manager for Isaac Hayes.

With Stax desperate for material, a variety of people associated with the label who were no longer active as artists, such as songwriter Mack Rice and engineer William Brown, found themselves back in the studio recording new material. The Fiestas record was one more example of this.

Bettye Crutcher and Frederick Knight teamed up, on Jim Stewart's recommendation, to create Knight's final Truth release, "I Wanna Play with You."

"I think everybody virtually knew or felt that things were bad," recalls Knight. "This was one of the few sessions that Jim Stewart was in on when I was there. Jim was actually 'hands on' on this particular date. He was trying desperately to take the reins of the company and pull it back out of the hole. Jim had given his life for that company. Understanding that, we all tried to rally around him for support."

---

8. As a CBS artist Taylor enjoyed a brief string of hits, including "Disco Lady," "Somebody's Gettin' It," and "Love Is Better in the A.M."

June also saw the release of Rance Allen's *A Soulful Experience* LP on Truth. Produced by David Porter and Ronnie Williams, *A Soulful Experience* was Allen's attempt to move beyond the gospel market. It had been preceded at the beginning of the year by a Porter-Williams single, "Ain't No Need of Crying," that had struggled its way to number 61 R&B. According to Ronnie Williams, in the final year of Stax's existence, "Ain't No Need of Crying" became the company's unofficial theme song.

Although a further eleven singles were scheduled for release between mid-June and December 19, there is some doubt as to whether all of these singles actually saw the light of day. Some may have gotten no further than disc jockey promotional copies while others may have just been assigned a catalogue number and release date but were never actually pressed. Increasingly operating with a bare-bones staff, Stax paperwork is extremely sketchy for the final six months of the label's life.[9]

During late winter and early spring, Stax's ability to meet its payroll continued to ebb and flow. After June 8, the company basically ceased being able to pay anyone. Unbelievably, many of its employees continued to work without pay, maintaining a near-religious belief that Al Bell would pull the company through.

At that point, Earlie Biles tried to talk her husband James Douglas into leaving Stax and getting another job while she continued to work for the record company without pay. "He said, 'No!'" recalls Biles, shaking her head a decade later. "He really had a lot of respect for Mr. Bell and he said, 'No way, I'm going to stay here and help him fight.'"

Earlie herself had been trying to leave Stax since January, when she told Al that she could no longer work day and night. In September she enrolled in law school in Inglewood, California. Her loyalty to Stax was so great that she attended school from Monday evening through Thursday, then flew back to Memphis, charging the plane tickets to her own credit card, worked at Stax over the weekend, and flew back to Inglewood for class on Monday. The whole while she was maintaining this backbreaking and nerve-wrecking pace, Stax was unable to pay her or anyone else. While Biles's commitment may seem extreme, there are similar stories from many of those who stood steadfast at Al Bell's side. Even as late as 1975, Stax remained a very special place for those who understood its spiritual and emotional core.

For those who weren't as emotionally committed to Stax Records, things were just a little bit different. As head of East Memphis Music, Tim Whitsett found himself in an adversarial position. The company-wide meeting the previous April had provided plenty of evidence of that. In June things got just a little bit crazier. Union Planters Bank was contemplating raising a few dollars by foreclosing on Stax's Union Avenue Extended building, legally owned by East Memphis, which, of course, Union Planters controlled due to Stax's inability to make the required payments on East Memphis's loans. Tim Whitsett was given the task of showing the building to two executives from the Memphis jingle company Pepper-Tanner, which already occupied an office building right across the street from Stax.

Given the current emotional climate at Stax, Whitsett was not looking forward to this assignment. To try to ease his task, he phoned Stax administrator J. Leonard Smith under the ruse that, because East Memphis was paying the insurance policy on the building, they

---

9. My best guess is that most of these records hit the market in one form or another, although the number of copies actually distributed was minimal. I physically have copies of a couple of the 45s, including the second-to-last record scheduled for release, and a few of the artists I interviewed had copies of some of the other records. In some cases, though, the artist in question was absolutely certain he or she had never seen a copy of the record and therefore it is unlikely it was released. Al Bell states emphatically that the company continued to release records right up to that fateful December day when it was forced into involuntary bankruptcy.

needed to see the blueprints. Smith consented, and a short while later Whitsett and the two Pepper-Tanner employees came by.

"I got over there," recalls Tim Whitsett, rolling his eyes, "with these guys on the pretext that they were from the insurance company and they're just inspecting the place so that the policy can be updated. We get around and they start unfurling blueprints [saying things like] 'Ah, this will make a good staff cafeteria, won't it.' 'Yes, yes, T.J.'"

It didn't take long for Smith to put two and two together and realize what was up. The next day, which was Friday the 13th, William Tanner of Pepper-Tanner told Whitsett that he and a few others wanted to make one final inspection of the building. They suggested that Whitsett sneak them in over the weekend. Not willing to go that far, Whitsett said he was going back to Jackson for the weekend and that they could wait until Monday for one final visit.

This time Stax security was on red alert. Consequently Whitsett and his guests were escorted the whole time they were in the building by Stax security man C. G. Kelly. "I remember Kelly following me around," continues Whitsett. "'What's up Tim? What you doing Tim? Y'all ain't selling the building is you Tim?'"

"By the time we were leaving the building," continues Whitsett, "word had filtered out to Al Bell's secretary what we were doing and I did get worried that I was a dead man. She had sent word to Kelly to stop me with a gun if necessary from leaving the building. He came and he told me, 'Miss [Earlie] Biles said for me to pull my gun on you, you better get out of here.'" Needless to say, Whitsett and company exited the building post haste. Tanner did not buy the building, and the Union Avenue office would not be foreclosed on until March 1976.

The same week that Whitsett was showing the Union Avenue building to the Pepper-Tanner executives, a memo from Robert Harris, former controller and current assistant to David Porter, was displayed prominently on the company's bulletin boards. In essence the memo condemned all "negative thinking employees." Those who wished to continue to gripe were told to "leave." It went on to say unequivocally: "We do not want you. Those who don't leave but continue to gripe, we will find you out and root you out and, don't be surprised if it's your co-worker who finds you out."

Another memo was posted on every door leading into both the Union Avenue and McLemore complexes. It stated that songwriters "Carl Hampton and Homer Banks are not allowed on the premises for any reason whatsoever, not as a guest or in any other capacity. Anyone who allows them in will be fired!"

Paranoia was running deep at "Soulsville U.S.A." as an "Us against Them" mentality began to prevail. This was a war, framed in nearly a religious context of good versus evil. You were either part of the solution or part of the problem. In Banks and Hampton's case, they had crossed the line and were now branded as the enemy.

In early May, Banks and Hampton had gone to East Memphis and requested a release from their songwriting contract. When other publishing firms realized that Stax was on its last legs, several began making overtures to the team that had created "If Loving You Is Wrong (I Don't Want to Be Right)," "I'll Be the Other Woman," "If You're Ready (Come Go with Me)," and "Touch a Hand, Make a Friend." After rejecting offers from Motown and ABC-Dunhill, the dynamic duo opted to go with A&M. The California-based publisher was offering them a pretty substantial deal and, as things stood at Stax and East Memphis, they were not receiving a penny. Tim Whitsett agreed and took their request to Shellebarger. By mid-month, East Memphis's two primary songwriters had their walking papers. By the end of the summer they had moved to California.

Meanwhile, Al Bell and Jim Stewart frantically phoned the pair, pleading for them to re-sign their songwriting agreement, reasoning that Stax desperately needed to maintain such key creative staff if it were to have any chance of survival. Hampton and Banks simply said at this point that they had to look out for themselves. They were duly informed that their Stax production contracts were being ripped up and they were banned from the premises. Although Banks felt that in his heart of hearts he was doing what he had to do, he was extremely depressed. "Stax was like my life," the songwriter opines.

On June 9 Stax bounced an $83,260.27 check to CBS. The wolves began circling the door. Nine days later, Al Bell sent a three-page memo to all Stax employees headed "THESE DAYS WOULD COME" that provides considerable insight into the state of mind of many of the company's employees. A beleaguered Bell began the memo by referring to statements and predictions he had made at three different general company meetings held since the settlement with CBS.

"I tried to make it as plain as I possibly could <u>that</u> these days would come. I explained that 'the battle was over but that the war had just begun.' We are in the midst of that war. Please try to reflect on that for <u>your</u> <u>own</u> <u>mental</u> <u>health</u> . . . My observations <u>were</u> and still <u>are</u> that we would experience some trying and painful times. Attention was called to some of the <u>extreme</u> sacrifices that would have to be made. <u>I</u> <u>also</u> <u>asked</u> <u>each</u> <u>individual</u> <u>to</u> <u>make</u> <u>his</u> <u>own</u> <u>personal</u> <u>decision</u> <u>as</u> <u>to</u> <u>how</u> <u>much</u> <u>he</u> <u>could</u> <u>take</u>.

"WE SHALL AND WILL WIN—ONLY THE STRONG SURVIVES."

Bell stressed that "Not one time did I promise a chicken in every pot, caviar in every dish or a cadillac in every garage. . . . no 'pie in the sky'—merely hard facts," adding that he believed that in such troubled times the onus was on a company like Stax to do everything it could to maintain its employee complement.

"To attempt this requires that business to make <u>many</u> corporate sacrifices. I hasten to say, however, that a business cannot accomplish this without the full and complete support of <u>all</u> persons employed by that business. In addition, and more importantly, there has to be UNQUESTIONED LOYALTY—IT IS A TWO WAY STREET . . .

"It is important that we, individually find security in our own being; and your motivation in this instance must be self motivation. GENERAL MORAL [sic] IS DETERMINED BY INDIVIDUAL MORAL [sic] , WHICH EMANATES FROM A SINCERE AND CARING SOUL . . . ENTHUSIASM? If you act (action) enthusiastic, you will be enthusiastic. All I am attempting to say here is . . . 'LET'S GET IT ON.' You can make the overall job easier by giving more—admittedly, under the circumstances, it is painful; but by getting it on—coming together—and doing what weak, lazy, careless and selfish people call <u>the</u> <u>impossible</u>, we rid ourselves of our frustrations, individually and collectively; and we, without even recognizing how it happened, will 'WIN THE WAR' . . . I argue that we have the people who can easily do this; however, ONE BAD APPLE CAN SPOIL the whole barrel. To sit and wait on things to happen and <u>not</u> do something to make things happen is to create <u>the</u> <u>impossible</u>."

The next two-thirds of a page consisted of a series of one-line comments that Bell said were made to him by various employees. The vast majority were supportive, one employee stating, "If the building should fall, look for me under the board, I will be there," another quoted as saying, "If I have to do two jobs to survive, I am with you to the end." Interestingly enough, Bell chose to include a couple of quotes that indirectly cast aspersions on some employees, representative examples including, "I don't know why you're killing yourself for these people, half of them are jealous of you anyway," and "Mr. Bell, these people don't appreciate you or what you are doing, they don't really care."

The memo's conclusion read like a sermon, placing the responsibility on the employees to prove their belief through appropriate action. "I say to you today, each and everyone of you, that if you are under a <u>CLOUD</u> that is <u>IMMOVABLE</u> it is because you have not demonstrated the will to move it. Where is the confidence in ourselves?

"The drive to survive and the will to live brings out the BEST or the WORST in a person. Check yourself out—your <u>REAL</u> character may be beginning to show.

"STAX WILL PREVAIL (FOR STAX IS AN ATTITUDE)—WILL YOU ?? . . .

"Recommended reading for understanding: <u>PSALMS 23</u>."

Stax was now down to under one hundred employees. For those remaining, *these days* had come and worse ones were just around the corner.

Just under a month after Bell's memo, on July 8, Al Bell's father, Albert Isbell, contributed $50,000 of his own money to give Stax badly needed working capital.[10] Toward the end of the month, Chicago lawyer W. Maudlin Smith held a press conference at the Holiday Inn Rivermont in Memphis to announce that a group of unnamed Chicago investors were interested in bankrolling a relocation of Stax Records to Gary, Indiana. The investment group, at least partially centered around Chicago's Guaranty Bank and Trust Company, reportedly was considering floating $10 million for operating capital for Stax. Much of the money was hopefully going to come via a multimillion-dollar loan from the Teamsters Pension Fund.[11]

Gary, Indiana, mayor Richard Hatcher's office was interested in Stax taking over three floors of an abandoned Holiday Inn highrise. To that end, his office met with Stax officials in early August to offer assistance in occupancy and financing. During the press conference, Smith repeatedly cited the "lack of interest of civic and business" organizations in Memphis as the prime reason that Stax might relocate. The offers to move to Gary had partially come about due to Stax's hiring of a Chicago-based company called Public Relations International, Inc., to spearhead a "Save Stax" campaign.

Only one 45 was issued in July, "Back Road into Town," from the final Staple Singers Stax album, 1974's *City in the Sky.* For many at the company it was becoming increasingly evident that Bell and Stewart stood very little chance of ever righting the good ship Stax. For those who had that foresight, it was simply too depressing to stay on and battle in vain. Shortly after the release of the Staples' single, the company's longest-tenured and one of its most loyal employees, Deanie Parker, packed it in, heading back to the university and pondering her future.

Two further 45s, Eddie Floyd's "I'm So Glad I Met You" and Little Milton's "Packed Up and Took My Mind," were released into a few stores in August.

Trying to generate product any and every way it could, in mid-July Stax released "Best of" packages on Isaac Hayes, the Staple Singers, the Dramatics, and Johnnie Taylor. These were the albums Bell had spoken of several months earlier in his conversations with Union Planters vice president William Dick. Their release was timely, because the Dramatics and Isaac Hayes were both enjoying hit singles for their new labels, and in the fall, the Staple Singers would release the number 1 pop and R&B hit "Let's Do It Again" on Curtis Mayfield's Curtom label. A Stax press release at the time claimed that Terry Manning was going through the Stax tape vaults to assemble a new Booker T. and the MG's album of previously unreleased material.[12] That same month Stax inked a deal with Dutch distributing company VIP to sell Stax product in the Netherlands.

---

10. Cashing in his certificates of deposits, Albert Isbell's $50,000 represented most of his life savings.

11. The exact amount of the capital that these investors were considering floating for Stax ranges in various reports from $3 to $13 million.

12. Although there were several hours worth of unreleased MG's material, this album was not released in 1975. In the late 1970s, an album of MG's outtakes, a number of them with overdubs provided at the time by Booker T. Jones, was released in Europe. Entitled *Union Avenue Extended,* it was somewhat disappointing. Much better is a compact disc assembled by Ace Records in the mid-nineties consisting of unreleased covers recorded by the MG's. Entitled *Booker T. and the MG's Play the Hip Hits,* it is a delight from beginning to finish.

While Stax tried to find a way to get its new releases pressed, onto radio, and into the American marketplace, it was forced to lay off its entire accounting staff. Consequently, after August 25, no entries were made in the company's books. Despite the shortage of staff, Bell formed a new subsidiary called Melody, Inc., to conduct mail-order sales of Stax catalogue. Activity at this level was penny ante stuff compared to the looming reality of Stax finances. Nonetheless, Bell, Stewart, and several dozen other employees heroically worked day and night clutching at any straw that would generate absolutely any funds that would help to relieve the increasingly desperate situation the company found itself in. Despite bravery in the face of what appeared to be insurmountable odds, Stax was losing ground. In late August the company's phone was disconnected for a few days as Bell and Stewart awaited various small pockets of money then due to them.

A few days later, on September 8, Al Bell was presented with a fourteen-count indictment by a Memphis federal grand jury. The indictment charged that Bell, in partnership with bank officer Joseph Harwell, had defrauded Union Planters National Bank of $1.8 million via fraudulent loans, credit extensions, and overdrafts. Harwell was already in federal prison, having been earlier convicted of embezzling $284,000 from the bank. Bell's bail was set at a $100,000 unsecured bond.

On September 20, in its report on Bell's indictment, *The Tri-State Defender* stated that "speculation is that Bell is the victim of a 'racist plot' by several influential Memphians who feel that he is getting too 'financially independent' for them."

Within a couple of weeks of Bell's indictment, the Al Bell Defense Fund had been set up, chaired by the dean of black radio in Chicago, E. Rodney Jones. Organizers of the Defense Fund referred to the situation as a "legal lynching" of Bell engineered by Union Planters. The press release announcing the formation of the group opened by asking: "What has Al Bell to do with Robin Hood or with the doctrine of economic strangulation as practiced in the modern day south?"

Further on, the release brought up the very real specter of racism. "In happier times it was possible to create a Wattstax and a Memphis sound. Stars could be made and gold records produced. It was believed that the company was white and loans were made to it. As the land changed hands [i.e., when Stax became black-owned through Al Bell's buyout of Jim Stewart] so too did the problems arise and when the news of a move from Memphis surfaced, so too did news of an indictment.

"Al Bell was indicted and charged with borrowing from the rich and giving to the poor. The strangulation now became a lynching but it was deified by the aura of the federal court and disguised as a federal indictment. . . . CBS has attempted on previous occasions to take over the company and had now manipulated Union Planters Bank into causing an indictment. . . . This is sophisticated corporate economic strangulation, the new legal lynching in the south.

"It is time that black people and liberal and fair thinking white people all over this nation should demonstrate their sense of justice and fair play by contributing to a legal defense fund that has been established by persons throughout the record industry who have been given assistance by Al Bell and Stax Recording Company."

Typically the rallying of support for Al Bell and Stax came from outside the Memphis city limits. The defense fund was being administered by the Guaranty Bank and Trust Company in Chicago, a business that W. Maudlin Smith described as a "black Muslim firm." To get the ball rolling for the defense fund, the National Conference on Minority Development honored Al Bell at that year's convention held in St. Louis in early October. Bell was saluted as America's "outstanding entrepreneur and humanitarian" and presented with an award for his "outstanding contribution to the entertainment industry and heroic struggle for minority development." It's hard to get an accurate reading on how much money was actually raised for the fund. Although $100,000 was its stated goal, it would appear that only $7,500 was ever raised.

At Al Bell's arraignment on September 24, approximately fifty supporters turned out to demonstrate, including the Southern Christian Leadership Conference's Dr. Ralph Abernathy. *The Tri-State Defender* reported that "Abernathy says charges [against Bell] are another attempt to destroy a black leader in Memphis" and that he was there to "prevent another assassination of a famous black leader." This would not be the last time that the persecution of Al Bell would be compared to that of Dr. Martin Luther King.

While the Al Bell Defense Fund and African-American press may have been playing the race card, to put the times in perspective it is worth recounting a few events that occurred in Memphis from the late 1960s through the mid-1970s. It is also important to keep in mind that all of these local events occurred within the context of sensationalized national media reports on the activities of black activists, such as the Black Panthers and Angela Davis. Memphis had its own advocacy group in the Black Invaders, one of whose members, Mad Lad lead singer John Gary Williams, along with three others was sent to prison in March 1969 for allegedly planning to ambush a white policeman as revenge for the arrest of a fellow Invader. Two weeks after Williams's conviction, fifty policemen stormed the Invaders headquarters.

The relationship of the Memphis Police Department to the area's black citizens was generally less than sanguine. Throughout this period, the mid-South's black newspapers contained innumerable articles about incidents of unbelievable levels of police brutality. Late in 1969, Memphis teachers protested the lack of black representation on the city school board. During one peaceful march, hundreds of people were gassed by the police. A staggering thirty-five African-American citizens were actually shot dead by Memphis police between 1970 and 1975.

Throughout this period, the busing of students to force the integration of the school system remained a constant issue. The insanity did not abate in the 1970s. In 1971, facing federal legislation that mandated that all public facilities—including swimming pools—be open to every citizen, the Memphis City Council, rather than allowing white and black children to swim in the same water, decided that they would simply close all public swimming pools. If they had to be integrated, nobody would swim in public facilities in Memphis, Tennessee. Although this was challenged in court, in June 1971, the Supreme Court ruled that the council's actions were legal.

The litany continued. In 1975 alone there were articles about white homeowners requesting real estate agents not to show or sell their properties to blacks; black policemen in Memphis filing a bias suit against the Memphis police force; and Memphis judge John P. Cotton refusing to marry a black man and a white woman. In the latter instance, disgusted and disheartened, the couple eventually moved to Denver to escape local harassment.

On a personal level, Al Bell recalls, "An IRS agent came in my office, sat down, lit a cigarette and did this [Bell pretends to blow out a long puff of smoke]. 'Mr. Bell, how does a *nigra* boy like you make this kinda money?' [Another IRS agent] stood on the steps on the sidewalk and told my attorney, 'I'm gonna *bust that nigger!*' "

It would seem that a number of people in white Memphis had a problem with the fact that Stax Records had become a black-owned company. Bell's ownership became public knowledge during the CBS/Stax lawsuits of the fall of 1974. The day it first appeared in the newspapers, Bell's yard was covered in toilet paper. "It disturbed people way beyond what you would think it would," asserts Larry Shaw. "As long as Jim Stewart owned it, it was no problem. We knew it was wise that we did not make Al the boss of the white folk. We were just little Negroes in the garage banging the guitars and playing the banjos. That proved to be wise. People resented it when they found out that [Al owned it]."

In the 1970s this was everyday hegemonic thinking in Memphis. The Civil Rights movement may have forced antisegregationist legislation but it had yet to raise the consciousness of a couple of generations of dyed-in-the-wool racist power brokers.

Although Al Bell was eventually totally exonerated of all charges brought against him, his indictment meant that the battle for Stax's survival raged on yet another particularly malicious front. There weren't many people left to help with the fight. With Stax unable to meet their payroll since early June, by the fall the company had been reduced to approximately fifteen employees.

Eight days after Al Bell was indicted, Jim Stewart tried yet one more route to raise the money that Stax so desperately needed to weather the storm. Stewart wrote a letter to one Allan Weston in Memphis. The letter proposed that Mr. Weston arrange a $50 million loan for Stax. The repayment scheme was rather complex. Stewart suggested that the loan would be repaid via a pledging of U.S. Treasury Bonds that would mature each year between 1994 and 2005. Stewart wrote, "Upon notification that $50,000,000.00 in U.S. dollars has been deposited in Manufacturers Hanover Trust, NYC, c/o a stated trust number, we will arrange for Manufacturers Trust to act as an escrow agent and coordinate the simultaneous transfer of the $50,000,000.00 for Stax's use, and in pledging $41,000,000.00 in U.S. Treasury Bonds to any account designated by the depositor of the funds. Bonds will remain in Stax's name for income tax purposes." According to Stewart's letter, the bonds would have a value of over $92.5 million in ten years. Unfortunately, Weston did not, or could not, arrange such a loan.

Two 45s were slated for issue by Stax in September. Desperate for a hit record to bring in some needed cash, Bell took a Johnnie Taylor–Carla Thomas duet, "Just Keep on Loving Me," that he had produced in 1969 for the *Boy Meets Girl* album, erased Thomas's performance, and put it out as a brand-new Johnnie Taylor record. Taylor actually refers to Carla on the entrance to the third chorus right before the ad lib, but it is so brief most people would miss it. It actually works just fine as a solo effort, but it was not the hit the company needed.

The second Stax 45 issued in September was by R. B. Hudmon.[13] Hudmon's first 45 was recorded when he was thirteen years old, and paid for by his father. It was released on the tiny Columbus, Georgia label Tomahawk Records. A few years later Joe South, of "Games People Play" fame, wrote and produced "Yo-Yo" for the still-teenage Hudmon. Released on A&M, the record generated a smattering of sales before the Osmonds heard it and turned it into a number 3 pop smash. Hudmon next recorded singles for Bill Lowery, initially on Capitol and later on Lowery's own 1,2,3 label. These releases were also unsuccessful, and Hudmon was dropped.

In the early seventies, Hudmon's parents broke up. Suffering from a heavy bout of depression, he wrote the therapeutic "How Can I Be a Witness" in just half an hour. The first version of the song was a sparse recording, featuring just Hudmon on keyboards and a hired drummer. About five hundred copies were pressed on Tomahawk Records. Columbus disc jockey Rudy Rutherford gave the record regular airplay, and local demand became strong enough for Gwen Kesler of Southland Record Distributors in Atlanta to become aware of it. Hudmon's cousin conveniently managed one of Southland's retail outlets and put Kesler and Hudmon together. For about a year noth-

13. Not "Hudman," as is often misspelled on record labels.

ing happened, except that Hudmon got a day job working for Southland.

Atlantic promotion man Larry King became Kesler's
silent partner and together they worked out a deal with Jim
Stewart at Stax. Stewart decided to recut the record with a
new A-side, "If You Won't Cheat On Me (I Won't Cheat
On You)." However, the newly recorded B-side, "How Can

(left to right) Reverend Walter Fauntroy, Al Bell,
E. Rodney Jones, and Ben Branch in the Stax stu-
dio at the sessions for Fauntroy's September
1975 album *The Congressional Record: The
Living Legacy of Dr. Martin Luther King, Jr.* COUR-
TESY DEANIE PARKER.

I Be a Witness," sporting an irresistibly catchy melody, was actually the better side of the Truth
release. Hudmon claims that initial orders were for 26,000 copies, and King remembers the
B-side becoming a number 1 record in Atlanta in the first week of December. According to
Jim Stewart it was also a big hit on the highly influential WVON in Chicago.

In mid-December King was working for Atlantic in Miami when he heard that Stax had
been forced into involuntary bankruptcy. On January 19, 1976, King and Hudmon went
to Memphis, where they appealed to the bankruptcy court to license the master tape to
them. The essence of their argument was that "How Can I Be a Witness" was, in effect, a
perishable item with a limited shelf life. If they had to wait the usual several months it
would take to process Stax's assets and debts, all momentum in the marketplace would
be lost. The court agreed with King and Hudmon, and on January 23, 1976, approved the
licensing of the master tape to Larry King and Gwen Kessler for $5,000. Atlantic subse-
quently sublicensed the record from them and rereleased it with "How Can I Be a
Witness" restored to A-side status. In March 1976, "How Can I Be a Witness" on Atlantic
reached number 73 on the national R&B chart.[14]

---

14. Hudmon continued recording for Atlantic with Bobby Manuel and Jim Stewart producing him. He had two
   more chart records on Atlantic and one on Cotillion through the spring of 1978.

Cash-strapped to the max, by the time of the Hudmon release, Stax was attempting to sell what few releases it could eke out on a C.O.D. basis. In addition to the Taylor and Hudmon singles, in September the company issued a double LP by Congressman Walter E. Fauntroy entitled *The Congressional Record: The Living Legacy of Dr. Martin Luther King, Jr.* The Fauntroy album was a bit of a departure. The congressman had long been an important member of the black clergy, and had played a significant part in the civil rights movement. In 1971 he was elected to the House of Representatives for the District of Columbia. Remaining on the board of the Martin Luther King Center for Social Change and as pastor of the one-hundred-year-old New Bethel Baptist Church in inner-city Washington, Fauntroy recorded this double album with the help of Operation PUSH bandleader Ben Branch. All proceeds were to be split evenly between the King center and Fauntroy's church.

In October Reverend Fauntroy held a special day for Al Bell at his Washington church. Bell spoke at length, his text entitled "Silver and Gold, Have I None: But Such as I Have, Give I Thee." The general theme of this talk was that black Americans should "get an excellent, formal, academic, business education." Although Bell did not mention his recent indictment in the course of his speech, he did refer to his current situation implicitly, at one point stating: "I must warn you that the waters of business are filled with killer sharks and piranhas, and sometimes it seems as though a repellent is nonexistent." Reverend Fauntroy closed the nearly four-hour service stating that "This has all been worth it. Al Bell can face the days ahead with his head high."

Bell and Stewart continued to display imagination and resourcefulness in their attempts to raise funds for the label. In late September they closed the studio down for a couple of weeks, and Bell, Stewart, and John Burton traveled to Switzerland, where they spent a month attempting to raise funds. "We were there with Dr. Mustapha Samy, a personal secretary to Anwar Sadat," recalls Bell. "He was trying to pull together some of his international connections to raise moneys for us at that time. We came really, really close on a couple of occasions but nothing ever materialized. I got a great education in international dealings with Dr. Samy."

The finances of both the company and its principals were so low at this point that the airplane tickets for the Switzerland adventure were paid for by Bell's personal secretary Earlie Biles and her husband, Stax salesman James Douglas. Al Bell's father, Albert Isbell, contributed $12,000 to cover most of the expense money needed by the trio of executives while in Switzerland.

Biles and Douglas had been contributing their personal finances in the service of Stax for quite some time. They had recently sold a house they owned in California, and most of the money realized from its sale went into Stax. The couple's personal credit cards were used to pay for everything from shipping records to hotel bills for promotion men. Due to their support of and faith in Stax, the young couple eventually were forced into personal bankruptcy and lost their Memphis house.

Not surprisingly, given the precarious state of the company's finances and the superhuman efforts Bell and Stewart were making to find outside sources of cash, rumors continually spread through the Stax community. One such rumor had one or another Mafia family coming in to save the company. "At the time," laughs Pete Bishop, "we were all saying, 'Well, I hope it's true because the Mafia's got money.'" That said, there is absolutely no indication that Mafia funding was ever remotely considered.

By the summer of 1975 David Porter had been put in charge of the McLemore studios with Stax's former controller, Robert Harris, handling the administrative duties there. For most of the 1970s, Porter had been lost in action, depressed over both the death of his mother and the loss of his songwriting partner, Isaac Hayes. Toward the end of 1974, he had begun to emerge out of an alcoholic haze. Newly cleansed, he began work on the Rance Allen Group's *A Soulful Experience* album, penning the autobiographical "Just Found Me." It was the strongest piece of songwriting Porter had been involved in for years.

Still enjoying the economic fruits of the catalogue of material he had written with Hayes, Porter was one of the few people left at Stax with any money. Believing in the company as much as Biles and Douglas, every Friday night Porter would gather together what was left of the McLemore crew. With everyone sitting on the leather couch in Isaac Hayes's old office, David would basically ask each individual what was the least amount that he or she needed to get through the week. In a gesture of extreme magnanimity Porter would then reach into his pocket and give them money to pay for groceries, the rent, or the light bill.

"It was difficult," recalls Porter. "I saw myself losing a tremendous amount of money [but] I was so into Stax Records until I felt that it was all going to work out. All this was gonna go away and Al and Jim were gonna pick up the money and it would all be fine. I believed that so much until I was paying money out of my personal moneys to people to keep them working, keep them trying, keep their spirits up." Porter continued to do this every week from the summer through December 19.

Considering the situation, the morale at Stax was incredibly high. As the engineer in charge of purchasing tapes and electronic parts, Pete Bishop for some time had been more aware than most as to how desperate things really were. "We'd been cut off from buying tapes and stuff from people for a long time," recounts Bishop somewhat wistfully. "I couldn't get any parts and everybody I talked to was hounding me about when they were going to get paid. I

Robert Harris and David Porter in the last days of Stax, fall 1975. COURTESY MISSISSIPPI VALLEY COLLECTION.

stayed until there wasn't anything else I could do. I really wanted to see it continue. Even when we were going under, there was still a strong family feeling. I think that's what amazed me more than anything else. Even while it was going down, people didn't just jump ship. And when they [did leave], very few people did it casually—it was [due to a] family's necessity or something. Everybody really tried to save it. It kept getting smaller and smaller and smaller and ended up being almost only the McLemore nucleus, back down to what it was. It was like saying good-bye to a family. I just wished it had gone on forever."

At the Union Avenue offices, there was no one able to help out any of the staff pay their bills. Nonetheless a number of individuals, such as promo man Mike Williams, kept on working without pay. "I believed in the company," says Williams, with his voice quietly shaking. "I believed in Al and Jim. At that point it wasn't about any money. I worked there without a salary. I wasn't the only one. There were quite a few more who just really believed that somehow or another this thing was gonna pass and were willing to hang in there. We hung in . . . but it didn't pass."

In October the bad news continued apace. Isaac Hayes once again sued Stax, claiming that the company had not paid him $150,000 due from his September 1974 Union Planters–engineered settlement with the label. In the meantime, Stax was experiencing difficulty getting any of its records pressed, and more artists continued to drift away, the most recent being O. B. McClinton, who signed a deal in late September with Mercury Records.

Stax's financial troubles paled beside the next bombshell to hit the beleaguered company. While Bell and Stewart were in Switzerland trying to raise funds, at 12:15 in the morning on Wednesday, October 1, Al Jackson, Jr., former member of Booker T. and the MG's and current Stax songwriter, producer, and session musician, was shot and killed execution-style at his home. Twenty-two years later the murder is still officially unsolved.

For some time, Jackson's relationship with his wife, former local R&B singer Barbara Griffin, had been extremely rocky. In fact, Al and Barbara had both long been romantically involved with other people and were most likely on the verge of separation. A year earlier Al had actually filed for a divorce but had then changed his mind. Things had gotten so bad at the Jackson house that Al had been shot and wounded in the chest by his wife on July 31. On September 6, a Memphis judge ruled that Mrs. Jackson had acted in self-defense in what had been a particularly vicious domestic fight. According to William Bell, at the time of his death Jackson was intending to move to Atlanta, where he and Bell were jointly going to form a production company.

On the night of September 31, Jackson had attended a closed-circuit broadcast of the Muhammed Ali–Joe Frazier "Thrilla in Manila" boxing match at the Mid-South Coliseum with his girlfriend. When the broadcast ended, Jackson was to head to the airport, where he was scheduled to board a plane for Atlanta. At the last minute, he decided to return to his spacious home at 3885 Central Avenue just down the road from Memphis State University. What happened next is unknown, and because there is no statute of limitations on murder, the case is officially still open, and the police file pertaining to Jackson's murder is unavailable for public inspection.

What is known unequivocally is that early in the morning of October 1, an off-duty policeman, Sergeant J. S. Massey, while driving home spotted Barbara Jackson screaming on her front lawn with her hands tied behind her back. She told the police that when she had come home that night, she found a man ransacking the Jackson household. According to Barbara, the alleged intruder tied her up, and when her husband came home, the intruder made him lie face down on the floor and then shot him five times. Jackson identified the assailant as black but also claimed that a white man was standing in the darkness outside of the house.

The October 11 edition of *The Tri-State Defender* ran a headline that screamed "PROBE UNDERWORLD 'TIES': HINT BARBARA PLOT VICTIM: MRS. JACKSON MAY HAVE BEEN USED: POLICE." Unfortunately, the article provides no real clues as to what "underworld ties" might have been involved in the murder or how Barbara Jackson may have been used. In the November 21 edition of *The Memphis Commercial Appeal,* police director E. Winslow "Buddy" Chapman was quoted as stating that the police know what actually happened, and that they could solve the case if the "black community would cooperate." Chapman went on to say, "We feel we have a clear case. But what we know and what we can prove in court are two different things. We feel there are some individuals who are probably in a position to know first hand or second hand what happened. They were either there or came on the scene. If we can get the black community to convince these certain people to come forward, the Al Jackson case could be solved."

If anyone did come forward, it's hard to know whether they told the police enough to arrest and convict those responsible for Jackson's death. Five months after Chapman's appeal to the black community for help, on May 1, both *The Tri-State Defender* and *The Commercial Appeal* printed articles that stated that indictments were about to be brought in Al Jackson's murder against Barbara Jackson, Denise LaSalle, and two men, including LaSalle's boyfriend, Nate Johnson/Nathaniel Doyle, Jr. *The Commercial Appeal* mentioned that LaSalle had been involved in recent federal litigation in which she was accused of harboring a criminal, Johnson/Doyle, who was wanted for armed robbery in Cincinnati when he was staying with LaSalle. Johnson/Doyle, it was believed, had killed Al Jackson.[15]

The indictments were never actually brought down, and very curiously no mention is ever made again of Jackson's murder in either Memphis daily newspaper or *The Tri-State Defender.* No one has a motive for the murder, and no one has any idea as to why the indictments didn't actually come down.

Several of Jackson's friends were very frustrated by the fact that his murderer(s) were never brought to justice. A few of these friends pushed the Memphis police on the matter for several months until it became plainly evident to them that "they had no intention of solving this particular case." The NAACP reached the same conclusion, sending a letter to various law enforcement agencies that in part stated, "We hereby protest what appears to us to have been a very shallow investigation on the murder of Mr. Jackson." The NAACP letter went on to list a number of "statements [made] in our office by associates of the late Mr. Al Jackson, Jr. who were the last persons known to be in his company before he arrived at his home." These statements concerned "inconsistencies and suspicious aspects surrounding the case which, in the opinion of many friends and relatives, have either not been properly investigated or possible conclusions from which could have been drawn [but] have been ignored." Among the many things these statements pointed out were the facts that the intruder at the Jackson's home allegedly entered a window in front of which there was a table holding several items, none of which were "disarranged" and that although the house contained numerous articles of great value, nothing of any significance was taken in what was supposedly a burglarly. Further casting doubt that Jackson's murder was in any way connected to a burglary was the fact that the jewelry Jackson was wearing at the time he was shot was not removed.

At various points in the last twelve years, I have made efforts to find out what happened to the indictments. Along with various intermediaries, I have spoken with several past and present members of the Memphis police and have been completely stonewalled, one officer advising us that some things were better left unknown. Several years later, after he retired, this same officer claimed that he didn't really remember anything much about the murder of a drummer named Al Jackson.

I was able to locate one of the two officers who signed the official report on Jackson's murder. Now retired from the force and engaged in another completely different line of employment, he was reluctant to speak to me. When I first contacted the officer, his voice started shaking as he told me that some things were just too horrible to want to remem-

---

15. Johnson/Doyle was twenty years old at the time of Al Jackson's murder. He had a long police record including arrests for arson, armed robbery, and shooting at a policeman.

ber. When pressed, he acknowledged the sequence of events as reported in the Memphis newspapers but stated unequivocally, "To be honest I really don't want to have no comment on it." When asked if there was a particular reason he wouldn't talk about it, he paused for several seconds before simply stating, "Nuh." This officer eventually agreed to take my phone number, and stated that, if he ever decided to speak with me, no one was ever to know. A few weeks later he agreed to a time to do an interview but when the time came, he stood me up, going fishing instead. Repeated subsequent attempts to contact him have been to no avail.

For those at Stax who loved Al Jackson, the fact that justice was never brought to bear on those involved in his killing leaves a very bitter taste in their mouths. Nate Johnson/ Nathaniel Doyle, Jr., ended up on the FBI's Ten Most Wanted list. He met his demise July 15, 1976, in Seattle, Washington, during a botched robbery attempt. Johnson/Doyle critically wounded a police officer before that same officer shot back and killed him.

At Al Jackson's funeral, Al Green sang "Jesus Is Waiting" and Shirley Brown contributed an emotionally draining version of "Amazing Grace."

It is one of the great ironies that after close to five years, the four members of Booker T. and the MG's had agreed on September 21, just over a week before Jackson's execution, that they would play together again. Plans were in place to start recording a new album on January 1.

Throughout September and October Stax had severe problems getting its records pressed. As well as can be determined, only two singles were scheduled for release in October, Rufus Thomas's "Jump Back '75" and an unfinished Staple Singers track entitled "I Got to Be Myself." Thomas is fairly certain that a few copies of "Jump Back '75" made it to the marketplace. As the title indicates, the song was a funky update of his 1964 classic "Jump Back." Mavis Staples believes that "I Got to Be Myself" was not actually issued in the fall of 1975. It is possible that, because the Staples were no longer at the company and very few copies would have been pressed, Mavis simply was never aware of it. Fantasy issued the performance in 1981 on an LP of Staples outtakes that they called *This Time Around*. At the time Mavis was none too amused because, whether issued first by Stax or Fantasy, the song was never properly finished by the Staples. As was the case with the previous month's Johnnie Taylor release, Stax was dredging the vaults for whatever they could find while the wolves were baying at the door.

On November 1 the handful of employees still left at the company received a piece of paper which read "You are no longer employed at Stax Records." This was done so that those left could collect unemployment insurance. Those who were willing stayed on and continued to work "officially" without pay (in reality this had been true since early June), collecting unemployment benefits while Al Bell and Jim Stewart continued to try to find a miracle solution. Many of the remaining employees, including controller Ed Pollack, resigned. By the Thanksgiving weekend, both Larry Nix and Pete Bishop had packed it in, leaving, of the engineers, only William Brown and Robert Jackson.

Those final days are ones that no one who was there will ever forget. "I can't imagine," recalls engineer Pete Bishop, "a company that could have had better solidarity. If there was a ghost of Otis Redding in the building, I think he would have been happy. The feeling did linger on there. People sacrificed towards the end. I lost my house and I left town with thirty dollars after not being paid for fourteen weeks or something like that."

The proprietor of the College Street Sundry, Ms. Ethel Riley Flowers, helped keep a lot of the company's remaining employees afloat, regularly offering them food without ever asking for financial remuneration. After the company closed in mid-December, Mary's Bakery also gave food to everybody still left because, in William Brown's words, "she knowed we didn't have no money. These people were surviving on the love of each other. They weren't surviving on waiting for that dollar to come around the corner. They knew it wasn't coming!"

Ever resourceful to the very last days, Bell partially solved the company's pressing problems on November 13 when he made a deal with Memphis's Plastic Products. Plastic Products president Buster Williams had worked with Stax when the label was just getting started and was willing to help out if he could in its last days. Williams officially agreed to press Stax product on a "press available" basis on the condition that he retain "a trust on thirty-one per cent (31%) of all moneys received by Stax Records, Incorporated from its sale of all records bearing the labels 'Stax,' 'Volt' and 'Enterprise,' pressed by Plastic Products." The trust account was set up at the National Bank of Commerce. Williams also had the right to invoice directly distributors of Stax product 17.5 cents for every single on the Truth, Gospel Truth, Partee, and Respect labels that Plastic Products pressed. Under this arrangement, the once mighty Stax was able to ship 144,000 records between Thanksgiving and the day it was padlocked, December 19. Deposits in the trust account on that December day totaled $15,092.

When Bell and Stewart had returned from Switzerland empty-handed, Stax's resident disc-mastering whiz Larry Nix knew the game was up. "I could see they had come back and that evidently nothing had been accomplished. I could see that it was not going to be," testifies Nix. "So, I got with John Fry and worked out a thing with putting mastering in [at Ardent]."

Eight days after the pressing agreement had been worked out with Plastic Products, as a result of the overtures Nix had made to Fry, Stax leased its disc-mastering system to Ardent for $700 a month plus 10 percent of the net profits Ardent received from the use of the system. Ardent never actually cut Stax a check. The rental fee was to be applied against Stax's existing $3,000 debt to Ardent for use of its studios.

As the Ardent deal was being consummated, Stax was informed by its insurance agent, Barry, Powell & Barnett of New York City, that its insurance was being canceled due to the nonpayment of premiums.

At about the same time, separate deals were made with both Randy Stewart and Mack Rice whereby Stax's existing and future royalty obligations to both men were canceled in exchange for their receiving certain master tapes. Stewart was given some unreleased Fiestas material he had cut and the second album, yet to be released, by a white pop group that he produced, the Round Robin Monopoly. Rice was given a handful of unreleased tracks he had been involved in. According to Union Planters lawyer Wynn Smith, it was upon learning that master tapes were leaving Stax's premises that the bank decided to foreclose.

Two final records were scheduled for November. Shirley Brown's third release on Truth was a wistful reading of a masochistic Bettye Crutcher lyric entitled "It's Worth a Whippin'." The track had been written during the sessions for the *Woman to Woman* album but had been left in the can. Although it received substantial airplay in Baltimore, Atlanta, and Chicago, the record was never worked to its best advantage by a now very crippled Stax.

The last waltz, or at least the last that was scheduled, was reserved for the Bar-Kays. The song in question was a James Banks–Henderson Thigpen–Eddie Marion composition entitled "Holy Ghost." Bassist James Alexander and lead vocalist Larry Dodson don't think "Holy Ghost" was actually ever released by Stax, but they do remember the group recording three or four different versions.

The story is interesting. In what seemed to be some rather odd maneuvering, the Bar-Kays were released from their contract in the first week of October. On October 8, they

The Bar-Kays as funksters at Wattstax. COURTESY FANTASY, INC.

then signed an agreement to deliver five masters to Stax with a song titled "Jam Motherfucker Jam" specifically designated as one of the tracks to be recorded. The titanic funk stomp "Holy Ghost" possibly came out of these sessions. The Bar-Kays signed another agreement with Stax on December 16, promising to deliver eight masters that would be recorded on sixteen specific days between December 17 and January 14. The song "Jam Motherfucker Jam" was again specifically mentioned as one of the songs to be finished.[16] It is possible that "Holy Ghost" did not come out in November, but was pushed back so it could be properly finished under the terms of this second agreement. My assumption would then be that the Bar-Kays had not delivered the five masters specified by the October agreement, which is why the December agreement became necessary.

If "Holy Ghost" was issued in those waning days of 1975, few people got to hear it. It is also not certain what version Stax would have picked, because the Bar-Kays attempted recording the song in several radically different grooves. In 1978 after the group had

16. Dodson recalls that at the time Al Bell was going through an overtly religious phase and had serious problems with the title "Jam Motherfucker Jam." Whenever the song came up in conversation, Bell inevitably referred to it as "That jam song."

become chart busters for Mercury, Fantasy took one of the versions of the song originally recorded for Stax, overdubbed timbales and horns, and turned out a number 9 R&B hit single. They then took a second version of the song, replete with a rhythm guitar lick lifted from David Bowie and John Lennon's September 1975 recording of "Fame," titled it "Holy Ghost (Reborn)," and included it on the *Money Talks* album, which was cobbled together from other Stax-era Bar-Kay outtakes. To this day it is one of the four or five most popular songs at Bar-Kays gigs. Whether "Holy Ghost" was the final Stax 45 in actuality or only symbolically, it is fitting that the label's story closes with such an extraordinary, mind-crushing recording.

Given the relative success of the Brown, Hudmon, and Bar-Kays' 45s over time (let alone that in January 1976, a month after its doors had been shut, Stax had 45s by Maceo Woods and Rance Allen listed in *Jet*'s Top Ten Gospel Hits), it is quite clear that Stax was more than capable of continuing to produce hits. It was just running out of financial means.

In early December everything started closing in. Chase Manhattan Bank of New York sued Al Bell for nonpayment of a $25,000 loan extending back to April 1973. This was small change. In late November Union Planters National Bank began foreclosure proceedings against Stax's most profitable subsidiary, the East Memphis Music publishing company, due to a default on a $3 million 1973 loan that had been secured with East Memphis's salable assets as collateral. Despite eleventh-hour attempts to block the auction by both Stax in Memphis and Otis Redding's estate in Nashville, on December 5 East Memphis's assets, including 3,360 copyrights, were put up for auction.

Prior to the auction, a number of physical threats were made by an unnamed militant black group that labeled Union Planters' actions "corporate racism." Consequently, an inordinate number of police, undercover agents, and plainclothes detectives surrounded the crowd that had gathered at the Shelby County Courthouse steps where the auction was scheduled to take place. With the bank retaining the right to reject any bids they deemed inadequate, at high noon James A. Cook, senior vice president of Union Planters, submitted the only bid. While the auctioneer shouted "going, going, gone," police rushed Cook and bank attorney James S. Cox into the courthouse and out a side door to an unmarked police car to drive them back to the bank. Union Planters National Bank had bought the assets of East Memphis Music Co. for the price of the outstanding $3 million loan.

Al Bell and Jim Stewart began to circle the wagons. On December 14 and 15 those employees still remaining began moving the furniture and files out of the Union Avenue Extended offices, taking them in a rented truck back to 926 East McLemore. Stax was now a very small group of people working out of an old neighborhood movie theater that had been converted into a recording studio. In what has to be an ugly irony, the situation eerily paralleled that of the company when Al Bell first arrived in the summer of 1965. As the offices were being moved, Bell began working on assembling an album of unreleased Staple Singers product that would surely generate some cash flow given the phenomenal success the group was currently enjoying on Curtom.

On the night of December 18, a meeting was held at Union Planters' head offices, with Bill Matthews, Roger Shellebarger, Tim Whitsett, Janice Harper, Joe Shamwell, Eddie Floyd, and Mack Rice in attendance. East Memphis, through Tim Whitsett, had been trying to entice Mack Rice and Bettye Crutcher to re-sign with the company. According to Rice, Matthews inquired as to what condition the studio was in, whether it would be profitable to work from that studio or whether it would be better to build a new one, whether the masters were safe, etc. He also wanted to know whether Rice and Floyd's interests were with UP or Stax and if either had a problem with Union Planters "taking over Stax." It would appear that the purpose of the meeting was for Union Planters to gather information so that it would be as prepared as possible for the planned foreclosure of Stax the next morning. Also a part of the discussion was a Martin Luther King memorial album that Matthews had conceived as a project that the bank could put together with former Stax personnel. Matthews, in his typically half-baked manner, thought that the completed record could generate enough cash flow that a bank-controlled Stax Records could then be sold to local black investors as a going concern.

On Friday, December 19, 1975, what remained of Stax was forced into receivership by an involuntary bankruptcy petition orchestrated by the bank and filed by three of Stax's creditors: Mayer Myers Paper Co. of Memphis; Star Photo Services, Inc., of Nashville; and Newark Electronics Corp. of Chicago. These creditors were chosen because there could be absolutely no dispute as to their respective claims. Union Planters senior vice president William Dick stated publicly that the bank played no direct role in the involuntary petition against Stax. All evidence clearly suggests that nothing could have been further from the truth.

Despite the heroic efforts of Bell, Stewart, and several others, Stax had only managed to generate gross sales of $1,363,552 for 1975. Even more telling is the fact that all but $300,000 of that had occurred prior to June 30. On the day it was shut down, Stax had $304.59 in the bank.

Once the court order had been obtained on the morning of the nineteenth, between 10:00 and 10:30 Roger Shellebarger's compadre, Burton Leman—who conveniently had been appointed receiver by bankruptcy judge William Leffler—a federal marshal,[17] and four Guardsmark security officers headed by Tom Weaver descended on 926 East McLemore.

Shellebarger understood that the way justice is meted out in our society is partially a factor of who can control public discourse. Consequently the media were not notified that Stax was about to be forced into receivership. Instead, Shellebarger elected to send out to Stax a privately hired industrial film crew, whose footage could then be parceled out to the media in whatever manner Shellebarger saw fit.

According to Al Bell, the federal marshal relayed to him that Shellebarger had told Judge Leffler when they obtained the bankruptcy order that "'there was going to be a death out there that day. Somebody was going to have to die.' This is what Shellebarger was telling the court. I was a black Mafia kingpin and I wasn't going to give it up easy and somebody was going to be killed." It was due to this level of hysteria that Leman decided to bring security guards to the foreclosure.

For the benefit of Shellebarger's film crew, Leman had everyone in the building, including Al Bell and Jim Stewart, ordered at gunpoint to vacate the premises within fifteen minutes. According to Leman's testimony in the subsequent Stax bankruptcy trial, "I met resistance from a number of people. Emotions were running high and tempers were fairly short and there was some shouting and screaming and a little pushing and a little grabbing here and there. But nonetheless I did the job I was sent out to do."

Upon exiting the building, everyone was searched, and no one was allowed to take any personal effects other than their coat or jacket. Everyone still working at Stax lost several personal possessions that by rights they should have been able to take. Eddie Floyd, for example, was never able to get his personal awards that were on display in his office

17. The federal marshal was identified as one Mr. Durham, who, according to Stax security guard Henry "Castro" Hopkins, had Georgia identification, suggesting that perhaps he had a long-standing relationship with Leman and Shellebarger.

returned. At twelve noon, Leman sent the guards to secure the Union Avenue Extended building.

In a truly macabre coincidence, just as everyone at Stax was being told they had fifteen minutes to vacate the premises, Eddie Floyd was frantically calling the company. His two-year-old daughter had been playing with his .32 derringer and had accidentally shot herself. Floyd needed information regarding the company's medical insurance policy. "The lady told me," recounts Floyd, still shaking his head, "'I'm sorry but we can't get off into that right now because the federal marshals are here right now and they're closing up the place!'"

A little later in the day, Bill Williams, unaware of the situation, headed in to work. "I drove up to the McLemore lot," says Williams, wincing a decade after the fact, "and pulled into the back gate like I would always do and there was a strange security guard standing there telling me, 'You can't come in here anymore.' I say, 'What?' He said, 'You can't come in here anymore!' I said, 'Hey, you better get out of my way or this Oldsmobile is going to run over you.' By that time Castro came out and said, 'Hey, he's right, Bill. The company is in receivership. The bank has taken it over so any of the old employees can't come on the property anymore. He's within his legal rights.' I said, 'Well, okay I'm glad you told me because he was about to be a dead security guard out here!'"

Robert Jackson and William Brown also found out about the company's closing after the fact. With sessions becoming increasingly infrequent, they had no real reason to be at the studio that morning. Later that day, though, they decided to drop by. "We were supposed to receive some money for the Christmas holiday," relates Jackson, the pain still clearly evident in his voice. "We walked up there and the sheriff told us we couldn't come in. It was closed. The checks that were written for us were on the desk. They'd taken them and we couldn't get them. We had a bad Christmas that year."

The mighty Stax was no longer in operation.

Epilogue

Angel of Mercy

The legal aftermath of the closing of Stax Records is incredibly convoluted and ultimately quite depressing. Stax immediately challenged the appropriateness of Berton Leman being named as its receiver given his close relationship and that of the company he co-owned with Roger Shellebarger, Crisis Management, Inc., to Union Planters, one of Stax's two main creditors. After much tussling and a lot of vicious rhetoric, the two sides agreed that, commencing January 5, 1976, former Criminal Court Judge W. Otis Higgs, Jr., would take over as receiver. Because Higgs was one of the leading African-American citizens in Memphis at the time, the principals at Stax felt that their company would be in good hands while they fought the bankruptcy proceedings.

No matter who the receiver was, Stax lobbied heavily for that person to have the authority to continue to conduct business through the pressing arrangement Bell had worked out with Plastic Products. From the label's vantage point, it was imperative to keep the business operating, thereby losing as little momentum as possible while they argued their solvency. As far as Leman and, of course, Union Planters was concerned, there was no business to be done at Stax Records. They simply wanted to shut the company down, move the bankruptcy through court as quickly as possible, and dispose of the assets. They had absolutely no interest in allowing Stax to work its way out of its financial hole.

"I think we could have worked our way up," says Jim Stewart somewhat wistfully. "We had cut down to absolutely bare nothing. A few people were staying there, all of them working for nothing. It had gotten back to that point and we were actually beginning to sell a few records."

The role Union Planters played in the earliest days of the bankruptcy proceedings seems extremely odd given the fact that the bank wasn't one of the three creditors who had filed the involuntary bankruptcy petition against Stax. It is even odder given William Dick's statement that Union Planters was in no way directly involved in bringing about the involuntary bankruptcy petition. However, contrary to Dick's public statements, quite clearly Union Planters was directing the whole show, and the original three minor creditors were serving merely as straw men. In fact, as Jim Stewart pointed out on the stand, if Stax was not allowed to continue, small unsecured creditors such as the three companies that filed the involuntary bankruptcy petition—Star Photo Services, the Mayer Myers Paper Co., and Newark Electronics Corp.—would not receive a penny by the time CBS and UP were finished carving up what was left of Stax. It was not at all in the interests of these creditors to force Stax into bankruptcy. Needless to say, Union Planters was holding the three creditors harmless from any expense involved in the litigation. What else Union Planters might have offered them is not known.

After stating that Stax was "not an ongoing business. It is a bankrupt sham operating on credit that they are incapable of paying off," on December 24, 1975, attorney James Irion suggested that Union Planters be attached to the original complaint. Despite protests from Stax's attorney Michael Pleasants,[1] Judge William Leffler agreed to this move. At this point UP attorney Wynn Smith[2] took over the case. The antagonists clearly became Union Planters/Bill Matthews/Roger Shellebarger versus Stax/Jim Stewart/Al Bell. The problem was that Al Bell was not able to testify on behalf of his own company.

"I believe that I could have prevailed in the bankruptcy court," affirms Bell, "but I had to make a decision between saving Stax and saving my life. If I had gone off into that bankruptcy court to fight for Stax, then these guys would have just destroyed me and it would have been all over the papers prior to me going to my criminal trial. . . . I made the decision to save my life and let Stax go. My counsel had advised me, 'You got a choice, your company or your freedom.'

"That was a difficult decision for me. This was what I had been working for and I had finally gotten Stax to the point where I could go on and build it and now I [had] to make the decision to give it up, just to try and maintain my freedom because the people on the other side are using this to collect on a bond claim to save a bank!"

If the jury had been sequestered in Bell's fraud trial, this would not have been an issue, but that was not an option Judge Wellford, who was presiding in the Bell and Harwell case, was willing to consider. Consequently, Al Bell sat on the sidelines throughout the bankruptcy trial of the company he had built from a small cottage industry to an R&B powerhouse.

Bell's attorney in his criminal case was James F. Neal, a former special Watergate prosecutor who had been recommended to Bell by Ruff Fant of Stax's Washington-based legal counsel, Cohen and Uretz.[3] It was Neal who had counseled Bell not to appear in bankruptcy court, which was probably good advice. Throughout the bankruptcy trial, Union Planters did everything it could to discredit and slander Al Bell.

One of the issues the bank focused on with regard to Bell was the $2.5 million paid to Johnny Baylor in late 1972 and 1973. Union Planters theorized that, when Al Bell borrowed the $6 million and executed the distribution deal with CBS, he already knew Stax was in trouble. Bell's plan was to simply pay Jim Stewart a substantial portion of the CBS money and then give much of the remainder to Johnny Baylor, who would launder it out of the company. At that point Bell could let Stax go down the tubes and declare bankruptcy, leaving Stax creditors such as CBS and UP holding the bag. Baylor meanwhile would hold the laundered money, most of which was destined for the personal use of Al Bell, who would end up a wealthy man. UP argued that this scheme fell apart when Baylor was stopped at the Birmingham airport on November 30, 1972. With the cash Baylor was being given effectively sequestered by the IRS, Bell changed his mind and attempted to save his own company.

This theory is ultimately ludicrous given the fact that at the time Baylor was stopped in Birmingham he had only been paid $500,000. If Bell was laundering money for himself through Baylor, why would he continue to pay Baylor another $2 million after the Birmingham incident? I don't believe for a minute that Al Bell ever intended for Stax Records to go bankrupt.

---

1. Of the law firm of Heiskell, Donelson, Adams, Williams & Kirsch.

2. Of the law firm of Canada, Russell & Turner.

3. In the Watergate trials, Neal prosecuted White House Special Assistant on Democratic Affairs John Erlichman and White House Chief of Staff H. R. Haldeman. Earlier in his career Neal had been brought in by Robert Kennedy to prosecute Teamsters Union President Jimmy Hoffa.

While Stax and Union Planters were waging their holy war, there were a number of minor side skirmishes brought to the table by other parties. Carrie McDowell sued for damages and the return of masters that she had cut under the auspices of Al Bell. Terry and Carol Manning filed suit for the return of masters and paperwork for their company, Privilege Records, which had been leasing three rooms from Stax at the Union Avenue office since October 1974. When Leman arrived at the Stax offices with his court order forcing the company into receivership, among the property he inadvertently seized was that of Privilege Records. R. B. Hudmon, as described in Chapter 17, pleaded with the court to allow the receiver to lease his Truth single "How Can I Be a Witness" so that he could capitalize on the limited shelf life of a record that was proving that it had the potential to hit big.

Outside the courtroom, a groundswell of enmity was beginning to develop around the role Union Planters played in shutting down what had been for years the economic hub and pride of black Memphis. The Memphis branch of Operation PUSH called for a boycott of UP, and picketers began to show up daily outside the bank's main offices distributing leaflets that accused the bank of being behind Al Bell's and Stax's troubles, as well as unrelated problems faced by Operation PUSH and African-American Congressman Harold Ford. The flyer concluded that "UP IS IN TROUBLE! Union Planters, because of the fact that their name was on a list of <u>TROUBLED BANKS</u>, and the vicious, mafia type tactics that it has employed, while pretending to be a viable financial institution does not deserve the support of the honest citizens of the City of Memphis!"

Operation PUSH asked Memphis citizens to turn in their "Annie" cards (UP's relatively new ATM cards), withdraw their money from UP, attend Saturday PUSH meetings, join the boycott against UP, and to support their local black bank.

Tensions were rife on a number of fronts. There were ongoing attempts to break into both McLemore and the Union Avenue offices after Stax was forced into involuntary bankruptcy. Because the master tapes were stored at McLemore, the receiver was paying for round-the-clock security at the studio, but Union Avenue was much more vulnerable and, in fact, was broken into a number of times.

On January 15, 1976, Stax lost its first court battle. After hearing six hours of heated arguments three days earlier, during which UP attorney Irvin Bogatin referred to Stax as a "disheveled, confused, mixed up, failing, defunct business that hasn't kept any records since last August," Judge William Leffler ordered receiver Higgs to cease the operation of any business at Stax Records. In effect, Leffler changed Higgs's role from that of an operating to a custodial receiver.

Bogatin was particularly vicious in his attacks on Jim Stewart, attempting to discredit him as an incompetent businessman and insisting instead that all he had ever been was an "artist." As he left the courtroom, Jim Stewart was shell-shocked. "I just don't understand," he muttered. "We were operating and could have done well. I just don't understand." Battered but yet to be knocked down, Stax lawyer Michael Pleasants filed a motion for a jury trial, which was then set for June.

In the interim Union Planters kept going for the jugular. On March 19, UP foreclosed on the Union Avenue Extended property, and then on April 14 the bank foreclosed on the East McLemore studio complex. A few days prior to the McLemore foreclosure, Bill Matthews and William Dick had met in Chicago with the director of Operation PUSH's Memphis contingent, Rev. Samuel Kyles, Rev. Jesse Jackson, George Johnson of Johnson Products, and Tom Louis, president of the Southside

The PUSH flyer urging a boycott of Union Planters National Bank. COURTESY TIM WHITSETT.

P.U.S.H.

BOYCOTT UP BANK

UP IS BEHIND AL BELL'S TROUBLES!
It is common knowledge that UP has sought to destroy Mr. Al Bell,
although officials of OPERATION P.U.S.H. have been told by
officials of the bank that Al Bell has done nothing which could
be deemed criminal.

UP IS BEHIND STAX'S TROUBLES!
While STAX RECORDING COMPANY is struggling for life, UP Bank is
in the process of liquidating the STAX property at 926 East
Mclemore Avenue, and using every method that can to destroy the
company, and the people behind it!

UP IS BEHIND P.U.S H. 'S TROUBLES!
Operation P.U.S.H. has knowledge that Union Planters Natl Bank
refused to give radio station WLOK a contract to broadcast the
LeMoyne Owen Basketball games because that station carried a de-
layed broadcast of the weekly meetings of OPERATION PUSH, on
Monday nights, at 9:30 p.m.

UP IS BEHIND HAROLD FORD'S TROUBLES
OPERATION P.U.S.H. has knowledge that a Union Planters official
vowed that he would see to it that Mr. Ford would not be re-
elected because Congressman Ford would not cooperate with them
in plans to erect a monument to the late Dr. Martin Luther King, Jr.

UP IS IN TROUBLE!
Union Planters, because of the fact that their name was on a list
of TROUBLED BANKS, and the vicious, mafia type tactics that it has
employed, while pretending to be a viable financial institution,
does not deserve the support of the honest citizens of the City of
Memphis!

ACTION SPEAKS LOUD!

WHAT CAN YOU DO TO HELP!

THE PUSH IS ON!

1. TURN IN YOUR ANNIE CARD
2. WITHDRAW YOUR MONEY FROM U.P.
3. ATTEND SATURDAY PUSH MEETINGS
4. JOIN THE BOYCOTT AGAINST U.P.
5. HELP SUPPORT IN ANY WAY YOU CAN IN YOUR COMMUNITY
6. SUPPORT YOUR LOCAL BLACK BANK!

FOR FURTHER INFORMATION, CALL P.U.S.H. 946-2529, OR 946-2520

BOYCOTT U.P. BANK

Al Bell and Reverend Samuel "Billy" Kyles.
COURTESY DEANIE PARKER.

Bank of Chicago and national treasurer of PUSH. The black business group proposed that Union Planters allow Stax to be placed under a board of directors headed by Kyles, which would administer Stax until the company's debts were paid off. Matthews rejected the idea and instead proposed that a nonprofit foundation be set up in honor of Dr. Martin Luther King, and that this foundation could operate Stax. Black businessmen could then buy up Stax's debt as a donation to the foundation, which could, in turn, produce records to pay back the businessmen. Obviously nothing came of Matthews's facile, half-baked idea.

In May, Otis Higgs approached the court asking that Judge Leffler either order those responsible for placing Stax in bankruptcy to pay the bills that had accrued since Stax had been shut down (security, the moving and storage costs of the master tapes, the cost of an audit, rent, utilities, Higgs's fee, etc., totaling $84,845) or dismiss the involuntary bankruptcy petition. Higgs pointed out that, although CBS and Union Planters had on a number of occasions stated that they would take care of these bills, funds had not been forthcoming. Attorney Irion accused Higgs of having "ceased to be a receiver and begun to be an advocate on behalf of Stax."

On May 28, it became public knowledge that Judge Robert McRae, before whose court the Stax bankruptcy trial was ultimately slated to occur, owned 1,214 shares of common stock in Union Planters. McRae amazingly commented that it "just dawned on [him] last night" that he owned such stock. Rather than step down, he stated that he intended to sell his UP stock, therefore supposedly removing all partiality he might have otherwise possessed. No matter that he clearly had close, personal fiduciary relationships with numerous directors, officers, and employees of Union Planters and no matter what personal knowledge McRae might have of the UP-Stax relationship. This was justice mid-seventies, Memphis, Tennessee style.[4]

In early June, Stax attorney Michael Pleasants asked McRae to step down anyway. McRae refused, and on June 16 denied Stax's request for a jury trial due to what McRae termed the delaying tactics of Stax's attorneys. He specifically noted delays in the answering of interrogatories filed by Union Planters, and said that some of the responses that Stax had filed were inadequate and others "were evasive in such a fashion that was insulting." He concluded by stating that he felt the jury request itself was a delaying tactic. McRae was obviously not a fan of Stax Records.

Pleasants argued that the problem in responding to the interrogatories was that Bell and Stewart did not have adequate access to Stax's records, which were either in the hands of the IRS or locked up at the McLemore location. UP's attorney Wynn Smith later stated that he felt that the delaying tactics employed by Stax were designed to postpone the bankruptcy trial until after Al Bell's criminal court trial.

The same week that Stax lost its right to a jury trial, Rev. Jesse Jackson launched an international fund-raising campaign to aid in the defense of Stax and Al Bell.

On June 21, Stax tried another tactic, filing a petition for Chapter 11, or voluntary bankruptcy. This statute allows the petitioner to formulate a court-approved plan so it can continue to do business while in an orderly fashion taking care of its indebtedness.[5] Bell and Stewart had already secured rent- and utility-free headquarters for Stax (in the offices of Memphis attorneys Walter Evans and George Brown, Jr., at the Tenoke building in downtown Memphis), and had several employees who stated that they would work, for an initial period, without a salary. At the outset, Stax was planning only on repackaging its back catalogue to minimize the production costs required to get salable product into the marketplace.

Union Planters, as could be expected, aggressively challenged Stax's request for Chapter 11 status and argued that, if it was approved, a $30 million bond should be posted. UP's lawyer, Wynn Smith, put an interesting new wrinkle into his rhetoric in court as he attempted to portray the bank as the true champion of the black artists whose work was being frozen by the bankruptcy proceedings. After railing about the many ways that Michael Pleasants had tried to delay the proceedings over the past six months, Smith stated, "These people simply should not be permitted . . . one minute longer to persist in the course of conduct they have followed in the past [i.e., use Chapter 11 proceedings to delay what Smith wanted the court to believe was inevitable bankruptcy] . . . in the interest of all the black artists and black writers and black performers whose work product is now languishing in the vault of C and I Bank.

"If the court please," added Smith for special effect, "we anticipate that the proof in this Cause will show that this loan made by Union Planters National Bank is the largest single loan ever made to a minority enterprise by a national bank."

Smith, on behalf of Union Planters, contended that Stax owed the bank $8.8 million, CBS $11 million, and had collective debts totaling $30.8 million with assets of approximately $9.7 million, leaving the label "financially dead or mortally wounded." Stax's prin-

---

4. Judge McRae previously had handled the separate criminal trials of former Union Planters employees Joseph Harwell, William Grissom, and Paul Grissom prior to revealing and selling his UP common stock.

5. The vast majority of bankruptcies then and now in the United States are of this nature. In fact, in 1978 (the closest date to the Stax bankruptcy that I could find statistics for), only one of every two hundred bankruptcy cases in the United States was involuntary. The involuntary bankruptcy that Stax was forced into under the auspices of Union Planters was the exception, not the rule.

cipals contended that these amounts were grossly exaggerated, pegging their collective debt at approximately $21 million. Stax attorney David Kennedy argued that, because a reorganized Stax would have no overhead and no payroll, there was no need for a bond. He went on to point out: "A large indemnity bond would force Stax into immediate bankruptcy. The purpose of Chapter 11 is rehabilitation."

A large point of contention with regard to the appropriateness of a Chapter 11 reorganization had to do with the value of the master tapes. Roger Shellebarger had earlier estimated their worth at between a half and $3 million, claiming that his figures came from former Stax employees Richard Salvador and Hy Weiss. Randy Wood, founder of Dot Records, testified in court on Union Planters' behest that the master tapes were worth between $4 and $5 million. George Schiffer, former vice president of Motown, testifying on behalf of Stax, came up with a very different figure, telling the court that the tapes were worth in the range of $21 million.

On July 8, Judge Leffler ruled that Stax could reopen under Chapter 11 if they posted a bond of $500,000 to cover the first thirty days of operation. In his decision, the judge described Stax's situation as a "financial holocaust" with little hope of success, and stated unequivocally that he would be "amply justified" in turning down the company's bid to reopen. The judge also complained that it had been difficult to get an accurate financial picture of Stax because the company's records were kept in a "very haphazard and non-businesslike manner since August 1, 1975" (the date Stax had been forced to terminate its entire accounting staff). He granted Chapter 11 only because the Stax plan met all statutory requirements. Leffler concluded by stating that if Stax did reopen, he would hold another indemnity hearing in thirty days to see if an additional bond should be posted to protect the firm's creditors. Leffler appears to have been anything but impartial.

On July 15, David Kennedy asked Judge Leffler to reconsider his imposition of the $500,000 indemnity bond. A crucial issue in this appeal was whether Union Planters was actually a secured creditor of Stax. Kennedy argued that a priority of liens had to be determined before a bond could reasonably be required. He then argued that UP did not have priority because the bank had subordinated its loans to Stax to that of CBS back in October 1972. If CBS was considered the first mortgagor, bankruptcy rules would make UP an unsecured creditor and leave the bank no standing to require a bond. At this point, CBS filed a motion stating that it felt no need for Stax to post an indemnity bond. Kennedy also objected to Union Planters' continued motions requiring "us to be in court every other day. Why doesn't the bank leave us alone . . . and give us time to file a plan? The bank, for whatever reasons, wishes to bury Stax Records."

Proving the validity of Kennedy's assessment, on July 17 UP immediately filed a motion to adjudge Stax bankrupt for failing to meet the deadline for the posting of the $500,000 bond. Attorney Wynn Smith argued that the motion to stay the bond requirement was just another in what he felt was a long line of delaying tactics by Stax. "We've heard this before," Smith complained. "Just a little more time, just a little more time, just a little more time and we'll walk on water." On July 22, Judge Leffler sided with Union Planters, valued the tapes at approximately $5 million, estimated Stax's debt as lying somewhere between $25 and $30 million, and ruled "the little label that could" irrevocably bankrupt.

As far as Stax was concerned all that was left was for the vultures to fight over the remains, which, of course, UP and CBS did with a vengeance, attacking each other with gusto. Along the way UP occasionally took a cheap shot at Al Bell and Jim Stewart. One of UP attorney Wynn Smith's more memorable lines was that CBS had made the distribution and loan agreement with Stax with full knowledge that the management at Stax was "inept, gullible and corrupt in the area of business administration."

On the same day that Stax was finally adjudicated bankrupt, the government rested its case in the fourteen-count bank fraud trial against Al Bell. Despite winning in bankruptcy court, Union Planters' malice was unabated. "When [Stax] was adjudicated bankrupt," recalls Al Bell, "it was in the middle of my criminal trial and Wynn Smith came in and said to me, [whispers] 'It was just adjudicated bankrupt' and did a thumbs-up thing on me."

The case against Al Bell, in essence, was that he had guaranteed several fraudulent loans drawn by Joseph Harwell for individuals who did not exist. In return, Bell received from Harwell, under both his and Stax's names, a number of loans when Bell and/or Stax could not meet their current debts. Further, it was alleged that Bell had provided cash kickbacks to Harwell in exchange for approving the bad loans to both Bell and Stax.

Bell's defense was simple. During the time that several of these fictitious loans were supposedly guaranteed by him, Stax was in very good shape and Union Planters was bending over backward to service the record company. Bell clearly had no need to conspire or guarantee fictitious loans to obtain credit from UP. Furthermore, handwriting experts had already proven that many of the documents Bell had supposedly signed were forged, which Harwell also admitted. With regard to the documents that he had actually signed, Harwell routinely had occasion to call on Bell to sign various documents; Bell signed whatever Harwell put in front of him, never taking the time to read these documents. Harwell had simply used Al Bell to defraud the bank. Harwell's testimony completely supported Bell, even though it would appear that doing so was not necessarily in his best interests.

"He told them in the witness stand," claims Bell, "that his life had been threatened in prison, that they wanted him to come into that courtroom and testify against me. If he had, he would have been out of prison a lot sooner, but he didn't do it."

Because both Harwell and Bell had nearly two years earlier made the same representations to Union Planters' attorneys, one has to wonder why was the bank so intent on having Al Bell criminally convicted. This seems especially odd in that there was no attempt to go after singer Al Green or Jim Stewart, whose names and signatures Harwell had also used to guarantee fraudulent loans.

One could cite race as one factor in the bank's desire to see Bell convicted; Bell's defense did just that when they called Delta Air Lines employee Keith Hagstette to the witness stand. Hagstette recounted racial slurs made in his presence by Shellebarger, claiming that in January Shellebarger had bragged about "getting all the niggers out of Stax, especially the head nigger, Al Bell."

While racism may partially explain some of the bank's viciousness and vehemence that often surfaced in court, the central reason for UP's behavior, as is commonly the case, centered around something as prosaic as money. Union Planters desperately wanted to collect that $10 million contingent receivable from its bonding company that was listed as one of its assets. The bank believed it had a much greater chance of doing so if Al Bell could be tied into Harwell's fraudulent activities. If Bell and Harwell had operated in collusion, then all Stax-related loans that were in default, theoretically, would be covered by the bonding company. If Harwell had acted alone in creating the fictitious loans to himself and had not received kickbacks from Bell and/or Stax, then the Stax loans would have to be interpreted as bad judgment on Harwell's part and would not be covered by Union Planters' bonding insurance. It's important to keep in mind that Harwell's loan limits were $10,000 for unsecured loans and $25,000 for secured loans; every loan he made to Stax had to be approved by his superiors at the bank. What was at issue here was that a conviction of Al Bell was worth several million dollars to Union Planters' board of directors.

"It was an unbelievable situation," says Jim Stewart. "It was [more] prudent for the

Attorney James F. Neal, unidentified person, and Al Bell outside United States District Court Room 3 during Al Bell's fraud trial in the summer of 1976. COURTESY THE STAX HISTORICAL PRESERVATION COMMISSION.

bank and profitable to prosecute him than to let the company try to work its way out. There was no way you could overcome something like that. Al Bell was innocent. I knew that and he knew it too and we knew why it was being done. Understood it very well. But it happened and nobody stood up for him, not even the black community. When all that happened everybody ran for cover that ever even had an affiliation with Stax. It was a leprosy colony over there."

Bell's attorney, James F. Neal, did everything he could to make Union Planters' motivations and goals as plain as day for the jury, and in fact stated directly in court what Neal's partner James Doramus described in an affidavit as "the appearance of unusual cooperation between the Government and Union Planters National Bank." Supporting this contention was the "apparent reliance by the Government on the bank's civil discovery in support of its criminal case." Union Planters made a number of depositions it had taken from Bell, Harwell, and others, as well as their bond claim of July 1975, available to the government, with the latter's indictment of Bell and Harwell including "substantially all the allegations of the bond claim." Doramus noted that further proof of this "unusual cooperation" was that Roger Shellebarger had easier and more complete access to Stax financial records in the hands of the U.S. government than Bell and his counsel enjoyed.

Doramus also pointed out the bank's attempts to "unfairly create pre-trial publicity which would unduly influence the trial," noting quotes by Bill Matthews in the Memphis press that UP was intending "to turn East/Memphis over to 'responsible blacks' thereby publicly inferring that Mr. Isbell was not a 'responsible black.'" Finally he pointed out that the bank was "using the indictment to enforce its civil claims by making Mr. Isbell choose between his Fifth Amendment rights and his property interests in his livelihood." In other words, because Judge Wellford would not sequester the jury in Bell's criminal trial, if Bell chose to testify in the bankruptcy trial, Union Planters would use his appearance there to prejudice in every way possible the jury that would be deciding his fate in criminal court.

Fortunately the jury saw through Union Planters' machinations, and on August 2, after some nine hours of deliberation, Al Bell was acquitted of all charges against him in federal court. He was now a free man. Harwell was not so fortunate. The jury found him guilty on two counts and sentenced him to two-and-a-half years in federal prison on top of the five years he was already serving for embezzlement.

At the conclusion of the trial, Bell's attorney, James F. Neal, told the vindicated executive, "Al, I'm going to have to bill you, I have a partner. Al, if you pay me in thirty days that's fine, if you pay me in sixty days, Al, that's fine, if you pay me in ninety days that's fine, but Al, if you never pay me that's fine too. I just want to be your friend for the rest of my life. I have prosecuted and defended a lot of people in my life but I've never prosecuted or defended anybody that I didn't see some criminal tendencies in them and I find none in you. I just want to be your friend for the rest of my life."

From Neal's vantage point, it had been an honor to defend a man of Al Bell's integrity in what had clearly been a sham from start to finish. His statement brought Al to tears.

Despite the acquittal of Al Bell, Union Planters did not abandon its efforts to collect on the bond claim. They eventually sued both Harwell and their bonding company, emerging with a judgment awarding them $4.5 million. While it was not quite the $10 million they had so boldly listed on their financial statement at the end of 1974, it was still a tidy sum whose existence they would use in attempting to defuse a malicious prosecution suit Al Bell would bring against them a year later.

By January 1977 Al Bell had moved to Washington and begun a new record label he optimistically dubbed the Independence Corporation of America (ICA). Working literally from a phone booth and a friend's car, Bell's very first release on ICA, Frank Lucas's "Good Thing Man," was an immediate success, breaking into the Top 10 on the R&B charts. Medium-sized hits followed by Margie Evans, Vernon Garrett, Lucas, and L. V. Johnson, but Bell ran into the age-old problems of an independent label. Despite a modicum of success, cash flow was low, getting paid by distributors was a problem, and, in June 1978, Bell decided that Washington was simply too expensive. Retreating to Little Rock, Al continued to try to run ICA on a shoestring, with releases trickling out through the early 1980s. All told, just over thirty singles were issued on ICA. In the mid-1980s, Bell was partners in the similarly short-lived Edge label, and in 1988 Berry Gordy appointed him president of Motown Records. After Gordy sold Motown, Bell once again decided to head his own company, founding Bellmark Records in September 1989, and hitting it big in 1993 with Tag Team's "Whoomp! (There It Is)."

On October 26, 1976, Otis Higgs stepped down as bankruptcy trustee, stating that the Stax case was not a simple bankruptcy but a matter of "deep seated long standing hostilities and hatred, overshadowed by tremendous problems of racism. I can't solve these problems." Higgs's position was immediately taken over by A. J. Calhoun. A week earlier, Bell had accused Higgs of being "a pawn of [Stax's] adversaries," because the former judge repeatedly ignored Bell's requests to ask for an investigation by the U.S. comptroller of the currency into the relationship between Stax, CBS, Union Planters, and the IRS. He also complained that Higgs was acting "irresponsibly" in going after funds that the IRS had just returned to Johnny Baylor.

As Higgs was resigning, a group of concerned citizens responded to Bell's call by forwarding a letter to nearly two hundred influential national and international leaders asking for support in pressuring the comptroller of the currency to launch an investigation into the relationship between Stax, CBS, Union Planters, and the IRS. The letter climaxed by stating, "What seems to be at stake here transcends the Stax Records and Al Bell issue; but rather involves the entire black race and more immediately the future of Memphis as a music capital. . . . In the name of justice, free enterprise and all that we hold sacred, let us pray for peace, love and an end to the crucifixion of Al Bell."

On November 24, new Stax receiver Calhoun, after being presented with a petition bearing 1,300 signatures, wrote then Acting Comptroller of the Currency Robert Bloom, forwarding the petition so that the comptroller could take "appropriate action," whatever that might be. Just before Christmas, Calhoun received a reply that simply said that the comptroller had no power to investigate the conduct of the IRS as it might relate to the IRS's own investigations. "Unless, therefore, you have information which indicates that a national bank may have violated the law, this Office is without jurisdiction to conduct any investigation." Neither Calhoun nor anyone else pursued the matter further.

Despite extensive investigations conducted over two-and-a-half years following the Johnny Baylor incident at the Birmingham airport in November 1972, the IRS never brought charges against Al Bell or Stax Records. According to a deposition filed by former U.S. Attorney John Mulrooney, prior to July 1975 the IRS had recommended that Stax, Al Bell, and other individuals associated with Stax be indicted for conspiracy to defraud the United States with regard to tax matters. In fact, the IRS, under the direction of agent Edward Keane, compiled what it estimated to be between forty and fifty thousand pages of documents pertaining to its investigation of Stax, concluding that Stax was guilty of 13 general areas of tax fraud totaling 159 overt acts. Most of these involved expense-account violations, the payments to Johnny Baylor's crew, payments for Baylor's apartment, the Herb Kole/Ewell Roussell kickback scheme, and instances of payola. Many of these supposed "overt acts" could have been successfully challenged in court. According to Mulrooney, the reason that no tax-fraud indictment was ever sought was due to the Department of Justice's policy that, if an indictment for Title 18 (General Crimes) offenses is returned first, the tax indictment is almost never sought. In other words, Al Bell's indictment on fraud charges effectively precluded any tax charges.

On January 26, 1977, Stax's master tapes, recording equipment, album, tape, and 45 inventory, and office fixtures were put up for bankruptcy sale. NMC, a subsidiary of Los Angeles–based professional liquidating company Sam Nassi and Associates, purchased the tapes for $1.3 million. The Nassi bid was accepted over $3.75 million offered by Al Bennett's Cream Records, because Bennett's bid involved only $200,000 up front, a further $200,000 after three years, and the balance, if possible, from royalties generated through the sales of reissued product through 1982. NMC sold their Stax holdings to Fantasy Records that June. Leonard Lubin, the manager of the Whiteway Pharmacy in Memphis, bought the recording equipment for $50,000, while the office furniture and equipment was sold to the Delta Auction and Real Estate Company for $36,000.

On February 25, 1977, Al Bennett purchased East Memphis Music and Birdees Music directly from Union Planters by putting $250,000 down immediately and agreeing to pay the remainder of the $1.8 million purchase price over a five-year period. This was considerably less than Union Planters might have been able to get for East Memphis, but for months now the bank had screwed up potential deals with any number of serious buyers. "They were asking prices way too high," comments Tim Whitsett. "They wanted to recover all the money they had lost. You had all these serious buyers coming in and they wasted a lot of time and money because they weren't going to come up with anything in the range [that Union Planters was demanding]."

Union Planters had been following the advice of New York City attorney Walter Hofer, who ran a company called the Copyright Service Bureau. Hofer suggested that UP sell East Memphis and Birdees to overseas buyers territory by territory, with one company buying the rights for the United Kingdom, another for France, and so on. The conclusion was that, if parceled off in this fashion, Union Planters could potentially get $7 to $8 million for the company, rather than the $3 million East Memphis was probably worth on the open market. Eventually UP ran out of prospective buyers and came to the conclusion that it had better dump the company as soon as someone made anything resembling a reasonable offer. Bennett was the lucky beneficiary. Six or so years later, he sold East Memphis to Irving Almo for somewhere in the range of $10 million.

In November 1977 the spoils of Stax itself were finally split, CBS getting approximately $750,000, Union Planters about a half-million, and about $100,000 being divided up between former employees and the IRS. While UP and CBS received pennies on the dollar, the employees, artists, producers, and writers at Stax were even bigger losers financially.

Words on a page can never adequately convey the human misery and suffering brought about by Union Planters' efforts to bury Stax. Isaac Hayes ultimately went bankrupt largely due to the funds that Stax was unable to pay him. In the process, Isaac lost his royalty position as a producer, songwriter, and artist at Stax; in the 1990s, with the Stax catalogue selling better than ever, Hayes receives not one penny for the wondrous music he created. Less wealthy nonstars such as Earlie Biles and Pete Bishop also found themselves in financial ruin, both losing their homes and almost everything else they owned of value. Other individuals went through one or two really bad years living hand to mouth as they attempted to adjust to life without Stax.

William Brown had first come to 926 E. McLemore when he was in his mid-teens. "When you come out of Stax," relates Brown, "you say, 'What now? It's closed, what now?' The bottom drops out of life and you learn how to live." Like many others, though, Brown ultimately realized that Stax had given him an education and a craft that was perennially marketable. "Stax made you know if you worked you could get it," affirms Brown. To this day he is a highly successful freelance engineer still based in Memphis.

For a while, to be associated with Stax was to be tainted in Memphis. Many higher-level former employees found it extremely difficult to find employment. "The city of Memphis was so jealous of Stax," concludes Robert Harris. "I felt that personally. That's why I'm not in Memphis now. After I went through that court hearing, I couldn't even get anyone to answer my calls. There was an attitude."

For some, those rough times have never abated, as they find themselves still being adversely affected some two decades later. Jim Stewart and Al Bell were wiped out. Whatever they had left was taken by Union Planters when they foreclosed on their personal holdings, based on the various guarantees Bell and Stewart had been forced to give UP to obtain the necessary operating capital loans of 1973 and 1974. Whatever the bank didn't get was sold to simply put food on the table. As far back as July 1976, Al's wife, Lydia Isbell, had been forced to sell her wedding and engagement rings to pay for the daily transcripts from Bell's fraud trial. For much of the late 1970s and some of the early 1980s, Al, Lydia, and their two sons were forced to live in an unfinished basement so squalid that Al's children to this day have marks on their legs and arms from spider bites.

This was the second time Jim Stewart, in effect, had lost his company. Not surprisingly, the emotional toll was grave. In the immediate weeks after Stax closed, William Brown,

Larry Nix, and Robert Jackson were at Jim Stewart's house practically every day. "He was so under," William Brown recalls. "We kept him afloat."

In the late 1990s Jim Stewart is still a broken man. Never seeing the need for drawing up a contract with himself as producer on the recordings made by his own company during its first seven years, Stewart to this day receives no royalty payments for his efforts in the creation of this music. Now in his retirement years when he should be able to enjoy himself, money to subsist is a never-ending worry. He deserves far better.

Stax ultimately was a victim of a number of forces. Its distribution agreement with CBS Records in theory might have paved the way to a significant increase in sales through the accessing of the white pop market. Unfortunately, neither Clive Davis nor Al Bell analyzed just how different their corporate cultures were. While the arrangement began on a positive note, these cultural differences eventually alienated all the players involved. When a small company becomes embroiled in a battle with a giant corporation, the smaller company is bound to lose out. When the going got rough, CBS played hardball, acting in its own self-interest, for example, by warehousing records that it wasn't working very hard at putting in the marketplace, thereby engaging Stax in economic strangulation. In corporate America that's an everyday activity known as a hostile takeover. It may not be pretty and it certainly is anything but fair, but to expect otherwise is not to understand the nature of capitalism.

Unfortunately, while battling the corporate giant CBS, Stax found itself on the losing end of simultaneous wars with two other major institutions. Union Planters was threatened with its own extinction. Their takedown of Stax and their attempted ruination of Al Bell were in the service of trying to save the bank's ass. From the bank's point of view, one might conclude that the actions of Bill Matthews made perfect sense. From a moral standpoint, they left much to be desired. But again, to expect anything else within a capitalist system would be foolhardy.

The United States government's continual harassment of Stax and then Al Bell in a way all stemmed back to Johnny Baylor. If Baylor had been less cavalier about boarding an airplane with approximately $130,000 in cash, Stax would most likely not have been the subject of a payola or IRS investigation, and the U.S. Attorney's office might never have sought a criminal indictment against Al Bell. As it happened, the fallout from Baylor's foolishness was immense, reaching deep into the core of the company's demolition.

Through it all, Stax was constantly let down by a judicial system that, in many ways, merely reflected the general attitude of the moneyed business community of Memphis, Tennessee. Stax was at war with Union Planters National Bank; UP's board of directors was inextricably connected to all the sources of regional power, including the judicial system. In retrospect, especially when you add in the possibility of latent racism, it is not surprising that Stax couldn't buy a break in a Memphis courtroom.

Stax might have been able to survive any one of these onslaughts, but their grand confluence was more than any company its size could be expected to bear. Not to be discounted in Stax's downfall was the label's own overexpansion during and immediately after its boom years. If Al Bell had been a little less bent on building an empire, the cash-flow situation of the company might never have gotten so extreme.

Stax was ultimately the victim of its own overexpansion, an ill fit with another corporate culture, the greed and self-interest of many different players, the mismanagement of a bank more powerful than itself, and the foolishness of Johnny Baylor.

On October 25, 1978, a federal jury found that Johnny Baylor had fraudulently been paid $2,541,409.54 "with the actual intent to hinder, delay or defraud the creditors of Stax." The jury agreed with Union Planters' earlier assertion that the money paid to Baylor was being laundered out of the company. The net result was that the money from Baylor could now be recovered to satisfy some of Stax's outstanding debts. Wynn Smith, now acting as the attorney for Stax trustee Calhoun, baldly stated in court that "Al Bell had a laundry service named Johnny Baylor, Johnny Baylor was a bag man for Mr. Bell, but the bagman got caught with bag in hand at the Birmingham airport."[6] Commenting on the fact that Baylor was ultimately forced to pay back what was left of his Stax earnings, Al Bell simply shook his head, stating quietly, "That was wrong. That should never have happened. That was Johnny Baylor's money."

On July 29, 1977, Al Bell filed a $20 million lawsuit against Union Planters National Bank for malicious prosecution. Bell charged that Union Planters had convinced U.S. Attorney Thomas Turley to indict him so that UP could collect $10 million from its bonding company. The trial was incredibly ugly. Wynn Smith imputed that Bell was involved with drug dealing and violations of IRS laws, introducing irrelevant and prejudicial material from the IRS Intelligence Division's report alongside inflammatory evidence with regard to the lawsuit brought by A. J. Calhoun against Johnny Baylor. Bell's defense team was barred from subpoenaing crucial evidence presented by Union Planters before the grand jury that Bell's attorneys contended ultimately led to Bell's indictment. At the end of this circus, Union Planters was found without fault by a jury on June 25, 1982.

On July 8, 1982, Michael Pleasants filed a motion requesting a new trial, claiming that Judge Wellford had erred in allowing inadmissible evidence, including the IRS Intelligence Report and information about the Calhoun-Baylor lawsuit. On August 3, the judge gave an order overruling the motion for a new trial. A notice of appeal was filed by Bell's team on September 1, but, alas, Bell was unable to raise the $25,000 in legal fees that were necessary to continue and, consequently, on October 7, 1982, the court of appeals ordered that the appeal be dismissed. Al Bell had finally reached the end of the line in what had been nearly seven years of legal battles.

In November 1977, Fantasy signed David Porter to relaunch the Stax label. Porter was to remain in Memphis, where he would sign and record new talent and oversee a reissue campaign that would simultaneously put together packages of previously released Stax classics and unreleased gems from the company's vaults. Porter signed six new acts: Fat Larry's Band, Rick Dees, Circle of Fire, Sho Nuff, Rhonda, and Kilo. Of these, only Fat Larry's Band and Sho Nuff managed to get on the charts. Porter did a little better re-signing proven Stax talent such as the Soul Children, Rance Allen, and Shirley Brown, and dredging the vaults for chart records by the Emotions and the Bar-Kays. The latter hit bigtime, with "Holy Ghost" scorching its way to the number 9 slot on the R&B charts in the winter of 1978–79. Although "Holy Ghost" was the only major hit, out of twenty-seven singles issued in the year-and-a-half that Porter ran the revamped label, he placed a very respectable nine songs on the R&B charts. He also put together albums of previously unreleased material by Albert King, the Emotions, Randy Brown, Isaac Hayes, and the Bar-Kays while recording new albums with the Soul Children, Rance Allen, Shirley Brown, Sho Nuff, and Fat Larry's Band.

In July 1980 Union Planters conveyed the McLemore studio to Memphis's Southside Church of God in Christ for ten dollars. At the time, the church stated that it wanted to renovate the studio to house recreation facilities, a counseling center, and other services. Such plans never materialized and, despite several offers by individuals within the com-

6. Neither Smith nor anyone else has ever offered any explanation for why, if their theory and accusations were correct, Bell would have paid Baylor over 80 percent of the money in question after Baylor was taken into custody and the funds impounded in November 1972.

munity, the church refused to sell it to anyone who wanted to turn it into a monument to Stax, their negative attitude stemming from a refusal to support what they saw as "the devil's music." Tragically, in 1988 the Stax building was torn down. What should have been a national historic site remains in the late 1990s an empty field containing rubbish and junkie needles. It's a disgrace, and speaks volumes regarding Memphis's treatment of its African-American heritage.

Over time, the value of the Stax masters and the East Memphis catalogue has grown beyond anything anyone ever imagined. In fact, the Stax catalogue has been subjected to the most in-depth, assiduous, and careful reissuing in the United States of any independent record label primarily engaged in rhythm and blues or rock and roll. The highlight of this reissue program has been a trilogy of boxed sets, coproduced and annotated by this author, containing every A-side of every R&B single ever released by Stax and its myriad subsidiaries. Together these sets total some twenty-eight compact discs, nearly thirty-seven hours of music, and are accompanied by over 120,000 words of liner notes detailing the stories of virtually every performance included. The first of these boxed sets is about to go gold. With one or two exceptions, every original Stax R&B album has also been reissued on CD, many with bonus cuts, and there are a number of CDs issued in Europe and the States containing previously unissued performances. More of these are to come as are a series of selected B-side reissues. None of this would be occurring if the music wasn't selling. In the late 1990s the sound of Stax Records has more currency than ever before. Such reissues have also spurred some interesting covers of material from the East Memphis catalogue. In 1993 Janet Jackson covered "What'll I Do for Satisfaction" from the first Stax boxed set, and in 1994 Salt-N-Pepa had a number 3 hit on both the pop and R&B charts with their cover of Linda Lyndell's immortal "What a Man" from the second Stax box.

While Otis Redding, Albert King, and O. B. McClinton have passed on, many of the company's great artists are still out there playing gigs and making great music. The Mad Lads, the Temprees, the Bar-Kays, and the Emotions all re-formed in the mid-nineties, and Isaac Hayes and Booker T. and the MG's both signed major recording deals in the same period. Ron Banks and A. J. Reynolds of the Dramatics and Rance Allen are both back recording for Al Bell on his Bellmark label. The Staple Singers, Eddie Floyd, William Bell, Sam Moore of Sam and Dave, Johnnie Taylor, Little Milton, J. Blackfoot of the Soul Children, and Rufus and Carla Thomas constantly play gigs throughout North America and occasionally in Europe. Smaller artists such as Mable John, Mack Rice, Ollie Nightingale, Little Sonny, Jean Knight, and Shirley Brown also remain active, playing gigs for the most part on a regional basis, occasionally getting offers to travel farther afield. Booker T. and the MG's, Sam and Dave, Rufus Thomas, Carla Thomas, Mable John, Eddie Floyd, Johnnie Taylor, William Bell, and Little Milton all have received Rhythm and Blues Foundation Pioneer Awards, and Booker T. and the MG's, Otis Redding, and Sam and Dave have been inducted into the Rock and Roll Hall of Fame.

The mighty Stax building at 926 E. McLemore Avenue, shuttered and closed by court order in 1976. COURTESY MISSISSIPPI VALLEY COLLECTION.

In every one of these artists, a little bit of Stax Records, the "little label that could," lives on. It's a legacy that makes the world just a little bit richer place to live.

Selected Bibliography

The first section of this bibliography contains works that were directly referred to in the course of writing this book.

Section One

Baker, Bob. "'Burn, Baby, Burn!!' What Began as a Radio Disc Jockey's Soulful Cry of Delight Became a National Symbol of Urban Rebellion." *Los Angeles Times,* August 12, 1985. Metro Section, p. 1.

Billboard magazine—close to twenty years of *Billboard,* the music industry's weekly bible, were consulted in the preparation of this work. A number of quotes from specific issues are cited in the course of the text.

Cantor, Louis. *Wheelin' on Beale.* New York: Pharos Books, 1992.

———. *Cinemania* CD-Rom. Richmond, WA.: Microsoft, 1995.

Dannen, Frederic. *Hit Men: Power Brokers and Fast Money Inside the Music Business.* New York: Times Books, 1990.

Davis, Clive, and James Willwerth. *Clive: Inside the Record Business.* New York: Ballantine Books, 1974.

———. *Encarta* CD-Rom. Richmond, WA.: Microsoft, 1997.

George, Nelson. *The Death of Rhythm and Blues.* New York: Pantheon Books, 1988.

Gordon, Robert. *It Came from Memphis.* Boston: Faber and Faber, 1995.

Gurlanick, Peter. *Sweet Soul Music: Rhythm and Blues and the Southern Dream of Freedom.* New York: Harper and Row, 1986.

Kinkle, Roger D. *The Complete Encyclopedia of Popular Music and Jazz 1900–1950* (four volumes). Westport, CT: Arlington House, 1974.

Knoedelseder, William. *Stiffed: A True Story of MCA, the Music Business, and the Mafia.* New York: Harper Collins, 1993.

Nix, Don. *Road Stories and Recipes.* New York: Schirmer Books, 1997.

Parker, Deanie ed., *Stax Fax*—all eleven issues of this magazine published by Stax Records in 1968 and 1969.

Pepin, John. *The Turnaround.* Oklahoma City: Western Heritage Books, Inc., 1980.

Rubin, Mike, and Derek Yip. "As Serious as a Heart Attack: A One-Way Conversation with Melvin Van Peebles." *Motorbooty,* no. 8 (Winter 1995): no page numbers given.

Sigafoos, Robert A. *Cotton Row to Beale Street: A Business History of Memphis.* Memphis: Memphis State University Press, 1979.

"A Study of the Soul Music Environment Prepared for Columbia Records Group," a report prepared by a team of masters students and faculty at the Harvard School of Business Administration, tabled May 11, 1972.

Tri-State Defender—close to twenty years of this weekly black newspaper were consulted during the preparation of this book. A few quotes pertaining to the murder of Al Jackson, Jr., and the ultimate demise of Stax are included in this manuscript. In all cases they are identified in the text.

Wade, Dorothy, and Justine Picardie. *Music Man: Ahmet Ertegun, Atlantic Records, and the Triumph of Rock'n'Roll.* New York: W. W. Norton & Co., 1990.

Watkins, Mel. *On the Real Side: Laughing, Lying, and Signifying—the Underground Tradition of African American Humor that Transformed American Culture, from Slavery to Richard Pryor.* New York: Simon and Schuster, 1994.

Westbrooks, Logan H., and Lance A Williams. *The Anatomy of a Record company: How to Survive the Record Business.* Self published, 1981.

Wexler, Jerry, and David Ritz. *Rhythm and the Blues: A Life in American Music.* New York: Alfred A. Knopf, 1993.

Whitburn, Joel. *Top Adult Contemporary 1961–1993.* Menomonee Falls, WI: Record Research Inc., 1993.

———. *Top Country Singles 1944–1993.* Menomonee Falls, WI: Record Research Inc., 1994.

———. *Top Pop Albums 1955–1996.* Menomonee Falls, WI: Record Research Inc., 1996.

———. *Top Pop Memories 1890–1954.* Menomonee Falls, WI: Record Research Inc., 1986.

———. *Top Pop Singles 1955–1990.* Menomonee Falls, WI: Record Research Inc., 1991.

———. *Top R&B Singles 1942–1995.* Menomonee Falls, WI: Record Research Inc., 1996.

Wittet, Bruce T. "Al Jackson: Memphis Backbeat." *Modern Drummer,* no. 96 (October 1987): 22–27, 84–88, 90, 92, 94, 96.

Also consulted heavily during the actual writing of this text were several file cabinets worth of court documents relating to the various court actions by and against Stax Records and/or Al Bell; several further file cabinets worth of contracts, sessions sheets, royalty statements, memos, letters, notes, and sundry other items in the possession of Fantasy Records, who bought Stax in 1977; several Al Bell speeches in the possession of one former employee who prefers not to be named; and company memos and a personal journal kept by another employee. Finally, I obviously made extensive use of my own published work on Stax entailing the liner notes for over sixty-five compact discs, three academic articles, and a number of popular press articles.

Section Two

The following books are long out of date and were not used during the actual writing of this manuscript in 1996 and 1997 but they were seminal to my earliest research on this music in the mid-1980s.

Garland, Phyl. *The Sound of Soul.* Chicago: Henry Regnery Company, 1969.

Haralambos, Michael. *Right On! From Blues to Soul in Black America.* London: Eddison Press Ltd., 1974.

Hoare, Ian, and Clive Anderson, Tony Cummings, Simon Frith. *The Soul Book.* London: Methuen, 1975.

Larkin, Rochelle. *Soul Music!* New York: Lancer Books, 1970.

Also important for my early research were multiple issues of the following soul music magazines: *Black Music, Blues and Soul, Hot Buttered Soul,* the *Otis File, Soul, Soul Bag, Soul Illustrated, Soul Suvivor,* the two Memphis daily newspapers the *Commercial Appeal* and the *Press–Scimitar* and the music collector's magazine, *Goldmine.* In addition, there were a plethora of magazine articles on Stax artists in a variety of publications ranging from *Essence* to *Shout* to *Rolling Stone* that were read in preparation for my interviews with various Stax personnel.

Index